East and Southeast Asia:
A Multidisciplinary Survey

East and Southeast Asia:
A Multidisciplinary Survey

Colin Mackerras (editor)

LYNNE
RIENNER
PUBLISHERS

BOULDER
LONDON

First published in the United States of America by

Lynne Rienner Publishers, Inc.
1800 30th Street
Suite 314
Boulder, Colorado 80301

Cover designed by Lyndell Board
Designed by Lyndell Board
Cover photography by: Market in Hong Kong – Richard I'Anson – Great Southern Stock
        Tibet – Richard I'Anson – Great Southern Stock
        Buddhist temple in Jinghong – Colin Mackerras
Set in Palatino
Printed in Australia by Australian Print Group

Library of Congress Cataloguing-in-publication data

East and Southeast Asia : a multidisciplinary survey / Colin Mackerras (editor).

 p. 24.2 x 17.8 cm
 Includes bibliographical references and index.
 ISBN 1-55587-612-9 (alk. paper)
 1. East Asia. 2. Asia, Southeastern. I. Mackerras, Colin.
DS511.E13 1995
950--dc20   95–8986
                            CIP

Contents

Preface

The writing of this book was motivated by the expanding importance of East and Southeast Asia in world politics and economics, and consequently in the curriculum. The Key Centre for Asian Languages and Studies is an Australian government-funded body located at Griffith University and The University of Queensland, both in Brisbane, Australia. One of its functions is to assist in curriculum development at all levels, and the present volume is one of its early contributions in the field of non-language Asian studies.

Since the topics covered in this book are so broad, it was thought to be desirable — indeed necessary — to involve quite a few scholars in its composition, so that each could write with a good degree of expertise. For the second edition, contributors have been asked to revise and update their contributions as appropriate. In addition, several new chapters have been added in order to give additional weight to the concept of 'Eastern Asia'. As general editor and contributor, I should like to thank my fellow contributors for their co-operation in the writing of this book. In addition, special thanks go to Susan Jarvis and Margaret Smith for their support, the first for her enormous editorial assistance and the second for typing and formatting the manuscript ready for publication.

The romanisation of the terms and proper names is based on internationally used systems, for example the *Hanyu pinyin* for Chinese and the Hepburn for Japanese. However, some exceptions have been made to the total linguistic implementation of these systems. Thus I have thought it unnecessary to include certain diacritic marks, such as the lengthening marks over o and u in Japanese. Those places and people with internationally accepted English-language spellings (e.g. Jakarta, Syngman Rhee, Kim Il Sung, Sun Yatsen and Chiang Kaishek) have been spelled in the way normally found in English-language publications, even where they differ from the standard romanisation systems used here. The order of personal names generally follows common practice in the relevant country. For example, in Japan and Korea, the surname is usually placed first. Again, exceptions are made as demanded by convention in the West (e.g. in the case of Syngman Rhee).

Colin Mackerras
Co-Director
Key Centre for Asian Languages and Studies
Griffith University Programme
Brisbane, Australia

Tables, figures and maps

Contributors

Professor Colin Mackerras, Co-director, Key Centre for Asian Languages and Studies, Griffith University (Chapters 1, 6, 7, 9, 20, 25, 33)

Dr Amitav Acharya, Associate Professor, Department of Political Science, York University, Toronto, Canada (Chapter 40)

Dr Reiko Atsumi, Faculty of Letters, Okayama University, Tsushima Japan (Chapters 4, 33)

Professor Colin Brown, Flinders University of South Australia, Adelaide (Chapters 23, 26)

Mr Jim Coughlan, James Cook University of Northern Queensland (Chapter 34)

Dr Robert Cribb, Department of History, University of Queensland (Chapters 6, 10, 18, 37, 38)

Dr Larry Crissman, Faculty of Asian and International Studies, Griffith University (Chapter 3)

Professor Paul Evans, Joint Centre for Asia Pacific Studies, York University and the University of Toronto, Toronto, Canada (Chapters 2, 41)

Professor Edmund Fung, University of Western Sydney, Nepean, Sydney (Chapters 14, 17)

Professor Helen Hardacre, Reischauer Institute Harvard University, Cambridge, Massachusetts, USA (Chapter 35)

Dr Julia Howell, Faculty of Asian and International Studies, Griffith University (Chapters 5, 36)

Dr Iyantul Islam, Faculty of Asian and International Studies, Griffith University (Chapter 29)

Dr Amarjit Kaur, Department of Economic History, University of New England, Armidale (Chapter 9)

Dr Anek Laothamatas, Assistant Professor, Faculty of Political Science, Thammasat University, Bangkok, Thailand (Chapter 31)

Dr Andrew MacIntyre, Graduate School of International Relations and Pacific Studies, University of California, San Diego (Chapter 31)

Dr Javed Maswood, Faculty of Asian and International Studies, Griffith University (Chapter 27)

Dr Tessa Morris-Suzuki, Department of East Asian History, Australian National University (Chapters 15, 28)

Dr David Schak, Division of Asian and International Studies, Griffith University (Chapters 5, 36)

Dr Glen St John Barclay, Department of History, University of Queensland (Chapters 22, 32)

Associate Professor Martin Stuart-Fox, Department of History, University of Queensland (Chapters 8, 16, 19, 42)

Dr Pradeep Taneja, China Australia Iron and Steel Industry Training Centre, Wuhan Iron and Steel University (Chapter 30)

Professor Nicholas Tarling, formerly of the University of Auckland, Auckland, New Zealand (Chapters 11, 12, 13)

Dr Russell Trood, Director, Centre for Australia-Asia Relations, Griffith University (Chapters 21, 39)

Associate Professor Peter Wicks, University of Southern Queensland (Chapter 24)

Acknowledgements

For permission to reproduce photographs and illustrations we would like to thank the following:

Australian War Memorial, Canberra, Photo 38;
Garuda Indonesian Airlines, Photo 5 & Photo 10;
Gedenkboek van Nederlandsch-Indie / Idayu Documentation, Photo 14;
The Herald & Weekly Times, Melbourne, Photo 36;
Historiographical Institute, Tokyo University, Photo 17;
Hong Kong Tourist Association, Photo 8;
Indonesian Embassy, Canberra, Photo 20;
Indonesian Promotions Board & Garuda Airlines, Photo 10;
Japan Information Service, Sydney, Photo 11, Photo 12 & Photo 33;
Koninklijk Instituut v.d. Tropen, Photo 7, Photo 22 & Photo 30;
Korean National Tourism Corporation, Photo 4;
Ministry of Foreign Affairs, Japan, Photo 16 & Photo 39;
National Army Museum, London, Photo 18;
New China Picture Company, Beijing, Photo 24;
News Ltd, Sydney, Photo 2 & Photo 13;
Peabody Essex Museum, Photo 3;
QANTAS, Photo 6;
Roger-Viollet, Photo 23;
The Age, Melbourne, Photo 31;
United Nations, NY, Photo 29;
Joseph Waters, Photo 1, Photo 27 & Photo 34;
Xinhua News Agency, China, Photo 37.

Other photographs:

Japan Information Service, Sydney, pp. 41 & 281;
News Ltd, Sydney, p. 1.

I | Introduction

1 | Introduction

In recent years the nations of East and Southeast Asia have come to occupy an ever more important place in the world, from strategic, political, social and economic points of view. In Australia this has been recognised in government, business, industry and education circles alike, and there has been a very substantial push towards Asian studies. Through this book, the authors hope to encourage, assist and facilitate this trend towards a greater and more general knowledge of Asia. In a way, this book itself forms part of the trend.

An understanding of the present requires and depends on a knowledge of the past. The principal aim of this book is to provide a reliable, coherent and interesting survey history of East and Southeast Asia from the sixteenth century to the present. It is not intended as pathbreaking or new research, even though some of the writers may indeed be presenting the summation of research which they have published elsewhere.

The main target readership is first-year university students. However, we expect that other students will also find it useful. Also, the authors hope that general readers wishing to gain an understanding of the history of East and Southeast Asia may find it interesting and suitable for their purposes.

The history which this book aims to provide is narrative and analytical. It is narrative in that it seeks to convey the kind of accurate information which the authors think necessary for a firm, basic grasp of East and Southeast Asian history. It is analytical in its division and arrangement of material and in the authors' approaches and interpretations.

The message which this book seeks to convey is that the history of East and Southeast Asia is not only fascinating in itself, and therefore well worth study, but also important in world historical terms. This is partly because it has produced cultures and ideas which continue to be influential today. But it is also because the immense significance of the region in the world today is to some extent tied to its history.

On the other hand, this book does not seek to present any general theory of history. In that sense there is no overall message. The authors may share a conviction about the importance of Asia and its history, but they do not necessarily agree with each other on the sorts of historical and political issues of focus in this book. For instance, some may support revolutions in the modern world while others may oppose them. The choice of authors was based on expertise, not on political or historical opinion.

History consists not only of facts, but also of trends. Precisely what information is necessary for an understanding of any historical period will depend on a particular point of view. There may be such a thing as an historical fact, like an event taking place at a specific time and place, but there is no absolute historical truth. There are perspectives and views about trends of the past, present and future. The assumptions which individual writers make about what is important in history will determine which information they consider it important to convey.

History is, in a sense, an amalgamation of the past, present and future. Unlike a drama or novel, history has no beginning or end. For the purposes of this particular book, we have decided to begin our focus with the sixteenth century. It was a period which saw the reunification of Japan and a time when Europe was beginning to expand its knowledge of and dealings with East and Southeast Asia. As for the ending, we have chosen the time when the present edition of this book was completed, that being 1994.

To begin our survey in the sixteenth century does not imply any view on when 'modern' history begins in Asia. Actually, historians have debated furiously on precisely what *are* the characteristics which mark out the 'modern' period in any culture. On the basis of their definitions, they have drawn conclusions — which may differ from country to country or culture to culture — on just when 'modern' times may be said to have begun. If the authors of this book were to debate the boundaries of 'modern' history, even for one of the countries covered here, it is quite likely that they would reach different conclusions from one another.

Except for Chapter 42, the Asian coverage here is mainly limited to those areas within the boundaries of six contemporary states: China, Japan, Indonesia, Korea, Vietnam and Thailand. Of course, not all these states have always had the same boundaries as they do today. For instance, the state currently called the Republic of Indonesia covers territory ruled in the past by a range of regimes, having varying degrees of control over areas which were different from time to time and which were not always clear anyway. The choice of these six contemporary states does not at all imply that the authors believe others like the Philippines or Myanmar (Burma) to be insignificant. That is clearly not the case. But it is impossible to be comprehensive, and the six countries selected are reasonable choices on historical, population, political, strategic and economic grounds for the limited space available. Even in discussing these six states, there are large areas which have not received as much treatment as they deserve.

Although the limitation to six countries is clear, in fact most of the chapters deal with topics across several countries, rather than discussing a single state. This theme-based approach has a great advantage over one based on particular countries in that it highlights commonalities and differences among the major civilisations of the region. A good illustrative example is Confucianism, which is very important in the histories of China, Japan, Korea and Vietnam. It has manifested itself similarly in all four countries in many important respects, but differently in others.

Historians are bound by their own sources, knowledge, experience and biases. In one sense we are all ignorant, since not even the most learned person knows more than a minute fraction of what there is to know on any subject. The authors of this book are specialists in their subject, but not all are specialists in all the subjects about which they write here.

The editor has quite deliberately abstained from placing ideological restrictions on the choice of authors and from imposing ideological viewpoints on the chapters after they were written. The assumptions which underlie research will influence the analysis and conclusions of that research. It is perfectly possible for excellent historical writing to emerge from a wide range of different standpoints and the reader will observe quite different standpoints in several of the chapters — for example, Chapter 22 on 'The Continuing Struggle in Indochina' is much less sympathetic to left-wing revolutionary movements, and attributes much less importance to their nationalist aspirations, than several of the other chapters.

Most of the material here comes directly from secondary rather than primary sources. Because of the nature of the book, the use of endnotes is generally limited to stating the sources of direct quotations, citations of a specific author or statistics. Each chapter is accompanied by a short but analytical 'guide to further reading' in order to assist students to undertake further research.

A study of history depends not only on knowledge and sources, but also on one's chronological vantage point. Thus an historian looking at the history of any people from the vantage point of 1994 is likely to have a different view from one who looks at it in 1950. This applies especially, but not exclusively, to recent history. One reason is that more or different sources may be available in 1994 than 1950. But it is more significant that somebody writing in 1994 knows how things have developed between 1950 and 1994. An important illustrative example lies in historical attitudes towards nationalism. We know now that the nationalist aspirations which were once so important did not on the whole produce anything like the results which Asian nationalists and their Western supporters hoped for, or in many cases even expected. It may be that nationalism and its enemy, colonialism, should at least in part be re-evaluated in the light of the historical experience of the last four and a half decades.

Not only is the present important in analysing the past, but historians, like many others, analyse the present and the future in the light of the past. Predictions may be dangerous, but it is natural to want to speculate about the future. We all make our decisions for the present based on how we think they will turn out, and our analysis of the past helps us to understand the present. Thus it is natural that our view of the past will undergo changes depending on how the present and future develop. It follows that this work does not claim or aim to be definitive.

The aims of the book's authors are thus strictly limited. But if this work helps students and others learn about the history of East and Southeast Asia, and develop a critical enthusiasm for understanding the problems the peoples of these regions have faced and the achievements they have made over the past four centuries or so, then it will have achieved its purpose.

2 | The concept of Eastern Asia

Textbooks which take a regional approach face special problems. Making the case that we need to focus attention on interactions beyond the nation state but below the global level is scarcely controversial at the end of the twentieth century. We need not be apocalyptic about the world economy breaking into three competitive economic blocs based in North America, Europe and Asia to see that regional interactions and institutions are major factors in contemporary international economics. Similarly in security matters, the ending of global strategic competition between the United States and the Soviet Union has given more importance to regional rivalries and opportunities.

The controversy begins when we try to define the boundaries and constituent principle of the particular region we have in mind. In it simplest terms, a region is composed of geographically contiguous units which share something in common. But what are the units? And what do they have in common?

In interpreting the part of the world which is the subject of this book, a wide array of words and phrases is in current usage. For academic purposes, definitions of the region can be based on geography, ethnography, cultural or civilisational forces, historical, linguistic, social, political and economic criteria. A recent review of the academic literature revealed more than 50 definitions, among them Asia-Pacific, Asian-Pacific, Asia Pacific, Asia and the Pacific, Asia/Pacific, Asian/Pacific, East Asia, East Asia and the Pacific, East Asia and the Western Pacific, Eastasia, Eastern Asia, Far East, Monsoon Asia, the Pacific, Pacific Asia, Pacific-Asia, Pacific Basin, Pacific Rim and Western Pacific. To make things more complicated, each of these concepts is subject to different interpretations. There are, for example, at least two dozen different definitions of what countries or territories can be included within the concept of 'Asia-Pacific'.

Identifying regions is an intellectual challenge, but it also has direct political implications in at least two ways. First, governments have immediate interests in how regions are defined, normally because they do not wish to be excluded from groupings they see as valuable. The definitions of region and the creation of new international institutions and processes go hand in hand. Large amounts of time and money are thus being spent in shaping vocabulary.

Second, the very process of selecting names tells us a great deal about the play of power and interest in societies and international relations. There is now a great deal of self-consciousness when academics come to the matter of applying names. Few scholars are content with the proposition that regions are discovered. Instead, they are aware that regions are more likely to be invented or constructed. In an era that is post-colonial, post-imperial and post-hegemonic, it is increasingly difficult to impose from the outside a definition of a region that is neither accepted nor understood by those who live within it. Rather, definitions are now created in great abundance and the fun begins in seeing what constellation of individuals and institutions will coalesce around any one of the alternatives. 'To define or to name,' writes one scholar, 'is to conquer.'[1] Viewed in slightly broader terms, to define or to name can also be an act of defence or, alternatively, an act of building new communities.

Precursors

Power relations and epistemological sensitivities were rather different in the first half of this century. Two main concepts — 'the Orient' and 'the Far East' — formed the basis for textbooks, academic organisations and policy analysis in much of the English-speaking world. The idea of 'the Orient' dates back to the Greeks and, according to the *Oxford English Dictionary*, refers to 'That region of the heavens in which the sun and other heavenly bodies rise . . .' More recently it has been referred to as 'That part of the earth's surface situated to the east of some recognized point of reference . . . usually those countries immediately east of the Mediterranean or of Southern Europe.' Note that the editors choose to add 'Now *poetic* or *literary*' to their recent entries.

'The Far East' too uses Europe as the 'recognised' point of reference — in this instance for the major imperial powers which extended their reach into Asia in the seventeenth century. The idea was popular in Europe and in the former colonies, including Australia, Canada and the United States. Up to and following World War II, regional courses at most American universities used the title 'Far East'. The *Far Eastern Quarterly* was first published in 1941 and the Far Eastern Association (now the Association for Asian Studies) was created in 1947.

In the immediate postwar period, scholarly opinion moved in new directions. Then, as now, changes in words reflected shifting analytic sensibilities and political forces. In the 1920s, the Institute of Pacific Relations attempted to create a Pacific-based definition which transcended imperial conceptions. But it was only in the decade after the Pacific War that a widely accepted alternative took hold. Two professors at Harvard University, John Fairbank and Edwin Reischauer, played pivotal roles. The concept of 'East Asia' had been used in scholarly circles since the 1920s, but jumped into the limelight after the publication of their influential textbooks *East Asia: The Great Tradition* (1960) and *East Asia: The Great Transformation* (1964). East Asia, they wrote,

> can be defined in three ways: in geographical terms as the area east of the great mountain and desert barrier that bisects Asia; in racial terms as the habitat of Mongoloid man (except for the Eskimo and American Indian branches of that race); and in cultural terms as the domain of what we call East Asian civilization. In this book the last definition is naturally the most important. We concentrate on the histories of China, Japan, Korea and, to a lesser extent, Vietnam, the areas that derived much of their higher culture and their primary system of writing from ancient China.[2]

The concept of East Asia interpreted as 'the Chinese culture area' was a significant new departure. It explicitly moved beyond a Euro-centric perspective and instead put China at the centre. The reference point was at last Asia, not Europe. While there have been disagreements about the territorial extent of East Asia, there developed broad agreement in academic and government circles about its boundaries and constituent principle.

The companion to 'East Asia' has been the concept of 'Southeast Asia'. It too was principally nurtured in American academic and policy circles. The phrase had first been used in scholarly work in 1839 but it was World War II and the Southeast Asian Command, not scholarship, that brought it into common usage a hundred years later.[3]

Where East Asia is largely based on civilisation commonalities, Southeast Asia is a largely political idea which uses nation-states as its basic components. In geographical scope it is widely understood to include the member states of ASEAN (now Brunei Darasalam, Indonesia, Malaysia, the Philippines, Singapore and Thailand), as well as Vietnam, Laos, Cambodia and Burma. The ASEAN member states and, more recently, the latter four have all found it of common advantage to see themselves as part of one Southeast Asia. And where East Asia was largely useful for analytic purposes, Southeast Asia also developed an institutional structure through such organisations as the Southeast Asia Treaty Organisation (1954) and in more mature form the Association of Southeast Asian Nations (ASEAN), created in 1967.

Beyond political advantages, there are links in historical experience. Though Southeast Asia is comprised of multiple racial, ethnic and linguistic groups, the two dominant cultural influences have come from India and China. There remain academic arguments about whether some of the Pacific islands (especially Papua New Guinea) and other countries or territories (including Taiwan and Australia) should be included within Southeast Asia, but the concept of Southeast Asia is no longer truly controversial.

Eastern Asia

In its simplest form, 'Eastern Asia' is a convenient device for referring to both East *and* Southeast Asia. It is based on the assumption that the lines of connections between the states and peoples of East and Southeast Asia are now so great as to encourage us to begin with what *links* East and Southeast Asia rather than what divides them.

One of the earliest references to Eastern Asia was in R. Calwer's *Introduction to the World Economy* (Einführung in die Weltwirschaft) published in 1906. Calwer's argument, approvingly cited by V.I. Lenin in his 'Imperialism: The Highest Stage of Capitalism', published five years later, made the point that 'Eastern Asia' was one of five main economic areas in the world economy at the time. There have been important connections between East Asia and Southeast Asia in the areas of trade, religion, migration and international politics for more than two thousand years. The Japanese effort to identify (and dominate) a 'Greater East Asia Co-Prosperity Sphere' in the 1930s in fact conceived of a territory closely resembling a combination of East and Southeast Asia.

This raises an important definitional point. A variety of authors in the twentieth century have used 'East Asia' in a rather different way from that popularised by Fairbank and Reischauer, referring instead to a geographical area roughly composed of what we have defined as East Asia and Southeast Asia and, in some accounts, also including Australasia. When Prime Minister Mahatir of Malaysia issued his call for the creation of an East Asian Economic Caucus, he had in mind a grouping including the countries of what we have defined as East and Southeast Asia. So what is in a word? Why prefer Eas*tern* Asia?

One reason is simply to minimise confusion and thereby keep Professors Reischauer and Fairbank happy. A second is because of current regional sensitivities. For three thousand years, China has been the principal and usually dominant political, economic and cultural force in East and Southeast Asia. The idea of Eastern Asia removes any possible implication that contemporary trends are a manifestation of re-emergent Chinese dominance or a pan-Asian assertion of Confucian values. So far as contemporary Eastern Asia has a dominant player, it is Japan, not China, although it is not clear if that will always be the case. More importantly, Eastern Asia suggests a regional order that is less hierarchical in cultural and political terms than in the past. One of the advantages of Eastern Asia is that it has not been embraced by any government or international institution. For the moment, at least, it has a political neutrality.

Just as Professor Calwer used the term at the beginning of the century, 'Eastern Asia' is primarily economic in character today It is much larger than the Confucian or Chinese culture area and encompasses a crescent arc running from Japan and China in the north to Indonesia in the south. Its geographical boundaries are subject to debate, though its core is centred in Japan, the economically advanced regions of China, South Korea, Taiwan, Hong Kong and the six ASEAN countries. Vietnam, and to a lesser extent Cambodia, Laos and Myanmar (Burma), are being integrated into the region. Only North Korea remains outside.

Boundaries, analytical or political, are necessary but produce controversy. With respect to Eastern Asia, several adjoining countries wish to see themselves as part of the region, among them Mongolia, a portion of Pacific Russia, some of the Pacific island states, and Australia and New Zealand. Australia in particular has made major efforts to become more deeply involved in Asia. Curiously, there is only limited interest in South Asia and in Eastern Asia in seeing the linkage between the two regions expand substantially in the near future.

As several recent studies reveal, regionalisation in Eastern Asia has been multi-dimensional.[4] It has been most visible in intra-regional trade. In 1980, intra-Eastern Asian trade was valued at about US$100 billion. By 1990 that figure had tripled; by 1993 it had almost doubled again to just under $550 billion. Significantly, Eastern Asia countries now do 42 per cent of their trade among themselves, a volume considerably higher than trade across the Pacific. In terms of investment, though the United States remains a major investor, Japan and other Eastern Asian countries provide more than 60 per cent of the investment in the region. The total Japanese investment in Southeast Asia in the past decade has surpassed $60 billion and has been supplemented by a rising level of investment from the Newly Industrialising Countries (NICs) of Northeast Asia, especially Taiwan and South Korea. Between 1987 and 1992, Taiwanese companies invested about US$12 billion in Southeast Asian countries. In the past three years, this has been supplemented by a new flow of investment *among* Southeast Asian countries, a flow that has also extended into China. In 1993 the largest single investor in mainland China was a Thai firm, Chaeron Pokphand.

In developmental assistance, Japan now disburses more than $8 billion annually within Eastern Asia; Taiwan and the Korea are responsible for an additional $1.5 billion. Intra-regional tourism has soared.

At the core of Eastern Asia is what can be described as a regionally integrated production complex. Behind the dynamic economic growth has been a fundamental restructuring of the economies and firms of the region. Contemporary Eastern Asia was born in September 1985 when the Plaza Accord among the Group of Seven Industrialised Countries permitted the Japanese yen to appreciate dramatically relative to the American dollar. Combined with the welcome mat in Southeast Asia, rolled out by a process of competitive deregulation among the ASEAN countries beginning in 1986, the ensuing wave of Japanese investment into Southeast Asia has produced a period of unprecedented economic activity. Not only was this investment unprecedented in volume, it was connected to production systems in several key industries which transformed basic industrial structures. Japan's trade with Southeast Asia has increasingly become intra-firm, intra-industry trade. Toyota, for example, has recently created integrated ASEAN operations involving production sites in Thailand, Malaysia, the Philippines and Indonesia. These are supplemented by inter-firm alliances. In its most advanced forms in electronics manufacturing, the company has become less important than the network, with firms producing component parts in production chains in geographically dispersed locations. It is not just the volume of trade and investment flows which are reshaping Eastern Asia but also their scope and intensity.

The process of economic integration has several significant features which differentiate it from patterns in North America and Europe:

- Investment has preceded trade.
- The principal players have not been governments (though they have played a vital role in creating the domestic arrangements necessary for economic growth), but private sector firms.
- The level of formal institutionalisation has been low. Regulatory frameworks to facilitate cross-boundary transfers have been produced by tacit and unilateral policy adjustments rather than formal regional institutions or formal trade arrangements along the lines of formally negotiated free trade agreements. The only indigenous free trade area — the ASEAN Free Trade Area, created in 1991 — is of only marginal importance to the overall economic flows within Eastern Asia, across the Pacific and to Europe.
- Economic integration has not produced or been supported by any common political aspirations to create an Asian commonwealth or supranational state. Economic integration has not been promoted as a path to other political objectives such as political unification or the eradication of war.
- The division of labour within the region has been explicitly hierarchical. Very little effort has been made to harmonise economic and social conditions across the region or reduce regional disparities.

- There has been a recent emergence of trans-national economic sub-regions created in response to still formidable barriers to the movement of goods, capital and labour across national boundaries. The focus is not countries but something that one scholar has described as 'natural economic territories'. These include the South China Growth Triangle (involving south China, Hong Kong and Taiwan), the Tumen River project, the Southern Growth Triangle (involving Singapore, the Johor province of Malaysia, and the Riau province of Indonesia), the Northern Growth Triangle (involving portions of Indonesia, Malaysia and Thailand), the Eastern Growth quadrangle (involving Mindano in the Philippines, Sulawesi in Indonesia, East Malaysia and Brunei) and the Greater Mekong Region (involving China, Myanmar, Laos, Vietnam, Thailand and Cambodia).

This new dynamic Eastern Asian capitalism has produced some dramatic results, the most obvious of them being extraordinary economic growth for a prolonged period of time. This growth has created a vastly expanded middle class, a new group of successful capitalists and the growing self-confidence of states and leaders in the region. But it has also produced unprecedented environmental degradation, political turbulence, a durable and hierarchical division of labour, and a series of daunting new problems including growing trade deficits with Japan, continued dependence on United States markets and Japanese technology, and increased vulnerability to the ongoing United States trans-Pacific trade deficit.[5]

The idea of Asia-Pacific

Eastern Asia, even in economic terms, cannot be understood as a world unto itself. Much of its economic dynamism has been a product of close trade and investment relations with Europe and across the Pacific, especially with the United States. Any understanding of Eastern Asia must thus be connected to a larger unit, something now most commonly referred to as 'Asia-Pacific' or one of its multiple variants. Again, to complicate the picture, 'Asia-Pacific' is sometimes used to refer to an area similar to what we have identified as 'Eastern Asia'. More frequently, however, inserting 'Pacific' into the label aims at constituting the region in broader fashion. 'Asia-Pacific' is based on identifying and enlarging the connections, primarily economic, between countries, firms and institutions in Eastern Asia with their trans-Pacific counterparts.

In the most ambitious configurations of 'Asia Pacific', the objective is to emphasise the economic, political and security interests which make Eastern Asia and its trans-Pacific partners a single unit; a kind of 'Pacific community'. In this conception, such countries as Australia, New Zealand, Canada and the United States do not just have interests in and connections with Eastern Asia, but are part of a common region. They enter such organizations as the Asia-Pacific Economic Cooperation (APEC) at the formal governmental level, and the Pacific Economic Cooperation Council (PECC) and the Council for Security Cooperation in Asia Pacific at the non-governmental level.

A narrower use of Asia-Pacific is to focus on the Asian side of the Asia-Pacific equation, specifically the more dynamic, growth-oriented economies. This narrower version recognises that the outward connection across the Pacific and into world markets is vital, but focuses on the Asian economies. In this respect, a visit to the Asia-Pacific does not include Sydney, Vancouver or Los Angeles.

Asia-Pacific in its broader sense aims at identifying and building upon trans-Pacific connections. Rather than treating the Pacific as a great body of water which divides, it looks at the sea as a medium which unifies or at least connects. Since the end of World War II, America has underwritten the security order of the region. Since the mid-1960s, the lines of connection across the Pacific have been essential to the market economies of East and Southeast Asia. Access to the American market has been the life-blood of the export-oriented industrialisation strategies of Japan, the NICs, the ASEAN five, and more recently China. Waves of Asian immigration have altered the demography of Australia, New Zealand, Canada and the United States. And the advent of 747 travel and satellite communication has shrunk the Pacific in ways scarcely imaginable at the turn of the century.[6]

The choice in this book to focus on Eastern Asia rather than the Asia-Pacific is partly one of convenience. There is a great deal to be said about a region of the world which is home to about a third of its population, contains some of its most dynamic economies, and represents rich and durable cultural traditions.

But so far as Eastern Asia is something more than a strictly economic concept, it raises the possibility of other lines of connection — political, social, civilisational. And here arise some perplexing problems. How deep are these non-economic connections? Can there be discovered or created, as is being attempted by many Asian intellectuals, a pan-Eastern Asia to lay the foundations for common regional institutions? We will turn to these questions in Chapter 40.

Guide to further reading

Segal, Gerald, *Rethinking the Pacific*, Oxford University Press, Oxford, 1990
    A fascinating but unsuccessful attempt to use the concept of 'the Pacific' as a meaningful unit of analysis in explaining political, social and economic developments.

McDougall, Walter, *Let the Sea Make a Noise: A History of the North Pacific from Magellan to MacArthur*, Basic Books, New York, 1993

A broad gauged and insightful geopolitical history of the North Pacific since 1528.

Dirlik, Arlik (ed.), *What is in a R?I?M?: Cultural Perspectives on the Pacific Region Idea*, Westview Press, Boulder, Col., 1993

A collection of dissenting essays on the nature and objectives of the proponents of the capitalist economic integration of the Pacific.

Evans, Paul M., 'The Emergence of Eastern Asia and Its Implications for Canada', *International Journal*, vol. XLVII (Summer 1992)

An early effort to define Eastern Asia on the basis of new patterns of production and economic interaction.

Notes

1 Arif Dirlik, 'The Asia-Pacific Idea: Reality and Representation in the Invention of a Regional Structure,' *Journal of World History*, vol. 3, no. 1 (Spring 1992), p. 76.

2 Edwin O. Reischauer and John K. Fairbank, *East Asia: The Great Tradition. A History of East Asian Civilization, Volume One*, Houghton Mifflin Company, Boston, 1960, p. 3. The concept remains influential. See, for example, Gilbert Rozman in his introduction to his edited volume, *The East Asian Region: Confucian Heritage and its Modern Adaptation*, Princeton University Press, Princeton, 1991.

3 The best examination of the concept of Southeast Asia remains Donald K. Emmerson, 'What's in a Name?', *Journal of Southeast Asian Studies*, vol. XV, no. 1 (March 1984).

4 Recent governmental studies include *East Asia: Regional Economic Integration and Implications for the United States*, published by the United States International Trade Commission in May 1993; *Economic Integration in the Asia-Pacific Region and the Options for Japan*, published by the Ministry of Foreign Affairs in Tokyo in April 1993; and *Australia and North-East Asia in the 1990s: Accelerating Change*, published by the East Asia Analytical Unit of the Australian Foreign Ministry in early 1992.

5 Mitchell Bernard and John Ravenhill, 'Beyond Product Cycles and Flying Geese: Regionalization, Hierarchy, and the Industrialization of East Asia', *World Politics*, January 1995.

6 For a fascinating but futile effort to identify a Pacific identity, see Gerald Segal's *Rethinking the Pacific*, Clarendon Press, Oxford, 1990. A recent history of a somewhat smaller area locates a sense of shared history (much of it conflictual) and future inter-connectedness, if not destiny. See Walter McDougall's *Let the Sea Make a Noise: A History of the North Pacific from Magellan to MacArthur*, Basic Books, New York, 1993.

3 The physical and ethnic geography of East and Southeast Asia

Introduction: Climate, weather and topography

Eurasia is by far the largest continental land mass on Earth and would still be so if its various large peninsular appendages, such as Western Europe, India and mainland Southeast Asia, were subtracted. The great size of the continent has a profound effect on its climate and weather patterns, which in turn are of primary importance to human settlement patterns in Eastern Asia. One consequence is that the interior is very dry, even in latitudes that are well watered in other continents, as the little rain that falls in central Asia comes from the remnants of weather systems that have originated over the Atlantic Ocean. The very large range of latitudes occupied by the continent also produces great ranges of variation in annual temperatures. In addition, marked seasonal differences in temperature are characteristic of continental climates and, as a result of having the largest land mass, the interior of Asia has the most marked alternations of heat and cold found anywhere on Earth.

Those seasonal differences produce monsoonal weather patterns throughout East, Southeast and South Asia, which is why the term 'Monsoonal Asia' is applied to those regions, as distinct from other parts of the continent. However, in terms of their climate, relatively small peninsulas such as the Korean and Malayan ones need to be considered in conjunction with the adjacent detached island groups, such as Japan, the Philippines and the Indonesian Archipelago, as the surrounding oceans and seas allow maritime influences to ameliorate monsoonal ones to varying degrees.

Although this is a simplification of very complex weather patterns, the cause of the reversal of prevailing winds that produces an alternation between wet and dry seasons, referred to as the *monsoon effect*, can be understood as follows. In winter, a vast, nearly stationary high-pressure centre forms in the northern interior of Asia in the region of Lake Baykal as the giant land mass becomes very cold and the air above it descends and flows outward. As this occurs in the interior, where there is no possibility of the northern winds picking up moisture, much of East Asia is very dry in winter except for the west coasts of the Japanese islands of Honshu and Hokkaido, which experience very heavy snowfalls as a result of moisture absorbed as the winter monsoon crosses the Sea of Japan. Although some interior regions of China, such as the Sichuan Basin lying to the south of the Qinling Mountain Range, are protected from the winter chill of the northern monsoon, its drying effects extend down into mainland Southeast Asia. However, these same prevailing winter winds which cross the South China Sea also bring winter rain to most of insular Southeast Asia and the Malay Peninsula.

In summer, the interior of Asia warms rapidly and transfers heat to the atmosphere above it, which rises and produces a region of low pressure over the Gobi Desert that attracts moist air from the oceans to the south. As the southern monsoon winds strike mountain ranges (e.g. the Himalayas, those in western Myanmar (Burma), Luzon in the Philippines and the western slopes of the Annamitic Cordillera), they shed a large amount of their moisture, producing areas of very high summer rainfall. The same effect occurs in smaller, dispersed parts of Japan and the Korean Peninsula. Southern China also receives regular summer rainfall as the southern monsoon rises over its hills and mountains. Summer rain on the North China Plain is far more variable, due to a lack of elevated land, whereas the Loess Plateau in northwest China is in the rain shadow of the Qinling Mountains and often suffers a shortage of rainfall in summer as well as having dry winters. Little or no moisture at all reaches the Gobi Desert itself.

In addition to the monsoon bellows that alternately suck in warm moist air off the oceans in summer and then blow out cold dry air from the north in winter, another factor influencing rainfall patterns in East and Southeast Asia is the pattern of cyclonic systems that migrate from the southeast to the northwest every week or so. They also draw in moisture from the South China Sea and account for the thunderstorms that provide most of the summer moisture on the North China Plain and in Manchuria. They are also responsible for the alternation between clear and rainy weather in Korea and Japan during the summer.

From time to time in summer and autumn, the warm surface waters in the South China Sea feed those cyclonic low-pressure systems with enough energy to generate tropical depressions, or typhoons, which then track erratically to the northeast. They can strike shore anywhere from Vietnam and the Philippines to Korea and southern Japan, with the southeast coast of China and Taiwan being particularly vulnerable. Although the heavy rains the typhoons bring add significantly to average annual rainfalls in much of East Asia, the flooding and wind destruction they cause make them much more of a bane than a boon.

Another major influence on climate is topography. Asia is very mountainous, particularly in the dry interior, although the fringing peninsulas and island arcs are also formed by mountains, often of recent volcanic origin. The dominant feature of the physiographic structure of Asia is the series of mountain ranges and plateaux north of India and Pakistan that has been, and indeed is still being, uplifted by the collision of the tectonic plate containing the South Asian sub-continent with the rest of Asia. They include the Pamirs to the east in Tadzhikistan, a republic of the former Soviet Union, and the Karakorum Range which fans out to become the Plateau of Tibet, a highland that actually extends throughout Qinghai Province as well. The southern rim of that Qinghai-Tibetan Highland, often also referred to as the 'Roof of the World', is formed by the Himalayan Mountain Range which contains most of the world's highest mountains, among which is the highest one of all, Qomolangma (or Mount Everest), nearly 8850 metres in height.

A series of other mountain ranges to the north of the Himalayas also radiates out of the Pamirs to the southeast and east, notable among them being the Kunlun Mountains which form the northern boundary of the Qinghai-Tibetan Highland in the west. The roughly parallel ranges defining the Highland run eastward before bending to the south in eastern Qinghai and western Sichuan Provinces, and their somewhat lower extensions then channel most of the major rivers of Southeast Asia through Yunnan Province into Southeast Asia. Despite containing the headwaters of almost all the major rivers of South, Southeast and East Asia, much of the Qinghai-Tibetan Highland is quite arid, particularly in the west and north where there are large tracts of uninhabited land. The southern slopes of the Himalayas are one of the wettest places on Earth because the moist South Asian monsoonal summer winds dump their moisture as they attempt to rise over them, and they therefore cast a vast rain shadow over the area to their north that extends all the way across Mongolia.

Another major mountain range, the Tianshan, is also linked to the Pamirs, but the range arcs to the northeast, dividing the Soviet central Asian republics from Xinjiang (which used to be called Chinese Turkestan, in contrast to Russian Turkestan on the western side, consisting of Kazakhstan and Kirghiziya). The Altai Mountains similarly define the border of Xinjiang with the Mongolian People's Republic to the northeast, which mostly consists of a vast highland desert of rolling hills and low, worn mountains west and north of the Gobi Desert Basin in its southeast, where the deserts are generally flatter as they give way to pasture lands on the Inner Mongolian Plateau.

A number of generally north–south mountain ranges radiate like fingers on a south-pointing right hand from the southeastern portion of the Qinghai-Tibetan Highland and its southern extension in southwestern China. Those 'fingers' define the coastlines of mainland Southeast Asia and separate the major drainage basins of the large rivers that originate on the Highland or the Plateau, just as mountain ranges and plateaux extending to the east in China divide it into distinct drainage systems. The large river systems of Eastern Asia have, over geological time, deposited expanses of alluvial soils, particularly in their lower reaches and delta regions, and it is on these rich soils that the civilisations of the mainland have prospered.

All the mainland Southeast Asian nations, with the exception of peninsular Malaysia, which is geographically and historically related to the adjacent islands of Indonesia, are centred in the plains or deltas of such drainage basins, while the 2300-year history of Imperial China consists, in its broadest outlines, of the conquest and incorporation of a number of such drainage systems which define China's physiographic macroregions and support its dense concentrations of population.

The mountainous insular and peninsular nations of East and Southeast Asia lack the large alluvial plains of the mainland, since the basins that their mountain ranges define are largely submerged. Nonetheless, their populations are still generally concentrated in the lowlands and narrow river valleys, where areas of alluvial soils that support intensive agriculture are found. This is also true for the southeastern coastal region of China, where some particularly dense populations are found in very small areas near the mouths of the relatively small rivers that drain the hilly interior. The major exceptions occur in Indonesia. Here the rich volcanic soils and high rainfall throughout the island of Java support a large majority of the population of the country, while the islands of Sumatra and Borneo, as well as Irian Jaya, have large areas of swamp and marsh along much of their coasts that have precluded extensive agricultural development although they are the remainder of only partially submerged aluvial basins.

Significant features of the geography of Japan

Japan now has four main islands as well as numerous small ones, including the Ryukyu Chain that extends to the southeast nearly to Taiwan. Hokkaido was only settled by significant numbers of Japanese in the late nineteenth century when it was developed agriculturally, resulting in the displacement and partial absorption of the indigenous Ainu people. In fact, even the northern part of the main island of Honshu was not fully a part of the 'Old Japan' of the feudal Tokugawa Shogunate. In addition to the Kanto Plain, by far the largest of Japan's lowlands which contains Tokyo and its port city of Yokohama, 'Old Japan' was centred on the smaller plains in the Kansai region of west-central Honshu at the eastern end of the Inland Sea, the southern and western shores of

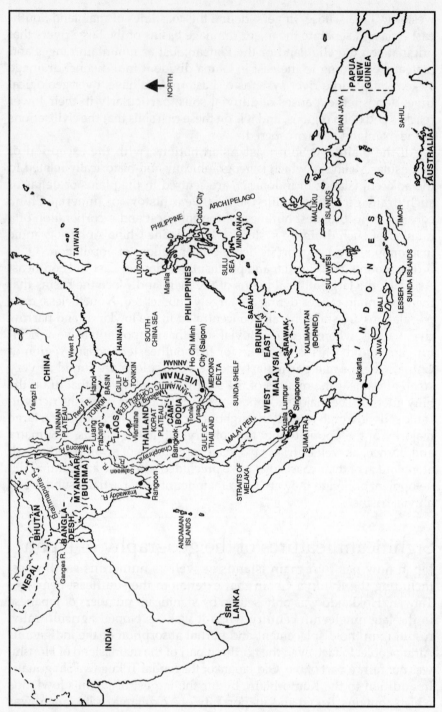

Map 3.1 Southeast Asia

which consist of the main islands of Shikoku and Kyushu, respectively. Kansai contains the heavily industrialised cities of Kobe and Osaka, which, like Tokyo and Yokohama, are now contiguous twin cities. The only other very large city in Japan is Nagoya, on the Nobi Plain in the heavily built-up and industrialised transport corridor between the two poles of contemporary, as well as traditional, Japan.

In fact, although Japanese society has been transformed since the Meiji restoration of the mid-nineteenth century by the development of what has become, since World War II, the world's second most powerful industrial and commercial economy, the distribution of the Japanese population has not been radically altered from what it was when Japan was a feudal agrarian society, the major difference being due to the aforementioned agricultural development of Hokkaido. When fully developed, arable land in Japan was limited to around 6 million hectares, or l6.5 per cent of the total land area, around a third of this being in a few major lowlands. The remainder of the agricultural land is found in patches where small rivers and streams leave the mountains and have formed limited alluvial deposits before reaching the nearby coast and where small terraces could be constructed in their ascending valleys. The agricultural population was densely packed into places where alluvium is present, the other soils — particularly in the mountainous interior — being too thin or of too poor a quality to have any agricultural potential. Fishing villages were also commonly found along suitable shorelines, particularly around the Inland Sea.

As in the rest of Asia, Japanese agriculture was — and to some extent still is — highly labour intensive, particularly where wet rice can be grown. In north-central Honshu and southwards, the growing season at low altitudes is long enough to allow more than one field crop per year, and the incidence of multiple cropping of paddy fields with a dry crop following the rice increases rapidly to the south. However, double cropping of rice itself is possible only in southernmost Kyushu, which has an almost sub-tropical climate despite its latitude because of maritime influences. The large incidence of irrigation of one kind or another is one factor in the very high yields of rice produced in Japan, meaning the country is still virtually self-sufficient in that staple food. Another factor is the very high use of chemical fertilisers and pesticides. Despite the small size of the fields, agriculture has become highly mechanised in Japan in recent decades; however, government policies (particularly rice subsidies) have continued to make it profitable, and the value of remaining agricultural land is very high.

The point of discussing the agricultural past and present of one of the world's most industrialised countries is that those places where the agrarian population of the feudal period was concentrated are precisely the places that have been developed the most intensively in the past hundred years. The mountainous interior of Japan is too rugged to be of much economic use, apart from exploitation of relatively low-grade timber resources, and as much as two-thirds of the total land surface is covered with bush, consisting of some remaining natural forests (particularly in Hokkaido and Northern Honshu), planted stands of pines and Japanese cypress, coppice stands of small broad-leaved trees, or once-logged brushlands. Industrial development in resource-poor Japan began, and has continued, where raw materials could be brought in and finished goods could be exported by sea, and where skilled labour was already available. As a result, the Tokugawa capital of Edo, which was remarkable for a pre-industrial city in having had a population of a million or more when Japan was 'opened' to the West in the mid-nineteenth century, has grown to become the Tokyo of today, with its enormous population. Essentially, apart from Hokkaido, the limited land areas that supported 50 million or so largely agricultural Japanese a hundred years ago now contain the 125 million largely urbanised Japanese of today.

The Korean Peninsula

During the last millenium, the northern boundary of the Korean state became fixed along the estuary of the Yalu River and was eventually extended upstream and over the mountains to follow the course of the Tumen River to the Sea of Japan, incorporating territory that is not really part of the geomorphic peninsula itself. During the Manchu (Qing) Dynasty, which dominated Korea as well as ruling China, the area to the north of the Yalu was prohibited to Chinese as well as Korean settlers, but the eastern part of the border was not well policed. Beginning then, but increasing substantially in the early twentieth century, a significant number of rice-growing Korean peasants moved into Manchuria's Jilin Province to become the ancestors of the two million or so Koreans living there in the 1990s; wheat-growing Chinese came to occupy the lands to the north of the Yalu in the west.

The physiographic structure of the Korean Peninsula is similar to that of Japan, although they are mirror images in that each has its mountain spine along the Sea of Japan with broader valleys and some lowlands on the opposite side. In the case of Korea, this is the western one fronting the Yellow Sea. Although lacking extensive plains, there are lowland areas that support intense agricultural activity in the northwest and the central-west near the cities of Pyongyang and Seoul respectively, as well as in the southeast and south. The percentage of arable land, around 20 per cent overall, is somewhat higher than in Japan. There are still extensive forests in the high mountains of the northeast, but the lower mountains and hills near settlement concentrations have for a long time been denuded of any growth apart from shrubs and young trees not yet cut for firewood, although some reforestation has been accomplished in recent decades.

Being surrounded by the ocean on three sides is not enough to ameliorate the continental character of Korea's climate, as the shallow Yellow Sea does not retain heat in the winter to the same extent as the Sea of Japan, and the peninsula itself is aligned with the prevailing direction of the winter monsoon. As a result, there is a very large range of temperatures between the warm to hot, moist summers and the cold, dry winters, particularly in the north. The growing season in the north is too short to allow double cropping, whereas a second, winter crop can often be obtained on the dry fields and drained paddies in the south. The greater agricultural resources of the south, in addition to the incidence of double cropping, allow a denser population to be supported. Whereas the north was developed industrially under the Japanese far more than the south, primarily because of its coal resources, the extensive economic development in the south in recent decades has made South Korea into a relatively wealthy country. It now has a population of over 40 million, while North Korea has around 20 million people.

The geographical structure of the People's Republic of China

According to its 1990 census, the People's Republic of China (PRC) has over 1.13 billion people (approximately one-fifth of the world's five and a half billion), making it the world's largest country in terms of population. However, its land area of 9.6 million square kilometres (6.4 per cent of the world's land area) made it in that year only the third most extensive country after the Soviet Union and Canada, and even since the collapse of the Soviet Union at the end of 1991, it still ranks only third after Russia and Canada. Moreover, much of that area is too dry or too cold or too rugged to support agriculture. Only 10.4 per cent of the land is arable, meaning that the peoples of China must rely for subsistence on a mere 1 million square kilometres (100 million hectares). That is less than .09 hectare (less than a quarter of an acre) per capita of agriculturally productive soil which, in addition, is very unevenly distributed throughout the country.

As China continues to have what is still fundamentally an agrarian economy with an inadequate modernised transportation system, the majority of the population must live where the food they eat is produced. Those stark facts and figures are central to an understanding of the economic and social geography of China. However, before one can begin to understand the ways in which the Chinese use their environment and to comprehend the organisation they have imposed upon it, it is necessary

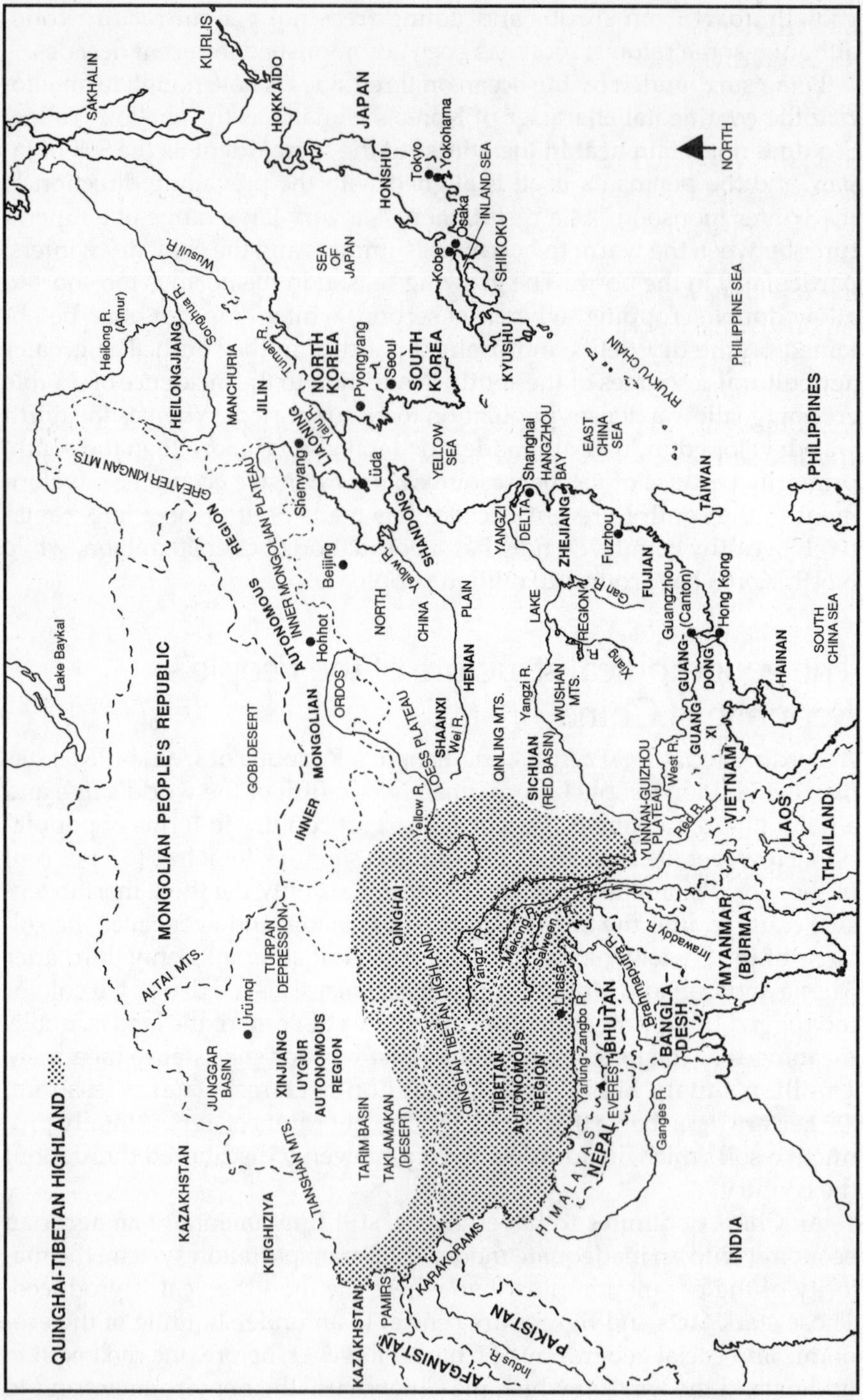

Map 3.2 East Asia

to have an overview of the physical structure and climatic features of the large and diverse territory controlled by the PRC.

The far west: Tibet and Xinjiang

That part of the cold and dry 'Roof of the World' contained in the PRC, the massive Qinghai-Tibetan Highland, is composed of several mountain ranges and plateaux which extend over 2.2 million square kilometres at an average altitude of over 4000 metres. That is high enough to produce arctic-like tundra conditions thousands of kilometres south of where they occur elsewhere at more normal elevations. Its central area contains numerous glaciers on the crests of ranges that often exceed 6000 or even 7000 metres, while the valleys often contain salt lakes, as only the southern and eastern portions of the Highland drain exteriorly. Although it does not match one's normal idea of what a desert is, because it is high and cold rather than low and hot, much of the Qinghai-Tibetan Highland should be classified as such because it supports little vegetation or other life.

> There are a series of mountain-ringed basins to the north of the Highland that receive virtually no rainfall. The mountain streams that flow into them, produced by the melting of sparse winter snows, have no outlet to any ocean, and eventually disappear into the deserts in their centres, such as the vast Taklimakan, a sandy desert which covers 330 000 square kilometres of the Tarim Basin. An eastern extension of the mighty Tianshan mountain range separates the Tarim Basin and the much lower and somewhat wetter Junggar Basin (Dzungaria) in the northwest of the Xinjiang Uygur Autonomous Region, which has a largely pastoral economy. Just to the east of those mountains, but surrounded by branch ranges, lies the Turpan (Turfan) Depression, the lowest point of which is a salt lake 154 metres below sea level. It is surrounded by gobi, a desert surface of stony gravel, which extends far to the east into the Inner Mongolian Autonomous Region, which itself lies along the southern circumference of the huge Gobi Desert itself in Mongolia proper, aptly named for its desolate surface.

Despite the barrenness and/or ruggedness of most of the western portion of the PRC discussed so far, which comprises roughly 60 per cent of the total land area of the country, it supports around 25 million people. However, the vast majority of them live in widely scattered pockets where, for one reason or another, agriculture is possible. There are a few nomadic pastoralists in western Tibet who take herds to mountain pastures in the summer, and other Tibetan pastoralists in western Qinghai. However, apart from the less than 100 000 Tibetans who live in the city of Lhasa, and others who inhabit a few other modest-sized towns, most of the 4.6 million Tibetans are peasant farmers who cultivate barley and a few other crops in isolated places as high as 3500 metres above sea level.

Although few Han, or ethnic Chinese, live in the Tibetan Autonomous Region apart from those in government or military service, about two-fifths of the approximately 15 million people living in the Xinjiang Uygur Autonomous Region are Han. Most of them have migrated or have been sent to the region since 1949. Many of them live in or in the vicinity of Ürümqi, a city of over a million inhabitants, nearby Shihezi city with a concentration of over half a million, and a number of other urban centres with populations between 100 000 and 300 000, making Xinjiang one of the most highly urbanised parts of the PRC. The indigenous Uygurs, who are a Turkic-speaking agricultural people numbering over 7 million, largely inhabit oases in the southern rim of the Junggar Basin and the western rim of the Tarim Basin, which are watered by underground channels carrying snow-melt from the nearby mountains to their irrigated fields. There are also around a million pastoralists in northern Xinjiang, such as the Turkic-speaking Kazaks and Kirghiz in the mountains west and north of the Junggar Basin.

The question must surely arise as to why the Tibetan and originally largely Turkic-speaking areas just discussed are today part of the People's Republic of China. Answers vary depending on their source, but a short one from a historical point of view is that the Chinese Communist Party (CCP), like the Nationalists before it, regards most of the territories that were still part of the Qing Dynasty (Manchu Empire) when it collapsed in 1911 to be part of its country, and has managed to reform military and political control over most of it. The major exception is the State of Mongolia (the Mongolian People's Republic from 1924 to 1991), occupying the territory that was once known as 'Outer Mongolia', which became an independent country in the 1920s under Soviet sponsorship.

Inner Mongolia

There is one other peripheral part of the PRC that should be discussed in conjunction with the mountains and deserts of the western 60 per cent or so of the country described so far, and that is the Inner Mongolian Autonomous Region, which was actually established in 1947, although its extent has varied from time to time, particularly during the Cultural Revolution of the 1960s and 1970s. It now extends from the Greater Khingan Mountains in Manchuria, across the Inner Mongolian Plateau north and west of Beijing, and on around the southern perimeter of the Gobi Desert almost to Xinjiang. Its northern boundary with the Mongolian People's Republic was only established definitively in 1962. The extremely dry western third is virtually uninhabited, while the Mongol pastoralists who once moved their herds across the plateau have now been settled and many have become agriculturalists. A large number of the nearly 5 million Mongols in the PRC in fact live to the north and northeast of Beijing. Some four-fifths of the total Inner Mongolian population of over 20 million are now Han Chinese, who farm irrigated areas along the upper bend of the Yellow River north of the Ordos Desert and mostly dry fields in the southern tiers of counties to the east of Hohhot, just to the north of the remnants of the Great Wall.

The so-called Great Wall of China, which according to the nonsensical imagination of some anonymous nineteenth century European was the only feature on Earth hypothetically large enough to be discerned from the moon, has always been a varying combination of a number of separate structures with numerous branches and parallel arms, and even in its heyday during the fifteenth and sixteenth centuries would have made less of a mark on the Earth's surface than a typical modern divided highway. Due to neglect during subsequent centuries, it has long since deteriorated into a series of low mounds, except where it has recently been restored as a tourist attraction near Beijing. Although not very successful as a military barrier, at least in the long term, various sections of the wall did run along the approximate long-term average dividing line between two ecologically distinct economies, separating pastoralism and agriculture. The wall's presence amplified their divergence, enhancing the trade in agricultural products and metals to the north and animal products and horses to the south.

'China proper' and the minority nationalities in the south

The wall thus formed the northern boundary of what was once called 'China proper', a term that applied to the eighteen provinces that once comprised the Ming Dynasty's (A.D. 1368–1644) territories and distinguished them from the remainder of the much larger domains of the following Qing, or Manchu, Dynasty (A.D. 1644–1911), which were regarded as 'outer China' by Westerners.

There was (and to a certain extent there still is) a frontier between Chinese farmers and indigenous peoples in south China as well as in the north, but instead of being sharply demarcated by a fortified wall dividing fundamentally different ecological adaptations, it was delimited largely by altitude. For some 2000 years Han Chinese have moved over the southern mountain ranges and settled in low-lying river valleys where their agricultural technology could produce higher yields than that the technology of the indigenous peoples. Although originally small in numbers, these pioneer Chinese farmers, protected by Imperial garrisons and ruled by Confucian bureaucrats, exerted a strong, if not irresistible, assimilative force on the locals, many of whom through intermarriage and acculturation eventually merged with or became indistiguishable from the Han Chinese.

The Sinicisation of indigenous peoples began early enough in Guangdong and Fujian Provinces, which in addition do not contain any extensive, agriculturally suitable highlands, so that apart from around

600 000 members of the She minority nationality living in Fujian and Zhejiang, and the more than a million Li on Hainan Island (formally made into a province in its own right in 1988), there are no clearly identifiable large communities of non-Han minority peoples left in southeast China.

The situation is quite different in the higher and more extensive mountains to the west and the rugged terrain in the upper reaches of the West River drainage system in southern China. The highland areas of central, southern and southwestern China contain a large number of minority nationalities with an aggregate population of nearly 50 million. Many of them are highly Sinicised, particularly the 15.5 million Zhuang in Guangxi Province, the 5.7 million Tujia in the Wushan Mountains, and the 1.6 million Bai in west-central Yunnan. Others, particularly those living in the higher altitudes like many of the 6.5 million Yi, have largely avoided or resisted assimilating with the Han. The significance of altitude in segregating people with different ethnic identities and ecological specialisations is particularly apparent in the steep river valleys of western Yunnan, where a number of nationalities are sometimes stacked like layers in a cake with the Tibetans farming at the highest altitudes and the Chinese usually occupying the available low areas, except for those where the Dai, ethnically Thai rice growers numbering around a million, have long been established.

Manchuria

The only extensive and relatively productive agricultural region of the PRC that was not part of 'China proper' is in the three northeastern provinces of Liaoning, Jilin and Heilongjiang, sometimes known collectively to foreigners as Manchuria. Although Han Chinese were supposed to be excluded by the Manchu government from the area beyond the portion of the Great Wall northeast of Beijing, some farmers had long been established to its north. As the Qing Dynasty became more and more Sinicised and Manchu military power became more and more ineffectual, increasing numbers of Chinese trickled into what was officially designated as the Manchus' tribal reserve. With the collapse of the Qing Dynasty in 1911, the trickle of Han Chinese infiltrating the Northeastern Plain became a flood of pioneering farmers from the North China Plain and the Shandong Peninsula, driven by the grinding poverty of their native areas. In the 1920s, more than a million of these Northern Mandarin-speaking immigrants came to Manchuria in some years, opening land within reach of the Russian-built Chinese Eastern Railroad that connected the Trans-Siberian Railroad directly with Vladivostok and the by then Japanese-operated South Manchurian Railroad that linked Port Arthur (Lüda) with Mukden (Shenyang). Chinese immigration slackened off after Japan took over Manchuria in 1931, but the Japanese continued to develop their puppet state of Manchoukuo both agriculturally and industrially, using local iron and coal resources. One reason given for using the atom bomb to compel Japanese surrender in World War II was that Japan's armies in Manchuria were supported by a self-sufficient industrial base and it was believed that they could fight on independently for some years after an invasion and conquest of the Japanese home islands.

Although many of the Japanese factories in Manchuria were carted off to Siberia by the Soviets after World War II, it remains the most industrially developed part of the PRC, in part because of the very dense pre-war rail and road networks. Agriculturally, the Northeastern Plain in central Manchuria is good spring wheat country, having a continental climate with cold winters but warm and relatively moist summers similar to the northern 'wheat belt' in North America. Almost 100 million people now live in the three provinces of Liaoning, Jilin and Heilongjiang.

The physiographic macroregions of 'China proper'

There are a number of different ways that the agricultural core areas of China, with their population of approximately 1000 million people, can be divided into distinctive geographical regions. In the present context of a geographical overview, the most informative regionalisation of China is the one defined by G. William Skinner in his article listed in the 'Guide to further reading'. He divides the agrarian Han Chinese domains into nine large regions, primarily on the basis of their physical structure — hence his term 'physiographic macroregions' (see Map 3.3). They are basically river drainage basins divided from one another by mountains or hills, although there are some anomalies. Due to the twentieth century developments discussed above, Manchuria now constitutes a tenth such division.

Each of the macroregions has a distinct and discrete core area of dense population supported by relatively productive agricultural resources that diminish in the peripheral areas dividing them, where significantly sparser populations are found. The core areas are also less rugged and have considerable advantages over the peripheries in terms of transport, whether by river, canal or road. As a result, in previous centuries the core areas became far more commercialised than the peripheries, and the industrial and economic development of recent decades has taken place in the cities and towns concentrated in them.

The core area of the northwest China macroregion embraces the Loess Plateau on its southern and eastern sides. Loess is a deeply fertile soil with an unusual vertical structure, so terraces can be easily constructed on the hills of the plateau, allowing a relatively dense peripheral population throughout the region despite its erratic and often marginal rainfall. Although it is one of the poorest regions of China, which is experiencing severe erosion and desertification, over 70 million people live in the

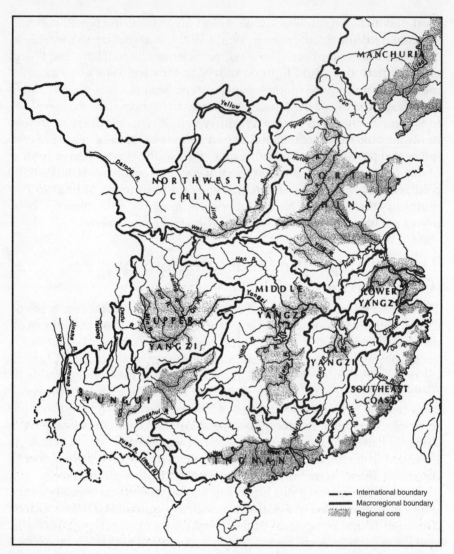

Map 3.3 China's physiographic macroregions, showing major rivers, and the extent of regional core areas, as defined by G.W. Skinner for the late nineteenth century

northwest. They include a majority of the country's 8.6 million Hui, or Chinese Muslims. Northern Mandarin dialects are spoken throughout the northwest as well as in the rest of north China.

The North China Plain, the core area of the North China macroregion, is the largest densely populated area on Earth. Due to the extent and fertility of its alluvial soils, it supports nearly 20 per cent of China's total population, making North China by far the most populous of the macro-regions, with over 320 million people altogether, including over 80 million in hilly Shandong Province. Beijing, China's capital, located on the northern edge of the plain, has experienced a major construction boom in the last decade, and now contains numerous large and tall buildings, completely altering the once low cityscape.

The Red Basin in Sichuan Province, the core of the Upper Yangzi macroregion, is now home to around 100 million people. As a result of its protected position south of the sheltering Qinling Mountains, the Sichuan Basin has a growing season of over 300 days per year everywhere and nearly 350 days in some places. Because the mountains to its southeast are not particularly high, the summer monsoon reliably brings in rainfall adequate to support intensive agriculture. Although a dialect of Mandarin Chinese, Southwestern Mandarin, is spoken everywhere in the province, small communities often use other dialects or languages, such as Hakka or Cantonese, brought in by ancestral settlers who repopulated the area in the seventeenth century following internecine genocide.

The 'lake region' in the central basin of the Yangzi River contains numerous lakes linked to the river. These act as natural flood-control reservoirs, although their function in that regard has been significantly impaired in recent decades by land reclamation projects. The core areas of two macroregions are contained in this 'rice bowl' of China, which produces significant surpluses of this basic food crop. The Middle Yangzi region, the periphery of which extends northwest into southern Shaanxi and Henan Provinces and southwest into Guizhou Province, is the second largest in terms of area as well as population, supporting nearly 130 million people altogether. The Gan Yangzi region is the smallest, being roughly equivalent to the province of Jiangxi, which had a population of 67 million in 1990. The Eastern Mandarin dialect is spoken along the Yangzi River and in the large cities in both regions, but distinctive Han Chinese languages, Gan and Xiang, are spoken in the peripheral parts of the river systems of the same names south of the two large lakes. The upper reaches of tributaries of the western rivers south of the Yangzi are inhabited by minority nationalities such as the Tujia (5.7 million), the Miao (most of their 7.4 million) and the Dong (2.5 million).

The lower Yangzi macroregion, home to some 93 million people, has a core area that encompasses the Yangzi Delta and extends to the south to encircle Hangzhou Bay. The Wu language is spoken south of the Yangzi. Although population densities in the core are very high, the Lower Yangzi macroregion is the most prosperous part of China, due in part to the long growing season and ample water, but also to the efficiency of its traditional water-borne transport system. The great metropolis of Shanghai grew from an insignificant eighteenth century administrative centre to become China's largest city in the nineteenth century under the treaty port system, and then became the most highly industrialised city in China during the twentieth century.

The Southeast Coast macroregion comprises the southern part of Zhejiang, all of Fujian and the eastern part of Guangdong Provinces. It has a population of around 63 million, concentrated in the most densely populated pockets in China (exceeding 1500 per square kilometre in some instances) spread along the rugged coast. As might be expected from its fragmented terrain, the Southeast Coast is the most linguistically diverse part of China, having a number of indigenous languages divided into Northern and Southern Min groups, the latter including Hailam spoken on the island of Hainan in addition to Hokkien (the pronunciation of Fujian in that language).

Lacking any potential for agricultural development in the extremely hilly interior, the Chinese of the Southeast Coast looked outwards to the sea for alleviation of the constant pressure of overpopulation. Drawing on a long tradition of coastal fishing, the Southern Min speakers in particular became the coastal traders and seafarers (and part-time pirates) of China, who established trading settlements in many parts of Southeast Asia several centuries ago. They were the ancestors of the hybrid communities of partially acculturated Chinese which played such an important role in the nineteenth-century commercial development of Southeast Asia. They were joined by Cantonese and Hakka (descendants of Gan speakers who migrated over the South China Hills) in the greatly increased emigration of overseas Chinese in the late nineteenth and early twentieth centuries.

There are two macroregions in South China: Lingnan (south of the mountains), comprising the West, North and East River drainage systems plus Hainan Island, with a population of nearly 100 million; and the comparatively sparsely populated Yungui, centred on the plateau region to the far west, containing around 65 million. The Cantonese-speaking core area of Lingnan is centred on the very densely populated Pearl River (Zhujiang) Delta area south of Guangzhou (Canton), where there is now very rapid development due to investment in factories by capitalists from nearby Hong Kong and overseas.

The upper reaches of the West River system in the Guangxi Zhuang Autonomous Region are largely inhabited by minority nationalities, such as the Zhuang themselves (15.5 million) and the Yao (2.1 million). Apart from the largely Han-inhabited core area on the plateau where Southwestern Mandarin is spoken, the Yungui macroregion is the home of large numbers of minority nationalities of many varieties, including the Yi (6.5 million), who are found scattered throughout, and the Bouyei (or Buyi, 2.5 million), who live in Guizhou. Yunnan Province has the largest number of distinct nationalities, some 24 in all, including the Bai (1.6 million), the Hani (1.25 million) and the Dai (1 million).

The province of Taiwan

Because it is of recent volcanic origin and experiences frequent small earthquakes, the island of Taiwan geologically belongs to the 'Rim of Fire' that surrounds the Pacific Basin, even though it was linked with the mainland during the last Ice Age. The central spine of Taiwan consists of rugged mountains, some of which are nearly 4000 metres high, while there are narrow alluvial plains in the west and small basins in the north that are home to the vast majority of the now-highly urbanised population of more than 20 million. Although the island of Taiwan lies only a hundred kilometres or so from the coast of Fujian Province, for reasons that are not entirely clear it only began to be settled by significant numbers of Han Chinese immigrants after the Dutch established a fort in the southern part of the island in the early seventeenth century.

After Qing imperial administration was established, increasing numbers of Hokkien-speaking pioneer settlers Sinicised and absorbed some of the indigenous Malayo-Polynesians and drove others up into the mountains. During the nineteenth century, the Hokkiens were joined by some Hakkas, many of whom came from Guangdong. Taiwan began to develop commercially during its period as a Japanese colony from 1895 to 1945 due to improvements in its transportation infrastructure, but recent decades of industrial development have transformed its economy into one of Asia's strongest and most advanced. The one thing that the Nationalist government (which retreated to the island after its defeat in 1949) and the Chinese communists can readily agree on is that the province of Taiwan is an inalienable part of China.

Insular and peninsular Southeast Asia

As recently as 10 000 years ago, before the continental glaciers of the last Ice Age melted away, the present islands of Sumatra, Java and Bali, along with Borneo and the Malay Peninsula, were part of a broad land area, the Sunda Shelf, which extended southwards from the mainland. The Philippine archipelago was one of its island outliers, while the Maluku Islands to the east were associated with the Sahul, the name used to refer to the prehistoric combination of New Guinea and Australia. The two prehistoric land areas were never themselves connected, thus preserving the unique Australasian fauna, although the biological divide called 'Wallace's Love' lies between Bali and Lombok in the Lesser Sunda Islands chain rather than between Timor and Australia where the geological division occurs.

The Philippines

As the mountains that define the Philippine islands are generally lower than those of much of the rest of insular and peninsular Southeast Asia, when the sea levels rose the land surface in that region became much more fragmented, producing the hundreds of islands that make up the country. The major lowlands, which were just barely too high to be inundated at present sea levels, are on the main northern island of Luzon to the north of Manila and in the northeastern valley between the central cordillera and the fringing mountains along the east coast. The major southern island of Mindanao is largely hilly or mountainous, and the second largest urban area in the country is Cebu City on the rather small central island of the same name. Ninety per cent of the population of over 60 million are Christians, due to the long history of Spanish colonisation. They grow rice in the lowlands or inhabit the cities, and speak one or more of the nine major Malayo-Polynesian languages indigenous to the islands, although up to 10 per cent of them have some Chinese ancestry. Some 5 per cent of the population belong to a wide variety of hill tribes, while another 5 per cent are Muslims living on the islands surrounding the Sulu Sea, which link the archipelago to the large island of Borneo.

Malaysia

The northwestern coastal region of Borneo was once occupied by a number of independent Muslim sultanates. The small Sultanate of Brunei continues as an independent country, largely because of its vast oil wealth, while Sabah and Sarawak have become part of Malaysia. Only 20 per cent of the 2.5 million or so inhabitants of East Malaysia are Muslim Malays, while approximately 45 per cent are indigenous Malayo-Polynesian tribespeople such as the Dyaks and Iban. Overseas Chinese make up the remaining 30 per cent or so, and are concentrated in the cities or on small holdings nearby. Chinese-dominated trading relations, channelled via Singapore, are the major link between East and West Malaysia.

The population of the lower part of the Malay Peninsula belonging to Malaysia is approximately 15 million. Only slightly more than half (55 per cent) are Bumiputras, or 'Sons of the Soil', the term used for in-digenous Malay Muslims. They are nonetheless still politically dominant, due to their traditional control over government institutions. The over-seas Chinese, who make up 35 per cent of the population, are economi-cally dominant due to their control over most commercial activities. They are concentrated on the western side of the peninsula in the states along the Straits of Melaka. This is the most developed part of the country and it contains the capital, Kuala Lumpur, which has grown greatly in recent decades. Around 9 per cent of the population have South Asian ancestry; a proportion of these are engaged in plantation labour. As little as 1 per cent of the population are tribal hill peoples inhabiting the mountainous interior, which is not suitable for plantation agriculture.

Indonesia

Extending around 5000 kilometres from its eastern border of Irian Jaya on the island of New Guinea to the northwestern tip of Sumatra, the island nation of Indonesia ranks among the world's most extensive, if not largest, countries. In addition to the abovementioned extremities, Indonesian territory includes the larger portion of the island of Borneo (which the Indonesians call Kalimantan), Sulawesi (The Celebes) and nearby small islands, the Maluku (Moluccas) Group in Indonesia's east, the Lesser Sunda Islands to the north of Australia (now including all of Timor) and last but not least, the island of Java. Although not a particularly large island, Java is by far the most centrally important one in Indonesia for a variety of reasons, most of which are related to its ample rainfall evenly distributed throughout the year and the widespread volcanic soils that are conducive to rice agriculture.

Near the end of the eighteenth century the islands previously dominated by the Dutch East India Company (the 'East Indies') were taken under the Dutch colonial umbrella. At that time the population of Java, which came under more or less direct Dutch control, was apparently relatively stable at somewhere around 5 million, although some estimates double that number. However, the island of Java became the focus of Dutch policies designed to increase the production of tropical commercial crops for the world market, which had the side-effect of promoting rapid population growth. By the time the Dutch relinquished control in 1949, the population of Java had risen perhaps tenfold to an estimated 50 million, around two-thirds of the total in the entire new Republic of Indonesia.

In the mid-1990s, the population of the whole country was around 190 million , of whom 90 per cent were Muslim. The five other officially sanctioned religions account for almost all of the remainder, there being the Hindus on Bali and Protestants like the Toba-Bataks, each of which make up around 2 per cent of the total. The Chinese, who make up perhaps 2.5–3 per cent of the Indonesian population, are usually, for official purposes anyway, registered as adherents of either Buddhism or Confucianism although a significant number (perhaps a third) are Catholics. A large majority of the Muslims are lowland wet-rice agriculturalists, such as the Javanese themselves, the Sudanese from western Java, and the Madurese and the Minangkabau on Sumatra. There are, however, also a fair number of 'coastal Malays', in eastern Sumatra and western and southwestern Kalimantan and the Makassarese and Buginese from Sulawesi, who inhabit the areas where the old independant sultanates had existed.

The countries of mainland Southeast Asia

Unlike the Malayo-Polynesians of the insular and peninsular countries of Southeast Asia, who were, apart from the Javanese and their 'Hinduised' neighbours, oriented towards the sea and trade across it, the lowland peoples of mainland Southeast Asia were river-oriented rice growers. Derivative, but ultimately distinctive, civilisations developed in the basins and delta regions of the major rivers, where broad expanses of alluvial soils remained unsubmerged by the post-Ice Age inundation of the rest of the Sunda Shelf and the present Gulf of Tonkin.

Vietnam

The Red River Valley in northern Vietnam (Tonkin) was conquered by the first emperor of all China in the third century B.C. It remained under the control of the following Han Dynasty and was also a part of a number of subsequent ones, giving Vietnamese culture a decided Confucian and Mahayana (or Chinese) Buddhist cast, despite a long tradition of resistance to Chinese rule. Annam, the coastal region along the east side of the Annamitic Cordellera, contains small areas of soil suitable for wet-rice cultivation; these were the locus of the traditional Vietnamese state that was, most of the time, successful in resistance to Chinese conquest. The Vietnamese, or Annamese, eventually reached the Mekong Delta, which was not heavily populated by the indigenous Chams, largely due to swampy conditions, although there was a long history of military conflict between them and the Vietnamese from Annam as well as the Khmers centred in the Lower Mekong Basin up-river. The French established themselves in Cochin-China, as they called the Delta region, in the mid-nineteenth century, and promoted drainage projects in order to increase rice production, encouraging increased settlement by Vietnamese, whom they regarded as being more industrious than the Chams or Khmers.

As a result, a bi-polar distribution of the Vietnamese population developed, with major concentrations in the Red River and the Mekong Deltas, which are separated by nearly 1000 kilometres of the relatively spottily inhabited Annamese coast. The Tonkin Basin around Hanoi is very intensely cultivated and elaborately irrigated from distributaries of the Red River, and supports one of the world's densest, and poorest, populations. The Mekong Delta around Saigon in the south supported roughly half the population on twice the area, and has been a rice surplus region, although yields are lower than in the north, partly because irrigation is far less developed. Around 85 per cent of more than 60 million people in the whole country are ethnically Vietnamese, with another 10 per cent or more belonging to a number of linguistically distinctive hill tribes in the cordillera. The remaining 3 per cent or so are Chinese, who were largely concentrated in Cholon, Saigon's commercial sister city.

Ethnic Chinese have comprised a majority of the refugees who left Vietnam by boat in the last decade or so.

Cambodia

By as early as the first century A.D., Hindic influence extended as far as the Mekong River, resulting ultimately in Theravada (Hinayana) Buddhism being established in all the countries of mainland Southeast Asia apart from Sinicised Vietnam and Islamic Malaysia. Khmer civilisation, which reached its height in the twelfth century city of Angkor, has long occupied the Lower Mekong Basin in Cambodia, which is noteworthy for the natural flood control system that annually fills and then drains the Great Lake in its centre as the Tonle Sap River, which links it with the Mekong, reverses its flow when the season changes from wet to dry and back again. Irrigation in the basin is largely uncontrolled, being reliant on the annual floods, and as a result rice yields are not high. Nor is cultivation intense, there being only limited areas of high quality soil; consequently Cambodia is not densely populated. Although reliable census figures have not been available for many years, due to the political and military situation in the country, it has been estimated that in the mid-1980s the population was between 6 and 7 million. Before the massacres of at least a million people associated with the regime of Pol Pot's Khmer Rouge in the 1970s (see Chapter 42), 85 to 90 per cent of the people were Khmer, 5 to 7 per cent were Vietnamese, and 7 to 8 per cent were Chinese, with the remaining 2 to 3 per cent being Chams or Thais.

Thailand and Laos

Thailand comprises a number of distinct regions, including the hilly to mountainous north, the central basin drained by the Chao Phraya and its tributaries, the peninsular region (Kra) in the south and the Upper Mekong Basin (Korat Plateau) in what is called the northeast because of its direction from the capital, Bangkok, located at the head of the Gulf of Thailand in the Chao Phraya Delta. Apart from the peninsula, which has a maritime monsoonal climate like insular Southeast Asia, Thailand, like Cambodia, has distinct wet and dry seasons produced by the monsoon effect. Most of the Chao Phraya region floods annually, providing both the water and the fertility for extensive rice growing, which is the basis of the economy.

In recent decades, Bangkok has experienced tremendous growth and development. This has transformed it into a major metropolis, the only major city in the country of nearly 55 million people. Eighty to 85 per cent of the population are ethnic Thais, with most minorities having the ethnicity of neighbouring nations, as there are less than a million tribal peoples. The exception is the Chinese, who have been coming to Thailand for many centuries. Unlike many other parts of Southeast Asia, where they have remained distinct for one reason or another, the Chinese immigrants in Thailand have tended to assimilate in the course of a generation or two, so that although up to 10 per cent of the Thai population have some Chinese ancestry, those who still regard themselves as ethnically Chinese are far smaller in number.

Most of Laos is mountainous, the northern bulge consisting of an extension of the Yunnan Plateau and the southern leg extending along the western slopes of the Annamitic Cordellera. There is a small area of alluvial soil suitable for rice growing around the old royal capital of Luang Prabang on the Mekong in the central north, and another near the present capital, Vientiane, but most agricultural land in Laos is found in small pockets in the Upper Mekong basin across the river from northeast Thailand. The Laotians are closely related in language, culture and religion to the northeastern Thais, and the country as it is today came into being when the French detached a portion of the northeastern Thai-speaking region in the late nineteenth century. As soils in the Upper Mekong Basin are generally very poor, and irrigation is difficult or impossible, only sparse populations can find a meagre livelihood. Northeast Thailand is by far the poorest part of that country, while Laos has less than 5 million people, 10 to 20 per cent of whom are members of various hill tribes practising shifting cultivation. As many as 2 per cent were Chinese before the Indochinese War.

Conclusion: Asian population patterns

The recurring theme of the foregoing, necessarily brief geographical descriptions of the countries of Eastern Asia and the regions of China is that populations are concentrated where grain and other food are produced abundantly. Such a pattern is opposite to that of places like Australia or North America, while that of Western Europe is only partially similar due to two centuries of industrialisation, transport improvements and food imports. Industrial development in Asia, which has only occurred during the last century or so in Japan and for less than half a century in most other places, has not had time to thoroughly modify long existing agrarian population distribution patterns despite recent massive population growth.

The major exception to the generalisation that Asian populations are concentrated on alluvial soils, in either broad basins drained by large rivers such as those in the interior of China 'proper' or relatively small or narrow deposits produced by smaller rivers and streams, is the island of Java in Indonesia which has widely distributed and rich volcanic soils. However, it also fits the general pattern in which each distinct area or set of contiguous areas of highly productive soil supports a more or less culturally homogenous population speaking the same language that is today under the control of the same national government. The mechanisms that have produced those national cultural and linguistic uniformities are largely historical conquest and subsequent assimilation of subjugated peoples to the dominant elites. Only in the less productive, hilly or mountainous peripheral areas does a significant amount of cultural and linguistic variability persist among groups of people now largely regarded as 'minorities' within their national contexts.

Guide to further reading

Cannon, Terry & Jenkins, Allen (eds), *The Geography of Contemporary China: The Impact of Deng Xiaoping's Decade*, Routledge, London, 1990
The twelve chapters in this British-edited volume range over most subjects of particular concern to geographers, but also include historical, demographic, economic and security perspectives.

Courtenay, Percy P., *Geographic Themes in South-east Asia*, Longman Cheshire, Melbourne, 1986
Although designed as a secondary education text, this is a useful introduction to the entire region for anyone with no prior background. It contains numerous photographs, maps and charts, as well as definitions of technical terms.

Noh, Toshio & Kimura John C. (eds), *Japan: a Regional Geography of an Island Nation*, Teikoku-Shoin Co., Tokyo, 1989
Translated from Japanese, this profusely illustrated volume is replete with detailed thematic regional and local maps. It tends to take an encyclopedic approach to the various parts of Japan.

Skinner, G. William, 'Presidential Address: The Structure of Chinese History', *Journal of Asian Studies*, vol. XLIV, no. 2, February, 1985, pp. 271–92
The utility of the macroregional approach to the study of China is demonstrated in an examination of regional differences in cycles of economic development and decline during the dynastic period of Chinese history.

II | Traditions

4 | Basic social structures and family systems

Introduction

This chapter attempts to show how domestic and communal life was organised in Asia in traditional times. It has three objectives. Firstly, it intends to familiarise readers with the variety of ways in which Asian people have organised their lives in traditional society. Secondly, it tries to show some of the ideas and values lying behind these different forms of domestic and community organisation in traditional Asia. Finally, it aims to introduce basic conceptual tools essential to an understanding of various forms of domestic and community organisation in Asian societies.

The chapter presents a generalised picture of the situation which existed before modernisation affected the lives of people in Asia. Here caution is called for, since what we sometimes read about other people's lives does not necessarily correspond to what they have actually *done* in daily life. Descriptions of the lives of a people are often mixed with their ideals — in other words, what they think they *ought* to do. To complicate the matter further, some of the ideals presented may not even have been the ideals of the ordinary people, but the ideals of the upper class or the elite of the time. We try to distinguish these two orders of 'reality' in this chapter, for they are conceptually different from each other.

This chapter is written on the basis of available anthropological literature. Discussions are limited to four Asian societies, namely Javanese society in the first half of this century, Minangkabau society (in central Sumatra) in the pre-twentieth century period, Chinese society before the twentieth century and Japanese society from the late nineteenth to the early twentieth centuries. The economies of all four societies were primarily derived from labour-intensive agriculture, and in this sense they share a common ground. Yet these societies are quite different from one another in their domestic and community organisation. The above time indications are by no means definitive, since no society is static; they should therefore be taken as a rough reference to the time framework of the societies discussed in this chapter, where the ethnographic present tense is sometimes used.

It is first necessary to clarify what we mean by *family* and how it differs from *household*. In the West, family and household are very often used interchangeably, a family meaning a nuclear family sharing a living. The concept of 'family', however, is not identical to that of 'household'. Firstly, family is a concept based on *kinship* (relationship through blood, marriage and adoption), while the concept of household is based on propinquity of residence or co-residence. Secondly, family and household do not always correspond to the same content. There are societies where a nuclear family (one type of family) does not form a household, as we will see later in the case of the Minangkabau, and there are other societies where a household contains members other than family, such as apprentices and servants as in the case of the traditional Japanese *ie*. In this chapter, the term *family* means a group of people who are related through kinship, but who do not necessarily share a common residence. *Household*, on the other hand, refers to a group of people who share a residence, in particular a hearth.

Family and household in Javanese society

Javanese people are the largest ethnic group in Indonesia. They inhabit the central and eastern regions of the island of Java, the most populous island in Indonesia. The majority live in village communities and engage in wet-rice agriculture, though in the mountainous interior they cultivate manioc in dry fields. They have a distinct language and culture, and the majority adhere to a non-puritan kind of Islam.

The basic unit of Javanese society is the nuclear family. When a woman and man marry, a nuclear family is created, and it expands when their children (natural and/or adopted) are added to it (see Figure 4.1). Marriage in Java is, in the majority of cases, *monogamous*, but *polygyny* (where a husband is shared by two or more wives) is permitted and, although rare, carries prestige. In the Javanese marriage an emphasis is placed on the establishment of a new, autonomous unit. Therefore, a married couple normally set up their household away from either of the parents' households. This practice is called *neolocal* (post-marital) residence. In general, two married couples seldom share the same house in Javanese society. Due to economic or other reasons, however, a young couple may delay establishing their own independent household by living in either of the parents' houses for a while. When they live with the husband's parents and share a living with them, the practice is called *virilocal* residence, while the practice of living with the wife's parents is called *uxorilocal* residence. Preference for *neolocal* residence in Javanese society results in the popular occurrence of nuclear-family households. The nuclear-family household is not only the most frequently observed form of domestic organisation, but also the ideal form in Javanese society.

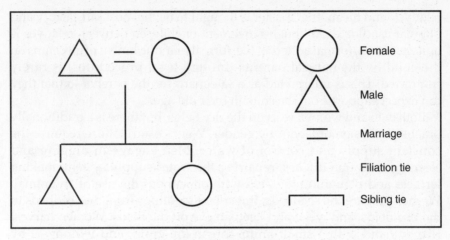

Figure 4.1 The nuclear family

Most marriages are arranged by parents. They start to seek a suitable marriage partner for their daughter soon after her first menstruation. Although the age of marriage for girls appears to be gradually rising, it is reported that in the 1950s most Javanese girls were married by the age of 16 or 17. Very few women remained unmarried in traditional Javanese society. Universality of marriage also applied to Javanese men, though boys usually waited until they could support themselves economically.

In the process of finding an appropriate marriage partner, parents take the wishes of their children into account. This is important, because the child's acceptance of the parents' choice of a marriage partner is interpreted as acceptance of their future responsibility towards the parents in old age.

In Javanese society a marriage partner ideally is chosen from a family of a comparable rank or class and of the same religious background, as inequality in status and a different religious orientation are thought to produce constant friction. There are very few kinship prohibitions in selecting a marriage partner, and step-siblings may marry. This suggests that the Javanese marriage encourages an *endogamous* tendency. *Endogamy* means that one is prescribed to marry someone from one's own group. (A group may be defined in terms of kinship, territory or other criteria.) *Exogamy*, on the other hand, prescribes that a marriage partner should come from outside one's own group. In Java, *exogamous* unions occur in the urban areas where people with different backgrounds and affiliations are likely to meet. Upper-class people, however, are in favour of *endogamous* marriages, as they wish to retain their status, wealth and tradition within their own group.

Children are very much desired by Javanese people. A childless couple, therefore, may ask a relative to lend them one of their children temporarily or permanently. It is felt better to lend or borrow a child between female relatives, and the mother's sister is thought to be the most satisfactory and popular candidate. Although movement of children between relatives is quite common, formal adoption (i.e. formal relinquishment of all claims on the child by the natural parents through legal procedures) is rarely contracted. This is interpreted as a safeguard for the parents so that they can expect support from the child in their old age.

Both men and women work in the rice fields, but there is a traditionally practised division of labour by gender. Wet-rice agriculture requires the constant supply and control of water. Men engage in digging and cleaning irrigation ditches, repairing the water supply system, making terraces and ploughing the field with or without the use of an animal. Women prepare the seedbeds, transplant seedlings from the seedbeds to the rice fields, and weed and keep an eye on the fields. Women harvest rice by hand with a small knife, thresh the grain, and winnow it by tossing it in the air.

A clear division of labour also exists in the Javanese household. Domestic work is all performed by the wife. This includes going to market, preparing meals, washing and ironing, sewing children's clothes and the care of children, as well as the financial management of the household. Javanese men are reported to be emotionally as well as practically dependent on women. Most Javanese men give all or a greater proportion of their earnings to their wives to manage, and ask for spending money. This pattern is endorsed by a common belief that women are endowed with thrift and foresight. Few men can actually manage and run the household satisfactorily by themselves. The above indicates that the Javanese wife has an equal or even dominant voice in decision-making in the household. In family relationships, an emphasis is placed on maternal connection (i.e. a woman maintains a close relationship with her family). Male relatives, on the other hand, tend to avoid each other. Thus a father and his grown-up son and adult brothers are not very close.

Divorce is quite prevalent in Javanese society, with nearly half the marriages ending in divorce. There are several reasons why divorce is so common in Javanese society. It carries no stigma, whereas spinsterhood does. As it is embarrassing for Javanese parents to have an unmarried daughter who is old enough to be married, such parents arrange a trial marriage for her in order to remove the stigma of spinsterhood. This kind of marriage is likely to end in divorce, but at least the woman was initiated and has become freer than before. Divorce is also quite easy to obtain.

There are two more important reasons for the prevalence of divorce. Firstly, Javanese women are not economically dependent on men. Women control the household finances, and participate in cultivation, disposal of produce and financial transactions. Most occupations are also open to Javanese women. A woman can own property (rice field, house, jewellery, etc.) in her own name and can dispose of any of it as she sees appropriate. Legally, Javanese women and men are given equal rights to inherit from either of their parents, although Islamic law allows twice as much inheritance for a man as for a woman. Secondly, Javanese women maintain firm ties with parents and sisters. Therefore, in case of divorce, they can easily go to one of their houses and mobilise their support.

The nuclear-family household is the basic unit of the Javanese village, and two types of family, *family of orientation* (family into which one [ego] was born) and *family of procreation* (family which one [ego] creates by marriage) are the basic kin groups in the life of the Javanese (see Figure 4.2). Members of these two types of family have major obligations towards one another, and they can expect maximum care and support from each other. Beyond these, the significance of kinship ties is very limited in Javanese society. Rights and obligations towards kin beyond these two types of family are less clearly defined and less strongly sanctioned. As a result, considerable individual variations are observed. It is for this reason that the Javanese village is sometimes described as 'loosely structured' by anthropologists. Despite this 'loose structure', there exists a definite conception of *kindred* (a network of ego-orientated, bilaterally related relatives) among the Javanese. A person's kindred consists of both *consanguineal* (blood) relations and *affinal* (in-law) relations and provides various kinds of aid and assistance when needed — for example, lodging and hospitality, assistance at a circumcision ceremony and so forth. Javanese villagers are also organised on the basis of residential proximity. Maintaining a good relationship with one's neighbours is very important, because neighbours are the ones who provide assistance at times of emergency and for tasks which require help from others. Reciprocity is the principle regulating these neighbourly relationships.

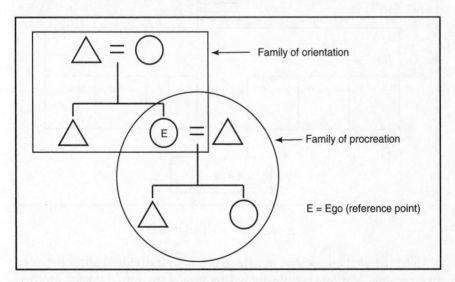

Figure 4.2 Family of orientation and family of procreation

Family and lineage in Minangkabau society

The highlands of western-central Sumatra are the homeland of the Minangkabau people, the fourth largest ethnic group in Indonesia. Minangkabau people live in village communities, engage in paddy-rice agriculture, and practise Islam. The Minangkabau village consists of various levels and units of *matrilineal* groupings. At the highest and largest level, there exists a *matrilineal clan* (a group of related lineages which share a common unknown female ancestor); at the next level is a *matrilineal lineage* (a consanguineal kin group whose members can trace their descent through females to a female ancestor); and below them there are matrilineal sub-lineages. People of a matrilineal sub-lineage live together in one house (*rumah adat*) which forms the basic economic unit of Minangkabau society.

Minangkabau people's daily life is centred around the *rumah adat* (*adat* house) which is commonly known as a long house because of its shape (see Figure 4.3). The *adat* house consists of two parts. The front half of the house is an open area used for dining, lounging and entertaining, holding ceremonies and meetings, and sleeping quarters for children and occasional guests. The back half of the house is partitioned off into small compartments called *bilik*. The size of a *bilik* is about 3 metres by 4 metres. These small cubicles are reserved as sleeping quarters for the female members of the *adat* house, especially for married women and their small children and women of marriageable age. The house could be quite large; the largest standing *adat* house is reported to have twenty *bilik*, but a normal *adat* house has about seven.

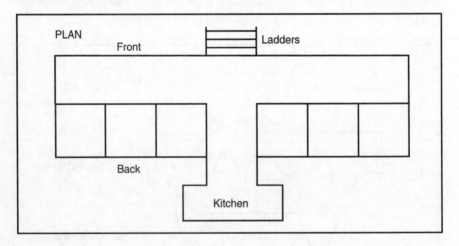

Figure 4.3 Plan of an adat *house*

In Minangkabau society, marriage is not an individual affair between two persons. Various people, including *mamak* (maternal uncle), mother, father and other relatives, participate in the process of selecting a suitable marriage partner. Proposals can be made from either the bride's or the groom's side, depending on the region. The most desirable marriage is between maternal *cross-cousins* (cousins whose connecting parents are sister and brother) — for example, a man marries his *mamak's* daughter (see Figure 4.4). In Minangkabau society, cross-cousins do not belong to the same lineage where *parallel cousins* on the maternal side are members of the same *lineage*, and thus a marriage between them is proscribed (*lineage exogamy*). A marriage which is not accepted by the relatives of a woman is likely to face difficulties later.

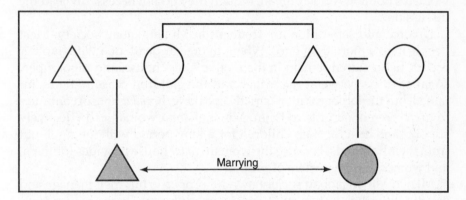

Figure 4.4 Maternal cross-cousin marriage

Traditionally the Minangkabau woman does not leave her *adat* house upon marriage, nor does her husband. Both of them continue to stay in their *adat* houses after marriage (*duolocal residence*). The husband visits his wife at night, and leaves her house in the morning. This assumes that both houses exist in close proximity and hence encourages *village endogamy*. As mentioned above, however, the marriage partner must come from another lineage, violation being severely punished by expulsion from the village community. The husband remains a regular and honoured guest in his wife's house, but he continues to belong to his *adat* house after marriage, and it is to this that his primary allegiance and responsibilities are directed. Therefore, the husband's position in his wife's house is rather marginal.

A newly born infant of the couple automatically becomes a member of the mother's *adat* house. The husband/father's economic and domestic responsibility towards his wife and children is minimal, except for gift giving on ceremonial occasions such as circumcision of his sons and marriage of his children. The wife and children's living is provided by their *adat* house, and the *mamak* is responsible for the conduct and welfare of his sisters and their children (*kemanakan*), and the harmony in the house. The most senior *mamak* in the house assumes the position of the house-head.

Minangkabau women do much of the agricultural work, and are also involved in home industries such as cloth and mat weaving and embroidering. Many also sell agricultural produce and craft products in a village market, and some even travel to an urban centre to do so in a larger market. Women participate extensively in household decision-making. Senior women of the house make most of the day-to-day decisions, which include matters regarding land use, lending and borrowing, and the sale of agricultural produce and handicrafts. Men are consulted in the decisions involving religious ceremonies and lineage matters, but senior women's opinions often prevail, though they do not necessarily lead the discussion.

Divorce and separation are frequent in Minangkabau society. Most people marry more than once. When divorce or death of a wife/mother occurs, her children remain in the mother's *adat* house, and regular personal contacts between the father and the children cease to be maintained, but the father (or more strictly speaking, his *adat* house) continues to give ceremonial gifts to them. Minangkabau women can effectively support and care for their children for a long period without any input from their husbands, because the woman's *adat* house provides for them, and women are the owners of property.

Men in Minangkabau society own no property, but they manage and expand it for their sisters and their sisters' children. There are four ways to obtain access to cultivated land, which is the most valued property in Minangkabau society:

1 by inheritance;
2 by money;
3 by labour; and
4 by gift.

Ancestral land is transmitted through the female line and considered inalienable. Both newly purchased land and land newly opened by a man becomes the ancestral property of his lineage after one generation. Gifts of property generally take place between a man and his children, because otherwise what he has acquired by his own effort goes to his sisters' children (*kemanakan*). If a man wishes to give what he has personally earned to his children, he may arrange it through gift. This arrangement, however, involves the agreement of all parties concerned and an expensive feast.

Men in Minangkabau society do not really have a house or a place of their own. Small boys (after the age of 6 or 7) begin to sleep in a prayer house attached to a village mosque where they learn to recite the Koran at night. They continue to sleep there until they marry. If a man is divorced, or widowed, he again lives in the prayer house. Even in the *adat* house of his origin, day-to-day affairs are carried out by women, which further reinforces his marginality. This lack of roots of the Minangkabau man intensifies in the case of a *mamak* who occupies no position such as the house-head or lineage elder. This marginality of men in Minangkabau society is one of the factors that has facilitated them to migrate or commute to other parts of Indonesia for educational and/or commercial pursuits. The economic opportunities available to men have changed the traditional pattern of marriage, and created a trend towards *uxorilocality* and *neolocality* in recent times, but traditionally important family relationships (i.e. the brother–sister relationship and the *mamak–kamanakan* (maternal uncle–sisters' children) relationship) are still significant.

Family and lineage in traditional China

Kinship provides the fabric of Chinese domestic and community organisation, where a household is the basic unit. The Chinese household is quite different in its structure and operation from those we have examined in the preceding sections. The main feature is the strong father–son relationship, the essential ingredient of which is filial piety. Ideally, the Chinese family forms an extended family household where parents live with their sons and their wives and their male descendants and their families under one roof. Members of this multi-generational extended family household share a common kitchen and finances, and are led by the most senior male. In reality, however, poverty and a high infant and premature mortality rate limited the family size. In addition, personal clashes within the household often resulted in the breaking up of the extended family household when the father died and the headship was transferred to the eldest son. Thus the most commonly observed household types in traditional China were the nuclear-family household and stem-family household. The stem-family household contains two or more nuclear families, but only one married couple per generation (see Figure 4.5).

The primary goals of a Chinese family are continuity and prosperity. Only male children can continue the family line, and transmit family property to succeeding generations. Accordingly, a Chinese family must have a son who continues the family line, performs rituals for the ancestors and provides for the parents in their old age. When a couple is not blessed with a son, the household head must adopt one. The ideal and most preferred adoption pattern is that transacted between *agnatically* related relatives (i.e. female and male descendants by male links from the same male ancestor).

Marriage was all but universal in traditional China. Nearly everyone married before middle age. Parents arranged their children's marriages through a go-between. In most cases young people were not consulted at all, and had not even seen their marriage partner until after the wedding was over. Sometimes children were betrothed before they were born or

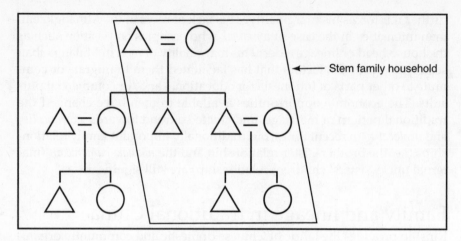

Figure 4.5 The stem family household

when they were small. A bride was chosen from outside the agnatically related people who usually shared the same surname. People with the same surname are believed to have descended from the same unknown ancestor *(clan exogamy)*. Marriage between paternal *parallel cousins* is strictly prohibited *(lineage exogamy)*. This is due to the fact that these cousins belong to a same *patrilineal lineage* (a consanguineal kin group whose members can actually trace their relationship to a common male ancestor through male links). When all of the villagers bear the same surname, a bride must be brought in from another village.

Before marriage is consummated, it is necessary for the husband's family to present a marriage gift to the wife's family. This gift is called *bride-wealth* or *bride-price* in anthropology, and must not be confused with *dowry*, which is a gift from the wife's family to the wife or the marrying couple. The meaning of bride-wealth is twofold. It compensates for the loss of a daughter's labour and fertility to the wife's family, and ensures the wife's and her offspring's status in the husband's family. Therefore, the larger the amount of bride-wealth, the higher the status of the in-marrying wife in the husband's family. Two families usually negotiate over the sum.

Post-marital residence in China is *virilocal* (i.e. the bride is brought into the husband's father's household). Daughters invariably leave their parental household upon marriage. Marriage of the eldest son produces a stem family household. If a family is lucky enough to have raised more than one son and can afford additional bride-wealth for succeeding sons, these other sons also bring their brides into the father's household. Then an extended family household is formed. Ideally a Chinese household should keep expanding in this way, but the death of the parents or the father often results in brothers splitting the estate and the household, thus failing to abide by the ideal.

The ideal of the five-generation extended family household originates in the Confucian teachings which emphasise firstly the father–son relationship and secondly the relationship between the elder and younger brother. Brothers are to work jointly and harmoniously for the welfare of the family as one group. Despite the ideal, personal conflicts and incompatibility within the extended family household often surface after the death of the father. As a result, brothers decide to divide up the family estate into equal pieces, each brother setting up his own nuclear family household.

The husband–wife relationship in the Chinese household is very much undermined by and sacrificed for other more important relationships. A married woman's first and utmost duty is towards her parents-in-law. Neglect of this duty can be a cause for divorce. Gender segregation also exists in the traditional Chinese household. A young wife is trained by her mother-in-law, and placed under her supervision. There is little communication between the wife and the husband. Chinese women existed for the benefit of the family, which placed the main emphasis on males.

This precarious position of the young wife in the husband's parents' household did not result in the prevalence of divorce, however. Legally a wife could have been divorced for almost any reason, but the following circumstances prevented a wife from seeking a divorce, even if she may have wished for one. Firstly, her own family (her parents and brothers) would not welcome her back. Chinese women were from the first day of their life meant to be married off. Secondly, the general public strongly disapproved of divorce and remarriage for women. Thirdly, the bride-wealth had to be returned totally or partially to the husband's family, which may not have been possible because it may have been already expended to acquire a wife for a son of the family. In any case, unmarried or divorced women had no means to support themselves in traditional Chinese society except by becoming a beggar, a prostitute or a nun. The above picture of women in traditional China looks dismal. Nonetheless, a woman's position in the household did improve with the birth of a son. As she matured and produced more sons, her position became firmer and her influence and importance in the household also grew. Recent studies reassessing the abovementioned classical model of Chinese family and kinship point out that departure from this elite model is not uncommon in Chinese villages and that uxorilocal marriage, duolocal marriage and 'small daughter-in-law' marriage had been their custom.

Let us now turn to the community organisation in the Chinese village, where the main mode of production was paddy-rice agriculture. Such villages are found in the southeastern provinces of China, especially Fujian and Guangdong (see Figure 4.6). In these provinces, *lineage* was a way of organising a village community. Therefore, in order to understand community organisation in these provinces, it is best to look at how a lineage functioned in the village.

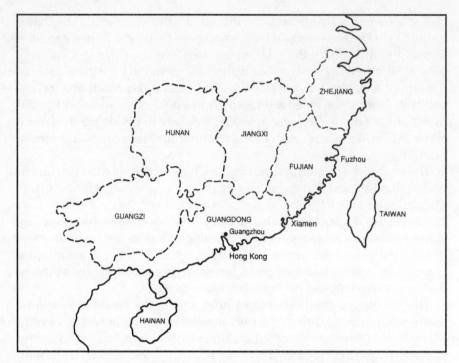

Figure 4.6 Sketch map of southeastern China

Chinese lineage *(zong)* is *patrilineal* or *agnatic*, and is localised. Members of a lineage all lived in one settlement, which sometimes meant that an entire village was composed of a single lineage. In such a case, the village was structured on the basis of consanguineal relationships. A lineage consisted of sub-lineages, each of them represented by a head, and further segmented into branches and smaller units. A man highest in generation and the oldest of his own generation automatically became the head of a lineage. A lineage collectively owned land (lineage trust or estate), and this corporate landholding played an important role in the economy of the village and in keeping lineage members together in the close vicinity. Profits from the lineage trust were used to the best advantage of the group. This included projects such as:

1 expanding and repairing the irrigation system of the area;
2 constructing lineage schools to educate male children in the lineage;
3 building and maintaining temples, shrines and halls for ancestral rituals;
4 performing ancestral worship services;
5 performing other rituals when a need arose (e.g. at the time of drought or flood);
6 digging a well, making a new road, building defensive walls and moats, and any other public works thought to be beneficial.

Lineage leaders organised these projects, mediated disputes, and settled internal conflicts and problems. The lineage protected the members from other lineages, and walls and moats guarded the lineage property from thieves and bandits. In this way, the identity and solidarity of the members were strengthened. As can be seen, the Chinese lineage performed many functions which were economic as well as political, religious and socio-psychological. A large lineage was very advantageous in these respects.

Domestic and community organisation in pre-war Japan

Pre-war traditional Japanese society was built around the unit called the *ie* (the two vowels are pronounced distinctly — *i* as in *'seat'* and *e* as in *'set'*). The *ie* system had developed among the upper stratum (warrior class) of society during the Tokugawa era (1603–1867). The *ie* is defined as a single, unbroken family line including the unborn living and the dead members. The *ie* is a corporate group which persists beyond the present generation. The *ie* has a number of attributes. Firstly, each *ie* has a name, tradition, occupation, property and an ancestral grave and altar. Secondly, each *ie* has a co-residential unit or a household which is usually formed by members related through blood, marriage and/or adoption, but which may also include unrelated people such as servants and apprentices. Thirdly, an *ie* ideally takes a form of stem family household. Fourthly, the *ie* is represented by the head, and its activities are organised under his leadership. The head of the *ie* is responsible for the behaviour and welfare of all the members, manages its property and occupation, and looks after the ancestral graves and tablets.

Since the *ie* must be perpetuated, one of the children (male or female) is designated for the task by remaining in the parents' *ie* throughout his/her life, and bringing his/her spouse into the parents' *ie*. *Virilocal* residence is more common and is preferred to *uxorilocal* residence, though the latter was quite frequent in the Japanese village. An heir apparent (mostly the eldest son) succeeds to the position of the head when the head of the *ie* dies or retires, at which point the status of housewife is also transferred to the younger wife from her mother-in-law. The transfer of these positions normally takes place years (and sometimes decades) after the heir's marriage.

When the *ie* has no children, or all of the children have died prematurely, the head of the *ie* arranges to adopt a son or daughter to continue the *ie*. An adopted child is preferably chosen from related people but may be an unrelated person such as an apprentice or servant who has proven to be hard-working and loyal to the *ie*. When the *ie* has no sons but only daughters, a husband is adopted for one of the daughters. This husband is called *mukoyoshi*, takes the name of his wife's *ie*, and moves into her parents' household (*uxorilocal* residence). Since the husband in the *uxorilocal* marriage is a non-inheriting son of his *ie*, which is usually lower in standing than the wife's *ie*, he resigns himself to the submissive status of adopted husband (*mukoyoshi*), although he eventually succeeds to the household head. When there is some reason for bypassing a son as heir — for example, he is too young, sickly or incompetent — the heir may be adopted from outside.

Other children (i.e. those who do not become or marry the heir) are expected to leave the natal household by marrying out or being adopted into another *ie* which lacks an heir, or migrating to an urban centre for non-agricultural employment. In cases where their *ie* is not wealthy, these other children do not inherit and are expected to contribute to their *ie*. If the *ie* head is a wealthy landlord, the other children are provided with a house and a portion of the land or tenant rights for the land in the adjacent area of the natal household to establish their own household. The household newly created by this process is called a branch house (*bunke*) and is under the supervision of the main house (*honke*).

Practices pertaining to marriage vary between strata of the society and regions. The most widely practised marriage pattern in pre-war Japanese villages was that of a woman marrying into her husband's *ie* (*virilocal* marriage). The best known form is a marriage arranged for the heir of the *ie* by the parents through a go-between. In selecting a suitable bride (*yome*) for the heir, compatibility in the status and wealth of the two *ie* is stressed rather than the personal wishes of the two individuals marrying. A great deal of adjustment is required of a bride who moves from her natal household to her husband's *ie*. For this reason, cousin marriage was popular in the Japanese village. In any case, it is important to ensure that a bride-to-be possesses the following qualities:

1 She must be able to adapt to a new environment and tradition.
2 She must be able to get along well with all the members of the husband's *ie*, particularly her mother-in-law (*shutome*) who will function as her supervisor.
3 She must be healthy and able to produce offspring for the *ie*.
4 She must be hard-working and take part in the *ie*'s occupation.

Marriage of this type was in many cases legalised only after the bride conceived or gave birth to a child. The birth of a child was the first step towards the stabilisation of her position in her husband's parents' household. In some cases, the bride was alleged to be unfit and sent back to her parents' house or even divorced. In the case of divorce, she had to leave her children with the husband's *ie*. The husband–wife relationship in this type of marriage is not very close, mainly because the relationship between the head and the heir took precedence over all other relationships in the *ie*. Another reason was the lack of privacy in the traditional Japanese house. The absence of an affective conjugal relationship fosters a very strong and close emotional tie between the mother and her children. This becomes a hindrance to the development of a good relationship with their own spouses when the children themselves grow up and marry.

The above type of marriage was common among wealthy farmers and landlords who had been strongly influenced by the warrior class ideals. But other marriage practices also existed in various parts of the traditional Japanese village before the turn of the century. Although there are many variations, the second type of marriage practice can be classified as a *duolocal-virilocal* marriage where the husband and/or the wife move(s) between the two households daily or periodically at the early stage of marriage. In one of the variations, for instance, the wife stays in her natal household even after marriage has been consummated with the proper ceremonies, and the husband visits her at night, continuing to do so until the first child is born. Even after the birth of the child the wife still leaves her personal effects such as her clothes in the natal household and often goes back there for an extended stay in order to 'change the clothes' or 'wash and mend clothes and bedding'. The wife is eventually settled in the husband's parents' household when her mother-in-law transfers the position of housewife to her. This type of marriage was practised among the people in the lower strata of society, and was particularly popular in the coastal and island villages where youth and daughter associations (a type of age-graded organisation) were active in facilitating and sanctioning open heterosexual relationships among the young villagers. In contrast to the first type of marriage, which tends to promote *village exogamy*, this second type encourages *village endogamy* and egalitarian husband–wife relationships.

Certain scholars of the Japanese family argue that the second type of marriage practice is older than the first. Whether this hypothesis can be substantiated or not is not our concern here. What is important is that in the second type of marriage the wife's otherwise stressful transition from her natal houshold to her husband's parents' household is very much eased. The existence of *duolocal* marriage practices reveals that the wife is not immediately incorporated into her husband's *ie*. The fact that the wife in a sense belongs to both *ie* in the early phase of the marriage and derives comfort and support from her own parents is conducive to forming a close interlocking relationship between the two *ie* involved in the village.

Let us now turn our attention to community organisation in the pre-war Japanese village. The economy of the Japanese village at the time was primarily based on paddy-rice agriculture which required corporate management of waterways and intensive labour at the time of transplanting and harvesting. A household contained five or six members on average and was too small to fulfil all the necessary agricultural and life needs in the village. In those days it was rare to hire labourers or to pay for services rendered. To meet the various needs of villagers, several *ie* were organised into a fairly constant corporate unit. These *ie* formed a community, and co-operated with one another through labour exchanges, mutual aids and assistance, and participation in festivals and other religious activities. Two common forms of such community organisation are *kumi* and *dozoku*.

In the Japanese village, houses cluster as a hamlet, and there develops a close relationship between neighbouring households. When the relationship between them takes on a permanent character and is formalised, it is called *kumi*, an egalitarian organisation the leadership of which rotates from one household to the next. All member households are expected to fulfil duties and obligations necessary for living in a village. One of the essential functions of the *kumi* is labour exchange. The member households help one another in the cultivation of rice at peak times. They also co-operate in community work such as road repairs, bridge building and fire fighting. Both men and women participate in these activities.

The member households of *kumi* also help each other by rendering aid and assistance at emergency situations like illness and death in the household and also on happy occasions like childbirth and marriage. One of the distinctive functions commonly performed by the *kumi* throughout rural Japan is mutual help at the time of death in a neighbouring household. *Kumi* takes over the entire responsibility related to death, which includes informing the relatives and other villagers, sending for a priest, digging a grave and catering for the mourners with food and drinks.

Every household in the village participates in seasonal festivities and sends a person (man or woman) to help prepare for them. Local sanctions are applied to the household which has failed to respond to *kumi* expectations and the norms of reciprocal obligations. The most severe form of community sanction is ostracism *(mura-hachibu)*. The ostracised household receives no assistance or co-operation from other households. *Kumi* members develop a strong sense of reciprocal obligation and group solidarity through helping each other and participating together in economic, social and religious activities. This mechanism of group sanction was effectively utilised by the government in the Tokugawa period and during World War II to control the populace.

In some regions of Japan, there developed another type of community organisation, *dozoku*, which was formed on a different principle. *Dozoku* is a group of households related in a network of main house *(honke)* and branch house *(bunke)* ties. Like *kumi*, members of a *dozoku* are bound to one another by reciprocal rights and obligations, but unlike *kumi*, *dozoku* is not an egalitarian organisation. Since the branch house is established by the main house's resources, the latter assumes a superior position to the former.

The *dozoku* performs similar functions to the *kumi* in the Japanese village. In addition to labour exchange, mutual aid and assistance and participation in various rites of passage of the member household, there are activities which are *dozoku*-specific. These are memorial services and ceremonies of ancestor veneration. The main house organises these ceremonies in which branch houses participate. The main house is also responsible for maintaining the ancestral altar, tablets and grave. Through these activities, *dozoku* members reinforce their identity with their *dozoku* and enhance their solidarity as a kinship group.

Dozoku and *kumi* are not mutually exclusive organisations. In some regions (e.g. northeastern Honshu and northern Kyushu) the *dozoku* has dominated the village organisation and acted as *kumi*, but in other regions (e.g. southwestern Honshu and coastal regions) it has never fully developed, but the *kumi* and other organisations have been more active.

Conclusion

We have examined ways in which four Asian societies organised their domestic and communal lives in traditional times. Principles of their organisation differ from society to society, but they all share one characteristic: the basis of the society is not the individual, but the household. Individuals existed for the sake of the unit to which they belonged. The degree and content of individual subordination to a unit varied greatly between societies, and within a society, according to a person's age, gender and status. We have also observed that the interaction between the forms of organisation and values and ideals upheld by the society served to reinforce the system as well as the ideology on which it was based.

With modernisation, many of the traditional structures have weakened, but certain ideals and values remain — for example, the preference for male children persists in contemporary China. However, it is not possible to understand the societies of contemporary Asia without a knowledge of those from which they have evolved.

Guide to further reading

Baker, Hugh D.R., *Chinese Family and Kinship*, The Macmillan Press, Sydney, 1979

This presents a general picture of the Chinese family that prevailed in 'traditional' (pre-twentieth century) rural China. The book includes discussions of household and family structure, lineage organisation, ancestor worship, inter-lineage relations and interactions between the family and the wider society.

Embree, John F., *Suye Mura*, University of Chicago Press, Chicago, 1939
This is the first ethnographical work on a Japanese village, which laid a basis for Japanese village studies. The first four chapters are particularly useful for gaining an understanding of the structure and function of the traditional Japanese family and household, hamlet organisation and other forms of village co-operation in pre-war rural Japan.

Fukutake, Tadashi, *Japanese Rural Society*, Cornell University Press, Ithaca, 1967
This book deals with the Japanese agriculture and village structure before and after World War II. Parts II and III, in particular, cover topics discussed in this chapter, such as family kinship and hamlet organisation in the Japanese village.

Kato, Tsuyoshi, *Matriliny and Migration*, Cornell University Press, Ithaca, 1981
This book is concerned with the adaption of the Minangkabau matrilineal system to changing times and circumstances. To pursue this theme, it first describes (in Chapter 2) how the matrilineal system was practised in Minangkabau society in the past. The rest of the book is devoted to an examination of Minangkabau migration patterns in a historical perspective and of how this migration has resulted in a new configuration in Minangkabau society.

5 | Religious traditions in Asia

Besides the family, another aspect of society is religion. People in Asia today practise many different kinds of religions, and not only religions that are native to the Asian region. Chinese people, who keep to their native religious heritage of Daoism (often spelled Taoism) and Confucianism, supplemented with Buddhism, have Christian and Muslim neighbours. Indonesian tribal peoples who perpetuate the home-grown traditions of their ancestors are under pressure from their own compatriots in more cosmopolitan farming and city areas to adopt religions of both Indian and West Asian origin (Islam, Christianity, Hinduism or Buddhism). Indeed, in all Asian countries, indigenous religious traditions have been supplemented by religions introduced from other regions of the world.

In order to understand this variety, it is helpful to begin our study of religion in Asia by identifying particular traditions and examining the historical processes through which these traditions originated in Asia or were introduced to the region. The historical overview will be prefaced, however, by a discussion of the major dimensions of contrast among religions. This will help to show general patterns of similarity and difference both among religions in Asia and between religious life in Asia and elsewhere. Chapter 36 summarises current patterns of religious affiliation that are the product of the historical processes reviewed in this chapter.

Some major contrasts in Asian religions

The most prominent religions in Asia today are the 'universalistic' religions (sometimes known as 'world religions' or 'salvation religions'). Some of these — Islam and Christianity — are of West Asian origin. Others — Hinduism and Buddhism — originated in India. Daoism is a universalistic religion indigenous to China.

Universalistic religions

The universalistic religions are open to anyone, regardless of their colour, customs or social prominence. These religions are 'held together' by shared beliefs that have been formulated as doctrines: those people who accept the core beliefs or doctrines are members of the religion; others are not. The doctrines identify some crucial problems in human existence (such as death, injustice or fundamental limitations in our ability to understand the world) and point to ways of transcending or rising above them. The faithful are taught to restrain selfish and thoughtless behaviour in order to please God or to experience the divine, in the present life or after death. They hope to rise above the problems of this world by placing hope in the reward of a better life beyond the grave or by radically transforming their attitudes towards and perceptions of the world.

The teachings of each of the universalistic religions about humanity's problems and prospects and about how to transcend this world are recorded in sacred books. These form fixed reference points for the lives of the adherents. However, differences in interpretation of the holy books and the admixture of core teachings with local customs make for considerable variations in the ways Asian peoples actually understand and practise the world religions. More will be said below about the growth and spread of the individual universalistic religions in Asia.

Community religions

Alongside the universalistic religions in Asia today are many diverse 'community' religions (sometimes called 'primal' religions). These are the religions that are the heritage of particular local communities (whether tribes or villages), going back to the distant past. One does not become a member of these religions; one simply 'owns' a tradition because one has grown up with it as part of the village or tribe in which it is practised. Everyone in the community shares roughly similar beliefs and has similar ways of celebrating crucial life transitions (birth, coming of age, marriage and death). And all families will be represented at rituals which concern the whole community, such as harvest celebrations and rituals in honour of guardian spirits of the community. These religions are not suitable for 'export' to people outside the area (unless they are considerably reworked) because they are so specific, or particularistic. They are concerned mostly with spirits attached to particular families and local groups: ancestor spirits, legendary heroes who taught farming and crafts, deities who guard a certain village, spring, mountain or crop, etc. Further, religious law is intimately interwoven with the host of specific rules governing everyday social life in each community. To accept the village's custom regarding acceptable marriage partners, the use of land, inheritance, punishment for wrongs and so on are all at once religious and social obligations. This is in some ways like the religious law of Islam or the more detailed laws followed by orthodox Jews. For Muslims and orthodox Jews, however, there is one law for all believers, no matter where they live, whereas for the community religions there are as many laws as there are villages. In Islam or Judaism (which may be practised in communities where there are also members of other faiths) infringement of the law brings punishment upon the individual who committed the wrong. Community religions, in contrast, place responsibility on everyone in the community for everyone else. Violation of custom will bring down the wrath of the spirits, not only upon the offender, but possibly upon the whole community. This reflects the intense need for mutual support in small, rural villages and tribes.

The community religions are kept alive not by holy books, prayer books and hymnals, but by living day to day with the village's customs, performing the rituals and listening to the stories and guidance of the elders. Believing particular teachings is by no means crucial to one's acceptance or even to the fate of one's soul after death. Many stories are told, and one believes this or that or nothing at all. What is crucial is behaving properly towards one's human neighbours, towards the animal and plant world upon which life depends and towards the spirits (whatever one thinks about them), giving each its due, humouring and cajoling the powerful and placating lesser beings to prevent them from making a nuisance of themselves. The spirit world is there, whether one likes it or not. (Or at least, enough people believe this to be so that individuals who do not are more or less obliged to play along with the idea.) One does not strive to know God, because the divine is constantly involved with everyday life in apparently obvious ways: sending a wild elephant crashing through a camp where someone committed incest, speaking through the mouth of a trance medium, ripening the grain in the field where the proper ritual has been performed. So the focus of community religions is not upon finding God and thereby transcending an unsatisfactory world, but upon creating and maintaining harmony amongst the spirit, human, animal, plant and mineral worlds of which we are all inescapably a part.

Chinese folk religion

Chinese folk religion has many of the same features as community religions. Although Chinese religion is often described in terms of universalistic religions such as Daoism and Buddhism, most of the religious behaviour that one sees among Chinese is most accurately described merely as Chinese folk religion. Chinese folk religion is comprised of practices that flourished long before people such as Confucius attempted to systematise them or draw on them as the basis for a philosophical system.

Followers of Chinese folk religion believe that nature and society are unified rather than dichotomised, which means in practice that what is done in society, especially by the sovereign, affects happenings in nature. They also believe that the dual forces, *yin* and *yang*, permeate the entire universe. *Yin* originally referred to the shady side of a hill. By extension it represents all that is dark, moist, yielding and female. *Yang* represented the sunshine and was extended to depict brightness, hardness and maleness. Together, these forces give birth to all things.

The most basic ritual of Chinese folk religion is sacrifice to the ancestors (often crudely referred to as 'ancestor worship'). Although ancestral spirits reside in the nether, or *yin*, world, they have the same needs — food, clothing, shelter, comfort and money — as the living do in this, the *yang* world. Thus sacrifices must be made in order to supply them with their needs. Otherwise they will become dangerous 'hungry ghosts', who will haunt and do harm to their descendants.

Worship takes place at various shrines, temples, graves and altars. It is most commonly found at what is called the domestic altar. This is located in the main room of a home and is a high table or a mantle on which pictures and statues of gods are placed on one side and ancestral tablets and perhaps photos of recently deceased ancestors on the other. There are separate censers for the gods and the ancestors. Usually families will sacrifice daily by placing the fare to be eaten by the family at the next meal on a table in front of the altar, lighting some sticks of incense and inviting gods and ancestors to partake of the spiritual essence of the food. A short time later, the family eats the physical essence. Ancestors are also worshipped annually at the grave site and, if there is one, at the ancestral hall.

Ancestors are worshipped only by their descendants; thus this activity emphasises the separateness of family and descent groups. Worship of gods, however, is done on a wider basis at the community temple, thus integrating disparate kinship units. Temples can be large or small, elaborate or simple, well-kept or dilapidated. Village temples house the main village deity and often a number of minor deities as well. Individual worship can be undertaken at any time a person feels the need or desire. The main community worship takes place on the main god's birthday. In addition, there are specialist folk temples which house gods regarded as efficacious in a particular function (e.g. healing, ensuring that one bears a son, academic success, etc.), and who are worshipped across communities.

Anomalous cases

Because the community religions are so much a part of each particular village and tribe that they are wholly identified with the community, they are not named. They are simply part of the customs of the place. Most of these religious traditions have never been codified into an official set of doctrines, nor do they have any officialdom linking people with similar beliefs across localities into anything like a church, brotherhood or other ecclesiastical authority. There is one very important exception, however: Shintoism.

Shintoism

Shintoism grew out of the indigenous community religious traditions of Japan and still has many of the qualities of community religions, but it has been formalised, somewhat like the universalistic religions, at different times in its history. In ancient times it existed simply as a folk tradition centred around village rituals and regional spirit cults. When Buddhism and Confucianism entered Japan in the sixth century A.D., the local traditions were named 'Shinto' (a word derived from Chinese meaning 'the way of the Gods') just to distinguish them collectively from the imported traditions. But at this same time the chiefly clan that had managed to dominate rivals and unite them under its rule began to synthesise Shinto, Buddhist and Confucian traditions into a cult that would lend support to the throne. This culminated in the seventh century in the Ritsuryo Synthesis, a kind of new official religion that drew from Shintoism beliefs in spirits *(kami)* of clan ancestors and cast the emperor as a living *kami* for the whole state. In the early tenth century, documents relating to Shinto were collected into the *Engishiki*, which became a guide for many Shinto practices performed or sponsored by the state. But by this time the state cult was already losing importance, as the central government weakened under challenges from the warlords. Unregulated, unco-ordinated folk Shinto remained a vigorous part of village life, but Shinto's part in a regulated, codified state cult diminished in significance.

This situation was only reversed in the late eighteenth and nineteenth centuries when the Tokugawa rulers and then the Meiji rulers again saw the usefulness of Shinto for boosting the image of the monarchy. The Meiji government, which came to power in 1868, brought Shinto under the sponsorship of the modernising state, not only using it in state rituals concerning the emperor, but providing it with an administrative bureaucracy drawing every temple throughout the country under the spiritual authority of the Japanese emperor. Borrowing heavily on Confucian ideas as well, Meiji State Shinto taught that Japan was a 'family-state' in which the Japanese people were one family descended from a single original ancestor, with the emperor as the closest descendant and chief celebrant of rituals relating the people to their ancestral spirit. From the early part of the twentieth century until the defeat of Japan in World War II, State Shinto was promulgated though the mass education system and the military.

Confucianism

Another anomalous case (neither a universalistic religion nor a community religion in any simple sense) is Confucianism. Strictly speaking, Confucianism is not a religion but a philosophy, especially for good governance. As such it is covered also in Chapter 7. In this chapter its religious features are introduced.

Confucius (or Kong Fuzi, 551–479 B.C.) simply advocated a moral philosophy for getting along in everyday social life (see also Chapter 7). This philosophy is basically a collection of ethical traditions and ideas about goverment already current in Chinese society in Confucius' time, but it was compellingly presented by the master. These ideas were recorded by his students in a number of works and attributed to him. Only one of the works associated with Confucius, *Lunyu (The Analects)*, was certainly written by Confucius himself. Subsequently his many students also added their own contributions to the Confucian canon.

Confucius believed that in this world we should strive for harmony with one another by observing strict hierarchical relationships within the family and between family units and the state. 'Filial piety', the respect shown by children to their parents, and particularly to their father, was to be extended by each subject to the emperor and his representatives. Here, as in the community religions, we see a concern for harmony (and Confucius clearly drew inspiration from such community traditions in China), but in Confucianism, unlike the community religions, ideas of harmony were gradually developed into a systematic philosophy and recorded in written form for use by people all over China and abroad.

Confucius refused to take a position as to whether or not there really were supernatural beings (the focus of concern for most religions), there being no hope, in his view, of ever knowing anything with certainty about the reality or otherwise of the spirit world. However, his philosophy was deeply rooted in traditional Chinese community values and he strongly believed in the importance of ritual in reinforcing social order. It is not surprising, then, that in time traditional family rituals concerned with honouring the spirits of the ancestors and court rituals celebrating the Chinese emperor as the 'Son of Heaven' came to be associated with the Confucian tradition. Confucius himself came to be honoured in temples dedicated to him, but he was seen as an object of reverence and respect rather than as a deity to be beseeched for favours.

In some ways, then, Confucianism eventually functioned very much as a religion — even a universalistic religion: it had yearly rituals on a uniform pattern and centred around written texts read and taught by Chinese all over their native land as well as in overseas Chinese communities in more recent times.

Interestingly, Confucianism managed to spread beyond the bounds of China, not only to overseas Chinese communities, but also into northern Vietnam, Korea and Japan, where it was adopted in the early centuries A.D. along with Chinese statecraft. Confucianism remains an important element in the Japanese and Korean outlook, along with another ancient import, Buddhism, some elements of Daoism and a more modern import, Christianity. In contrast, Shintoism has never spread beyond the bounds of its native land. It is very much a religion of Japanese local communities and of the Japanese people as a national community. As such it is intimately associated with the Japanese cultural identity.

The history of the universalistic religions in Asia

Let us look more carefully now at the universalistic religions, which have so widely absorbed or displaced community religions in Asia. We will be concerned with their historical origins and with their spread in East and Southeast Asia.

Daoism in China

Daoism is a Chinese tradition. Its legendary founder Lao Zi (Lao Tzu) is fictional, but its historical origins can be dated to about 300 B.C. Like Confucianism, Daoism began simply as a philosophy, only later developing features of a religion. In contrast to Confucianism, however, there emerged in Daoism an explicit interest in cultivating the supernatural, not only through ordinary rituals of worship and petition, but through occult and alchemical practices which in many ways paralleled those which occupied European fringe groups at the dawn of modern science.

Early Daoism sought harmony, as did Confucianism and the community religions upon which both drew. But where Confucianism strove for harmony in society, Daoism taught that harmony was achievable only by living in harmony with nature and the universe as a whole. Its central concept, the *Dao*, was the way of doing this. Whereas the Confucians wanted to make society easily governed by ensuring that all would be loyal to the sovereign, the Daoists wanted to make it unnecessary to govern at all; people would live in small, self-contained groups, obtain all their needs in a 'natural' way, and have no desire to intervene in the affairs of others.

The Daoist philosophy, however, soon developed into a religion. Ritualistic and occult elements were drawn into Daoist practice and it incorporated and expanded upon a number of religious principles then current in Chinese culture, principles such as *yin–yang* and the Five Forces. It also became active in areas such as the search for immortality and eternal youthfulness, which led to dietary and medical experimentation as well as to the use of breathing exercises and meditation. Daoists attempted to turn lead, mercury and cinnabar into gold, and tried to summon spirits and communicate with deities. Over the course of time they found themselves dealing with an enormous pantheon of deities and immortals.

In the late Han (206 B.C.-A.D. 221) period, and probably under the influence of Buddhism, Daoism developed collective worship and organised sects. Two of these, the Five Pecks of Rice and the Yellow Turbans, revolted against the Han rulers in A.D. 184. Although the rebels were defeated, the government still imposed very strict bans on organised religious activity. The rulers also attempted to channel popular religious activity into government-approved cults and to suppress any religious expression which might present a danger to them.

Although Daoist beliefs and practices have for millenia been an important element of folk religion all over China, Daoism never achieved the success that Confucianism or Buddhism did. It lacked the official acceptance of Confucianism and the organisational strength of Buddhism. Although it was embraced and sponsored by various emperors, it was never able to become established as a unified organisation. This may be because of the sometimes bizarre behaviour associated with it or because it occasionally presented a mocking alternative to the powerful Confucian orthodoxy. In the villages there were hereditary *daoshi* (Daoist masters) who made their living performing rites and exorcisms, making charms and amulets and directing funerals. And it did develop a sort of hereditary priesthood headed by a 'papacy' descended from the founder of the Five Pecks of Rice cult, Zhang Ling. Yet, despite this, it lacked overall leadership and direction.

Daoism spread to Korea and Japan along with Buddhism, Confucianism and Chinese culture in general. But by the time this cultural exchange was made, Daoism no longer had the organisational strength required to make a lasting impact. Many practices and ideas associated with Daoism were accepted in Korea and Japan, but no Daoist school was established and no Daoist practitioners set up shop. Thus these practices and ideas were simply absorbed into local folk practices, where their origins were forgotten.

Indian religions: Hinduism and Buddhism

Hinduism (sometimes called 'Brahmanism' after its brahman priests) is actually a congeries of Indian religious traditions only loosely linked by reverence for a common set of holy books, the Vedas, and by worship of a common set of deities, the most prominent of which since classical times have been Brahma, Vishnu and Shiva. Until the Muslim and then European conquerors brought the radically different West Asian religions to India, the Indian people did not see their own diverse traditions as a single religion. The word 'Hindu' itself was introduced by the Muslim invaders who derived it from the Greek and Persian word for India. (This is reminiscent of the origins of the word 'Shinto', denoting the native Japanese traditions in a Chinese word.) 'Hindu' simply meant the religious traditions of native peoples of the subcontinent who had not converted to Islam. The British colonials, who also used the term, helped to generate an awareness amongst Indians that their non-Muslim and non-Christian traditions were more similar to each other than they were to foreign religions. The British Christian presence also prompted nationalistic identification with Hinduism to counter colonialism.

Long before Indian peoples forged a conscious Hindu identity, as early as the first centuries A.D., Indian priests and artisans came to Southeast Asia where they were patronised by the native rulers. These rulers seem to have benefited from Indian ideas of statecraft and from the use of Indian religious ideas. The Indian cults of the gods Shiva and Vishnu spread the idea that the spirit guardians of all the numerous native tribes and lands were ruled by a supreme deity. (The Shaivites believed this was Shiva, the Vaishnavites believed it was Vishnu.) The kings who sponsored these cults also put themselves forward as regents or incarnations of Shiva or Vishnu. These were potent ideas. Where once in Southeast Asia there had been only fragmented tribal groups and petty chiefdoms, great kingdoms emerged. We see evidence of this in the beautiful stone temples erected in Indian styles to celebrate the rites of Shiva or Vishnu or of lesser deities associated with those principal gods, and to commemorate the kings who claimed to incarnate those deities. In ancient manuscripts from the Indonesian islands of Java and Bali, we also find evidence of a very sophisticated understanding of Hindu theology and of Indian mystical practice developed to a high standard by native masters or gurus. Further, surviving texts mention the Indian words for the four castes, but there is little evidence that the caste system significantly modified Southeast Asian village life.

At about the same time that Shaivite and Vaishnavite cults were introduced into Southeast Asia, Buddhism, an offshoot of Hinduism, also appeared. Burmese and Thai traditions hold that Buddhism was brought to Southeast Asia from India by missionaries of King Asoka in the third century B.C. However, the first historical evidence of Buddhism there comes from stone inscriptions found in the ruins of the Indian-influenced kingdoms that formed in Southeast Asia early in the first millenium A.D. It appears that Buddhism played a very similar role to Hinduism in justifying the expansion of power of local rulers. Such magnificent temples as those of Angkor Wat in Cambodia and Borobudur in Indonesia testify to the grandeur of ancient Southeast Asian Buddhist realms.

Buddhism originated in the teachings of a holy man of Mongolian stock, Prince Siddhartha, who was born in the northeast of India around 563 B.C. As a prince, Siddhartha was a member of India's warrior (*kshatriya*) caste, and so was a person of considerable dignity in society, though not of as great dignity or 'ritual purity' as members of the priestly (*brahman*) caste. According to tradition, he left his father's palace to search for spiritual knowledge, following the time-honoured pattern of Hindu renunciates. When this proved fruitless, he decided to modify his practice according to his own inspiration, creating what was later called 'The

Middle Way'. Thereafter he achieved enlightenment, the ecstatic experience of true knowing or true being, the highest goal of all Indian religious-seeking. From this he became known as the Buddha Gautama.

His teachings, later recorded in Buddhist holy books called the Tripitaka (in the Sanskrit language) or Tipitaka (in the Pali language), preserved with some modifications earlier Hindu ideas such as reincarnation and *karma* and the idea of the illusory nature of the world as we ordinarily experience it. However, he took this notion of the illusoriness of the world much further than most Hindus did: he taught that even the human personality and the gods we imagine in human form are no more real than dreams. Further, he rejected the Hindu caste system, with its hierarchy of social value and religious worth, and dispensed with the rituals of the brahman priests. The monk, the person who leaves family, village and court to seek enlightenment, replaced the priest as the central focus of the princely holy man's religion. The community was supposed to support the monks and their monastery, meeting their material needs and offering them protection. This relationship was later elaborated, with the monks in some parts of Asia taking on roles in family, village and court rituals, though these were always regarded by the learned as secondary functions. Nuns were allowed a grudging place in monastic life at a distance physically and socially from the monks. This reflected values in the wider environment of ancient India where women were sharply subjected to the authority of male family members. Today, just as in male-dominated Christian churches, there are some initiatives both in Southeast Asian and Western Buddhist communities to undo this bias.

In the last centuries B.C., Buddhism spread widely across India from its place of origin in the northeast and became firmly established in Sri Lanka as well. However, just when we start to see firm evidence of the spread of Buddhism into Southeast Asia and China — that is, a century or so after the time of Christ — it began to decline in India. For reasons that are not entirely clear, it began to lose royal patronage and the villagers failed to sustain the material welfare of the monasteries. Muslim conquests from the eighth century also contributed to Indian Buddhism's gradual demise. The closure of the last of India's great Buddhist universities in the twelfth and thirteenth centuries A.D. marked the end of Buddhism as a significant social phenomenon in pre-modern India.

Although Buddhism had virtually disappeared from India by the twelfth century A.D., it remained vigorous in Sri Lanka, and a distinctive form of Buddhism that developed there, the Theravada tradition, was enthusiastically imported into mainland Southeast Asia by Burmese and Tai rulers. (The Tai people later evolved into the Thai, Lao and Shan groups whom we know in Southeast Asia today.) Theravada Buddhism quickly displaced earlier Buddhist traditions as well as old Hindu cults in the mainland, not only in the Burmese and Tai areas, but also in the Cambodian kingdoms. Northern Vietnam remained under the influence of Chinese forms of Buddhism in the less demanding, mass-oriented Mahayana tradition. Today the 'southern' Theravada tradition of Southeast Asia contrasts with the 'northern' Mahayana tradition of China, Korea and Japan in placing greater responsibility on individuals for their own salvation. The Mahayana tradition has evolved schools which treat buddhas and *bodhisattvas* (people who hesitate on the brink of enlightenment to aid their fellow beings) as god-like and which consequently encourage people to ask those elevated beings for both worldly favours and help in achieving salvation.

In island Southeast Asia, also, the pattern of relationships between Hinduism and Buddhism changed in the second millenium A.D. However here, rather than displacing Hinduism, Buddhism was assimilated with Hinduism. From the tenth century the native religious and artistic genius of the Indonesian islands began to absorb the Indian traditions, giving rise to an original, Indonesian architectural style and a distinctive theological synthesis. This was facilitated by the fact that Buddhism was by this time represented in the islands by the Mahayana and Vajrayana traditions (the latter a variant of Mahayana Buddhism developed in Tibet) that were much closer theologically to local Hindu traditions than the Theravada tradition was. Even though the Javanese monarchs, who dominated the region, continued to support individual Shaivite, Vaishnavite and Buddhist temples and monasteries, the courts made simultaneous use of Hindu and Buddhist rituals, as well as rituals of a wholly indigenous character.

The rise of Buddhism's popularity in China seems to have depended on the decline of strong central control of the state in the third century A.D. In this time of constant warfare, banditry and famine, Confucian notions of finding the good life through filial piety and reverential obedience to the emperor must have sounded painfully naive and offered little comfort or direction to people's lives. In contrast, Buddhism made the problem of human suffering the centre of its teachings and offered solutions individuals could use on their own. Monasteries were established and numbers grew rapidly. By the sixth century, Buddhism was sufficiently influential to play a role in the foundation of a new dynasty, the Sui (A.D. 581–618), and it reached the height of prestige in the succeeding Tang dynasty (A.D. 618–907).

Early on, the individualistic tenor of Buddhism, as well as the size and strength of the monasteries, came to be seen as a threat to the government. It was not until the ninth century, however, that elements hostile to Buddhism were able to take decisive action. In 845, the government, egged on by the Confucianists, sacked a number of monasteries, seizing their riches and forcing hundreds of thousands of monks and nuns to forsake monasticism for secular life. Thereafter Buddhist power was curtailed by limiting the number of persons who could enter a monastic order. Confucianism once again enjoyed ascendency, though mixed with some elements of both Buddhism and Daoism.

Despite its reduced stature, Buddhism remained important in Chinese life and distinctively Chinese understandings of the Buddha's teachings continued to evolve. This was necessitated in part by the need to translate those teachings into Chinese. There were no words in Chinese to translate many Buddhist concepts; indeed, the equivalent concepts in some cases did not even exist. Thus the Chinese either transliterated these terms (e.g. *pusa* for *bodhisattva)* or, more often, translated them with a word they considered to be similar in their own language. For example, the Buddhist term for morality was translated as *xiao*, which means filiality. But while filial behaviour is certainly moral behaviour, the original Sanskrit term was much broader. Thus the Chinese gained an understanding of Buddhism that differed in important ways from Indian Buddhism. In fact, the Chinese had developed a number of native Buddhist sects of their own, including Chan, which spread to Japan as Zen.

Buddhism spread to Korea by the third century A.D., and then to Japan in the sixth century. In each case it was imported as part of a complex of Chinese culture, together with Daoism and Confucianism and a variety of Chinese folk customs. Whereas Confucianism was attractive to the rulers because of its emphasis on public morality and obedience to authority, Buddhism was appreciated for its mystical practice and metaphysics. In Korea, Buddhism came to incorporate several native deities and folk religious practices. Syncretism of Buddhism with local traditions also occurred from time to time in Japan. For example, in the eighth century the *Jinenchishu* (Nature Wisdom School) of Buddhism, drawing on the Shinto feeling for the sacredness of nature, developed the notion that enlightenment was to be found through physical discipline in the wilds and meditation.

In both Korea and Japan, Buddhism was sometimes seen as a threat to governments and sometimes supported by them. At the height of its fortunes in Korea, during the Koryo Dynasty (918–1392), Buddhism became the state religion. Zen Buddhism achieved something like that status in Japan in the Ashikaga period (1337–1573). The political and military might of its monasteries was crushed at the end of this period and it was subject to firm restrictions on religious activity in the following Tokugawa period, but the basis of its present pervasive influence in society was laid in that same period by the government's use of Buddhist temples to register the population. Every family had to be registered with a temple. The government also gave the Buddhists charge over cemeteries, giving them a very visible role in what is probably the most important rite of passage and laying the foundation for the present association Japanese people have of Buddhism with funeral rites.

West Asian religions: Christianity and Islam

Christianity

Christianity is the religion that purports to represent the teachings of Jesus of Nazareth, a Jew whose birth marks the beginning of the 'Christian' or 'Common Era' (the centuries A.D.) in what is now Israel. Christians regard Jesus as the 'Son of God' and as the *Messiah* (originally in Judaism a hoped-for king who would free the Jewish people from foreign oppressors, but in Christianity, God born as humankind to save believers from damnation for their sins). Independent historical records attest to the ministry of a rabbi (or learned Jewish religious teacher) named Jesus and to his execution by the Romans in 30 or 33 A.D. 'Christ' is a Greek term meaning 'Anointed', from which we derive the word 'Christianity'. It was used in Jesus' time, though not by him, to suggest his divine identity as Son of God. The Christian holy book, the Bible, contains both Jewish scriptures (the Old Testament) and later writings (the Gospel or New Testament) by his apostles about Jesus. It also tells how the churches formed after his death and ascension should conduct themselves, and about his expected miraculous return to Earth at the end of time.

Present-day Christian communities in Asia have their origins in missionary activities associated with European and North American colonial expansion from the sixteenth century. However, the religion had first reached China by the seventh century. Christianity was one of several universalistic religions that filtered into China when the Tang dynasty expanded Chinese rule west into Central Asia. This revived the overland trade with India, Persia and regions farther to the west. The traders brought their religions with them: not only the Nestorian form of Christianity but also Zoroastrianiasm and Manichaeism from Persia and Islam from the Arabian peninsula. Until the middle of the ninth century, Christianity was practised freely in China, but it was confined to communities of foreigners in the larger trading centres. Then, in 845, when Buddhism and other foreign religions were being suppressed, Christianity was made illegal.

Nestorian Christianity reappeared in China under the patronage of the Mongol rulers who invaded and dominated the native Chinese or 'Han' peoples in the thirteenth and fourteenth centuries. Christianity benefited from the Mongol strategy of controlling the ethnically distinct Han by promoting non-Han to prominent positions. The large numbers of Christians in China in this period indicate that the church had expanded beyond foreign enclaves, but the religion disappeared completely when the Mongols were defeated in the mid-fourteenth century. When the

Jesuits arrived in China in the sixteenth century they found no evidence of descendants of the earlier churches.

In the age of European geographical discovery, Christian missionaries travelled to the East both in association with armed instruments of expansion (armies of conquest and armed trading companies) and as independent witnesses to the faith. The Italian Jesuits, who arrived in Japan in 1549 and in China in 1583, came without military support. In China they were allowed to settle and convert local people whilst exchanging knowledge of science, mathematics and geography with Chinese literati. Acceptance of the Christian presence waxed and waned, however, and by the time the first Protestant missionary arrived in 1807, church membership was only about 200 000. Both Christian religions made more headway in China after the fall of the Qing dynasty in 1911 in the atmosphere of political disunity and greater openness to European ideas. In Japan, Christianity was vigorously suppressed after a short period of tolerance in the sixteenth century. It only revived in the later nineteenth century when the new Meiji government 'opened its doors' to exchanges of all kinds with foreigners. Christianity remains very much a minority tradition in both China and Japan; however, its influence in Japan is somewhat disproportionate to its numbers insofar as it draws many intellectuals into the fold.

Christianity first came to Korea in the seventeenth century through a number of Korean intellectuals who had come into contact with Jesuits in China. Some of their fellow Koreans showed interest, but the Choson court opposed Catholicism because of its opposition to ancestor worship; Confucianism was the official ideology. However, French missionaries were smuggled into Korea, and despite periodic persecutions, Catholicism grew rapidly. In 1866 Korea (like Japan) adopted an open-door policy towards the West and ceased its persecution of Christians. Protestantism came to Korea in 1885 with the arrival of two American missionaries. There has been a steady growth in Christianity, especially since the arrival of Protestantism; in fact, Protestants now outnumber Catholics by about four to one. Both Catholicism and Protestantism doubled their numbers in the 1970s, exemplifying the far greater acceptance of Christianity in Korea than in either China or Japan.

In Southeast Asia, Christianity spread along with colonialism. Spanish colonisation of the Philippines and Portuguese colonisation of some of the small islands of eastern Indonesia introduced Christianity in a particularly martial context: conquest was pursued as a means of 'civilising and Christianising'. The majority of Filipinos and Timorese (Timor is now part of Indonesia) today still follow Catholicism, the religion of the conquistadors. However, Protestant missionaries, particularly American Protestants, are making a dramatic impact in the Philippines (as they are in predominantly Catholic Latin America).

Christianity made less of an impact on the English and Dutch colonies in Southeast Asia (in present-day Burma, Malaysia, Singapore, Brunei and Indonesia). Not only did the northern European colonialists not use the churches as instruments of domination in the way the Spanish and Portuguese did, but all the regions into which the English and Dutch expanded had already embraced one or more of the universalistic religions: Buddhism in Burma, Hinduism in Bali and Islam in much of Malaysia, Brunei and other parts of Indonesia. The need for a religion that was adaptable to many different places and situations and which could draw together people of different backgrounds in relationships of trust and acceptance was already met by their own universalistic religions. Further, the sophisticated intellectual traditions and vigorous networks of religious institutions in Southeast Asian Buddhism and Islam enabled those religions to defend themselves from Christian assaults on their worth. Before the present century, Christianity made a major impact only on a few parts of the British and Dutch territories where people were still 'pagans' — that is, where they held to their indigenous community religions. Other converts were small numbers of Chinese resident overseas in the colonies and a few natives closely associated with the Western sector of the colonial economies.

Islam

Islam is the name of a religion founded in the Arabian peninsula in the seventh century A.D. by the Meccan merchant, Muhammad. Followers of the religion are called 'Muslims', not (as is often heard) Muhammadans, for they do not wish to give the impression that Muhammad himself is an object of worship. They accept Muhammad only as a prophet of God. Indeed, the central teaching of the religion is that there is only one God. This belief they share with Jews, upon whose traditions they draw in part, and with Christians, whose founder, Jesus, they consider a great prophet, but not an aspect of God. Muslims call God by the name 'Allah', using the name of a deity, a creator god, who was but one of many clan gods and other spirits worshipped by the Arabs of Mecca when Muhammad was a youth. In Islam Allah is recast as the single, transcendent divine being and sole creator of all.

In his fortieth year (A.D. 610), whilst on a retreat in the desolate mountains near Mecca, Muhammad saw a vision of an angelic being who called him the Apostle of God and identified itself as the archangel Gabriel. Later Muhammad dreamed of Gabriel and saw visions of him in which the angel related writings from a heavenly book. These writings, Gabriel said, were from God and related God's intentions for humanity. Although tradition has it that Muhammad could not read, he transmitted the contents that he had understood in his visions to others, who wrote them down. These now form the Muslim holy book, the Quran (also and more usually spelled Koran). The Quran enjoins Muslims to abandon all idols and worship only the one true God (much like the Old Testament teachings of the Jews and Christians). The Quran pictures a Day of Judgment (again, very like the Jewish and Christian one) and a heaven and hell to which the soul is assigned after a single passage through the world of mortals. It also contains many rules for daily living (concerning, for example, marriage, divorce and inheritance) and for ritual observance (praying, fasting, avoiding impure acts, etc.) to form the basis of a new community in place of the old Arabian clan organisations.

In the Prophet Muhammad's lifetime and the century after his death, Islam spread amazingly rapidly. By the time the prophet died in 632, his armies had carried the new religion throughout the Arabian peninsula; a century later Muslims had conquered territory stretching from Spain and the western shores of North Africa to West Asia as far as the Indus River, even touching on the northwest frontiers of China. Beyond these Muslim dominions, Islam had undoubtedly spread east across the Indian Ocean (though we have no concrete evidence). But we must imagine that the faith was carried here by traders, not armies as it had been further west. For centuries, since before the birth of Christ, Yemeni traders had sailed to India and Southeast Asia, just as Indian, Chinese and Southeast Asian peoples had sailed west. Once the West Asian traders converted to Islam, they must have created a Muslim presence in Southeast Asia, where they traded and waited for the change of monsoon winds on their way to and from China. Evidence of Muslims in southern China, to which they must have come through Southeast Asia from the beginning of the eighth century, lends credence to the scenario.

Unlike the first spread of the faith in the Western regions, however, the building of Muslim communities in Southeast Asia was a slow process, taking many centuries. Only in the thirteenth century did Muslim kingdoms appear there, beginning with Pasai on the east coast of Sumatra. With maritime trade by then dominated by Muslims, Muslim sultanates that participated in that trade quickly came to dominate the politics of the region. Islam replaced Hindu-Buddhist traditions in the Malay Peninsula up into what is now southern Thailand, and in the Indonesian islands, except for Bali. Further east, the southern islands of the Philippines, never significantly Hinduised, came under the sway of local Muslim rulers.

Muslims who came to western China overland via the silk route were also mostly merchants, though the first Muslim settlers were actually Arab mercenaries in the pay of the Chinese court. Then, in the thirteenth century, the Mongolian conquerers of the Han Chinese state imported Muslims from West Asia (amongst other non-Han peoples, including Christians) to help administer the state. These migrants intermarried with Han women, swelling the size of the community. But despite this blending with local people, the Chinese Muslim community remained distinct, with its members drawing a clear boundary between themselves and other Chinese by refusing to participate in ancestor worship or to eat pork. Today most of the Muslims in China are from the minority nationalities who live in the northwest and west, Xinjiang, Qinghai and Ningxia. They are culturally and linguistically distinct from the Han who live within the Great Wall, in China proper. They and other recognised ethnic minorities are given certain privileges, such as exemption from the one child per family policy and, in the case of the Muslims, the pressure to relinquish their religion.

Conclusion

All over East and Southeast Asia, community religions of purely local origins have been practised since time immemorial. There is no reason to believe that they are exactly the same as they were in the distant past, and yet historical records sometimes show striking continuities in community religious traditions over long periods of time. This is true, for example, of Chinese folk religion, the origins of which can be read in the archeological remains of civilisations two to three millennia distant from us in time, as well as in written records from the more recent past. As we have seen in the case of Shintoism, however, some community religions have undergone dramatic changes in their institutional structure over time whilst preserving many of their age-old belief systems and rituals.

We have also seen how indigenous Asian community traditions have been reworked to form the basis of universalistic philosophies (early Confucianism and Daoism) and religions (Confucianism and Daoism in their later forms). Asian peoples have made a place for these sophisticated forms of religion alongside their village traditions, as they have for other universalistic religions originating in India (Hinduism and Buddhism) and West Asia (Christianity and Islam). The extent to which the universalistic religions have replaced, as opposed to merely augmented or partially displaced, indigenous community traditions differs considerably from place to place. Further, all these processes unfold over time, and it is important to seek out why these processes have proceeded rapidly or slowly in different times and places.

The variety of religious traditions, both community and universalistic, and the complex relationships of traditions with each other make the map of religious affiliation in Asia today a real 'crazy quilt'. However, some broad patterns can be discerned, as discussed in Chapter 36. The extent to which secular philosophies which have arisen in Europe since the eighteenth century have displaced religions as means of understanding the world and shaping moral action will also be considered there.

Guide to further reading

Caldarola, Carlo (ed.), *Religion and Societies: Asia and the Middle East*,
    Mouton, The Hague, 1982
    A country-by-country survey of the development and present state of
    religious life in Asia, including West Asia, edited by a sociologist. This
    work contains both historical and sociological perspectives on Asian
    religious life.

Eliade, Mircea, *A History of Religious Ideas*, University of Chicago Press,
    Chicago, 1982
    An exploration of the development of religious thought from the
    beginnings of human history to modern times by a doyen of the
    history of religions. This multi-volume work covers both universalistic
    religions and reflections on the nature of the community religions
    which preceded them.

Kitagawa, Joseph M. (ed.), *The Religious Traditions of Asia*, Macmillan
    Publishing Co., New York, 1989
    Excerpts from *The Encyclopedia of Religion* (Mircea Eliade, editor in
    chief). Comprehensive historical treatment on selected topics from the
    Encyclopedia by prominent authors. Emphasises institutional and po-
    litical history rather than the history of religious thought.

Smart, Ninian, *The World's Religions: Old Traditions and Modern Transfor-
    mations*, Cambridge University Press, Cambridge, 1989
    A leading historian of religion provides an historical overview of
    religious history, taking regions rather than universalistic religions as
    the main organising device for his discussion. Much contemporary
    material.

6 | Literature and the arts

In the precolonial period, the arts and literatures of East and Southeast Asia were extremely different from each other in their natures, their forms, their content, their traditions and in the societies which produced them and reflected them. For this reason, it has proved necessary to treat them in quite separate sections. The only major link between the two is Vietnam, a Confucianised country in Southeast Asia which is heavily influenced by Chinese traditions. Yet even in this case it is essential to remember the strong indigenous characteristics of Vietnamese arts and literature.

East Asia

In East Asia, the influence of Chinese culture has been very strong indeed, not only on society and ideology (especially through Confucianism), but also on literature and the arts. Nevertheless, while there are branches of Korean and Japanese literature and arts which show very great Chinese influence, there are also those which demonstrate the strong individuality of Korean and Japanese cultures. If the period of focus is the sixteenth century on, then Chinese influence is at its greatest in such aristocratic arts as history-writing, Confucian philosophy and calligraphy, but weakest in those favoured by other classes of society, such as certain forms of drama. The influence of China in the field of traditional literature and arts is substantially greater over Korea than over Japan. In the seventeenth century in Japan there was a flowering of bourgeois culture centred on Osaka and later Edo which was to exercise an enormous influence over the Japanese arts, and which was more or less entirely Japanese in origin.

The aristocratic arts

From the point of view of creativity, the Chinese aristocratic arts were in decline by the sixteenth century. This was partly due to the stereotypical attitudes spawned by the heavy Confucianism of the examination system. Those who appreciated the aristocratic arts belonged to an educated class in which the scholar-gentleman was critic, connoisseur, collector and amateur artistic technician, rather than creator. These were highly aesthetic men whose private appreciation went as much to Daoism or Buddhism as to Confucianism. It was part of their education to be able to paint, play the seven-stringed zither *(guqin)* or write poetry, but they rarely dared strike out in new directions.

The court patronised the aristocratic arts. From the 1730s, the Qing court had its own special drama troupes. Painters worked at court, and most of the emperors strove to be good painters themselves. Outside the court, the main centre for the arts was in the south, specifically the lower Yangzi valley, in which the provinces of Jiangsu, Zhejiang, Anhui and Jiangxi were paramount.

Possibly the most distinguished and innovative Chinese painter of the late imperial age was Dong Qichang (1555–1636), a southerner whose style later became regarded as 'orthodox'. He carried on the tradition of landscape painting, in which the earlier Song dynasty (960–1280) had represented a high point, but his style was more individualistic and personal. Dong was typical of the traditional Chinese painter in being quintessentially a nature-lover and admirer. He strove to capture not the external realities of his subject, but its essence, as he himself conceived it. This kind of thinking was actually more Daoist than Confucian; it expressed the amateur's attempt to escape the realities of the everyday official world represented by Confucianism.

The Korean painting of the Yi dynasty tended strongly to follow the subjects and style of Chinese models. Landscape painting in the Chinese style remained a strong feature of Korean art throughout the Yi dynasty. In Japan, also, many painters retained the influence of traditional Chinese landscape painting, and of Dong Qichang in particular.

A major branch of literature sponsored by the Chinese court was the ancient art of history-writing. The most important task of the court historians early in each dynasty was to write the 'standard history' *(zhengshi)* of the previous dynasty from the detailed records kept by the historians of the earlier era. The first standard history was the *Records of the Historian (Shiji)*, mostly by Sima Qian, who began working on his *magnum opus* in 104 B.C. The standard history of the Ming *(Mingshi)* was completed early in 1736. It is extremely long, but follows exactly the style of earlier models. The essence of this style is that there is an enormous quantity of detailed information, with facts accurately dated, but very little to distinguish what the authors considered important, and virtually no interpretation outside brief and highly stereotypical Confucian moral judgments. The standard histories, especially the later ones, are characterised by a cut-and-paste method of writing. In other words, the historian copied down extracts from his sources character by character with very little critical evaluation of why certain matters should be included and others excluded.

The Koreans took up the same style of history-writing, and it became one of the most important branches of Korean literature. In 1451, the *Koryo sa (History of Koryo)* was completed at the Yi dynasty court. Designed to record the official account of the preceding dynasty's history, it was very much in the style of traditional Chinese scholarship. At that time formal Korean literature was always written in Chinese characters.

History-writing was assisted by the introduction of movable-type printing early in the fifteenth century. The motive was mainly to facilitate the introduction of Confucian texts to the scholar class, but in fact this was the first time anywhere in the world that movable-type printing had been extensively used. The widespread use of printing in Japan dates from the late sixteenth century.

The spread of Confucianism in Japan in the Tokugawa period brought with it attention to various kinds of Confucian writings, including moral, philosophical and historical. Tokugawa Ieyasu's descendants were in the forefront of bringing Confucian works to the *samurai* class. One of his grandsons, Tokugawa Mitsukuni (1628–1700), started to compile a Chinese-language history of Japan on the model of Sima Qian's *Records of the Historian*, but he never completed the task.

The folk and bourgeois arts

In all three countries of East Asia, the most important developments in literature and the arts from the sixteenth century on were in the popular arts. In China and Japan, this was especially so in the theatre. Although the Chinese scholarly class had patronised its own form of drama through private troupes drawn from slaves and servants in private mansions, the most flourishing theatre was that of the regional popular drama. Each area had its own style of music with the dramas sung in the local dialect. The main development of the regional theatre in China took place from the sixteenth century on, both in the north and south. Wandering companies would take popular stories from place to place, with the largest number of performances being on festival days. Popular theatre was highly integrated with society as a whole, and this was one of its greatest strengths. Its stories and characters were familiar to all people and part of their upbringing, no matter what their class. They created images of good and evil in the minds of the people and thus exercised a considerable influence over Chinese attitudinal patterns.

The most spectacular development of Chinese popular theatre was in the capital, Beijing. From the late eighteenth century, groups of actors from Sichuan in the southwest, and Anhui and other parts of the lower Yangzi Valley took the capital by storm with their art, the various styles combining to form the Beijing Opera. The earliest phase of this art emphasised boys or men performing the roles of women, but this changed in the 1830s towards a more heroic form of theatre in which older men, generals, statesmen and rebels took over the stage. Nevertheless, the performance of female roles by boys or men, which was actually already old in China, continued to be practised in the theatre not only in Beijing, but elsewhere in China as well, until the twentieth century.

Although a fully developed professional drama tradition did not emerge in Korea until the twentieth century, the distinguished *no* drama had been known in Japan since the fourteenth century and had already developed a fine literature by the time the urban bourgeois culture of Japan refined the *kabuki* and spawned the puppet theatre in the seventeenth century. The theatres, along with brothels, bathhouses and restaurants, were part of the thriving amusement quarters which formed a stark contrast to the prevailing and highly disciplined Confucianised *samurai* society of the Tokugawa period.

As in China, men played female roles. This was because the government banned women from the stage, believing them responsible for the dissoluteness of the lives of many of the patrons of the theatre. It was not Chinese influence that led to the custom of men's playing female roles; indeed there is hardly any sign of Chinese influence in the Japanese drama.

Japan's most famous dramatist is Chikamatsu Monzaemon (1653–1724), who is credited with the creation of the Japanese puppet theatre. The topics of Chikamatsu's plays are of basically two kinds: historical dramas and domestic pieces. The former 'transmitted without noticeable alteration the values of the *samurai* and were replete with scenes of his drama and battle'.[1] The domestic plays are about sexual love, a topic hardly found in *samurai* writing, and frequently end in double suicides. Chikamatsu's view of art was that it lay 'in the slender margin between the real and the unreal. It is unreal, and yet it is not unreal; it is real, and yet it is not real.'[2]

In the course of the eighteenth century, Edo reached maturity and even overtook Osaka as a cultural centre. The *kabuki* replaced the puppets as the main theatrical attraction. Nevertheless, the style and topics of the puppet theatre were at first very influential in the *kabuki*. In the course of time, however, there was a gradual shift in taste which no doubt reflected the maturing urban society. The most popular dramas were those on erotic, grotesque or mysterious subjects, or on the exploits of outlawed heroes. There was also a move from stylisation to realism.

The art of story-telling is very ancient in China. The famous stories of Chinese history were transmitted by the story-tellers and were written down to become novels. In the fourteenth century there appeared full texts of novels such as *The Romance of the Three Kingdoms (Sanguo yanyi)*, which records heroic stories of the warlike period of the second and third centuries A.D. Being popular literature, they were subject to variation, and numerous versions were published over the centuries.

Although aristocratic Korean literature continued to be written exclusively in Chinese, the Koreans did indeed develop their own writing system. Known as *hangul*, it was devised by King Sejong and completed in 1443, being officially adopted by royal rescript in 1446. It originally consisted of 28 simple symbols (although only 24 are now in use), which in combination could represent any sound found in Korean. The invention of the *hangul* system enabled the birth of a genuinely Korean literature.

The first major literary work to be written entirely in *hangul* was a novel, *The Tale of Hong Kil-tong (Hong Kil-tong jon)*, a satire attacking discrimination against concubines and their children. It became a model for quite a few later novels. Though at first even novels were mostly written in Chinese characters, eventually fiction came to be written exclusively in *hangul*. The main themes were love or family stories. To this day the most famous and popular of all Korean folk romances is the anonymous *Tale of Ch'unhyang (Ch'unhyang jon)*, a love story about the son of a provincial magistrate and Ch'unhyang, the daughter of a courtesan *(kisaeng)*.

Just as in China, the relationship between the story-teller and novelist in Korea was a close one. A Western source of the very late Yi dynasty says:

> If a gentleman of means wants to 'read' a novel, he does not ordinarily send out to a book-stall and buy one, but he sends for a professional story-teller, who comes with his attendant and drum and recites a story, often consuming an entire day or even two days in the recital.[3]

The great age of the Japanese novel was the eleventh century. Although none of the prose writings of the Tokugawa urban merchant culture could rival that earlier period, the seventeenth century did produce its own genre of novels which mirrored its society well and attracted a substantial readership in its own time. An early example, and perhaps the most representative, is Ihara Saikaku (1642–93), who in a precise and undeclamatory style wrote realistic accounts of merchant families and of the amusement quarters. His best known work is *The Life of an Amorous Man (Koshoku ichidai otoko)* (1682), which describes in detail the numerous heterosexual and homosexual love affairs of its hero. No doubt it says something about Tokugawa merchant society that, in contrast either to Western or Chinese counterparts, the main character of such a novel receives no punishment for his exploits, and does not come to a bad end.

Despite the continuing influence of Chinese traditional painting in Japan and Korea, there grew in those two countries styles of painting which were actually much more innovative and much more characteristic of their own particular cultures. In Japan from the late seventeenth century, professional painters in the employ of the rich, including the emerging merchant class, developed a form of genre painting known as *ukiyoe*, which became very popular in the form of wood-block prints. Although they were initially monochrome, they soon developed into polychrome so that the term *ukiyoe* became synonymous with colour prints. In the early period, the main themes were popular actors and famous beauties of the day, but in the late Tokugawa period, they turned back to landscape painting. Ando Hiroshige (1797–1858) painted familiar landscapes of the main routes of travel from unusual perspectives and won enormous popularity among many sections of society. To this day, Hiroshige remains one of the most famous of all Japanese painters. In Korea, also, the eighteenth century saw a move towards independence of Chinese models with the growth of genre painting. The two most famous painters of this kind were Sin Yun-bok, who painted the daily life of the urban upper class, and Kim Hong-do, whose speciality was the manners and customs of peasants, shopkeepers and artisans.

Southeast Asia

Southeast Asia in the sixteenth century presented a picture of astonishing cultural diversity. No single power, local or foreign, had ever controlled the whole region or managed to impose its cultural norms, and the visitor who travelled from island to island in the archipelago, or from river valley to ridge top in the peninsula, would pass through a multitude of distinct cultures and civilisations on his or her journey.

Historians of the old school tended to emphasise the outside elements in these cultures. Southeast Asia's key position on the maritime trade route between China and India and the West made it open to ideas and influences from outside. Scholars, therefore, could see a complex inter-weaving of foreign cultural elements, especially Indian, Chinese and Arab. Vietnam, moreover, was under direct Chinese rule for many centuries to A.D. 939 and Chinese culture left a deep imprint on government, daily life and civilisation. Today, however, we have become more conscious of the indigenous Southeast Asian role in selecting different elements of foreign culture and moulding them into thoroughly indigenous forms, with no more relation to the culture of origin than, say, *Macbeth* has to Scottish history.

Southeast Asia's oldest recorded cultural tradition is musical. Great bronze kettledrums were cast in Vietnam from 300 B.C. and soon afterwards spread to the archipelago. On some remote islands, similar drums can still be seen in ritual use, but on Java they diversified into a percussion ensemble of tuned *gong* (a Javanese word) and chimes of different sizes, in which the interweaving of notes from different instruments was more important than the melodic line. Ensembles of this tradition, generally called *gamelan*, can be found throughout the western archipelago, and probably influenced the development of the *pi phat* ensemble of the Thai courts.

Gamelan was never a static tradition. Musical notation was sparingly used, and musicians experimented with different forms and combinations of instruments. Chinese and West Asian instruments — the Chinese zither, for instance, and the Turkish *zurna* or oboe — were adopted, sometimes to embroider a melodic edge over the percussion ensemble, sometimes largely displacing it. Perhaps because the older bronze instruments were associated with rituals of power, they were commonly reserved for men, whereas women often seem to have been the conduit by which new instruments were first assimilated by Southeast Asian cultures. The largely string *mahori* ensemble of the Thai courts, for instance, is the special preserve of women. In Vietnam, the indigenous drum tradition was largely displaced, except amongst hill tribes, by Chinese musical forms, though instruments such as the monochord *(dan bu)* were local inventions.

One of the main roles of music was to accompany various forms of dance and drama. Community entertainment was highly valued and early European visitors to the region were often struck by the frequency of public performances and festivities. Except to some extent in Vietnam, where Chinese influence was strong, there was no sharp distinction between court and popular culture. Performing artists began their careers in the village and moved widely as times and talent permitted to regional and central courts without significantly changing their cultural form. Drama told a variety of stories. Most widespread were two epics, the *Ramayana* (known as the *Ramakien* to the Thai) and the *Mahabharata*, as well as the Buddhist *Jataka* stories, but the details of these originally Indian tales were extensively changed to give them a Southeast Asian setting and to make their protagonists the ancestors of local dynasties.

Dance drama also had a more serious purpose. The movements of the dancer and the story performed put him or her in special contact with the cosmos and were a means both of attracting benevolent spirits and of accumulating spiritual power. This was particularly so in forms of drama where the humanity of the artist was partly concealed, as in the masked theatre (*topeng* in Indonesia, *khon* for the Thai), or the shadow puppets *(wayang kulit)* of Java, an ancient form which had spread to the mainland by at least the fifteenth century. *Wayang kulit* performances telling an episode from the *Mahabharata* begin some time after dusk and continue until dawn, a single puppeteer *(dalang)* manipulating the puppets, improvising the dialogue and cueing the *gamelan* for the whole performance. Shadows on the screen, flickering in the light of a coconut oil lamp, symbolise the state of the world — half illusion, half reality — while the *dalang* who controls all becomes a metaphor for the cosmic forces governing human existence.

Shadow puppets were also a powerful tool in shaping popular attitudes. The shadows were understood not only to represent the puppet behind the screen but to symbolise living figures in society, from kings to local identities, and a deft *dalang* could transmit a strong social or political message by the episode he (or occasionally she) chose and the words given to the characters. In the fourteenth century, this was one of the means by which Islam spread in the interior of Java. Vietnamese opera *(hat boi)*, too, had a political tinge. Its forms were closely based on Chinese models — according to legend, the Vietnamese learnt opera from a Chinese opera troupe captured in battle in 1285 who were offered their lives in exchange for teaching young Vietnamese their art — but the plots commonly described episodes from Vietnam's ancient feud with China and so tended to strengthen national consciousness.

Except in Vietnam, the peoples of Southeast Asia wrote in scripts derived directly or indirectly from Sanskrit. In the archipelago, literacy was remarkably widespread, partly because many languages were written in relatively simple scripts of fourteen to seventeen letters and partly because literacy was intimately involved with courtship customs. In a great many regions of the archipelago, young women and men would court by exchanging four-line poems or *pantun*, often suggestive or humorous. The need to secure a desirable partner created an enormous incentive in young people to learn to read and write while the everyday involvement of women and men in recording details of commerce, noting messages and the like ensured that the literacy acquired in youth survived long enough for a woman to pass it on to her children.

On the mainland, literacy was much more restricted. In Thailand, reading and writing were closely associated with Buddhist religious scholarship, which was in turn largely reserved for males. In Vietnam, the complicated Chinese script was a barrier to literacy amongst all except those with the wealth and time to enjoy an extended education. The tonal system of both languages presented special difficulties in preparing easily remembered scripts. Thai was systematised in about 1283, when King Ram Kamheng devised a workable script, while only in the fifteenth century did Vietnam evolve a still-complex demotic version of Chinese script called *nom*. Sadly, too, literacy diminished in the archipelago with the introduction of Islam and Christianity, both of which tended to reserve education for males and were actively suspicious of the sexual freedom which courtship rituals seemed to give to women.

Southeast Asians in the archipelago wrote on *lontar* palm leaves, etching the characters into the surface of the leaf and rubbing it with charcoal to make them stand out. Most documents, such as *pantun*, were short, occupying a single leaf, but histories and long literary or religious works could be written on thick bundles of leaves; in Thailand palm leaves were common, but parchment was also used; the Vietnamese had learnt the use of paper from the Chinese by the third century. Although there was no sharp cultural difference between court and village, long written works were invariably commissioned by a king from his corps of writers and were generally intended mainly to reflect glory on his name. In contrast, the epics told in villages at night, like music, were not written down but were passed from story-teller to story-teller over the generations.

Oral traditions are fragile and the vast bulk of such stories have been lost as story-tellers died without the chance to pass them on to later generations. *Lontar* leaves, for their part, perish rapidly in Southeast Asia's tropical climate. Even the better materials and more benign climate of Vietnam have left us with remarkably little literature from before modern times. Those works which remain have survived either because they were copied and re-copied over the centuries under the auspices of courts or temples, or because they survived in oral form until Southeast Asians or Westerners took the initiative to have them recorded. What remains includes several gems. The *Nagarakertagama* by Prapanca is an epic poem describing Javanese civilisation in the fourteenth century. The Malay Annals or *Sejarah Melayu* purport to trace the founding of the Sultanate of Melaka (Malacca) from Alexander the Great and the powerful Sumatran kingdom of Srivijaya and is the outstanding Malay work of the fifteenth century.

From the sixteenth and seventeenth centuries, however, the legacy is far richer, partly because rising wealth in the port cities of the region created a host of new patrons amongst the merchant class. A remarkable group of rulers, too, many of them authors in their own right, encouraged a literary flowering which went beyond the old panegyric histories. The tragic romance *Pra Lo*, retold by the Thai king Narai (r. 1656–88), is still a major work of Thai literature, while the cosmopolitan Karaeng Pattingalloang (1600–54) turned seventeenth century Makassar into a major consumer of literature. It was in this era that Malay, formerly restricted to the Malay Peninsula, the eastern coast of Sumatra and adjacent islands, expanded to become the *lingua franca* of the archipelago and the coasts of the mainland, not just as a traders' pidgin but as a sophisticated language of religion and philosophy. Authors such as Nuruddin al-Raniri and Hamzah Fansuri, who was born in the Thai capital Ayutthaya, typified this cultural florescence, producing outstanding poetry and prose strongly influenced by Muslim mysticism.

The numerous contemporary tourists who carry home woodcarvings from Bali are sharing in a tradition of artistry with origins that can be traced back as far as Southeast Asia's musical traditions. As with literature, we have only a fragmentary record of this tradition. Southeast Asia's tropical climate is as voracious a consumer of wood carvings, cloth and painting as it is of *lontar* leaves, and for centuries our record is limited to stone carving and metalwork.

Stone carving, however, does shed some light on other artistic forms. The representation of daily life on monuments such as the Borobudur, a massive ninth-century Buddhist *stupa* in Central Java, tells us not only important information on the assimilation and transformation of Indian sculptural and architectural forms but also fascinating details about the culture of early Java: clothing and ornaments, music and dance, warfare and technology, even social hierarchy and diet. On the mainland, the great

Khmer temple complex of Angkor in modern Cambodia is our principal record of early Khmer civilisation, which heavily influenced the development of Thai culture, especially after the capture of Angkor in 1369.

Amongst the Thai and their predecessors in the valley of the Chao Phraya, bronze was a favoured artistic medium and some of the finest Southeast Asian artworks in existence are Buddha images which take Indian models and transform them, by a twist of the eyelid, a turn of the hand or a new decorative motif, into works of unmistakably Southeast Asian origin. In the archipelago, by contrast, bronze had a more functional role, in musical instruments and weapons, and the finest artistry was in rarer metals, especially gold. Metalwork even blended with weaving in the form known as *songket*, in which fine gold and silver threads were woven into cloth, giving it a special lustre and beauty.

Although the climate permitted Southeast Asians to wear relatively few clothes, cloth had a special cultural significance, both as a bearer of symbolic or magical designs and as a status symbol. Cloth such as *songket* drew its significance both from the enormous labour input required to create it and from the fact that it blended the arts of weaving and metalwork, traditionally the preserve of women and men respectively. *Ikat* and double-*ikat*, in which the threads of the cloth are tie-dyed before weaving, carried greater meaning in its patterns than in its means of production, as was true of *batik*, the technique of decorating cloth by painting its surface with wax and immersing the whole cloth in dye so that the waxed portions remain unaffected. Batik seems to have emerged in Java in the seventeenth century from a much older tradition of cloth painting, and became a sophisticated and diverse art.

Even more so than in music or drama, Vietnam followed China in its visual arts. Lacquerware and silk were specialities of the Vietnamese craftsmen and part of the trade with more southerly states.

Vietnam, too, was ahead of the rest of the region in the production of ceramics and joined China in meeting the enormous demand for crockery utensils in the rest of Southeast Asia between the tenth and sixteenth centuries. From late in the thirteenth century, however, Thailand became a major producer, with kilns outside the capital, Sukhothai, producing the celebrated fine celadon ware for local use and export.

Conclusion

In the seventeenth century, Asian literature and culture presented a kaleidoscopic picture of diverse cultural endeavour. The twin impacts of imperialism/colonialism and modernisation were to exercise a profound impact on this picture and transform it dramatically. At the same time, it was a mark of the strengths of the existing traditions that they survived this onslaught, in some ways even gaining new life from it. Tradition and modernity confronted each other, but were also forced to accommodate to one another, and in some ways even to learn from one another.

Guide to further reading

Brandon, James R. (ed.), *The Cambridge Guide to Asian Theatre*, Cambridge University Press, Cambridge, 1992

This extracts, rearranges, revises and updates those contributions dealing specifically with Asian theatres in *The Cambridge Guide to World Theatre*, edited by Martin Banham and published by Cambridge University Press, Cambridge, 1988. It covers both the traditional and modern periods and includes all the traditions relevant to this chapter.

Kato, Shuichi, *A History of Japanese Literature, Volume 2, The Years of Isolation*, trans. Don Sanderson, Macmillan, London and Basingstoke, 1983

This is the relevant volume of a three-volume general history of Japanese literature, the first covering 'the first thousand years' and the third 'the modern years'. The coverage is broad, but simply presented. There are biographical notes on the main authors considered, and a glossary of terms, but documentation for the text itself is very sparse.

Liu Wu-chi, *An Introduction to Chinese Literature*, Indiana University Press, Bloomington and London, 1966

Still an excellent general survey of Chinese literature from the earliest times to the first part of the twentieth century. There are three chapters on drama.

Reid, Anthony, *Southeast Asia in the Age of Commerce 1450–1680: Volume 1: The Land Below the Winds*, Yale University Press, New Haven and London, 1988

This is a fine survey of Southeast Asian culture in the era immediately before significant European influence.

Swann, Peter C., *Art of China, Korea, and Japan*, Praeger, New York, 1963

The beauty of this well written and well-illustrated book is that it covers all three countries of Eastern Asia. It is comprehensive from a chronological point of view, except that there is hardly anything on the twentieth century.

Notes

1 Shuichi Kato, *A History of Japanese Literature, Volume 2, The Years of Isolation*, trans. Don Sanderson, Macmillan, London and Basingstoke, 1983, p. 89.

2 See Ryusaku Tsunoda, *Sources of Japanese Tradition*, Wm Theodore de Bary and Donald Keene, comp., Columbia University Press, New York, 1958, p. 448.

3 Hulbert, Homer B., *The Passing of Korea*, Yonsei University Press, Seoul, 1969 reprint, p. 312. This work was originally published in 1906.

7 | Administration and rebellion in East Asia

The fourteenth century saw the establishment of strong and lasting centralised secular states in China and Korea. In China, the Ming (1368–1644) and Qing (1644–1911) dynasties and in Korea, the Yi dynasty (1392–1910) headed highly stable governments which, until their last decades, eschewed change of virtually all kinds. The ideological basis of these states was Confucianism, which, in its political manifestation, belongs in this chapter rather than in Chapter 5. In Japan, the Tokugawa Shogunate (1603–1868) founded a centralised and Confucianised feudal state, which placed such a high priority on stability that it tried to prevent all political change and to that end introduced a formal policy of isolation from the outside world, or 'closed country' (sakoku).

Confucianism

Despite their differences, Confucianism was enormously important as a bulwark of government in all three of these East Asian countries. In all of them it had been either dominant or influential for centuries before, but reached its height in the period preceding the Western impact of the nineteenth century.

Confucius, who is discussed from the religious point of view in Chapter 5, specifically disavowed primary concern for the next life. His main interest was in how good government could be secured and how people should relate to each other in the interests of that objective.

Confucius worked in a specific context. It was of a China divided into numerous different states, where the ruling Zhou dynasty had lost all effectiveness even though it was still theoretically at the head. Real power lay with feudal rulers and smaller feudal fiefdoms. Confucius spent much of his life going from feudal ruler to feudal ruler giving advice on good government. He also offered his own services as adviser, but few appointed him for long. In terms of his personal career, Confucius was not a success. On the other hand, in historical terms he was supremely successful in that an ideology of such extreme influence in East Asian and Vietnamese history bears his name.

The ideas of Confucius rest on ethical concepts. The 'five ethics' are humanity, righteousness, propriety, wisdom and faithfulness, of which the first is probably the most important. Asked by a disciple to define 'humanity' *(ren)*, Confucius answered: 'to be able to practise five virtues everywhere in the world constitutes humanity', the five virtues being courtesy, magnanimity, good faith, diligence and kindness.[1]

Another key concept is filial piety, discussed in Chapter 5. The emphasis on this virtue is probably stronger in Confucianism than in any other Chinese or non-Chinese system of thought. It is obviously related to the central position of the family in Chinese traditional society (see Chapter 4).

The person who has acquired these various virtues is called a gentleman *(junzi)*. The significance of this concept reflects a generally slighter concern in East Asian philosophy with abstracts or with eternal verities than with how people should behave and treat each other. Some aphorisms concerning the gentleman are that he does not specialise, practises what he teaches, is fair and impartial to all and does not form his own clique, and, in contrast to the small man whose love is for material gains, loves virtue. The fact that the term *junzi* is readily and accurately translated as 'gentleman', not 'gentleperson', emphasises the male-centredness of Confucianism, and indeed of traditional East Asian civilisation as a whole.

The Confucian passion for order, stability and proper hierarchy is obvious in the stress Confucius placed on correct titles. When one of his disciples asked Confucius what he would do first if asked to govern a state, he replied: 'I would rectify titles'. His justification for such a priority was as follows:

> If titles are incorrect, orders will not be carried out; and if orders are not carried out, then nothing can be achieved. That means that rites and music will not flourish, laws and punishments will be wide of the mark, and people will not know what to do.[2]

It is clear from this comment that one of the mechanisms for ensuring the sustenance of all virtues, indeed a virtue itself, is the rites or ceremonial. As in other societies, rites functioned as an outward manifestation of power and propriety in traditional Confucian societies. Confucius' strong approval of the ceremonial was nothing new in China, and he was in this, as in so much else, a transmitter rather than a creator: 'If a ruler can administer his state with the rites and courtesy, then what difficulty will he have?' and again, 'a man who is not humane, what has he to do with rites?'

It is through education that virtue and proper conduct are inculcated. Confucius believed that education should be available to all without class discrimination, an ideal which Confucian societies were generally unable to put into practice. The factor of political power should not be ignored. What Confucianism really meant by its stress on education was that the educated, and hence the virtuous, should rule. It is a political doctrine which in practice places power in the hands of those of the correct ideological persuasion, because education always means a particular type of education, the nature of which is determined by those already in power.

One of Confucius' leading disciples of a later age was Mencius (c. 372 B.C.–c. 289 B.C.), who developed several major Confucian doctrines more fully than the master himself. Among them is the political notion of the Mandate of Heaven. According to this idea, the vague supernatural force termed Heaven *(tian)* bestows on the virtuous the right to rule. Should he or his descendants turn wicked, cruel or corrupt, then Heaven withdraws the Mandate. When that happens, the people have the right to rebel and replace the wicked ruler with the man of virtue on whom the Mandate has devolved.

In China itself, Confucianism was suppressed during the reign of the tyrannical but strong Emperor Qin Shihuang, who reunified all the feudal states under his own sway in 221 B.C. His state ideology, termed legalism, held in essence that people behave properly not because of humanity or Confucian ethics, but through fear of laws and savage punishments. The legalists saw war as an appropriate instrument for the gaining of political power and strongly opposed the Confucianist tendency always to look to the past, rather than the present or future, for models. Qin Shihuang is famous in East Asian history not only for completing the building of the Great Wall, but also because in 213 and 212 B.C. he had Confucian books burned and Confucian scholars buried alive, hoping thereby to uproot the influence of Confucianism.

Qin Shihuang believed his dynasty would last ten thousand years. However, it outlasted his death in 210 B.C. by less than four years. The succeeding Han dynasty (206 B.C.–A.D. 220) revived Confucianism and took over some of the elements of legalism, such as savage laws, but also tried to eliminate its overall influence. The great Emperor Wudi (r. 140 B.C.–87 B.C.) banned all students of legalist philosophy from court and showed a definite bias in favour of the Confucian tradition. From this time on, the government paid for much of the lower bureaucracy to receive a Confucianist education, and Confucianism became recognised as the state ideology.

Confucianism's impact sank in China from about the third century A.D. Its fortunes suffered ebbs and flows, with Daoism and Buddhism competing for the minds of China's educated and influential men. In the ninth century, Confucianism began a strong revival while, with gathering intensity from 842 to 845, Buddhism was subjected to persecution which affected it so deeply that it never fully recovered. The Confucian revival absorbed many important Buddhist and metaphysical elements, although the family-centred ethical and political strand definitely remained the core of the ideology.

This Confucian revival is known as Neo-Confucianism. It spawned a whole series of highly significant philosophers, the most famous of whom was Zhu Xi (1130–1200), who is credited with the synthesis of the moral and metaphysical strands of Confucianism. In both Korea and Japan, it was in its Neo-Confucian form that the ideology had its most profound effect.

Administration and bureaucracy in East Asia
China

The period from the time the Mongols reunified China in 1280 to the fall of the Manchu dynasty in 1911 was one of absolutism in China. The Mongol invasion had the permanent effect of reducing checks on imperial power. This was a foreign dynasty which had achieved authority in China through a particularly brutal conquest, a people used to giving total power to the head man.

The Ming and Qing emperors retained this greater imperial authority over courtiers and officials. The Ming retained the Mongol custom whereby the emperor could have senior officials flogged while the court watched. In 1380 the first Ming emperor Hongwu abolished the post of prime minister permanently because he believed the occupant was plotting against him. The contemporary historian Charles Hucker explains this shift of power in class terms:

> The disappearance from Chinese society of the early imperial age's entrenched hereditary aristocracy accounts in large part for the new absolutism. The disposition of military forces in the later dynasties gave military leaders no power bases from which they might threaten the throne. Members of imperial families and imperial relatives by marriage, who in former times could have counted on being appointed to the highest civil and military offices, were now systematically excluded from any governmental positions of importance and were normally even kept at a distance from the capital. By entrusting governmental administration increasingly to nonhereditary bureaucrats who were subject to promotion, demotion, and dismissal at the imperial pleasure, emperors protected themselves from the rise of any new entrenched power group that might threaten them.
>
> The newly dominant civil service bureaucracy of the later imperial age was thus no threat to the throne; rather, it gave the later dynasties greater efficiency and durability than had been known previously.[3]

The Ming and Qing developed a three-sided administration based on earlier precedents which even the Mongols had retained. The three were a civil bureaucracy under six ministries, a centralised and hierarchical military bureaucracy, and the censorate. The third of these consisted of a Board of Censors, the function of which was to watch over, and if necessary investigate, the other officials, and in addition a censorial staff attached to each of the ministries. These censors were very powerful and had direct access to the emperor. They could accuse other officials, and in theory criticise the emperor, although in fact this was extremely dangerous and few dared to do so. The bureaucracy existed at regional, provincial, district and county levels, as well as centrally. An estimate for 1469 suggests that there were altogether more than 100 000 civil and over 80 000 military officials in the Chinese bureaucracy.

The selection of these officials was through an examination system based on Confucianism. It operated on three levels, the lowest being the county and the highest the capital. Those who did the best at the lowest level, according to a quota, could proceed to the next level upwards. The most outstanding candidates were those who succeeded in the highest level triennial examinations in Beijing and thus became 'presented scholars' (*jinshi*).

Successful candidates were appointed to bureaucratic posts, the level depending to some extent on how well they did and at which level. Even after they were actually in office, they had to continue undertaking the examinations, and their promotion depended on how well they performed.

The system, which was managed by the Board of Rites, had the advantage that it brought the best scholars into the running of the country. China was in theory a meritocracy, a state run by the educated and virtuous, just as Confucianism had always advocated. But this also had very serious drawbacks. Perhaps the most important of these was that it became very conservative and self-perpetuating. China was stable, indeed too stable, and therefore resistant to change, and the examinations were partly responsible. They were designed to test knowledge of a limited number of Confucian books. In 1487 the famous 'eight-legged essay' style was set down as standard; eight major headings for writing examination papers. This stereotypical approach produced a deadening effect on the minds of the officialdom and the people who were supposed to be the country's intellectual cream, and it grew worse as the centuries of late imperial China wore on. The examinations held extreme social prestige and bestowed the same on those who did well in them. Education thus became in theory a source of power and social status.

In fact, these examinations were not really the only means of entrance to the bureaucracy. Depending on the actual stability of the particular period, various forms of corruption grew stronger or weaker. Nepotism was quite standard. Under the Qing dynasty, the practice of buying office became more and more widespread. Merchants may in theory have been low in the social scale, but their wealth came to be able to buy them power and hence prestige.

Another source of power under the Ming was the eunuchs. Emperor Hongwu had made a conscious and largely successful attempt to keep eunuch power in check, but they were one of the groups who moved in to take advantage of his abolition of the prime ministership in 1380. After a special school was set up to train them in the 1420s, the number of eunuchs at court increased greatly, rising to many thousands at any one time. Their power was considerable outside the court as well, and there were even men who had themselves deliberately castrated to gain power. The worst period for eunuch power was the 1620s, when the notorious Wei Zhongxian was able to terrorise not only the court but the whole empire with his secret service and his enormous influence over the emperor himself. According to the Manchu Kangxi Emperor, late-Ming eunuchs 'obtained the power to write endorsements on the emperors' memorials' and then 'passed the memorials on to their subordinates to handle',[4] in this way gaining control over the court.

Although the Manchu emperors had hundreds of eunuchs at court, they were never able to attain the power they had held in the late Ming period. The Kangxi Emperor stated that he limited their number to about 400 and kept them working at menial jobs. There were no eunuchs in either Korea or Japan.

Korea

The Mongol invasion affected not only China, but also Korea. Mongol armies attacked that country in 1231, beginning a long conflict which resulted in the submission of Korea to the Mongols in 1258. However, the Mongols never actually overthrew the ruling Koryo dynasty, as they did the Jin and Song respectively in north and south China. Instead, they totally dominated the Koryo and imposed Mongol institutions, administration and official titles on Korea. They also used Korea as the base for two attempted but unsuccessful invasions of Japan, the first in 1274 and the second in 1281. In the event, Koryo even outlasted the collapse of the Mongol empire in the middle of the fourteenth century and the rise of the Ming in China in 1368. It succumbed finally to a revolt by one of its own generals, Yi Song-gye, who seized power in 1388 and four years later formally set up his own Yi dynasty, becoming known as King T'aejo.

Zhu Xi's interpretation of Confucianism had been introduced into Korea during the late Koryo period when the Mongols held sway over the country. Yi Song-gye had been careful to surround himself with Confucian advisors even before actually ascending the throne. The structure of Yi dynasty government was established in the early decades of its rule and was based closely on the Chinese model. There was a State Council, a Royal Secretariat and six ministries or boards, of personnel, revenue, ritual, war, justice and public works, named after the corresponding boards of Tang dynasty (618–907) China. The function of the Royal Secretariat was to draft orders and decrees; there were six secretaries in it, one responsible for each board. Initially, the State Council supervised the six boards, but when these were later placed under the King's direct control, the State Council was relegated to an advisory role only.

In addition, there were two censorial offices, that of the Inspector-General and of the Censor-General. Their functions were, respectively, to scrutinise and supervise government policy and the actions of government officials, the royal court and the king himself. In time, these bodies became extremely powerful.

The ruling official class in Korea was termed *yangban*. This word means literally 'two groups', specifically the civil and military officials. It was part of the aristocracy from the tenth century on. Under the Yi dynasty, each *yangban* family had to have at least one member in office to remain within the class and retain its wealth, so the term designated the whole of the aristocratic, land-owning and official class.

In 958, the Koryo government formally adopted the Chinese examination system to choose its officials. This grew in importance over the following centuries and Yi Song-gye immediately adopted it for his own dynasty. The format, style and content of the Korean examination system was closely modelled on China's, including the emphasis on Chinese Confucian books and ideology. The only major difference was that in Korea the system was less open — in effect, only members of the *yangban* class were eligible to sit.

Not only the examination system in particular, but the government structure in general was thus based closely on the Chinese model. However, it was by no means merely a replica. Indeed, King Sejong (r. 1418–50), who was the grandson of T'aejo and possibly the dynasty's greatest monarch, 'remarked that the political organisation of his kingdom was not and could not be a blind imitation of Chinese ways'.[5] Two major but related differences were the far weaker power of the Korean king by comparison with the Chinese emperor, and the correspondingly greater power of the aristocracy and *yangban* than of their counterparts in China. The Chinese emperor was the Son of Heaven and consequently enjoyed a quasi-religious authority. This was not the case with the Korean kings. The censorial offices functioned in Korea with considerably greater real authority than was ever the case in China.

Japan

The Confucian bureaucracy, chosen through examinations which characterised administration both in China and Korea, ensured civilian dominance. In Japan the situation was entirely different. The form of administration which prevailed from the late sixteenth century on was a centralised feudal state in which the military *shoguns*, based in Edo (today's Tokyo), held effective power, while the emperors, all in one dynasty and living in Kyoto, were figureheads who merely did as they were told.

The period is known as the Tokugawa because the founder of the shogunate was Tokugawa Ieyasu (1542–1616). After several decades of attempts by several leaders to reunify Japan, he completed the process by winning the great Battle of Sekigahara in 1600, and in 1603 getting the emperor to formally appoint him as *shogun*. The Tokugawa system of administration was more or less totally in place by the middle of the seventeenth century and remained virtually unchanged for over two centuries.

The highest class in this system was the *samurai*, who were warriors and also administrators. Below them were the peasants, artisans and merchants, in that order. Intermarriage between the *samurai* and lower classes was prohibited so as to prevent people moving upwards on the social scale. The greatest of the *samurai* were called *daimyo*. These functioned as military feudal lords over domains termed *han*, which gave their *daimyo* power and status according to several criteria, the main one of which was how much rice they could produce.

In theory, these *daimyo* had a considerable degree of autonomy within their own domains, but in practice the Tokugawa shogunate exercised substantial effective control over them. The Tokugawa not only arranged political marriages between itself and the main *daimyo*, but even prohibited direct contact, and especially marriage, among the *daimyo* families themselves unless they first obtained the express permission of the central government. Disloyalty was among the crimes which could lead the Tokugawa shogunate to confiscate a *daimyo's* domain or reduce its size.

Another mechanism whereby the Tokugawa shogunate could keep the *daimyo* in line was that all of them were forced to spend about half of their time in Edo itself attending on the *shogun*. Most of the *daimyo* went into Edo every other year and all kept mansions and retainers there. They were compelled to leave their wives and children there as hostages even when they returned to their own domains. Very detailed and expensive ceremonials were prescribed according to which the *daimyo* undertook large-scale processions from their own domain to Edo, and paid homage to the *shogun* when they were in residence there. In addition to ensuring that the military feudal lords would be subservient to the Tokugawa shogunate, this system enforced the building of a very fine network of roads throughout Japan.

Most of the officials of the shogunal government were chosen from the personal retainers of the *shogun* and, most importantly, from among the ranks of particular *daimyo* who had recognised Tokugawa Ieyasu as their overlord before 1600 and were thus considered more loyal than the others. These loyal *daimyo* contributed members of the *shogun's* main advisory group and two main administrative bodies, the latter of which functioned as cabinets under him. Although talent was sometimes a factor in selection or promotion, hereditary feudal status was much more important.

The philosophical basis of the Tokugawa political order was Confucianism. It was a secular order based on moral precepts of loyalty, obedience and hierarchy. It encouraged warriors to become the scholar-officials needed for the political system. For the Tokugawa, Buddhism, which had earlier been so very powerful in Japan, held comparatively little appeal, and even though the Japanese masses continued to believe in Buddhism, the Tokugawa was a period of decline for it. The Tokugawa was quite specific that the class structure it wanted for Japanese society was perfectly consistent with Confucianism. It was in the ethics and the social relations of the period that this moral ideology of Chinese origin exercised its greatest impact on Tokugawa Japan.

Confucianism also gained a strong following among Japanese scholars and philosophers of the Tokugawa period, especially in the Neo-Confucian synthetic form of Zhu Xi. Just as in the China of the Song period, the metaphysics of Neo-Confucianism appealed to scholars. But what was most attractive was the emphasis on the moral and secular foundation of political authority, the strong and hierarchical family and social order, the male-centredness, the moderation and conservatism in all things. The cultural influence of China was strong among the educated, even though Japan never saw fit to introduce the examination system.

Peasant rebellion

The emphasis on Confucian conservatism and law and order in China, Korea and Japan did not prevent the existence of opposition in the form of peasant uprisings. These were certainly not new either in Korea or Japan. Yet it is China which has the longest history of peasant revolts, and on the largest scale. The overwhelming majority of these peasant revolts failed in all three countries. But on the other hand, two of China's main dynasties, the Han and the Ming, were formed as a result of peasant uprisings, and their founders were of peasant origin.

There are several reasons why China's history is more studded with peasant revolts than either Korea's or Japan's. One is that the country is much larger and thus more difficult to govern. It is more disparate and less concentrated in language, ethnic or geographic terms. Imperial rule never extended below county level, and the remote regions far from provincial capitals were especially difficult for officials to control, so rebels could gather opposition forces there with a good chance of escaping the eye of the authorities. Another reason is ideological. The Mencian idea that it was right to rebel against a wicked ruler who had lost the Mandate of Heaven became very important in Chinese history, but was never accepted in either Korea or Japan.

A rebellion which fails is tantamount to treason, so horrendous punishments were prescribed for this crime in all three countries. In line with the family-centredness of Confucianism, the rebel's relations were also accorded some responsibility and hence punishment. From a practical point of view, to punish the family members also gave them a good reason for refusing protection to any potential rebel and thus dissuading him.

There were similarities in the sources of rebellion in all three countries: oppression by the rich or officials, extreme poverty blamed on the fiscal screws of landlords, droughts or other natural disasters, or epidemics. In Confucianism, comets, earthquakes, droughts or other natural disasters were omens of a change of rule, so in China they might be considered signs that the Mandate of Heaven had changed hands so that the situation was ripe for a rebellion and a new ruler.

In Confucianism, the peasants were supposed to be a reasonably high class. Yet they were so poor that they could see no match between their supposed status and their poverty. In China, peasants formed the backbone of opposition to the government. In Korea, the king was often actually more afraid of factionalism at court than of peasant rebels. In Japan, the way the government was structured suggests that the *shogun* feared opposition more from rival *daimyo* than from peasants. Urbanisation was a major social feature of eighteenth century Japan, and urban riots occurred from time to time during the eighteenth and nineteenth centuries, an important example being in 1837 in Osaka.

A significant similarity between the uprisings of the three countries was the importance of various kinds of folk religion as a source. These religions were often messianic and very much more egalitarian than the traditional Confucianism which dominated the political order, including in their attitudes towards the relations between the sexes. In Japan, the Tenri religion was founded by a woman named Nakayama Miki in the 1830s. It was one of a spate of rebellions which showed that 'peasants sensed something drastically wrong with their world and were trying to radically restructure their lives'. She blamed what a modern-day Westerner might describe as the Confucian tradition for the immoralities of the world and taught that all people should be 'brothers and sisters', equal and related.[6]

Although peasant rebellions reached a peak in the nineteenth century in all three countries, they were far more devastating in China than in Korea and much more serious in Korea than in Japan. Incomparably the largest in scale and historically most important rebellions in East Asia took place in China, and in late imperial times the Taipings take pride of place. These were numerous revolts in many parts of Korea during the nineteenth century but the Tonghak was the most serious of them.

The Taiping rebellion lasted from 1851 to 1864 and was led by Hong Xiuquan (1814–64). It was based on a form of fundamentalist Protestant Christianity, mixed with traditional Chinese religious ideas. Although its attempt to overthrow the Qing dynasty ultimately failed, it is still regarded as a forerunner of the modern-day revolution for its egalitarian policies. It held a major city, Nanjing, as its capital from 1853 to 1864, a longer period than any other unsuccessful rebellion in Chinese history. Its core area of activity included the provinces of Jiangsu, Zhejiang and Jiangxi, but it affected most of the south and for a brief period even parts of the north of China. The number of people who died as a result of the Taiping rebellion was very large, in the range of 20 to 30 million.

Tonghak means 'Eastern Learning', and the religious basis of the rebellion was syncretic with values and beliefs drawn from Christianity, Confucianism, Buddhism and Daoism. The founder was Ch'oe Cheu (1824–64), but he was not the leader of the main phase of the rebellion. An uprising began in 1862, but Ch'oe was arrested the following year and executed in 1864, which he had predicted would be a good year for Tonghak members. His martyrdom merely inflamed the situation. However, it was not until 1894 that the rebellion reached its peak, seriously threatening the Yi government itself. The court called on China for help and the landing of Chinese and Japanese forces in Korea provided the opportunity for the Sino-Japanese war of 1894–95.

Conclusion

Confucianism provides a common core of significance in the administration, politics and ideology of China, Korea and Japan in the hundreds of years preceding the nineteenth century. All countries were centralised states; all were secular. Confucian family-centredness and male-centredness provided a powerful force for social cohesion in all three.

However, the Chinese Confucian influence was very much more pronounced in Korea than in Japan, and although Korea had its own culture and was not just a copy of China, the differences between Japan and Korea were substantially greater in political and administrative terms from the fourteenth to the the nineteenth centuries than those between Korea and China. The two essential Japanese characteristics dividing its government and social system from China or Korea were its military bent and the persistence of classical (as opposed to Marxist) feudalism with lords and domains.

Not surprisingly, the later years of late imperial China, Yi-dynasty Korea and Tokugawa Japan were less stable and prosperous than the earlier periods. The process of decline was much slower in Korea than in either China or Japan, and much more thorough in China than in Japan, partly because Japan suffered no population explosion from the early eighteenth century on.

Of the three countries, Japan was incomparably the most successful in coping with the Western impact and the modern ideas and technology which it brought. Probably the higher status of the military in society, and the lack of the deadening effect of the examination system on the intellectual cream of society, were among the many reasons for this fact. Like Korea, but quite unlike China, Japan saw the growth of an entrepreneurial merchant class which helped it respond to, and even rival, Western capitalism, but as a very small nation, Korea was caught between the giants of China, Russia and Japan itself, and for a period succumbed to Japan as a colony.

Guide to further reading

Gernet, Jacques, *A History of Chinese Civilisation,* trans. Foster, J.R., Cambridge University Press, Cambridge, 1982 (hardback), 1985 (paperback)
This covers all periods from the earliest times to the death of Mao Zedong in 1976, and is topically comprehensive with sections on politics, economics, culture and foreign relations. It also provides an excellent balance between interpretation and description. It includes a detailed chronological table and bibliographies by period of coverage.

Han Woo-keun, *The History of Korea,* trans. Lee Kyung-shik, Eul-yoo Publishing Company, Seoul, 1970, 12th printing 1981
This work is a very useful compendium of information covering the whole of Korean history from the earliest times to 1948. There are seven parts, ranging from 'The Primitive and Tribal Societies' to 'The Contemporary Period'. The author writes as Professor of Korean History at Seoul National University.

Mason, R.H.P. & Caiger, J.G., *A History of Japan,* Charles E. Tuttle, Tokyo, 1972, 14th printing 1988
This covers all periods from the earliest times to the American occupation which followed the end of World War II. It is written in a clear and accessible style, and is fairly comprehensive without being excessively detailed.

Reischauer, Edwin O. & Fairbank, John K., *East Asia, The Great Tradition,* George Allen & Unwin, London, 1958
Together with its successor volume, Fairbank, John K., Reischauer, Edwin O. and Craig, Albert M., *East Asia, The Modern Transformation,* Houghton Mifflin, Boston, 1965, this outstanding work has been through numerous editions, including being broken up into China and

Japan volumes; for example, *China: Tradition and Transformation* and *Japan: Tradition and Transformation* were published in revised editions by Allen & Unwin, Sydney, London and Boston, in 1989. The virtue of the East Asia volume is that it includes all three countries of concern to this chapter: China, Japan and Korea. It is comprehensive and fair in its treatment and is still of enormous value, even though first published so long ago.

Notes

1 See the translation in de Bary, Wm Theodore, Wing-tsit Chan & Watson, Burton, *Sources of Chinese Tradition, Volume I*, Columbia University Press, New York and London, 1964, p. 26.

2 Szuma Chien, trans. Yang Hsien-yi and Gladys Yang, *Selections from Records of the Historian*, Foreign Languages Press, Peking, 1979, p. 20. This work is the first of the 'standard histories'. It was written mainly by Sima Qian (145 B.C.–86 B.C.).

3 Hucker, Charles O., *China's Imperial Past, An Introduction to Chinese History and Culture*, Stanford University Press, Stanford, 1975, pp. 304–5.

4 Spence, Jonathan D., *Emperor of China, Self-portrait of K'ang-hsi*, Vintage Books, New York, 1975, p. 46.

5 Han Woo-kueun, trans. Lee Kyung-shik, *The History of Korea*, Eul-yoo Publishing Company, Seoul, 1970, 1980, p. 229.

6 Hashimoto Mitsuru, 'The Social Background of Peasant Uprisings in Tokugawa Japan', in Tetsuo Najita and Koschmann, J. Victor (eds), *Conflict in Modern Japanese History, The Neglected Tradition*, Princeton University Press, Princeton, 1982, pp. 159, 160.

8 | Political patterns in Southeast Asia

Southeast Asia today comprises ten nation-states, each with well defined, internationally recognised borders, within which systems of laws are enforced by centrally appointed bureaucracies. All are modern states, despite differences in their political institutions.

However, the formation of modern states in Southeast Asia has not been the indigenous development it was in East Asia, as discussed in the previous chapter, or in Europe. The states of Southeast Asia are relatively recent formations, constituted in response to the enforced imposition of European colonialism and to the exigencies of the modern world order. In the process, traditional polities have been swept aside, even if some traditional political forms and concepts have been (sometimes rather self-consciously) woven into the modern political fabric.

Because the modern notion of the state carries with it a strong Euro-centric component, historians of early Southeast Asia have been reluctant to apply the term to traditional Southeast Asian polities lest the wrong impression be given of how these early political systems worked and were legitimated and sustained. To refer to the 'state' of Majapahit or Ayuthia is to conjure up an image of government and bureaucracy that is very far from applying to fifteenth-century Java or Siam (Thailand), let alone to earlier kingdoms.

To avoid potential anachronisms of this kind, historians have sought an alternative term drawn from the political traditions of the region, the definition of which would make clear the difference between indigenous polities and the modern state. One such term is *mandala*, a diagram of relationships; another is *negara*, meaning 'town', and by extension the region controlled by an urban centre. Both terms derive from Sanskrit, the sacred language of India, and reflect the Indian origins of political institutions and statecraft throughout most of Southeast Asia. The term *negara* was first used by Geertz to refer to what he has called the 'theatre state'.[1] In using this designation, Geertz drew attention to the important role of ceremonial and ritual in ordering social relations and legitimating the exercise of power in Southeast Asia.

Mandala, like 'polity', is a neutral term, free of the Eurocentric reson-
ances of the term 'state'. The *mandala* best known to the West refers to
those sacred diagrams of Buddhas identified with the four or eight
directions depicted in Tibetan Buddhism. But the word has a more
general application in that it defines a set of spatial relationships around
some central point, hence its meaning as 'wheel' or 'rim' or 'circum-
ference'. In the Indian political treatise known as the *Arthasastra*, ascribed
to the fourth century B.C. sage Kautilya, the term *mandala* is used to refer
to the circle of surrounding kingdoms with which a ruler must necessarily enter into relationships to ensure the security of his own realm.
Adjoining kingdoms are taken as potential enemies; those beyond again
as potential friends with whom common cause can be made to limit the
ambitions of common enemies.

Mandala in this sense stands as a model of interstate relations. It was
used by O.W. Wolters in a paper published in 1968 to illustrate the way
in which statecraft was practised between Southeast Asian kingdoms.[2] In
a later influential study, Wolters modified the meaning to refer to those
polities which originated prior to and developed subsequent to the
introduction of Indian influence.[3] He suggested that a *mandala* represented a particular and often unstable political entity in a vaguely
definable geographical area without fixed boundaries in which smaller
centres tended to look in all directions for security. *Mandalas* would
expand and contract in concertina-like fashion. Each one contained
several tributary rulers, some of whom would repudiate their vassal
status when the opportunity arose and try to build up their own networks of vassals.

Here the term is virtually synonymous with *negara*. Both refer to a
single polity whose centre of political gravity lies in its capital, and whose
political influence is progressively reduced the further one travels from
that centre. The boundaries of such a polity are not fixed, but fluctuate
with the power available to the centre. Outer, regional centres of population and power may be weakly held in political orbit. When the centre
is weak they may be lost entirely, to become independent centres in their
own right or to gravitate under the political control of an alternative
power centre. One can see from this model the justification for Tambiah's
description of such states as 'galactic polities'.[4] However, the spatial
relationships of the *mandala*, and the fact that this was a term used by
people at the time, make it more appropriate than the model of dynamic
equilibrium implied by the term 'galactic polity'.

The contrast between a Southeast Asian *mandala* and the European
notion of a state is evident. *Mandalas* and states have different geographical and spatial connotations. The full meaning of *mandala* can only
be understood, however, by elucidating all the elements comprising this
kind of political system. We need to know what sources of power the

centre was able to draw upon, and what role the king played; what held the system together and what rendered it unstable; and what enticed some tributary rulers to repudiate their vassal status and others to remain loyal. Answers to these questions can be discovered by tracing the process of *mandala* formation in Southeast Asia from its earliest stages.

Throughout much of Southeast Asia — on the Khorat plateau of Northeastern Thailand, in the lower Chao Phraya and Mekong flood plains, in the Red River Delta and the plains of coastal Vietnam, on the central Irrawaddy, and on Java and other islands — domestic communities became well established from the early third millenium B.C. on. Excavation sites reveal the development of advanced cultures characterised by polished stone implements in their early phases, and bronze metallurgy and fine pottery from as early as 2000 to 1500 B.C. Rice was already the staple food crop and animals had been domesticated. Most sites varied from 1 to 2.5 hectares in extent, with a population not exceeding 500 people.

Some time around the last two or three centuries B.C., or somewhat later in some areas, previously autonomous domestic communities began to group together into chiefdoms — by what process, or under the impact of what influences, it is hard to know. What we can deduce from the archaeological evidence is that this change was accompanied by the spread of iron metallurgy, the growth of trade, and increasing social differentiation as reflected in the wealth and poverty of houses and burials. Available evidence suggests that the impetus for all three developed locally, rather than being due to the diffusion of technology from either China or India. Outside influences, when they were brought to bear, further stimulated processes that were already underway.

The centralisation of power which commenced with the rise of chiefdoms and developed more intensively with the evolution of those more complex social and political entities we are calling *mandalas* was brought about by a number of interacting causes. These we may distinguish analytically, though the details of their interaction in particular cases can only remain speculative. One crucial component was the shift from broadcast sowing of rice in natural swamps and flooded areas to irrigated wet rice cultivation requiring the transplanting of seedlings. A first step in this transition seems to have been the construction of retaining dykes to slow the loss of floodwater from natural rice fields. Thereafter permanent paddies were constructed. The new growing technique was less economical in terms of return from effort expended than broadcasting or shifting cultivation, but was far more productive in terms of yield. Irrigation allowed two, or even three, crops to be grown each year.

Wet-rice cultivation was probably encouraged by, and in turn itself promoted, population growth. Though it required increased labour, it permitted production of substantial surpluses from limited areas. For this reason, wet-rice cultivation was encouraged by powerful families who appropriated the surplus in return for protection and security. Accumulated wealth was then exchanged for luxury trade goods or the products of specialist artisans. This further stimulated social differentiation within domestic communities. Trade developed in iron implements and weapons, bronze, salt, ceramics, shells, horns, tusks, precious stones and other prestige items. Itinerant traders were protected by local elites who sought their goods. In this way, a network of trading contacts developed, linking neighbouring power centres.

Trade gave an economic advantage to communities with access to coveted resources, such as salt or metallic ores (iron, copper, tin), to communities of skilled artisans (making ceramics, weapons or personal ornaments) and to communities strategically situated at key points on trading networks (at the confluence of rivers, portage points, or where established trade routes intersected). Important trading relationships grew up not only between settled communities, but also between tribal minorities practising shifting (slash-and-burn) agriculture in the forested highlands and the peoples of the valleys and plains. In exchange for forest products (fragrant woods, benzoin, sticklac), hides, horns and antlers, the plains people bartered iron, salt and cloth.

Intensified agricultural production and increased trade provided the economic basis for the evolution of the earliest *mandalas*. Larger, wealthier communities either established satellite settlements of their own, or extended their control over smaller surrounding communities by offering protection from slave raiding or forced relocation of the population in return for tribute. Ties were developed through reciprocal obligations and redistributive economic relationships. Chiefs or kings demanded payment of regular tribute in the form of rice or luxury goods, corveé labour to build the earthen walls and moats of their cities and contingents of troops to fight when called upon.

Mandalas originated as expanding circles of political control built on economic exchange and reciprocal obligations, which were often reinforced by ties of blood and/or marriage. Affinal relationships were crucial for the cohesion of early *mandalas*. New settlements would be founded by the sons of chiefs, accompanied by a few designated families. Their loyalties would be to the founding settlement and the family line — and to the ancestors they revered in common. Marriage ties were another principal means of reinforcing the power and prestige of chiefs and kings. The daughters of the king would become the principal wives of important tributary chiefs, while their daughters in turn joined the harems of the king as minor wives.

The dynamics of early *mandala* formation in Southeast Asia thus rested on increased economic production and accumulation, social differentiation and elite intermarriage and family relationships. They did not, as in China, entail central administration of extended irrigation networks as postulated by Wittfogel in his conception of the 'hydraulic state'.[5] The mandala's wealth rested on the extraction of 'tribute' from regional chiefs, a process legitimated by common acceptance of a world-view which defined relations of power that were continually reinforced through ritual and ceremonial means.

As far as scholars can determine, the principal elements in the world-view of early settled communities in Southeast Asia comprised belief in a natural order permeated by unseen forces in the form of spirits associated with significant natural features and phenomena. These spirits required propitiation by means of which the demonic and dangerous could be tamed or overcome with the assistance of the more benevolent. Of the benevolent powers, the most important were the Earth itself, which brought forth its bounty for human consumption, and ancestors who retained a lively interest in the welfare of the living. Ancestral spirits had differing powers. Powerful chiefs and kings would become powerful ancestral spirits. Conversely, powerful kings and chiefs clearly enjoyed the assistance and support of powerful forebears. Such influences operated primarily at an individual and family level, but in the case of royal ancestors came to extend beyond the family to the community, and eventually to the *mandala* as a whole. The welfare of the *mandala* therefore depended on rituals which the king alone could perform. Ceremonies were held where the confluence of powers was greatest. Thus we find a prevalence of prehistoric religious sites in high places, or where nature demonstrated some extraordinary power.

In broad outline, these were the factors responsible for the evolution of proto-*mandalas* throughout Southeast Asia during the late centuries B.C. Of course, there were regional variations, depending on geographic and economic differences, cultural factors, particular cults and the idiosyncrasies of individual kings. But major elements existed in common: wet rice cultivation and iron technology, widespread trading relations, ancestor worship and fertility cults and chiefs and kings who owed their positions to family and marriage ties, to redistributive relationships with their immediate followers (in return for service and loyalty) and to their personal charisma. All these factors were already present in the increasingly sophisticated indigenous cultural and political situation at the time when external influences began to impact on the region, influences which had the effect of stimulating the development of larger and far more powerful *mandalas*.

These influences came from the two great civilisations to the west and east, India and China, whose appetite for luxury products — spices, precious timbers, ivory, gold — brought Southeast Asian merchants to their ports. Chinese, and particularly Indian, merchants sailing to Southeast Asia brought with them fine textiles (silks and muslins), ceramics and other luxury goods. Exchange of trade goods led to exchange of religious beliefs, of icons and art, and ideas of what constituted good government and the proper role of kings.

Brahmans and their books eventually followed adventurers and traders. From these, the rulers of coastal or riverine settlements learned of ideas that strangely parallelled their own — of the great fertility god, Siva, worshipped in the high Himalayas in the form of his phallic symbol, the *lingam*. They learned how the power or divine force of Siva could be tapped through concentrated meditation and the performance of austerities *(tapas)*. They learned too of the glory of Indian kings, of the great Mauryan empire whose administration had been recorded by the sage Kautilya to serve as a model for subsequent kings. From this exuberant source, Indian religious beliefs, and Indian concepts of statecraft and inter-*mandala* relations, were selectively borrowed by Southeast Asian rulers as and when they were needed or could be used to bolster their own royal pretensions and unify their realms.

Though southern China was closer than India to most of Southeast Asia, and the political dominance of China was widely acknowledged, the usefulness of Indian ideas for the developing *mandalas* of Southeast Asia is attested to by their extension throughout the region. Even on what is now the coast of central Vietnam, the Cham population drew upon Indian rather than Chinese religious and political thought. Only in the Red River Delta of northern Vietnam did the actual extension of the Han empire lead to imposition of the Chinese administrative model.

Confucian forms of ancestor worship did little to enhance local cults, and Heaven *(Tian)* was too nebulous a concept to serve as a ritual focus for Southeast Asian kings. As for Chinese administration in the form of a centrally recruited and appointed bureaucracy of mandarins educated in the Confucian classics, this was a model inapplicable in kingdoms held together by family ties and tribute which possessed no such tradition of government. The Chinese model was eschewed by Southeast Asian rulers because it could only be adopted *in toto*. The Indian model was acceptable because it could be endlessly modified in relation to local needs.

Paradoxically, however, it is from Chinese records that we have knowledge of the earliest significant power centres in Southeast Asia. Funan in the delta of the Mekong, the first of these Chinese-recorded *mandalas*, was visited by two Chinese officials around A.D. 250. Later we find reference to Zhenla, a Chinese name for what seems to have been a shifting sequence of *mandalas* situated on the Tonle Sap Plain and the Middle Mekong. Kingdoms in these regions were known to the Chinese as 'water' and 'land' Zhenla. Both seem to have been loose groupings of subsidiary centres or chiefdoms ruled either by sons impatient for their opportunity to claim supreme power, or reluctant tributaries forced temporarily to accept the overlordship of a powerful ruler and awaiting an occasion to renounce their allegiance.

Chinese records, however, are couched in explicitly Sinocentric terms. Chinese emissaries who made contact with local rulers at coastal trading ports naturally assumed that what they saw conformed to their notion of what a government was — that is, it took the form, in miniature, of the Chinese empire in the relation of its parts. There is little evidence, however, that Funan or Zhenla constituted stable kingdoms as the Chinese understood the term. From Chinese accounts we know that succession disputes were frequent and destructive. Although Indian laws were promulgated and an Indian script was used to inscribe stone stelae in the worship of Indian gods (the *Siva-lingam*) in what was clearly a royally endorsed cult, power was relatively weakly centralised and had often to be reimposed by force of arms wielded by powerful and charismatic rulers. Any weakening of central authority merely encouraged regional rulers to claim independence, leading to political instability at best and fragmentation at worst. The picture is one of competing centres of power, each intent on dominating other centres to extend its tributary domain.

In pursuit of these goals, rulers increasingly appealed to Indian gods in Sanskrit inscriptions proclaiming their power and majesty and their devotion to the god in question — almost always Siva — and the omnipotent creative force of his *sakti*, his power or energy, as symbolised in the *lingam*. To draw upon this power, rulers needed either to devote themselves to the worship of Siva through meditation and ascetic practices *(tapas)*, or to call upon the services of Indian brahmans or ascetics able to perform the necessary rituals and practices. Claims to legitimacy thus increasingly came to rest upon the ability of kings to draw upon the power of Indian gods. The relationship between god and king was demonstrated in elaborate consecration ceremonies centred upon the possession of royal regalia, and in the construction and endowment of shrines and temples as concrete evidence of the devotion of the king and the majesty of Siva.

Throughout Southeast Asia, the political pattern from about the fifth to the ninth centuries was similar, whether on Java, Sumatra and other islands, or on the mainland. Everywhere numerous small centres of regional power existed, each with its own ruler intent on expanding his personal domain to include neighbouring power centres. What was built by one local ruler through sheer ability and charisma was all too easily destroyed in struggles for his succession or the revolt of tributary chiefs seeking to reassert their independence. The 'personal polities' created by particular rulers were thus highly unstable. None constituted 'states' or 'kingdoms' in either the European or Chinese sense of these terms. They were instead *mandalas*, whose spheres of influence expanded or contracted 'in concertina-like fashion' depending on the ability of the ruler, his family connections and marriage contracts, and the resources contingently available to him.

By the early ninth century, however, conditions existed in a number of regions — on the central coast of Vietnam among the Cham, on the Tonle Sap plains among the Khmer, in central Java and elsewhere — which permitted the rise of larger, imperial *mandalas*, whose rulers were able to claim a more universal legitimacy. In doing so, kings of these *mandalas* constructed some of the most remarkable buildings in brick and stone to have survived in Southeast Asia — the sequence of temples constructed from the ninth to the twelfth centuries at Angkor in Cambodia, the Borobudur and Prambanan temple complexes in central Java, the Cham sanctuaries of central Vietnam, and the temples at Pagan on the upper Irrawaddy in Burma.

In all of these *mandalas* we find a similar political pattern. In all ambitious kings extended their tributary domains through force of arms, reinforced their dynasties through intermarriage with powerful families and established their legitimacy through royal patronage of cults claiming universal authority centred on impressive religious monuments. Though the Sailendras of central Java and the great King Jayavarman VII of Angkor were Mahayana Buddhists, the principal impetus for these legitimising cults of the ninth to twelfth centuries came either from Hinduism or from Theravada Buddhism. Thereafter, on the mainland of Southeast Asia, legitimation associated with the Theravada Buddhism of Pagan and the Mon *mandalas* of Dvaravati and Haripunjaya in modern-day Thailand provided the ideological support for kingship not only in Burma, but also in Siam (in the imperial *mandalas* of Sukhotai and Ayuthia), in Laos (the imperial *mandala* of Lan Xang), and in Cambodia. Further east, the Sinicised Vietnamese progressively extended their rule to the south at the expense of the Cham and subsequently the Khmer. We cannot follow the fortunes of all these imperial *mandalas,* so we will take one example each of Hindu and Buddhist *mandalas* in order to bring out significant similarities in the political implications of their rather different legitimising cults.

The founder of the Angkorean empire was Jayavarman II in A.D. 802. He was probably a member of the ruling family of a minor *mandala* on the lower Mekong, and seems to have spent some time in central Java. From there he took the idea of kingship as divine rule, and of the king as a reflection of Siva ('king of the gods' or *devaraja*) on Earth. Just as the power of Siva remained unchallenged on Mt Meru, the abode of the gods at the centre of the world, so the power of the god-king *(devaraja)* would go unchallenged as the symbolic representative of Siva at the centre of the worldly *mandala*. The identity of god and king rested on a belief in macrocosm–microcosm parallellism. The shrine of the god on the temple mountain at the centre of the *mandala* was identified with Mt Meru itself.

There god and king were one. More precisely, the deceased king merged with the person of the god, as the living king would do in his turn. Thus the cult of Siva, worshipped on his temple mountain in the symbolic form of a *lingam* named after the king himself, coalesced with the indigenous worship of deified ancestors. The king thus drew his legitimation both from his divine status representing Siva at the centre of the *mandala*, and from his kingly forebears, the line of powerful ancestors whose state cults were still maintained.

It took some time for this legitimating ideology to become formalised and widely accepted. In A.D. 802, Jayavarman II established in his own coronation the cult of the *kamraten jagat ta raja*, of 'the god who is king', centring on the possession of ritual regalia. In doing so, he staked a claim to divinity on which the welfare and prosperity of the *mandala* rested. The king in effect became the point of contact between Heaven and Earth, the conduit of divine influence from macrocosm to microcosm. It was he alone who could ensure not just the prosperity of his own ritual centre, but also the welfare of all who lived under its influence. However, the process was a two-way one. The great Siva, the royal ancestors, had to be satisfied with their worship. Hundreds, even thousands, laboured for the upkeep of the great temples. A network of regional temples was linked to those of the centre; they sent their offerings to the capital, contributing to maintaining the armies of priests and artisans.

Successive kings at Angkor built ever larger and more elaborate temple-mausoleums for their own worship as ancestors of subsequent kings. The building program of a new king usually began not with temples, but with the vast 'tanks' that are such a prominent feature of water conservation at Angkor. These huge rectangular tanks did not play any essential part in the irrigation of surrounding lands, though they undoubtedly provided water for the needs of the city population. More important than their economic role was their symbolic significance as the surrounding 'ocean' of each microcosmic Mt Meru. Next in order of precedence for a ruler was the cult of the royal ancestors, the completion of temple-mausoleums dedicated to the posthumous worship of close relatives, or construction of additional shrines. Only after his palace and city were built and embellished did an Angkorean king begin construction of his own temple-mausoleum.

Even these elaborate cults to which enormous resources were devoted were insufficient to guarantee political stability, for they did nothing to resolve the problem of succession. Furthermore, they sowed the seeds of their own replacement by reducing over time the resources available to the king to maintain his military and economic superiority. From the king's many sons came numerous contenders for the succession. Some of the Angkorean kings were remote relatives of previous monarchs. Others were actual usurpers. All claimed legitimacy by the same means — the cult of 'the god who is king' backed by construction of a temple-mausoleum in the form of a mountain signifying the centre of the world.

After the Cham sacked Angkor in 1177, the legitimacy provided by the *devaraja* cult was thrown into question. Jayavarman VII turned to Mahayana Buddhism in place of the Hindu gods who had failed to protect the realm. But he retained the structure of legitimation — the temple-mausoleum that stood as Mt Meru at the centre of the new city of Angkor, temples to his ancestors, tanks and palaces. The last vast building program of Jayavarman VII exhausted the Khmer imperial *mandala*. Temple endowments undermined the tax base. New *mandalas* in the further reaches of the empire rose to challenge the old centre. And in the heartland itself, a new religion took hold, a religion of personal salvation that depended on no god-king, and required no hereditary caste of priests. In Theravada Buddhism it is open to any man, the son of any peasant, to join the monastic order and elevate his standing above that of kings. Yet Theravada Buddhism provided its own legitimation of kingship, one with a political significance that continues to this day in the status it gives to the Thai monarchy.

Classical Siamese kingship of the Ayuthia period sought to emulate the ideal Buddhist king, the *chakravartin*, or universal monarch, whose rule would be coextensive with the Buddhist Dharma, or truth. In furthering that truth through his patronage of the Buddhist monastic order, the Sangha, the king was a *Dharma raja*, a king who ruled in accordance with the truth. And since each gift — each new temple or stupa or consecrated Buddha image — added to the store of the king's merit, or positive *karma*, each such action reinforced the belief of his subjects that he was well advanced along the path to Buddhahood and thus reinforced his status in their eyes.

Belief in *karma*, the universal law of moral cause and effect which determines the status of one's next reincarnation, is common to both Buddhism and Hinduism. In both, birth into a royal family is predetermined, such exalted status being earned in previous existences. Kings are kings, therefore, through their own deserts. The difference lies in the power attributed to the gods. In Hinduism, the *sakti* or power of Siva can be tapped by various means. The king is one on whom the gods smile. In Mahayana Buddhism, the cosmic *bodhisattva* (those already with the potential to be Buddhas) played much the same role. But in Theravada Buddhism the gods one may call upon wield far less power. Those who achieve Buddhist enlightenment do so through their own efforts, through the slow accumulation of merit over many lifetimes.

Belief in the ineluctable working of *karma* provides a powerful support for the established social order in Theravada Buddhist countries. Not only a king, but every member of society, is born according to his or her previous *karma*. Further merit could, of course, be accumulated, and social standing had to be constantly reinforced through meritorious acts. Kings had to demonstrate their continued right to rule by the continual making of merit on a scale superior to everyone else. Thus great kings in Burma, Laos and Siam undertook elaborate building programs to the glory of the Buddha and for the benefit of the Sangha as demonstrations that their store of merit remained greater than any of their subjects (including tributary kings and rulers), thus guaranteeing them their legitimate right to rule.

Through his patronage of the Sangha, the Buddhist king upheld the moral order of the Buddhist Dharma. Even aggressive wars, such as those waged by Burmese kings against Siam in the sixteenth and eighteenth centuries, were conceived of as 'righteous conquests' designed to further purely religious ends — proselytisation of the Dharma, seizure of texts, or famous Buddha images or relics. On their return, kings built stupas or temples to commemorate their conquests. Upholding of the moral order extended to upholding the civil and social order. Laws were Buddhist laws. The just society was one that was prosperous and ordered, in which everyone knew their place, and in which the Dharma could flourish. A king who maintained such social order proved his right to rule.

The ideal of the *chakravartin* was a powerful one for Buddhist kings. Each ruler set out to enhance his store of merit in the hope that he too could attain the status of a *chakravartin*. His ambitions would be encouraged by such symbolic indicators as the capture of a white elephant. The adverse side of Buddhist legitimation was that if a ruler showed few signs that he possessed great merit, and had none of the charisma that was its outward manifestation, then others who believed themselves the possessors of greater *karma* might challenge his rule. If successful, the case was proved.

Thus Buddhist, like Hindu, legitimation effectively functioned only in support of great and powerful kings — those who were militarily strong, or had the power and wealth to undertake great building programs or indulge in elaborate ceremonial celebrations of themselves and their realm, or had proved their divine powers or *bodhisattva* status through the course of a long and prosperous reign. When rulers were weak, they were open to challenge. Powerful families could always transfer their allegiance, as outer tributaries could renounce theirs altogether. No central bureaucracy functioned in Southeast Asian *mandalas* as it did in the Chinese empire to prop up weak and incompetent rulers. Thus, ingenious and elaborate as the systems of legitimation were, they were never able to prevent challenges to any authority at the centre deemed to be weak or vulnerable, to lack military power or economic resources, or to have failed to marshal the ritual and ceremonial means of legitimation potentially at his disposal.

These examples of political structures are taken from the mainland states of Cambodia and Siam, but similar *mandalas* were constructed by the Hindu successor dynasties to the Sailendras in central and east Java. Meanwhile a rather different form of *mandala* developed in southern Sumatra. Known as the empire of Srivijaya, its political centre was situated in the Palembang area, with subsidiary centres straddling the trade routes passing through the Melaka and Sunda Straits. Srivijaya was a trading empire, whose wealth derived from control over trade routes and the forcible imposition of levies on vessels using its ports. Any merchant ship attempting to bypass Srivijayan ports was waylaid and forced to berth by fast Srivijayan warships. Most made port as a matter of course, however, as Srivijaya provided the finest trading opportunities available, as entrepôt and market for an extraordinary range of rare and valuable products — spices, perfumes, aromatic woods and precious metals.

As trade developed and the wealth of other ports grew, so Srivajayan power declined. By the time the Portuguese arrived in Southeast Asia at the end of the fifteenth century, Melaka had supplanted Palembang as the major entrepôt in the region — a development due in large part to the influence of Islam. Melaka was the pre-eminent example of a prosperous and powerful Muslim state, whose ruler derived his legitimation from the encouragement he gave to the propagation of the faith. Other Muslim trading ports from Aceh to Brunei and south to the spice islands of Ternate and Tidore were prosperous trading centres, each with its own ruler, each an independent, or semi-independent *mandala*. At times a powerful imperial *mandala* such as Majapahit in central Java would extend its overlordship over surrounding islands, but the moment a succession dispute or rebellion weakened central power, island rulers regained a degree of independence.

It was the wealth of Srivijaya that permitted its rulers to wield their authority over smaller trading ports on the 'offshore' islands and coasts of the region. The generosity of the Maharaja bought the loyalty of his subjects. Only more distant ports with access to their own resources chafed under Srivijayan domination and sought opportunities to assert their independence. Srivijaya was a *mandala*, therefore, like the inland states, but without the need to extract surplus production from a large peasant population, or therefore to establish legitimate grounds for doing so. Though Srivijaya was known as a centre of Buddhist learning, the Maharajas undertook no elaborate program of temple construction to reinforce their claims to *chakravartin* status. The fabled wealth of Srivijayan rulers was legitimation enough of their right to be accorded overlordship by petty coastal rulers whose ports and palaces were only too vulnerable to retribution from the Srivijayan fleet.

The only markedly different political system in Southeast Asia was that of Vietnam. As Taylor and others have shown, there are important 'Southeast Asian' elements in the political legitimation of the early Ly dynasty (eleventh century) whose emperors ruled as 'men of virtue' with the support of supernatural powers over subordinate regional power centres awaiting only the occasion to assert themselves.[6] Subsequent dynasties hewed more closely to the Chinese model of a centralised bureaucratic state. Border marches seized from the Cham were colonised and incorporated into the centrally administered state. Difficulties were encountered only where Vietnamese colonisation was limited and power rested in the hands of local rulers. Attempts to incorporate what is now the Plain of Jars in Laos into the Vietnamese state by designating it a province and appointing mandarins to oversee the administration generated immediate resentment and political opposition. The solution, to give local rulers Vietnamese titles, could hardly disguise the fact that, where unsupported by Vietnamese migration, emperors seeking to expand their control into non-Vietnamese areas were forced to play by the political rules of their neighbours to the west. In a Southeast Asian context, Vietnam was forced to act as another *mandala*. Its advantage lay in the administration of its ever-expanding Vietnamese core area where, despite the division into northern and southern dynasties, no contraction ever occurred.

Into this shifting system of fluctuating power relationships between larger and smaller Southeast Asian *mandalas*, European traders and colonisers brought their own ideas of effective administration, and fixed boundaries and legal contracts. At first the Portuguese, British and Dutch merely represented additional trading interests, but increasingly they imposed their own political values. Local rulers were deposed (as in Burma), reduced to becoming territorial administrators for imperial powers (as in Indonesia), or were left as powerless figureheads while their realms were administered by colonial officials (as in Cambodia and Laos). In every case, the colonial state was a European state. In areas of little economic significance, local rulers were virtually ignored as late as the late nineteenth century, permitted to play out their political struggles in traditional but by then irrelevant ways. The political future of Southeast Asia lay with those indigenous nationalists who understood and could manipulate European political values and institutions. The independent states they shaped and led were players in an international order, membership of which was never open to polities constructed on the model of traditional Southeast Asian *mandalas*.

Guide to further reading

Two excellent general surveys of the pre-historic background to *mandala* formation in Southeast Asia are: Bellwood, Peter, *Prehistory of the Indo-Malaysian Archipelago*, Academic Press, New York 1985; and Higham, Charles, *The Archaeology of Mainland Southeast Asia: From 10 000 B.C. to the Fall of Angkor*, Cambridge University Press, Cambridge 1989.

In addition to the works by Geertz, Tambiah and Wolters cited in the endnotes, two important recent studies are: Hall, Kenneth R., *Maritime Trade and State Development in Early Southeast Asia*, Allen & Unwin, Sydney, 1985; and Hagersteijn, Renée, *Circles of Kings: Political Dynamics in Early Continental Southeast Asia*, KITLV/Foris, Dordrecht, 1989.

Useful collections on early Southeast Asian political patterns include the following:

Smith, R.B. and Watson, W. (eds), *Early South East Asia*, Oxford University Press, Oxford, 1979

Mabbett, Ian (ed.), *Patterns of Kingship and Authority in Traditional Asia*, Croom Helm, London, 1985

Marr, David G. & Milner, A.C. (eds), *Southeast Asia in the 9th to 14th Centuries*, Institute of Southeast Asian Studies, Singapore, 1986

On ceremonial and symbolic aspects see Gesick, Lorraine (ed.), *Centers, Symbols, and Hierarchies: Essays on the Classical States of Southeast Asia*, Yale University Press, New Haven, 1983

Two collections of papers of interest in placing developments in Southeast Asia in comparative perspective are:

Claessen, Henri J.M. & Skalnik, Peter (eds), *The Study of the State*, Mouton, The Hague, 1981

Claessen, Henri J.M. & van der Velde, Pieter (eds), *Early State Dynamics*, Brill, Leiden, 1987

Notes

1 Geertz, Clifford, *Negara: The Theatre State in Nineteenth-century Bali*, Princeton University Press, Princeton, 1980.

2 Wolters, O.W., 'Ayudhya and the Rearward Part of the World', *Journal of the Royal Asiatic Society*, nos 3 & 4, 1968, pp. 166–78.

3 Wolters, O.W., *History, Culture, and Region in Southeast Asian Perspectives*, Institute of Southeast Asian Studies, Singapore, 1982, p. 17.

4 Tambiah, S.J., *World Conqueror and World Renouncer: A Study of Buddhism and Polity in Thailand Against a Historical Background*, Cambridge University Press, Cambridge, 1976.

5 Wittfogel, K.A., *Oriental Despotism: A Study of Absolute Power*, Yale University Press, New Haven, 1957.

6 Taylor, Keith, 'Authority and Legitimacy in 11th Century Vietnam', in Marr, David G. & Milner, A.C. (eds), *Southeast Asia in the 9th to 14th Centuries*, Institute of Southeast Asian Studies, Singapore, 1986, pp. 139–76.

9 | Interstate relations in traditional Asia

As suggested in Chapters 7 and 8, China was the dominant country in Eastern Asia. It also had the largest population and the most centralised and powerful government. So it is not surprising that the Chinese court tended very strongly to see the world from its own point of view. One of the most important features of China's foreign relations, or the 'Chinese world order', as it has come to be known, was its Sinocentrism.

China may have been a single state, but given the diversity within Southeast Asia, historians have debated whether that region can be considered as a unit of study at all. Indeed, for a long time, Southeast Asia was seen as being shaped by external influences — first Indian, Persian, Islamic or Chinese and later European. Studies since World War II, and especially the independence of its countries, have accorded the region its autonomous identity and there is now an increased sensitivity to the cultural distinctiveness of the region as a whole and to its component parts.

From the earliest historical and archaeological records of the region, trade appears to have been an integral part of economic life, and indeed may well have been a major stimulus to the development of politics in Southeast Asia. Situated on the great East–West trade route, with its accessibility by sea and with the role of the monsoons in providing their twice-yearly pattern of contrary winds which solved the needs of traders coming and going, the region was naturally destined as a halfway house for trade in transit. Added to this, its own natural resources and its fame as a source of spices made the region a goal for traders in its own right. Trading links within the region bound the peoples of Southeast Asia tightly to one another and to outside influences. During the sixteenth to eighteenth centuries, these maritime links were particularly active, and there were profound and momentous changes in the region which have led one scholar to label this period as 'the age of commerce'.[1]

At the same time as these trading links were flourishing so well in Southeast Asia, Japan was even more self-sufficient than China. In the 1640s, the Tokugawa shogunate adopted a policy of 'closed country' (*sakoku*), by which it sought to exclude virtually all foreign influences and cut off all non-economic dealings with the outside world. However, this self-imposed isolation was not complete, and trade continued at quite a substantial level with such countries as China, Korea and the Netherlands. Despite the trade, the 'closed country' policy makes it appropriate to focus more or less entirely on China and Southeast Asia in the present chapter.

China

The ideological basis of the traditional Chinese world order was Confucianism. This fact had several implications. The first was that the strongly ethical nature of Confucianism noted in Chapter 7 was reflected in China's foreign policy. Of course, neither the military nor commercial aspects were negligible, but it was China's moral authority that the court considered most important. In particular, the emperor's virtue *(de)* should shine not only throughout China, but other countries, whether he was in fact virtuous or not.

The second point to note is that Confucianism was by its nature hierarchical and anti-egalitarian. The modern notion that nations should be treated as equals would have been regarded as absurd by an old-style Chinese emperor. So foreign nations were ranked according to their 'merit' *(gong)* towards China, meaning the value they themselves placed upon Chinese culture.

A third implication of the Confucian nature of Chinese traditional foreign relations was the importance of education, especially in the Chinese classics. What this really meant was that the more thoroughly a foreign ruler or dignitary knew Chinese culture, the better able he was to deal with it. China was called *tianxia*, that is, 'all under Heaven'.

Confucianism was a very authoritarian philosophy which ordained that one person only should be in control. The emperor, or 'Son of Heaven', was thus not only in control of all China but was the central figure to whom foreign rulers should pay homage. In return, it was in him that the authority should be enshrined. It was his duty to treat all with impartiality, not to take sides or become involved in squabbles among foreign powers.

The Chinese world order was based not on any notion of the nation-state, but upon the superiority of Chinese culture. Even though the whole of China was ruled by two foreign dynasties, that of the Mongolians, called Yuan, from 1280 to 1368, and that of the Manchus, the Qing, from 1644 to 1911, it succeeded not only in preserving its own culture more or less intact, but in exerting a powerful influence over the culture of its conquerors: 'Political subjugation may have been feared, but cultural conquest was unimaginable.' In order to distinguish Chinese pride in their dominant Chinese culture from 'nationalism' with all its overtones of the modern nation-state, the distinguished historian of imperial China,

John King Fairbank, has adopted the term 'culturalism' to designate the traditional Chinese view.[2]

The traditional Chinese world order is extremely ancient. From very early times the Chinese were forced to a particular view of the world because of their geographic position. It was a country with long and ill-defined borders, and some of the neighbours frequently caused it trouble. In particular, the inhabitants of what is today Mongolia were a frequent threat to China. True, China did expand its own borders. The China of the Qing dynasty was enormous by comparison with that of the Han (206 B.C.–A.D. 220). Yet the increase in the size of China's territory was anything but gradual; it varied sharply from dynasty to dynasty. The China of the Tang era (A.D. 618–907) was considerably larger than that of the succeeding Northern Song (A.D. 960–1126), as was Yuan territory greater than Ming. Moreover, the extent of Chinese territory could even vary within dynasties.

The fact that the Mongols did become the first people to conquer the whole of China proved that the threat was a very real one and produced a profound effect on China's foreign relations. Here was an example where force and not virtue had won the day. Was this an argument for no longer accepting the idea of a moral superiority prevailing over force? The answer was no, because the Mongol rule of China lasted less than a century. Once the Ming dynasty was established, the Chinese could argue that, after all, it had been moral authority, or Chinese culture, which had won out against the 'barbarians', despite all their military power. Of course, it was foolhardy to ignore military power, but it was still not as important as virtue or moral authority. As one contemporary historian has put it, 'the Mongols had reminded the Chinese of what had been the winning combination in the past, a hard core of *wei* [power] surrounded by a soft pulp' of virtue.[3]

Vital to the traditional Chinese world order — indeed, almost synonymous with it — was the 'tribute system'. Countries surrounding China would send to the court what was termed 'tribute' *(gong)*, generally gifts of some product or other of their own country. The despatch of special envoys to bring the tribute was a sign of the foreign ruler's recognition of the Chinese emperor's superiority to him. But recognition of superiority did not bring with it any acknowledgment of control. The frequency of tribute varied sharply, generally in accordance with the importance of a country within the system. So in the early nineteenth century, Korea, which was the most important of all the tribute states, sent in four missions per year while Siam despatched only one in three years.

There were no permanent embassies or representatives of foreign countries in China. When a state had business to do with China, it sent a special embassy, which carried out its task and then returned home. In being granted audience by the emperor it undertook a very special and elaborate ritual, which included the famous kowtow. The term is derived from a word which in Modern Standard Chinese is *ketou*, meaning 'knock the head'. The ritual of audience with the emperor included kneeling down and knocking the forehead on the ground in order to symbolise reverence for the authority and person of the emperor.

Despite the dominance of the political and ethical sides of the tribute system, trade was also involved. Merchants usually accompanied envoys bringing tribute and commerce could take place on a reasonably large scale after the tribute rituals were completed. It was possible to carry on trade without tribute, but on the whole it was those countries which did render tribute to China that traded most with it. When trade did take place, it tended to be carried out through specific trade ports, mostly on the borders, but if connected with tribute, it also frequently took place in China's capital city. The imperial court saw both tribute and trade as ways of defending China's boundaries against unruly 'barbarians'.

Although Western Europe had for centuries known about, and from time to time had dealings with, China, it was Russia which loomed largest among European countries for the Qing dynasty before the nineteenth century. Russia and China had both been part of the Mongol Empire, but with its collapse in the middle of the fourteenth century, relations were cut off for over two centuries. From the late sixteenth century, Russia expanded eastwards in Siberia, the founding of the town of Irkutsk in the early 1650s signalling the completion of the most important phase of the process. Cossack troops then began to threaten the Manchurian borders. Meanwhile, the Manchu Qing dynasty had only recently taken over China. In 1685, the Kangxi emperor, who had by then consolidated his rule in the rest of China, ordered a military campaign in Manchuria against the Russians to overcome the threat on the northeast boundary. The campaign resulted in the Sino-Russian Treaty of Nerchinsk of 1689, the first China had ever signed with a European nation. It laid down the borders and gave Russia a base for economic privileges and trade. In 1727 China and Russia signed the Treaty of Kiakhta which laid down further details on the joint border and added to the number of ports where trade could take place.

Russia occupied a very special position in early Qing China. It was the only foreign country with which China maintained treaty relations. It was the only European country to which China sent ambassadors and the only foreign state to which China granted educational, commercial and religious privileges in Beijing. With Russia's conquest of Siberia, it had become just too big and powerful and its border with China too long for it to be treated or regarded in any other way but as an equal.

The Opium War of 1839 to 1842 signalled the beginning of the incursions into China by the newly industrialised and confident nations of Western Europe, and consequently of the disintegration of the traditional Chinese world order. One of the many major issues raised by Western penetration was the stationing of permanent representation in foreign capitals on an equal basis. The Chinese resisted this strenuously at first, because it was flatly contrary to their traditional ways of handling foreign relations. However, in June 1858 China was forced to sign four treaties with the powers, Russia, the United States, Britain and France, ceding them the right to send envoys to reside in Beijing, as well as to send missionaries into China's interior.

As the nineteenth century progressed, the tribute system grew weaker and weaker, moving to a final collapse with the Treaty of Shimonoseki in April 1895, which ended the First Sino-Japanese War. By forcing China to recognise Korea's independence (see Chapter 20), the treaty in effect detached its most important member from the tribute system and prepared the way for Korea to become a Japanese colony.

Southeast Asia c. 1500–1800

To the south of the gigantic unified state which was China was a series of much smaller countries, among which two forms of states have traditionally been recognised — the coastal riverine state and the inland agrarian state. The agrarian state was based on the land and the yield of the land. It was organised and controlled by a centralised hierarchy of officials and headed by a ruler who was absolute. The coastal or riverine state was centred on some estuary or on the lower reaches of a broad river which provided safe anchorage and protection. Its trading network extended into the hinterland and along the coast, where tropical products such as resins, beeswax, tin and gold were collected. The coastal/riverine states developed at strategic points commanding trade routes which allowed them to act as collection centres for the long-distance trade between eastern Asia and the West, as well as the intra-regional trade of the immediate region. The rise and decline of such states depended upon their ability to control the trade route.

Nonetheless, there was some overlap in the basic economic functions of these two types of state. A large number of riverine and coastal states, though commercially based, were supported by a rice plain economy, two examples being Ayuthia and the Sultanate of Kedah. The functioning of riverine and coastal principalities such as Jambi, Siak and Indragiri in East Sumatra, which were based on the collection of jungle and mineral produce in the hinterland, also grew more complex with the introduction of a cash crop economy — in this case, pepper. They also began to emphasise cultivation. Conversely, many inland states, though primarily agrarian based, had trade as an important arm for obtaining additional revenue, and maritime outlets were crucial to their economies.

On the periphery of these two types of state — the land power with its agrarian base, and the sea power founded on trade — flourished a host of smaller communities. The variable nature of the physiogeographic terrain contributed to a fragmented distribution of polities which were relatively small and isolated from each other because of the difficulty of communication.

The fifteenth century witnessed the emergence of a rich cluster of maritime states which owed their power largely to the wealth and military expertise which accompanied trade. Some of them, such as Laos, Aceh and Banten, formed themselves into states for the first time only in the 'age of commerce'. Others, like Siam, Burma, Mataram (Java) and Cambodia, assumed something like their modern shape under strong absolutist rulers.

Chief among these maritime states was Melaka. To quote Tomé Pires, it rose to become 'of such importance and profit that it seems to me it has no equal in the world'.[4] Melaka was a 'gateway city' controlling economic and political relations with the interior and its surrounding regions. From the very beginning, its rulers sought and received vassal status from China, thereby gaining the assurance of protection and respectability. They also safeguarded their position by acknowledging themselves as vassals of their powerful neighbours, Ayuthia and Majapahit. To promote Melaka's vantage point as a centre for trade, the rulers certified loans to provide an efficient legal and administrative system. The needs of traders and storage, shipping and banking services were also assured, and a cosmopolitan marketplace was created at the entrepôt. An important factor determining Melaka's success as an entrepôt was the dual role it played as the principal collecting centre for cloves from the Moluccas and nutmeg and mace from the Banda Islands and as an important redistributing centre for Indian textiles from Gujerat Coromandel, Malabar and Bengal.

The revenue from trade enabled Melaka's rulers to transform it into a territorial power. Other Malay states on the peninsula were forced to acknowledge Melaka's suzerainty and two east coast Sumatran states, Kampar and Indragiri, became Melaka's vassals. Melaka was thus able to obtain access to the rich pepper and gold of the Minangkabau interior. With its vast trading network, Melaka eclipsed smaller Muslim trading communities, which changed from general trading centres to stapling ports — for example, Pasai became a staple port for pepper.

After Melaka embraced Islam, some time in the early fifteenth century, it persuaded or compelled its vassals in the Straits area to accept Islam. Its growing prestige and commercial success were also responsible for the Islamisation process in the archipelago. Its influence as a cultural centre was also evident in the widespread use of Malay as the language of many of the maritime states in the archipelago. When Melaka fell to the Portuguese in 1511, there was a temporary dislocation of the centre of the kingdom shortly afterwards; it later reconstituted itself under a new name in another part of its extensive territories. Its smaller vassals sought to preserve their independence and security. Other powerful and ambitious maritime states in the archipelago, including Brunei, Aceh and Johor, sought to inherit Melaka's mantle of power and to establish their own entrepôts. However, they were thwarted in their attempts by the Portuguese and the Dutch, who also sought to dominate trade in the area. The activities of these Europeans prevented the rise of another Malay power.

In Southeast Asia the ruler of the state played a unique role. Effective administration was not via a central bureaucratic structure, as it was in China, but through the ruler's exercise of patronage and reciprocal relations with the elite. Relations between the centre and component ports of the state were fragile and dependent on the ruler's military strength.

The focus of the maritime capital, like the agrarian capital, was the palace, which stood in the vicinity of the royal mosque or temple. The layout of the township was generally similar. The court, public buildings and residences of the royalty, nobility and merchant elite were generally built of stone. The rest of the city consisted of wooden structures divided into separate sections for the different communities.

Taxes on trade were the main source of revenue, so that control of trade and of the goods traded by the ruler or ruling class was important. An element of coercion was associated with most trade and entrepôt activities. Nonetheless, the importance of exhibiting an environment of peace and order to attract trade was also recognised, as factionalism and disorder often led to the unseating of well-established entrepôt states. The desire to expand and monopolise trade also caused local and intra-regional hostilities.

Control over the right to trade was jealously guarded by the ruling class. Although foreign merchants played a significant role, participation by the local people was very limited. This was due in part to a virtual monopoly held by the rulers over non-local trade so that goods traded were heavily taxed. Generally, the institutional arrangements and facilities offered were a major contributing factor in the smooth functioning of the market.

Trade had developed far beyond 'peddling trade' in luxury items between basically self-sufficient communities. For centres such as Melaka and Aceh in their heyday, self-sufficiency was not a serious consideration. They were dependent on imported rice and other foodstuffs. The bulk trade in commodities like rice, dried fish, pepper and timber was an integral part of the Southeast Asian trading system.

The international status of states like Melaka, Ayuthia, Banten and Makassar was an indication of their general prosperity. They were not only political and commercial capitals, but the cultural centres of their kingdoms. Under the patronage of the ruler, there was a diversity of people in the entrepôt and a variety of linguistic communication. There was also a large community of merchants, money changers, etc.

Religious change was an important influence during this period. As noted previously, the adoption of Islam by the major maritime states resulted in the spread of Islam not only along the trading route from Ternate to Tidore in the east to Melaka and Sumatra in the west but also northwards from Melaka to Patani and Champa along one of the routes to China. Christianity was adopted by most Filipinos in the latter part of the period and also by a proportion of eastern Indonesians and Vietnamese. At the same time, Theravada Buddhism emanating from Ceylon (Sri Lanka) and spreading over the states of mainland Southeast Asia had more appeal than the old Brahmanic and Mahayana traditions. Religious change fashioned the outlook of people in Southeast Asia and became a vital force in their social and political development.

While there was a concentration of population in the agrarian rice plains, the maritime states also accumulated relatively large populations in times of prosperity. Reid estimates that the populations of Ayutthaya, Pegu, Hanoi, Demak and Melaka in all possibility exceeded 50 000 people in the early sixteenth century while Ayuthia, Aceh, Banten, Surabaya and Makassar certainly did so in the first half of the seventeenth century.[5]

Control of people rather than control of land was the main indicator of power, and revenue from trade was seen as a way of attracting and maintaining followers. The legal codes of the period also indicate the monetary value of human beings who could be bought outright as slaves or could be bonded through debt. Society was vertically organised through reciprocal patron–client relationships. Patrons offered protection to their clients, who in turn owed labour or service to their patrons, the ultimate patron being the ruler of the state. Ideological sanction for this arrangement was provided by concepts of rulerless chaos, deriving from early Hindu influences. Obligations to provide labour or service could be defined by craft or other abilities so that such industry or manufacturing as there was was tied into the hierarchical structure of society.

Generally, the presence of Chinese power has always been a factor of very great political significance in the politics of Southeast Asia. This power has waxed and waned according to the conditions of unity and stability within China itself.

From early historical times, there are records of many of the smaller Southeast Asian states becoming tributary to China and sending embassies to the Chinese court. At the end of the fourteenth century, China entered a period of expansion in wealth and popularity. The demand for Southeast Asian products was given a boost by the six state trading expeditions of the Ming Emperor Yongle (1403–24). These resulted in imports of enormous quantities of pepper, spice, sappanwood and often forest products into China. At the same time, the China trade also stimulated Southeast Asian production and left a number of 'crucial communities' of Chinese (often Muslim) traders in the Southeast Asian entrepôts. One of the initial advantages of these traders was their ability to form links with officials of the state. They often combined the task of tax collecting and trading with holding a provincial office and with intermarriage. Such marriages reportedly occurred in the history of the Brunei Sultanate and also in those of Melaka and Patani.

Consequently, by Ming times, trade between China and Southeast Asia had become so established that two routes to the region had developed. The first was an easterly route which went to the Philippines, the Sulu Archipelago, Brunei and Western Indonesia, while the second was a westerly route which included the port cities of the Malay Peninsula as well as of Siam and the Isthmus of Kra. Chinese trading interests in the region were particularly boosted when the imperial embargo on the junk trade with Southeast Asia was lifted in 1729. China became not only a consumer of ever greater significance, but also a producer of similar importance and an even greater trading state with its rich merchant corporations extending their commercial networks beyond China to Mongolia, Central Asia and all of Southeast Asia.

There was a boom in trade due to other factors as well. In 1345, reliable purchases of spices in Alexandria by the annual galley fleet from the Adriatic were assured when Venice signed a treaty with the Mameluke rulers of Egypt. Control over other caravan routes serving Beirut and Damascus was also secured by the Mamelukes, which resulted in progress towards peaceful conditions for the caravans taking Asian commodities to the Mediterranean from the Red Sea and Persian Gulf ports. This led to a sharp upturn in trade travelling by sea from and through Southeast Asia to the Mediterranean in the latter part of the fourteenth century.

The Portuguese voyages to Asia via the Cape of Good Hope and their expansion into Asia in the sixteenth century resulted in regular shipments of Southeast Asian pepper and spices to Europe. Trade by the two sea routes also led to increased production in Southeast Asia, especially after the Dutch and the English joined in the competition for pepper and spices in the seventeenth century. Reid states that four variables were crucial to Southeast Asian prosperity over the period from the fifteenth to the seventeenth centuries. These were 'the exports from Maluku to Europe of clove and nutmeg; the likely Southeast Asian share of pepper exports to Europe; the import to Asia (here Southeast Asia cannot be separated) of silver and gold and the import to Southeast Asia of its most important item of luxury consumptions in Indian cloth'.[6]

Conclusion

Southeast Asia entered a phase of sustained export growth at the beginning of the fifteenth century. This growth was stimulated by spices from Moluku and included pepper and various other commodities. The spread of Islam and the accompanying trade expansion resulted in the emergence of a rich cluster of maritime states. These prosperous urban centres which lay athwart the main sea routes exhibited common characteristics which included a dense population, a pluralistic society, dependence on trade revenues, high military organisation, a large-scale bulk trade in rice imports which supplemented the peddling trade in high value luxury goods, and their role as centres for cultural dissemination.

In the sixteenth century, despite an initial disruption by the activities of the Portuguese, trade grew more rapidly, particularly during the period 1570–1630. From the second half of the seventeenth century, the Dutch East India Company's economic and political policies resulted in the most lucrative aspects of this long-distance trade passing out of the hands of Southeast Asians. Thereafter, the maritime ports gradually lost their prominence in commerce which led to their political decline as well.

The texture of international relations for China and Southeast Asia was in marked contrast. China differed enormously from the Southeast Asian states in size and, except for Vietnam, in culture. For its rulers, external trade was not at all important. On the other hand, Confucian moralism based on the status of its emperors was very high in the priorities which governed its international relations. Contacts with Europe from the sixteenth century at first touched Southeast Asia much more vitally than China. But just as the nations of Western Europe were eventually able to colonise almost every country of Southeast Asia, so their expansion was to challenge the Chinese world order so greatly that it ultimately brought about its end.

Guide to further reading

Fairbank, J. King, *The Chinese World Order, Traditional China's Foreign Relations*, Harvard University Press, Cambridge, Mass., 1968
   This is the standard work on traditional China's foreign relations, the focus being on the Ming and Qing periods. Fairbank himself provides the introductory framework, and there are thirteen other essays, on topics such as the tribute system and China's relations with specific countries and regions, including Korea and Vietnam.
Kathirithamby-Wells, J. & Villiers, John (eds), *The Southeast Asian Port and Polity: Rise and Demise*, Singapore University Press, Singapore, 1990
   This is a collection of twelve essays which concentrate on describing the growth of trade and statehood and the inherent links between the two in a few key areas. Kathirithamby-Wells herself provides the introductory framework and an article on Zanten in the sixteenth and seventeenth centuries. Villiers provides an article on Makassar.
Reid, Anthony, *Southeast Asia in the Age of Commerce 1450–1680*, Yale University Press, New Haven, 1988
   This is the standard work on the subject and is part of Reid's larger work on the topic. See also Chapter 11.

Notes

1 Reid, Anthony, *Southeast Asia in the Age of Commerce 1450–1680: The Lands Below the Winds*, Yale University Press, New Haven, 1988.

2 Fairbank, John K. & Reischauer, Edwin O., *China: Tradition & Transformation*, rev. edn, Allen & Unwin, Sydney, London, Boston, 1989, p. 178.

3 Wang Gungwu, 'Early Ming Relations with Southeast Asia: A Background Essay', in John King Fairbank (ed.), *The Chinese World Order, Traditional China's Foreign Relations*, Harvard University Press, Cambridge, Mass., 1968, 3rd printing 1974, p. 49.

4 Cortesâo, Armando (ed.), *The Suma Oriental of Tomé Pires*, vol. 2, Hakluyt Society, London, 1944, p. 285.

5 Reid, A., 'An "Age of Commerce" in Southeast Asian History', *Modern Asian Studies,* vol. 24, no. 1, 1990, p. 3.

6 ibid., p. 12.

III | Asian responses to the Western challenge, sixteenth to mid-twentieth centuries

An early twentieth-century Vietnamese nationalist cartoon depicts peasants routing French colonial troops. The peasants are shouting: 'Wipe out the gang of imperialists, mandarins, capitalists and big landlords!'

10 | Imperialism in Asia: A comparative perspective

While trade within Southeast Asia was extensive, linkages with Europe through the spice route of the Indian Ocean formed only slender, although mutually profitable, threads of trade. At the end of the fifteenth century, however, this distant relationship began to change with the arrival of European military and commercial power in Asia. In a vast process stretching from the late fifteenth to the mid-twentieth century, Europeans explored, examined, plundered, converted, traded, conquered, settled and ruled in Asia. Europe's penetration of the continent was uneven — parts of Java were under direct colonial rule for nearly three and a half centuries whereas Japan was never colonised — but it brought far-reaching changes to Asian societies. Ancient states were dismantled, patterns of commerce were transformed and the cultural and intellectual assumptions of Asian civilisations were challenged.

Historians have tersely described the three motives for European expansion as 'Gold, Glory and God': Europeans came to Asia to acquire wealth from plunder and trade, to win prestige both as individuals and nations, and to win converts to Christianity and later to Western civilisation. For each European power, as we shall see in the following chapters, these motives were important in different ways, and to different degrees. The Spanish and Portuguese in the sixteenth century, for instance, brought a Christianising zeal to their activities which was much less strongly felt by the Dutch and English traders a century later. British, Dutch and French colonialists who had disregarded uneconomic and marginal territories in Southeast Asia at the end of the eighteenth century snapped them up eagerly for prestige and strategic reasons towards the end of the nineteenth. A careful calculation of the interests at stake led the British and Americans to grant a high degree of self-government to their colonies in the first half of the twentieth century and eventually to accede more or less graciously in the transition to independence; different calculations led the French and Dutch to keep the reins of power well away from indigenous hands, and eventually to resist the transition to independence by force of arms.

Explaining motives, however, does not tell us how it was possible for Europeans to impose their will on Asia for so long. Traditional Asian states were no less expansionist in principle than their European counterparts. China had grown by military conquest from a heartland in the northern plains around the Yellow River to encompass a huge East Asian empire which included Tibet and Mongolia, and had an elaborate tributary system which extended its influence to outlying regions such as Korea and Southeast Asia (see Chapter 9). The states of Korea and Japan were the product of long periods of warfare in which a multitude of small states were eventually subordinated to a single conqueror. During much of Vietnam's history, its people have been pushing steadily to the south along the coast of Indochina, displacing existing populations. Both Siam (Thailand) and the early states in the Indonesian archipelago were determinedly expansionist, seeking to extend their dominance over surrounding states. The means which enabled European expansion, therefore, rather than the motives which drove it, need to be our starting point in discussing the age of imperialism in Asia.

One major area in which Europeans generally enjoyed a significant advantage was that of military and naval technology. Gunpowder was a Chinese invention, and primitive cannons had appeared like a rash across most of civilised Europe and Asia during the fourteenth century, but it was Europe which took the new technology furthest in applying gunpowder to military purposes. After initial experiments which produced little more than noise and smoke, cannons developed into a significant element in European battlefield technology. On land, the big guns shook the former importance of castles in defence and contributed to the steady decline of cavalry, though their effect was limited by their low manoeuvrability. At sea, however, cannons transformed naval warfare — once a modified version of land warfare in which huge ships acted mainly to provide a platform for foot soldiers — into a specialised art using small mobile vessels and firepower rather than manpower. This innovation gave the Portuguese a sudden, catastrophic advantage when their vessels arrived in Asia at the end of the fifteenth century:

> They eat a sort of white stone [wrote an observer in Ceylon] and drink blood . . . and besides, they have guns with a noise like thunder and a ball from one of them, after traversing a league [about five kilometres], will break a castle of marble.[1]

Guns with a noise like thunder, together with small, highly manoeuvrable ships able to out-run and out-fight the larger, cumbersome vessels of the Javanese and the Chinese, helped the Portuguese to establish their maritime empire in Asia, but these were only the first of a long series of military and related innovations which gave the West an advantage in its periodic confrontations with Asia. Hand-held muskets and improved ships made the Dutch and English dominant in the seventeenth century. Steam-powered gunboats forced open unwilling Asian societies and subdued defiant Asian rulers in the nineteenth century. In the twentieth century we have seen not only the full range of modern destructive technology — from napalm and machine-guns to submarines and the atomic bombs dropped on Japan — employed to assert the West's military dominance over Asia, but also a vast array of technical support, from radio and radar to refrigeration and photography.

Asian societies were quick to recognise European military pre-eminence. In the sixteenth and seventeenth centuries, European guns and European mercenary gunners were in great demand by rulers wanting protection against their seaborne enemies. In the nineteenth century, apprehensive rulers like Siam's King Mongkut and Japan's Meiji Emperor sent army and naval officers for training at the best European military academies. In the twentieth century, Asia is a major market for the international arms trade, which is still dominated by the West.

Often enough, Asian societies were able to develop tactical initiatives or to make the most of local advantages which enabled them to stave off Western predators. The history of Western intervention in Asia is littered with costly and humiliating defeats of European forces by Asians, from Sultan Baabullah's capture of the Portuguese fort at Ternate in Maluku (the Moluccas) in 1575 to the defeat of the French at Dien Bien Phu in northern Vietnam in 1954. Until Japan's industrial expansion in the twentieth century, however, no Asian society was able to match the West idea for idea when it came to technological advances. This is puzzling, for all the advanced societies of Asia had both developed and assimilated advanced technology in the past. China's legacy of technological innovation had been especially impressive, while in areas like metalworking, Southeast Asian societies had pioneered many basic techniques. In the late sixteenth century, Korea became a major producer of artillery, mainly in order to ward off Japanese invasion. However, Asia never overtook Europe as a creator of military technology.

The reasons for Asia's technological lag after the arrival of European power in the region are complex and much debated by historians. The main arguments fall into two broad categories. Some, as we shall see later in this chapter, have suggested that Asia's technological backwardness was a consequence of economic changes imposed by Europe. Others have argued instead the importance of the cultural and political differences between Asia and Europe. They have pointed out the importance of state sponsorship of technological research in Europe. New weapons were not simply developed by entrepreneurs who hoped to find a market amongst ambitious rulers; rulers themselves directed and initiated research, actively recruiting fertile minds and eagerly acquiring unproven inventions. At least until the nineteenth century, Asian rulers seldom did such things. Perhaps Europe's steady retreat from the idea that human history was determined by God gave it greater incentive to seize the means to make history, while Asian rulers remained confident for much longer in the efficacy of cosmological formulae. The Nguyen rulers of nineteenth-century Vietnam declined to move their imperial palace from Hue, close to the coast, into the interior and away from French gunboats, because they did not want to leave what their priests told them was a spiritually favourable site. In dozens of battles in the Indonesian archipelago, Dutch troops mowed down opponents who leapt upon them believing that a charm or spell had given them invulnerability.

It is probable, too, that Asian rulers were apprehensive about the possible political consequences of new military technology. All the traditional rulers in East and Southeast Asia rested their power on the command of people en masse. Firearms and associated developments, however, diminished the importance of sheer numbers in warfare; with cannons, a small well-trained army could destroy a multitude. The risk to royal and imperial power was that new weapons would require a different kind of army, an army whose need for technical expertise would turn the ruler from a commanding general into a figurehead commander-in-chief. If technology rather than numbers were permitted to become the central principle of military organisation, rebellion would become easier, because anyone with funds and initiative could command the best in military technology. Moreover, the army itself could become a challenger for political power, because of its increasing independence of central command. Such apprehension was well founded: military modernisation in China, Japan and Siam in the nineteenth and twentieth centuries was followed by an unprecedented intrusion of the new, confident armies into national politics.

Whatever the reasons for Asia's technological lag, Asians remained at a consistent disadvantage in comparison with the Europeans throughout the long encounter between their two worlds. Even when they managed to keep Europe at arm's length, they were never in a position to counterattack by sending their own fleets to menace the coasts of Western Europe.

The Europeans, however, were more than conquerors. They came to Asia to trade, and the key to their success was their ability to use military force to support their commercial ventures, while using commerce to finance their armed pre-eminence. This powerful formula, however, took shape only gradually. Portugal's discovery of the sea route between Asia and Europe around the Cape of Good Hope gave its traders an unprecedented opportunity to carry spices directly from Indonesia to Europe, bypassing the long, expensive chain of intermediaries in India and the

Arab world. The Portuguese, however, took surprisingly little advantage of this opportunity. Although Portuguese vessels sailing home around the Cape always carried a rich cargo of spices and other wealth from Asia, the Portuguese chose to base their Asian empire on tax collection and piracy. Asserting their sovereignty over the seas, the Portuguese insisted that all ships travelling along the Asian seas should carry a *cartaze* or safe-conduct pass, which they had to purchase from the Portuguese authorities. From fortified bases at key points along the coast — Ternate in Maluku, Melaka on the Straits, Goa on the western coast of India — armed Portuguese ships would sail out to patrol the seas and to plunder any ship seeking to sail without Portuguese authorisation.

There was nothing new about this regularised piracy: many traditional Asian states used heavy-handed methods to extract fees from passing merchants. The rulers of Srivijaya, which had dominated the Straits of Melaka between the seventh and thirteenth centuries, routinely sent out their navy to capture any ship which attempted to pass without calling at the main port. What distinguished the Portuguese operation was its extent — no Asian power had ever dominated from the Arabian to the South China Sea — and its thoroughness. The plunder of ships made an appreciable impact on the volume of trade passing through Asian ports and changed, if only slightly, the balance of economic power in the region.

Historians have long debated whether the arrival of the Portuguese should be regarded as a turning point in Asian history. In traditional European histories of Asia, the appearance of the Portuguese navigator Vasco da Gama in the Indian port of Calicut in 1498 in search of 'Christians and spices' has often been taken to mark the opening of a new era in the continent's history. More recent historians have shown that the maritime power of the Portuguese, although impressive, left the land-based power of most Asian states largely untouched and have pointed out the absurdity of Asian history which takes as its central actors a relatively small group of foreign interlopers. Perhaps we should take a middle view: although the Portuguese brought little that was new to Asia apart from military technology, their activities began the gradual weakening of Asia in the face of Europe. Portugal's capture of Melaka in 1511, in particular, destroyed the greatest of the Malay sultanates and although Melaka's removal cleared the way for imitators, none was able to recover the sultanate's might in the face of Portuguese naval power.

The first clear sign of the powerful interweaving of military and commercial organisation by European commercial innovation in Asia arrived with the Dutch and English in the seventeenth century. The English East India Company and the Dutch United East Indies Company (VOC) were themselves a commercial innovation: they were joint-stock companies, in which a number of investors pooled their resources to undertake a major trading venture. Companies had an advantage over individual traders because they could call on greater reserves of capital and because they developed a durable organisational structure capable of enormous expansion. This bureaucratic structure made the companies somewhat like states in their organisation and in fact both companies received charters from their home governments which gave them the right, like states, to administer and to make war in Asia.

This commercial advantage, however, would have counted for little without the backing of military power. The companies used military power to overcome the two major problems faced by Asian traders at the time. The first of these was the Portuguese, whose depredations were a permanent drain on commercial profitability. Rejecting Portugal's claim to sovereignty of the seas, the companies took military force into their own hands, and in a series of bitter conflicts during the seventeenth century broke the maritime power of the Portuguese in Asia. For the first time, traders controlled the seas.

The second problem traditionally faced by Asian merchants was the unreliability of markets. Irregular harvests, uncertain winds, changeable demand and the vast numbers of other traders in the market all made trade in Asia an unpredictable and risky business. An individual trader faced ruin if he arrived in port with, say, nothing but a load of pepper, only to find that dozens of other traders had preceded him and the price was pitifully low. The companies not only brought to the market greater capital reserves, which gave them the resources to survive market fluctuations, but they also took hold of the market directly, using their military power to establish a network of monopolies, excluding their Asian and European competitors. The Dutch in particular were ruthless in driving competitors from the seas and in forcing Asian rulers to grant them exclusive trading rights, at least over specific commodities. In 1664, for instance, the VOC extracted from the Thai King Narai a monopoly over the export of deer hides, then in great demand in Japan. In order to secure a monopoly over lucrative nutmeg production, for instance, the company virtually exterminated the original inhabitants of the Banda Islands and regularly patrolled neighbouring islands to uproot any wild nutmeg trees which might have germinated. Neither the Dutch nor the English ever controlled every route or every commodity, but the partial monopolies which each enjoyed gave them access to enormous wealth on which the glittering prosperity of seventeenth-century Amsterdam, London and other cities of the North Sea was constructed.

In the eighteenth century, military might underpinned Western economic power in much the same way. Dutch military power gave the VOC control of most of the island of Java and they installed a plantation economy growing sugar and coffee for the world market. The commercial success of this plantation economy, however, lay less in economic innovation than in the fact that the Dutch were able to preside over a political regime under which Javanese peasants laboured for pitifully low returns. Uprisings, whether by desperate peasants or by frustrated local elites, were firmly crushed. Of the regions covered in this book, only Java and Maluku were thoroughly subjected to this debilitating phase of European domination, though elsewhere Bengal and the Philippines suffered under their own versions of colonialism.

When discussing the reasons for Asia's technological backwardness earlier in this chapter, we raised the possibility that Asia's problems might have been a consequence of economic changes imposed by Europe's presence. In the case of Indonesia, the evidence for this is fairly strong. Dutch policies systematically destroyed the indigenous states of the archipelago whose active promotion of economic development would have been necessary if their people were to prosper. The Dutch continued to make use of indigenous elites, but they made those elites politically dependent on them, so depriving them of the capacity to make decisions which might have damaged Dutch interests. The Dutch also deliberately stifled the activities of Indonesian merchants who might otherwise have been the basis for continuing commercial prosperity. European influence on China and the rest of East and Southeast Asia, however, was far less malign, and it is difficult to attribute, for instance, China's failure to develop military technology at this stage to the economic influence of the West.

In these other regions, the first three centuries of European penetration of Asia worked mainly to alter, if only subtly, the political balance of power. The cities of the coast were weakened, along with traders and rulers who had successfully tapped trade. Strengthened, if only by contrast, were aristocracies of the interior and those whose wealth was based on agriculture. In China and Vietnam, with their long traditions of suspicion towards foreign trade and foreign values, Europe's presence simply confirmed the value of isolation and cultural self-reliance. In Japan, the general exclusion of Western traders after 1641 strengthened the power of the Tokugawa shogunate at the expense of the regional lords or *daimyo*.

Perhaps the most significant consequence of European penetration of Asia, however, was its contribution to the Industrial Revolution in Europe and especially in Britain. Industrial development needed capital and markets. The steady flow of wealth to the West, bolstering the power of trading cities and trading states, helped to lay the basis for capital accumulation which eventually produced the Industrial Revolution. The unrestricted access enjoyed by British manufacturers in particular to Britain's global empire (India and, at least until 1789, North America, rather than East or Southeast Asia) were decisive in absorbing the first abundant productions of the new factories.

Industrial production utterly changed the scale of values by which humankind worked. Tools and consumer items such as cloth, which were once the product of weeks of painstaking labour by craftspeople, could now be turned out by factories in a matter of hours or days. Suddenly Europe had goods at a price which could compete in Asian markets without need for monopoly or any other coercive aid. The United States, too, as a rising industrial power, became enchanted by the prospect of selling to the huge markets of Eastern Asia. The Industrial Revolution fundamentally changed the dynamics of Europe's activities in Asia. In the seventeenth and eighteenth centuries, Europeans had profited in Asia by buying cheap in markets which they controlled by force of arms and selling dear in Europe and in the rest of Asia. With the Industrial Revolution in Europe, the emphasis was suddenly reversed and the greatest profits were to be made from selling the products of Europe's flourishing factories to and in Asia.

Industrialisation initially gave the West a greater advantage in military technology than ever before and armed force was now used to secure access to markets which would otherwise have been closed. Thus Britain became the foremost advocate of free trade and insisted on its freedom to trade opium in China in the Opium War of 1839–1842. The Americans, represented by Commodore Perry, were not far behind in forcibly opening Japan to foreign commerce in 1853. Glory and God, too, continued to provide a motive for intervention. Considerations of national prestige and concern for the welfare of Vietnamese Catholics, as well as an interest in trading and investment opportunities, all contributed to France's decision to seize Vietnam in the late nineteenth century.

Historians have debated at great length, however, just how significant a role industrial capitalism played in the final decades of European imperial expansion before World War II. In 1915, Lenin offered the classic view that imperialism in the non-European world was driven by the needs of European capitalism: that European capitalists, hungry for markets and raw materials and having exhausted the possibilities for investment in their own countries, led their governments to annex new territories as an outlet for investment. Lenin's influence on subsequent analysis has been substantial — as a result of his writing, the term 'imperialism' is now closely associated with the concept of economic domination rather than simply with the notion of conquest — but the details of his analysis shed only limited light on Eastern Asia. The last surge of colonial annexations in Asia, which included the French conquest of Vietnam and Japan's seizure of Korea in 1909, as well as Japan's prolonged military invasion of China and Southeast Asia from 1937 to 1945, was motivated by a complex collection of factors, including — but not dominated by — capitalist considerations, while the division of China into spheres of influence by the European powers fell short of the kind of partition Lenin predicted.

On the whole, moreover, we find in both East and Southeast Asia signs of the growing independence of economic power from a direct military presence. One early sign of this development was the growing reliance of the Dutch in Indonesia on indirect rule as a strategy for domination. Instead of sweeping away the pre-colonial order and establishing their own institutions of government, as they had done in Banda and in parts of Java, the Dutch showed an increasing preference for leaving indigenous rulers in place and for making the most of what was assumed to be their greater acceptability to the mass of the people, while the Dutch themselves got on with the task of making profits. The most productive plantation area in the colony in the first half of the twentieth century was East Sumatra, where traditional sultans remained formally in power as a political underpinning for the vast foreign-owned estates.

The so-called unequal treaties which Britain and other European powers imposed on China, Japan and Siam appeared at the time to bring them perilously close to colonial rule, but we can see them now as offering the colonial powers an appealing alternative to annexation: the advantages of free trade without the expense and difficulty of direct administration. With their humiliating provisions for extra-territoriality (the right of Europeans abroad to be tried by their own courts and under their own laws rather than by the courts and laws of the country where they lived), they simply accelerated the assimilation of Asian countries to Western models. The agreement by the United States in 1920 that its citizens in Siam should at last be subject to Siamese law was meant as an acknowledgment that Siam had, as it were, passed a test of civilisation by bringing its legal system up to European standards. But with its new laws, Siam had acquired a legal environment which favoured its economic opening to the outside world.

In the same way, too, the retreat of Western powers from colonialism — the British and Americans beginning even before World War II, the others joining in with varying degrees of reluctance after the war — was by no means a wholesale disaster for Western commercial interests. Rather, it opened the opportunity for economic relationships relatively unencumbered by open political domination, in which a key element was an alliance of Western capital with indigenous elites: modernising traditional aristocracies in the case of Siam/Thailand, quasi-aristocratic administrators in former British and Dutch colonies, and landed oligarchies in the Philippines.

One of the great issues of modern international politics is whether this kind of relationship represents an extension of imperial exploitation by other means, with Western military hardware now wielded by indigenous client armies rather than by Western troops themselves, or whether economic co-operation is the best means for promoting economic development and introducing beneficial social change. Both Westerners and Asians have often been enthusiastic about the transplanting of Western or modern values concerning issues such as human rights, the position of women, private property and so on into Asian societies. Others have seen such introductions as a tragic and destructive intrusion into Asian cultures. Some see the continued openness of Asian economies to the industrialised West as destroying all prospects for national resilience; others see it as bringing a prosperity which creates strength.

For 30 years after the end of World War II, Asian communists and socialists were determined opponents of continued outside economic involvement in their countries and to describe the comfortable arrangement between foreign powers and local elites they had contemptuous words: neo-colonialism and neo-imperialism. The long struggle by communist China and communist Vietnam, as well as the shorter struggle by Sukarno's avowedly socialist Indonesia, against the United States — struggles in which the West once again deployed its superior military technology — were at least partly based on this fundamental assessment of the costs of continued Western economic predominance in Asia.

In the 1990s, this apprehension has been somewhat overtaken by the spectacular industrial growth of the 'Little Tigers' — Taiwan, South Korea, Hong Kong and Singapore — in the 1980s and 1990s (see Chapter 29), and the rapidly accelerating growth of Thailand and Indonesia, all of them following on the older achievements of Japan. The experience, on the other hand, of those countries which chose to exclude the West — China, Vietnam, Burma and, for a briefer period, Indonesia — has hardly been encouraging. Depressed living standards and generally tight political control have been a significant price to pay for national dignity and greater social equality.

Europe, however, no longer has a special position in Eastern Asia. The great wave of imperialism which swept the shores of the continent from the sixteenth century has finally retreated. Independent Asian states are making their way in a new and complex world; these themes will be taken up again in Part IV of this book.

Guide to further reading

The question of Europe's military and technological superiority in its encounters with Asia has been discussed by many authorities. Carlo M. Cipolla, *European Culture and Overseas Expansion*, Penguin, Harmondsworth, 1970 is a major contribution. More recently, Michael Adas, *Machines as the Measure of Man*, Cornell University Press, Ithaca, N.Y., 1989, has examined the relationship between Europe's technological advantage and the ideologies of European dominance.

Portugal's empire in Asia is discussed by Boxer, C.R., *The Portuguese Seaborne Empire*, Penguin, Harmondsworth, 1973; van Leur, J.C., takes issue with the Eurocentric view in *Indonesian Trade and Society*, van Hoeve, The Hague and Bandung, 1955; while Steengaard, Niels, *The Asian Trade Revolution of the Seventeenth Century*, University of Chicago Press, Chicago, 1974, provocatively analyses the structural innovations made by the European joint-stock companies in the seventeenth century.

The literature on imperialism in the Industrial Age is enormous. Useful surveys of the field are Lichtheim, George, *Imperialism*, Penguin, Harmondsworth, 1974, and Owen, Roger & Sutcliffe, Bob (eds), *Studies in the Theory of Imperialism*, Longman Cheshire, Melbourne, 1972.

Similarly, the writings on underdevelopment and its relationship to imperialism are too vast to summarise. A valuable collection compiled at the height of the debate is Rhodes, Robert I., *Imperialism and Underdevelopment: A Reader*, Monthly Review Press, New York, 1970. For a more recent discussion of the state of the debate, see Chilcote, Ronald H., *Theories of Development and Underdevelopment*, Westview, Boulder, Col., 1984.

Notes

1 Emerson, James, *Ceylon*, Longman, Green and Roberts, London, 1859, vol. 1, p. 418.

11 | Mercantilists and missionaries: Impact and accommodation

A sixteenth-century Spanish historian called the Iberian voyages of discovery 'the greatest event in the history of the world, apart from the incarnation and death of Him who created it'.[1] A modern historian, C.R. Boxer, uses rather different language: the Portuguese and Spanish ventures 'first made humanity conscious, however dimly, of its essential unity'.[2] Indeed, together with other European adventurers (Dutch, English, French, Russian), by land as well as sea, they made the world one. By so doing they brought benefits and drawbacks to its peoples and its resources. These voyages can be seen as the gestation period of the imperialism which was the subject of the previous chapter.

The extraordinary development which was the Iberian voyages was indeed related to the economic expansion that caught up both Asia and Europe from the fourteenth century on as they recovered from the Black Death plague epidemic, which in the middle of the fourteenth century had killed nearly one-third of the population of Europe. But it is still necessary to explain why it was the Europeans who took the initiative that eventually also drew the Americas into what became a worldwide relationship and which made Spain's the first empire upon which the sun never set. The change was not merely of economic origin: it was political in nature and to some extent religious too.

The greatest state in the world was indeed not in Europe but in Asia. The Chinese empire was uniquely populous, sophisticated, prosperous and inventive. However, its own ventures in this phase of expansion were limited, though striking. These were the voyages of Zheng He to Southeast Asia and beyond into the Indian Ocean undertaken in the early years of the Ming dynasty. But after this China was more important for the inspiration it gave others: the writings of the thirteenth-century Venetian visitor Marco Polo were studied by Henry the Navigator and by Columbus in the fifteenth century. In a sense China provided a goal that was ultimately disappointing. But other opportunities opened up.

'Only the hope of great profit and the courage of reckless adventure could induce men to undertake voyages on which the prospect of safe

return was at best fifty-fifty.'[3] An inspiring goal was all the more important for Europeans who had few obvious advantages in their favour.
Their expansion, particularly in its early days, cannot be explained by
capitalism or industrialisation. Portugal and Spain, the countries most
involved in the sixteenth century, were indeed not even the most commercially advanced of the European states: the former in particular was
a small country with a population of only 1 million in the year 1500. Nor,
clearly, was it a matter of surplus population. Probably there were never
more than 10 000 able-bodied Portuguese overseas in the whole vast empire they built in Asia, Africa and America. There was a flourishing textile industry in England and the Netherlands. But these countries did not
at first play a major part in the overseas voyages, and when they did, their
cloth exports were largely unsuccessful.

Nor can it be said that the expansion was the necessary result of
advances in technology or geographical knowledge. The Portuguese had
the compass (probably in fact derived from the Chinese through Arab
and Mediterranean sailors), and the astrolabe and quadrant in simple
forms. But navigation at sea remained somewhat haphazard. There was
no preliminary development of geographical knowledge. The Portuguese
patiently explored the west coast of Africa, only then leaping from the
Cape to the coast of India. Columbus, it may be argued, was more moved
by ignorance than knowledge. He would not have 'discovered' America
had he not thought it was not there. Later sea voyages were indeed to
have advantages over earlier. They built on the experience which had
been acquired, on the work of mathematicians like Digges, Stevin, Dee
and Nunez, and of cartographers like Mercator. But the early venturers
depended all the more on courage and determination, and the accounts
of their exploits show the tension that resulted, with their evidence of
death and disease, of disputes and mutinies. Less than 60 per cent of the
Portuguese who left Europe ever reached Goa, let alone got home again.

Profit was certainly a stimulus, and it was a stimulus both to the individual and to the state. The European Renaissance, in its attempt to re-
capture the glories of antiquity, in fact created a new culture, which
offered new ways of spending wealth. The Italian city-states, which profited from the initial development of overland and trans-Mediterranean
trade, set an example, and their culture was admired throughout Europe.
With its overseas wealth, Portugal was able to build Renaissance Lisbon
and create a splendid culture. The fact that states and not only individuals were involved may have been crucial.

In every case, European expansion in this early period was backed by
the state, in the Portugal that employed Genoese to outwit Venetians, in
the Spain that patronised another Genoese in Columbus, in a Russia that
chartered Novgorod merchants, in the Netherlands that set up the VOC.
The breakup of Europe into individual states is surely a prime explanation for its expansiveness. Each state sought to better itself outside

Europe. European fighting and privateering indeed extended to the rest of the world as a result. A power like Spain might seek to dominate Europe by its adventitious acquisition of American wealth. Others would seek to preserve their independence or to check its advance and were thus stimulated themselves to engage in extra-European expansion. Spain used its wealth to try to dominate Europe. England sought to undermine it by privateering. Muscovy sought to mobilise wealth and power against Poland, which was backed by Spain.

China remained something of a legend, but other places proved more accessible. Spaniards reached the 'West Indies', Mexico and Peru, even though it was to interest themselves in China, Japan and Southeast Asia and to establish control in islands (the Philippines) named after their future King Philip II that they first set sail. Though they found Brazil by accident, the Portuguese (like their successors, the Dutch) were to find that their main source of wealth was Asia. Europe had few goods to trade to Asia, but offered a market for goods from Asia, particularly spices, necessary in an era when winter-fodder was short and cattle had to be slaughtered, but refrigeration did not exist. That market had been supplied overland and through Venice. By going to Asia, the Portuguese might undermine that trade. They could not expect to do it by mere conquest, but violence would be needed to build up their commercial position. This would be based on securing a share of the trade within Asia more generally, and on establishing a monopoly, Venetian-style, of its more important elements. To this end they established factories or trading agencies and, where they were strong enough, fortified them. The Dutch, displacing the Portuguese, followed their example in pursuing an Asia-wide trade. The English, a lesser commercial power in the seventeenth century, found it difficult to do so. The Russians, though concentrating on the fur trade, renewed the land contacts between Europe and Russia which had existed at the time of the Mongols but had been broken off by the plague and the fall of the Yuan dynasty. Russia was to be the first European state to make a treaty with China. Tea — and the samovar — became and remained part of Russian culture.

These ventures were undertaken at a time of economic expansion in Europe and Asia. They contributed to further expansion, by encompassing the world, by throwing American precious metals into circulation, by opening up new routes and connections. The ventures were accompanied by violence and destruction, but all the same, this was a boom time, one which continued into the seventeenth century. However, from about the 1620s, a long period of economic recession set in with the exhaustion of the American mines. Competition intensified and with it more authoritarian approaches to the state, and to state intervention, both in Europe and Asia. The Dutch sought to intensify their control of the major items in Asian trade. Rival powers sought to destroy the Dutch hold on the carrying trade in Europe.

Wealth and power had not been the only objectives. There were religious motives too, particularly with the Portuguese and the Spaniards. When Affonso de Albuquerque attacked Melaka early in the sixteenth century, he gave his soldiers two reasons for the action:

> the first is the great service which we shall perform to the Lord in casting the Moors out of this country . . . And the other reason is the service we shall render to the King Dom Manoel in taking this city, because it is the source of all the spiceries and drugs which the Moors carry every year hence to the Straits [of Bab-el-Mandeb] . . . Cairo and Mekka will be entirely ruined, and Venice will receive no spiceries unless her merchants go and buy them in Portugal.[4]

Not surprisingly, missionary endeavour was closely tied to state enterprise, and the Portuguese and Spanish kings enjoyed extensive clerical patronage. In the days of economic decline — the era also, it is true, of Counter-Reformation and Jesuit militancy — they might be tempted to rely more upon religious than secular activity. But it could be counterproductive. Christian missionary endeavour helped to provoke the expansion of Islam in the archipelago and the exclusion of foreigners from Japan. The Dutch were assisted in their struggle against the Portuguese by their virtual abstention from missionary activity. In the two centuries of the VOC's existence, fewer than 1000 predicants left to serve in the East. The Dutch sought to avoid open conflict with Islam and were able to continue to trade at Nagasaki.

Politically China was less affected by these ventures than their original focus and inspiration had suggested it might be. It did not provide wealth for the taking, like the newly discovered empires of Mexico and Peru. Moreover, even when the ruling Ming dynasty was at odds with the Manchu invaders who were to displace it, it was, again unlike the American empires, politically resilient. Nor did it prove in the sixteenth and seventeenth century to be a great market. It was remarkably self-sufficient and European goods simply did not compete with Chinese products. Indeed, the Europeans bought Chinese goods — silks and porcelain, for example — with precious metals from the Americas, which were increasingly to monetise the Chinese economy and to make its merchants more specialised. The economic effects on China of the worldwide ventures of the Europeans were indeed considerable, if indirect. The peasants began to plant American crops, like maize and sweet potato. The long-term results included, from the eighteenth century, substantial population increases based on the utilisation of marginal land and so leading to substantial erosion.

China was, of course, part of the trade network within Asia — a traditional market, for example, for the jungle and marine products of Southeast Asia. The Europeans expanded that trade again indirectly rather than directly. The Portuguese established themselves in Macao, though only by 1553. The Dutch failed to dislodge them, and they continued a limited trade in the seventeenth century. The Dutch did not establish themselves elsewhere on the mainland, but only offshore on Formosa (Taiwan). The Chinese responded to the changes the Europeans brought to Southeast Asia in another way, too. Emigrant Chinese communities found new opportunities in the towns the Europeans set up in Java and Luzon, and they made themselves useful as artisans, intermediaries and tax-farmers.

The Manchus handled the European missionaries successfully. Italians were important in the commercial enterprises of the Europeans; they were even important in their missionary ventures. The Church accepted the need to work with the monarchies of Portugal and Spain. But it recognised that its duties went further. It had a duty, it conceived, to bring the Christian message to lands where the secular powers failed to penetrate or to control; in particular, its Italian servants recognised that it might not always be advantageous to rely too much on those powers or to be entangled too closely with their politico-commercial activities. The Italian Alessandro Valignano, visitor of the Jesuits in the late sixteenth century, advocated a policy of 'accommodation'. The missionary orders should accommodate their teaching to the customs and traditions of the elite of China and Japan. The policy enjoyed some success, partly because Jesuits had skills that were useful to the Manchu rulers. But it was criticised within the Church — for example, by the Franciscans, who thought the 'accommodation' went so far that the Christian message was unrecognisably diluted. The controversy was to bring about Papal intervention against the Jesuits. It also wearied the Manchu rulers, who were able to limit missionary activities. Even two centuries later, only 1 per cent of the Chinese were Christians.

The Manchu dynasty also dealt successfully with the Russian venture, though here there was some compromise. Its view of the world differed from the view that was emerging in Europe. Among the Europeans, the concept was developing of a world of sovereign states, equal in theory, if not in power. In East Asia, by contrast, China's predominance was represented in a view that saw it as the pinnacle of a state system, the Middle Kingdom between Heaven and Earth, other states finding their position in the world in relation to China. The maritime Europeans had more or less been fitted into the tributary pattern of foreign relations that was the corollary of this view. But the Russians did not quite fit.

Russian expansion eastwards began with the capture of Kazan in 1552, and it was very rapid: Muscovy reached the Pacific before it gained an outlet on the Baltic or the Black Sea. The mixture included the Stroganov charter, state backing, Cossack enterprise, weak native resistance and the lure of fur (another way, beside spices, of making winter bearable). Krasnoyarsk was founded in 1628, Yakutsk in 1632. A Cossack group reached the sea of Okhotsk in 1642 and continued to the Amur. Luxury fur was sought, and in each successive area quickly exhausted, but the state needed the revenue: it drew about 11 per cent of its total income from fur in 1605. Fur was to Russia what silver was to Spain. The Cossacks acted violently in the Amur. In 1651 Khabarov, for example, attacked a settlement of 1000 people on the Amur: 'with God's help . . . we burned them, we knocked them on the head . . . and counting big and little we killed 661.'[5] The Manchus sent an army against the Cossacks, first being defeated by them, then defeating them. Meanwhile the Tsar had sent a number of missions to Beijing. The most successful was that of Spathari, who in 1676 drank tea with the Kangxi emperor, and began negotiations through a Jesuit intermediary. There were further Cossack–Chinese clashes at Albasin in the 1680s. Yet another embassy, that of Golovin, was sent in 1685. Conducted through Jesuit interpreters, negotiations led to the Treaty of Nerchinsk (1689). The Russians withdrew from Albasin and the Amur, but secured commercial privileges, to be further defined in the Treaty of Kiakhta in 1727–28. These were the first treaties between China and a European power. In many ways, it was the Russians who benefited, and the Chinese who made concessions. Siberia gained in security and Russia could trade fur to China as well as to Europe. The Manchus had compromised, though it was only with a remote power and in a remote region.

Exhausting fur, and lacking food, the Russians were to look further east, to Kamchatka, the Aleutians, Alaska and America. But in the later eighteenth century these activities were to alarm the Japanese. Earlier their concern had been over the maritime European powers. The earliest contacts, those of the Portuguese, and then the Spaniards and the Dutch, had found Japan in a phase of civil war. The initial welcome the Portuguese received was indeed due to the fact that they brought firearms. But the Japanese quickly caught up, making their own arquebuses in imitation. Firearms ceased to be important in Portuguese trade, but silk and silver did not. For the Japanese, trade was a weapon in the struggle of one *daimyo* against another, and in the struggle to re-establish central authority which was carried on by Nobunaga, Hideyoshi and then, successfully, by Tokugawa Ieyasu.

The civil war also helped to explain the attitude to Christian missions. Francis Xavier, the Jesuit, was enchanted with what he heard of Japan, and went there in 1549. There were successes, but there were also doubts. Should missions concentrate on the poor? Or should they concentrate on the elite and thus all the more need to 'accommodate' to Japanese culture? Both courses had risks. The poor were dependent, and Christian communities might not survive if the elite turned against them. The elite might turn to Christianity, not only less fully, but more out of political expediency. By 1583 Valignano estimated that there were 150 000 Christians in Japan, and 600 000 in Asia as a whole. But by the end of the decade Hideyoshi was apprehensive that Christian influence would undermine social order. Persecution was stayed only by his fear he would lose the Portuguese commercial connection, but then renewed at the end of the decade, when Franciscans began to come from the Philippines.

Ieyasu was initially anxious for trade. He encouraged the Dutch to establish themselves at Hirado in 1609, and the English followed them in 1613. That gave Ieyasu a commercial alternative to the Portuguese and Spaniards. In turn he felt free in 1614 to expel the missionaries, close the churches and prohibit Christianity. The establishment of a new central regime in Japan reinforced the move towards seclusion. Japanese Christians were martyred or apostatised: overall some 5000–6000 were killed. Disaffection in western Japan came to a climax in the Shimabara rebellion, masterless *samurai* stirring up opposition in an old stronghold of Christianity. The Dutch bombarded Shimabara castle at the *shogun's* request. It was indeed the Dutch who were to best survive this crisis which faced the Europeans.

Already the Tokugawa had begun to take steps, not only against subversive missionary activity, but even against foreign commercial contacts. Macao, the City of the Name of God, tried vainly to dissociate itself from missionary activity: in 1639 its trade was cut off, and most of the members of a mission it sent to plead for the reopening of its trade the following year had their heads cut off. The trade of the Dutch, confined from 1641 to Deshima, a peninsula constructed in Nagasaki Harbour, was the only European trade allowed to continue. The Dutch, once established, used their position to ensure the failure of the Portuguese and the English and to resume contact. But the Tokugawa needed little persuasion. Seclusion was the price of stability at the end of a civil war in which one family had come out on top, but not so conclusively that it had eliminated its rivals. It had checked them and had to go on checking them.

In a sense, the Japanese, like the Chinese, dealt successfully with the European ventures. But there was a penalty. Coupled with their own determination to ensure stability, the threat of the Europeans led them to resort to a policy of seclusion that had no precedent in their past history and which strikingly affected their future. While the old pattern of East Asian relations, with China at its centre, remained essentially undisturbed, Japan could pursue this negative foreign policy. But its disruption was to show that an emphasis on internal stability might mean international insecurity. For some the advance of the Russians was already a source of alarm in the late eighteenth century. The British defeat of China in the 1840s was to bring the lesson home to all.

In mainland southeast Asia, again, the impact of the Europeans was limited, though not negligible. Dai Viet (Vietnam) was another state in the Confucian ambit of the Chinese, seeking to maintain its effective independence of its great neighbour by borrowing from it and confessing allegiance to it without being absorbed by it. Like Japan, Dai Viet suffered in this period from a civil war which opened the way to European commercial and religious influences. In the sixteenth century the country had become divided between two great feudal families, Nguyen and Trinh. In the period of conflict that lasted some 50 years from 1627, Trinh and Nguyen welcomed merchants, Portuguese and Dutch, especially as a source of munitions, and they welcomed missionaries, lest arms supplies should be cut off. The first mission was founded under Portuguese auspices in Tourane in 1615 after the exclusions from Japan. Later the Jesuits determined to work for French help and the Société des Missions Étrangères began to work in Vietnam. The conclusion of civil war by stalemate led to persecutions, which damaged but did not stop missionary activity.

In other states, Europeans played only a limited role. In Burma the Portuguese were mercenaries or adventurers — used, for example, by Tabinshweti and Bayinnaung in their attempts to reunify the kingdom, and by Arakan in an endeavour to secure independence. The Thai kingdom of Ayuthia, surviving Burman attacks and retaliating, was the leading mainland kingdom in the seventeenth century. It initially welcomed VOC merchants as a counter to the Portuguese, and later it called in the French as a balance against the Dutch. But it was never dependent on any of them. A French embassy of 1685, looking for large-scale conversion to Christianity, and also for the right to station troops in Bangkok and to settle at Mergui, was well received by Constance Phaulkon, a Greek adventurer at the Ayuthia court. But he had over-reached himself and was executed in 1688. French troops were withdrawn and for a while missionaries were treated with great severity.

It is difficult to conclude that the Europeans, even in the seventeenth century, had much impact on mainland Southeast Asia, where the main struggles were along traditional lines and over long-standing issues: the tension between Burmese and Thais, the ethnic divisions within the Burma state, the fragmentation of Dai Viet. Their impact in island Southeast Asia was much greater, though its history did not become merely colonial.

The capture of Melaka by the Portuguese in 1511 certainly struck down the major Muslim commercial entrepôt. The Portuguese sought to build their own trading empire in the archipelago, as part of a wider network in Asia as a whole. 'The years were filled with piracy and naval warfare by the Portuguese, defense against assaults, and attacks on trading ships, war fleets, and fortresses.'[6] They sought a foothold on Java, but their action provoked the ruler of Banten, who was to create an independent sultanate in subsequent decades. In Maluku, the source of fine spices, they finally established themselves at Ambon, where cloves were grown, but they never occupied Banda, the source of nutmeg and mace. And in general their incursion tended, as in West Java, to prompt the spread of Islam, and the creation of new states under its banner. In northern Sumatra, Aceh emerged as a rival for Melaka, and as a major participant in the pepper trade that expanded in the sixteenth century. The exiled ruling family of Melaka created the new sultanate of Johor at the tip of the Straits. Patani became a major commercial and political centre on the east coast of the peninsula. Other Muslim traders moved to Makassar in Sulawesi and to Brunei and Sulu. The Portuguese were in fact only one element in an archipelago marked by commercial expansion, political fragmentation and demographic diversity. Their major impact may have been to spur on the expansion of Islam. A latter-day emphasis on conversion could only add to the reaction against them. Another legacy was the creation of the first Eurasian communities in southeast Asia. The short-handed Portuguese did not discourage intermarriage.

When the empire fell apart, the Indies Portuguese were largely left to look after themselves, to 'sustain and enrich themselves from the advantages of the Indies as though they were natives and did not have any other fatherland', as a Dutch observer put it.[7] The Dutch played a major role in destroying the empire, but its weakness was already apparent. Indeed the VOC, though initially finding allies among the Asian states and abstaining from Christian propaganda, was essentially in rivalry with them. This became particularly evident in the intensely competitive post-1630s recession.

Already, however, the Dutch, based at Batavia from 1619, had made a determined bid to monopolise the fine spices. Banda was conquered, and the English driven from Maluku. In the next period they endeavoured with less complete success to control the far more widespread cultivation of pepper. They began by taking Melaka from the Portuguese in 1641. They brought the Sultans of Makassar, Tidore and Ternate under their control. They intervened in Bantam, which granted them exclusive trading rights and secured coastal territories from the ruler of the inland Javanese state of Mataram. The VOC obtained no monopoly of archipelago trade, except in fine spices, and it established no substantial colony. But its impact on the archipelago could not be denied. It was evident, too, that it could not be easily dislodged.

The most striking transformation in maritime Southeast Asia was in Luzon and the Visayas, where no state structures existed by the time the Spaniards arrived, and where no major world religion could compete with the Christian missionary activity they sponsored. Manila, taken in 1571, became the capital of a realm built on conquest, conversion and co-option of existing leaders. Only in 'Filipinas' did the Europeans construct what might be called a colony. But, perhaps paradoxically, its commercial role was limited. The Spaniards were few in number and did not seek to develop the resources of the islands themselves. They concentrated on the galleon trade. Goods from China were purchased in Manila with silver brought from New Spain. 'This trade is so great and profitable and easy to control that the Spaniards do not apply themselves to, or engage in, any other industry,' Antonio de Morga wrote in 1609.[8] The larger plans of the Spaniards — which so alarmed the Japanese — got nowhere; however, despite Dutch attacks, particularly in the 1640s, they were not dislodged from the Philippines. They did, however, fail to incorporate the

Islamic Sultanates of Sulu and Mindanao into their realm, despite their attempts to do so. In this part of Southeast Asia, however, the spread of Islam had been brought to a halt by a European adventure.

Guide to further reading

C.R. Boxer has written extensively on this period, particularly on the Portuguese. His books include *South China in the Sixteenth Century, Being the Narratives of Galeote Pereira, Fz Gaspar da Cuiz, O.P. Fz Martin de Rada, O.E.S.A. (1550–1575)*, Kraus Reprint, Nendeln, Lichtenstein, 1967 and *The Portuguese Seaborne Empire 1415–1825*, Hutchinson, London, 1969.

Meilink-Roelofsz, M.A.P., *Asian Trade and European Influence in the Indonesian Archipelago between 1500 and about 1630*, Martinus Nijhoff, The Hague, 1962
This work is still authoritative.

Reid, A.J.S., *Southeast Asia in the Age of Commerce, 1450-1680*, Yale University Press, New Haven, 1988
An exciting attempt to approach Southeast Asian history in a way influenced by modern French historians.

Scammell, G.V., *The World Encompassed*, University of California Press, Berkeley and Los Angeles, 1981
A commanding account of the expansion of Europeans overseas from the medieval period.

Tarling, Nicholas (ed.) *The Cambridge History of Southeast Asia, Volume One, From Early Times to c. 1800* and *Volume Two, The Nineteenth and Twentieth Centuries*, Cambridge University Press, Cambridge, 1992
These two volumes range from the earliest times to the present; it is written in thematically organised chapters by a group of world authorities.

Notes

1 Elliott, J.H., *The Old World and the New,* Cambridge University Press, Cambridge, 1970, p. 10.
2 Boxer, C.R., *Four Centuries of Portuguese Expansion*, Witwatersrand University Press, Johannesburg, 1965, p. 1.
3 Fitzgerald, C.P., *The Chinese View of Their Place in the World*, Oxford University Press, London, 1964, p. 50.
4 Hudson, G.F., *Europe and China*, Arnold, London, 1931, reprint 1961, p. 201.
5 Golder, F.A., *Russian Expansion in the Pacific 1641–1850*, P. Smith, Gloucester, reprint 1960, p. 45.
6 van Leur, J.C., *Indonesian Trade and Society*, W. van Hoeve, The Hague, 1955, p. 164.
7 Schrieke, B., *Indonesian Sociological Studies I*, Sumar Bandang, The Hague, 1948, p. 45.
8 Schurz, W.L., *The Manila Galleon*, Historical Conservation Society, Manila, 1985, p. 59.

12 | Free-trade commercialism: Tradition under pressure

The European ventures of the nineteenth century had more effect on Asia than those of the earlier period. They were also more marked by British leadership. In the sixteenth and early seventeenth century phases, the English Company had played a relatively limited role: in maritime Southeast Asia it had, for example, been driven out of Maluku, then out of Banten, and retreated to the remote Bengkulu in west Sumatra. But in the later seventeenth and early eighteenth centuries it began to enjoy more success. Its mercantilist measures against Dutch monopoly worked. The Union of Scotland and England in 1707 added to the effective power of the state. In Asia the company took up relatively new trades, the export to Europe of Indian textiles and China tea. In these areas the VOC was perhaps surprisingly an ineffective competitor. Its policies were better adapted to the recession of the second half of the seventeenth century than the more expansive conditions that followed. It still concentrated more on spices than on the products for which there was now a demand in Europe. Its chief contribution to world trade was to domesticate coffee in Java, where its increasing territorial power was turned to account by securing deliveries of export produce through the native elite.

The position of the British, the nature of their policies and the impact they had is hard to understand, however, without reckoning with the growth of their territorial as well as their commercial power. Eighteenth-century overseas ventures, like earlier ones, were stimulated by rivalry among the Europeans. Another contender had joined in. Like the English, the French had played a relatively minor role in the sixteenth and seventeenth centuries — a time of domestic strife. Unified under Cardinal Richelieu and Louis XIV, the French monarchy was more active in the recession of the later seventeenth century. But its power was less commercial than that of the British. France's power lay in its diplomacy, its armed forces, its prestige. It was indeed the French who precipitated political intervention in India, where the Moghul empire was disintegrating. But they were in the end outmanoeuvred and outfought by the

British and their native troops and allies. They precipitated the creation by the East India Company of a territorial state on the Indian sub-continent, a unique event in the story of European expansion in Asia, and one of which an understanding is required for the rest of the story to be comprehensible. India gave Britain additional resources, but also additional responsibilities. Possessing an empire on land in Asia affected in particular the policy the British pursued towards the other great European land-power in Asia, Russia, as well as the Asian states themselves. Indeed, in some ways India had to have a policy of its own, not one identical with the policy a commercial power like Britain might otherwise pursue.

The empire there, however, was certainly a contributor to the world-wide influence of the British in the nineteenth century. The rivalry that had spurred on its creation was also followed by British triumph. The wars of the French Revolution and Napoleon were the climax of the Anglo-French struggles of the eighteenth century as well as a contribution to the restructuring of European politics and political ideas. Britain's success was marked at sea by Trafalgar (1805) and on land by Waterloo (1815). It gained a security in Europe beyond that enjoyed by previous powers. It did not seek to use its power to conquer, but sought to uphold a balance of power on the Continent which would avoid the dominance of any power which might move into a position where it could threaten Britain by accumulating naval and military strength. Overseas, as a result, it did not seek to eliminate the activities of other Europeans. Their rivalry remained a factor in European expansion. Britain tolerated it, partly as a guarantee of security in Europe, and did not fear their commercial success.

Britain's position had indeed been vastly improved by another development, the Industrial Revolution, in which it had the advantage of being the first in the field. That redoubled its power from the later eighteenth century, economic success helping it to build a modern navy and to finance allies against the French. The advantages it enjoyed enabled Britain to contemplate continued overseas rivalry without alarm, as a useful counterpart to a balance in Europe. The only requirement was that British trade should have opportunities overseas and not be subject to exclusive policies. That indeed came to be the aim of the British, in respect to non-European as well as European powers overseas. What the British saw as reasonable treatment for their trade was what they sought from overseas regimes. If that was provided, there was no need for further intervention or for additional political responsibility. Commerce, some indeed believed, would transform the world, and bring about a world state system like that of Europe. If it did not do so, limited and temporary intervention might still suffice to put countries on the track to modernisation. Britain could confine itself to protecting the main routes as its contribution to a stable world in which trade could be safely carried on.

Britain's eighteenth-century Asian trade was still largely trade *within* Asia, and so it remained into the nineteenth century. The Industrial Revolution did not abruptly transform its nature. What the East India Company took to China, for example, was the produce of India and Southeast Asia. In this trade, indeed, opium came to play a significant and sinister role. Indian opium, not European goods, was the main means of paying for China tea, and it was a monopoly of the East India Company as ruler of British India. That complicated the relationship with the Chinese empire. The propagation of a vice that sapped the people's welfare was unacceptable to its rulers. But the concept of a free trade was unacceptable, too. Even if British merchants, now sanguinely believing their goods could compete in China's markets, had distinguished their objectives from those of the opium-traders, there would surely still have been a clash with the Chinese.

For a while, indeed, it was avoided. The Manchus allowed the company to trade at Canton (Guangzhou), a kind of exception to prove the rule, like the overland trade at Nerchinsk and Kiakhta. The company, for its part, was content to accept the compromise. It had its inconveniences, but it also fitted in with its monopoly of British China trade under its charter. That monopoly was, however, removed in the charter of 1833, and Britain's relations with China taken over by the British government. Pressed by private merchants, it sought to put British trade with China on what it saw as a more modern footing. The opium issue precipitated a crisis. Britain's success in the ensuing war prompted the Manchu government to assent to the Treaty of Nanjing (1842). A number of treaty ports were opened to British trade, consular jurisdiction applied to British traders, Hong Kong made over and Chinese tariffs limited. Other European powers, like the French, followed the British example, and the Americans secured a similar 'unequal' treaty.

Whatever Britain's hopes, it was unlikely that this blow would lead the Chinese government to 'reform' China. Faced with the crisis, Manchu officials, anxious to save the dynasty, had patched up a compromise with the barbarians. A longer resistance might have led to full-scale war in which the dynasty could have been displaced. But, if such a prospect could not be risked, it was also difficult to promote change. The Manchu dynasty depended upon the Chinese gentry and the relationship required the maintenance of Confucian ideology. The gentry indeed rallied to the dynasty against the Taiping rebels, who challenged that ideology. 'How can that be a change that concerns only our Ch'ing [Qing] dynasty?' asked Zeng Guofan: 'How can anyone who can read and write remain, quietly seated, hands in sleeves, without thinking of doing something about it?'[1] But this only made Westernisation more difficult for the dynasty to contemplate. The Western powers used the occasion to press for more concessions from it, rather than taking up the cause of the Taipings (despite their Christian-influenced teachings) against it. 'We do not wish to revolutionise the country,' Frederick Bruce was to write, 'for I am convinced that we are more likely to get on with a Manchu than with a purely Chinese dynasty.'[2] The Treaty of Tianjin (1858) granted the right to maintain an ambassador in Beijing. In 1860 the barbarians entered the capital itself in order to ensure ratification. The Russians returned to the Amur.

The Japanese reaction to the West differed. They saw what happened to the Manchu empire and they came to terms with the West without conflict. But (though admittedly only after an internal struggle) they also went on to transform themselves and, with the Meiji restoration of 1868, to put their country on the path of modernisation. They were fortunate in that the attitude of the outside powers to Japan also differed from their attitude to China. They did not press Japan so hard. It gained time to resolve its internal conflicts. While those conflicts risked the intervention of the outside powers, they also provided an advantage. From them Japan emerged with a leadership determined to carry out a program of modernisation. China had a leadership determined not to do so.

The Tokugawa regime had sought to rivet its power on Japan by a policy of seclusion which would in particular cut Western *daimyo* off from resources that might enable them to renew their opposition. Within Japan it pursued, indeed, a policy of checks and balances, one important element of which was the hostage system that required *daimyo* to reside in the Shogun's capital, Edo, and to leave members of their family there when back in their fiefdom. The system's main aim was to preserve internal tranquillity. The ability to concentrate on that depended, of course, on the preservation of Japan's external security by other means. It was possible only while the traditional pattern of East Asian relationships was preserved. Already, however, other powers were penetrating into the region, the integrity of which Manchu China (despite making some compromises) had substantially preserved.

Blocked off from the Amur, Russian expansion had pursued a more northerly course. But one part of Bering's expedition of the 1730s and 1740s that explored Alaska and the Aleutians explored the Kuril islands, and a Polish exile, Benyovsky, told the Deshima Dutch in the 1770s of a supposed Russian plan to conquer Japan. In 1792 an expedition under Laxman, designed to return some castaway Japanese, but also to open up trade, met with failure. The Japanese regime was indeed prompted to reaffirm its policy of seclusion. The Krusenstern expedition in the following decade also met with a negative response. The envoy, Rezanov, thought it might be a mistake to prod the Japanese into change. 'If there will rule over this populous, intelligent, dexterous, imitative and patient nation, which is capable of everything, a sovereign like our great Peter, he will enable Japan, with the resources and treasures which she has in her bosom, in a short number of years to lord over the whole Pacific Ocean. . . .'[3] So far, indeed, the Tokugawa confined themselves to edicts. They seemed to work: the Russians went away.

The attitude changed when the power of the West was demonstrated in the first Anglo-China war, and the Japanese realised that the pattern of relationships on which their security depended had been dislocated. It was necessary, they concluded, to take steps to defend Japan from the Western intrusion: indeed, it might have to take the lead in defending the whole region if China could no longer do so. But if that was a common conclusion among the Japanese elite, many sources of dispute remained. How should Japan react to the West when it sought unequal treaties? At what point should it commence to strengthen and modernise? In what way and to what extent? Nor was it a matter merely of political argument. The Tokugawa system was one in which power was diffused. Change was difficult to carry through because it would disturb the checks and balances on which it relied.

The system had certainly become more difficult to sustain two centuries after it had been inaugurated. There had been change within Japan as well as outside. The *samurai* or feudal warriors were idle, discontented, adversely affected by inflation. Merchants, benefiting from the growth of internal commerce, lacked status. Peasants, bound down, erupted increasingly in millennialist movements. Alternative leadership was, moreover, available from imperial court nobles, who had lacked power since the *shogun's* court monopolised it, and from the western clans, like Satsuma and Choshu. The leadership took advantage of the crisis into which the British victory over China plunged Japan.

Despite the loss of prestige involved in abandoning seclusion, the Tokugawa negotiated unequal treaties, first with the United States then with the other powers, Britain and Russia among them, the last including a frontier clause covering the Kuril Islands. Opponents of the Tokugawa took advantage of its temporising with the West to advance their own power. The *daimyo* and the imperial court sought to claim a share in policy-making, and the lower ranks of the feudal hierarchy identified the redemption of Japan with enhancing their own status. Initially the call was for the expulsion of the foreigner. That indeed embarrassed the Tokugawa to the maximum. But it was also manifestly impractical. The recognition of this, and the divisions of its opponents, seemed for a time to mean that the shogunate might survive. It would, however, be at the price of not asserting its leadership. When it did, its opponents were prompted, under Satsuma-Choshu court noble leadership, to overthrow it in the name of the Meiji emperor in 1868. The Meiji rulers pursued modernisation with determination, not only because they wanted to preserve Japan's independence, but because they wanted, like their predecessors, to firmly establish their power within the country.

The shogunate had begun to seek French help in its last years, and that had indeed been an argument for finally destroying it. Perhaps Japan came closer to falling under colonial control that its subsequent history suggests. But the West had after all behaved far more moderately than it did with respect to China. Though the *Edinburgh Review* claimed that 'the compulsory seclusion of the Japanese is a wrong not only to themselves, but to the civilised world',[4] the leading Western power, Britain, had indeed displayed little interest in 'opening up' Japan, and Commodore Perry and the 'black ships' of the United States Navy had been left to demand the first 'unequal treaty'. When the shogunate sought to delay the full implementation of the treaties, the British assented. But it was no doubt fortunate that the leadership that finally triumphed was that in Satsuma and Choshu, with which British relations were good. Vietnam, by contrast to Japan, did fall under colonial control. The course of its history was quite different.

For much of the eighteenth century, it was true that Vietnam, like Japan, had been secluded from the West. That was partly because Western nations had less interest in the country than before, but it was also the result of the stalemate in the Nguyen–Trinh struggles that had marked much of the seventeenth century. The French, however, began to interest themselves in the Nguyen region, Cochin-China, from the 1740s, and considered that Vietnam could have a role in their plans to undermine the growing British predominance in India and China. Vergennes argued that the French should pre-empt the British in Cochin-China:

> If they decide on that place before us, we will be excluded for ever and we will have lost an important foothold on that part of Asia which would make us masters by intercepting in time of war the English trade with China, by protecting our own in the whole of India, and by keeping the English in a continual state of anxiety.[5]

The disintegration of Trinh–Nguyen Vietnam under the onset of the Tayson rebellion of the 1770s opened up an opportunity to intervene, or so the head of the French missions argued. In 1787, Louis XVI's government made a treaty with the Nguyen representative, offering aid in return for the cession of Danang. The Nguyen, however, triumphed without any official French support. Once reunited, Vietnam tended to oppose foreign intervention, associated as it was with civil conflict. Furthermore, the emperors sought to maintain the integrity of their realm by insisting on the Confucian ideology they had borrowed from the Chinese. Foreign contact seemed disruptive.

The British had shown some interest in Vietnam. One reason for this was their concern about French influence during the period of their rivalry. But, even under the first Nguyen, Gia Long, and still more under Minh Mang, his successor, it was realised that such influence could not flourish. The other motive for British interest was commercial. Before the revolutionary war, Vietnam had been seen not only as a possible strategic threat in the hands of the French, but as a means of amplifying the trade with China. After the war, it was of less interest, since Indian opium supplied the East India Company's investment in China. The Indian government sent the Crawfurd mission to Vietnam in 1822. Minh Mang refused to receive him, the envoy of a mere governor-general. But Crawfurd did not recommend any action as a result, and the British did nothing.

It can be argued, at least with hindsight, that the Vietnamese should have taken the opportunity to come to terms with the major European power, since that would have stood them in good stead when they fell out with the French. Such a quarrel was indeed increasingly likely. Minh Mang redoubled attacks on Vietnamese Christians, as well as attempts to exclude Catholic missionaries. By the 1840s France had a navy in East Asian waters, following the opening of China. With little commerce to protect, it took up the cause of the missions. The government of Napoleon III took it up formally in the 1850s, and finally, with some Spanish co-operation from the Philippines, mounted an expedition against Vietnam. This did not in the event attack the Nguyen capital, Hue, but to the disappointment of the missions, moved south and seized Saigon in 1859. It became the basis of the French colony of Cochin-China. Little interested in Vietnam, and finding the Vietnamese rulers unresponsive to the approaches they had made, the British did not impede the French venture. 'It will lead to the expansion of Trade,' Sir John Bowring commented in Hong Kong, 'and there is perhaps no locality where less mischief will be done as regards our interests.'[6] The integrity of Vietnam, unlike that of China, was not important to the British. So long as the French did not expand into Siam (Thailand) and Laos, their expansion could be tolerated.

Siam and Laos were important to the British because of their interests in Burma and Malaya, but above all because of their interests in India. Siam, as Crawfurd had put it, was 'within the pale of our Indian diplomacy'.[7] The East India Company wanted a peaceful relationship with Siam. Its aim was to allay its fear of British conquest, and to develop a satisfactory commercial relationship with it. That line indeed received a more positive response from the Thais than it did from the Vietnamese. The Chakri dynasty in its new capital at Bangkok was outward-looking, interested in trade, and realistic enough to sign a treaty with Henry Burney in 1826, which allowed free trade to the English provided they did not 'molest, attack or disturb' states of the region.

Recognition that Siam was a feudatory of China, the source of its tea trade, had also been a restraining factor in the company's policy. But the restraint continued even after Britain's victory over China in 1840–42. Then new missions to Siam, as well as to Japan and Vietnam, had been advocated. After some doubt, the British government had rather reluctantly yielded to commercial pressure, and sent Sir James Brooke on a mission to Bangkok in 1850. Dissatisfied with his reception, he advocated an ultimatum and the seizure of the capital. No such policy was followed. The new king, Mongkut, made a treaty with Bowring in 1855, conceding much of what China had been forced to yield, and accepting British diplomatic representation in his capital. In this he anticipated the Japanese as well as the Chinese. The moderation of the British was matched by the responsiveness of the Thais. Once a treaty was made with the British, furthermore, it was both safe and advisable to make treaties with other Western powers. It was not necessary to give them more than the British had secured, and it was not desirable to develop relations only with the British.

The Burmese pursued a very different course. The British approach to them was also different. The contacts arose out of the Anglo-French rivalry of the mid-eighteenth century. From a base in Burma, the French could render British possessions on the opposite shore of India insecure, particularly in the northerly monsoon, and when they established a post at Syriam, the British established one at Negrais. This, however, was attacked by Burmese troops in 1759. The new king of Burma, Alaungpaya, was putting down opposition in the south, and thought the British had supported the Mons.

Over the next generation there was relatively little contact between the British and the Burmese. But meanwhile the British became a major territorial power in India, while the Burmese kings invaded Siam and, more successfully, incorporated Arakan. That brought the frontiers of the two realms together. But the issues which arose as a result were peculiarly difficult to settle. The Burmese kings found it difficult to accept a view of the world in which other countries were not placed in some sense in an inferior status. The British feared that this attitude would undermine their hegemony over Indian princes on the sub-continent. The British hoped for the extension to Burma of the Indian 'subsidiary alliance' system, but there was little chance of that. While in the revolutionary and Napoleonic wars the French were unable to make any use of Burma, there were bitter disputes on the Arakan frontier. The real issue was that Burma could not accept what Britain, as ruler of India, saw as an appropriate position, one of modified independence.

The first Burma War was fought in a sense to teach Burma that lesson. But it did not bring the quick and telling victory that was necessary. Britain's supremacy had therefore to be marked by the acquisition of Arakan and Tenasserim. It failed to produce the required effect: King Bagyidaw considered that to accept a British Resident at his capital would be 'a proof of our supremacy and a badge of his servility and vassalage'.[8] His successor refused to recognise the treaty of Yandabo: 'I am determined to place the relations between the two countries on precisely the same footing as they were previous to the reign of the late King . . .'[9] Burney, the Resident, withdrew in 1837.

Trade was a source of disputes that were, like those on the frontier, difficult to solve in the context of such an Anglo-Burmese relationship. A dispute at Rangoon late in 1851 escalated into a second war. Richard Cobden published a pamphlet about it, *How Wars are Got Up in India.* But Governor-General Dalhousie was by no means anxious for war, and still less was he anxious to acquire territory. The war became necessary because 'the Government of India could never, consistently with its own safety, permit itself to stand for a single day in an attitude of inferiority towards a native power, and least of all towards the Court of Ava'.[10] The acquisition of Pegu was a way of demonstrating the 'inferiority' of Burma. Dalhousie hoped the Burmese would accept that outcome. He realised he could not get a treaty that formally acknowledged it, though the new king, Mindon Min, was conciliatory.

The decisions the British took about island Southeast Asia were quite different. The Dutch were allowed to prevail in what they came to see as Netherlands India. The British sought to provide for their interests, strategic and commercial, without taking territorial control. European considerations reinforced their moderation: an independent Dutch state in Europe enhanced Britain's security, and such a state would be supported by the possession of an empire. It was only necessary to ensure that Britain's strategic interests in the defence of India and the route to China were provided for, together with its commercial interests in the products of the maritime world. The acquisition of Penang in 1786 helped to provide for these interests, but the British still sought to acquire Riau at the other end of the Straits. In the revolutionary and Napoleonic wars, when the French influence prevailed in Europe, Dutch authority overseas was displaced. But on their victory, the British restored their conquests in the Malay world. They did not even seek to acquire Riau. By pointing to the insecurity of their commerce, but particularly of the route to China, Raffles secured the authority that he used to found Singapore in 1819. By the subsequent treaty of 1824, the British withdrew from Sumatra and undertook not to sustain political relationships in the archipelago. The Dutch dropped their opposition to Singapore, transferred Melaka, and agreed to give British trade commercial opportunity in islands where they had authority or treaty relationships.

Subsequently the Dutch concentrated on Java, intensifying its export production and drawing off a substantial surplus for the benefit of the Netherlands. The British, by contrast, did not take over on the peninsula. Their relationship with Siam restrained them, and they developed a pattern of working with Malay rulers so as to put down piracy and create stable conditions for commercial development. The opening up of tin mines in Perak and Selangor — with Malay rulers encouraging the immigration of Chinese labour — was to produce problems for which this approach was an inadequate solution.

In the Philippines, as in Indonesia, the British dislodged, but restored, a European power. They captured Manila in 1762, but they returned it soon after. Thereafter, the Spaniards, like the Dutch, developed their policy in some sense with an eye on the British. Though no treaty required it, they gave them the commercial opportunities they sought, opening Manila, and later other ports, to foreign commerce. British capital and entrepreneurship indeed helped to transform the economy of the Visayas, and thus to produce the lively *mestizo* elite that was increasingly to claim a share in the governance of the colony.

To the south, the Spaniards had not succeeded in establishing control over the Muslims or Moros. In the 1760s and 1770s, the East India Company had taken steps to establish an entrepôt there, but had not persisted in the face of opposition from the Sulus and the Spaniards and due to the incompetence of its own officers. In 1849, James Brooke, whose venture in Brunei and Sarawak had received limited support from the British government, made a treaty supporting the independence of Sulu. But the British government, diminishing its support for him in Borneo, did not ratify his treaty with Sulu. Relations with Spain came first.

Guide to further reading

Lensen, G.A., *The Russian Push towards Japan, Russo-Japanese Relations 1697-1875*, Princeton University Press, Princeton, 1960
   A work by a major authority on a topic too often ignored.
Tarling, N., *Imperial Britain in South-East Asia*, Oxford University Press, Kuala Lumpur, 1975
   Collects together a number of papers on British relations with governments, indigenous and European, in Southeast Asia.
Sansom, G.B., *The Western World and Japan: A Study in the Interaction of European and Asiatic Cultures*, Knopf, New York, 1950
   This is a wonderful book, still worth reading.
Greenberg, Michael, *British Trade and the Opening of China 1800-42*, Cambridge University Press, Cambridge, 1951
   This is a careful and well-written study, based substantially on Jardine Matheson papers.
Mo, Timothy, *An Insular Possession*, London, 1986
   An account of the first Anglo-China War which should appeal to those who like 'faction'.
Tarling, Nicholas (ed.), *The Cambridge History of Southeast Asia, Volume One, From Early Times to c. 1800* and *Volume Two, The Nineteenth and Twentieth Centuries*, Cambridge University Press, Cambridge, 1992

These two volumes range from the earliest times to the present; it is written in thematically organised chapters by a group of world authorities.

Notes

1 Spector, S., *Li Hung-chang and the Huai Army*, Introduction, F. Michael, Seattle, 1964, p. xxxix.

2 Banno, Masataka, *China and the West 1858–1861. The Origins of the Tsungli Yamen*, Harvard University Press, Cambridge, Mass., 1964, p. 237.

3 Lensen, G.A., *The Russian Push Towards Japan, Russo-Japanese Relations 1697–1875*, Princeton University Press, Princeton, 1960, p. 252.

4 Beasley, W.G., *Great Britain and the Opening of Japan*, Luzac, London, 1951, p. 89.

5 Lamb, A., *The Mandarin Road to Old Hué*, Chatto, London, 1970, p. 64.

6 Tarling, N., *Imperial Britain in South-East Asia*, Oxford University Press, Kuala Lumpur, 1975, pp. 124–25.

7 Crawfurd, J., *Journal of an Embassy from the Governor-General of India to the Courts of Siam and Cochin China*, Colburn and Bentley, London, 1830, I, p. 472.

8 Desai, W.S., *History of the British Residency in Burma*, University of Rangoon, Rangoon, 1939, p. 196.

9 ibid., p. 296.

10 Hall, D.G.E., *The Dalhousie–Phayre Correspondence*, London, 1932, p. xviii.

13 | Intensive capitalism: The domination of Asian societies

The latter half of the nineteenth century, in particular its last two decades, was marked by a phase of 'imperialism' that saw both the establishment of new colonial frontiers and a redirection of economic activity. The rivalry of Europeans played a part in this development as in the earlier phases of European expansion overseas. In the period of British predominance that rivalry had been diminished or accommodated. That had by no means always been to the advantage of the non-European states, like those left to the Dutch, the Spaniards or the French in Southeast Asia. But a new phase of rivalry was still less to their advantage. The Europeans sought to pre-empt each other. The British accepted compromises with others, sometimes at the expense of Asian states, or moved to establish their influence more formally, where their interests seemed to require it. Nor were the Europeans now facing rivalry merely with one another. The period, unlike the earlier period, was marked by the emergence into world affairs of centres of power outside Europe. The chief of these was, of course, the United States. But the most striking novelty in Asia was the emergence of Japan as a modern and expanding state.

The British, who had enjoyed an unusual predominance in the previous period, found themselves overburdened and forced to unwelcome prioritisation. First, still, was a concern for their own security in Europe. That had rested, in large part, on their supremacy at sea and on the balance of power on the Continent. But the latter was challenged, if not entirely overthrown, by Bismarck's unification of Germany in 1871, while the former was challenged, initially by the French and Russians in potential combination, but then by the Germans themselves. Not surprisingly, the British, while pegging out their own claims, also came to terms with others. It was easier indeed to come to terms outside Europe than inside. The rise of the United States did not seem to present as direct a threat as Germany, and compromise could be reached in the Caribbean.

It was also easier to come to terms with Japan than it was with Russia, even though both threatened the integrity of China and British interests in that country.

The reasons for these challenges are paradoxically to be found in part in Britain's very success. Its foremost role in industrialisation depended upon the opening-up of markets elsewhere. Its approaches were imitated and indeed, rival industries might be organised on more up-to-date lines, with newer techniques and higher capitalisation. While other states remained anxious lest Britain, faced by rivals, would abandon free trade and put up protective barriers, they were not slow to protect their own nascent industries by such means. The Germans adopted a protective tariff in 1879, the Americans and the Russians in 1891. By the 1890s, the United States and Germany surpassed Britain's industrial capacity in a number of fields. Britain's pre-eminence had passed, economically as well as politically.

The relationship between the economic and political thrusts of Western states in the earlier period was, perhaps, more simple than it was in the later nineteenth century. To describe the 'imperialism' of this period as the mere product of 'capitalism' is insufficient. For one thing, some of the economic changes that affected the world were international. The inventive technology of the Industrial Revolution inspired dramatic changes in the world's communications, including the building of railways, the establishment of the electric telegraph, the opening of the Suez and Panama Canals and the introduction of coal- and later oil-fired shipping. In some cases, of course, such changes were clearly backed by the state, which saw them as a means of integration or expansion, and thus of more effective rivalry, one with another. But an international canal or telegraph service was open to other interests. A more complex network of economic, as well as cultural and political, relationships became possible, and indeed inevitable.

Secondly, the relationship between capital and government differed from state to state. In Germany, a new power, it was probably closer than it was in Britain; certainly, there remained in the latter (perhaps in part as a legacy of the days of predominance) something of a tendency to insist that merchants must take risks and not expect government to bail them out. There was also something of a desire to set up administrations concerned with 'law and order', but not to intrude further. In the French case, as in the Japanese, government intervention might be greater. Indeed, capital in France tended not to be imperial at all: if the French invested in foreign countries, it was in Russia. In Japan, capital followed government initiatives, and the connection remained close.

The other half of the story helps to exemplify and even perhaps to explain some of these differences. How did the extra-European world meet these challenges? The penetration of new economic interests —

those searching for minerals, for land to grow tobacco or sugar for world markets, or for raw materials — might prove too much for the existing frameworks to cope with; it certainly presented them with a challenge, often initially in the form of adventurers and concessionaires of no great scruple or reputation. Behind them, though not necessarily squarely backing them, lay political ambitions, fuelled by the more intense rivalry among states. The outcome would differ from country to country. Some might be able to uphold their political independence, perhaps with the assistance of an interested outside power or powers. Others might succumb, an outside power deciding that it was essential to foreclose the intervention of others. Only rarely could a state hope to survive in this dangerous new world without a patron.

Within the boundaries that might thus be at least partially redrawn, the play of economic forces would be worked out in the context of the administrative and political structures set up and the policies followed under them. The economic effects of these changes thus differed from area to area because of the political context. But areas differed still more because of the nature of the economic changes themselves. As in the past, but still more in the new period, economic transformation was a patchy affair. It centred on coastal towns, on plantations, on mines, on products with a market 'niche'. The patterns of economic life became more variegated. So did the patterns of social life, particularly in parts of Southeast Asia always open to Indian and Chinese migration — the ethnic patterns.

When force and diplomacy had done all they could legitimately effect, Lord Elgin, who led the force which sacked Beijing's Old Summer Palace in 1860, wrote, 'the work which has to be accomplished in China will be but at its commencement'. How far could the foreigners develop their trade in the country?

> The machino-manufacturing West will be in the presence of a population the most universally and laboriously manufacturing of any on the earth. It can achieve victories in the contest only by proving that physical knowledge and mechanical skill, applied to the arts of production, are more than a match for the most persevering efforts of unscientific industry.[1]

In fact, though a market of 400 million beckoned, it did not yield the returns expected: by 1895 the total foreign trade of China was only worth 53 million pounds. Merchants tended to blame their failure on obstructive regulations and unsympathetic bureaucrats. Their attempts to secure further backing from their own governments had limited success. The major power, Britain, recognised, in Elgin's phrase, that there was a limit to force and diplomacy: it had no wish, as *The Times* put it in 1875, to make China another India. The Foreign Secretary wrote:

The true policy to be advocated, is that which, by mutual forbearance, shall combine the suffrage of both parties in some common system, which, though it may not be the best in the abstract, yet may have in its favour that it does not, without some palpable advantage to Chinese interests, clash with their existing habits and fixed opinions.[2]

The suppression of the Taiping rebellion had, in Rutherford Alcock's view, arrested China in that course of renovation which nations could often effect only by civil war and revolution. Was the old system 'susceptible of a regeneration, and a new life of adaptation to modern exigencies and foreign civilisation', or was it to be 'dissolved by a process of decomposition and degradation, more or less progressive and complete with all their consequences within and without the Empire'?[3] Merchant pressure added to the anti-foreignism that seemed likely to answer Alcock's question. It was further stimulated by the increase in Catholic missionary activities after 1860. The suspicion and resentment they aroused, together with the imprudence of the French consul, produced a massacre at Tianjin in 1870. War was avoided, partly because the French were soon engaged in war with Germany and British policy remained moderate. But the influence of the reactionary Empress Dowager grew in Beijing, and worked against even the limited change promoted by the Tongzhi restoration of the 1860s. Li Hongzhang, one of the Tongzhi figures, carried on military Westernisation as Governor-General of Zhili. But military Westernisation on its own was unlikely to be effectual, and Li Hongzhang in any case worked to strengthen himself rather than China. The impact of imperialism was limited:

Chinese diplomats and Chinese society had adapted to the irruption of the West by minor changes in a highly sophisticated system and had contained it thereby so successfully that there was no stimulus left to bring about major structural innovation.[4]

The weakness of their response was shown up by further defeats at the hands of outside powers in the 1880s and 1890s. The Chinese went to war with France in response to appeals from the Nguyen dynasty in Vietnam, but failed to avert French control in Tonkin. In the north, the Russians reasserted their interest in the Far East in the 1890s after two decades of concentration on the Balkans and Central Asia and began to construct the Trans-Siberian Railway, with a terminal at Vladivostok, in 1891. That brought the future of Manchuria and Korea into question, and in turn precipitated Japanese intervention. Japanese success was a further humiliation for China, and this, together with further subsequent concessions to foreign powers, including the Germans in Shandong, prompted a new, but brief, phase of imperial reform, and stimulated those who, prompted by the defeats of the 1880s, had begun to work for the overthrow of the dynasty, drawing support in particular from overseas Chinese who had never sympathised with it. It now seemed that the answer to Alcock's question would be the breakup of China, as a result of the combination of its failure to effectively modernise and increased pressure from outside.

Britain's policy was to uphold the integrity of China. It had adopted this when it had hoped, in the days of its predominance, to enjoy commercial success over its rivals. Now the policy was designed to uphold China against their territorial ambitions. But Britain could not sustain the policy on its own. In 1894–95 it was unable to intervene effectively. In subsequent years, particularly concerned about the Russian threat to China, it looked to Japan to offset it. But the alliance of 1902 encouraged the Japanese more than it restrained them.

The period of the Meiji restoration in Japan is covered in greater detail in Chapter 15 in order to explain Japanese nationalism. Since European 'intensive capitalism' affected it greatly and it was the most successful of all Asian nations in its response, it is also covered here. The intrusion of the West and the failure of China to meet it had been elements in Japanese thinking before the Meiji restoration, and they continued to exist after it. Should Japan work with China to limit the Western intrusion? Or should it unilaterally seek to defend the region? Given China's weakness, the latter course increasingly seemed the one that had to be followed, though some hankered after the 'pan-Asian' program. If need be, the course had to be followed at China's expense. As early as 1873, the ruling oligarchy resolved to intervene in the Ryukyus, and they were annexed as Okinawa in 1879. It differed over the policy to be followed in Korea. That state had so far enjoyed seclusion and, rather ironically, it was Japan that broke in upon it by forcing on it the commercial treaty of 1876. The Chinese, who had been unable to assist the Koreans, became more active after the Japanese annexation of the Ryukyus. They first advised the Koreans to make treaties with other powers, then became more interventionist themselves. That played a part in determining the Japanese decisively to intervene in 1894. Annexation was to follow in 1909.

Within Japan, these policies had been the source of some dispute. The ruling elite was agreed that Japan must be strong and prosperous, the equal of other nations in the new multi-national world it had now entered. There was substantial agreement on some of the ways in which this goal might be attained. Though the restoration had emerged from a feudal background, it overthrew feudalism, so preparing the way for a strong central government, at once benefiting the new leadership, and enabling it to mobilise Japan's resources and sustain its independence. The *daimyo* were induced to surrender their lands to the emperor. In the face of rather more opposition — and, in Satsuma, rebellion — the *samurai* were ungenerously pensioned off, clearing the way for a modern army, first on the French and then on the German model, and for a navy on the British model. Perhaps even more significant for the future, the oligarchy began the industrialisation of Japan, not only by creating an infrastructure, railways and telegraphs, but also by setting up model factories, drafting female labour into them, importing foreign expertise and ensuring its application. The differences within the elite were less about the major aim than about tactics and timing. Should Japan wait until these changes had been carried out before attempting a more active foreign policy? The question was the source of some division within the oligarchy. The outcome was to concentrate on internal modernisation and the undoing of the unequal treaties.

Others wanted a more active policy and they wanted it sooner. These should not be identified simply or even mainly as right-wing or militarist elements. Those who argued for 'popular rights' in Japan, like Itagaki Taisuke and Okuma Shigenobu, indeed argued for them as a means of strengthening Japan:

> Everyone thought . . . on the basis of the conviction that national unity and independence should take precedence over all other things. This was as true of the oligarchs as of their opponents. They differed only in respect of the methods to be used, in achieving the common goal.[5]

They did not advocate democratic values for their own sake; popular participation, they believed, was a better means for achieving strength and prosperity than the Satsuma–Choshu oligarchy. Nor did they do much to tap the unrest of the peasants who, bearing the major burdens of the new state as of the old, paid heavy taxes, but who, like *samurai* rebels, could be contained by the new conscript army.

The oligarchy sought to counter opposition by a number of other means. Effective systems of local government and police were installed. Shinto was played up as the state's ideology. The new national education system came, under Mori Arinori, to lay a heavy stress on the state:

> The goal of our educational administration is purely and simply the service of the state. The administrators of our various schools should at all times be mindful of the fact that the undertaking is on behalf of the state, not on behalf of the individual student.[6]

The oligarchy also thought it expedient to set up a constitution which, in addition to establishing Japan's modernity with other powers, and so expediting the end of the unequal treaties, would also enable it to deprive the popular rights movement of the initiative. The country Ito Hirobumi found it most appropriate to imitate was the Second Reich, where the Bismarckian constitution provided for an elected Reichstag, but preserved imperial power. As Inoue commented:

> To put into effect a Prussian-style constitution, is an extremely difficult task under existing circumstances; but at the present time it is possible to carry it out and win over the majority and thus succeed. This is because the English-style constitution has not become firmly fixed in the minds of the people.[7]

Ito and his colleagues, however, went further. The army and later the navy leaders were given 'the right of supreme command', that is of direct access to the Emperor outside the bounds of the cabinet. That was a final defence against any democratisation of the state, let alone the introduction of a Republic.

Despite all their precautions, Ito Hirobumi and his colleagues found the governments they led or sponsored to be often at odds with the Diet after it was inaugurated in 1890. That tension was diminished when the oligarchy shifted away from its cautious foreign policy and embarked on the war with China of 1894–95, for an elected Diet was not a source of moderation in foreign policy. There was widespread disappointment with the oligarchy when it agreed, under pressure from France, Russia and Germany, to hand back its gains in Manchuria. Even Okuma, though pan-Asianist when out of power, was to be aggressive towards China when he came to power in World War I. It was the oligarchy, even when dominated by the militarist Yamagata rather than the civilian Ito, that was the source of caution.

While Japan had escaped imperialist intervention more narrowly than is sometimes assumed, Vietnam had fallen out with the French. Established in three southern provinces in the south, they extended over the rest of Cochin-China during the 1860s, as well as intervening in Cambodia. The fall of the Bonapartist regime in France did not bring a halt to the imperialist enterprise it had begun. Much of the initiative had indeed been, and remained with, the naval and colonial authorities on the spot. The government of the Third Republic was initially unwilling to fully back such initiatives and sought a compromise with the Nguyen regime. But by the end of the decade, Republican leaders were emphasising a vigorous colonial policy, in Africa as well as Asia, as a means of demonstrating, at least to the French people, that France was still a world power, despite its defeat in Europe. This, they hoped, would undercut right-wing nationalist opposition to the regime. The local authorities had, in the 1870s, displayed an interest in the Red River when they realised that the Mekong did not provide access to the interior of China. Now their superiors backed them. In 1882 a small expedition was sent to deal with disorder obstructing traffic on the Red River, and a further expedition in 1883 secured control over lower Tonkin. The French quickly established a protectorate over Tonkin and the remainder of Vietnam. In the following decade, Paul Doumer, later President of France, was to incorporate

Tonkin, Annam, Cochin-China, Cambodia and Laos into a federation called French Indochina. He was himself Governor-General of French Indochina from 1897 to 1902 (see Chapter 19). But the move into Laos had provoked a crisis with Siam and the British.

Unlike Japan, Vietnam lost its independence. But the contrast between the history of the two countries in this phase is even more striking than this simple statement suggests. The Vietnamese mandarins, and indeed the masses, were ready to resist the foreigner, but the dynasty was unwilling to enlist or encourage that resistance. The partisans in Cochin-China in the 1860s were disavowed. Facing a challenge in the north, the dynasty compromised with the invaders, and the initial hesitation of the Third Republic perhaps raised its hopes of regaining territory by negotiation. When this policy changed, however, the dynasty still hesitated to evoke patriotic resistance. Instead it invoked the help of its old suzerain the Chinese, albeit in vain. Only belatedly did Emperor Ham Nghi identify his cause with resistance. It was as if the dynasty hesitated to place confidence in the mandarins and the people, perhaps because, despite all its emphasis on Confucian orthodoxy, it was seen in the Vietnamese heartland in the north as the creation of southern pretenders.

In any case, the French had been able to find collaborators in the south — though they could argue that their collaboration could in the end profit Vietnam, since it was a means of acquiring the Western knowledge that it had so lamentably lacked — and they were now, at least nominally, to work through a dynastic figurehead at Hue. Though, like all colonial regimes, they relied on collaborators, their rule was increasingly direct, even outside Cochin-China which they actually termed a 'colony'. But while it favoured French interests, there was no great inflow of capital. French imperialism, in Indo-China as elsewhere, was connected more with French greatness in the world than with trade or investment. That was perhaps to make it more difficult for France to abandon its colonies, not less.

In Vietnam, the French retained a puppet ruler; in Burma, the rest of which the British finally acquired in 1886, the Konbaung kings were displaced. No satisfactory relationship had ever been established between them and the British: the views of the relative status of Burma and British India differed too widely. Mindon Min took a realistic view in the earlier years of this reign. But, realising that Siam had established diplomatic relations with a range of European powers, he tried to do the same, and in 1873 sent an embassy to France and to other countries. This was, however, a risky policy for a close neighbour of British India to pursue. The death of the king, moreover, left the way open for still riskier policies. A problem arising in 1875, the so-called 'shoe question', diminished contacts between the Burmese monarch and the British Resident, and the Resident was withdrawn altogether in 1879. An opportunity to put the relationship on a new footing was missed in 1882. Relations with the British were increasingly the subject of intrigue among court factions and the concessionaires and adventurers who now came to Mandalay in greater numbers and from a wide range of countries.

Increasingly it seemed that the kingdom could not cope with the additional economic pressures of the 1880s. It was indeed an incident involving the Bombay–Burmah Trading Corporation that was to precipitate the third Anglo-Burman War in 1885. But it is unlikely that economic motives were a priority with the British government. Burma had never quite acknowledged the kind of semi-independent status the British considered it should accept once they had built their own territorial dominion in India. Now, moreover, the threat from the French was being revived as a result of the establishment of their protectorate in Tonkin. Their approach to the Burmese frontier, coupled with the activities of their consul in Mandalay, prompted the British to act. 'It is French intrigue which has forced us to go to Burmah,' Lord Randolph Churchill insisted. 'If you finally and fully add Burmah to your dominions before any European rights have had time to be sown, much less grow up, you undoubtedly prevent forever the assertion of such rights.'[8]

Annexation was to involve ending the monarchy. In contrast to their practice in much of India, and in Malaya, the British did not seek to rule through a puppet king. Lord Dufferin dismissed the idea, partly in the hope that direct administration would make Burma easier to incorporate in the empire. In fact it extended the already considerable opposition the British were meeting: a long program of pacification had to follow. The establishment of British authority in the minority areas was also a long process, though by contrast it was effected with systems of indirect rule. The British settled a frontier with the Chinese and, with greater difficulty, with the French.

Siam, unlike Vietnam and Burma, preserved its independence from the colonial powers, though it was a close call, and compromises and concessions had to be made. It was assisted in its task by the failure of its neighbours. The British had seen Siam as an outlier of their Asian empire, with which if possible they wished to remain at peace. The establishment of the French in Vietnam and Cambodia made the independence of Siam still more important to the British. But a buffer state cannot rely for survival merely on its position: it has to have stability. This the Chakri kings recognised. In particular, as the imperial powers intensified their activities towards the end of the century, King Chulalongkorn carried through a range of reforms designed to modernise Siam and also to centralise control over it. Rather paradoxically, perhaps, his realm became in some respects like the colonial territories, but he retained an essential independence. Foreign advisers were appointed, but they remained advisers, and came from a range of countries. Administrative reform followed Prince Devawongse's visit to Britain for the 1887 jubilee and Prince Damrong's tour of 1891. The reform of the legal system was begun in the hope of ending extraterritorial jurisdiction. Telegraph construction commenced in 1875 and railway construction in 1891. The Royal Survey Department was set up in 1885, partly in the hope of avoiding boundary clashes. But they still occurred.

'It is sufficient for us to keep ourselves within our house and home,' Maka Mongkut (King Rama IV) had said in 1867; 'it may be necessary for us to forego some of our former power and influence.'[9] In fact, in order to preserve its independence, Siam had not only to make commercial, administrative and jurisdictional changes: it had also to make territorial concessions. Already in 1863, France had asserted a protectorate over Cambodia. In the new phases of expansion, France moved into northern Vietnam and into Laos. Its claim to extend to the Mekong produced a crisis with Siam in 1893, and Chulalongkorn had to renounce his claim to the Laotian territories on the left bank. The British congratulated themselves on getting the French to 'disgorge' Siemreap and Angkor, but the Siamese felt their help had fallen short. In 1896 France and Britain established a frontier between British Burma and French Indochina in the Shan states to the north. To the south, each agreed not to advance into the Chao Phraya Valley without the other's consent, but even that was hardly a guarantee. Still further south, peninsular Siam was the following year the subject of a secret agreement with the British. Siam promised to cede no rights there without British consent, in return for Britain's backing against third-power intervention. The area had long been sensitive — a canal might be cut across Kra, as through Suez or Panama, and undermine Singapore — and the active policy of Germany made it more so.

In the Malay states that were the subject of the Burney treaty, British economic interests had expanded. But, before the development of rubber in the earlier years of the twentieth century, the main focus was on the tin-mining states of the west coast, and indeed the infrastructure that was developed there as a result was to focus on rubber-growing too. But the success of the Resident system adopted in Perak and Selangor — at least after the first Resident in Perak had been murdered, and a punitive expedition had reminded Malay rulers of the wisdom of following British advice — encouraged the Singapore government to contemplate extending it to other states; and the increased activity of concessionaires suggested that it was desirable to establish orderly forms of government and economic development. Governor Weld extended the system to Pahang in 1888, and in 1895 the states with Residents were combined into the Federated Malay States (FMS), with an administrative capital at Kuala Lumpur. That, it was agreed, would contribute to greater efficiency in administration, though it was likely to reduce the role of the rulers still further. It was also one of a number of consolidatory moves made within the British empire at this stage as means of strengthening it in a changing world. The establishment of the Commonwealth of Australia was the most striking.

The other states were not included in the FMS. That was partly because they were not the scene of tin-mining or, like the states that were, the recipients of extensive Chinese immigration. It was also because the rulers of the states were effective enough to cope with the problems they faced, particularly when, like the rulers of Kedah and Johore, they were much influenced by the neighbouring Straits Settlements. Yet a further restraint was provided by Siam's claim over the northern states. Any British attempt to upset that would encourage the French in their challenges on the other side of the buffer state. Even when deals were struck — first with France in 1904, then with Siam in 1909 — the British were unable to bring the transferred states into the FMS. They, like Johore, stood outside it, and what was called 'British Malaya' was a political patchwork. So was 'British Borneo': Sarawak, Brunei and North Borneo all became protectorates in 1888, but they were not integrated.

What the Dutch called 'Netherlands India' was a political patchwork, too. In this period, however, their wish to develop the Outer Islands, and still more their wish to avoid the intervention there of other powers, led them to assert their control over the many indigenous principalities so far virtually untouched by colonial government. Their dealings with the sultanate of Aceh were politically perhaps the most significant. Even after the 1824 treaty with the British, the Dutch had not managed to bring it into the normal contractual pattern they had established with other Indonesian states. But in the 1860s they began to develop the east coast of Sumatra, which proved capable, with imported labour, of producing a kind of tobacco that secured a special niche in the world market. That drew attention to Aceh, which had claims over some of this territory. But the major concern of the Dutch was that another power might intervene, and it was this which drove them into a conflict with Aceh after 1873. 'As long as it does not recognise our sovereignty foreign intervention will continue to threaten us like the sword of Damocles.'[10] The conflict proved difficult to resolve, partly because it inflamed Islamic resistance of the kind the Dutch had long wished to avoid. The war was indeed only brought to an end early in the new century by compromise with Acehnese leaders who did not rely for their authority on Islam so much as on *adat* or custom. The Aceh war affected Dutch activity elsewhere. It prompted attempts to play down the political role of Islam which might be stimulated by improved contact with Cairo and Mekka following the opening of the Suez Canal. It was an argument for caution in dealing with Lombok, for example, but the argument for intervention prevailed. The Aceh war also prompted the development of the 'short contract', a form of relationship with native rulers that stressed their obligation to abide by Dutch authority. By the early twentieth century, 'Netherlands India' stretched from Sabang, off Aceh, to Merauke, in western New Guinea. Within it there still remained many 'self-administering' districts, but colonial authority was more firmly established.

The desire to avoid foreign intervention also encouraged the Dutch to adopt an 'open door' policy. Earlier the British had abandoned any aspirations to acquire territory in the archipelago in return for a promise of fair commercial treatment. That deal, though dented, had continued to run. In the new period, the Dutch applied the same approach to the other imperial powers now interested in the area. In 1911 they were to extend most-favoured-nation treatment to Japan. Well established in the previous period, however, the Dutch did not lose their economic grasp on Netherlands India. From the 1870s, the cultivation system in Java was progressively dismantled and private capital gained the right to lease village and 'waste' land. There, and elsewhere, investment by other countries was not unwelcome: it diminished the risk of undue British predominance.

The Spaniards in the Philippines, like the Dutch in Netherlands India, sought in the period both to avoid foreign intervention and to limit the role of Islam. The focus of their apprehension was Mindanao and Sulu. In the former they were more successful than in the latter. Spurred on by a fear of British and German intervention and of Islamic revivalism, the Spaniards resorted to a policy of great violence in Sulu in the 1870s, and some British officials were indeed alarmed that it might harm the relations between Europeans and Muslims in Asia more generally. Their violence, in any case, brought only limited success. Even in the 1890s, their settlements in the Sulu islands were no more than forts, the subject of Muslim attack. And that was the case even though, by a tripartite convention of 1885, they had brought the British and German challenge to their claim over Sulu to an end, while themselves agreeing not to take up Sulu's claims over North Borneo.

In the 1890s, the Spaniards faced revolt from their Christian subjects and not merely continued opposition from Muslims they claimed to rule. Unlike the Dutch, they had relied on foreign capital to develop their possessions, and burgeoning exports of sugar and abaca had enhanced the wealth of the *mestizo* elite. The *ilustrados* — those who had gained advanced Western education (which, unlike the Dutch, the Spaniards provided in their colony, and which in any case they could not prevent their subjects acquiring overseas) — wanted a share in government at the regional and national level. This the Spaniards refused to concede. Revolution broke out in 1896. Whether the Filipinos would have won is uncertain. For the Spaniards faced what they had feared at least since the 1760s, a combination of domestic revolt with foreign intervention. At odds with Spain in the Caribbean, and aspiring to a greater role in East Asia, the United States intervened in the conflict. The British would have preferred the continuance of Spanish rule. But if that could not be secured, they preferred American rule to German. In any case, what counted was American power. Buying out Spanish claims, the United States proceeded to establish its authority in the Philippines, by conflict then compromise with the *ilustrados*, and by compromise then conflict with the Sulus.

A new member had thus joined the ranks of the colonial authorities in Southeast Asia. It was one sign of the redistribution of power in the world at large in this period. In a way, however, it insulated Southeast Asia against further change among those authorities. That was to come only 40 years later, when the Japanese determined to overthrow them. In the meantime, most of Southeast Asia underwent a phase of colonial rule more intense than anything it had previously known.

Guide to further reading

Wright, M.E., *The Last Stand of Chinese Conservatism*, Stanford University Press, Stanford, 1957, is a classic study of the Tongzhi restoration.
Several books on Japan take a biographical approach, for example:
Hackett, Roger F., *Yamagata Aritomo in the Rise of Modern Japan 1838-1922*, Harvard University Press, Cambridge, Mass., 1971
Hall, Ivan P., *Mori Arinori*, Harvard University Press, Cambridge, Mass., 1975
Iwata Masakazu, *Okuko Toshimichi*, University of California Press, Berkeley and LA, 1964
Jansen, Marius B., *Sakamoto Ryoma and the Meiji Restoration*, Stanford University Press, Stanford, 1971
Chien, F. Foo, *The Opening of Korea A Study of Chinese Diplomacy, 1876-1885*, Shoe String Press, Hamden, Conn., 1967
This book tells a story which is too often neglected.
An overall view of Southeast Asia can be found only in general histories. However, the origins of the third Anglo-Burma War are well set out in Keeton, G.L., *King Thebaw and the Ecological Rape of Burma*, Manoher Book Service, Delhi, 1974.

Patrick Tuck has published an interesting collection of documents, *French Catholic Missionaries and the Politics of Imperialism in Vietnam, 1857–1914*, Liverpool University Press, Liverpool, 1987.

Notes

1 Pelcovits, N.A., *Old China Hands and the Foreign Office*, Octagon Books, New York, 1969, p. 18.
2 Wright, M.C., *The Last Stand of Chinese Conservatism*, Stanford University Press, Stanford, 1957, p. 270.
3 ibid., p. 10.

4 Adshead, S.A.M., *The End of the Chinese Empire*, Heinemann, Auckland, 1973, p. 12.

5 Narasimha Murthy, P.A., *The Rise of Modern Nationalism in Japan*, Ashijanak, New Delhi, 1973, p. 119.

6 Hall, I.P., *Mori Arinori*, Harvard University Press, Cambridge, Mass., 1975, p. 397.

7 Pittau, Joseph, *Political Thought in Early Meiji Japan*, Harvard University Press, Cambridge, Mass., 1967, p. 166.

8 Keeton, C.L., *King Thebaw and the Ecological Rape of Burma*, Manohar, Delhi, 1974, p. 243.

9 Moffat, A.L., *Mongkut, the King of Siam*, Cornell University Press, Ithaca, 1961, p. 124.

10 Reid, A.J.S., *The Contest for North Sumatra*, Oxford University Press, Kuala Lumpur, 1969, p. 95.

14 | Chinese nationalism in the twentieth century

Since the eighteenth century, nationalism has become one of the most powerful and widespread political forces of modern times. It has survived the challenge of many other political ideologies such as anarchism, fascism, communism and internationalism because of its protean ability to accommodate the interests of diverse groups and elements in the name of the state or the national interest. Unlike communism or fascism, it is not bound to specific dogmas, classes, religions, periods or historical conditions, and it remains a powerful political force in many nations in contemporary times.

'Nationalism,' writes Boyd Schafer, 'is what the nationalists have made it; it is not a neat, fixed concept but a varying combination of beliefs and conditions.'[1] Indeed, no other political ideology has been able to manifest itself in so many different forms, and in so many different societies. One would search in vain for a single version of nationalism or for some 'genuine' doctrine or 'true' movement to act as a prime criterion for judging what exactly nationalism is. Since its eighteenth-century origins, different conceptions of nationalism had found expression in the writings of Burke, Montesquieu, Rousseau, Jefferson, Herder, Fichte, Mazzini and others. And in 1931 Carlton Hayes was able to write on its historical evolution showing its ideological richness and variety.[2]

It is this richness and variety that has enabled nationalism to be identified with many political causes in modern times: movements for national unification, national liberation and self-determination, anti-colonialism, anti-imperialism, the autonomy of 'home rule', modernisation, expansionism, militarism, even racism. It has been used by its protagonists so often and so effectively to unify disparate and diverse elements in support of their varying causes.

Since the French Revolution of 1789 and the emergence of such new states as Germany and Italy in the nineteenth century, nationalism spread to other parts of the world and underwent many transformations. It led to the formation of many new nation-states, especially after World War II. While it also suffered many temporary setbacks, it remains today a powerful instrument for popular mobilisation in support of national causes that transcend class, political, provincial and religious boundaries.

Yet, despite its variety and the different circumstances in which it asserts itself, nationalism is based on a varying combination of beliefs and conditions. First, there is a people inhabiting a territory — the historic land or the homeland — which is more or less clearly demarcated and which may be under foreign occupation or control. They share a common history and a distinctive culture, some common dominant social and economic institutions, an independent and sovereign government (or the desire for one), a love or esteem for fellow nationals, a devotion to the well-being of the land as a nation-state and a common pride in its achievements (or a common concern for its problems and predicament), and a hostility to any outside force that threatens its political and territorial integrity. Above all, nationalism entails a vision of the nation both as a free and independent political entity and as a member of the family of nations. Each nation is distinctive and unique in some ways, especially in a historical sense, and each is entitled to exercise its sovereign rights and contribute to humanity and the world community.

For analytical purposes, nationalism can be understood either as a condition already in existence, or as a process of coming into being. If it is considered to be a static condition, its emphasis is on the consciousness of nationality. If it is considered to be a process, its emphasis is on the forces that cause the formation of nation-states and the circumstances under which cultural or ethnic groups of people are transformed into national citizens. It is important to differentiate between national consciousness and national movement. Nationalism is more than an abstraction or a state of mind; it is more than a sense of patriotism and local loyalty, and it does not consist of or in xenophobia or anti-foreignism that is primitive, unorganised and fraught with mob violence. Modern nationalism entails a political movement underpinned by an ideology — a body of ideas which may or may not be coherent but which serves as a guide for political action. The ideology is articulated by a political elite and propagated both orally and through published materials, while the nationalist movement is led by a political organisation. There is a more or less well defined political platform, or program, designed to achieve a set of national goals; it is carried out with the support, or in the name, of the people whose solidarity is essential for its success.

While Europe and West Asia saw the collapse of such empires as the Habsburg and the Ottoman under the weight of national self-determination, the nationalism of the European powers, coupled with international rivalries, also proved to be a motor force behind empire building and neo-imperialism in Asia and Africa. The scramble for Africa is a familiar story that need not be told here. In Asia there stood the British colonies of India, Burma and Malaya, the Dutch colony of the

Netherlands East Indies (Indonesia), and the French colony of Indochina. The United States occupied the Philippines and 'opened' Japan, and to some extent Korea, to foreign trade. And in China, after the Opium Wars (1839–42), the imperialist forces, led by Great Britain, rapidly built up a formidable foreign regime that maintained itself on the basis of gunboat diplomacy and a series of what came to be known as the 'unequal treaties'. Though not a colony in the fullest sense of the word, China was reduced to what Sun Yatsen called a 'sub-colony' — a status lower than that of a colony, as China was controlled by a host of imperialist powers.

If the emergence of new nation-states in nineteenth-century Europe was the result of the breakup of empires after the French Revolution and the Napoleonic Wars, the growth of Asian nationalism was largely a response to Western intrusion. To be sure, foreign imperialism was not the sole cause of Asian nationalism. But it provided the initial impetus to change and aroused the political consciousness of the indigenous elites about the foreign menace and their countries' weaknesses vis-à-vis the great powers. The pace at which Asian nationalism grew varied from country to country, but in all of them it gathered momentum after World War I, thanks in large measure to the lofty principle of national self-determination espoused by United States President Woodrow Wilson. The Revolution of 1917 in Russia furthered encouraged the growth of nationalism in many Asian states as part of a worldwide anti-imperialist movement inspired, though not controlled, by the Bolsheviks and the Comintern.

Yet, before the turn of the century, Japanese nationalism had already found full expression in the determination and purposefulness with which the Meiji leadership sought to transform Japan into a modern nation-state, one that would be an equal to Great Britain, with which an alliance was formed in 1902. Thanks to a successful modernisation program, Japan was on its way to becoming an imperialist power in its own right. In 1894-95 it was able to humiliate China in a war and establish a controlling influence in Korea. In 1904–15, much to the surprise of the West, Japan defeated Russia in Manchuria and, in 1909, proceeded to annex Korea, becoming a fully fledged imperialist power in the East.

Meiji Japan's quest for wealth and power also made the Japanese more aggressive and expansionist in the twentieth century. Ultra-nationalism developed among Japan's civil and military leaders, taking the form of militarism which led to the invasion of China in the 1930s and a southward thrust into Southeast Asia in the 1940s. Once again the Chinese were victims of the foreign imperialism begun many decades before.

Owing to historical and cultural factors, modern Chinese nationalism was a slow development. Until the mid-nineteenth century, the Middle Kingdom had indulged in 'culturalism' (see also Chapter 9), a sublime form of ethnocentrism which placed China at the centre of the world as representing a superior civilisation rather than a narrower political entity within a larger polycentred world. The concept of nationhood did not evolve in pre-modern times as the Chinese treated all foreigners as barbarians and conducted their external relations within the framework of the tributary system. Unlike the British empire, the Chinese empire was not economically driven; it did not use the tributary states as markets for China's manufactured goods, as sources of raw materials or as targets for capital investment. Nor did imperial China possess a powerful navy which otherwise could have extended its writs beyond the waters of Asia.

Traditionally, moreover, the Chinese felt no particular identification with the state, their loyalty being due to the family and the clan first, the locality second and the state last. The Chinese state was coterminous with Chinese culture, and China's Confucian society was remarkable for its cohesiveness and tradition of unity, despite its vast size, geographical diversity and a population several times larger than that of Europe. In a broad sense, loyalty to Chinese culture took precedence over loyalty to the emperor, even though his authority was duly acknowledged. This explains why alien dynasties such as the Qing could enjoy the support of Chinese scholar-officials, provided the alien rulers followed the Chinese system of government, Chinese traditions and Chinese cultural values.

Modern nationalism could not evolve in China until two preconditions were met. One was the realisation on the part of the Chinese themselves that China was not the centre of the world and that foreigners who came to their country did not always wish to be Sinicised. The other was the development of a sense of citizenship; the Chinese would have to learn to identify themselves with the state and to accept its supremacy over the family, the clan and the local community. The fulfilment of these preconditions required a cultural and psychological reorientation of the Chinese people.

It is difficult to say exactly when modern Chinese nationalism was born. Some have traced its origins to the Opium War (1839–42), others to the aftermath of the first Sino-Japanese war. It is possible also to speak of the pre-modern roots of Chinese nationalism, but no doubt it was Western intrusion that provided the initial impetus to its growth in the nineteenth century.

China's defeat in the Opium War signalled the end of the Chinese world order. A new framework of Sino-foreign relations — the framework of the 'unequal treaties' — was being set up, which would last for the next hundred years. China's external problems had just begun. In 1856 she went to war with the British again over the '*Arrow* Incident'. In 1860, Anglo-French forces occupied Beijing. In 1874 the Japanese invaded Formosa (Taiwan) and, five years later, annexed the Liuqiu (Ryukyu) Islands. In 1875 the British attempted to open Yunnan to foreign trade. In

1871–81 the Russians occupied Yili in Xinjiang. In 1884–85 the French seized Annam and went to war with the Chinese, and in 1894 the Japanese expanded into Korea, an action which led to war with China. To crown it all, a foreign scramble for concessions in 1897–98 reduced China to a semi-colonial state.

Yet it would still take the people of China a long time to evolve the concept of nationhood. Throughout the latter half of the nineteenth century, there were numerous anti-foreign and anti-missionary manifestations in the hinterland, where the presence of foreigners was blamed for all the problems in the rural communities. Ignorance and fears, combined with traditional xenophobia, fuelled the anti-foreign movement, culminating in the Boxer Uprising. Such anti-foreign activities represented a form of proto-nationalism, but they were violent, negative and devoid of political values. Worse still, they created the circumstances in which the allied forces, reacting to the Boxer Uprising, invaded Beijing and pillaged the Forbidden City in 1900.

Only then was the idea driven home that China's very existence as a nation was threatened. At long last, even conservative scholar-officials realised that China was not quite the Middle Kingdom they had been brought up to believe in, and that the foreign threat was real and very different from what imperial China had ever experienced. This led to a series of reforms in the post-Boxer decade which were designed to prepare China for the challenge of the modern world on the one hand and to strengthen the imperial government against the domestic challenge on the other.

The change from traditional culturalism to modern nationalism was a long and painful process. In that process, Chinese nationalism became intertwined with war and revolution throughout the twentieth century. The bottom line was the survival of the state, while the long-term goal was national wealth and power. The idea of national wealth and power (*fuqiang*) stemmed from the theory of social Darwinism, articulated first by Herbert Spencer in the West and then by the Japanese scholar, Kato Hiroyuki, whose Japanese translations of Spencer's works were read by a few Chinese. It provided the theoretical underpinning of Meiji Japan's recponse to the West and also had a profound impact on such Chinese intellectuals as Yan Fu (1854–1921) and Liang Qichao (1873–1929). Liang, an influential figure, believed that nationalism was the necessary precondition for the power of modern nation-states and that therefore it must be developed among the people of China. Stressing the imperialist threat, he called for an energetic and nationalistic China that could survive in a world of rampant imperialism, join the world community and take the universal path to modernity. With its emphasis on natural competition, the rights of the strong and the survival of the fittest, social Darwinism was present in the very origins of Chinese nationalism in the nineteenth century.

The anti-Manchu movement that led to the overthrow of the Qing Dynasty in 1911 was a nationalist one aimed at building a strong and united China capable of warding off the foreign threat. The Manchu rulers had failed not because they were Manchus, but because they had been unable to roll back the tide of foreign imperialism. However, as soon as the Manchu rulers came under attack, the revolutionary movement took on a racist dimension and became a conflict between the Han and the Manchu minorities. For many, Chinese nationalism meant the revival of the Han more than the establishment of a modern, democratic republic. In the short term, anti-Manchuism was the dominant theme of the revolutionary movement.

The revolutionary leader, Sun Yatsen (1866–1925), a Western-educated doctor by training, gave up his medical profession for a cause that many others would follow. Sun's contributions to the Chinese revolution lay not in his ideology or organisational skills, but in his patriotising optimism and self-confidence. More than any Chinese before him and in his time, Sun instilled a sense of modern nationalism in a people who had for centuries been politically apathetic and who had behaved, in his words, like a 'pool of scattered sand'. He was the first in a line of Chinese nationalists who sought by every possible means to unite the Chinese people in the pursuit of national goals. He urged them to identify themselves with the nation-state, not with the local communities to which they were attached. He had a program of national reconstruction based on his thought, the Three Principles of the People, encompassing nationalism, people's rights and people's livelihood. For the first time in China's history, a modern nationalism, positive and goal-oriented, was asserting itself.

Sun's nationalism was firmly anchored in the politics of national survival, and in this regard he was no different from the reformer, Liang Qichao. Although Sun regarded himself as a republican and saw the need for a fundamental reordering of the Chinese political system by first overthrowing the Manchus, he was not a liberal. He saw China's predicament as resulting not from a lack of freedom but from an excess of it. The individual, he would insist in his later years, should not have too much liberty; rather, the state should have complete liberty, because only then could China become strong and united and thereby free herself from the foreign yoke. Sun placed national liberation ahead of personal freedom, a position which reflected the Chinese traditional thought that the public good must always take precedence over private interests.

External events accelerated the growth of Chinese nationalism in the post-imperial era. China's shabby treatment by the great powers at the Paris Conference in 1919 touched off the May Fourth Movement when the news was brought home that Japan had refused to relinquish its possessions of the Shandong concessions seized from Germany during World War I. Chinese nationalism now assumed a distinctly anti-imperialist character, helped also by the emergence of Soviet Russia as a new international force after the Bolshevik Revolution of 1917. Urban-based, postwar Chinese nationalism was supported by a wide spectrum of the city population, especially the small but growing middle class. It was a movement of students and intellectuals, many of whom had been educated abroad and who had engaged in a search for a new political form for China that would lead to a revival of her past glory and greatness. It was largely confined to the treaty ports, schools, colleges and universities. New ideas were disseminated in journals, magazines and books which only the well-educated could read. All this took place at a time of warlord rule, political instability, chaos and competing ideologies from liberalism to anarchism. But the students and intellectuals were all concerned about China's fate, and were anxious to find ways and means of national regeneration.

Chinese nationalism after World War I reflected a Chinese intellectual dilemma towards the West. For many years, the advanced Western nations, representing progress, science and democracy, had been a source of inspiration for the modern-educated Chinese. But after Versailles the Chinese could not but perceive the Western powers as oppressors and aggressive imperialists threatening the very existence of their country. Many Chinese intellectuals still looked to the West for guidance, but not without scepticism and reservations; others were attracted to socialist theories that were critical of Western liberal thought which sanctioned the existing capitalist-imperialist order.

The May Fourth Movement also saw a cultural revolution aimed at transforming Chinese culture as a means of national regeneration. There was an iconoclastic rejection of the cultural past. Confucianism and the traditional family system, regarded as obstacles to progress, were under attack by a new intellectual elite — those who had received a modern education either at home or abroad. Prominent among them were the Japanese-educated Chen Duxiu (1879–1942), later first General Secretary of the Chinese Communist Party, who was well known for his advocacy of science and democracy as the two pillars of a modern society. Another important figure was the American-educated Hu Shi (1891–1962), a respected educationalist, philosopher and liberal, who launched a *baihua* (common language) movement to reform China's written language as a first step towards educating the Chinese masses. Both Chen Duxiu and Hu Shi were nationalists; both had a common concern about China's predicament. While Chen was politically active, Hu was sceptical, if not disdainful, of political engagement. One proceeded to become a communist, the other remained a liberal and philosopher throughout his life.

In the wake of the May Fourth Movement, two political parties came to dominate China's political life in the next three decades. One was the Guomindang (GMD, Nationalist Party), successor to the Revolutionary Alliance which had overthrown the Qing Dynasty. Until his death in

March 1925, the GMD was led by Sun Yatsen, who had failed repeatedly to secure Western aid for his revolutionary movement against the military regime in Beijing which was recognised by the foreign powers. It enjoyed the support of patriotic students in south China. The other political party was the fledgling Chinese Communist Party (CCP), formed in 1921, which was connected with the Bolsheviks and the Comintern. Despite their ideological differences, the two parties formed a united front in 1923. What held them together temporarily was a common desire to rid the country of warlord rule and foreign imperialism, the twin enemies of the Chinese revolution. This led to a reorganisation of the GMD along Soviet lines and the establishment of the Soviet-trained Whampoa Military Academy, which laid the groundwork for the Northern Expedition that ultimately brought the country under Nationalist rule.

The GMD rode to power in 1928 on a wave of nationalism under the leadership of Chiang Kaishek (1887–1975). It inherited Sun Yatsen's ideology and program of national reconstruction. It formed a new government in Nanjing, the most modern one China had ever had. It consisted of a number of very well-educated ministers who appeared capable of leading China to modernity. The Nationalist leaders were convinced that they were equipped to achieve national wealth and power once all the 'unequal treaties' were revised or abrogated. During the Nanjing era, the campaign for treaty revision was vigorous and successful insofar that some foreign concessions and settlements had been recovered, as had tariff autonomy. Negotiations with the great powers on the thorny issue of extraterritoriality were well underway until the Manchurian crisis came to a head in September 1931.

Japan's actions in Manchuria and north China presented an opportunity for the Nationalist government to consolidate itself on the basis of nationalism. Yet the GMD leadership, instead of seizing upon that opportunity, showed itself unwilling to fight the Japanese before the Communists were eliminated. Chiang Kaishek was more concerned about the communist challenge to his authority than about the external threat. In trading space for time, he alienated many patriotic elements and non-communists. There were numerous student demonstrations and protests against both Japan and Nanjing's 'weak-kneed' foreign policy, with repeated calls for a united front against the external foe. Chinese nationalism was seething once again in the cities and the educated class. Yet the vast majority of the people who lived in the rural areas remained politically passive, much as they resented Japan's actions.

When the Nationalist government eventually went to war with Japan in 1937, a second united front between the GMD and the CCP was formed, one that enjoyed the support of the minor political parties and groups that had sprung up since the Manchurian crisis. Chinese nationalism then underwent a significant change. Transcending all party lines, it had a strong appeal to the students and all other patriotic elements. More importantly, it was now drummed up to an unprecedented height by the Communists, who had managed to fill many of the power vacuums created by the government forces that had retreated to Chongqing, the wartime capital. As Chalmers Johnson has argued in his seminal study of the Chinese communist movement, the CCP owed much of its success to the Japanese invasion which enabled it to mobilise the rural population as never before. It took an eight-year war — marked by extreme Japanese brutality and Chinese suffering — to galvanise the Chinese population into action, and it took the Communists considerable efforts to bring an urban-based nationalism to the countryside. The bourgeois nationalism of the May Fourth period was now changed both qualitatively and quantitatively. The 'pool of scattered sand' that Sun Yatsen had lamented was cemented through mass mobilisation and popular participation in the struggle against the Japanese. Thus, in Johnson's view, Chinese communism during the wartime period was 'a particularly virulent form of nationalism' — peasant nationalism — and the communist rise to power was 'a species of nationalist movement'.[3]

But the communist revolution was not abandoned. In fact, while fighting the Japanese behind enemy lines, the Communists also carried out land reforms in some areas under their control and continued a revolution that promised to transform China from what they described as a 'semi-feudal' and 'semi-colonial' society into a modern nation-state. It was these promises and hopes that China would be united under communist rule that ultimately won the CCP the support of the people and the liberal intellectuals who had lost faith in the Nationalist government.

The CCP leaders were communist and nationalistic at once. They were Chinese and proud of it. While they vehemently attacked Chinese traditions that were 'semi-feudal', they had no intention of emulating the Soviet model wholeheartedly. The Chinese communist movement was not directed by Moscow, though the early leadership had consisted of a number of Soviet-trained Bolsheviks. Mao Zedong had never liked Stalin, was always suspicious of Soviet intentions in China, and rose to power with little Soviet aid. That the People's Republic, as soon as it was established, leaned to one side (the Soviet Union) in its foreign policy was a Hobson's choice forced upon a China which the United States had failed to accommodate. China under communism was as anxious as ever to be a free and independent nation, and Beijing's leaders had no desire to be dominated by the Russians or anyone else. It was this sense of national assertiveness as much as ideological differences which eventually brought about the Sino-Soviet split in 1959, a division which lasted for the next 30 years.

Furthermore, for many CCP leaders, communism was a means to an end as well as an end in itself. They believed that communism could succeed where Western-style democracy had failed. Communism, not liberalism, provided solutions to China's pressing socioeconomic problems. It had succeeded in uniting the population during the War of Resistance. And if Marxism-Leninism was an alien ideology, it had been adapted to suit China's conditions, as the thought of Mao Zedong formed an integral part of the Chinese communist ideology. The communist revolution was to serve the interests of China first and foremost.

The aspirations of Chinese nationalism were consistent throughout the twentieth century. The prime consideration was national survival — the defence of China's political and territorial integrity — no easy task for any Chinese government before 1949. When Chairman Mao declared on 1 October 1949 that the Chinese people had stood up, at long last, it was the proudest moment in his life. The people of China had reason to rejoice that the days of foreign imperialism were gone.

Yet, while its survival was assured, China remained a very poor and backward country. What lay ahead for the Chinese leadership was the task of modernisation. The Communists did not use the term 'modernisation' as freely as it was used in the West, because 'modernisation' had served as justification for imperialist actions in China and other semi-colonial societies. The new government conceived of modernisation in terms of socialist construction. But, like the late Qing reformist intellectuals and the Nationalists before them, Beijing's leaders regarded the pursuit of national wealth and power as a long-term goal. How it could be achieved was, however, not always clear. Nor was there agreement as to how much China should borrow from the West and to what degree it should remain distinctively Chinese. Nevertheless, it had been argued by many thinking Chinese such as Hu Shi that to be wealthy and powerful, China needed to put her house in order first. It was no help to the country and the people to blame all China's problems on foreign imperialism, for China's problems were essentially China's own and had to be solved in domestic terms. Unfortunately, for the greater part of the twentieth century, China was in a state of chaos and civil strife. Chinese political life was steeped in violence, war and revolution. The Nationalists had failed to restore peace and order; if anything, they had aggravated existing social antagonisms by ignoring the needs of the rural population. The Communists after 1949 were able to maintain peace for a decade, but civil disorder was renewed with a vengeance during the Cultural Revolution. Mao's continuing revolution, while laudable in theory and in some of its goals, did not help the cause of national wealth and power.

In the post-Mao era, the Chinese leadership launched an ambitious program aimed at achieving basic modernisation in the fields of agriculture, industry, science and technology, and national defence by the year 2000. The term 'Four Modernisations', introduced in the Chinese vocabulary as part of continuing socialist construction, may have been new, but essentially it means the same thing as national wealth and power, an echo of nineteenth-century reformist thought and a remarkable continuity with the past. Furthermore, the modernisation program, as China's leaders have emphasised time and again, is one with Chinese characteristics. This means that wholesale Westernisation is not, and will not be, embraced and that Western values and systems will be used discriminately to suit China's conditions. Given China's distinctive culture and historical experience, the attitude of its leaders is not difficult to understand.

In conclusion, Chinese nationalism has undergone several phases and manifested itself in different forms. It has changed from primitive anti-foreignism through anti-Manchuism in the nineteenth century to organised anti-imperialism in the twentieth. It spread from the treaty ports to the countryside during the war against Japan. And it was transformed from an urban-based, bourgeois phenomenon to a mass movement involving the peasants and popular participation. Throughout the first half of this century it shared a common trait with the nationalist movements in some other Asian countries such as India, Vietnam and Indonesia in their struggle for national liberation and independence, though each struggle was waged in its own way and guided by a different ideology. Unlike Japanese nationalism in the inter-war period, China's was not oriented towards militarism. Rather, it stemmed from the need to liberate China from foreign domination. And, as it grew over time, it became interwoven with war and revolution. It united the Chinese people in the War of Resistance and also contributed to the ultimate success of the communist revolution.

After 1949 Chinese nationalism was subsumed in the program of socialist construction under the communist leadership. But its central themes remained unchanged: national independence, political and territorial integrity, and China's place in the world. China's survival is no longer at stake, and foreign imperialism is a thing of the past, but ultimately the real index of great power status is still national wealth and power. Whether or not China remains under communism in the next century, nationalism will continue to be a powerful force in reshaping its future.

Guide to further reading:

Chow Tse-tsung, *The May Fourth Movement: Intellectual Revolution in Modern China*, Harvard University Press, Cambridge, Mass., 1960
A balanced, authoritative account of the Chinese intellectual revolution in which nationalism played a crucial part.

Hayes, C.J.H., *The Historical Evolution of Modern Nationalism*, Smith, New York, 1931
An early scholarly account of modern nationalism focusing on its richness and diversity.

Johnson, Chalmers A., *Peasant Nationalism and Communist Power: The Emergence of Revolutionary China, 1937–1945,* Stanford University Press, Stanford, 1962

A provocative thesis that interprets the nature of Chinese nationalism and the ultimate triumph of the Chinese Commnist Party during the Sino-Japanese War in terms of an appeal to the national, rather than the revolutionary, feelings of the peasantry.

Schafer, Boyd C., *Nationalism: Myth and Reality,* London, 1968

A scholarly study of nationalism debunking some of its metaphysical, 'physical' and cultural myths.

Smith, Anthony D., *Nationalism in the Twentieth Century,* Australian National University Press, Canberra, 1979

An interesting book exploring the fundamantals of twentieth-century nationalism and its enduring appeal in the modern world.

Schwartz, Benjamin, *In Search of Wealth and Power: Yen Fu and the West,* Harvard University Press, Cambridge, Mass., 1964

A stimulating account of Yan Fu, a nineteenth-century Chinese intellectual who was profoundly influenced by Western liberal thought.

Wright, Mary C. (ed.), *China in Revolution: The First Phase, 1900-1913,* Yale University Press, New Haven, 1968

A collection of scholarly essays on the Revolution of 1911, with an introduction by Mary Wright on the growth of Chinese nationalism at the turn of this century.

Notes

1 Shafer, Boyd C., *Nationalism: Myth and Reality,* London, 1968, p. 7.
2 Hayes, Carlton J.H., *The Historical Evolution of Modern Nationalism,* Smith, New York, 1931.
3 Johnson, Chalmers, *Peasant Nationalism and Communist Power,* Stanford University Press, Stanford, 1962, p. ix.

15 | Japanese nationalism from Meiji to 1937

In Japan, as in other Asian countries, the challenges of Western expansion encouraged the rise of nationalism and the formation of the modern nation-state. The political commentator Tokutomi Soho (1863–1958) described this process vividly, though with some simplification, when he wrote that:

a threat from abroad immediately directs the nation's thoughts outwards. This leads immediately to the rise of a spirit of nationalism. This directly induces national unification. The concept 'foreign nations' brought forth the concept 'Japanese nation'.[1]

The process of nation-building in Japan, however, was in some ways very different from the emergence of national consciousness in most other Asian countries. For one thing, Japan escaped the fate of colonisation by the Western powers. In Japan, therefore, nationalism was not associated with a struggle against foreign rule — though it was associated with efforts to overcome the economic and military gap between Japan and the West. These efforts came to be inextricably connected to the issues of overseas expansion and the creation of Japan's own empire in Asia. Japanese nationalism thus led eventually to confrontation, not only with the West, but also with the other Asian nations over which Japan sought to assert economic or political domination.

Social change in late Tokugawa Japan

During the latter part of the Tokugawa period, a variety of new political and social ideas began to develop in Japan. The official ideology espoused by the Tokugawa shoguns was largely based upon Chinese Confucian thought, and particularly on the neo-Confucian ideas of the Chinese philosopher Zhu Xi. This philosophy, with its emphasis on order, loyalty and spiritual self-improvement, was eminently well suited to the interests of the Shogunal government (see Chapter 7). From about the middle of the eighteenth century, however, new intellectual currents emerged to challenge the dominance of Confucian orthodoxy.

One source of new ideas was the West. Although Japan's contacts with the outside world were severely limited, the Dutch trading post at Nagasaki provided a window through which Western scientific ideas could filter into Japan. In fact, from the second decade of the eighteenth century onwards, the shoguns themselves began to encourage the study of Western astronomy and cartography, although books containing Western social or religious ideas were still strictly prohibited. Inspired by this new learning, some Japanese scholars, like Honda Toshiaki (1744–1821), not only studied the Dutch language, but also advocated the opening of Japan to foreign trade.

As Japanese thinkers became more conscious of the Western world, however, they also became more conscious of the need to strengthen Japan itself. Honda Toshiaki, for example, favoured not only trade but also the expansion of Japan's political control over the nearby islands of the Pacific. Growing emphasis on the economic and military strengthening of Japan was accompanied by efforts to redefine a sense of Japanese national identity. From the mid-eighteenth century onwards, a number of Japanese intellectuals began to study the indigenous religion, Shinto, which had wide popular influence in Japan, but had previously attracted little attention from scholars. Motoori Norinaga (1730–1801), a leading figure in this Shinto revival, spent many years researching early Shinto myths, which he saw as embodying the true essence of Japanese culture and spirituality. One consequence of his research was a new interest in the Japanese imperial family, which figured importantly in Shinto mythology and ceremony, but whose political role in Tokugawa Japan was purely symbolic.

Meanwhile, Confucian thought itself was not static. By the early nineteenth century, for example, many Confucian scholars were emphasising the importance of *jitsugaku*, the practical application of ideas to the improvement of society. This approach helped to reconcile Confucian tradition with the Western scientific ideas which were becoming familiar to Japan's ruling classes.

The intellectual ferment of late Tokugawa Japan was influenced by developments within Japan, as well as by challenges from abroad. The development of new crops and handicrafts, the spread of the money economy and the growing urbanisation of society all served to weaken the supposedly rigid status system. Merchants, in theory the most lowly members of society, sometimes managed to amass substantial fortunes, while the *daimyo* and their *samurai* followers faced increasing difficulty in adapting to economic change, and often became indebted to merchant money-lenders. In the countryside, too, wealthier farmers invested money in new commercial activities such as *sake* brewing and silk production. The widening gap between the successful few and the impoverished many was one of the factors behind the peasant revolts of the late Tokugawa period (see Chapter 7).

Until the 1850s, though, the questioning of neo-Confucian orthodoxy did not produce any major or direct challenge to the rule of the Tokugawa shoguns. The event which speeded the pace of political change, and led to the eventual fall of the Tokugawa shogunate, occurred in 1853, when Commodore Matthew Perry sailed into Uraga Bay near Edo, with a message from United States President Fillmore demanding trading rights in Japan.

The Meiji restoration

The intrusion of the West upon Japan's seclusion was not a wholly unexpected event. During the half-century preceding Perry's arrival there had been several unsuccessful attempts by the Western powers to secure the opening of Japanese ports to foreign shipping, and the Japanese government was well aware of the Opium Wars, which had so dramatically demonstrated Britain's growing economic and military influence in Asia. Just one month after Perry's arrival, another foreign envoy, Admiral Putyatin, arrived in Japanese waters with a request from Russia's Tsar Nicholas I for the opening of trade. Matthew Perry's uncompromising negotiating style and his evident military strength, however, were particularly impressive: his 'black ships' included one of the largest and most modern naval vessels afloat. The combination of these challenges forced a reluctant shogunate to reassess its approach to foreign relations.

The shogunate's first reaction to the foreign intrusion was to send a memorial to all the *daimyo* asking for advice in dealing with the foreigners. This unprecedented action immediately made it clear to their rivals that the Tokugawa shoguns were losing their grip upon the affairs of state. The new crisis forced the shogunate to increase its defence spending, further weakening its already precarious financial situation. Clearly, fundamental political changes were called for, yet the shogunate was unable to carry through far-reaching reforms without endangering the complex political structure on which its own survival depended.

The opening of Japan upset the delicate power balance between the shogun and the powerful *daimyo* who controlled large outlying fiefs such as Satsuma and Choshu. Under the energetic though short-lived *daimyo* Shimazu Nariakira, who ruled the domain from 1851 to 1858, Satsuma introduced Western-style arsenals and blast furnaces, while the domain of Choshu secretly sent a group of five young *samurai* to Britain to study Western knowledge. These outlying domains, which had a long tradition of passive hostility to Tokugawa rule, thus acquired technological and military know-how which strengthened their hand in the coming confrontation with the shogun.

In 1858 the shogunate signed a series of treaties with the major powers, opening more Japanese ports to foreign merchants and allowing international trade to occur without official interference. The treaties also included two clauses which aroused profound resentments in Japan, and which led them to be popularly termed 'the unequal treaties'. Firstly, they allowed foreign residents in the treaty ports to be subject to the laws of their own countries, rather than to the laws of Japan, and secondly, they deprived the Japanese government of the right to determine the level of tariffs, which came to be fixed at the low rate of 5 per cent of the value of imports. These conditions, all too reminiscent of those imposed on China by the Western powers, provoked widespread hostility both towards the shogunate and towards the Western 'barbarians'. This anti-foreign feeling at times boiled over into physical attacks on Westerners in Japan, and on two occasions led to armed skirmishes between foreign forces and the domains of Satsuma and Choshu.

By the middle of the 1860s, resistance to the shogunate was becoming increasingly active and articulate. The rallying cry which united the anti-shogunal movement was the slogan 'revere the emperor; expel the barbarians!' *(sonno joi)*, but the ideology of the movement was more complex and less single-mindedly xenophobic than these words might suggest. The aim of its leaders was not so much to give supreme political power to the emperor, but rather to use the emperor's name as a means of legitimising their actions. This legitimation was very important in a society like Tokugawa Japan, which had no tradition of recognised opposition to the existing political order. Further, the use of the slogan 'expel the barbarians' did not mean that all the opponents of Tokugawa rule were hostile to foreign trade and foreign ideas. On the contrary, as we have seen, the domains of Satsuma and Choshu, which played a leading role in the restoration movement, had been particularly receptive to Western technology. Within these and other domains, debate on the proper attitude to the foreigners raged throughout the early 1860s. An increasing number of leading intellectuals, however, were coming to the conclusion that, in order to resist the military and economic threat posed by the 'Western barbarians', it would first be necessary to learn their secrets.

In 1866 the domains of Satsuma and Choshu signed a treaty creating a united opposition to the shogunate, and a brief skirmish between shogunal forces and troops from Choshu, though it proved indecisive, demonstrated the military weakness of the government. The end was not far away; when it came, it proved remarkably swift. In 1867 the last shogun, Yoshinobu (also known as Keiki), voluntarily surrendered his power to the emperor in Kyoto, hoping to remain as chief adviser. This concession, however, was not enough to appease his enemies. Troops led by Satsuma and Choshu surrounded Kyoto, forcing the shogun to leave the city. After some fierce fighting in the early months of 1868, the city of Kyoto fell to the rebels, who announced the abolition of the shogunate and the 'restoration' of power to the young emperor Meiji. The emperor himself was taken from Kyoto to the Shogunal capital of Edo (now renamed 'Tokyo', or 'Eastern Capital'), and symbolically installed in the former shoguns' castle.

Westernisation and nationalism in Meiji Japan, 1868–1912

The Meiji restoration of 1868 is generally seen as one of the great watersheds in Japanese history. The underlying nature and meaning of the restoration, however, remains a topic of great debate among historians. Some Japanese historians have emphasised the role of the newly emerging mercantile interests in the overthrow of the old regime. They see the restoration, therefore, as being somewhat like the 'bourgeois revolutions' which ushered in constitutional political systems in Western Europe (although they also accept that there were many differences between political conditions in Japan and Europe). Others, on the contrary, regard the restoration as being essentially a conservative revolution, through which the existing ruling classes tried to preserve their own positions in the face of threats both at home and abroad. These debates affect our interpretation of political developments in Meiji Japan, and of the upsurge of Japanese nationalism in the first half of the twentieth century.

Certainly the main architects of the restoration movement came from the warrior class. For the most part, however, they were not *daimyo*, but rather low-ranking, well-educated and ambitious *samurai*. Although anxious to preserve order, stability and their own power, these new leaders were also aware that wide-ranging reforms would be necessary if Japan wished to meet the challenges of the late nineteenth century world order, and they moved quickly to put their ideas into action. Taking advantage of the political confusion of the age, and of the perceived threat from the Western powers, they introduced a number of major political changes. Administration was centralised, with the domain governments being abolished in 1871 and their powers concentrated in the hands of a council of ministers made up of a handful of *samurai* from the leading restorationist domains. The four-tier Tokugawa status system was abolished and official restrictions on occupation and geographical mobility were removed. However, the ex-*daimyo* and a few leading *samurai* retained some privileges, as they became the core of a new Western-style aristocracy with titles which approximated to the Western terms 'Viscount', 'Baron', etc. The disappearance of the *samurai* as a hereditary caste of warriors paved the way for the creation of a conscript army along Western lines, which was established in 1873. At the same time, the tax system was also overhauled. The private ownership of land was formally recognised for the first time, and the rice tax replaced by a monetary tax based on the value of landholdings.

Despite these great changes, however, it is important to remember that human ideas and attitudes were not transformed overnight. Many of the policies put into practice in the Meiji period derived inspiration from ideas which had been developing in Japan well before the restoration. Even the slogan 'a rich country and a strong army' *(fukoku kyohei)*, which became the guiding principle of Meiji government policies, was not new. Its origins go back to the Chinese classics, and it had been revived and popularised by nationalist writers of the late Tokugawa period. Similarly, the idea of government action to establish and support new industries, which the Meiji leaders pursued with great vigour, owed much of its inspiration to policies pursued by the domains of Tokugawa Japan.

Throughout the Meiji period the question of how best to combine the necessary Western knowledge with Japanese culture and traditions was a topic of intense debate. Newly established newspapers and journals, like the *Meiroku zasshi*, carried articles discussing issues such as Western education, the role of elected parliaments, the rights of women and the possibility of writing Japanese in the Roman alphabet. A leading figure in these debates was Fukuzawa Yukichi (1835–1901), a scholar of low ranking *samurai* origin who had travelled to the United States and Europe in the 1860s. Fukuzawa became a tireless advocate of the ideals of Westernisation, which he preached both through his many publications and through the Keio Gijuku, the college which he founded in Tokyo. Reformers like Fukuzawa, strongly influenced by mid-nineteenth century British liberal thought, argued that Japan could only hope to achieve economic development and international respect if it wholeheartedly embraced Western social and scientific 'enlightenment'.

The Meiji government itself, however, took a more cautious approach to Westernisation. Although eager to learn foreign military and industrial techniques, government leaders recognised that the foreign ideologies of political liberalism posed a threat to their own power. They therefore preferred the approach suggested by the late Tokugawa philosopher Sakuma Shozan (1811–64), who had argued for a combination of 'eastern ethics and western science'. In practice, of course, such a simple division between 'ethics' and 'science' could not be maintained, but Sakuma's formula did provide a basis for a selective approach to foreign borrowing — one in which the relatively authoritarian model of countries like Prussia came to be regarded as 'more appropriate' to Japan's circumstances that the relatively liberal model of countries like the United States.

Debates about the suitability of Western theories affected economic as well as political thought. Many of the earliest works of economic thought to be introduced to Japan put forward the *laissez faire* ideals which were influential in Britain and the United States at that time. By the late nineteenth century, however, many Japanese intellectuals were reaching the conclusion that these theories were unworkable for a latecomer to industrialisation like Japan. Instead, they turned increasingly to the ideas of the German historical school, which recognised the need for the state to play an active role in promoting the economic development of late-industrialising nations.

By the 1880s, indeed, the current of early Meiji Westernisation was losing some of its impetus. Enthusiastic Westernisers like Fukuzawa Yukichi began to grow disillusioned as they realised that the Meiji reforms were failing to secure a respected place for Japan in the hierarchy of the world powers. International prestige, it seemed, was won less through political enlightenment than through military might. By 1882 Fukuzawa was writing that 'the one object of my life is to extend Japan's national power . . . Even if the government be autocratic in name and form, I shall be satisfied with it if it is strong enough to strengthen the country.'[2]

Ideas in practice: Political and economic change in Meiji Japan

The fluctuating fortunes of Westernisation and nationalism are reflected in the evolution of Meiji government policy. The most important area of practical debate during the 1870s and 1880s concerned the drawing up of a constitution. Demands for the creation of an elected parliament began to be heard in the 1870s. Support for the concept of parliamentary government came both from disaffected *samurai* who had failed to gain positions in the new government, and from sections of the peasant population, who wanted a forum for expressing their grievances on issues such as taxation and rural poverty. This People's Rights Movement (as it was called) was successful in forcing the government to accept the notions of a constitution and a parliamentary system. The constitution which was finally promulgated in 1889, however, made only very limited concessions to notions of democracy. The parliament which it created was to be responsible to the emperor rather than to the people, and voting rights (for men only) were to be based on a property ownership requirement which excluded the vast majority of the population.

A similar mixture of liberal and authoritarian views helped to shape the development of the Japanese education system. Education was recognised by Japan's leaders as a vital element in the acquisition of Western scientific knowledge and the modernisation of the nation, and as early as 1872 the Meiji government had laid the foundations for the creation of a universal system of primary schooling. Selective middle schools, high schools and universities were also established, and foreign teachers recruited to staff the top levels of the educational pyramid. In the initial stages, schools relied heavily on the use of translated Western texts, including such nineteenth-century classics as the works of Samuel Smiles. Not surprisingly, this eventually provoked a reaction, particularly from conservative Confucian intellectuals. To counteract the supposedly subversive foreign concepts of liberalism and individualism, the Education Department was given sweeping powers to control the content of school texts, and an Imperial Rescript on Education, issued in 1890, defined the aims of study as being to promote loyalty and filial piety, and thus to enhance the glory of the Empire.

The development of education was, of course, part of a broader strategy of using Western technical knowledge to promote economic growth and industrialisation. The Meiji government played an active and interventionist role in the Japanese economy. It established the infrastructure of an industrial economy, including a central bank, a telegraph system and the nation's first railways; it also set up several of the earliest modern factories in Japan, importing foreign equipment and technicians to train Japanese employees. During the 1880s, a number of these enterprises were sold to wealthy private entrepreneurs, so helping to lay the foundations of the great business conglomerates, known as the *zaibatsu*, which were to dominate the Japanese economy in the early twentieth century.

Government policy on its own, however, was not enough to create the basis for an industrial revolution. Industries like silk and cotton textiles developed relatively rapidly, not just for political reasons, but also because Japan possessed a relative abundance of skilled labour and an adaptable entrepreneurial class. A majority of workers in the early textile factories were women from farm families, many of whom had some experience of spinning or weaving in the home. The business skills developed by the urban and rural merchants in the Tokugawa age also undoubtedly proved useful as Japan's industrial and commercial businesses expanded. The import and adaptation of foreign technology were also supported at regional level by local governments and groups of merchants who, in some areas, set up colleges and research laboratories to assist the modernisation of traditional industries. The effects were impressive: between 1880 and 1915, industrial production in Japan increased more than fourfold, and the production of textiles almost tenfold.

Japan's emergence as a colonial power, 1868–1912

'In my opinion,' wrote the Japanese Foreign Minister Inoue Kaoru in 1885, 'what we must do is to transform our empire and our people . . . To put it differently, we have to establish a new, European-style empire on the edge of Asia.'[3] For political leaders like Inoue, imperial expansion was part of the process of imitating and learning from the great Western powers. Japan, they argued, would be able to win the respect of nations like Britain and France only when it too had demonstrated its ability to acquire overseas territories through conquest and diplomacy. Overseas expansion into the neighbouring regions of continental Asia would also help to provide a buffer, protecting Japan from potential rivals such as the Russian Empire.

Even during the Tokugawa period, Japan had been gradually extending its northern limits, imposing even tighter Japanese control over the Ainu people who inhabited most of Hokkaido, the Kuril Islands and Southern Sakhalin. Within a decade of the Meiji restoration, the Japanese government had also asserted its control over the Ryukyu and Bonin Islands to the south of Japan (areas where Japan had exerted some economic influence since the Tokugawa period), and in 1875 Japan claimed formal sovereignty over the Kuril Archipelago to the north of Hokkaido. The annexation of the Ryukyu Islands provoked conflict with China, which had traditionally received tribute from the king of the Ryukyus, and this antagonism intensified as Japan turned its attention to another and more important tributary of China: the kingdom of Korea.

In 1894 rivalry for political influence in the Korean Peninsula led to outright war between Japan and China, a war which Japan won, to the surprise not only of the Chinese government, but also of many Western observers. The Sino-Japanese War (1894–95) was the first test of Japan's new conscript forces in an international conflict, and their victories fuelled the ambitions of Japanese nationalists for further overseas expansion. The Treaty of Shimonoseki, signed at the end of the war, gave Japan extensive territorial gains, including control of the island of Formosa (Taiwan) and of the Liaodong Peninsula in Manchuria. China was also made to pay a large indemnity to Japan (part of which was invested by the Japanese government in the development of the steel industry). The major Western powers, however, were by now thoroughly alarmed by the emergence of Japan as a rival to their interests in East Asia. In the so-called Triple Intervention, France, Germany and Russia joined in forcing Japan to return the Liaodong Peninsula to China. This incident was to prove a lasting source of Japanese grievance towards the Western imperial powers.

The outcome of the Sino-Japanese War failed to satisfy Japan's ambitions towards Korea. The Treaty of Shimonoseki had affirmed Korean independence but, having disposed of one competitor in the region (China), Japan now became increasingly nervous of another — Russia. In 1904, tension between the two countries flared into war. Japan's annihilation of the Russian fleet in the Straits of Tsushima led to the first modern victory of an Asian nation over a European great power, and left Japan firmly in control of Korea, which was made a Japanese protectorate under the terms of the Treaty of New Hampshire in 1905. The Treaty also gave Japan control of the southern half of the island of Sakhalin, a lease on the Liaodong Peninsula, and control over the South Manchurian Railway, which had been constructed by Russia in an attempt to increase its influence in the Manchurian region. By 1910 Japan had converted its protectorate in Korea into outright annexation, and Korea had become a fully fledged colony of Japan.

Strategic and political factors may have been the principal motives behind Japan's creation of its colonial empire, but many Japanese politicians and businesspeople were also quick to grasp the economic gains to be made in the colonies. The Asian colonies were seen both as potential sources of agricultural imports, and as markets for the Japanese manufactured goods which were not yet sophisticated enough to compete in the developed markets of Europe and North America. The building of ports and railways in Taiwan and Korea helped to open up the economies of the colonies to Japanese control, and by the end of the Meiji period many of the major *zaibatsu* companies already had substantial interests in Japan's overseas territories.

The effects of war and military expansion on Japan's own economy and society are controversial. Victory in the conflicts with China and Russia was made possible only by a massive human and financial investment in the armed forces, and between 1880 and 1912 about 30 per cent of government expenditure was directed to military purposes. Some historians believe that this provided an important stimulus to Japan's industrialisation. The army and navy were major customers for the products of Japan's newly emerging steel mills and shipyards, and even for its woollen textile factories, which provided cloth for army uniforms. Government arms factories also provided a channel through which advanced foreign knowledge of engineering techniques was introduced to Japanese industry. Others, on the contrary, suggest that military expansion imposed a heavy economic burden on ordinary Japanese people, particularly the farmers, whose tax payments provided a major source of Meiji government revenue. These burdens increased the gaps between rich and poor, distorted the development of the Japanese economy and created the basis for the social and political problems which Japan was to face in the 1920s and 1930s.

Social change in Taisho Japan, 1912–1916

Despite the impressive industrial growth of the Meiji period, Japan in 1912 was still a predominantly agrarian society. About 60 per cent of the workforce was engaged in farming, and most of these were very small-scale farmers, working holdings of little more than 1 hectare. Agriculture was very much a household activity, with all members of the family helping out in the busy seasons of the year. Farm labour was hard, and the hardship was increased by the high rents which landlords charged to those farmers (more than half of the total) who had to rent all or part of the land they farmed.

In the years which immediately followed the death of the Emperor Meiji in 1912, economic and social change was rapid. Industry expanded vigorously, and there was a steady flow of population from the country-side to the major cities (although farming would continue to employ over 40 per cent of the workforce until after 1945). An important factor behind these phenomena was the outbreak of World War I in 1914. Japan participated in the war on the side of the Allies, but was involved in relatively little actual fighting. However, the conflict in Europe disrupted trade links between the European powers and their Asian colonies, and left Japan — as the most industrialised nation in Asia — with un-expectedly expanded markets for its manufactured goods. As well as light industrial goods like textiles, Japan began for the first time to export more sophisticated products like cement and chemicals. It was at this time that a number of Japan's larger firms began to establish branches in places like the Philippines, Malaya and the Dutch East Indies, and that the Japanese media and public began to develop a greater interest in the Southeast Asian region.

The Treaty of Versailles (1919), concluded after Germany's surrender in 1918, left Japan with an expanded empire, now including a mandate over a group of Pacific islands which had previously been German colonies. But the treaty also provoked criticism in Japan, particularly when the Australian delegate, William Hughes, blocked a Japanese proposal for a declaration on racial equality to be included in the charter of the newly established League of Nations. The end of the war also restored economic links between Europe and Asia, and led to a postwar slump in Japan's exports. Industries which had expanded in the war years now entered a period of recession, and some of the enterprises faced collapse. Economic instability, indeed, continued throughout the 1920s, and was exacerbated by the disastrous earthquake of 1923, which killed about 100 000 people in the Tokyo-Yokohama area.

In the urban life which revived as earthquake damage was repaired, the economic uncertainties of the age were often concealed by new-found signs of prosperity. Work in the factories, or in the many small urban shops and workshops, was hard, and wages were still very low by comparison with most industrialised countries. Western electrical gadgets like cooking-stoves and fans, however, were beginning to appear in the homes of the middle classes; electrical trams ran along the streets, and the first underground railway line was established in 1920. Leisure activities were changing too: by the late Taisho period, radio and cinema were rivalling the popularity of traditional forms of theatre and storytelling.

The situation in the countryside, however, was very different. After World War I, the government encouraged the import of food from the colonies to meet the needs of Japan's growing population. This depressed agricultural prices at home, and reduced the incomes of many farm families. During the 1920s, some farmers were able to supplement their incomes by producing cocoons for Japan's large, and still growing, silk industry, but with the onset of the world depression in 1929, silk prices crashed and many parts of rural Japan experienced real hardship. In areas which were not far from towns, farmers could often find part-time or seasonal employment in industry, but in more remote areas this was rarely possible.

The resentments caused by these gaps in wealth are captured by the agrarian radical Shibuya Teisuke, who wrote in 1926:

> I return home. The house is not lit and it is pitch dark. My sick father is groaning . . . The children are crying. Oh, what misery! . . . The 'people of culture' enjoy the glory of life while the producers of essential goods for human life — food, housing and clothing — have to live like this. The skies of Tokyo light up the eastern horizon. You [town-dwellers], together with the landlords, are the leeches who bleed us.[4]

Radicalism, reform and repression

The response to the social problems of the day encouraged the growth of a wide range of conflicting political ideologies. By the end of World War I, party politics had become well established in Japan, and the parliament was dominated by centre-right parties which enjoyed the support of business and of landlord-farmers. During the 1920s, however, the policies of these parties were challenged from both left and right.

Socialist ideas had been introduced to Japan in the early twentieth century, and the influence of socialism was increased by the success of the Bolshevik revolution in Russia in 1917. The growth of industry during the first two decades of the century encouraged the emergence of trade unionism, and high levels of inflation in 1918 caused widespread strike activity and rioting. A Friendly Society established in 1912 to assist factory workers was converted, in 1919, into the General Federation of Labour and played an important role in co-ordinating trade union activities during the 1920s. Together with left-wing political parties, it campaigned not only for higher wages, but also for political reforms, including an extension of the right to vote in general elections. In the countryside, tenants' associations were set up to demand lower rents and to present the grievances of peasant farmers to the landlords. New ideas were also influencing other areas of Japanese life. In the early part of the Taisho period, women's organisations like the Bluestocking Society (established in 1911) and the New Women's Association (1919) began to demand improved social and legal rights for women, and campaigned against a law of 1900 which had debarred women from participating in political activities.

Radical politics in prewar Japan, however, faced many difficulties. Repressive laws meant that anyone suspected of harbouring revolutionary ideas could be arrested. As a result, left-wing groups in Japan tended to be sharply divided between radicals and moderates, with the moderates seeking to distance themselves from extreme views in order to avoid the risk of prosecution. Trade unions, peasants' groups, women's groups and socialist parties all suffered from this tendency towards factionalism and fragmentation. The structure of Japanese society also made it difficult to create effective workers' organisations. In the 1920s, only about 16 per cent of the Japanese workforce was employed in manufacturing, and many of these worked in very small, family-run enterprises, and were therefore unlikely to join trade unions. Peasant farmers, too, were often reluctant to join militant peasants' associations. However hard their lives might be, traditions of respect and community ties inhibited them from criticising the landlords, who were often neighbours and prominent figures in village life.

The political left was also weakened by the way in which government and business leaders responded to its protests. This response could be described as a carrot-and-stick approach. In large enterprises, including some of the *zaibatsu*-owned factories, strikers were often subject to dismissal, but loyal workers were rewarded with some improvements in working conditions during the 1920s. Bonuses for good performance, wage rises based on length of service, and a variety of fringe benefits — indeed, many of those features which are now regarded as typical of 'Japanese style' management — began to appear in the largest factories at this time.

At the political level, the government reacted to demands for change by extending the franchise. A new law, introduced in 1925, gave the vote to all men over 25 years of age. At the same time, however, the introduction of a sweeping *Peace Preservation Law* gave the police the power to arrest people for a wide range of vaguely defined political offences. In the late 1920s and 1930s, this law was used with increasing severity to restrict political dissent. As a result of these measures, left-wing political activity was effectively stifled, and there was consequently little basis for political opposition to the nationalist ideologies which were gaining increasing publicity and support in the latter part of the Taisho period.

Nationalism triumphant

The resurgence of nationalism in interwar Japan did not simply mean a revival of the ideas of Tokugawa and Meiji on Shinto mythology and the strengthening of the state. Instead, the ideologies which were popularised in the 1920s and 1930s involved a combination of traditional ideas with concepts borrowed from a wide range of modern and Western sources.

Very broadly, these ideologies can be divided into two types. At one extreme, there was the radical nationalism which is well represented by the works of the famous propagandist Kita Ikki (1884–1937). Kita, who had spent several years in China, was influenced by the revolutionary ideals of socialism as well as by the myths of imperial divinity. He argued for radical reforms to redistribute land to peasant farmers and purge Japan of corrupt politicians and big business. At the same time, he believed that such changes could only be achieved by enhancing the power of the emperor, whom he saw as an embodiment of the true will of the Japanese people. After the death of the sickly and feeble-minded Emperor Taisho in 1926, and his succession by the Emperor Hirohito (Showa), Kita and his supporters began to speak of the need for a 'Showa restoration', which would strengthen imperial authority in a way which had not been achieved by the Meiji restoration. These calls for domestic reform were linked to demands for the expansion of Japan's overseas empire. Kita envisaged Japan as leading a Pan-Asian revolutionary movement which would free the continent from the yoke of Western colonialism. How these ideals of liberation were to be reconciled with Japan's own colonialism, however, was never satisfactorily explained.

Radical nationalism appealed particularly to many poor peasants and small businesspeople, and to low-ranking army officers who often came from humble backgrounds. On the other hand, the higher ranks in the Japanese military tended more often to espouse a conservative form of nationalist ideology. They had little interest in revolutionary economic and agrarian reforms. However, like the radical nationalists, they were eager to extend the political influence of the armed forces, to rid Japan of the inefficiency and corruption which they associated with civilian control and, above all, to expand Japan's overseas empire in Asia.

In Japan, therefore, there was no single, powerful extreme right party which might be compared to the Fascists in Italy or the Nazi Party in Germany. The political right, like the political left, was divided and factionalised, and nationalist thought exerted an influence over a wide assortment of groups, ranging from intellectual think-tanks to small terrorist bands. It was these latter groups which were the first to put their ideas into action, carrying out a number of physical attacks on politicians and businesspeople whom they saw as lacking in 'national spirit'.

In 1921, both the Prime Minister, Hara Kei, and a leading Japanese industrialist, Yasuda Zenjiro, were assassinated by fanatics. In 1930 Prime Minister Hamaguchi was shot and fatally wounded by an extremist protesting against a naval agreement with the major Western powers. The following year both the Finance Minister and the chief manager of the Mitsui *zaibatsu* were assassinated, and a group of junior officers in the military staged a bungled attempt at a *coup d'etat*. The most serious challenge, however, came on 26 February 1936, when two army detachments murdered a number of leading politicians and occupied the centre of Tokyo, demanding the government's resignation. The rebellion was eventually put down by troops brought in from other parts of Japan, and the leading conspirators committed suicide or were arrested. Among those executed for their part in the plot was Kita Ikki, who was seen as having inspired the activities of the rebels.

The defeat of the so-called '26 February Affair', however, did not mean the defeat of nationalism in Japan. The events of 1936 may have represented a setback to radical nationalism, but they did nothing to weaken the power of the conservative nationalists in the army's leadership. Meanwhile, the actions of the rebels made Japan's political leaders more and more cautious of pursuing any policy which might provoke the hostility of the armed forces. Not only was the army itself increasingly taking the initiative in foreign affairs; it was also exerting an extensive influence over domestic policy. The inability of the political parties to control events is illustrated by the fact that a growing number of cabinet ministers were drawn from the armed services — indeed, four of Japan's ten prime ministers in the 1930s were senior military officers.

Why were nationalism and militarism able to gain such influence in interwar Japan? Some historians answer this question by going back to the roots of Japan's political modernisation in the Meiji era. They argue that the Meiji restoration failed to provide a sound basis for the development of Japanese democracy. Political and economic power was left in the hands of a small elite group of ex-*samurai* and wealthier landlords. Business came to be concentrated in the hands of a few *zaibatsu* families who had close links both to senior politicians and to the military leadership. There was, therefore, never a strong independent middle class which might have provided a sound basis of support for liberal ideologies.

Other writers place greater emphasis on the political and economic problems which Japan faced during the 1920s and 1930s. In the international arena, a number of perceived insults and frustrations encouraged the belief that military strength was essential to secure Japan's place as the dominant power in Asia. Multilateral negotiations to limit naval expansion in the 1920s had imposed limits on the Japanese fleet which many people felt to be unacceptable. Diplomatic frictions were also aggravated by an American law of 1924, which stopped the flow of Japanese migration to California.

Within Japan itself, economic instability and rural hardship provided a fertile ground for the spread of radical nationalism. With the onset of the world depression in 1929, Japan's industrial production fell sharply, but recovered relatively quickly. Agriculture, however, remained depressed, and in the early 1930s there were even famines in some of the poorest and most remote parts of Japan. The economic crisis also provoked the rise of trade protectionism throughout the world. As other imperial powers moved to restrict the entry of foreign goods into their domestic and colonial markets, so pressure increased for Japan to carve out for itself a larger economic empire in Asia. The vision of Japan as a resource-poor, overcrowded nation, whose only hope for survival lay in overseas expansion, was one which was readily accepted by many Japanese people in the years before the Pacific War. As an American sociologist who worked in a Japanese village in the 1930s observed:

> In every classroom is a world-map or map of Asia which shows Japan in red as a very small land indeed, compared to the mainland nations of Asia . . . In a perfectly bland manner some villager, on looking at such a map, will suggest how nice it would be to appropriate a bit more of China.[5]

The slide into war, 1926-1937

Ever since its victory in the Russo-Japanese War, Japan had been enlarging its economic and political influence in China. During World War I, the Japanese government had taken advantage of the international turmoil to demand a series of sweeping concessions from China. These 'Twenty-One Demands', as they were called, included articles granting Japan mining and railway concessions in central China and strengthening Japan's position in South Manchuria. The newly formed and weak Chinese republican government was reluctantly forced to bow to Japan's pressure. The Twenty-One Demands, however, not only left a legacy of bitterness in China, but also caused suspicion and hostility towards Japan in many Western countries.

By the late 1920s Japan had extensive trading and investment interests in China, and as civil war spread throughout China, Japanese nationalists were able to use the threat to these economic assets as an excuse for demanding military intervention. A key factor in any move to expand Japan's role in China would be the Japanese Guandong Army — the troops who were assigned to protect Japanese interests in the Liaodong Peninsula and Manchuria. Throughout the 1920s, these soldiers had become increasingly influenced by radical nationalist ideologies, and increasingly involved in political intrigues on the continent, among them the assassination of the Manchurian warlord Zhang Zuolin in 1928.

The decisive move came in 1931. In September of that year, a group of soldiers from the Guandong Army staged an explosion on the South Manchurian railway line. They then claimed that the attack had been the work of Chinese terrorists and, on this pretext, the army seized political control of Manchuria. These events had occurred without the approval of the Japanese government, but cabinet lacked the will and power to repudiate the army's action, and in 1932 Japan established a puppet government in Manchuria, which was then declared to be the independent state of Manchukuo. The events in Manchuria provoked international outrage. A League of Nations commission under the leadership of Lord Lytton was sent to investigate Japan's actions, and issued a highly critical report. Japan's response was to withdraw from membership of the League.

At home, however, the takeover in Manchuria received widespread popular support. Not only did it bolster nationalist pride, but military spending associated with the activities in Manchuria also helped to pull the Japanese economy out of the recession which had followed the world slump of 1929. In the period 1931–37, indeed, Japan's economy grew rapidly, with particularly high rates of growth being recorded in industries like steel and shipbuilding, which were closely linked to military demand. At the same time, important changes were taking place in the nature of Japan's economic policies. Manchuria itself was to provide a sort of testing ground for the new economic approach favoured particularly by the army. There, economic policy was largely devised by Japanese military 'advisers' to the Manchukuo government, and large sums of government money were pumped into the expansion of military-related heavy industries, most of which were controlled either by the government or by the South Manchurian Railway Company. In 1937 these enterprises were transferred to the hands of the newly established Manchukuo Heavy Industries Development Company, which was financed partly by the Manchukuo government and partly by the private industrial conglomerate Nissan.

In Japan itself, state control of the economy was less direct, but was nevertheless expanding throughout the 1930s. During the depression of 1929–31, the government had created state-supervised cartels in major industries to regulate production and prices. This was initially intended to be a short-term measure to deal with the economic crisis, but was renewed and strengthened in the mid-1930s as the military increased its influence over policy-making. At the same time, a number of schemes were introduced whereby the government used licensing and subsidies to encourage the development of selected heavy industries such as steel, vehicle manufacture and the aircraft industry.

The establishment of Japanese domination in Manchuria and the growth of military power at home, however, failed to satisfy the demands of the army. Japan's burgeoning strategic heavy industries needed ever-expanding imports of raw materials such as coal, iron ore and oil, and this encouraged Japanese nationalists to turn their attention to mineral-rich regions of China, and even to Southeast Asia, as potential areas for Japanese expansion. Tensions along the Manchurian–Chinese border were high, and Britain and America were growing increasingly hostile to Japan's aggressive policies in China. Japan's main source of support in the West was Germany, with whom Japan signed the Anti-Comintern Pact in 1936. By now it was clear that only a minor incident would be needed to trigger an international conflict in East Asia.

That incident occurred on 7 July 1937, when a contingent of Japanese troops conducting manoeuvres near Beijing came into conflict with Chinese soldiers. The clash rapidly flared into a full-scale battle. Once again the military had pre-empted cabinet decisions by engaging in a conflict which the government then felt obliged to support. Some 150 000 Japanese troops were rapidly dispatched to the region, and the war with China had begun.

In a book published in English in 1938 to justify Japan's actions in China, a Japanese spokesman put forward several explanations for the war in East Asia — explanations which were very similar to those being used within Japan to rally popular support for the war. In part, he presented the conflict as an economic necessity, whose aim was to find new 'living space' for Japan's expanding and overcrowded population. At the same time, he saw Japan's actions, as many contemporaries did, in terms of cycles of the rise and fall of nations. The once-powerful Chinese nation was now weakened and corrupt, and it was inevitable that it should succumb to the domination of the vigorous, dynamic Japanese state. Japan's presence, he claimed, would save China from falling prey to the more alien and exploitative forces of Western colonialism. Lastly, he wrote, Japan was 'compelled to take proper measures' to combat the growing threat of communism in China: 'Japan as the champion of East Asia, leading the crusade against Communism, has a mission of vital significance in history.' The outbreak of war in China was thus depicted as 'the dawn of a new era in Asia'.[6] In fact, of course, it was the start not only of a period of tremendous suffering for most Chinese people, but also of the greatest catastrophe in Japan's modern history.

Guide to further reading

Good general surveys of this period are provided in Beasley, W.G., *The Rise of Modern Japan*, Weidenfeld and Nicolson, London, 1990 and Hunter, J., *The Emergence of Modern Japan*, Longman, London, 1989, both of which also cover Japan's postwar history.

Wray, H. & Conroy, H., *Japan Examined: Perspectives on Modern Japanese History*, University of Hawaii Press, Honolulu, 1983, contains brief essays on a number of major debates in Japan's modern history. Parts 5, 9 and 10 deal specifically with Japanese nationalism and imperialism.

A further useful source on Japan's overseas expansion is Myers, R.H. & Peattie, M.R. (eds), *The Japanese Colonial Empire 1895–1945*, Princeton University Press, Princeton, 1984.

Gluck, C., *Japan's Modern Myths: Ideology in the Late Meiji Period*, Princeton University Press, Princeton, 1985, offers thought-provoking insights into the origins of twentieth-century Japanese ideologies.

Welfield, John, *An Empire in Eclipse, Japan in the Postwar American Alliance System: A Study in the Interaction of Domestic Politics and Foreign Policy* , Athlone, London, Atlantic Highlands, N.J., 1988 is a masterpiece on this subject.

Notes

1 Quoted in Myers, R.H. & Peattie, M.R. (eds), *The Japanese Colonial Empire, 1895–1945,* Princeton University Press, Princeton, N.J., 1984, p. 64.

2 Quoted in Blacker, C., *The Japanese Enlightenment: A Study of the Writings of Fukuzawa Yukichi,* Cambridge University Press, Cambridge, 1969, p. 134.

3 Quoted in Myers, R.H. & Peattie, M.R. (eds), *The Japanese Colonial Empire*, p. 64.

4 Quoted in Hane, M., *Peasants, Rebels and Outcasts: The Underside of Modern Japan,* Pantheon Books, New York, 1982, p. 36–37.

5 Embree, J.F., *Suye Mura: A Japanese Village*, University of Chicago Press, Chicago, 1939, p. 67.

6 Kawai, T., *The Goal of Japanese Expansion*, Hokuseido Press, Tokyo, 1938.

16 | The nature and causes of revolution in Asia

The 'greatest catastrophe in Japan's modern history' with which the previous chapter concluded was also a major catalyst and cause of revolution in Asia. 'Revolution' is a word with many meanings and to which many definitions have been given. A revolution is a single complete orbit or rotation. It also refers to a radical development producing a new situation.

This meaning of 'revolution' is applied to many quite different phenomena. We talk of revolutions in science or technology or thinking, of revolutions in art or culture or social mores. Political-social revolutions are complex historical changes which result in fundamentally new social structures and political institutions, with new leadebs, policies and programs — just as scientific or artistic revolutions are fundamental changes in the way natural phenomena are understood and explained, or cultural phenomena are expressed. We would not, however, use the term 'revolution' to refer to slow processes of change, even though the outcome represented a fundamentally new development. Implicit in the meaning of revolution is that such changes occur relatively rapidly.

Revolutions so understood are defined neither by the means by which they are carried through nor by those responsible. In modern definitions of revolution, however, one means is often stressed — and that is the use of violence. For example, Samuel Huntington defines revolution as a 'rapid, fundamental, and violent domestic change in the dominant values and myths of a society, in its political institutions, social structure, leadership, and government activities and policies'.[1] As soon as we include violence as a defining characteristic of political-social revolutions, however, we do two things: we sever the connection with other kinds of revolution — scientific, artistic — which do not entail violence; and we include such political revolutions in an entirely different category of political and social phenomena — those entailing the use of violence or force. Among this latter category would be included revolts, rebellions, riots, mutinies, insurrections, *coups d'etat* and counter-*coups*, civil conflict, even acts of terrorism. Nor should state-sponsored repression of political opposition or non-violent protest be forgotten. Eckstein groups all such acts under the category of 'internal war' which he defines as 'any resort to violence within a political order to change its constitution, rules, or policies'.[2] Such events have occurred in every country in the world, in Asia as elsewhere, but few have brought about lasting change, and few could be categorised as revolutions in terms of results achieved.

Another problem encountered the moment we make resort to violence as part of the definition of revolution is that we have to find some other word to denote those complex historical processes which result in profound and rapid change in political leadership and institutions, and social policy without the use of violence, or where violence is minimal. The political and social changes which occurred in Japan after the Meiji restoration in 1868 were every bit as rapid and fundamental as those which occurred in China between 1911 and 1949. We can hardly claim that events in China were revolutionary while those in Japan were evolutionary, for the difference between revolution and evolution hinges not on the use of violence but on the speed of change.

Nevertheless, if we look at the history of Asian states, especially during the twentieth century, violence has undoubtedly played a significant role in bringing about radical political and social change. We need to understand why this is so while recognising it as a contingent rather than a necessary component. In other words, we need to understand both why violence has figured so prominently in twentieth-century Asian revolutions, and why it has taken the form it has. These are empirical questions to be answered through historical analysis. But they are questions that tend to be lost sight of, if violence is taken as a defining characteristic of revolution.

Other definitions of revolution emphasise not violence *per se* but those social groups responsible for bringing about the change. Thus Skocpol defines social revolutions as 'rapid, basic transformations of a society's state and class structures; and they are accompanied and in part, carried through by class-based revolts from below'.[3] The social classes credited with fulfilling a revolutionary role, at least in the twentieth century, are the proletariat or working class, and the peasantry. But to define social revolutions in terms of classes involved is again to confine the reference of the term in a way which may limit both its usefulness and our understanding of why such rapid changes occur. For the purposes of this discussion, therefore, revolutions will be taken to be complex political-social responses to a combination of internal and external circumstances which result in rapid and fundamental changes in political institutions and social relations.

Class responsibility and violent means have entered into the definition of political-social revolution in the twentieth century through the influence of Marx, and after him Lenin and Mao, largely because the Marxist theory of revolution has acted as the motivating ideology inspiring movements for rapid and fundamental change that have occurred in countries such as China and Vietnam, and because Marxist revolution has often been used as a paradigm against which events elsewhere must be measured to determine whether or not they constitute 'revolutions'. Because of the influence of Marx on Asian revolutions, it is essential to understand what Marx taught.

Marx and revolution

Marx's theory of revolution forms an integral part of his theory of history. Marx believed the course of history to be driven by economic productive processes. As human beings have striven to increase production, they have developed new technologies. For each level of technology there is an appropriate mode of production and relations of production between social classes which permit one class, the ruling class, to appropriate the economic surplus produced by an exploited class of slaves, serfs or workers. It is in the interest of a ruling class to:

1 develop a given mode of production to its maximum productive capacity; and
2 maintain its own social dominance.

When new productive technologies come into play, and a new mode of production develops requiring new relations of production, what Marx called 'contradictions' arise; that is, social tensions develop as a result of the competing economic interests of different social classes. For example, in a feudal society, serfs are tied to the land, but early industrialists needed to be able to recruit free labour to work their factories. The interests of the landed gentry class therefore conflicted with those of the rising bourgeoisie, or class of capitalist industrialists and entrepreneurs. Resolution of this conflict could only come about through a struggle for political power which ultimately, Marx believed, had to take the form of violent revolution. The paradigm example of such a bourgeois revolution for Marx was the French Revolution of 1789. Thus, to Marx, revolution was both necessary and inevitable. Moreover, since a ruling class would always fight to maintain its privileged position and guard its interests, only violence, the use of force, could overthrow the old order and replace it by one characterised by a new mode of production in which new social relations were exploited by a new ruling class. Thus, for Marx, revolution resulted from economic causes and entailed radical social structural change.

Marx was not merely the pre-eminent sociologist and political economist of nineteenth-century capitalism, he was also the prophet of revolution. Future revolutionary change would come about, he believed, as a result of the contradictions that would inevitably develop in capitalist societies as wealth became concentrated in fewer and fewer hands and the life of the workers, the proletariat, became increasingly miserable. When the working class realised that its own interests lay in appropriating the means of production for itself through a forceful transfer from private to social ownership, Marx predicted that it would rise up and seize political power. The capitalist mode of production would give way to the socialist mode where workers, no longer alienated from the product of their labour because it was owned by someone else, would joyfully work each according to his (or her) ability to provide for each according to his (or her) need. No ruling class would expropriate surplus value from the workers. For the first time in human history, societies would be classless communities of free men and women whose willing increase in productivity would ensure the equal prosperity of all. It was a heady vision, appealing to the finest of human aspirations, and it inspired not only the intellectuals and workers of Russia, but countless others in the countries of Asia after the Russian Revolution.

To this utopian vision, Lenin added his own particular contribution. By the end of the nineteenth century, even before Marx's death in 1883, it was evident that the contradictions that Marx had foretold were not occurring. The working class in advanced capitalist countries, rather than becoming impoverished, was decidedly better off than it had been half a century before. Lenin diagnosed this as being due to the net transfer of wealth from their colonies to the metropolitan imperialist states of Europe. Imperialism was the last advanced stage of capitalism. This net transfer of wealth permitted the capitalist ruling class to bribe the workers of the metropolitan countries with higher wages at the expense of indigenous workers in the colonies. The principal contradiction in this process of economic exploitation was transferred from the metropolitan power (where both capitalists and workers shared an interest in maintaining the system) to the colonies where the exploitation of workers was far more blatant. It was the workers in the exploited colonial periphery who must and would rise up first and drive out their imperialist masters. Only when this had been accomplished could contradictions in the metropolitan societies develop as Marx had foreseen, and result in their own domestic revolutions.

The appeal of Marxism as modified by Lenin to intellectuals throughout Asia smarting at colonial repression and exploitation is easy to understand. To begin with, it offered a plausible explanation of why Europeans had imposed their control over most of the rest of the world. It was a law of capitalism to seek the most lucrative opportunities for investment. Marxist theory revealed the global forces at work behind local developments, the historical pattern behind events. More importantly, it showed what political activists would have to do to break the system at its weakest point — they would have to educate and mobilise colonial

workers in order to convince them that their true interests lay in committing themselves to overthrowing colonial domination. This would require
extraordinary dedication and organisation, but Marxism-Leninism provided both the means and the justification to achieve this.

The revolutionary overthrow of colonial power would be brought
about at the direction of an elite revolutionary party acting as the
conscious vanguard of the proletariat, a vanguard buoyed up by the
conviction that their victory was, firstly, inevitable, because it conformed
to the laws of history that Marx had discovered, and secondly, would
provide the means whereby their countries, backward as they perceived
them to be in comparison with the imperial powers, would surge forward
through the superior productive power of socialism to catch up and
overtake European capitalist states — just as they believed the Soviet
Union had done.

To recapitulate, then: Marx's theory of revolution, as interpreted by
Lenin, saw revolutions as occurring at certain necessary points in the
historical process when the objective conditions were right. That is,
revolutions would occur when contradictions developed which would
arise not in advanced capitalist states, but in peripheral agrarian societies
exploited by imperialism and capitalism. These revolutions would be
brought about through violent struggle between social classes — initially
between those whose interests lay with maintaining colonial exploitation
and the imperial powers plus their local agents (whom Marxist-Leninists
called the 'comprador bourgeoisie') and all other classes in colonial
society whose interests lay in getting rid of the imperialists. Once this, the
nationalist phase of revolution, had been accomplished, the subsequent
socialist phase could be embarked upon; during this, the class struggle
would pit the indigenous proletariat against the indigenous bourgeoisie.

One problem with this scenario was that in agrarian countries in Asia,
the working class was numerically small and was concentrated in the
cities where repressive authority was strongest. Uprisings by urban
workers could be relatively easily suppressed, as in Shanghai in 1927. It
was Mao Zedong's contribution to Marxist revolutionary theory and
practice to transfer the responsibility for revolution in agrarian societies
from the proletariat to the peasantry, and the arena of revolutionary
action from the cities to the countryside. Marx believed the peasantry
possessed no social cohesion as a class. They were, he said, like potatoes
in a sack. Mao, steeped in a knowledge of Chinese history, recognised the
potential of the peasantry as a revolutionary force to bring about political
change. All they needed was leadership and direction, and this would be
provided (as always in Chinese history) by an educated intellectual elite
— not a Confucian elite, but the Chinese Communist Party.

Communist parties were therefore central to the revolutionary process.
Their vanguard role was to direct and organise the revolutionary struggle.
Only a strong, disciplined and dedicated communist party could ensure

a successful revolutionary outcome against either a colonial regime or a national bourgeoisie, supported as both were by international capitalism. And since neither could be expected to relinquish power voluntarily, force, in the form of morally justifiable 'revolutionary violence', would have to be used. Violence, its organisation and judicious application, was thus an essential component of Marxist revolution.

But violence, as we have seen, is not a necessary component of all forms of political-social revolution. Marxism-Leninism owed its extensive influence in Asia to the impact of the October Revolution in Russia in 1917. Prior to that, revolution was carried out in the name of liberal principles with nationalist fervour that sought to redress indignities suffered by proud and ancient civilisations at the hands of European imperialists. Such was the impetus behind both the Japanese and Chinese responses to the challenge of Western capitalism. In 1868 in Japan and in 1898 in China, reformist members of traditional elites set out to initiate rapid and fundamental political change in the leadership of their countries, in their political institutions and in government policies. In China they failed, but the members of the *samurai* class responsible for the Meiji restoration in Japan brought about a 'revolution from above', whose effect was every bit as far reaching in terms of the political and social changes it initiated as later revolutions successfully carried through in the name of Marx.

The extent of revolutionary change

We should recognise that traditional societies throughout Asia changed radically in terms of political leadership, policies and institutions, first through the imposition of colonial rule, and subsequently through the impact of World War II. The changes that the French brought about in Vietnamese society during the last two decades of the nineteenth century were nothing if not revolutionary. The traditional leadership was eclipsed, its mode of recruitment (through competitive examination in the Confucian classics) abolished and its policies, particularly as these determined social relations and the economy, entirely changed to facilitate French domination and the investment of French capital. The emperor remained in place, but as a mere figurehead.

The British seizure of upper Burma was no less revolutionary in its impact, and in parts of Indonesia the extension of Dutch rule during the same period was just as rapid and destructive of traditional political institutions. Even in Thailand, which escaped direct European rule, the impact of European imperialism both in its penetration of the Thai economy and in the pressure exerted on the frontiers of the Thai state was such as to force a series of changes in the way the country was governed in the late nineteenth century that were hardly short of revolutionary.

World War II also had a revolutionary impact on the countries of Asia. Colonial leadership and colonial institutions were overthrown to be replaced by Japanese military regimes. It was precisely the revolutionary impact of Japanese occupations that made it so difficult, and ultimately impossible, for former imperial powers to reimpose colonial regimes after the war. In some cases the impossibility was recognised, as in the British decision to leave Burma. In others it was not, notably by the French in Indochina. In such cases, the use of force was resorted to on both sides. We need to recognise, however, that the change in political leadership, the modification of colonial political institutions, and above all the radical reassessment of government policies that occurred in Burma (where virtually no fighting took place between British and Burmese) were just as revolutionary as those that occurred in Indonesia. It is difficult to see what, apart from three years of warfare, made the Indonesian revolution any more revolutionary than Burmese independence in terms of its political and social impact.

The case of Vietnam, and ultimately after 1975 of Cambodia and Laos too, was different only insofar as the political changes were arguably more far-reaching, and were accompanied by changes in the class structure of those societies. We shall return to the structure of agrarian societies below. What needs emphasising here is that the revolutionary changes that have taken place in Asia cannot be understood if they are confined to events accompanied by the use of violent means by less privileged socio-economic classes. We must instead understand the different forms of rapid and fundamental political and social changes that have occurred in different countries in relation to the specific set of historical conditions each responded to, and seek in this conjuncture the causes of the revolutionary events that have occurred.

The causes of revolution

As complex sequences of historical events, political-social revolutions are always due to a variety of causes. Marx, of course, recognised this, though he believed economic causes to be fundamental, and all other causes to be determined by economic conditions. More recently, political scientists and sociologists of revolution have sought other 'basic' or 'essential' causes — psychological, sociological, political. All such attempts to define a fixed hierarchy of more and less important causes risk, like definitions of revolution, fitting only certain cases. Those that do not fit the model tend to be ignored, and this distorts our understanding of the broad currents of historical change, and why on some occasions such change has been more rapid and fundamental than at other times.

Rather than define a hierarchy of causes, some students of revolution have attempted to define a set of necessary and sufficient conditions or causes of revolution. Some scholars, building on Marx, have emphasised economic causes (poverty, extreme differentials of wealth, tensions between traditional and modern economic systems). Others have focused on psychological factors that might lead individuals or groups to join a revolutionary movement, such as the anger and frustration brought on by unfulfilled expectations. Some have pointed to social causes (insufficient opportunities for social mobility, the rise of new social classes); others to intellectual factors, as when intellectuals among the ruling elite withdraw assent to traditional forms of legitimation and proclaim alternatives that advantage opponents of the regime in power. Others again have laid stress on political causes (response to and by oppressive and incompetent governments, especially where democratic forms of political action are not available) or to structural tensions produced by rapid and uneven economic and social change.

Theories of the causes of revolution also differ in the emphasis they give to the actions of the protagonists involved. Some stress the role of revolutionaries (revolutions are civil conspiracies by fanatics determined to destroy all properly constituted political authority); others see revolutions in competitive terms as both insurgents and governments struggle to mobilise the resources each needs to triumph over the other; and some focus on sins of omission, on the failures of established governments leading to the breakdown of regimes that provide the opportunities for opponents to act. Let us look briefly at some of these theories about how and why revolutions occur.

Whether we accept Marx's theory of history or not, it is evident that economic factors are important causes of revolutions. The rapid penetration of Western capital in colonial states caused the disruption of traditional social relationships and consequent disorientation and destruction of traditional values. These tensions resulting from the economic integration of agrarian states into a predominantly capitalist world order are, in the view of such influential theorists of revolution as Barrington Moore, the key underlying determinant of the direction and outcome of political-social revolution (see below).

Psychological theories of revolution accept that economic conditions are important, but go on to ask why men and women take the decision to rebel. The emphasis is placed on individual motivation: of what we might call the revolutionary elite (the leaders, both theorists and activists) and the revolutionary masses (the followers prepared to support a revolutionary movement). Few useful generalisations can be made about what makes individuals become revolutionary activists. Of more interest to students of revolution is what motivates the mass following without which no revolutionary movement can contest the power of a ruling regime. Misery would not seem to be enough. Subsistence farmers in many parts of the world endure miserable conditions year after year without rising in mass protest. One has only to think of India and parts of Africa. Davies suggested that those who rebel are not the poorest of the poor, but people who have come to expect some improvement in their living conditions.[4] When this fails to occur, expectations are frustrated, and frustration finds expression in support for a revolutionary movement. An extension of this expectation–frustration theory changes the focus from material conditions to political participation. Expectations of political reform may be frustrated, leading people to believe that there exists no alternative but revolution.

Sociologists influenced by Talcott Parsons have taken revolutions to be symptomatic of disequilibrium between the various subsystems — economic, political, etc. — that make up the overall social system. In 'healthy' societies, these sub-systems are fully integrated: change occurring in one produces compensating changes in the others in such a way that the equilibrium is maintained. During periods of crisis, such as war or economic depression, however, strains occur which disrupt the equilibrium and undermine the legitimacy of the regime. At such times, revolutionary movements flare up, like some disease in the body politic, to challenge the existing system. Few students of revolution would now subscribe to such a view.

Other sociological explanations of revolution focus on tensions generated by the rise of new classes or 'class factions', especially where political power is monopolised by one social group — a traditional aristocracy, single party, military officer corps, or minority tribe as in some states in Africa. Such tensions may arise as a result of economic development, leading to an increase in the size and importance of the national bourgeoisie (as has happened in Thailand, and to a lesser extent in Indonesia); or they may arise as a result of increased opportunities for education (as in Cambodia in the 1960s). In either case, new social groups resent what they perceive to be their lack of political influence and social status, and demand increased participation in government and policy-making. Where these demands remain unmet, intellectuals (the 'communicators' in society: journalists, clerics, teachers, lawyers, writers, academics) begin to question the legitimacy of narrow ruling elites. Eventually the majority of intellectuals withdraw their support for the regime and join the opposition — as happened in Eastern Europe in the late 1980s.

Then there are obvious political causes which have to be considered. What avenues are open for different social groups to make known their political aspirations, to influence the political process? How is opposition handled by the government — through compromise, through oppression? What forms of political action are available to minority groups in society? In examining such political causes in specific cases, we need to take account of the political culture of the society under study. Demands for democratic reform are less likely to be made, and less likely to elicit popular support, in a society with no tradition of popular participation in government, and where the prevailing world-view lends powerful religious legitimation to autocratic rule.

All these various causes of revolution have primarily to do with the conditions for revolution. They emphasise the grounds for popular discontent with and opposition to ruling regimes. But there is no basis on which to argue that because certain conditions pertain, a revolution will, firstly, break out, or be successful. The external observer adding up the causes creating conditions for revolution might easily conclude that revolution is inevitable, and be entirely wrong. Much depends on the strength of the ruling regime and how this is perceived by its citizens. All the conditions for revolution may be present, but the oppressive apparatus of the state — the means of coercion available to the authorities, the police, the military — may still be sufficient to prevent its outbreak. The balance may be a fine one. The outbreak of revolution may occur as a result of some accidental 'trigger' or 'precipitant', some incident which acts as a spark to light the conflagration.

The success or failure of revolution

While early students of revolution focused on the stages through which revolutions progressed, and subsequently on the causes giving rise to conditions for the outbreak of revolutions, later theorists have shifted attention to what makes revolutions fail or succeed once they have broken out. Tilly and his followers have emphasised in this respect the means of mobilisation of resources available to both sides.[5] Mobilisation theorists believe that frustrated expectations and political discontent are always present in any society. So too are social tensions and economic inequalities. Whether or not a potential alternative political leadership is able to carry through a successful revolution depends not on conditions that are always present, but on whether or not it is possible to mobilise sufficient resources to defeat the regime in power.

Resources for revolution can be divided into social, economic, political and military means. A revolutionary movement must enjoy popular support among the broadest possible cross-section of the population. To this end, Vietnamese communists formed the Vietminh Front, behind which the role of the party remained hidden, so as not to alienate non-communists. Economic resources include financial backing, food supplies for guerrilla fighters, means of transportation and the logistics of providing basic material requirements. Methods include 'taxation', corvée labour, commandeered items and so on. Where 'liberated areas' can be established, alternative administrations function as in government-controlled areas to provide the economic basis for revolutionary activity.

Political resources include revolutionary institutions, such as mass organisations to mobilise popular participation, and policies of mass appeal. Revolutionary ideology and effective propaganda are essential to generate political commitment to a revolutionary cause. In this respect, too, the Vietminh provide an excellent case study. Military resources have either to be won from the government through attacks on isolated outposts or ambushing patrols, purchased on the arms market if finance is available, or provided by a sympathetic foreign power. The Vietminh gained some arms during World War II from the Americans and more from the Japanese, but they also seized a lot from French or French-officered Vietnamese forces. Nevertheless, the tide of struggle really only turned in early 1950, when Chinese communist weapons began flowing to the Vietminh.

Two other resources should also be mentioned: diplomatic or international, and geographic. Examples of the former are the diplomatic recognition accorded to Ho Chi Minh's government in 1950 by communist states, or the substantial international support given over the years by many countries to the African National Congress (ANC). Geographic resources refer importantly to cross-border sanctuaries provided by sympathetic neighbouring countries where revolutionary movements can organise and regroup. Examples would be the Cambodian sanctuaries used by the Vietcong during the Second Indochina War, or the sanctuaries enjoyed by the ANC in front-line African states. How effectively a revolutionary organisation mobilises and uses all such resources available to it, and how effectively a ruling regime responds by mobilising and utilising the resources at its disposal will determine the outcome of any attempted revolution.

The recognition that revolution depends on the relative capacities of ruling regimes and revolutionary movements to mobilise resources together with studies of the nature of the modern state has led to an alternative approach to revolution, particularly in the work of Theda Skocpol.[6] She has argued that so great are the resources available to modern states, revolutionary movements would, under normal circumstances, never be in a position to mobilise equivalent resources. Only where paralysis or breakdown of state administrative or coercive functions occurs could revolutionary movements possibly succeed. Subsequently Goodwin and Skocpol have argued that certain kinds of state are particularly vulnerable, namely those authoritarian regimes that are both repressive and exclude all but a small ruling group from political participation.[7] Such regimes fall into two broad categories: personalistic dictatorships such as those exercised by Ngo Dinh Diem in South Vietnam or Ferdinand Marcos in the Philippines; and directly ruled colonies, such as French Indochina. Colonies ruled indirectly, particularly where indigenous participation was permitted, as in British Burma or the Philippines under United States administration, were less vulnerable. Students of revolutions should therefore seek the causes of revolution not in reasons why revolutionary movements challenge ruling regimes, but in what makes states incapable of suppressing them. So just as mobilisation theorists hold that discontent and political frustration are always present to some extent and therefore cannot explain the actual occurrence of successful revolutions, state breakdown theorists take it for granted that violent revolution is always an option in the pursuit of political goals. What needs explaining is why the revolutionary path was chosen and succeeded in one case rather than another, and that depends primarily on the capability, or incapability, of the government to which it was opposed.

Revolution and the modernisation of agrarian societies

During most periods of history the maintenance of established forms of government and political systems has been the norm. Revolutions are exceptional. Why then have so many taken place, or at least been attempted, in the twentieth century? Those who have addressed this problem have focused on the impact the capitalist international order has had on traditional agrarian societies — something particularly relevant to the study and understanding of Asian revolutions. The process by which changes occurred in the class structure and political organisation of traditional states as they accommodated to the evolving world capitalist order has been called modernisation. Revolution and modernisation are thus clearly linked.

According to Barrington Moore, there are three kinds of revolution giving rise to modernisation, depending on which class comes to power. In agrarian societies there are two major classes: a traditional landed elite which wields political power, and the peasantry. The political dominance of the landed elite is threatened by the rise of the urban bourgeoisie, whether as an indigenous development or as stimulated by capitalist penetration from external sources. A modernising response can lead to one of three possible outcomes, in Moore's view: the landed elite may be overthrown by or make common cause with the dominant bourgeoisie (as happened in France or England); or the landed elite may retain political power through engineering its own modernising 'revolution from above' (as in Germany or Japan); or the peasantry itself may seize power through the revolutionary overthrow of the landed elite (as in Russia or China). While the first leads to democracy, the preferred form of government of the bourgeoisie, Moore argues, the second leads to fascism, and the third to communism.[8]

Jeffrey Paige addresses himself specifically to the study of revolution in agrarian societies. He argues that whether or not conflict in such societies leads to revolution depends on the kind of agricultural production that dominates, for this determines the nature of exploitation (surplus extraction) by what he calls 'the non-cultivating class'. Revolution is most likely, Paige argues, where sharecropping and tenant farming are the principal form of cultivation. Where rural workers are attached through patron–client bonds to commercial hacienda, revolts may occur, but there is little incentive to join revolutionary movements. Where rural smallholdings or plantation agriculture prevail, it is in the interest of proprietors or major companies to negotiate compromise agreements — in other words, to prefer reform over revolution.[9]

Both Barrington Moore and Paige have focused on agrarian class structure and economic production processes in putting forward general theories to explain the occurrence of political-social revolutions in agrarian societies. All Asian societies in the mid-nineteenth century were overwhelmingly agrarian. Only in late Tokugawa Japan had some of the foundations been laid for subsequent development of an industrial and commercial capitalist state. Yet in Japanese society, as everywhere else in Asia, the majority social class comprised peasant farmers producing at barely above subsistence levels. Particularly from the second half of the nineteenth century on, these agrarian societies were subjected to the disruptive impact of capitalist penetration of their economies. This was the last great period of European imperial expansion which witnessed, in addition to the carving up of Africa, the extension of British, French and Dutch rule throughout Burma and Malaysia, Indochina and Indonesia, as well as the 'opening up' of China and Japan. The impact of industrial capitalism through the *mise en valeur* (as the French so nicely put it) of colonial possessions was very much greater than had been the earlier impact of mercantile capitalism. The shift from self-sustaining village agriculture to agricultural production for export, particularly in areas such as the Mekong Delta and the lower Irrawaddy, had a profoundly disorientating effect on peasant life and values. In both areas, mass movements developed which sought to respond to these pressures. In Cochin-China, two religious sects rapidly gained adherents in the 1930s. The Cao Dai drew all divinities into an eclectic pantheon and defined for believers their place in a socio-religious hierarchy. The Hoa Hao promised a millenarian future in the kingdom of Maitreya. Neither preached violence. In Burma, however, the Saya San rebellion called for expulsion of the British and recreation of a Burmese Buddhist political order. In looking to the past for political solutions, Saya San was responding to the impact of colonialism in a way his peasant followers intuitively understood, for it was couched in an idiom they recognised and could relate to.

Peasants and intellectuals

The effect of Western capitalist penetration on agrarian societies is clearly central to an understanding of Asian revolutions. But structural explanations do not provide an adequate understanding of the complexity of the historical processes at work. We need, in addition, to take account of two factors often overlooked in explanations of revolution. The first is how revolutionary alliances are formed between workers and peasants on the one hand and what we might call the revolutionary elite, the educated intellectual leadership of the revolution responsible for forging the revolutionary organisation, strategy and goals on the other. The second is peasant mentality, the thought world of the peasantry itself which predisposes it to participate in or stand aside from political struggle.

Revolutionary movements in Asia, as elsewhere, are based upon revolutionary alliances between different social groups and classes, each of which has its own interests to pursue. To be effective, a revolutionary alliance has to bring together as wide a cross-section of social groups as possible. Mao included not only workers and peasants, but also artisans and traders (the petit bourgeoisie), middle and small capitalists, oppressed minorities, all kinds of intellectuals, and even 'enlightened gentry' and overseas Chinese. Where a revolutionary alliance failed to transcend ethnic and/or religious differences, its success was unlikely. Membership of the Malayan Communist Party was almost entirely limited to urban Chinese, and no revolutionary alliance was formed between this group and the predominantly rural Muslim Malay community — a failure that was the principal underlying reason for British success in defeating the MCP during the 'Malayan Emergency'.

Of all the alliances formed in a revolutionary movement, that between the peasantry and intellectuals has been the most crucial, since it is the latter that has for the most part formed the revolutionary leadership which the former has followed. If for the rural peasantry the impact of colonialism was disruptive and disorientating, for the intellectual elite it was humiliating and degrading. While some compromised with their new masters, others sought a philosophy of resistance, in refurbished traditional beliefs and institutions, in the adoption of European liberal and democratic values, or in Marxism. For all, however, the goal was the same — to build, as rapidly as possible, new social structures and political institutions based on new values that would permit Asian societies to escape the humiliation of colonial domination and compete with Western capitalist powers.

Throughout Asia the circumstances that created the conditions for revolution were remarkably similar. The stimulus came from Western imperialism: the response was on the part of agrarian societies composed of a numerous peasantry, a limited working class and a small landholding and intellectual/religious elite. It was the highly nationalistic intellectual elites in particular who articulated revolutionary responses to the Western challenge. But if their goals were broadly the same, the means were not, and the relations these elites forged with the numerically dominant class, the peasantry, were different in different societies.[10]

In Japan the elite engineered its 'revolution from above', taking little account of a compliant peasantry with no tradition of intervention in political processes. In China the radical modernising elite was too weak to overcome the opposition of conservative and regional interests and, after turning first to the urban working class, was forced in the end to mobilise peasant support. That they could do so depended very much, as we shall see below, on the historical understanding the peasantry possessed of their occasional revolutionary intervention in the political process.

In Southeast Asia, Thailand was the only country to escape colonial domination. There the traditional elite took the lead in initiating change with no reference to the peasantry. Where the peasantry did respond to new and disorientating pressures, it was in localised and traditional ways (such as the traditionalist millenarian 'Holy Man' revolts in north and northeast Thailand). In the colonised societies of Southeast Asia, fundamental changes were first brought about by the colonisers themselves. We have noted already how far-reaching many of these changes were. Thus, in a sense, in these countries modernising elites had much of their work done for them. They could either accept the new values and institutions, or modify them, or reject them entirely.

How indigenous elites responded to the challenges posed internally by colonialism and externally by the capitalist world order dominated by industrialised states depended on how they conceived of their own countries in relation to the industrialised West. They might, like Japan, set out to compete with Western imperialism on its own terms; or, recognising their limitations, be content like the Philippines to fulfil the role the major capitalist states (particularly the United States of America) assigned to them; or they could, like Burma, withdraw into isolation; or like Indonesia under Sukarno chart their own idiosyncratic non-aligned way. Or they could be more ambitious and attempt, like China, like Vietnam and (in the most extreme form) like Cambodia under the Khmer Rouge, to leapfrog forward in the march of history and to bypass capitalism altogether by advancing immediately to what they believed to be the economically superior mode of production of socialism.

Which path to take was a matter of intense debate which split the political and intellectual elite into opposing factions, each of which sought to mobilise opinion in support of its own position. Which faction had its way depended upon specific conditions in different countries, including the nature of the colonial regime, the kinds of innovation it had introduced, and the strength of the administrative and coercive institutions in place. It also depended on the political goals of the dominant elite faction, how these were formulated and communicated, and what means were available to mobilise mass support.

Elite goals included seizure of political power, elimination of foreign domination, and rapid modernisation as the means to reassert national pride and prestige. For these to be accepted by a peasantry often suspicious of urban intellectuals required a twofold approach: education in national issues, and the relation of peasant interests to these — both with a view to developing political consciousness and commitment. Peasants needed to be assured that participation in a revolutionary movement was going to be of benefit to them. The Vietcong were particularly adept in linking the struggle for national unity to the discontent of particular villages over the unpopularity and corruption of South Vietnamese officials with whom they came in contact.

The means of mobilising mass peasant support include effective organisation, participation and motivation through appeal to deeply held cultural values and historical traditions. Organisation has been best provided through a disciplined revolutionary party. Such a party provides leadership structure, policy formulation and direction, and the solidarity that comes from belonging to a powerful semi-secret organisation. Participation in such an organisation often begins with limited involvement — providing information on government whereabouts, joining a mass organisation (farmers, women, youth), or simply failing to report the presence of revolutionaries in a village. From there it becomes more active and committed, to the point of joining the party or a guerrilla unit. Again the techniques developed first by the Vietminh and later by the Vietcong in Vietnam provide good examples of how such participation was encouraged at the village level.

Mentality and patterns of violence

A further important means of mobilisation of the peasantry comes from appeal to cultural values and historical traditions. Cultural values shape the response of peasants to situations which seem to them to be insupportable and unjust. Such values form part of a shared world-view derived from myth and legend, oral tradition and popular culture.

Peasant mentality influenced the nature of elite–peasant interaction. How effectively elite goals could be communicated within the parameters of the peasant world-view largely determined the nature and extent of peasant commitment to movements seeking to bring about rapid and fundamental political and social change. It also influenced (and this is a crucial consideration) the extent to which violence would or would not be central to the process. The scholar who has come closest to recognising the significance of the peasant world-view in determining responses to potentially revolutionary situations is James Scott in his studies of the 'moral economy' of peasant societies.

In Japan, Confucian values reinforced the monopoly of power by an hereditary aristocracy by limiting education and office to that elite. Power struggles were fought out by *daimyo* and their *samurai* with little participation from a passive peasantry. In China, by contrast, mass action was the principal means by which Heaven made known its displeasure. A dynasty enjoyed the Mandate of Heaven for so long as harmony and prosperity prevailed. Warnings of moral laxity might be given by natural phenomena — earthquakes, floods, strange happenings — but the ultimate sign of Heaven's displeasure was when conditions became so bad that a peasant rebellion broke out, either to be put down, in which case the mandate was temporarily restored, or to be successful, in which case the mandate passed to a new dynasty. Mass peasant participation was thus a feature of the Chinese political process. In the Chinese peasant world-view, such participation was part of their historical tradition, as it never was for Japanese peasants (see Chapter 7). In the final apocalyptic struggle between Guomindang (GMD) and CCP forces between 1946 and 1949, the notion of the Mandate of Heaven shaped the response to the fortunes of war by whole peasant armies, some of which defected *en masse* from the GMD in the belief that Heaven favoured Mao's communists, that Chiang Kaishek had lost the mandate to govern.

In Vietnam too we find traditions of peasant participation in political resistance movements. While the Vietnamese Nationalist Party adopted the model of Chinese secret society opposition to the Qing dynasty to get rid of the French, the communists tapped the rich tradition of mass peasant participation in violent action, both against foreign, historically Chinese occupation, and in support of anti-dynastic rebellions, such as the successful eighteenth-century Tay Son rebellion. It is salutary to recall that in China secret societies like the Triads degenerated into criminal gangs. It was mass peasant uprisings such as the Taiping Rebellion that threatened the Qing. The communists in both China and Vietnam were effective in mobilising peasant support because they drew upon historical traditions of peasant involvement in violent protest and resistance movements, and it was that peasant mobilisation which assured the success of their respective revolutions.

In the Theravada Buddhist states of mainland Southeast Asia, by contrast, no such tradition of violent peasant involvement in the political process has existed. What we do find are two very different patterns of violence: struggles for control of ritual centres by rival elite contenders for power, and millenarian attempts to create utopian theocratic polities. Violent attempts to control centres of power occurred primarily under one or other of two sets of circumstances: either upon the death of an incumbent when the succession was disputed, or when an incumbent's power was weak enough for tributary rulers to assert, or attempt to assert, their independence. Both sets of circumstances derived from the political structure of Southeast Asian *mandalas* (see Chapter 8).

The other pattern of violent opposition to authority most characteristic of Theravada Buddhist societies in Southeast Asia took the form of millenarian peasant uprisings in the name of establishing a utopian kingdom to be ruled over by a divine saviour. Such revolts were almost always led by some charismatic figure claiming supernatural powers and knowledge, or divine grace and protection, who called upon his followers in the name usually of Maitreya, the next Buddha-to-be. Such uprisings sought a utopian order, not the restoration of efficient government, and collapsed as quickly as they had arisen once their charismatic leadership was destroyed.

The significance of these differing traditions of violence in East and Southeast Asia lies in the way in which each is embedded in peasant mentality, and predisposes peasants to respond to revolutionary movements in tradition-sanctioned ways. To leave peasant mentality or world-view out of account, as both mobilisation and state breakdown theoriests tend to do, is to fail to recognise an important causal dimension in Asian revolutions.

Summary

An understanding of Asian revolutions rests on analysis of three intersecting sets of factors: actual circumstances (economic, social, political), including the balance of resources available to each side; the goals and intentions of the revolutionary leadership and its relations with other classes, especially the peasantry; and the cultural values and historical traditions that shape the responses and actions of those who support revolutionary movements. It is not enough to focus, as many students of revolution have done, on material/economic or social-structural causes alone to explain revolutions in Asia. These are essential components of actual circumstances, but they are insufficient in themselves to explain why revolutions in different countries have taken the courses they have. For that, we need to examine the actual historical conditions, including the mentalities and intentions of those involved.

Guide to further reading

Of the works cited already in this chapter, those by Moore, Paige, Scott, Skocpol and Tilly are all important studies.

Dunn, John, *Modern Revolutions: An Introduction to the Analysis of a Political Phenomenon*, 2nd edn, Cambridge University Press, Cambridge, 1989, and Kimmel, Michael S., *Revolution: A Sociological Interpretation*, Temple University Press, Philadelphia, 1990, are good general studies of revolution. Also of interest is Eisenstadt, S.N., *Revolution and the Transformation of Societies: A Comparative Study of Civilizations*, Free Press, New York, 1978.

On the theme of 'revolution from above', centreing on a case study of Japan, see especially Trimberger, Ellen Kay, *Revolution From Above: Military Bureaucrats and Modernisation in Japan, Turkey, Egypt, and Peru*, Transaction Books, New Brunswick, 1978.

On the causes of revolution from a psychological perspective, the best study is Gurr, Ted Robert, *Why Men Rebel*, Princeton University Press, Princeton, 1970. Tilly has brought his ideas together in *From Mobilization to Revolution*, Addison-Wesley, Reading, Mass., 1978

Samuel Popkin has challenged James C. Scott's approach to peasant motivation in *The Rational Peasant: The Political Economy of Rural Society in Viet Nam*, University of California Press, Berkeley, 1979. On the Vietcong, see Pike, Douglas, *Viet Cong: The Organization and Techniques of the National Liberation Front of South Vietnam*, MIT Press, Cambridge, Mass., 1966 and Race, Jeffrey, *War Comes to Long An: Revolutionary Conflict in a Vietnamese Province*, University of California Press, Berkeley, 1972.

On peasants and revolution, Wolf, Eric R., *Peasant Wars of the Twentieth Century*, Harper & Row, New York, 1969, and Migdal, J.S., *Peasants, Politics, and Revolution in Asia*, Stanford University Press, Stanford, 1974, are both worth consulting.

Notes

1 Huntington, Samuel P., *Political Order in Changing Societies*, Yale University Press, New Haven, 1968, p. 264.

2 Eckstein, Harry, 'On the Etiology of Internal Wars', *History and Theory*, vol. 4, 1964, p. 133.

3 Skocpol, Theda, *States and Social Revolutions: A Comparative Analysis of France, Russia and China*, Cambridge University Press, Cambridge, 1979, p. 4.

4 Davies, J.C., 'Toward a Theory of Revolution', *American Sociological Review*, vol. 27, 1962, pp. 5–19.

5 Tilly, Charles, 'Revolutions and Collective Violence' in Greenstein, F. & Polsby, N. (eds), *Handbook of Political Science*, vol. 3, Addison-Wesley, Reading, Mass., 1975, pp. 483–555.

6 Skocpol, Theda, *States and Social Revolutions*, Cambridge, 1979.

7 Goodwin, Jeff and Skocpol, Theda, 'Explaining Revolutions in the Contemporary Third World', *Politics and Society*, vol. 17, 1989 pp. 489–509.

8 Moore, Barrington, *Social Origins of Dictatorship and Democracy*, Lane, London, 1967.

9 Paige, J.M., *Agrarian Revolution: Social Movements and Export Agriculture in the Underdeveloped World*, Free Press, New York, 1975.

10 Scott, James C., *The Moral Economy of the Peasant*, Yale University Press, New Haven, 1976.

17 | The Chinese revolutions

Are there numerous revolutions or just one long revolution in the history of modern China? The answer to this question depends firstly on how the term 'revolution' is defined and, secondly, on whether one takes a long view of China's modern history. The writer's inclination is to see the momentous changes that have taken place in China since the turn of this century as part of a continuing revolution to transform China from a weak and divided country into a strong and united one. Despite the differences of opinion among Chinese leaders and intellectuals on ways and means of achieving that goal, there was general agreement that the ultimate objective of the Chinese revolution was national wealth and power. From a broad historical perspective, therefore, the Chinese revolution may be understood as a continuing movement that underwent several phases. It brought about fundamental change in important aspects of Chinese society, but in many ways China today remains the same old and 'semi-feudal' society that the Communists sought to change many decades ago.

For a start, revolutions must be distinguished from peasant uprisings, military coups, revolts, dynastic changes and civil disturbances. A revolution is not merely a change of rulers and governing personnel. More importantly, it aims at an overthrow of the existing social order as well as the political power structure. The basic criterion for judging a revolution is its aspirations to fundamental change in society (see Chapter 16).

It is customary to call revolutions by the years in which they occurred — for example, the English Revolution of 1688, the French Revolution of 1789, the Chinese Revolution of 1911 and the Russian Revolution of 1917. But these dates only refer to the years in which established authorities were overthrown. They do not indicate when the revolutionary movement started and when and where the revolution finished. It should be borne in mind that revolution in any form has a period of gestation and a subsequent period of maturation. At many points, a revolution can be aborted either because those promoting it are incapable of the task or not yet prepared for it, or because the conditions for it are not present, or because the forces defending the status quo have been reinforced. Consequently, many revolutions in retrospect appear either abortive or failures because their medium- or long-term goals were not achieved; some became counter-revolutionary as soon as their immediate aims were accomplished. In many cases, because the 'first' revolution was a failure, a 'second' revolution became a necessity and, because it failed again, a 'third' one was in order, and so on.

Every succeeding revolution inherits a legacy of the immediate past. In this sense, the revolution moves into a new phase, perhaps taking a different form, with a different emphasis, and under a new leadership. Each new generation of leaders owes a debt to the one before it. It is the cumulative results of their endeavours over a long period of time that determine the long-term outcomes of revolutions.

While the chief criterion for judging a revolution is its aspirations to fundamental change in society, it must be appreciated that such change cannot be brought about simply by a decree of the new regime or an act of parliament. For any social change to have a lasting effect, there must be a transformation of thought on the part of the intellectual elite and a change of habit on the part of the masses. A revolution does not occur in an intellectual vacuum. Rather, it often takes place in the midst of an intellectual movement that calls into question a whole range of old values and beliefs. An appreciation of the intellectual movement around the time of the revolution is useful in understanding the revolution itself.

In the case of China, one can speak of the Revolution of 1911, the Nationalist Revolution of 1926–28 and the Communist Revolution of 1949. But they should not be understood as separate and distinct events. Nor should they be studied without reference to the intellectual movement in modern China.

The revolutionary movement that resulted in the overthrow of the Qing Dynasty can be traced back to the late nineteenth century when Dr Sun Yatsen, a Western-educated medical practitioner born in China but brought up overseas, turned himself from a reformist into a revolutionary. His desire was to replace the corrupt and incompetent Manchu government with a modern democratic republic. His early support came from students in Hong Kong and Honolulu where, in 1894, he organised a revolutionary society called the Restore China Society (*Xingzhong hui*), as well as from the secret societies in south China which had maintained an anti-Manchu tradition since the fall of the Ming dynasty. Independently, other revolutionary societies were later formed by radical students and intellectuals in the middle and lower reaches of the Yangzi River region. The revolutionary camp was made up of diverse and disparate elements who had different ideas about the ideology of the revolution and its strategy. It was not until 1905 that a Revolutionary League (*Tongmeng hui*) was formed in Tokyo among the Chinese students there who elected Sun as the leader. But the revolutionary movement remained fragmented and factionalised. The only thing that united the revolutionary protaganists was opposition to Manchu rule.

The Manchu rulers had failed in many ways, especially in regard to the defence of China's political and territorial integrity in an age of imperialism. Since the Opium War of 1839–42, China had suffered a series of defeats and humiliations at the hands of the foreign powers, culminating in the foreign scramble for concessions in 1898 and the allied pillage of Beijing in 1900. Consequently, China was reduced to a 'semi-colonial' status, controlled and dominated by the foreign powers which maintained their privileged positions by force. The imperial government, already shaken to its foundations by the Taiping Rebellion (1850–64), showed a lack of capacity to ward off the ever-increasing foreign threat. The Self-strengthening Movement in the latter half of the nineteenth century, with its emphasis on military reforms and acquisitions to the neglect of institutional change, was a major disappointment, as evidenced by China's humiliating defeat at Japanese hands in 1894–95. It took the disaster of the Boxer Uprising to galvanise the imperial court into launching a series of new reforms. But the reforms failed to stem the revolutionary tide, as the Manchu rulers' sincerity and efforts were called into question by those who had lost faith in them.

The fact that the Qing was an alien dynasty gave rise to a new wave of racist anti-Manchuism. The Manchus, though they had adopted the Chinese system of government and had been assimilated culturally in many ways, remained a privileged class, and became a scapegoat for China's problems. Not only were they accused of selling out China to foreigners and castigated for corruption and incompetence, but they were also ridiculed as an inherently inferior race incapable of good government. To save China from national extinction, the revolutionaries argued, Han rule must be restored because only a Han government could roll back the tide of imperialism. There was a resurgence of Han nationalism which became a motif of the anti-dynastic movement.

The Revolution of 1911 was a political revolution, not a social one; its immediate aims were the overthrow of the Manchus and the establishment of a republic. It was relatively brief and non-violent, and it succeeded in putting an end to the imperial system, a change that was irrevocable despite later attempts by President Yuan Shikai and warlord Zhang Xun to restore the monarchy. To the extent that the political system was fundamentally altered, the events of 1911 were profoundly significant. Yet, despite Sun Yatsen's long-term plans for China's reconstruction and his emphasis on improving the people's livelihood, little attention was given to the real problems facing the rural masses. Nor was there any attempt to change the existing social structure. Chinese society, which had for centuries been Confucian, authoritarian and dominated by the landlord gentry, remained basically the same in the post-imperial era. The new republic did not emancipate the poor people of China from landlord exploitation or from the fetters of tradition and authoritarianism.

Historians in the People's Republic of China have interpreted the Revolution of 1911 as a 'bourgeois-democratic revolution' led by 'progressive bourgeois forces' and supported by 'petit bourgeois elements'. Sun Yatsen and his educated followers represented a new generation of political activists who were anxious to extricate China from its predicament and embark on a journey to modernity. They were influenced by Western ideas, even though their understanding of republicanism, liberalism and democracy was far from profound. Yet the bourgeoisie as a class was diverse and small in the first decades of the twentieth century. Even though capitalism had made a start in China, it was advancing slowly and unevenly in the provinces, concentrating as it did on the treaty ports, especially Shanghai. The bourgeoisie was only in the early stages of formation, consisting of elements drawn from the local gentry as well as entrepreneurial merchants and officials. Until the revolution was well underway and showed signs of succeeding, the support of the business community was not always forthcoming.

The revolutionary leaders had attempted to enlist support from other social classes and groups. One important source of support was the progressive segment of the gentry whose concerns had extended beyond the local and provincial boundaries to the national level. Most of the revolutionary students had recently returned from Japan and, to a lesser extent, Europe; many had also received a traditional education. Another source of support, especially regarding the rank and file, was the secret societies which provided the sinews for armed uprisings. However, they were badly organised, poorly equipped and totally unreliable as a fighting force. After a series of unsuccessful revolts, the revolutionary party turned to the government's New Army, subverted it, and succeeded in winning over large sections of it. Eventually the revolution began as a military coup in Wuchang in Hubei Province, which enjoyed the backing of other provinces where the military and the newly formed gentry-dominated provincial assemblies promptly formed a coalition to maintain law and order. At the time of the revolutionary outbreak, Sun Yatsen was in the United States.

The Revolution of 1911 was not a peasant revolt; although the rural masses were available for mobilisation, they had not been mobilised — the peasant revolution was not to unfold until a decade or so later. Nor was it a bourgeois revolution in the eighteenth and nineteenth-century European sense. Even though Sun Yatsen and the overseas students could be classified as bourgeois elements imbued with Western thought, the Chinese bourgeoisie as a class was not a powerful political force. The merchants, industrialists, bankers, financiers and entrepreneurs — the business community — were both too weak in numbers and too passive politically to play a significant role in the events of this period. They did not represent the kind of political and social values commonly ascribed to the European middle class. It would be wrong, for example, to assume that they necessarily believed in liberalism and democracy, even though they favoured constitutional government, a broadening of political participation and economic advancement through science and technology. The bourgeoisie was not the motor behind the Chinese revolution — not in 1911, nor in the years that followed. And Sun Yatsen, in spite of his advocacy of a republic and people's rights, was not a liberal in the European sense. He believed in a strong state more than individual rights and personal freedoms.

Nor was the revolution an 'upper-class' revolt against the Qing. To be sure, the gentry's decision to withdraw its support from the throne was ultimately decisive in sealing the fate of the dynasty. But the anti-Qing movement encompassed a diversity of classes, elements and issues, and the final episode was played out by many different actors. The gentry, like the bourgeoisie, was a diverse class in which cleavages existed in social, economic and political terms.

In the sense that the Revolution of 1911 did not change existing social relationships, it was a failure. The new republic was filled with former goverment officials who had little idea about the meaning and practice of republicanism. Few people outside Beijing and the major provincial cities could distinguish between an emperor and a president; few cared anyway. Life in the rest of the country went on as usual. If anything, conditions in China became worse in the immediate post-imperial period. Chaos again ruled supreme following the death of Yuan Shikai, who had presided over a republic which could only be described as a travesty of democracy. Not only had Yuan suspended the Provisional Constitution of the Chinese Republic and assumed dictatorial powers, but he had proclaimed himself emperor shortly before he died in 1916.

Although democracy had failed in the early years of the Chinese Republic, the Confucian basis of Chinese society was being eroded. Already in the late nineteenth century there had been attempts by traditional but reformist scholars, notably Kang Youwei, to reinterpret Confucianism in a way that would make it more responsive to change in modern times. Confucius was understood to be a reformer who would have endorsed reform were he still alive. Aspects of Chinese society, such as the examination system, the traditional family, the status of women and so on were called into question. Yet a full-scale assault on Confucianism was not to unfold until the New Culture Movement of the mid-1910s.

The New Culture Movement grew out of the chaos and political instability that followed the death of Yuan Shikai. Seeing China's predicament in a cultural light, concerned Chinese students and scholars engaged in a search for a new culture that could serve as the basis for a new socio-political order. They represented a new generation of intellectuals who were anxious to exercise their responsibilities as social elites. Just as the late Qing reformer, Liang Qichao, had called for a 'New Citizen' over a decade earlier, so this new generation of students — mainly returned from overseas — called for a 'New Youth', which became the title of an influential magazine under the editorship of Chen Duxiu. The new youth was to be dynamic, cosmopolitan, enterprising, progressive, utilitarian and so on. Above all, he or she was to have faith in science and democracy, the secret of success of the advanced nations of the West. A few other magazines also appeared, expressing a spectrum of reformist views of the new intellectuals. Confucianism now came under heavy attack in the name of science and democracy. The slogan 'Down with Confucianism', chanted by radical students, carried with it a distinct iconoclasm as never seen before, though it did not mean an assault on Chinese culture in totality. Their activities were encouraged by the reforms at Beijing University, whose president, Cai Yuanpei, was a liberal with an anarchistic bent. The old order was discredited and repudiated. It was a time of intellectual dissent, of competing ideologies, and of cultural transformation. Indeed, an intellectual revolution was taking place in China.

When the May Fourth Incident of 1919 occurred in Beijing in protest against China's shabby treatment by the great powers at the Paris Peace Conference even before the Treaty of Versailles was signed on 28 June 1919, the intellectual revolution quickly became politicised. Not only did the new intellectuals emerge as a self-conscious force in Chinese public life, upholding the time-honoured tradition of remonstrance against the authorities on behalf of a passive people, but they desired to assert themselves as a modern nationalistic force in order to bring about change through a cultural transformation and, for many, political engagement also. It was against this background that some intellectuals were attracted to Marxism in 1919, leading to the formation of the Chinese Communist Party (CCP) two years later.

The turn of the decade saw a renewed revolutionary movement in south China. Sun Yatsen and his Nationalist Party (Guomindang, GMD) had secured a base in Guangzhou (Guangdong Province), where a military government was set up in opposition to the Beijing warlord regime. In 1923, Sun, having failed repeatedly to obtain Western support for his revolutionary cause, accepted aid from Soviet Russia and formed a united front with the fledgling Chinese Communist Party (CCP). By the time of Sun's death in March 1925, the GMD had been reorganised along Soviet lines and a Soviet-trained military academy established in Whampoa (outside Guangzhou). In July of that year, a self-proclaimed national government, which struck some foreign observers as the best administration in the entire country, was formed in Guangzhou. The Nationalist movement, highly indoctrinated with a powerful ideology, equipped with Soviet arms, and supported by patriotic students from south China, was fast developing. Anti-warlord and anti-imperialist at once, it was the only political force that seemed capable of achieving the goals of national unification and national independence.

However, like the Revolution of 1911, the Nationalist revolution was more political than social. The rural masses were not mobilised to a significant extent. Where they were mobilised, it was largely the work of the Communists operating within the framework of the united front. Peasant associations were formed in the rural areas, while a labour movement was afoot in Guangzhou and other provincial cities. But the CCP, small in number, was the junior partner in the alliance and was, moreover, under the influence of the Comintern and Soviet Russia. The ideological differences between the two parties were never out of sight, as the united front was intended to be no more than a temporary measure, despite common nationalistic concerns. Indeed, no sooner had the Nationalists consolidated themselves in the lower Yangzi region following the successes of the Northern Expedition in 1927 than a purge of the Communists was launched, which signalled the beginning of a counter-revolution. Many Communists were arrested and executed; others were forced to flee to the hinterland. The Nationalists then proceeded to dislodge the Beijing regime and proclaimed the National Government of China in Nanjing in the summer of 1928. China was once again reunified, albeit little more than nominally.

Over the next ten years, the Nationalists ruled China from Nanjing, but they effectively controlled less than one-third of the country. During the Northern Expedition, most of the warlords had been won over without a fight, but they owed little loyalty to the GMD, and less to Chiang Kaishek. They retained their powers, jealously guarding their regional or provincial interests. In the meantime, the GMD leadership was challenged by its own left wing and others who had broken away to form new political groups. Nanjing's position was precarious from the start.

The Nationalist movement had entered upon a new phase — that of political tutelage — during which the country and the people would be prepared for constitutional rule while Nanjing's leaders undertook a formidable task of national reconstruction. The idea of political tutelage was that of 'guided democracy', based as it was on the assumption that the Chinese people required a preparatory period in which to learn the practice of democracy before constitutional rule could commence. But the Nanjing decade turned out to be one of authoritarian rule, of continued chaos, political instability and ever-increasing foreign threat. Under combined domestic and external pressures, the GMD leaders discovered that the only way to keep themselves in power was to rely on the use of force, coercion and intimidation. Political tutelage, a euphemism for party dictatorship, became a source of political and intellectual dissent; it was not brought to an end until December 1946 when a constitution was adopted and promulgated.

While in government, the Nationalists had to confront a host of old and new problems. Some of these, such as chaos, political infighting, poverty, backwardness, the vastness of the country and its huge population, corruption at all levels of society (not just the government) — traditional problems that had brought down many previous regimes and which continued to plague the Nanjing government — were inherent in the Chinese situation. Others, such as the domineering personality of Chiang Kaishek, the militarisation of the ruling party, factionalism, official corruption and a lack of political will to attack vested interests and to solve China's socioeconomic problems were the fault of the new leadership.

In the end, the Nationalist revolution failed because it did not aspire to fundamental social change. The GMD, as a political party, did not have a class base. It did not represent the interests of either the landed gentry or the capitalists, as it claimed to represent the interests of all the citizens of the state in an 'all-people revolution'. In fact, it was an autonomous regime responsible only to itself and its leaders. Yet the support of both the landed gentry and the commercial bourgeoisie was needed for its survival. Consequently, the urban-based Nationalist government managed to neglect the countryside and all the pressing problems confronting the rural population. Despite some appreciable growth in the treaty ports and in some parts of rural China during the Nanjing decade, the gulf between the city and the countryside remained as wide as ever.

It was left to the CCP to continue the Chinese revolution for the people and by the people. The communist revolution had started in the 1920s. During its early phase it was allied to the GMD as a result of Comintern and Soviet influence. It was argued at the time that conditions in China were not ripe for a socialist revolution, not only because the bourgeoisie was still in the early stages of formation, but also because the proletariat was far too small to be the revolutionary vanguard. In order to promote revolution, it was necessary first for the CCP to support the 'bourgeois-democratic revolution' under the leadership of the GMD. Only when the 'bourgeois-democratic revolution' had been accomplished were the conditions ripe for a socialist revolution to be carried out by the CCP with the support of the proletariat and the peasantry.

The collapse of the united front, and the Nationalist purge of the Communists, split the Communist leadership into two distinct entities.

One was the CCP's Central Politburo under the leadership of Moscow-trained communists who went underground in Shanghai. The Politburo followed the Comintern tactics of strikes, sabotage and urban uprisings, using the city working class as the mainstay of support. On 1 August 1927, an uprising was launched at Nanchang, capital of Jiangxi Province. The Communists seized the city and held it for a few days before giving it up to government forces. The failure of the uprising, blamed on the party general secretary, Chen Duxiu, led to a change of leadership in Shanghai. The new leader, Qu Qiubai, a Stalin protege, held the position briefly before being ousted and replaced by Li Lisan in June 1929. Over the next few months, Li fomented strikes and sabotage and, in July 1930, launched the Changsha uprising, which proved to be another diaster. The failure of the 'Li Lisan line' led to Li's immediate downfall and the rise to power in January 1931 of Wang Ming (Chen Shaoyu) and Bo Gu (Qin Bangxian), who headed the 'international wing' of the CCP consisting of 28 returned students who had studied at Moscow's Sun Yatsen University from 1926 to 1930.

The other faction in the CCP leadership consisted of Mao Zedong and Zhu De, who pursued an independent course in the countryside of Hunan and Jiangxi Provinces. They adopted a different revolutionary strategy of mobilising the rural masses by addressing the problems of land tenure and landlord exploitation. In 1927 a revolutionary base was set up in Jinggangshan, a remote mountain region bordering on the provinces of Hunan and Jiangxi, and the Red Army was being formed from local peasants and vagabonds. In 1931 the Chinese Soviet Republic was established in Ruijin in southern Jiangxi. It was during this Jiangxi period that the Maoist strategy of an agrarian revolution originated. Local peasants were recruited through the appeals of a radical program of land confiscation and redistribution; they were to be the mainstay of the revolutionary force.

The Communists in Jiangxi were to survive a series of 'extermination campaigns' launched against them by the government between 1931 and 1934. On the fifth campaign, they were almost annihilated and were forced to go on the historic Long March — about 9500 kilometres — in October 1934. The Long March was, in the words of Edgar Snow, 'an Odyssey unequaled in modern times'.[1] It was one of the great exploits of military history, unparallelled in the last three centuries of world history. Of the approximately 100 000 men and 50 women who embarked on the tortuous trek with Mao Zedong, only about 8000 survived to arrive a year later in Yan'an, Shaanxi Province. When they reached Yan'an, they found a dreary and impoverished market town of around 10 000 people. But they used it as a new revolutionary base, from which they rebuilt their power and organised armed resistance against the Japanese behind enemy lines in an eight-year war (1937–45). It was in Yan'an that an extraordinary revolutionary spirit, characterised by hard work, discipline, frugality, altruism, self-sacrifice and self-reliance, was nurtured. The Yan'an spirit was underpinned by the Thought of Mao Zedong, which was to have a profound impact on the future of the communist movement.

Mao was an extraordinary revolutionary leader. When he was converted to Marxism in 1919, his understanding of it was informed by a revolt against China's old culture and traditions. He shared with the new intellectuals of the May Fourth era a hostility towards Confucianism, especially the traditional family, the privileged landed gentry and the social and economic inequality associated with it. He had been influenced by the liberal thought of Liang Qichao on the one hand and the anarchist thought of Liu Shipei on the other. Like Liang, Mao was a nationalist but, unlike him, did not believe in evolutionary change through gradual reforms. And, like the anarchists, Mao believed in progress, justice, equality and the role of the peasantry in the Chinese revolution.

Mao was a populist in the sense that he, unlike Sun Yatsen, went to the people, tried to understand their problems, and then mobilised them in support of revolution. He desired a revolution from below, one in which popular participation was imperative. One of his greatest contributions to revolutionary theory and strategy was his emphasis on the role of the peasantry in underdeveloped societies. He turned Marxism on its head by making it more relevant in a society where the bourgeoisie was least powerful. In his view, a Marxist revolution was possible in China not because of the strengths of the working class — the Chinese proletariat was in fact a very weak force — but because of 'the revolutionary potential' of the rural masses.

While acknowledging the importance of objective forces in socio-historical development, and subscribing to some extent to the deterministic view of the inevitability of a socialist future, Mao believed that the decisive factor in history was human consciousness — the ideas, determination and actions of people. Given these subjective forces and a correct ideology, as well as the leadership of the CCP, the Chinese revolution was a real possibility that did not depend on any predetermined levels of social and economic development. In other words, China's economic backwardness was no obstacle to revolution. On the contrary, the peasantry, once their 'proletarian consciousness' was aroused, could be a most powerful revolutionary force. In Mao's opinion, 'proletarian consciousness' was a potential inherent in the people as a whole, regardless of their social class. Everyone was capable of acquiring a true 'proletarian spirit' and a socialist world view through revolutionary action and ideological transformation. Thus the making of a socialist revolution in China was not a privilege of the industrial working class, but a task that could best be accomplished by a coalition of social forces, especially during a time of foreign aggression.

The Japanese invasion brought the external dimension of the Chinese revolution into sharp relief. A second united front was formed in 1937 between the CCP and the GMD in order to prosecute the War of Resistance successfully. But the Japanese advance could not be stopped, forcing the Nationalist government to retreat to Chongqing in Sichuan Province, the wartime capital. As a result, the CCP managed to fill the power vacuum in areas previously under GMD control and thereby provide military and political leadership. The brutality of the Japanese army also helped them to whip up Chinese nationalism and call on people of all classes to join in a grand alliance against the Japanese. The radical land policy of the Jiangxi period was shelved in some places, though in others land reforms in terms of rent reduction were effected. The communist revolution then assumed the character of a nationalistic peasant movement directed against the Japanese more than the class enemy of China.

The communist revolution was not abandoned, however; it gathered fresh momentum as soon as the Japanese had surrendered. Yet it must be noted that the fundamental social change envisaged by the Communists did not include the immediate elimination of the bourgeoisie. Mao Zedong had conceived of the Chinese revolution in terms of a two-stage development. The first stage was that of 'new democracy', the Maoist version of the Marxist concept of 'bourgeois-democratic revolution', in which the capitalists were to make a contribution to China's economic development and the creation of a genuine national market and polity. This stage was suited to the particular needs of China and to the conditions of colonial and semi-colonial societies in general. It was, Mao argued, 'vastly different from the democratic revolutions of Europe and America in that it results not in a dictatorship of the bourgeoisie but in a dictatorship of the united front of all the revolutionary classes under the leadership of the proletariat'.[2] When the 'bourgeois-democratic revolution' was completed, the conditions would be ripe for the second stage — socialist revolution. Yet the conditions for socialism had not yet ripened by 1949. When the establishment of the People's Republic was proclaimed in that year, Mao proclaimed not a dictatorship of the proletariat, not a socialist state, but rather a 'people's democratic dictatorship'. This was an ambiguous term to be sure, but one that nevertheless conveyed the Maoist view that the Chinese state was then based on a coalition of four social classes: the national bourgeoisie and the petty bourgeoisie as well as the proletariat and the peasantry. Socialism in China, which would be under the leadership of the proletariat, was to take place later.

The communist revolution succeeded in destroying the landlord gentry class and reshaping the face of rural China. With the implementation of a series of land reforms in the post-1949 era, landlord exploitation became a thing of the past, and new social relationships were established. The communist revolution also succeeded in resolving a perennial problem of chaos and foreign threat. Not only was China reunified by 1950, but the conditions that had been conducive to military rule and foreign intrusion were removed. For the best part of the 1950s, political stability and internal order were restored, the government was good, and the country was cemented into a powerful modern nation-state with a strong sense of national purpose.

But the communist revolution was a failure in other respects. Like the Nationalists before them, the Communist leaders had inherited the legacy of the past, and were faced with some of those problems which had bedevilled previous regimes: intraparty strife, power struggles, a huge population, poverty and a high illiteracy rate among the people. They succumbed to the same forces that the CCP had sought to eliminate many decades before — authoritarianism, corruption, bureaucratism and so on. Worst of all, they failed to establish the rule of law, a responsible government that guaranteed personal freedoms and the rights of the citizens of the state. The violence that accompanied the Cultural Revolution of the 1960s, and more recently the Beijing tragedy of 1989, illustrates the continued reliance on force as a means of conflict resolution. Clearly, China's leaders have not stripped themselves of the 'feudal' thinking that they had attacked.

After decades of revolution, China still lacks a system whereby political succession, or transfer of political power, could be achieved in a legal and peaceful manner. The ideas of political pluralism and power-sharing still evade the present Chinese leadership. The dominant state idea remains authoritarian. In short, the Chinese revolution has still not achieved the kind of liberation of which the advanced countries of the West speak — that is, personal freedoms. While China is today free from foreign control, it is a far cry from the prosperous and democratic society for which many revolutionary leaders sacrificed their lives.

Guide to further reading

Eastman, Lloyd, *The Abortive Revolution: China under Nationalist Rule, 1927–1937*, Harvard University Press, Cambridge, Mass., 1974
   An authoritative work critical of the Nationalist leadership during the Nanjing period.
Esherick, Joseph W., *Reform and Revolution in China: The 1911 Revolution in Hunan and Hubei*, University of California Press, Berkeley, 1976
   An excellent socio-political study of the revolution, concentrating on the gentry and reformist elite.

Fung, Edmund S.K., *The Military Dimension of the Chinese Revolution: The New Army and its Role in the Revolution of 1911*, Australian National University Press, Canberra, 1980

A scholarly work on military reform in the late Qing period and the role of the New Army in the Revolution of 1911.

Johnson, Chalmers A., *Peasant Nationalism and Communist Power: The Emergence of Revolutionary China 1937–1945*, Stanford University Press, Stanford, 1962

A provocative thesis on the nature of Chinese communism and the reasons for the ultimate victory of the Communists during the war against Japan.

Seldon, Mark, *The Yenan Way in Revolutionary China*, Harvard University Press, Cambridge, Mass., 1971

A scholarly work which challenges the Johnson theory on the nature of Chinese communism during the War of Resistance by emphasising the land reforms introduced in the rural areas under Communist control.

Snow, Edgar, *Red Star over China*, Random House, New York, 1938

Among an enormous amount of material on the CCP in the 1930s, this contains an extremely interesting and informative autobiography of Mao Zedong, as told to the American journalist, Edgar Snow, in 1937.

Notes

1 Snow, Edgar, *Red Star over China*, Random House, New York, 1938, p. 177.
2 Quoted in Meisner, Maurice, *Mao's China: A History of the People's Republic*, Free Press, New York, 1977, pp. 60–61.

18 | The Indonesian revolution

The rolling tide of Japanese imperialism reached Indonesia in early 1942 and the fragile colonial hegemony of the Dutch collapsed forever. Seven days after Japanese troops landed on Java, the Netherlands Indies commander-in-chief surrendered and the Japanese began a systematic process of dismantling the Dutch empire. The Dutch population was interned, the Dutch language was banned and the new authoridies set about teaching Japanese and otherwise imposing their image on what they imagined to be the malleable Indonesians. As the war drew on, the physical signs of colonialism also began to disappear. The prim settlements of houseproud colonial expatriates decayed under the drab war economy, railway lines were pulled up and shipped to Burma and forests were plundered for fuel and timber. The tea plantations which had once supplied a quarter of Europe could no longer reach their markets and the once-prized shrubs were grubbed up in their thousands, to be replaced with castor, rami and other crops to serve the war economy.

The Japanese occupation of Indonesia, lasting until August 1945, was a fearsome, uncertain and sometimes tragic time for Indonesians, but it was only the first half of a decade of disruption. On 17 August, two days after the Japanese surrendered, Indonesian nationalists declared their country's independence, heralding four and a half years of fighting and negotiation with the Dutch, who had rallied for a time after their defeats in Europe and Asia. The protagonists fought a protracted war, which ranged from ferocious street fighting and bitter guerrilla operations in mountain and jungle to tedious stalemate and distasteful compromise until a grudging final settlement was reached at the end of 1949.

The way people think of the Indonesian revolution has changed during the half-century since it took place. Hindsight gives us the chance to view the revolution in context, not only as a consequence of what came before, but also as an influence on what came after. To the Dutch at the time, the two half-decades of occupation and revolution were a single tragedy, the destruction of a colonial endeavour which dated back to the early seventeenth century, and they brooded resentfully on what might have been. To Indonesians, the decade was split by the gleaming symbol of independence, and they responded by celebrating 17 August, and even the 17th of every month, as a day of national pride. For each of them, the 1940s was a time when history suddenly changed direction. Historians at first agreed, and early accounts of the revolution bristle with excitement at the drama of the struggle and the significance of the issues at stake. In the 1990s, however, different things impress us. In an age when there is hardly a formal colony left on the face of the globe, we can say with confidence that Indonesia would have become independent sooner or later. More important to us now is to understand the form which independence took, the shape of the politics which have governed Indonesia since 1945; it owes many of its contours to the experience of the struggle for independence. The growing trend towards regional economic integration, moreover, draws our attention to the remarkable process by which the peoples of the archipelago became Indonesians in the first place.

The revolution which made Indonesia was a revolution in the minds of people as much as it was an armed conflict. The main obstacle to eventual Indonesian independence was not the Dutch, although they were no mean adversaries, but the novelty of the idea of Indonesia. Each of the other Asian countries discussed in this book entered the modern era with a long and proud tradition of nationhood. Despite this sense of identity, three of them — China, Korea and Vietnam — have spent long periods divided into hostile, rival states. Scholars may debate whether the sense of common identity which bound, say, the Vietnamese or the Chinese was nationalist in the classical sense, but the political and cultural frameworks within which the modern nations of China and Japan developed were ancient entities. It is all the more remarkable, then, that the sprawling Indonesian archipelago, home to hundreds of disparate ethnic groups from two main ancestral stocks, the Austronesians in the west and the Melanesians in the east, should have become a nation. Until the Dutch arrived, no empire had ever united more than a small portion of the region under a single jurisdiction. Even the name Indonesia was an invention of European anthropologists in the late nineteenth century. What created Indonesia was the sudden realisation by the people we now call Indonesians that a large, united country offered them the best chance of solving the numerous problems of existence in the modern world. In doing so, they changed the balance of power in Southeast Asia and created what is now the world's fourth most populous nation.

Dutch colonialism played a key role in clearing the way for Indonesian nationalism by destroying or crippling the indigenous states which might, under radically different circumstances, have formed the basis for nations in their own right. During their long, slow conquest of the archipelago, the Dutch confronted and defeated one state after another. The sea warriors of Ternate and Tidore were curbed in the seventeeth century. The powerful Javanese state of Mataram was steadily ground down and reduced in territory until its heartland was dismembered in the mid-eighteenth century. The rich trading principalities of the Sumatra coast succumbed during the nineteenth century, the toughest of them all, the proudly Muslim state of Aceh, finally going under in a 30-year welter of blood which lasted until early this century. Then it was simply a matter of completing Dutch administrative penetration of the mountains and jungles in the interior of large islands like Kalimantan (Borneo), where forest tribes were not in a position to offer more than brief resistance. The fate of indigenous states under the Dutch varied enormously. Some were utterly destroyed, like Banda, whose people were exterminated in the seventeenth century for opposing the Dutch nutmeg monopoly. Others survived, especially in remote corners of the archipelago, because their rulers abdicated military power, followed Dutch administrative advice and generally offered no threat to colonial authority. Some were actively sustained by the Dutch, who realised that using traditional rulers as the agents of their rule softened the appearance of colonialism. Collaboration with the Dutch did not necessarily taint these states morally — capable rulers could retain their own self-respect and a degree of influence over government — but collaboration was a poisoned chalice nonetheless because it created the habits and structures of dependence, leaving the old indigenous states financially, militarily and politically unfit for life without Dutch backing. One way or another, therefore, colonial rule fatally weakened the old political order in the archipelago, opening the way for new structures.

There was nothing predestined, however, about the extent of the Dutch empire. Dutch colonial authorities followed their economic interests — spices at first, later coffee, tea and sugar, and finally rubber and oil — and in doing so cast a proprietorial net over much of the archipelago, but the final outline of the Netherlands Indies depended more on Dutch negotiations with their colonial neighbours, Britain, Australia, Portugal, Spain and America, than it did on the ethnic and social make-up of the people whose allegiances were being divided. The border between British Malaya and Dutch Sumatra ran along the Straits of Melaka, dividing a region that had formed a single economic and cultural unit for 2000 years. The almost-straight line which divided Dutch New Guinea from the German and British (later Australian) parts of the island separated Papuan tribes who, though they expended a good deal of energy in warring with each other, at least had more in common with each other than they had with, say, the urban Muslim merchants of the Sumatra coast. The simple destruction of older alternatives to the Netherlands Indies, therefore, was not sufficient on its own to create Indonesia.

The first glimpses of an archipelago which was neither under Dutch rule nor under the sultans and rajas of the pre-colonial era came in the late nineteenth century. The colonial endeavour was growing increasingly complex. Whereas once colonial profits had depended largely on monopolistic trading practices and on extracting hard work for little pay from Javanese peasants, global competition now demanded increasing technical expertise and administrative efficiency on the part of private firms in the Indies, and it demanded increasingly sophisticated intervention in the economy by government. In the Netherlands, moreover, public opinion had become convinced by the beginning of the twentieth century that Holland had a debt of honour to repay to the Indies for the centuries of exploitation, and the colonial authorities responded to this by launching programs dedicated to raising indigenous welfare in areas such as health and education. Although the Ministry of Colonies continued to keep a firm hand on the basic principles of colonial policy, the Netherlands Indies increasingly appeared in world affairs as a distinct legal identity. It became possible to imagine that the interests of the Netherlands might not always prevail in colonial decision-making. The colonial connection still had immense practical significance, as well as deep emotional meaning to the Dutch, but to the outside observer the Netherlands Indies appeared to have embarked on a journey towards separation from what colonial settlers still called the Fatherland.

The colony's gradually increasing distinctiveness in international affairs was parallelled by a growing internal resilience. For the complex governmental tasks of the early twentieth century, a new cadre of capable officials was needed, and to find it the colonial government turned to Indonesians. An expanding education system took bright Indonesians and turned them into clerks, physicians, lawyers and engineers, and the colonial bureaucracy opened its lower doors to them. By 1928, a quarter of a million Indonesians worked in the colonial civil service, making up 90 per cent of the total staff. Although these Indonesians generally served only in the lower levels of the colonial bureaucracy, their experience of education and their access to some of the levers of power gave them the makings of an elite status. As they gained experience, too, the conventions of colonial discrimination which reserved top administrative positions for Europeans came to appear increasingly unreasonable. Exacting standards at higher levels of schooling ensured that the best Indonesian graduates matched their counterparts anywhere in the world, even though the absolute number of such graduates was tiny in proportion to the population. As the twentieth century wore on, this elite chafed under the legal and social discrimination embedded in the colonial order: legal discrimination which gave Europeans preferential treatment under the criminal code, economic discrimination which saw European officials taking home salaries vastly greater than those enjoyed by Indonesians doing exactly the same work, and the simple but galling social discrimination which excluded Indonesians from fashionable clubs and swimming pools. The existence of this elite made it possible to imagine, for the first time, that the Netherlands Indies could exist without the Dutch connection. The disadvantages that it suffered gave it a powerful reason to want that connection severed.

It was this elite, too, which determined that the framework for independence would be the entire territory encompassed by the Netherlands Indies. This was no automatic conclusion: in the history of decolonisation, large colonial units — British India, French Indochina, Spanish America — have commonly broken up into smaller independent states. Like many other colonies, the Netherlands Indies had its potential fracture lines — between islands or ethnic groups, and along the frontier between directly ruled territories and the surviving subordinate native states — but from early on in the movement against the Dutch, the elite decided to seek independence as a single country, to which they gave the name Indonesia. The key event was the Second National Youth Congress in 1928, which formally accepted Indonesia as the nationalist goal and adopted what became the national language, flag and anthem. This enthusiasm for unity had several sources. Firstly, the political traditions of the archipelago recognised the weakness of divided action. Seeing the Dutch as a powerful and cunning opponent, the new movement reasoned that only united action could remove colonial rule. The elite aspired, too, to make Indonesia an important voice in world affairs, and they recognised the importance of size in international political influence. This was a lesson learnt directly from Dutch observers, who resisted the loss of the colony on the grounds that it would reduce the status of the Netherlands in international affairs 'to the level of Denmark'. A second reason for preferring Indonesia as the framework for independence was that the new elite consisted of men and women trained to be a part of a modern, Westernised society. Chafing under the discrimination which prevented them from rising to the top in the Netherlands Indies, few of them favoured constricting their own prospects in just one of a number of separate successor states. Moreover, such successor states were likely in several cases to be based on the remnants of earlier kingdoms and sultanates, and this would have given greater political power to aristocratic and princely forces from the old order. In a united Indonesia, the remnant aristocracies would be reduced to regional elites, forced to participate in national politics on terms defined by the centre.

The mass of the Indonesian people, too, found much to resent in colonial rule. For Muslims, a large majority of the population in most regions, rule by Christians was basically unacceptable, though the passion with which Muslims registered this unacceptability varied enormously from region to region; peasants throughout the archipelago had suffered from systematic exploitation and control and town-dwellers from neglect by colonial authorities. We should not imagine that Dutch colonial rule, especially in the twentieth century, was irredeemably wicked: the colonial service contained many dedicated, unselfish officials who regarded the welfare of Indonesians as their highest goal; the broad thrust of colonial policy, at least after 1900, took explicit account of the impact of policies on the Indonesians; and the peace and order which colonial rule brought came to be valued in retrospect almost as a golden age during the turbulent politics of the 1940s, 1950s and 1960s. Even at its best, however, the colonial order remained authoritarian and condescending, unable to recognise the growing maturity and capacity of Indonesians to which Dutch rule itself had contributed. To all those Indonesians who thought about such issues, it was abundantly clear that Dutch rule would not end of its own accord, but that its demise would have to be struggled for.

But how to win independence? The question of strategy vexed the nationalist movement until the final formal transfer of sovereignty by the Dutch in 1949, and the history of the nationalist movement is in many ways a history of experimentation with techniques for winning independence. So dominant, in fact, was the question of strategy, that the question of the political form of independent Indonesia tended to be set to one side, leaving a host of issues unresolved by the time independence was finally achieved.

The earliest nationalist exploration of strategy was in the form of an intellectual questioning of the basis of colonialism. Budi Utomo (Glorious Endeavour), founded in 1908 and generally regarded as the first nationalist organisation, included in its aims equality of opportunity for Indonesians passing through the colonial education system. The most celebrated example of this direct questioning of colonialism is a sarcastic essay by Suwardi Suryaningrat, published under the title, 'If I were a Dutchman'. Suwardi, like many Indonesians, was deeply offended in 1915 when the Dutch organised festivities in the colony to celebrate the centenary of Holland's liberation from Napoleonic rule. 'If I were a Dutchman,' he wrote, 'I would not organize an independence celebration in a country where the independence of the people has been stolen.' Disturbing though this rebuke may have been to liberal-minded Dutchmen, it brought no change to colonial policy. Neither, on the other hand, did the earliest mass mobilisation against colonial rule go any distance towards dislodging the Dutch. The Sarekat Islam, or Islamic Association, emerged in 1911 or 1912 out of an earlier organisation set up to organise indigenous Indonesian batik traders in Central Java in competition with their Chinese counterparts, but under the charismatic leadership of Umar Said Cokroaminoto it developed into a mass movement with a large following amongst the people of Java. Its political aims were diffuse, and its leadership divided into many factions, radical and conservative, religious and secular, so that it was never able to launch a sustained political program. The broad public appeal it enjoyed at first, moreover, simply prompted the colonial authorities to tighten political repression. The experience of Sarekat Islam, however, established clearly that the Dutch would not crumble before popular dissent and confirmed the place of strategy at the centre of nationalist debate.

During the following decades, three broad strategies emerged. The first of these was confrontation with the Dutch. If the mass of the Indonesian people, it was believed, simply stood up to their colonial rulers, then weight of numbers and force of principle would see them victorious. The Indonesian Communist Party (PKI) adopted this strategy in its most enthusiastic form, launching abortive rebellions against the Dutch in 1926 and 1927, but the total failure of the uprisings led later nationalist politicians, especially Sukarno and his Indonesian Nationalist Party (PNI), to adopt a more careful strategy based on non-co-operation. Armed rebellion might have failed, it seemed, but if Indonesians staunchly refused to have anything to do with the colonial power, it would be bound to wither. Even this gentler strategy, however, foundered during the early 1930s, when the efficient colonial political police arrested and gaoled or exiled Sukarno and his colleagues. Although confrontation remained dear to the hearts of many nationalist leaders, the prospects for any kind of enforced removal of the Dutch seemed very remote.

The evident strength of colonial power made a second strategy of co-operation with the Dutch seem prudent to many. Dutch intransigence notwithstanding, there were some encouraging signs in the 1920s and 1930s of progress at least towards greater autonomy. Not only were the neighbouring colonies of Burma and the Philippines moving rapidly towards internal self-government, but powerful forces in the Dutch colonial establishment were moving towards a partial separation of the colony from Holland. Perhaps the most encouraging sign was the formation in 1918 of a kind of proto-parliament in the colony, called the Volksraad, or People's Council. In the Volksraad chamber, Indonesian representatives could freely raise matters of concern, and even exercised some legislative power, though the weighting of non-native representation was against them. Without the intervention of World War II, the Volksraad might well have become the beneficiary of a more extensive transfer of power to Indonesian hands, but for the late 1920s and most of the 1930s it remained a rather circumscribed and ineffective watchdog, sadly second best to confrontation in the eyes of most nationalists.

Under such circumstances, there was much appeal in a third strategy, which was to retreat from direct politics, postponing the struggle for independence in favour of social upliftment. This was a strategy which recognised that there was more to national fulfilment than simply removing the Dutch, and it was an element of the programs of all major nationalist organisations. The organisation which adopted it with greatest consistency, however, was the Muhammadiyah, founded in 1912; its program emphasised the promotion of Muslim religious life and the provision of education which combined Islamic religious principles and the best of Western science and technology. The Muhammadiyah made no political demands, but it set out to equip Indonesians morally, intellectually and technically for the rigours of life in the twentieth century and so made a major contribution to sustaining nationalist awareness.

So it might have gone on until global pressures for decolonisation eventually caught up with the Dutch. The Japanese invasion of 1942, however, swept the colonial order away before that could happen, confirming, if nothing else, that armed confrontation was indeed an effective way of removing the Dutch, if only it could be arranged. Japanese military government was a time of trial for all Indonesians: the new rulers were a largely unknown quantity with a style of operation very different from that of the Dutch. Gone were the meticulous legalists and slow but capable bureaucrats of the colonial era; in their place were military men in a hurry, ignorant of the country, dangerous when crossed, aware that in order to win the war Japan had to win quickly, and above all convinced that energy and spirit could overcome all obstacles. New political, economic and social initiatives flashed on the scene; the glittering but indistinct prospect of independence was held before the Indonesian people, never quite defined, never quite promised, but never dismissed with the resounding finality which the nationalists had been accustomed to hear from the Dutch. Fear and a sense of opportunity helped persuade a majority of nationalists that wherever the Japanese military machine might be carrying them it was at least in the general direction of independence, and for most of the occupation Indonesia's leaders lent their skills in support of the Japanese, mostly as part of one or other publicity or mass mobilisation organisation.

As the war turned against Japan, this optimism seemed both justified and unwise. Facing defeat, the Japanese began preparations for independence in Indonesia, preparations which accelerated as the Japanese army retreated. For Indonesian nationalists, the last months of the war were a race against time: would independence be granted before the impending Allied victory? When independence day was set for late August, the consummation of nationalist striving seemed imminent. Japan, however, collapsed too soon, surrendering abruptly on 15 August 1945 after the bombs fell on Hiroshima and Nagasaki. Nationalist disappointment and frustration were tempered by two considerations. First, Japanese-sponsored independence on the eve of Japan's defeat was hardly likely to count for much in international affairs, and in any case independence as a gift from Japan was less desirable than independence seized by the Indonesian people themselves. Second, and more important, at the time of the surrender, the victorious Allied forces, which included Dutch contingents, were far away from Java and other centres of power in

Indonesia. Indonesian nationalists were left suddenly with what seemed like a golden opportunity to take their future into their own hands and to declare an independence which was by the grace of neither Japanese nor Dutch. After intense discussions in the 48 hours following the surrender, the leading nationalists, Sukarno and Mohammed Hatta, agreed to declare independence in a brief ceremony in Sukarno's garden in Jakarta on the morning of 17 August 1945.

Independence quickly took on enormous symbolism: in the new Indonesian Republic and in Sukarno and Hatta as its president and vice-president, the Indonesian people had a tangible symbol of the final achievement of freedom. Independence, however, had virtually no content. The Japanese remained in formal control as temporary agents of the Allies, and the new 'government' had no army, no money, no officials and no territory. The construction and acquisition of all these attributes of statehood took place during the next four years and the conduct of the revolution thus had enormous impact on the basic institutions of politics in independent Indonesia.

The sudden seizure of independence also left the political identity of the new state largely undecided. During the pre-war independence struggle, the question of the ideological identity of independent Indonesia had been set to one side. Not only was the question of strategy more pressing, but the issue of ideology threatened to destroy the already fragile unity of the nationalist movement. Within that movement, however, were many opposing streams of thought. There was a liberal stream, made up of intellectual decendents of Suwardi Suryaningrat, who saw the creation of a Western-style liberal parliamentary democracy in Indonesia as a logical consequence of Indonesia's encounter with modernity. Alongside this stream, however, was a powerful nationalist left which regarded liberal democracy as an aspect of colonialism and which saw socialism or communism as the only philosophy which could bring justice and prosperity to the Indonesian people. Other nationalists, though not of the left, rejected liberal democracy because it seemed to institutionalise division and conflict; these nationalists preferred strong, even authoritarian, leadership and an active cultivation of distinctive Indonesian political values. Many Muslims, for their part, aspired to create either an Islamic state or at least a state in which Islamic principles would receive special protection and encouragement.

These streams of thought had not yet coalesced into rigid political blocs, but the potential for deep division within the nationalist movement was so clear that the small nationalist committee drafting the new republic's provisional constitution chose to avoid a firm decision on the philosophical basis of the state, accepting instead a suggestion by Sukarno that the Indonesian Republic should be based on five principles which, he said, could be accepted by all Indonesians, no matter what their political orientation. These five principles were enshrined in the preamble to the constitution and were given the name Pancasila, which means 'five pillars':

- belief in God;
- national unity;
- humanitarianism;
- people's sovereignty;
- social justice and prosperity.

Although Muslims were unhappy that the Pancasila referred to 'God' (*Tuhan*) — thus equating the God of Christianity and Islam's Allah — and communists were not pleased with any recognition of God, the vagueness of the Pancasila, together with the pressing need for unity at a crucial time in Indonesia's struggle for freedom, led them to accept it.

The course of the revolution against the Dutch, however, was still very difficult. In many parts of the country, nationalists were able to cajole or intimidate the demoralised Japanese into giving up power, and even into handing over weapons, but the republic was unable to prevent Allied (mainly British Indian) troops from landing in the main cities of Java and Sumatra and winning control of most of the other islands. The heaviest and most destructive fighting was for the East Javanese capital, Surabaya, in November 1945, but even there the Indonesians were forced to give way. Hesitant nonetheless about risking their troops in a war in the countryside, the British pressed the Dutch and Indonesians to negotiate towards an agreed independence program and the two sides finally reached a grudging settlement in the mountain resort of Linggajati in West Java in November 1946. Although agreeing in principle that Indonesia should become independent as a federation of the republic (on Java and Sumatra) with new federal states in Borneo and eastern Indonesia, the brief rapport between the two antagonists soon disintegrated in a spate of misunderstanding, accusation and counter-accusation, and ended in a Dutch military operation which seized half the republic's territory on Java, along with the richest regions of Sumatra. In the seventeen-month ceasefire which followed, another treaty was signed and broken, much like that of Linggajati, before the Dutch launched a second attack in December 1948 designed to wipe the republic off the face of the archipelago.

The Dutch miscalculated. Although the republic's provisional capital at Yogyakarta in Central Java was captured, along with Sukarno, Hatta and most of the cabinet, guerrilla resistance in the countryside quickly bogged down the Dutch military machine. The United States, fearing that a protracted guerrilla war would open the way to communist revolution, successfully pressed the Dutch to restore the republic and to hand independence to it in the last days of 1949.

The revolution left Indonesia with a complex legacy. First, it compounded the destruction previously wrought by the Japanese occupation. The armed struggle left much of Indonesia's economic infrastructure in ruins, making the tasks of post-revolutionary construction difficult. Even more important, it left the country's civilian bureaucracy weakened and demoralised. The physical destruction and displacement of people as a result of hostilities was partly responsible. In the early revolution, however, the bureaucracy had also had to face a storm of popular fury over its role in Japanese oppression, which had included the arbitrary seizure of rice from peasants and the enforced recruitment of labourers for work on defensive and other projects under conditions where tens of thousands died of disease and malnutrition. The bureaucrats, too, most of them former officials of the colonial regime, were widely suspected of favouring a return to colonialism. The result was an outbreak of social revolution in the countryside of Java and Sumatra which saw hundreds of local officials killed or chased away and replaced by popular but administratively inexperienced local leaders. This weakening of the bureaucracy opened the way to the emergence of powerful rival political forces, foremost amongst them the army.

The army had come into existence on the initiative of the new republican government soon after the declaration of independence. During the first months of the revolution it had been kept in the background: the republic's leaders were reluctant to send a barely formed army against the battle-hardened Allies and indeed hoped that refraining from violence might make a swift, peaceful transition to independence possible. From late 1945, however, the republic's defence ministry under Deputy Prime Minister Amir Syarifuddin devoted a large proportion of the national budget to building up the armed forces in order to prevent the Dutch from simply marching in and seizing the country. Even 50 per cent or more of the budget, however, was not enough to maintain what rapidly developed into an army of half a million men on Java, and both local units and the high command began developing techniques of self-reliance, funding their operations by trading ventures and by levying local taxes, so that a tradition began to emerge of military autonomy from the civilian authorities.

Within the army, too, there were many who were deeply sceptical of the government's willingness to negotiate with the Dutch. Believing in their own strength, despite successive defeats by the Dutch, they saw any compromise or hesitation as a betrayal, and gradually came to see themselves as the only true guardians of the principles of independence. This feeling was strengthened especially by the Dutch capture of the civilian cabinet in December 1948, after which the army fought on its own to defend the nation, and indeed played a crucial role in preventing the Dutch from turning their early military victories into a political triumph. A major legacy of the revolution, therefore, was a large and experienced armed force which enjoyed a strong sense of its own importance, a tradition of independence from the government and a solid scepticism about the capacity and nationalist commitment of civilian politicians. Especially in the absence of an effective bureaucracy, this was to be the basis for repeated military intervention in politics after 1949.

Political parties, however, also benefited from the revolution to a considerable extent. The political restrictions of Dutch and Japanese times were lifted, allowing parties to campaign widely and freely for public support. The weakness of the bureaucracy enabled parties, especially when they were in government, to place their own members in key administrative positions, where they remained well into the 1950s. The continuing threat to national independence, moreover, led to the formation of hundreds of 'people's armies' *(lasykar)*, irregular armed units outside the official armed forces. The *lasykar* remained apart from the army partly because they mostly had less military training and less respect for formal military conventions than did the official units. They also stayed separate because many of them were committed not just to independence but to a particular kind of independence, leftist, rightist, Islamic or other, whereas the army was officially neutral on such issues. As a result, many of the *lasykar* were affiliated to varying degrees with political parties, giving many parties what amounted to an armed auxiliary with which to strengthen their position in national politics or their authority in particular regions.

No single party, however, took charge of the revolution. The Socialist Party, which provided the country's first Prime Minister, Sutan Syahrir (1945–47), was strong amongst urban intellectuals but lacked a base in the countryside. It was, moreover, heavily infiltrated by the Communist Party, and indeed the Defence Minister Amir Syarifuddin, who became Prime Minister in July 1947, turned out later to have been a PKI member since 1927. The Communist Party's strategy in fact contrasts sharply with that of its counterparts in Vietnam and China. At the start of the revolution, the PKI shared the widespread elite belief that Indonesians were not prepared to fight an uncompromising revolutionary war. Instead the party aimed first to secure independence and only then to seek radical social change. In order to make the republic as acceptable as possible to international opinion, especially that of the Allies, the early governments which the communists supported and of which they were clandestine members presented as mild as possible a face, promising to guarantee the safety of foreign economic interests in the country and accepting the idea of a federal Indonesia in which Dutch influence would persist. Only having secured independence, they believed, would they then be able to push ahead with a more radical social agenda.

This strategy was enormously unpopular amongst the mass of the Indonesian people, particularly once it had proved ineffective. The banner of uncompromising revolution was taken up instead by opposition politicians, especially a maverick former PKI leader, Tan Malaka, who assembled a huge coalition of social and political forces in protest against what he saw as the government's betrayal of the revolution. Tan Malaka, however, lacked the backing of a party organisation, and he was unable to turn his mass support into political authority before he was arrested and gaoled by the government.

Only after a constitutional sleight of hand — in which Amir Syarifuddin resigned the prime ministership in January 1948, expecting to be re-appointed, only to find his rival the vice-president, Mohammed Hatta, appointed in his place — did the PKI adopt the rhetoric of revolutionary struggle. But this was too late for the party. Not only did its conversion look suspiciously like political opportunism, but others such as the radical Muslims in West Java headed by S.M. Kartosuwiryo already had much more impressive revolutionary credentials. Still more important, the party had grown accustomed to government patronage and protection. When the Hatta government began to demobilise leftist army units and to channel funding towards its own supporters, the party saw its power base shrink without any immediate prospects for recovery.

Uncertain of tactics, the party accepted the leadership of a new leader, Musso, who had actually been a leader of the party at the time of the 1926–27 uprisings and who had spent several years underground in the Indies during the 1930s. Clandestine party members in other organisations came into the open and the party adopted a thoroughly militant program, calling not just for confrontation of the Dutch but for a revolutionary transformation of Indonesian society and for the installation of a workers' state. The workers had indeed much to complain about as a Dutch blockade of Central Java attempted to strangle the republic into submission. Savage austerity measures by the Hatta government led to mass unemployment, while inflation pushed the price of food and other goods to unprecedented heights.

In this environment of economic decay, political tension and national crisis, tempers exploded in the East Javanese town of Madiun. After days of intensifying skirmishes between leftist and rightist army units around the town, local communists abruptly declared a soviet republic. Forced to choose between disowning their colleagues and embarking on revolution, Musso, Amir Syarifuddin and their colleagues chose the latter, launching a stinging attack on the alleged treason of Sukarno and Hatta and calling for a workers' revolution. A brief but bloody civil war followed, with leftists massacring Muslims in regions they controlled and

Muslims in turn massacring party members as government troops crushed the revolt. Musso and Amir Syarifuddin were killed in the fighting and the party's prospects for the rest of the revolution were utterly destroyed. Paradoxically, the main effect of the Madiun uprising was to help persuade the United States that the Hatta government, having defeated communists in battle, could be entrusted with independence, and United States pressure on the Dutch to withdraw after the second military action of late 1948 was in large part based on American confidence in the republic as a bulwark against communism.

Even so, the independence which the Dutch grudgingly acknowledged in December 1949 was qualified. Indonesia remained within a loose Netherlands–Indonesian Union, continued Dutch military and business interests were guaranteed and, most galling for the nationalists, the Dutch retained control of West New Guinea, previously an integral part of the colony, on the grounds that its inhabitants were ethnically unrelated to other Indonesians and would face no more than a new kind of colonialism if they were transferred to Indonesian rule.

The national revolution won Indonesia its independence, but it left a great deal of unfinished business. During the 1950s and after, Indonesians had to grapple with the issue of their country's ideological and philosophical basis, with the struggle for power between older but weakened institutions such as the bureaucracy and newer forces forged in the heat of the revolution, with the running sore of bad relations with the Dutch over West New Guinea (now Irian Jaya), and with social tensions and antagonisms deeper than ever after the decade of destruction.

Guide to further reading

The classic account of Indonesia's struggle for independence, and still a good read, is Kahin, George McTurnan, *Nationalism and Revolution in Indonesia*, Cornell University Press, Ithaca, NY, 1952. Scholars working piece by piece on Kahin's overall picture of the rise of Indonesian nationalism have found a good deal to challenge in the detail of his interpretation and information, without dramatically altering the broad way we approach the problem.

Amongst the more important works on aspects of the movement are Legge, J.D., *Sukarno: A Political Biography*, Penguin, Harmondsworth, 1973; Ingleson, John, *Road to Exile: The Indonesian Nationalist Movement 1927–1934*, Heinemann, Singapore, 1979; and Takashi Shiraishi, *An Age in Motion: Popular Radicalism in Java, 1912–1926*, Cornell University Press, Ithaca, N.Y., 1990.

A particlarly stimulating study which sets Indonesian nationalism in the context of nationalism in general is Anderson, Benedict, *Imagined*

Communities: Reflections on the Origins and Spread of Nationalism, Verso, London, 1983.

On the years of revolution itself, Kahin's work has been supplanted as a standard text by Reid, Anthony J.S., *The Indonesian National Revolution, 1945–1950*, Longman, Melbourne, 1974.

Anderson, Benedict R.O'G., *Java in a Time of Revolution: Occupation and Resistance, 1944–1946*, Cornell University Press, Ithaca, N.Y.,1972, is a strong evocation of the struggle over strategy in the early part of the revolution, while Frederick, William H., *Visions and Heat: The Making of the Indonesian Revolution*, Ohio University Press, Athens, Oh., 1988 describes the origins of the revolution in the city of Surabaya.

19 | Indochina to 1954

The first Europeans to arrive in Vietnam were the Portuguese in 1535. In 1615 a permanent Catholic mission was established, to which the French missionary priest Alexander of Rhodes came in 1626. Though he was expelled from the country four years later, Rhodes managed not only to establish a thriving Catholic community in Tonkin, but also to perfect a system of romanisation for Vietnamese, known as *quoc ngu*, which remains the writing system used to this day (see Chapter 37).

Responsibility for the Catholic evangelisation of Vietnam was given over to the French Society of Foreign Missions, established in 1664, the year the French East India Company was founded. A close link between Christianity and commerce was to mark the next two centuries of French contact with Vietnam. Missionaries were determined in ministering to their converts, and looked to metropolitan France for support. In their advocacy of French intervention, prospects for trade were regularly invoked. The French government, however, showed little interest and it took the activities of another remarkable French churchman to bring Vietnam once again to French attention.

Bishop Pierre Pigneau de Béhaine reached Vietnam in 1767. A decade later he was deeply embroiled in Vietnamese politics. In 1772 a peasant rebellion broke out, led by three brothers from the village of Tay Son. In a series of brilliant campaigns they overthrew both the Nguyen lords in the south and the Trinh in the north, who for a century and a half had divided power between them in the name of the powerless Le emperors. One young Nguyen prince managed to escape the massacre of his family. Pigneau de Béhaine became his early protector and trusted adviser. With the support of French mercenaries hired by Pigneau, Nguyen Anh in 1802 defeated the last of the Tay Son brothers, unified the country and, as the Emperor Gia Long, founded the Nguyen dynasty, the last to rule Vietnam. Pigneau did not live to see the triumph of his protégé, nor did he manage to convert him to Catholicism, but he did revive both the Christian community in Vietnam and French interest in the country.

The Nguyen rulers modelled themselves on the earlier Le dynasty. The court orthodoxy was an austere and dogmatic Confucianism, which left no room for alternative loyalties. The growing European challenge was dealt with by ignoring it and isolating the country from all foreign contact. Christianity was systematically suppressed, and missionary priests expelled. Their persistent attempts to smuggle themselves back into the country led to more severe persecution. The martyrdom of foreign and native Christians under Gia Long's successors provided both the Catholic Church and the colonial lobby in France with just the cause they needed to argue for French intervention. The imperial policy of isolation, the arrogance of the mandarins and the lack of any interest in foreign trade all served only to increase mutual misunderstanding between Vietnam and France, and to bring about the eventual French conquest of Indochina.

The French decision to mount a military expedition against Vietnam was made in July 1857, after a series of incidents involving the rescue of French priests and the rejection of attempts to open diplomatic contacts with the court at Hue. A Franco-Spanish fleet captured Danang, the nearest port to the imperial capital, but there the landing party was pinned down by Vietnamese forces. Hundreds of French troops died of disease. After six months the main fleet sailed south and seized Saigon. Further French penetration met with strong guerrilla resistance, but Emperor Tu Duc believed that if the French were given a piece of territory (as the British had been at Hong Kong), they would be satisfied. In a treaty signed in June 1862, Saigon was ceded to France along with three adjacent provinces.

As popular resentment over the French presence grew, fighting between French forces and Vietnamese guerrillas escalated, much to French annoyance. Faced as he was by rebellion in the north, Tu Duc adopted a conciliatory attitude towards the French. The naval governors of Saigon, however, were determined on aggressive expansion. In December 1863 a French protectorate was declared over Cambodia, the western provinces of which remained tributary to Siam. In January 1867, French forces seized the rest of Cochin-China. An attempt in 1873 to secure Hanoi and Tonkin, coming as it did in the wake of French defeat in the Franco-Prussian war of 1870, was, however, repudiated by the French government.

Ten years later a French force was again sent to Tonkin, this time to stay. A French fleet bombarded Hue, where Tu Duc had recently died. In June 1884, a Treaty of Protectorate was signed, terminating the independence of Vietnam. A belated protest by China and skirmishes between French and Chinese troops were resolved in 1885 through Chinese recognition of French suzerainty over China's former vassal. But if international recognition of France's colonial conquest was forthcoming, Vietnamese acquiescence was not. It took the French another twelve years to pacify Vietnam.

Urged on by the faction at court opposed to the French, the young Emperor Ham Nghi called for popular resistance. Known as the Can Vuong (Support the Emperor) movement, this national insurrection, led by traditional mandarins, succeeded in tying down thousands of French troops long after Ham Nghi had been captured in November 1888, banished and replaced by a pliant successor. Opposition was concentrated in northern Annam and Tonkin, and not until 1890 was the Tonkin Delta brought under French control. Resistance leaders such as Pham Dinh Phung and De Tham held out in the mountains until 1896 and 1897 respectively. That 'pacification' eventually succeeded was due in part to the sheer brutality of the French forces, in part to support given by Vietnamese Catholics, and in part to what was known as the 'policy of the races', the deliberate exacerbation of racial antipathy on the part of upland tribal minorities in north and northwestern Vietnam, such as the Tai and Muong, for their traditional Vietnamese oppressors. By the time the new colony had been brought under French control, military action had cost the government the enormous sum of 750 million francs.[1]

Even before the final pacification of Tonkin, France was seeking to expand its Indochinese empire. The protectorate over Cambodia gave the French access to the Mekong River and raised hopes of a possible trade route into southern China. The Mekong expedition of 1866–67 proved this to be impossible, but excited ambitions to bring the Mekong Basin, and perhaps even Siam itself, under French jurisdiction. However, in the latter part of the nineteenth century, Siam was itself extending control over both the Lao principalities of the Mekong Basin and the Tai Highlands covering what is now the border regions between northeastern Laos and northwestern Vietnam. In the power struggle that followed, France clearly held the upper hand. In 1893, Siam was forced to cede all territories east of the Mekong to France, and to neutralise a strip of territory 25 kilometres wide the length of the west bank. In subsequent treaties culminating in 1907, France gained control of the provinces of western Cambodia and two territories west of the Mekong in Laos in exchange for the recognition of Siamese suzerainty over the rest of the west bank.

Thus, by 1907, French Indochina had achieved its final form, consisting of five separate entities grouped into a single union. These were: the French colony of Cochin-China (whose French citizens elected deputies to the French parliament), and the protectorates of Annam (where the Vietnamese emperor still nominally ruled from Hue), Tonkin (directly administered by French officials), Cambodia (where the monarchy survived) and Laos (the northern part constituting the kingdom of Luang Prabang and the southern part French administered).

The organisation of French Indochina in its final form was the work of Governor-General Paul Doumer who served from 1897 to 1902. Doumer

set himself to achieve three major tasks: organisation of the government
and administration; organisation of finances to ensure that Indochina
paid for itself at no further cost to the French exchequer; and organisation
of a system of public works to lay the basis for profitable economic
development. In the face of opposition from the Colonial Council in
Cochin-China, which ran the colony for the benefit of French residents,
Doumer concentrated power in a central government which was responsible for deciding policy throughout the union. Doumer as Governor-
General was advised by a Conseil Supérieur whose membership
included, apart from French officials, the heads of the French Chambers
of Agriculture and Commerce and two mandarins. The advice it gave
was administrative and economic rather than political. The union government was responsible for customs, communications, public works,
judicial matters and internal security. Each constituent territory had its
own Résident Supérieur (or Lieutenant Governor in the case of Cochin-
China), and was responsible for matters such as health, education and
local affairs.

To pay for his new central government, Doumer introduced a number
of financial reforms designed to place the whole union on a firm financial
basis. These included additional indirect taxes and improved efficiency
of collection. Importantly, however, he divided tax receipts so that direct
taxes (head taxes and land tax) went to finance local budgets while
indirect taxes were reserved for Union use. Since direct taxes had to be
paid in silver piastres, the cash economy penetrated even to the most
remote villages. At the same time, supervision of council elections and
population registers undermined the traditional autonomy of the villages. Of the indirect taxes, most revenue was derived from customs dues
and from the three state monopolies that Doumer established — in salt,
alcohol and opium. All three proved highly profitable, though all three
engendered considerable popular discontent. Opium, imported mostly
from India, was cynically sold to Chinese addicts. Alcohol previously
brewed by villagers from surplus rice was made illegal so as to increase
rice exports and enforce the state alcohol monopoly. The indigenous salt
industry was also destroyed. Prices for these commodities increased
steeply, and the monopolies could only be enforced through giving an
army of officials the right to search private houses and shops — to the
anger of those subjected to such intrusion.

Doumer's third concern was with public works. A projected 3000
kilometre rail network proved too ambitious, but a start was made on
both the coastal line that eventually linked Saigon and Hanoi, and on the
Tonkin–Yunnan line. Road and bridge construction, port facilities,
irrigation works and the construction of public buildings were undertaken as part of a massive public works program designed to facilitate
the *mise en valeur* of Indochina for the benefit of France. Labour was

provided by the indigenous peoples, often in the form of corvée, performed under appalling working conditions. Some 24 000 of the 80 000 Chinese and Vietnamese workers engaged died during the construction of the Tonkin–Yunnan rail line alone.[2] French colonisation was encouraged through easily available land grants, and attractive opportunities were provided for French investment. Only industries which competed with French imports were discouraged, a policy which both delayed and distorted the colony's industrial development.

Doumer's policies extended to Cambodia and Laos, for the French administered Indochina as a whole. Opposition to reform by King Norodom in Cambodia gave way to co-operation upon succession of his brother Sisowath. The king was relegated to a pliant figurehead as the French administration, staffed primarily in its middle levels by Vietnamese, increasingly took control. Laos, meanwhile, was viewed by the French both as an economic liability and as a potentially productive hinterland for Vietnam. Disruption of traditional social relationships, heavy taxation and forced *(corvée)* labour demands provoked a series of uprisings by ethnic minorities in both southern and northern Laos. Once these were quelled, French development plans centred on construction of a railway from coastal Vietnam to the Mekong river, plus large-scale Vietnamese migration to provide a workforce. Luckily for the Lao, neither eventuated.

Doumer's reforms set the pattern of administration for the next 40 years. There were, however, two things Doumer failed to do: reduce the size of the French bureaucracy and reverse the policy of assimilation. These problems were linked and their impact was disastrous. About ten times as many French bureaucrats were employed to administer the same population as in either Dutch Indonesia or British India. Many performed lowly paid work which could easily have been done by indigenous civil servants, at salaries far in excess of more highly qualified Vietnamese. The effect was to reduce job opportunities and contribute to misunderstanding between the races, as most minor French bureaucrats in Indochina, unlike the Residents responsible for provincial administration, made no attempt to learn the local language. Thus, in 1911, of almost 5500 French bureaucrats in Vietnam, 90 per cent could not speak Vietnamese.[3]

That so few French officials could speak Vietnamese hardly mattered, however, for it was believed to be far more valuable for Vietnamese to speak French. The goal was assimilation of the Vietnamese to the French way of life, French values and French civilisation. This was France's *mission civilisatrice*, whose logical outcome, had it been successful, would have been to destroy Vietnamese culture. Within a decade of Doumer's departure, however, this unrealistic policy was abandoned, as more perceptive administrators had recognised it would have to be, in favour of a policy of association. France and Indochina each possessed their own unique history and culture, it was agreed, but they still shared a commonality of interests, and that was what counted.

Not many Vietnamese were convinced of this common interest. While some were prepared to collaborate with the French on a long-term basis, many more sought only to learn from France what they needed to strengthen their country and gain independence. One of the leading figures in the next phase of resistance to French rule, which gained momentum after Japan's victory over Russia in their war of 1905, was the scholar-patriot Phan Boi Chau, who set up a secret network to assist young Vietnamese nationalists to study in Japan. Another was the mandarin Phan Chau Trinh, who agitated for improved opportunities for education in Vietnam. Both recognised the importance of a modern Western education, but both also drew upon the best of Vietnamese tradition — its history and culture — in their appeals to their compatriots. The Chinese Nationalist Revolution of 1911 inspired Phan Boi Chau to form the League for the Restoration of Vietnam, uniting most nationalist groups, though both he and the League remained in exile in China.

In Vietnam itself, all forms of nationalist agitation were severely repressed by the French Sûreté. In 1916 the 18-year-old Emperor Duy Tan led a short-lived revolt, only to be captured, deposed and exiled to the French Indian Ocean island of Réunion. His co-conspirators were either executed or deported. Even the most moderate political demands were rejected, and no political parties were allowed to exist except in Cochin-China, where a group of moderates formed the Constitutionalist Party in 1923.

The refusal of the French authorities in Indochina to countenance any political reform designed to bring about even a modicum of representative government in Vietnam left Vietnamese nationalists no legal outlet for their political energies and ambitions. They were forced instead to organise covert political associations along the lines of Chinese secret societies. In 1927 the young nationalist school teacher Nguyen Thai Hoc founded the Vietnam Nationalist Party (Viet Nam Quoc Dan Dang or VNQDD) modelled on the Guomindang in China. The party was organised in the form of separate cells to minimise the danger of infiltration by the Sûreté. Its goal was the violent expulsion of the French from Vietnam, which Nguyen Thai Hoc hoped to achieve by means of a co-ordinated uprising by Vietnamese troops of the Garde Indochinoise together with acts of terrorism directed against French citizens. The arrest of many nationalist activists following the assassination of a French labour recruiter triggered a premature uprising by the VNQDD in February 1930. The uprising was quickly put down, and its leaders arrested. Nguyen Thai Hoc, and eleven other VNQDD members were guillotined. Hundreds more VNQDD members were imprisoned or deported. The few who avoided arrest fled to China, where they remained until 1945.

In 1930 a very different mass peasant uprising broke out in the provinces of Ha Tinh and Nghe An, and was put down with even greater severity. Although the initial outbreak seems to have been a spontaneous reaction to deteriorating conditions brought about by economic depression and high levels of taxation, it was quickly exploited by communist organisers and became known as the Nghe-Tinh Soviets. French suppression of the revolt was brutal and unrelenting. Peasant demonstrations were bombed from the air, and hundreds of peasants were summarily executed as the Foreign Legion was sent in to 'clean up' the rebellion. Thousands were killed and another 10 000 imprisoned.[4]

Earlier in the year, representatives of three regional communist organisations in Vietnam had met under the chairmanship of Ho Chi Minh in Hong Kong to form what became known as the Indochinese Communist Party (ICP). Ho was then known by his pseudonym of Nguyen Ai Quoc, or Nguyen the Patriot. He had left Vietnam almost twenty years earlier, settled briefly in France after World War I, then moved to the Soviet Union where he became a Comintern agent. In southern China in 1925 he had formed the Revolutionary Youth League, the forerunner of the ICP. The Nghe-Tinh uprising took the party unawares, but taught it a great deal. Here was proof (if proof were needed) of the revolutionary potential of the Vietnamese peasantry. Poverty and economic distress had created deep resentment against French rule. All that was needed was for the leadership of the party to channel this into an organised and disciplined mass revolutionary movement.

By 1930 the principal effects of French economic penetration and exploitation were apparent. In the Mekong Delta area of Cochin-China, some 2 million hectares of land had been brought into production through massive drainage and irrigation schemes. Canals had been dug and opened up to navigation so that harvests could more easily be marketed. As a result, rice production increased 90 per cent between 1900 and 1937 to 6310 thousand tonnes, making Vietnam the third largest rice-exporting country in the world. Rubber production had increased dramatically from less than 300 tonnes in 1915 to 70 000 tonnes from more than 100 000 hectares in 1940. By 1939, Vietnam boasted 3372 kilometres of railways and about 30 000 kilometres of roads, while modern ports had been developed at Haiphong, Danang and Saigon.[5]

However, this economic development and increasing prosperity benefited relatively few people. Vietnam was an area of profitable investment for French capital and a market for French products. Factories catering for mass consumption — alcohol, sugar, cement, textiles, etc. — were French owned, as were most mines and plantations. While a small, increasingly wealthy Vietnamese bourgeoisie benefited from the French presence, the majority of Vietnamese suffered from the high taxation needed to pay for the massive public works programs and for French salaries, and from declining living standards and quality of life. The most impoverished, the landless peasants of the Tonkin Delta and Annam, were forced to hire themselves out to labour contractors to work in the plantations and mines just in order to pay their capitation tax. Others were forced to sell their miserably small holdings as rural indebtedness rose dramatically. Land became concentrated in fewer and fewer hands. Wealthy families also seized control of communal lands which had previously provided some measure of social welfare at the village level. Already, by 1900, only about one in eight families in Cochin-China owned any land of their own. The rest worked as tenant farmers or rural labourers.

In Cochin-China especially, as the land area under cultivation increased, it became concentrated in the hands of a few wealthy, mostly absentee landlords. And while the level of rice exports increased and the population increased even faster, the levels of consumption fell. The depression of the 1930s was particularly severe. By 1937, average peasant rice consumption had dropped to 182 kilograms compared with 262 kilograms consumed in 1900.[6] The increasing poverty and misery of rural Vietnam in the 1930s provided fertile ground for any movement promising a better life and a more just society.

Marxism owed much, but not all, its appeal to these conditions, but it attracted adherents for a number of other reasons too. It appealed to members of the intellectual elite by virtue of its concern for social values and responsibilities which echoed those of Confucianism, for the comprehensive explanation it provided of European imperialism and economic exploitation, and for the certainty it offered of ultimate victory and a better society. It appealed to workers and peasants because, at a time when the moral obligations of Confucianism no longer tempered the greed and exploitation of the rural elite, only the communists took up their cause for improved working conditions and higher wages; only the party sympathised with their complaints and gave them leadership.

The methods and attitudes of the ICP were dramatically different from those of the VNQDD. Whereas the latter was elitist and secretive, imbued with the belief that revolution, like government, was the preserve of the educated on behalf of the masses, the former was far more democratic and open, drawing upon the strength and anger of the peasantry. The party took upon itself the leading role, but set out to generate a mass movement. Revolution was to be carried through not on behalf of the people, but *by* the people, through mass popular mobilisation drawing on strong nationalist sentiments. It was a recipe which was to prove remarkably effective.

The ICP was not the only organisation in the 1930s with mass appeal to a disoriented and suffering peasantry. In southern Vietnam, two popular religious movements sprang up offering their own millenarian solutions to present problems. The first of these was the Cao Dai, founded in 1926 but only gaining a mass following some years later. It offered the security of membership in a mutually supportive graded hierarchy of believers worshipping an eclectic hierarchy of divinities. The second new religion was proclaimed in 1938 by Huynh Phu So, known to the French as 'the mad bonze'. His Hoa Hao sect of Buddhism simplified ritual and offered hope for the future in the form of apocalyptic defeat of the French and arrival of Maitreya, the Buddha-to-be. Both movements were confined to the Mekong Delta region of southern Vietnam where the penetration of French capital had been most disruptive and where Vietnamese social institutions were less securely established than in the longer settled north and centre.

Election of the Popular Front government in France in 1936 had led to some relaxation of political controls in Indochina. The strong urban-based Trotskyite party won municipal elections in Saigon, much to the consternation of French officials, while the ICP was able to strengthen its leadership of the labour movement. When, at the outbreak of World War II three years later, political freedom was again suppressed, the ICP was well prepared to go underground.

After the fall of France, the Vichy regime in Indochina concluded an agreement with the Japanese permitting Japanese troops to be stationed in Indochina in return for continuation of French administration. A communist uprising in the south went ahead when orders cancelling it failed to reach southern leaders. Its savage suppression by French authorities seriously weakened the ICP in the Mekong Delta where it already had to hold its own against alternative, equally strong, popular movements such as the Cao Dai and the Hoa Hao.

No such diversions undermined nationalist unity in the north. In 1941, from a revolutionary hideout on the mountainous Chinese–Vietnamese border, the ICP announced formation of the Viet Nam Doc Lap Dong Minh Hoi, the Revolutionary League for the Independence of Vietnam, better known as the Vietminh. Its leader, the veteran communist Nguyen Ai Quoc, took a new *nom de guerre* — Ho Chi Minh (He who Enlightens), the name by which he became known to the world. Apart from extending its political organisation inside Vietnam, the Vietminh co-operated with Nationalist Chinese forces and with the American Office of Strategic Services (OSS). In return for intelligence and assistance in rescuing downed airmen, the Vietminh received American weapons and training.

The Vietminh exploited the opportunity provided by the war to build up a mass following. Their appeal was to all classes in Vietnamese society: to the peasantry they promised land and a reduction of taxes; to the middle class economic opportunities denied them by the French; to the intelligentsia the possibility of contributing to creating a new culture and society. And to all they appealed to a sense of history, patriotism and national pride. In 1944–45, the Vietminh gained much popular support in the north for their attempts to alleviate the disastrous famine of that winter by forcibly distributing hoarded rice. Even so, between one and two million were estimated to have died of starvation.

In a lightning move on 9 March 1945, following the liberation of France, the Japanese interned all French civilian and military personnel in Vietnam. Two days later, Emperor Bao Dai, last ruler of the Nguyen dynasty, declared the independence of Vietnam, but within the Greater East Asia Co-prosperity Sphere. But while the Japanese enforced their hold over key cities and towns and Bao Dai announced the formation of a new government, the Vietminh were free to step up their political and military mobilisation in the rural areas. Thousands joined the organisation, particularly from the intelligentsia — teachers, writers and civil servants.

When Japan surrendered on 15 August 1945, the Vietminh immediately organised a series of massive demonstrations in Hanoi, Hue and Saigon, in the face of which Bao Dai's government resigned and the emperor himself agreed to abdicate on 24 August. On 29 August the Vietminh formed a 'provisional government' with Ho Chi Minh as president, and on 2 September Ho solemnly proclaimed the independent Democratic Republic of Vietnam. So was the 'August Revolution' achieved.

Under the terms of the Potsdam Agreement of July 1945, Nationalist Chinese forces accepted the surrender of Japanese troops north of the sixteenth parallel in Indochina while British forces accepted their surrender to the south. Over the next few months, the British facilitated the return of the French to Cochin-China, while the Chinese gave assistance to non-communist nationalists in Tonkin. The Vietminh were thus forced to compromise with both. In the first elections, won comfortably by the Vietminh, seats were reserved for other nationalist parties, and when the Chinese withdrew, Ho agreed to the temporary stationing of French garrisons in central and northern Vietnam.

In a series of conferences and negotiations lasting throughout much of 1946, Ho struggled to preserve Vietnamese independence in the face of equally strong French determination to reoccupy Vietnam — as they had already reoccupied both Cambodia and Laos. Still smarting from their defeat in 1940, many Frenchmen believed that to re-establish France as a great power they needed to re-establish the French Empire. This was certainly the attitude of the French administration in Saigon, which believed that six months of internment under the Japanese had changed nothing and which wanted to deal with the Vietminh as it had dealt with every previous nationalist movement — through military action and police repression.

The inevitable showdown came with all the inexorable finality of a Greek tragedy. In response to a minor incident, French warships bombarded Haiphong, causing heavy civilian casualties. Even so, the Vietminh held back. A last-minute attempt by Ho to appeal to the new French government in Paris to avert war was deliberately delayed in Saigon. No answer was received. Convinced that French forces in Hanoi were about to attack, the Vietminh decided to move first. On the evening of 19 December, Vietminh forces attacked French positions in Hanoi and other cities in Indochina. As the Vietminh rearguard fought street by street in Hanoi against superior French forces, the main body of Vietminh forces withdrew north to prepared base areas near the Chinese border. The First Indochina War was underway.

The outbreak of war polarised political options in Vietnam. French attempts to find a 'political solution' were nullified by their refusal to permit a succession of non-communist nationalist governments any real political autonomy, let alone the independence that might have undermined the nationalist appeal of the Vietminh. For their part, the Vietminh denounced all such governments as the puppets the French obliged them to be, and selectively assassinated leading political opponents while building up their own political organisation and perfecting their techniques of guerrilla warfare.

For the first three years the war was inconclusive, but in October 1949 Mao Zedong proclaimed the People's Republic of China, and by December communist Chinese forces had fought their way to the Vietnamese border. The nature of the war from this point changed. Even then the French made only grudging political concessions. The colony of Cochin-China was at last reunited with the protectorates of Annam and Tonkin to form the unitary state of Vietnam, a condition stipulated by Bao Dai for his return from the French Riviera to become the country's chief of state. But France still refused to grant Vietnam full 'dominion status' as a free and independent state. As always, French concessions were too little too late. The 'Bao Dai' solution — the creation of a semi-independent state within the French Union, with important powers still reserved to France — was a fiasco before it began.

In January 1950, China and the Soviet Union recognised Ho Chi Minh's Democratic Republic of Vietnam. In response, Britain and the United States recognised the governments of the states of Vietnam, Cambodia and Laos. Chinese weapons and supplies began reaching the Vietminh, and American military assistance was stepped up to France and the Indochinese states. In September and October of 1950, the Vietminh attacked a number of isolated French garrisons near the Chinese border, inflicting the worst defeat suffered by French forces since World War II. However, an attempt to seize the Red River Delta proved too ambitious, and Vietminh commander General Vo Nguyen Giap was forced to revert to picking off French outposts and ambushing relief columns.

Over the next two years the Vietminh improved their military and political position vis-à-vis the beleaguered French. General Giap extended Vietminh control over the Tai Highlands south of the Black River along the border with Laos, and built up his stocks of Chinese weapons. Vietminh 'parallel administrations' took control of villages even behind the French de Lattre line of strong points protecting the Tonkin Delta. French-endorsed village chiefs became mere figureheads while real power was wielded by the Vietminh. At the national level, the politicians who continued to collaborate with the French were entirely discredited in the eyes of the mass of the population. Both militarily and politically, the advantage was shifting in favour of the Vietminh.

In the rest of Indochina, too, France's days were numbered. In both Laos and Cambodia, nationalist forces had opposed the return of the French. In Laos the Free Laos Movement (Lao Issara) had set up a government-in-exile in Bangkok which split at the end of 1949. Moderates returned to take part in the semi-independent government of Laos, while radicals formed the Pathet Lao in alliance with the Vietminh. In Cambodia, the Free Khmer (Khmer Issarak) refused to accept the concessions of 1949. Only after the Cambodian king, Norodom Sihanouk, negotiated full independence from France in 1953 did the Khmer Issarak split with the moderate majority accepting that what they had been fighting for had been achieved. The radical minority was forced to reorganise and rethink its strategy.

Complete independence for Laos and Cambodia by October 1953 came in part at least in response to the deteriorating French position in Vietnam. Earlier in the year the Vietminh had expanded their area of operations by striking deep into Laos, carving out areas which were then handed over to Pathet Lao control. It was to forestall another such thrust that French troops in November occupied the remote highland valley of Dien Bien Phu. It was a fatal military mistake. By March the battle was joined and the garrison surrounded. Despite supplies of American arms (the United States was by 1954 meeting some three-quarters of the cost of the war in Indochina), after two months of resistance French forces at Dien Bien Phu were overwhelmed and surrendered to the Vietminh on 6 May 1954. The following day, the nations assembled at Geneva to seek a settlement of the war in Indochina held their opening plenary meeting. The failure of the Vietminh to win at the conference table in Geneva what their troops had won at such sacrifice in the jungles and rice paddies of Vietnam set the scene for subsequent direct intervention by the United States which led to the Second Indochina War.

Guide to further reading

Though beginning to be dated, Joseph Buttinger's books still provide a useful introduction to Vietnamese history. *The Smaller Dragon: A Political History of Vietnam*, Frederick A. Praeger, New York, 1958, in fact only covers the period up to the French conquest of Indochina. Events since

1900 are covered in a summary and chronology. This period since 1900 is treated in detail in two subsequent books — *Vietnam: A Dragon Embattled,Volume 1: From Colonialism to the Vietminh,* and *Volume II: Vietnam at War,* Frederick A. Praeger, New York, 1967.

French colonial policy is covered in Chapter XI of Roberts, Stephen H., *The History of French Colonial Policy 1870–1925,* Frank Cass, London, 1963, and in Ennis, Thomas E., *French Policy and Developments in Indochina,* Russell and Russell, New York, 1973, first published in 1936.

For the economic impact of French colonialism see Robequain, Charles, *The Economic Development of French Indo-China,* Oxford University Press, London, 1944, and for a Marxist perspective, Murray, Martin J., *The Development of Capitalism in Colonial Indochina, 1870–1940,* University of California Press, Berkeley, 1980.

The plight of the peasantry under French rule is examined by Ngo Vinh Long, *Before the Revolution: The Vietnamese Peasants under the French,* MIT Press, Cambridge, Mass., 1973, and Pham Cao Duong, *Vietnamese Peasants under French Domination,* University Press of America, Lanham, 1985.

On Vietnamese resistance to the French, the best studies are Marr, David G., *Vietnamese Anticolonialism 1885–1925,* University of California Press, Berkeley, 1971, and its sequel, *Vietnamese Tradition on Trial, 1920–1945,* University of California Press, Berkeley, 1981.

For the rise of the Vietminh, two good studies are McAlister, John T., *Viet Nam: The Origins of Revolution,* Alfred A. Knopf, New York, 1969 and Hodgkin, Thomas, *Vietnam: The Revolutionary Path,* St Martin's Press, New York, 1981. Also useful are McLeod, Mark W., *The Vietnamese Response to French Intervention, 1862–1874.* Praeger, New York, 1991; and Tuck, Patrick J.N., *French Catholic Missionaries and the Politics of Imperialism in Vietnam, 1857–1914: A Documentary Survey,* Liverpool University Press, Liverpool, 1987 and Huynh Kim Khanh, *Vietnamese Communism 1925–1945,* Cornell University Press, Ithaca, 1982. A perceptive study is McAlister, John T. and Mus, Paul, *The Vietnamese and their Revolution,* Harper and Row, New York, 1970; and for Vietnamese nationalism, see Duke, William J., *The Rise of Nationalism in Vietnam, 1900–1941,* Cornell University Press, Ithaca, New York, 1976.

On the sects of southern Vietnam, see Werner, Jayne S., *Peasant Politics and Religious Sectarianism: Peasant and Priest in the Cao Dai in Viet Nam,* Yale University Press, New Haven, 1981; Hue-Tam Ho Tai, *Millenarianism and Peasant Politics in Vietnam,* Harvard University Press, Cambridge, Mass., 1983 (on the Hoa Hao); and Woodside, Alexander B., *Community and Revolution in Modern Vietnam,* Houghton Mifflin, Boston, 1976.

For the impact of Japan on events in Indochina, see Truong Buu Lam, 'Japan and the Disruption of the Vietnamese Nationalist Movement' in Vella, Walter (ed.), *Aspects of Vietnamese History,* University of Hawaii

Press, Honolulu, 1973, pp. 237–69, and Marr, David G., 'World War II and the Vietnamese Revolution' in McCoy, Alfred W. (ed.), *Southeast Asia Under Japanese Occupation*, Yale University Press, New Haven, 1980, pp. 125–51. The crucial years of 1945 and 1946 have been examined in detail by Tonnesson, Stein, in *The Vietnamese Revolution of 1945: Roosevelt, Ho Chi Minh and de Gaulle in a World at War,* Sage, London, 1991; and *The Outbreak of War in Indochina*, International Peace Research Institute, Oslo, 1982.

Finally, the First Indochina War is covered in O'Ballance, Edgar, *The Indo-China War 1945–1954: A Study in Guerrilla Warfare*, Faber and Faber, London, 1964, Irving, R.E.M., *The First Indochina War*, Croom Helm, London, 1975 and Dalloz, Jacques, *The War in Indo-China 1945–1954*, translated by Josephine Bacon, Barnes and Noble, Savage MD, 1990; while the Geneva Agreements are discussed in Randall, Robert F., *Geneva, 1954*, Princeton University Press, Princeton, 1969; and Cable, James, *The Geneva Conference of 1954 on Indochina*, St Martin's Press, New York, 1986.

Notes

1   Cady, John F., 'The French Colonial Regime in Vietnam', *Current History*, vol. 50, no. 294, 1966, p. 75.

2   Murray, Martin J., *The Development of Capitalism in Colonial Indochina (1870–1940)*, University of California Press, Berkeley, 1980, p. 173.

3   ibid.

4   Hodgkin, Thomas, *Vietnam: The Revolutionary Path*, New York, St Martin's Press, 1981, p. 258.

5   Economic statistics can be found in Robequain, Charles, *The Economic Development of French Indo-China*, trans. Isabel A. Ward, Oxford University Press, 1944, London, and in Murray, *The Development of Capitalism*.

6   Buttinger, Joseph, *Vietnam: A Dragon Embattled, Vol. 1: From Colonialism to the Vietminh*, Frederick A. Praeger, New York, 1967, p. 171.

20 | Korea to 1950

The period from the early nineteenth to the mid-twentieth century was not a happy one in Korea. The long-lasting Yi dynasty succumbed in 1910 not to an independent republic nor to a constitutional monarchy, but to the rule of a foreign power, Japan. When independence eventually came with Japan's defeat in 1945, the Korean nation was more or less immediately split into two parts under circumstances entirely beyond its control. Yet again a fairly small nation was prey to the whims and dictates of great powers.

The decay of Yi dynasty Korea

By the second half of the nineteenth century, the social, political and economic fabric of Yi dynasty Korea was beginning to fall apart. Corruption was rampant, and the social system showed few signs of being able to regenerate itself. The country had for centuries been a tributary state of the Chinese empire, but this also was coming under challenge from a variety of quarters, including the Western countries from the beginning of the nineteenth century and, from the 1870s, especially from a resurgent and aggressive Japan. The initial Korean response was to continue to resist change. Christianity spread quite widely in the second half of the eighteenth century. The government tried to prevent this development (including, from 1801, through the use of persecutions and executions).

From the second half of the eighteenth century, power at court fell more and more into the hands of the king's relations and the queen, turning the king into a figurehead. The crisis became acute during the reign of King Kojong (r. 1863–1907). Because he was only 12 at the time of his accession, his father Yi Ha-ung (1820–98) took over as regent and was given an honorary title of the king's father, *Taewongun* (meaning literally 'Prince of the Great Court'), by which he is normally known to history. A decade later, with Kojong's maturity, he was forced to resign, and a faction headed by the king's wife, who belonged to the powerful Min clan, seized power.

In the policy struggle which developed at court, the Taewongun represented resistance to all change and defence of isolationism, Confucianism and the Korean tradition. Queen Min, on the other hand, quickly came under strong Japanese pressure and in 1876 Korea was forced to sign a treaty with Japan which opened three ports to Japanese trade.

In 1882 a conservative and anti-foreign *coup d'état* took place in the Korean capital Seoul, supported by the Taewongun. Both China and Japan sent troops to suppress it, and China arrested the Taewongun, sending him to Tianjin in China. Two years later, a group of reformers favouring modernisation along Japanese lines attempted another coup, but they were defeated by Chinese troops led by Yuan Shikai. Although this was a victory for China and Chinese influence increased over the next decade in Korea, in fact it was Japan that ultimately emerged the winner. As a result of the Treaty of Shimonoseki, which ended the Sino-Japanese War of 1894–95, China recognised the 'full and complete independence and autonomy of Korea'. Although Korea was already independent, China had regarded the country as part of its tribute system, in fact the jewel in the crown of that system. So the Treaty of Shimonoseki implied the death both of the Chinese tribute system and of Chinese influence in Korea.

In the aftermath of the Sino-Japanese War, a faction in Seoul, led by Queen Min, turned to Russia as a balance against Japan; as a result, Japanese agents murdered her in October 1895. This outrage did not change policy at the Korean court and for a while Japanese influence was balanced by that of Russia.

Korea as a Japanese colony

With the defeat of Russia in the Russo-Japanese War of 1904–05, Japan asserted itself more strongly than ever. Only a few months after victory over Russia, it made Korea into a Japanese protectorate and took over total control of Korea's foreign policy. Finally, in August 1910, Japan made Korea a formal and total colony by declaring that the government-general of Korea would be organised as an agent of the government of Japan. Throughout the period the Japanese ruled Korea (1910–45), all governors-general were either generals or admirals, and the nature of Japanese administration was military.

There was nationalist resistance to Japanese rule right from the start. By far the most famous and important opposition came in the uprising of 1 March 1919. Over 30 prominent people issued a proclamation of independence in Seoul, and very large but peaceful demonstrations flared all over the country. About two million people took part in several thousand demonstrations throughout the rest of 1919.

The Japanese reaction was twofold. In the first place, Japanese police and soldiers fired at the crowds during many of the demonstrations and the numbers killed over the year ran into quite a few thousands. In addition, numerous thousands were injured, houses were burned and people were arrested and imprisoned. The other reaction was to soften its policy on Korea, replacing 'military' by 'cultural' rule. However, historians both of the north and south of Korea nowadays agree that in fact the change in policy was superficial only and altered nothing essential.

The 1 March incident also gave a spur to the labour and communist movements in Korea. The Workers' Mutual Aid Society of Korea, set up in April 1920 in Seoul, was the first mass labour organisation in Korea. There were over 330 fairly large workers' strikes between 1920 and 1925, with about 27 000 workers taking part. Although the Communist International attracted some interest in Korea, its role there was not significant. There were several left-wing or Marxist-Leninist-influenced Korean groups established, both inside and outside Korea. One of them was the Communist Party of Korea, set up in April 1925; however, it lasted only three years.

One historian has described the 1 March Movement not as a milestone, but as a landmark. His reason is that for all its scale and significance, the movement had no real predecessors or follow-on. Although the movement 'rises up like monolith, it is yet a monolith with no ranges leading up to it or away from it'.[1] Japanese control was just too strong for the Koreans. Moreover, it was primarily the victors in World War II who eventually broke Japanese control over Korea, not the Koreans themselves.

The Japanese attack on Manchuria in September 1931 did provoke a limited degree of armed struggle against Japan in Korea, which continued throughout the period of Japanese colonialism. Kim Il Sung has become the most famous of the anti-Japanese guerrilla leaders and his activities had some effectiveness and gained support, though it should be added that he spent very little of the period 1925–45 in Korea itself. He set up the Anti-Japanese People's Guerrilla Army in April 1932, which was able to organise guerrilla bases inside Korea. It was reorganised into the Korean People's Revolutionary Army in March 1934.

The Japanese domination of Korea was a particularly comprehensive form of colonialism. For a start, the Japanese government-general controlled everything and took the initiative for virtually all new developments in Korean society, politics and the economy. In 1937, about 246 000 Japanese in public and professional positions ruled some 21 million Koreans. This ratio of colonisers to local people was far higher than for the French in Vietnam in the same year, which was itself much higher than for the British in India.

According to Bruce Cumings, 'the primary effect of Japanese rule' in the countryside was 'to perpetuate, not eliminate, Korea's traditional landed aristocracy'.[2] The old aristocracy was thrown out of the administrative positions, which were taken over by the Japanese, but did not give up its landholdings. On the contrary, land became its last bastion of strength.

The Japanese carried out large-scale development. Under them, rice production, although not necessarily overall food consumption, grew. They built railways, roads and ports. They developed industry, and Mitsui, Mitsubishi and other large-scale companies developed enterprises from the late 1920s on. They tried to increase literacy and expand educational opportunities. When the Japanese colonialists were expelled from Korea, there was an infrastructure which had not existed in 1910 and which had the potential to contribute greatly to Korea's economic development.

It must be added, however, that the Japanese policies and actions were designed to meet Japanese, not Korean, interests. According to one authority, 'by 1933 more than half of the annual rice crop was being sent to Japan, while rice consumption by the average Korean dwindled in proportion'. Koreans had to supplement their diet with millet and other products, mostly imported from Manchuria.[3] This says a great deal about who benefited from any expansions in rice production. The Japanese aim in promoting industry was to assist the needs of Japan's expanding military–industrial complex. The Japanese used the educational system to keep the Koreans subordinate. Official policy demanded that the language of instruction in the public schools should be Japanese, not Korean. Japanese everywhere attempted to downgrade the Korean language and culture and to promote their own.

Japanese rule was responsible for massive population shifts and dislocations. Millions of peasants left their homes to move into cities, to another province or out of Korea altogether, mostly because Japanese policy rendered them landless. Of those peasants who migrated to the cities, many worked in the newly established Japanese industries. By 1944, 11.6 per cent of all Koreans lived outside Korea itself, an amazingly high figure. The main country of destination was, of course, Japan, where they were forced to go as cheap and dispensible labour, but many went also to Manchuria. Most returned home after the Japanese defeat.

Bruce Cumings argues that the fundamental fact about the colonial period is not so much the extent of Japanese-fostered change, though that was great enough, but that 'the changes did not run their course'. What he means is that peasants were not destroyed as a class and integrated into industry — as happened in, for example, England — but 'instead they were introduced to industry and then spewed back upon Korean villages'. In the process of this enforced Japanese-style modernisation and economic development, Korean society was torn apart.[4]

The division of Korea

The Cairo Declaration was issued on 1 December 1943 as a result of a meeting in Cairo between the United States President F.D. Roosevelt, British Prime Minister Winston Churchill and Chinese leader Chiang Kaishek. The first great-power statement of support for Korean independence since 1910, it declared that in due course Korea should become free and independent. Although the issue of trusteeship for Korea was discussed at the two meetings near the end of World War II by which the great powers planned out the shape of the postwar world, those of Yalta in February 1945 and Potsdam in July the same year, the Cairo Declaration contained the only international agreement to be reached by the Allies over the future of Korea by the end of World War II.

On the night of 10–11 August 1945, a meeting at the Pentagon in Washington decided to divide Korea into two parts. Knowing that the Soviet Union would occupy the northern sector, it planned that the United States should do the same for the southern. According to one account, two senior military officers, including Colonel Charles Bonesteel,

> wanted to follow provincial boundary lines north of Seoul, which would violate political divisions as little as possible and would place the capital city in the American zone. The only map immediately available was a small-scale wall map of the Far East, and time was pressing. Bonesteel noted that the 38th Parallel passed north of Seoul and almost divided Korea into two equal parts. He seized on it as the proposed zonal boundary.[5]

It is remarkable that a nation could be divided on the basis of such a unilateral meeting, where no non-American, let alone Korean, interests were represented at all, but the outlines are not in doubt. Unlike Germany, Korea was in no sense an enemy of the United States or anybody else. It was a colony of a defeated enemy. It should have been regarded as a victor against Japan.

Stalin chose to observe Washington's unilateral decision. It satisfied Soviet security interests. He did not care about Korea, and there were far more pressing and important matters and places to consider. In any case, Soviet troops occupied the northern part of Korea on 12 August, but did not move south of the thirty-eighth parallel.

On 15 August 1945, the Japanese surrendered and Koreans greeted their consequent independence with expressions of extreme delight. On 6 September, the Korean People's Republic was established with its capital in Seoul and headed by the nationalist Yo Un-hyong. His government's policies were mildly leftist, though essentially neutralist in terms of the new Cold War between the Soviet Union and the United States, but firmly anti-Japanese. Immediately on the collapse of Japanese power, people's committees emerged, apparently more or less spontaneously, throughout Korea. In general these were radical and on the side of the poor, but by far the most important criterion for headship of them was a history of opposition to the Japanese.

On 8 September, American troops landed at Inchon in south Korea. General John Reed Hodge, their commander, quickly made known his suspicion of the People's Republic and corresponding sympathy not only for Koreans who had collaborated with the Japanese, but even with the defeated Japanese themselves. According to Bruce Cumings, 'in August and September of 1945, Koreans changed to quasi-enemies, and Japanese to friends, in the eyes of the American Occupation'.[6] Hodge's position was that the United States Military Government Office was the sole government of Korea for the time being. After attempting negotiations with People's Republic leaders centring on whether it could be regarded as a government or not, he denounced it and its activities as unlawful on 12 December 1945.

Meanwhile, in the north of Korea, the Red Army occupation encouraged the people's committees, and the moderate nationalist Cho Man-sik recognised the Korean People's Republic government in Seoul. Kim Il Sung held the Inaugural Congress of the Korean Communist Party in Pyongyang from 10–13 October 1945, and the next day a large-scale ceremony was held to welcome him as leader. Although he had much support, it is extremely doubtful whether he could have assumed this position without the support of the Soviet occupying military.

In December 1945, the foreign ministers of the United States, Soviet Union and Britain met in Moscow to discuss a range of postwar problems, including Korea's division. The United States and Soviet Union put forward alternative proposals to cope with the problem, the United States wanting trusteeship, the Soviet Union a joint United States–Soviet military commission which would advise on the establishment of a provisional united government of all Korea, but the Soviet proposal was adopted by the meeting, with slight amendments. Meanwhile, the American military government in the south of Korea had its own views. It did not think much of either the United States proposal or the one which was eventually adopted. The American military regime was trying to sponsor two old and exceedingly ambitious right-wing nationalists, Syngman Rhee and Kim Ku, with the eventual aim of establishing a pro-American government in the south. In December 1945, to Hodge's extreme annoyance, Kim Ku attempted a *coup d'état* against the United States, so Syngman Rhee became the pro-United States frontrunner. When the United States set up a Representative Democratic Council in

February 1946, Rhee was chosen as chairman. It looked very much like the first step in the establishment of a separate southern government.

In the north, the Soviet troops behaved very badly indeed in the last months of 1945, but did nothing against the People's Republic or the people's committees. The Communist Party had organised a General Federation of Trade Unions in November 1945 and a Peasants' Union in January 1946, but it regarded these as national bodies and still assumed that reunification would soon follow. The failure of the Korean People's Republic was a matter of great concern in the north. Shortly after the Representative Democratic Council was announced, the north responded by setting up its own counterpart, the North Korean Interim People's Committee, with Kim Il Sung as chairman. According to Bruce Cumings, 'there is simply no evidence to support the assertion that the Soviets or their allies planned for a separate regime in the north before February 1946'.[7] However, from this point on, reunification became more and more difficult to achieve.

Two separate governments solidify division

As a result of the Moscow Agreement of December 1945, a Joint United States–Soviet Commission had been set up. Although meetings continued to take place in an attempt to implement the Moscow Agreement, in practice none of them made real progress and it was a dead letter almost immediately. The trend over the following years in the south was increased domination by the American military and its client Syngman Rhee.

In October 1947 the Soviet representative in the Joint Commission, General T. Shtikov, proposed the withdrawal of all foreign troops from Korea as a prelude to agreement among the various Korean factions on a provisional government which would lead the whole country to reunification and independence. But American policy, strongly supported by Syngman Rhee, was to internationalise the problem of a split Korea and involve the United Nations (UN), in which it had a clear majority against the Soviet Union. On 14 November 1947 the UN voted to set up the UN Temporary Commission on Korea, the functions of which were to supervise and conduct elections throughout the whole of Korea to establish the government of a unified and independent Korea. The Soviet Union opposed the measure, arguing that UN intervention was unnecessary and that the withdrawal of foreign troops should be the first step in reuniting Korea. Both the United States and the Soviet Union knew perfectly well that the United States would dominate any UN procedures and that the communists would lose any UN-supervised election for the very simple reason that the population of the south was substantially larger than that of the north.

The problem was that, with the American-dominated UN determined to press on with elections against Soviet opposition, the result could only be the holding of elections in the south alone, which would have the effect of permanently splitting Korea, precisely what all parties had in theory been trying to avoid since 1945. In March 1948 the entire South Korean opposition issued a joint appeal against the holding of separate elections in the south.

The elections duly took place, in the south only, in May 1948. Charges of corruption, intimidation and various forms of vote-rigging were levelled by the opposition. Syngman Rhee and his followers won and the result was accepted by the UN Commission as valid, although it did not recognise the resultant Assembly as national or able to form a government for the whole country. In July a Constitution was adopted for the Republic of Korea, which stated among many other points that its government represented the whole of Korea, not just the south. In the same month the Assembly elected Syngman Rhee as president of the new state. Finally, on 15 August 1948, the Republic of Korea, was formally inaugurated, and the American military government ended. Most of the United States troops withdrew by the middle of 1949, but about 500 stayed behind as advisors.

The period from 1946 to 1950 was an extremely unstable one in the south. The American military government suppressed the people's committees which had emerged at the end of the war. The social background to the political developments just discussed was of uprisings, strikes and permanent conflagration in large areas of the south. In the autumn of 1946, peasant uprisings erupted in the areas where the people's committees had been especially strong; the peasants were trying to reverse the effects of the American occupation. In September 1946, some 40 000 railway workers went on strike demanding better living conditions and democratic reforms and protesting against suppression by the United States military government. Hundreds of thousands of industrial workers, students and office employees supported them with strike action. The reaction of the authorities to these various actions was to put them down with varying degrees of force, and many people were killed, wounded or arrested. As the right-wing forces consolidated their power in the south, the left-wing leaders there moved north.

The establishment of the ROK hardly improved the situation. One authority sums up the situation thus:

> Between 1948 and the middle of 1950 the whole of South Korea was seething from one end to the other. The army was not entirely reliable. The workers and farmers were outright hostile to the régime. The guerrillas could operate with a strong base of popular support. Even in the capital, Seoul, Rhee was under attack, and retaliating with violence and torture. When the National Assembly

launched an investigation into Rhee's financial affairs, Rhee had his police raid the Assembly: 22 people were arrested, of whom 16 were later found to have suffered either broken ribs, skull injuries or broken eardrums.[8]

Although Kim Il Sung encountered political challenges in the north in the period from 1945 to 1950, they were not nearly as intense or complicated as those in the south. Moreover, the Soviet troops were much more disciplined from early 1946 on and withdrew completely in 1948. At no time was Soviet domination of the north anywhere near as extensive as that of the United States in the south.

On 5 March 1946, 'The Law on Agrarian Reform in North Korea' was promulgated. This ushered in the period of land reform, by which land was redistributed from the landlords to the peasants. Meetings to denounce traitors who had collaborated with the Japanese were held. This process was thorough but not nearly as violent as similar land reforms in China or North Vietnam. Even an American government source could state that 'from all accounts, the former village leaders were eliminated as a political force without resort to bloodshed, but extreme care was taken to preclude their return to power'.[9]

There are several reasons why the north Korean land reform was comparatively non-violent. The Japanese landlords had already left, and many of the Korean landlords had already fled south. Landlordism had never been as bad in the northern part of the peninsula as in the south. In contrast to China, the approach adopted by Kim Il Sung was for the authorities to organise land reform from the top down, rather than giving the masses their head to carry out the land reform and seize land for themselves.

There were also other measures for social reform. In June 1946 a labour law was introduced, which provided for an eight-hour working day, social security benefits and equal pay for equal work, irrespective of gender. In July came a law stipulating equality for women and outlawing concubinage, prostitution and female infanticide, among a number of other practices which for centuries had discriminated against women. While these laws did not change everything immediately, they certainly did destroy the *yangban* class in north Korea and improve the situation for lower classes of society and for women. Similar reforms had not been adopted, let alone carried out, in the south.

On 28 August 1946 the Inaugural Congress of the Workers' Party of North Korea was held in Pyongyang. It was formed as a merger of the former Communist Party and a variety of other left-wing parties functioning in the north. It is in effect the same party which, as of 1995, still ruled north Korea, despite the death, in July 1994, of Kim Il Sung who had dominated it ever since its beginning.

The northern authorities watched the preparations for the Soviet-opposed UN-supervised separate election in the south with growing alarm. In April 1948, Kim Il Sung convened a joint north–south conference in Pyongyang to call for the withdrawal of all foreign troops and to oppose the holding of the election planned for the south. Not only the northern leaders, but (except for Syngman Rhee) virtually all the main southern ones, attended, even the rightist nationalist Kim Ku.

In response to the May 1948 election in the south, the northern authorities held their own in August. It was claimed as a nationwide election, with the United States and south Korean authorities suppressing and arresting voters. Needless to say, Kim Il Sung and his Workers' Party won it handsomely and set up a Supreme People's Assembly, the first session of which took place on 2 September 1948. It adopted a Constitution and elected Kim Il Sung as Premier and Head of State. Exactly one week later, on 9 September, he declared the establishment of the Democratic People's Republic of Korea (DPRK). Like its southern counterpart, it claimed to be the only legal government of all Korea.

What is striking is that, in all the moves which began and maintained the division of Korea between 1945 and 1948, it was the southern side which moved first. It was the United States which issued the unilateral statement to divide the country at the thirty-eighth parallel; it was the United States which suppressed the Korean People's Republic and the people's committees in the south; it was the south which moved first to establish a provisional regime in February 1946; and, most important of all, it was the south which moved first to set up a formal government in 1948.

Conclusion

The reason for the choice of dhe year 1950 as the terminal date for this chapter is, of course, the outbreak of the Korean War in June. This is covered in Chapter 21. Yet any understanding of the Korean War must take into account how Korea had developed in the recent period and especially in the crucial years following the defeat of Japan and the collapse of Japanese colonialism in Korea, when Korea was split and kept asunder through no fault of its own. Indeed, the main issues over which the Korean War was fought were already obvious in 1945 and led to various forms of conflict and fighting in a 'cold' war which killed over 100 000 people even before the 'hot' Korean War broke out in the middle of 1950.[10]

> In other words, the conflict was civil and revolutionary in character, beginning just after 1945 and proceeding through a dialectic of revolution and reaction. The opening of conventional battles in June 1950 only continued this war by other means.[11]

Guide to further reading

Cumings, Bruce, *The Origins of the Korean War, Vol. 1, Liberation and the Emergence of Separate Regimes, 1945–1947*; *Vol. 2, The Roaring of the Cataract, 1947–1950*, Princeton University Press, Princeton, New Jersey, 1981
This brilliant work takes a comprehensive and very fair look at the impact of Japanese colonialism on Korea and the two crucial years which followed its collapse. It relies on a quite extraordinarily wide range of Korean (both north and south), American and other sources. Among its other strengths, it is written in a readable style, which never fails to interest. It is the definitive work on Korea in the first half of the twentieth century.

Han Woo-keun, trans. Lee Kyung-shik, *The History of Korea*, The Eul-yoo Publishing Company, Seoul, 1970, 12th printing 1981
This large and scholarly work covers the whole of Korean history from the earliest times to 1948. The author writes as Professor of Korean History at Seoul National University. Despite obvious political bias in the seventh part on 'The Contemporary Period', this is a very useful compendium of Korean history.

Kim Han Gil, *Modern History of Korea*, Foreign Languages Publishing House, Pyongyang, 1979
This very well documented work covers the history of Korea in the twentieth century down to the mid-1970s. There are three parts: 'Anti-Japanese Revolutionary Struggle', 'Building of a New Korea: The Fatherland Liberation War', and 'Socialist Construction and Struggle for National Reunification'. There is a strong pro-northern bias, and Part 3 deals almost exclusively with the Democratic People's Republic of Korea, but the book contains a great deal of material which is otherwise difficult to access.

Lee Ki-baik, trans., Edward Wagner, with Edward Schultz, *A New History of Korea*, Harvard University Press, Cambridge and London, 1984
This is a translation of a book which first appeared in 1961 and has been revised several times and printed numerous times since then. It is an integrated history which weaves cultural, social, economic and political material together. It covers material from the most ancient times down to April 1960. Although it uses some Japanese and north Korean sources, it more or less ignores the rise of Korean communism and developments in north Korea after the Korean War.

Lone, Stewart, and McCormack, Gavan, *Korea Since 1850*, Longman Australia, Melbourne, St Martin's Press, New York, 1993
This excellent study contains chapters on the late years of the Yi dynasty, the Japanese colonial period, the Korean War and general development both in south and north Korea.

Notes

1 Wells, Kenneth M., 'Background to the March First Movement: Koreans in Japan, 1905–1919', *Korean Studies*, vol. 13, 1989, p. 7.

2 Cumings, Bruce, *The Origins of the Korean War, Liberation and the Emergence of Separate Regimes 1945–1947*, Princeton University Press, Princeton, 1981, p. 48.

3 Han Woo-keun, trans. Lee Kyung-shik, *The History of Korea*, The Eul-yoo Publishing Company, Seoul, 1970, 1981, p. 480.

4 Cumings, Bruce, *The Origins of the Korean War*, pp. 66–67.

5 See Collins, J. Lawton, *War in Peacetime: The History and Lessons of Korea*, Houghton Mifflin, Boston, 1969, pp. 25–26.

6 Cumings, Bruce, *The Origins of the Korean War*, p. 128.

7 ibid., p. 393.

8 Halliday, Jon, 'The Political Background', in McCormack, Gavan & Gittings, John (eds), *Crisis in Korea*, The Bertrand Russell Peace Foundation, Nottingham, 1977, p. 17.

9 United States, State Department, *North Korea: A Case Study in the Techniques of Takeover*, Washington DC, 1960, p. 57.

10 The terminology is Gavan McCormack's. See *Cold War Hot War, An Australian Perspective on the Korean War*, Hale & Iremonger, Sydney, 1983.

11 Cumings, Bruce, *The Origins of the Korean War*, p. xxi.

IV | Asia since the mid-twentieth century

21 | The Cold War in Asia and the Korean conflict

In 1945, as the war in Europe was drawing to a close, there were signs that the wartime alliance between the United States, the United Kingdom and the Soviet Union was coming under increasing strain. Within two years the partnership was to collapse completely as the Cold War closed in on Europe. 'From Stettin in the Baltic to Trieste in the Adriatic,' Winston Churchill remarked, 'an iron curtain has descended across the Continent.'[1] In Asia these events did not initially attract the close attention of either colonial administrations or the governments of the newly independent states of the region. After four years of war in the Pacific, most regimes were struggling with the problems of postwar economic reconstruction and the growing dilemmas of widespread political change. The outbreak of war in Korea added a new dimension to this struggle. America's response to the invasion by the Democratic People's Republic of Korea (North Korea) of the Republic of Korea (South Korea) in June 1950 brought the Cold War to Asia; as in Europe, it was to change profoundly the geo-strategic landscape of the whole region. Over the next 25 years the struggle between East and West periodically broke into conflict as it continued to shape the political and economic life of all Asian countries as well as those with interests in the area.

The advent of the Cold War

By the end of 1944 an Allied victory in Europe seemed assured. After five years of conflict, Germany alone among the Axis powers was able to offer any resistance to the Allied advance through Europe and even that seemed destined to crumble, forcing Hitler's swift capitulation. For the most part the wartime alliance between the 'big three' powers, the United States, Great Britain and the Soviet Union, had been a relatively harmonious association. Although divided from its allies by a fundamentally different political ideology and consequently a vastly different system of government, the Soviet Union had nevertheless been accepted as a partner in the alliance and had co-operated effectively with Washington and London to achieve the defeat of the common enemy. Now that the war was nearing its end, the three governments were looking to the future and the foundations of a new peacetime order. From President Roosevelt's perspective, the close personal relations forged between the leaders of the three countries during the war were expected to serve as a sound basis for future co-operation. In London, Churchill, as Britain's wartime leader, fully recognised the value of continued co-operation and was determined that this should be a primary objective of Britain's postwar policy towards the United States, but when it came to future relations with Moscow, the British leader's inherent distrust of Soviet policy made him far more guarded. In retrospect it has also become clear that Stalin also held serious doubts as to whether his wartime alliance with the West could survive the transition to peace.

Apprehensions notwithstanding, as the war in Europe drew to a close, the 'big three' continued with their planning for the postwar era. At Yalta in February 1945, the items under discussion between Roosevelt, Churchill and Stalin included: the progress of the war against Japan, which Stalin agreed to enter once the European conflict had ended; the establishment of a postwar collective security organisation, later to become the United Nations; and the future of Germany, which was to be temporarily divided, it was agreed, into three zones of occupation pending a more complete determination of its status. But in the context of the differences that were to emerge later between the three governments, the most important item on the agenda was Poland.

As a result of having carried the burden of the war on the Eastern Front, Soviet troops had liberated Poland from the Germans and now occupied the country. At Yalta, Stalin made a determined effort to preserve the Soviet presence as a means of establishing a territorial buffer between his country and its historic enemies in Western Europe. In pursuit of this aim, Stalin had already moved to establish a pro-communist government in Lublin and to redraw the country's territorial boundaries. While Roosevelt and Churchill raised objections to both Stalin's actions and his long-term plans, and managed to secure his agreement to hold postwar elections in the country, the Soviet leader nevertheless came away from the meeting believing that the issue had been settled in the Soviet Union's interest. He appears to have regarded the British and American opposition as being for domestic consumption in the West.

The differences over Poland were part of a pattern of disagreement that began to emerge as the war ended. For example, Britain and the United States also took exception to Soviet policy in Romania and Bulgaria where, in apparent disregard of an Allied agreement to hold free and open elections to establish postwar governments, the Soviets had moved quickly to create communist administrations. At the Potsdam conference in July 1945 the three allies not only found themselves in continued discord over these issues, but also at odds over a range of other matters, among them the future of Germany and the cost of war reparations.

Efforts to reach solutions to this growing list of problems were made more difficult by the fact that the personalised form of diplomacy which had been practised by Roosevelt, Churchill and Stalin during the war, and which had helped to bind the alliance together, was no longer possible. In April 1945, Roosevelt died in office and the presidency was assumed by Harry Truman, a man with little experience of international affairs and with decidedly hardline views about the Soviet Union. A few months later, during the Potsdam conference, Churchill was removed from office at a British general election and replaced by Clement Atlee. Like Truman, Atlee's experience of foreign affairs was also extremely limited and his distrust of the Soviet Union deep-seated. These changes brought to office in the United States and Britain a group of men who shared their predecessors' commitments to finding solutions to the emerging problems of the postwar period, but who were unwilling to be as patient as their predecessors with the perceived manoeuvrings of Soviet policy.

As 1945 drew on, relations between the former allies continued to deteriorate. Japan's capitulation in August did little to improve the situation. Indeed, Washington's acquisition and use of the first atomic bomb underscored its postwar strategic ascendency and increased Moscow's own apprehensions over the future of American policy. At the same time, relations between Washington and London were not entirely harmonious. In August 1945 the United States terminated without warning its wartime credit (lend lease) arrangement with Britain, thereby adding to the nation's already difficult economic situation. A year later relations began to be more strained when Washington decided that the United States would no longer co-operate in the development of Britain's postwar atomic energy program. This, of course, was after the British had co-operated freely in the development of an American atomic bomb.

But on the subject of the Soviet Union the two Western allies remained as one. As Stalin moved to consolidate his power throughout Eastern Europe, their anxiety over his long-term ambitions became acute. Both countries had been strongly opposed to the Soviet government since the success of the communist revolution in 1917 and had even taken steps to try to topple the regime. With Germany now defeated, their long-held fears about the expansionist nature of the Soviet state had resurfaced and been powerfully reinforced by Moscow's postwar diplomacy. That the West's own moves to consolidate its position in Western Europe had much the same impact in Moscow did not occur to political leaders in either London or Washington. Their image of the West, under increasing threat from an ambitious leader at the head of a brutal and repressive regime with an expansionist political ideology, became an integral part of their world-view. As a consequence, their rhetoric against Soviet policy grew increasingly strident. A huge ideological gulf now divided the former allies, each new move was interpreted with suspicion and overall relations were marked by increasing hostility and mistrust.

Events in 1947 served to confirm the depth of the differences between East and West and so underscore the reality of the Cold War. In March, Truman argued before Congress that the United States had a responsibility 'to support free peoples who are resisting attempted subjugation by armed minorities or by outside pressures'.[2] The president was referring specifically to the threat posed by a communist insurgent movement in Greece, but his speech had much wider implications. It established what later became known as the Truman Doctrine and it committed the United States to resisting the expansion of the Soviet Union and communism around the world. Expressed most frequently as the policy of containment, the doctrine became the central pillar of American foreign policy around the world for the next 25 years.

A few months later, in June, Washington took another step towards a complete break with the Soviets when it announced the Marshall Plan. Designed to assist reconstruction of the shattered postwar economies of Europe through a massive injection of financial aid, the benefits of the plan were offered to countries in both Eastern and Western Europe. Under Soviet pressure, however, the former were forced to decline. Moscow's rejection of Marshall aid added yet another divide between East and West. With the benefit of American capital and technology, Western Europe began its recovery from the ravages of war much more quickly than the East. This not only served to underpin the maintenance of capitalism in the West; it was to underwrite a high level of political stability in the area and ensure the retention of America's postwar influence and power on the continent.

By the end of 1947 the advent of a struggle between East and West was no longer in doubt. Fear and mistrust on both sides had completely wrecked the wartime alliance against Germany and created a situation in postwar international affairs that few had envisaged. Instead of the great powers co-operating to produce order in the postwar environment, the protection of their competing interests had generated a fierce hostility that presaged a new and (given the advent of nuclear weapons) potentially far more serious conflict in international politics. Nor was the struggle merely a passing one. After 1947, a succession of new confrontations only served to deepen the rift and the mistrust which had come to characterise the breach. In 1948 there was a serious confrontation over the conduct of elections in Czechoslavakia and later in the year the most serious postwar crisis to date occurred when the Soviets blockaded Berlin, attempting to cut its lifeline to the West. When Moscow finally capitulated in May 1949, the West had already moved to reinforce its security in Europe by the creation in April of the North Atlantic Treaty Organisation (NATO). In 1955 the Soviets were to establish their version of the alliance in the Warsaw Pact. The new security alliance in Western Europe institutionalised America's postwar military presence in Europe and gave the hard military edge to containment that Washington's policy-makers believed it should have.

Postwar security in Asia

Despite this highly charged atmosphere, the first military confrontation of the Cold War did not occur in Europe, but in Asia. On 25 June 1950 the armed forces of communist North Korea launched a full-scale attack on the American-backed government of Syngman Rhee in the south and signalled the start of the Korean War.

The outbreak of war in Korea followed half a decade of postwar turmoil and political instability in Asia. Although the wartime allies in the Pacific had made few plans for the postwar future of the region, there was a general expectation, both in Europe and America, that there would be an orderly transition to peace and thereafter steady progress towards postwar reconstruction. The reality was very different. While the war in the Pacific had ended Japan's hegemonial ambitions in the region, it had also served as a catalyst for profound political change. Throughout Asia, and in Southeast Asia in particular, the postwar era was one in which the old prewar political order was under constant challenge from an array of new pressures and forces. The most notable of these was nationalism, which was to become a force for change in nearly every country of the area, but the war had also encouraged the evolution of communism and this was also to be a potent element in postwar Asian politics.

European administrators returning to their prewar colonies confronted the danger of communism by attempting to repress it. Influenced by the deteriorating situation in Europe, their efforts became more urgent as local communist parties went on the offensive to offer a more radical path to independence. In Malaya, British efforts to contain the threat of communism were broadly successful, but elsewhere — in Vietnam, for example — they were an abject failure and overall there was a perception among Western governments that the threat posed by communism was becoming increasingly acute. This impression was reinforced as the communist revolution in China gained momentum in the late 1940s, leading Western governments, and the Truman administration in particular, to re-evaluate their interests and strategy in the region. Thus, in Washington as elsewhere, concern over the future stability of Asia in the light of a growing communist menace had by the late 1940s elevated issues of Asian security to a newly important place on America's foreign policy agenda.

Seen against this background, the escalation of the war in Korea from its beginnings as an attack on the south by the communist regime in the north to become a seminal conflict in the Cold War was perhaps not surprising. Yet the immediate origins of the conflict were largely unrelated to the deteriorating situation in Europe. They are to be found in events at the end of World War II and after (see Chapter 20). It was anticipated on both sides that the country would be unified and eventually achieve its independence. But as the 1940s wore on, the prospect of unification steadily receded. In the north of the country a communist movement led by Kim Il Sung became firmly entrenched with Soviet backing, while in the south the strongly right-wing government of Syngman Rhee maintained an uneasy alliance with the United States. Efforts by the United Nations to try to bridge the growing divide between north and south were to little avail. National elections were attempted in 1948, but failed when the United Nations Commission which was to oversee them was denied access to the north. When the postwar occupation of the Korean Peninsula ended in 1949 with the withdrawal of most American and Soviet forces, the two communities were growing increasingly antagonistic towards one another.

Tensions between north and south Korea increased appreciably during the first half of 1950. Yet the actual invasion early on the morning of 25 June caught the government of Syngman Rhee under-equipped and ill-prepared to offer an adequate response. Fearing that its client might be inclined to use heavy military equipment to go on the offensive against the north, United States policy during the late 1940s had been to restrict the nature of the war material it delivered to the south. Now, lacking the military capability necessary to resist the north's determined attack, the south Korean army was overwhelmed by vastly superior forces and soon in retreat. Seoul, the south Korean capital, was quickly over-run, and within a matter of weeks the army had been forced to retreat to the Pusan perimeter, a small enclave in the far southeast corner of the country near the provincial city of Taegu. Near collapse, the only thing that was to preserve the south from complete defeat was intervention of an allied land, sea and air force under the authority of the United Nations.

United Nations involvement in the conflict came largely at the behest of the United States. Although absent from Washington when news of the north Korean attack first reached the United States, President Truman moved quickly to register America's strong opposition to the invasion. At a diplomatic level, the Security Council of the United Nations was called into emergency session and met at 3 a.m. on the morning of 25 June, New York time. In the absence of the Soviet Union (which was boycotting meetings of the Council in protest at the People's Republic of China being denied the 'China' seat on the Council), America secured the passage of a resolution declaring that north Korea had caused a breach of the peace and calling for the cessation of fighting as well as the withdrawal of all troops from the south. Two days later, the United States secured the passage of a further resolution calling on members of the United Nations to help south Korea repel the armed attack and restore international peace and security to the area. This was followed on 7 July by the passage of a British-sponsored resolution recommending the creation of a unified United Nations command to provide all necessary military assistance to south Korea. The United States was asked to supply a commander for the force and General Douglas MacArthur was duly appointed.

The main effects of this diplomatic activity were twofold. First, by approaching the United Nations, the United States had secured international condemnation of north Korea's actions and so established a basis for action to repel the attack. Second, it had secured United Nations participation in a military action to defend the peace for the first time since the organisation was established in 1945. As a consequence, the United States was now able to seek the support of members in defending south Korea. With the passage of the resolutions, the British, Canadian, Australian and New Zealand governments, among several others, began preparations to send ground, air and naval forces to Korea, while many others agreed to contribute other forms of aid. Thus the conflict in Korea was quickly internationalised.

Although the resolution of 27 June secured United Nations authorisation for the allied 'police action' in Korea, the main burden of the campaign against the north was assumed by the United States. Partly as a result of its own concerns and partly as a response to the pleas for urgent assistance from the Syngman Rhee government, Washington moved quickly to try to reinforce the south's deteriorating position. Ahead, in fact, of any United Nations authority, Truman directed American military aid to south Korea and a short time later agreed to a range of other measures including the dispatch of air and naval forces. American ground forces quickly followed and thereafter a steady buildup of forces continued.

United States policy

The speed with which Washington had responded to the north's invasion of south Korea reflected the seriousness with which the Truman administration viewed the attack. As well as believing it to be an unprovoked attack on a peaceful country friendly to the United States, American policy-makers saw events in a wider context with broad international implications. In his memoirs, President Truman recalled thinking that:

> if South Korea was allowed to fall Communist leaders would be emboldened to override nations closer to our own shores. If the Communists were permitted to force their way into the Republic of Korea without opposition from the free

world, no small nation would have the courage to resist threats and aggression by a stronger Communist neighbour. If this was allowed to go unchallenged it would mean a third world war, just as similar incidents had brought on the second world war. It was also clear to me that the foundations and principles of the United Nations were at stake unless this unprovoked attack on Korea could be stopped.[3]

Truman's analysis of the conflict in Korea was widely shared in the United States. It was also common in London, Canberra, Ottawa and among other countries that rallied to the south's aid. But in the American capital perceptions of the danger were especially acute and reflected the growing paranoia of policy-makers and others over the communist threat. Having recently met, at least for the moment, the communist challenge in Europe, American officials now saw themselves facing the spectre of an equally dangerous situation in Asia. The monolithic nature of communism meant that the two threats were integrally related. 'What was developing in Korea,' Truman told his advisers, 'was a repetition on a larger scale of what had happened in Berlin. The Reds were probing for weaknesses in our armour; we had to meet their thrust without getting embroiled in a worldwide war.'[4] It was perhaps the first round in Moscow's drive for global domination. In fact there was no evidence that the Soviet Union had orchestrated the attack on the south, and still less that there was any direct Soviet military involvement. Nevertheless, the Soviet Union's complicity in the attack was assumed. One effect was to heighten the perceived danger, but it also made Truman and his advisers anxious to contain the conflict. Although it might be argued that there were times when United States policy could easily have endangered this objective, as over the atomic weapons incident mentioned below, the Korean War was nevertheless to remain a limited conflict.

American fears at the outbreak of war in Korea were acute and had been reinforced by several recent international developments. One was the explosion of a Soviet atomic bomb in August 1949. This occurred well before American officials had thought it possible and, since it signalled the end of the West's nuclear monopoly, the incident created great anxiety in Washington. In an attempt to offset the military capability Moscow had now gained, the United States decided to press ahead with the development of a hydrogen bomb. Equally unwelcome was the success of Mao Zedong's communist revolution in China a few months later. Hoping to prevent the collapse of the nationalist government of Chiang Kaishek, the United States had given massive amounts of military aid to the failing regime, but to little effect. The communist victory in October 1949 was not merely a severe blow to American prestige; it was seen as undermining the nation's strategic position in Asia. The Truman administration was accused of having 'lost' China and, in an increasingly bitter domestic political atmosphere, a witch hunt began to find those responsible. By the time the Korean War broke out, the seriousness with which Washington viewed these developments — against, of course, the background of the Cold War in Europe — was reflected in a new appraisal of American strategy in Asia. In a National Security Council paper of late 1949, the emphasis was on America's need to 'contain and where feasible to reduce the power and influence of the Soviet Union in Asia' and 'support the non-communist forces to take the initiative' in the region.[5] The administration's policy on Korea was a clear reflection of these objectives.

The course of the conflict

Initially United Nations forces did little to arrest the advance of the North Korean army. Understrength and with insufficient heavy armour and material, they were consistently being forced on to the defensive and retreat. The Pusan perimeter held firm, but during the first weeks of the war Allied successes were few. In September, however, the north suffered a spectacular reversal of its fortunes when the commander of the UN forces, General Douglas MacArthur, successfully landed a large force of United Nations troops at Inchon, several hundred kilometres behind communist lines. Caught by surprise, the north Korean army retreated in disarray and by early October had been driven back across the thirty-eighth parallel.

This daring manoeuvre achieved the objective that the United Nations had set when it had first intervened in the war, namely to repel the north Koreans from the south. It also satisfied America's original war aims cast in much the same terms. But the triumph did not end the conflict. Persuaded by strong interventions from MacArthur and Syngman Rhee, the Truman administration decided to press the military advantage which the United Nations had now attained and seize what all saw as an historic opportunity: to drive communism completely from the Korean Peninsula and to unify the country under democratic rule. To this end, MacArthur was authorised to continue the advance northwards towards the Chinese border. As a precaution against a possible widening of the war, Washington's instructions came with the proviso that the advance was to be halted if there was any sign of substantial Chinese or Soviet intervention. MacArthur thought this no more than a slight risk, and spoke confidently of victory when he had a personal meeting with Truman on the Pacific Island of Guam in mid-October.

MacArthur's reassurances notwithstanding, American officials were troubled by the danger of an expanded conflict, and with good reason. In late September, the Chinese Premier Zhou Enlai had said that the Chinese would not 'supinely tolerate their neighbours being savagely invaded by imperialists'[6] and repeated the message several times over the following weeks. While these statements may have been an attempt at bluff on the Chinese part, confirmation of their position emerged from other sources such as the Indian ambassador to Beijing. After a meeting with senior Chinese officials he reported that if United Nations forces crossed into north Korea, China would intervene with its own troops. While this opened the possibility that a south Korean drive north of the thirty-eighth parallel might be allowed to go unchallenged, while a United Nations advance would not, dividing the Allied force in this way had never been the American intention: both UN and south Korean forces were to drive forwards. Supremely confident, MacArthur was drawn to making rather ill-advised predictions about the success of the campaign, declaring, for instance, that the north would collapse by the end of November and American forces would be back in Japan by Christmas. In Washington, MacArthur's increasing outspokenness on political issues had begun to cause deep anxiety. Some of America's allies, Britain and Australia among them, were also alarmed at the influence MacArthur seemed to be exercising over the direction of strategic policy. Nevertheless, Washington was still able to secure a fresh vote of confidence for its policies when the General Assembly of the United Nations resolved that the aim of its actions was to establish a 'unified, independent and democratic Government of Korea'.

The United Nations advance north towards the Yalu River and the border with China proceeded rapidly until 25 October. Then, as Zhou Enlai had warned, the Chinese entered the conflict. China's initial intervention was small and short-lived, but a month later the Chinese launched a much larger offensive with a force of over 300 000. MacArthur's troops were unable to hold their ground and were soon in retreat back to below the thirty-eighth parallel.

China's intervention marked a significant escalation of the conflict in Korea and caused a crisis within the Truman administration. Not for the first time in the conflict, Truman found that he and MacArthur held strongly differing views as to how the war should be pursued. At a press conference in late November, Truman had rather unwisely conceded that his administration had at one point in the war contemplated the use of atomic weapons. The admission caused a furore in the press and encouraged the British Prime Minister Clement Atlee to seek urgent consultations with Truman. These took place early in December and concluded with the British prime minister being assured that the option was no longer being considered. Rejection of the nuclear option underscored the fact that throughout the conflict Truman and his political advisers had been determined to limit the danger of escalation as far as possible. Now that the Chinese had entered the war, this became imperative. MacArthur, however, viewed things differently. Far from urging greater caution on his political masters in Washington, he sought permission to expand the war, advising (among other measures) the mounting bombing raids into China in an effort to meet the new circumstances. Nor was MacArthur content to render his advice in private. Throughout the latter part of 1950 and the early months of 1951 he publicly advocated policies at odds with those of his government. Truman attempted to bring his wilful commander to heel, but to no avail. Exasperated by MacArthur's continued refusal to obey directions, Truman dismissed him in April 1951 and appointed General Matthew Ridgway to command the United Nations forces.

Just as the command of the United Nations forces changed, the war began to enter a new phase. During the first nine months the main battle front of the war had moved hundreds of kilometres up and down the Korean Peninsula. By the spring of 1951 it was in the vicinity of the thirty-eighth parallel, with both sides finding it difficult to make any substantial gains. From this point forward there was to be a new pattern of struggle. As Robert O'Neill has noted, 'the rally of massive offensives and counter-offensives of 1950–51 was followed by two years of limited probes and holding actions while the two sides negotiated slowly towards a settlement'.[7] These probes and actions were costly in human terms, but they availed little territory to either side. Over the two years the front did not move very far from the parallel, nor did the confrontations ever promise either side a decisive battlefield victory with which they could end the conflict. The only realistic prospect was a negotiated settlement.

The negotiations which eventually led to the end of the war began in July 1951. They were the result of an agreement between the American and Soviet governments and followed an initiative by the Canadian Foreign Minister and the Secretary General of the United Nations. With the two parts of Korea and the Chinese included as participants in the talks, the two sides quickly divided over two main issues: the location of the ceasefire line and the exchange of prisoners. Despite regular meetings of the negotiating teams at Panmunjom on the border between north and south Korea, these issues obstructed the progress of the negotiations for nearly two years and simultaneously prolonged the fighting.

On the first issue the communists pressed for adoption of the thirty-eighth parallel, but eventually accepted the existing battle line together with a two-and-a-half-mile demilitarised zone as a means of separating the two armies. The issue of prisoners proved more difficult to resolve. Both sides had captured large numbers of enemy forces but were unable to agree on the conditions under which they should be repatriated. The United States was opposed to forcible return on the grounds of free choice and concern over the fate of those who had been critical of communist governments, while the Chinese and the north Koreans did not wish the West to gain the propaganda victory that would result from large numbers of their troops deciding to remain behind. The impasse over this matter continued until the spring of 1953 when the communist side began to show some flexibility in its position. Whether this was a reflection of new Soviet foreign policy priorities following the death of Stalin in March of that year or the result of other factors remains unclear. The change, however, was crucial in bringing the talks to a relatively swift conclusion. On 27 July 1953, the parties signed an armistice agreement which included the provision that no prisoners would be repatriated against their will and that each side would have an opportunity under United Nations supervision to persuade their own nationals to return. Eventually 30 000 of the 95 000 North Korean prisoners elected to remain behind while 5000 of the 21 000 Chinese decided to do so. The armistice agreement brought an end to the fighting in Korea but it did not end the political conflict between North and South. In Geneva in 1954 an attempt was made to conclude a formal peace agreement, but after several weeks the talks collapsed without progress. All efforts to finalise a peace settlement since then have also failed.

The impact of the war

The Korean War began with the north's invasion of the south in June 1950. There can be little doubt that the government of Syngman Rhee contributed to the conflict by its aggressive and provocative stance towards the North, but the wider question of outside complicity is more difficult to answer. One author has argued that the United States engineered the conflict, hoping to start a big war by neglecting a stop a small one.[8] While this, as O'Neill notes,[9] lacks plausibility, the issue of the Soviet and Chinese roles in starting the war is less straightforward, largely because of the difficulty of gaining access to records. While it is possible to ascribe an interest in starting the conflict to both countries, the weight of evidence tends to support the view that their roles were limited. While the Soviets in particular helped the Kim Il Sung government develop its massive military capability and they (together with the Chinese) were probably aware of its plans for the attack, the initiative appears largely to have been Kim's.

Considerations of responsibility to one side, the war ended with neither side gaining any significant territorial advantage and with each having sustained heavy casualties: an estimated 300 000 south Koreans lost their lives along with 52 000 from the north. In addition, the country suffered massive physical destruction. Politically, the legacy has been equally painful. Korea became a long-term divided country after the war: two communities separated from each other by a mutual and deep-seated hostility. Not only has Korea not been reunified as of 1994, but Koreans on both sides of the thirty-eighth parallel have been denied contact with one another while the border itself has remained one of the most heavily fortified areas on Earth. In the south, the United States became guarantor to a succession of repressive right-wing governments whose conception of democracy until recently was far from the high ideals for which the United Nations had fought. In the north, the Kim Il Sung regime received strong economic and political support from its fraternal communist allies. For most of the decades since the signing of the armistice, the prospect that there might be a reconciliation between the two sides has seemed extremely remote. It is only in the last few years that changes in the international environment, as well as in Korea itself, have encouraged a more optimistic outlook.

That these changes are now occurred as the Cold War came to an end serves to underscore the point that the Korean War was one of the most important conflicts of the Cold War period and had a profound impact on postwar international politics. At the outbreak of the conflict, the United States had relatively limited interests in Asia. Having 'lost' China, the Truman administration had begun to pay closer attention to the region, but the focus of United States policy was firmly on the postwar reconstruction and demilitarisation of Japan. Korea had barely entered the American foreign policy consciousness and was deemed by senior officials early in 1950 to be outside the key area of United States interests in Asia. The outbreak of war was to change all this. Committed by virtue of the Truman Doctrine to the defence of Western interests against the advance of communism wherever it should threaten, American policy-makers saw within the conflict an orchestrated communist attack on their country's interests. Not to have responded forcefully to the challenge would have been to display weakness, to play the role of appeaser and almost certainly to encourage further communist adventurism. Neither Washington nor any of its Western allies doubted that this would be a mistake with potentially fatal consequences. By committing themselves to the defence of South Korea they were making a stand for the future.

They also brought the Cold War to Asia. America's military involvement in Korea elevated the ideological confrontation between East and West to a new level of intensity. In Europe, where the Cold War had begun, the threat had become institutionalised and to some degree less acute as a consequence of the massive military capability now deployed there on either side of the Iron Curtain. In Asia, however, the situation was more fluid. As the outbreak of fighting in Korea demonstrated, the communists might periodically seek to probe the West's weaknesses. At the same time, China was now a communist power posing a clear and recognisable threat. American intervention in Korea was part of a strategy to deter these dangers, but Washington also went much further. To reinforce its new deterrent posture in Asia and 'contain' communism, the Truman administration expanded its military aid program in Southeast Asia, extending access, for example, to the French in their efforts to subdue a communist (but also nationalist) revolution in Indochina. At the same time, it entered into a series of new security agreements with friendly countries in the region: bilateral arrangements with Japan and the Philippines and a tripartite pact (ANZUS) with Australia and New Zealand. The war also hastened Japan's international rehabilitation. Determined to turn the country into a bastion of liberal democratic political and economic values, and thus a strong friend of the United States in Asia, a peace treaty was signed in September 1951, economic aid was increased and the Allied military occupation was wound down. Simultaneously, America's relations with China deteriorated and became increasingly hostile, precluding any chance of reconciliation. Overall, one of the clear effects of the Korean War was that the United States built a massive stake in Asian security, one which brought the doctrine of containment to Asia, led it into Vietnam in the 1960s and ensured that it remained militarily committed on the mainland of Asia for the next two and a half decades.

As in Europe, the coming of the Cold War had a profound effect on the politics of the region. Few relationships either within the region or between local countries and outsiders were unaffected. Over the next 25 years the history of Asia became the history of political instability and confrontation as time and again in places like Malaya, Vietnam, Laos, Thailand and China the ideological struggle that was the Cold War manifested itself in a contest for strategic position and territorial advantage.

Guide to further reading

Cumings, Bruce, *The Origins of the Korean War, Vol. 1, Liberation and the Emergency of Separate Regimes, 1945–1947; Vol. 2, The Roaring of the Cataract, 1947–1950*, Princeton University Press, Princeton, 1981
   The definitive scholarly account on the origins of the Korean War.
Goulden, Joseph C., *Korea: The Untold Story of the War*, Times Books, New York, 1982
   A very able popular account that makes use of recently released documents.
Lowe, Peter, *The Origins of the Korean War*, Longman, London and New York, 1986
   This is one in a series devoted to the origins of modern wars. Apart from covering the history of Korea from the beginning of the Japanese colonial period to the months after the outbreak of the Korean War, this book considers the world situation which led to foreign intervention, including the rise of the Chinese Communist Party in China and the Cold War in Europe.

McCormack, Gavan, *Cold War, Hot War: An Australian Perspective on the Korean War*, Hale and Iremonger, Sydney, 1985
This account focuses on Australian participation in the Korean War. It takes a view which is somewhat more sceptical of the United Nations position than most in the English language.
Rees, David, *Korea: The Limited War*, W.W. Norton, New York, 1965
An account of the war from a military perspective.
Yergin, David, *Shattered Peace: The Origins of the Cold War and the National Security State*, Houghton Mifflin, Boston, 1977
One of the best scholarly accounts of the origins of the Cold War focusing on the evolution of American policy.

Notes

1 Quoted in Knapp, Wilfrid F., *A History of War and Peace 1935–1965*, Oxford University Press, Oxford, 1967, p. 107.
2 Quoted in Yergin, David, *Shattered Peace, The Origins of the Cold War and the National Security State*, Houghton Mifflin, Boston, 1977, p. 283.
3 Truman, Harry S., *Years of Trial and Hope 1946–1952*, Doubleday and Co., Garden City, New York, 1956, p. 333.
4 ibid., p. 337.
5 National Security Council Paper 48/2, approved at the end of 1949, quoted in Yergin, David, *Shattered Peace*, p. 405.
6 Quoted in Knapp, Wilfrid F., *A History of War and Peace*, p. 229.
7 O'Neill, Robert, *Australia in the Korean War 1950–52*, AGPS, Canberra, 1981, p. 202.
8 Stone, I.F., *The Hidden History of the Korean War*, Monthly Review Press, New York, 1952.
9 O'Neill, Robert, *Australia in the Korean War*, p. 16.

22 | The continuing struggle in Indochina

'It is hopeless,' United States Army Chief of Staff General Matthew B. Ridgway told fellow-members of the Joint Chiefs of Staff Committee on 2 August 1954, 'to expect a US training mission to achieve success unless the nation concerned is able to effectively perform governmental functions.' A 'reasonably strong, stable, civil government', he considered, would have to be in control before the United States should assume any military responsibilities towards any country in what had been French Indochina.[1] Such a description could not possibly be applied to the government over which Ngo Dinh Diem had been presiding since he became first Prime Minister of the Republic of (South) Vietnam on 7 July 1954, after having been chosen by Washington for that role during the Geneva Conference. His government might indeed have been termed a racket rather than a regime. Diem himself was indisputably honest. But he insulated himself from the world outside, living 'like a monk behind stone walls', immersed for up to eighteen hours a day in the minutiae of administration relying for political advice on his sinister younger brother Ngo Dinh Nhu, who ran a secret police force to protect his interests in illegal gambling, drug trafficking, waterfront rackets, fraudulent deals in foreign currency, prostitution and extortion.[2] Another brother, Ngo Dinh Can, operated a smuggling ring shipping rice to the communist enemy in North Vietnam, as well as a drug syndicate dealing in the archdiocese of a fourth brother, the Archbishop of Hue, who was himself engaged in suspect deals in real estate in Vietnam and Australia.

A corrupt government is not necessarily unpopular, or even inefficient. But Diem adopted policies calculated to inspire the greatest possible opposition. Nearly three-quarters of South Vietnam's population of rather more than 14 million in 1960 were Buddhists; another 2 million or so were members of the Cao Dai, an eclectic blend of Christianity and Asian religions; 1 million were adherents of the Hoa Hao, a schismatic Buddhist sect; and a little more than 1 million were Catholics, their numbers increased considerably by refugees from the North. But it was the Catholics who had always enjoyed privileged positions because of their readiness to co-operate with the French, and Diem and his family were Catholics. He now proceeded to establish his co-religionists as a ruling elite in South Vietnam, despite their constituting less than 8 per cent of the population. He also restored the properties of land to land-lords dispossessed by the communists before 1954, and replaced elected village councils with official appointees whose conduct towards the peasants was characterised by 'arrogance, capriciousness, dishonesty and cruelty', according to alarmed United States military observers.[3] Australian journalist Denis Warner reflected that Diem was only giving the Vietnamese people a choice of terrorisms, and that the terrorism of his government troubled them more than that of the communists.

Such a government met none of Ridgway's criteria. It did not even control its own capital, where gangsters ran the police force. And the Army of the Republic of Vietnam (ARVN) reflected the deficiencies of the Diem regime. It had been developed in the first place by the French as a kind of auxiliary to their own Expeditionary Force. It accordingly lacked any logistic capability of its own and was quite unable even to organise the huge amounts of equipment left behind by the French. Nor did it exhibit anything like a professional standard of conduct. Senior officers routinely supplemented their income by selling on the black market, embezzling official funds, exploiting prostitution and dealing in drugs, as the official United States Army historian recorded; and the lower ranks continued to steal from the local population until the very end of the war. Nor was this surprising. Commander of the Australian Advisory Team, Colonel F.P. Serong, observed that they were 'neglected by their officers, inadequately paid and provided with a ration allowance no higher than that for a dog'.[4]

All this might seem to make South Vietnam indefensible in every sense of the word. But successive Administrations in Washington felt compelled to try to defend the indefensible. Dwight D. Eisenhower had already spelt out, on 10 February 1954, the horrific prospect of communist control of Indochina leading to the progressive fall of other regional countries, so that the entire Western Pacific region would become strategically endangered, forcing the United States to concentrate on the defence of its own hemisphere, even to the point of having to abandon Western Europe. This would mean that the communists had won the Cold War. Such an analysis, of course, rested on two assumptions. One was that the Soviet Union and the People's Republic of China constituted a gigantic communist monolith, applying a concerted strategy of global domination. The second was that every communist-led national liberation movement in the region was acting as an agent of such a strategy. Intelligence agencies such as the CIA itself insisted that they were unable to discover any evidence to support either of these assumptions. But the Joint Chiefs could hardly have imagined how hopeless the situation really was. The officers of the United States Military Assistance Advisory Group (MAAG) were, for example, appalled to discover that their counterparts in the ARVN were totally unfamiliar with concepts like regimental honour of loyalty from the top down and the bottom up, articles of faith at West Point, The Citadel or the Virginia Military Academy. But even more serious was the fact that the Americans themselves were totally unfamiliar with the kind of war which the ARVN was actually going to have to fight. The immediate threat to Diem's regime was internal subversion and insurgency, directed largely by former members of the Vietminh, now known as Vietcong, or 'Vietnamese Communists'. Counterinsurgency was thus the order of the day. But the very term 'counterinsurgency' was all but unknown in United States military circles. Four hours' basic training in what was called 'counterguerilla warfare' was considered sufficient for all practical purposes. There was plenty of first-hand experience to be drawn on from the British and the French. But American military planners tended to assume that admitting that anything could be learned from people so obviously less successful in war than themselves could lead to a subtle sapping of the American character. In any case, MAAG Commander General Samuel T. 'Hanging Sam' Williams was convinced that the real threat to South Vietnam would take the form of a conventional invasion by the North, and all indications to the contrary were merely part of a communist plot to weaken the capacity of the ARVN for conventional warfare. And there was no future in trying to argue with Hanging Sam.

General Williams might indeed have viewed the situation differently if he had been receiving any intelligence about it. But this was another fatal problem. The MAAG had no intelligence unit of its own. Diem's government had six, all working against one another and all unreliable. Reports of successes were invented to protect the reputations of the officers involved. Failures were not reported at all. Even reports suggesting that conditions in any combat zone were less than ideal were likely to lead to the demotion of the commander responsible. British journalist David Hotham wrote despairingly in 1957 that it was 'not that the Communists have done nothing because Diem is in power, rather Diem has remained in power because the Communists have done nothing'.[5]

They had done nothing much at that stage for two reasons. Perhaps the more important was that the communist leadership in North Vietnam was preoccupied with the immediate tasks of building socialism in its own half of the country. But in any case, communists in both the North and South had expected that Vietnam would soon be united under their control, either as a result of the collapse of the Diem regime or through the nationwide elections provided for in the Geneva Accords. But wholesale arrests and other government countermeasures were threatening the very existence of the Vietcong, and Diem was simply ignoring calls from the North or anywhere else to allow such elections to take place. The Vietnamese Communist Party (Lao Dong) accordingly decided at its 15th Congress in January 1959 to adopt a triple program of intensified political organisation, the extermination of government officials and collaborators and the use of the armed struggle as a means of overthrowing the Diem regime. A series of patrol-type engagements followed, in which the ARVN showed itself consistently ineffective against often less numerous and less well-equipped Vietcong insurgents. Diem nonetheless assured General Williams in September 1959 that the strategic victory against the Vietcong had been won. He could well have been correct, in the sense that the strategy being applied might well have brought victory if only the tactics had been effective. But perhaps nobody had told Diem that they were not.

Throughout 1960, the Vietcong routinely attacked government installations and routed ARVN patrols. New United States President John F. Kennedy despatched his vice-president, Senator Lyndon B. Johnson, in May 1961, to report on the obviously deteriorating situation. Johnson sent back a call for urgent action. Vietnam and Thailand, he told Kennedy, were:

> the immediate — and most important — trouble spots critical to the US. The basic decision in Southeast Asia is here. We must decide whether to help these countries or throw in the towel in the area and pull our defenses back to San Francisco.[6]

Kennedy felt that he could hardly afford to concede another round to the communists. His policies were failing in Laos, where the pro-American faction was losing ground to the pro-communist one; and he had been gravely embarrassed by the Bay of Pigs fiasco in Cuba. He nonetheless delayed taking any action until the Vietcong crowned their record of unbroken success against the ARVN by seizing and holding the provincial capital of Phuoc Vinh, only 90 kilometres from Saigon, in September 1961. Kennedy then sent his personal military adviser, General Maxwell D. Taylor, and presidential aide Walt Whitman Rostow to Vietnam, to report on possible courses of action that might be taken by the United States. They advised that the situation might still be salvaged if Washington acted promptly to shore up South Vietnamese morale by reinforcing the ARVN with American combat troops. This was further than Kennedy was prepared to go. However, he agreed to despatch 33 helicopters with 400 United States Marine Corps aviators to fly and maintain them. Their ostensible role was to enhance the training and logistic capabilities of the ARVN. But the Marines predictably rigged helicopters up with machine guns and rocket launchers and proceeded to strafe the jungle hideouts of the Vietcong, driving the insurgents out into the open where they could be overrun by ARVN armoured infantry in United States-supplied M-113 personnel carriers. A critical threshold had been crossed. The Americans were no longer just trying to advise the South Vietnamese how to fight. They were starting to do their fighting for them.

It was soon evident that they would have to do more. The new tactics were brilliantly successful at first. But ARVN forces supported by USMC aviation, M-113s and artillery were totally defeated by outnumbered and outgunned Vietcong at Ap Bac on 2 January 1963, chiefly because of the almost insuperable reluctance of ARVN commanders to do anything that might provoke the Vietcong to retaliate. One ARVN armoured cavalry unit took three and a half hours to advance 1500 metres against largely ineffective small arms fire. And South Vietnam itself began to collapse into chaos when Diem allowed Catholics in Hue to fly flags in honour of the birthday of his brother, the Archbishop and dubious dealer in real estate, but refused to allow the vast majority of the population to observe the birthday of the Buddha in the same manner. Riots flared throughout the country. Seven Buddhist monks burned themselves to death in protest. United States Ambassador Henry Cabot Lodge reported help-lessly that 'there is no possibility, in my view, that the war can be won under a Diem administration', and suggested that 'at this juncture it would be better for us to make the decision to get out honourably'.[7] Diem himself was indeed removed from office by a military coup on 1 November and assassinated, along with his racketeer brother Ngo Dinh Nhu. But this led only to more coups and more defeats. Lyndon Johnson, now president after Kennedy's own assassination three weeks later, sent General Taylor back to Vietnam, accompanied by Defense Secretary Robert S. McNamara, for more advice. They reported in March 1964 that things were unquestionably growing worse, but that disastrous con-sequences were likely to ensue for the United States should South Vietnam fall under communist control. Washington should therefore make it clear to all concerned that it was prepared to furnish assistance and support to South Vietnam for as long as it took to bring the in-surgency under control. General Taylor said later that it never occurred to him to recommend that the United States should just cut its losses and get out.

Johnson would have found it difficult to furnish support of the order that was obviously going to be necessary unless the Vietnamese com-munists were so unwise as to take some action directly hostile to the United States itself. They obliged on 4 August, when two North Viet-namese patrol boats attacked an American destroyer carrying out an intelligence-gathering mission in the Gulf of Tonkin on behalf of the South Vietnamese. A second attack was reported two days later. It was concluded later that in fact the radar operators on the American vessels might have mistaken the wakes of their own ships for the outlines of supposed enemy craft. Johnson had no cause to doubt the genuineness of the original report at the time, however. He seized the opportunity to unleash massive air strikes against North Vietnamese naval bases and to obtain from Congress a resolution authorising him to take all action necessary to protect United States Armed Forces and to assist nations covered by the SEATO Treaty. The Vietcong responded by attacking American bases at Bien Hoa, Pleiku and Qui Nhon. Johnson hit back with more air strikes. Then, in the last week of December 1964, the Vietcong gained their most spectacular victory yet, seizing the village of Binh Gia on the coast near Saigon. New Commander of the United States Military Assistance Command Vietnam (MACV), General William C. West-moreland, considered that it was 'the beginning of an intensive military challenge which the Vietnamese Government could not meet within its own resources'.[8]

The most serious implication of this was that the ARVN could no longer be relied upon even to defend United States bases, as was demon-strated by successful Vietcong raids on Pleiku and Qui Nhon in February 1965. But such bases had to be secured if the Americans were to apply their new strategy, which was to carry out severe reprisals for spectacular operations by the Vietcong, while gradually increasing the pressure of air strikes until the North Vietnamese were forced to stop assisting in-surgency in the South. This meant that United States combat troops would have to be deployed, if only for defensive purposes. Operation Rolling Thunder, the sustained aerial bombardment of selected military targets in North Vietnam, commenced on 2 March. USMC Landing Team 3/9 splashed ashore at Da Nang on 8 March, to protect the United States Air Force bases and facilities from which Rolling Thunder was launched. It was the very last job on Earth suited to the training and disposition of shock troops. Nobody could doubt that the Marines would not remain long in such a passive role. It could only be presumed that the time of 'Advice and Support' was over, and that the United States was at last going openly to war in Vietnam.

It was not going to war alone. Eisenhower himself had laid down as a basic principle that the United States should never become involved again in a war on the Asian mainland except with regional support. This had been assured by the government of Australia, which had supplied 30 military instructors to South Vietnam on 24 May 1962, and had indicated in December 1964 that it would be prepared to send combat forces if the United States were to do so. Prime Minister Robert G. Menzies duly announced on 29 April 1965 that he would be sending a battalion of the Royal Australian Regiment to Vietnam. New Zealand Prime Minister Keith J. Holyoake followed suit on 27 May. A South Korean combat division began landing in October. But that was about the extent of significant support worldwide. On 23 April 1964, Johnson had expressed the hope that he would see some other flags in South Vietnam. It was all the more important that this should happen, because the president and his advisers were convinced that Vietnam would be seen generally as a touchstone of United States commitment in the rest of the region. But the fact was that most regional countries remained resolutely uncommitted, as did the Latin Americans and Africans. Even the British and Canadians made it quite clear that military assistance was out of the question, and the West Europeans plainly regarded the whole enterprise as a disastrous distraction from the area of truly critical importance — namely Europe. Only 39 nations in all provided assistance in even the most minuscule form in response to Johnson's repeated appeals for more flags in Vietnam. Only five sent military forces and only four actually engaged in combat — only Australia and New Zealand at their own expense. They were also the only other democracies in the world to fight in support of American intervention in Vietnam.

Domestic support was no more heartening. Fifteen thousand anti-war protestors marched on the White House on 15 April 1965, even before United States ground forces had become involved. Rallies against the war swept the nation in October and November. Two men burned themselves to death in protest, after the manner of the Buddhist monks in South Vietnam. Then 35 000 marchers converged on the White House on 27 November 1965. Perhaps no war was ever undertaken in the face of such active discouragement at home and abroad.

This made military success all the more desirable. United States strategy was effectively to maintain pressure through air attacks, while United States ground forces dealt with the major communist insurgency, leaving the ARVN to counter local guerilla operations and generally pacify the countryside. But the major problem with the air offensive was that it was not being directed against the only targets which might have neutralised the capacity of North Vietnam to support insurgency in the South, like the rail link with China, port facilities in Haiphong and other harbours and the administrative and industrial centre of Hanoi. Johnson feared that striking at these might have created problems with the Russians and Chinese, who were supplying the North with essential military equipment, and would also risk causing heavy civilian casualties, thereby adding fuel to the protest movements which were now active in Europe and Australia as well as in the United States. Nor was it possible to press for anything like the complete overhaul of the officer corps of the ARVN which was obviously required to bring it to something approaching a satisfactory level of efficiency, because any South Vietnamese government was so dependent upon the support of the officer corps that it would have been impossible to carry out major changes in the latter without causing the former to fall apart even more than it was doing anyway.

The results were predictable. United States ground troops continued to inflict losses on the communists out of all proportion to their own. However, even McNamara considered that the enemy could continue to sustain casualties of that order almost indefinitely. And meanwhile, pacification in the countryside was actually going backwards under the impact of continuing ARVN defeats. A renewed wave of strikes and coups swept through South Vietnam in the New Year; open civil war between Catholics and Buddhists raged in Hue; and there was no evidence that the bombing offensive was having the slightest impact on either the morale of the North Vietnamese, or their capacity to continue infiltrating forces to the South. McNamara proposed in despair that Johnson should 'consider terminating the bombing in all of North Vietnam . . . for an indefinite period in conjunction with covert moves toward peace'.[9] There was no alternative but for the United States and its allies to shoulder even more of the burden of the war than they were carrying already, while the South Vietnamese tried to set their own house in order. This would mean more American troops and more United States casualties at a time when total United States strength in Vietnam had already reached a figure of 385 000.

This might well have seemed too politically hazardous for Johnson to accept. He did so, nonetheless, rather than admit what he regarded as defeat. Another 100 000 American troops were despatched to Vietnam during 1967. Also present by the end of the year were 48 000 South Koreans, 7353 Australians and New Zealanders and 2205 Thais. Combined United States and ARVN forces carried out ever larger and wider ranging search-and-destroy operations, inflicting casualties on the enemy of the order of 10 to 1, according to official body counts. These were of course notoriously unreliable in conditions of guerilla warfare, where the dead were all too likely to include hapless civilians caught in the crossfire. Nor was there any question that the communists could easily support losses of between 40 000 and 50 000 dead a year, especially as there was no need to be concerned about popular feeling in a totalitarian society where the leadership controlled all the media of information and misinformation, and did not tolerate protest movements anyway. At the same time, communist victory could not be assured as long as the Americans were still in South Vietnam.

It was accordingly decided in Hanoi that an all-out offensive should be launched in the hope of setting off a general uprising in the South that would topple the rickety regime in Saigon and convince the Americans that their mission was indeed impossible. As United States Military Historian Charles B. MacDonald put it:

A catastrophic military defeat in an American election year, an immense increase in American and South Vietnamese casualties, a demonstration that the South Vietnamese were incapable of shouldering the burden of the war: all these together, might prove the equivalent of a Dien Bien Phu. The US might decide that there was no way to victory except at a price that the American people were unwilling to pay.[10]

Surprise and deception were essential. North Vietnamese officials hinted at a diplomatic reception in Hanoi in December 1967 that they might be prepared to enter into negotiations on a peace settlement if the United States air offensive were stopped. Johnson eagerly took the bait and halted the bombing in the vicinity of Hanoi, making it easier for the North Vietnamese to infiltrate men and materials to their bases in ostensibly neutral Laos and Cambodia. As a further ruse, the Vietcong announced a truce for the period of the sacred holiday of Tet, the lunar New Year, from 27 January to 3 February. North Vietnamese forces then opened a massive bombardment of the United States base at Khe Sanh on 21 January, to divert American attention from the real intended targets.

On 30 January 1968, some 80 000 Vietcong and NVA regular troops struck across the length and breadth of South Vietnam at 36 of the country's 44 provincial capitals, five out of six autonomous cities, 64 of 242 district capitals and 50 hamlets. It was the greatest communist operation of the war to date and it was a total military disaster. There were no popular uprisings; the ARVN fought back more resolutely than expected and most of the initial communist gains were wiped out in two or three days, and almost all within a fortnight. The NVA and Vietcong lost some 45 000 dead, most of them Vietcong, ten times as many as the Americans and South Vietnamese combined. The Vietcong were indeed almost annihilated, thereby leaving a vacuum in the countryside which enabled the government forces to renew their pacification program almost unhindered by guerilla activity. It was a tremendous victory, and it broke the will of the victors in Washington.

Credit for this paradoxical result must go to the United States media. Tet demonstrated vividly the incapacity of television to tell the truth, given its reliance upon a battery of visual images selected for shock effect. Television coverage of South Vietnamese cities damaged in the fighting gave an impression of total devastation by showing only what had been devastated. Commentators without any sense of history stressed the ability of the communists to launch a major offensive after years of war, overlooking the fact that the Germans had done the same in 1918 and 1945, and had also been totally defeated. This blatant attempt of the media to represent an unmitigated communist disaster as some kind of great Allied defeat did indeed have the unintended effect of rallying popular support in the United States behind the government, in the expectation of strong retaliatory action. But this support soon evaporated when it became evident that no such action was going to be taken. Decisive measures to follow up the victory of Tet would have required a still greater United States military effort. Some of the president's advisers considered that it would be too inconvenient to have to explain to the American people in an election year why this should be necessary, after three years of allegedly successful operations against the communist enemy. Others argued that it would be impossible to augment the commitment to Vietnam without seriously impairing the ability of the United States to respond to threats to areas of far greater strategic importance, such as Western Europe.

If it was inexpedient to augment the United States' military effort in Vietnam, and if it was demonstrably inadequate at its present level, there was nothing left to do except to disengage from Vietnam entirely. The question was how to do this while avoiding the appearance of having lost a war for the first time in American history. The CIA suggested that the North Vietnamese might be prepared to negotiate peace terms if the air offensive were stopped unconditionally. They had of course last pretended to be interested in peace talks as a cover for their preparations for Tet. Johnson nevertheless announced on 31 March 1968 that bombing north of the twenty-sixth parallel would cease from 1 April. He also said that he would not be a candidate in the forthcoming presidential elections. Hanoi responded by offering to discuss peace terms in Paris. Johnson agreed on 3 May. North Vietnamese troops and the remnants of the Vietcong thereupon launched a whirlwind series of attacks on 109 towns and hamlets in South Vietnam the following day. Their efforts, however, were on a far smaller scale than during Tet and made no significant impression. Negotiations began in Paris on 13 May, after it became evident that this second bid for a military solution by the communists had failed too. Agreement would be reached over the next four years on little more than the shape of the conference table. Johnson meanwhile announced that he would end the bombing of North Vietnam entirely from 1 November. This was only a week before the date set for the presidential elections, and it was suggested that Johnson might have been trying to improve the chances of the Democratic candidate. It made no difference, as it happened. Richard M. Nixon swept into office on the Republican ticket with a commitment to end United States military involvement in Vietnam.

To Nixon, this meant that some arrangement would have to be found to avoid giving the impression of complete surrender by Washington. Formal truce negotiations began on 25 January 1969, just five days after his inauguration. The North Vietnamese decided to test his resolve immediately, carrying out mortar and rocket attacks against 115 bases, towns and cities in the South over 23–24 February, while some 40 000 NVA troops massed secretly inside the border of officially neutral

Cambodia. Open retaliation would have caused trouble for Nixon with Congress, as he would have had to explain why he was extending the scope of the war when he was supposed to be winding it down. His solution was to unleash B-52 Stratofortresses in mass attacks against the communist sanctuaries, without telling Congress. What he did announce publicly on 8 June was that he would be withdrawing 25 000 American combat troops from Vietnam. He followed this on 16 September by announcing the impending withdrawal of another 35 000 troops.

But the public relations effect of these statements was blunted by a series of less popular developments. United States and ARVN forces stormed a Vietcong position on Ap Bia Mountain on 20 May, after six days of heavy fighting, only to abandon it a few days later because the Vietcong had escaped across the border of officially neutral Laos. The operation was a tactical blunder and was represented by the United States media as typifying the futility of the whole Vietnam operation. Far more serious still was the revelation of the massacre of 347 Vietnamese civilians by United States troops at My Lai on 16 March 1968. Invest-igations discovered that another 50 civilians had been similarly murder-ed in a nearby hamlet on the same afternoon. Atrocities by one's own side in wartime are, of course, normally concealed, denied or held to be justified by the far worse atrocities that the other side is supposed to have committed. It was the peculiar quality of the Vietnam War that the My Lai outrage inspired far greater public indignation in the United States than the more than 17 000 murders of civilians known to have been carried out by the communists in South Vietnam since 1964, even though these had formed an essential part of overall communist strategy, while nobody seriously suggested that atrocities like My Lai were part of official United States policy.

But the protestors found even more to object to in what was un-doubtedly the official policy of the Nixon administration. In March 1970, the vehement anti-communist Lon Nol had ousted compliant Prince Norodom Sihanouk in Cambodia, which the NVA and Vietcong had long been using as a supply route and staging base, with Sihanouk's acqui-escence (see Chapter 42). The North Vietnamese accordingly increased pressure on Cambodia to the point where it was clear that Lon Nol would soon be overthrown. Some 26 000 ARVN troops, with United States support, swept into Cambodia on 29 April in an attempt to eliminate communist bases and command centres before the inevitable takeover. There might have been a certain encouragement in seeing the ARVN actually undertake an offensive operation, even against a supposedly neutral country, and large quantities of material were certainly captured, even though the Vietcong leadership proved elusive. But the forward moves were tentative and badly co-ordinated, and ARVN commanders showed a most disquieting disposition to rely on United States aviation

Photo 1: (Ch. 3) Loess country in North China.

Photo 2: (Chs 3, 4) Harvesting rice in Java.
Photo 3: (Ch. 4) An old-time Chinese woman seated in a chair, showing her bound feet, Courtesy, Essex Institute, Salem, Mass.

Photo 4: (Ch. 5) The ancient Bulguksa Buddhist Temple near Kyongju, Korea.

Photo 5: (Ch. 5) A traditional Minangkabau house.
Photo 6: (Ch. 5) Balinese women making an offering to the gods.

Photo 7: (Ch. 5) Muslim women at prayer in Indonesia.

Photo 8: (Ch. 6) Traditional Chinese ribbon dance.

Photo 9: (Ch. 6) Wayang figure.
Photo 10: (Ch. 6) Highlight of an Indonesian dance, where the men simulate stabbing themselves with the ancient kris.

Photo 11: (Ch. 6) Traditional Japanese no *drama.*

Photo 12: (Chs 6, 37) Traditional Japanese orchestra.

Photo 13: (Ch. 7) The Dacheng Hall of the great Confucian Temple in Qufu.

Photo 14: (Ch. 8) During the days of Dutch colonialism in Indonesia, local Dutch and Indonesian heads move towards the latter's palace.

Photo 15: (Ch. 10) A cartoon from the age of European and Japanese imperialism in China.

Photo 16: (Ch. 15) The Emperor Meiji.
Photo 17: (Ch. 7) A feudal lord's escort enters the outskirts of Edo.

Photo 18: (Ch. 12) The signature of the Sino-British Treaty of Nanjing in 1842.

Photo 19: (Ch. 22) A group of Communist guerrillas using captured American weapons during the Vietnam War.

Photo 20: (Ch. 26) President Sukarno addressing a religious meeting at Indonesia's Presidential Palace.

Photo 21: (Ch. 8) Traditional court dress in Solo, Java.

Photo 22: (Ch. 18) The annual opening of the People's Council in 1930, during the period when the Dutch controlled Indonesia.

Photo 23: (Ch. 17) Yenan, centre of the Chinese communist movement in 1935–36 after the Long March.

Photo 24: (Ch. 25) A view of Tangshan, Hebei province, after its destruction by the great earthquake of 28 July 1976.

Photo 25: (Chs 25, 30) Community construction work in China.

Photo 26: (Ch. 29) Symbols of the various parties in Jakarta, Indonesia, during the 1955 elections.
The largest one reads 'Choose PKI'.

Photo 27: (Ch. 25) Chairman Mao, Lin Bao and Red Guards.

Photo 28: (Ch. 28) Part of Tokyo, showing the observation tower, which is also used as a television and radio transmitter, and reclaimed land.

Photo 29: (Ch. 26) Indonesia and the Netherlands sign the agreement on West New Guinea (West Irian), August 1962.

Photo 30: (Ch. 38) Rice fields in Indonesia.

Photo 31: (Ch. 26) Fretilin leaders in East Timor hail East Timor's independence.

Photo 32: (Ch. 27) Television assembly lines in a Tokyo factory.

Photo 33: (Ch. 27) The port of Yokohama, one of Japan's largest postwar trading ports.

Photo 34: (Ch. 30) Peasants in Guangdong province, China, are improving their water-lifting equipment.

Photo 35: (Chs 33, 35) Meal time in a Japanese family, showing the combination of Japanese and Western dress and Western mechanical gadgets.

Photo 36: (Ch. 33) A group wedding in the People's Republic of China.

Photo 37: (Ch. 38) Part of the spring afforestation campaign in Sining, Chinghai province, China.

Photo 38: (Ch. 44) Australian soldiers in Vietnam during the Vietnam War.

Photo 39: (Ch. 15) The last shogun of the Tokugawa proclaiming his relinquishment of power on 7 November 1967 in Kyoto.

for fire support and transport, as well as for casualty evacuation, instead of making appropriate use of their own field artillery or indeed their own feet. And of course this apparent extension of the war into territory where the communists had been operating for years revitalised the protest movement in the United States. Some 100 000 demonstrators marched on Washington and anti-war rallies enlivened over 400 college campuses, including that of Kent State University, where four students were shot dead by units of the Ohio National Guard on 9 May. This tragedy impelled Congress to take drastic action to speed disengagement. United States troops were withdrawn from Cambodia on 29 June. On 31 December, Congress voted to deny funding for the deployment of United States combat troops in Laos and to repeal the Tonkin Gulf Resolution.

The ARVN forces had meanwhile been driven out of Cambodia by the NVA. South Vietnamese President Nguyen Van Thieu, however, ordered another offensive sweep on 8 February 1971, this time into Laos. Operation LAM SON 719 was named after historic Vietnamese victory over China in 1427, but it ended on 9 April with very mixed results. An enormous amount of material was captured, and communist dead were estimated at some 19 000, against a total of 10 000 ARVN casualties. But nearly half the NVA casualties had been inflicted by supporting United States aviation, without the help of which the ARVN invaders might not have been able to escape at all. And this further extension of the war set off a new wave of protests in the United States. Some 200 000 demonstrators besieged the White House. Public dissatisfaction with the whole business was inflamed still further when the *New York Times* began on 13 June to publish the official record of United States–Vietnam relations compiled by the Defense Department for Secretary McNamara and illegally made available to the press by one of his public servants. Their narrative certainly revealed some deliberate deception on the part of preceding administrations, as any revelation of official documents is likely to do. But what it showed most significantly was how Johnson and his advisers had sought to find some middle way of limited action between the recommendations of their military experts who wanted the United States to use its sea and air power in the most effective manner possible in Vietnam, and those of its intelligence agents and diplomats who doubted the wisdom of intervening at all. It also demonstrated how United States officials in the field had reported bitterly year after year that the middle way chosen by the administration was not working and things were getting worse all the time.

What was truly ironic was that things were in fact starting to get better at last. There was no challenge to Thieu's authority in prospect; pacification was proceeding satisfactorily, in the absence of the devastated Vietcong, and improved farming techniques were providing ample supplies of food, as well as markedly improving the incomes of the peasants.

The Green Revolution was leaving the Red one for dead. A communist uprising in the South was no longer a reasonable expectation. There was no way for the North to gain control except through force of arms.

In the Easter Offensive of 30 March 1972, the North Vietnamese unleashed the outstanding weapon of the ground war in Vietnam. Russian 130 mm field guns far outranged the American 105 mm How-itzers with which the ARVN was equipped, as well as having a quicker rate of fire. South Vietnamese fire support bases were blown away, as six NVA divisions stormed from North Vietnam, Laos and Cambodia in a three-pronged offensive, striking at Hue in the North, Kontum in the middle of the country and Saigon in the South. It was not a very well managed campaign. Any one of the three thrusts might have been fatal, if it had been successful, but striking at all three targets at once meant that the NVA never had sufficient force at the decisive point to take any of them. NVA armour moved cautiously into rubble-strewn towns, became bogged down and was picked off easily by ARVN soldiers using Ameri-can M-72 Light Anti-Tank Weapons. And NVA infantry massed behind the armour, waiting patiently for the breakthrough that never came, were devastated by American aviation in the most brilliant display ever of the use of tactical air power in a defensive role. Nixon found a role for strategic air power, too, doing what the Joint Chiefs had vainly implored Johnson to do from the start. B-52s struck deep in North Vietnam for the first time since November 1967, blasting power plants, factories, com-munications and supply dumps around Hanoi and Haiphong. Mean-while, the United States Navy mined Haiphong and six other North Vietnamese harbours on 8 May, cutting off seaborne supplies from the Soviet Union and China.

Success was complete. The Easter Offensive petered out in May. It was an even greater disaster than Tet, costing the NVA some 120 000 dead. Nixon meanwhile continued the withdrawal of United States combat troops, the last leaving on 12 August. Bombing north of the twentieth parallel was halted on 23 October, in the belief that a ceasefire was now certain. Secretary of State Henry Kissinger declared that peace was at hand. Then, on 23 December, the North Vietnamese walked out of the negotiations. Two days later, Nixon ordered Linebacker II, a maximum effort by the B-52s, supported by F-111s and the Naval Air Service, to destroy North Vietnam's capacity for waging war. Over eleven days, pausing to celebrate Christmas, United States Air Force and Navy aviators delivered the most concentrated bombing attacks against the most heavily defended targets in the history of air war. By 28 December the air defences of North Vietnam had been totally suppressed and its industrial capacity destroyed. It had been achieved with surgical pre-cision, at a cost of fifteen B-52s and only 1300 civilian lives. It brought the North Vietnamese back to the conference table, where a ceasefire was finally signed on 23 January 1973, but it was denounced by Australian politicians as the most brutal and indiscriminate massacre of women in living memory, and by the *New York Times* as 'Shame on Earth'. The United States had won the war. It had lost the peace.

South Vietnam had a chance of surviving only if it were defended against further Northern invasions by United States air and naval support of the kind which had shattered the Tet and Easter Offensives. Nixon had promised Thieu that this would be assured. But the Fulbright Amendment in July 1973 denied funds for any United States combat action in or over Indochina. Nixon himself resigned the presidency over the Watergate scandal on 8 August 1974. Congress voted on 8 October to cut appropriations for South Vietnam to only $700 million for the year ending 30 June 1975. This meant, among other things, that the South Vietnamese would be unable to re-equip their Air Force with more modern aircraft capable of dealing with the Soviet anti-aircraft weapons with which the NVA was being supplied. And this meant that they would not be able to carry out air surveillance of NVA movements. It also meant that they would be unable to provide sufficient cover for their helicopters, which they had come to rely upon excessively for a wide range of military purposes.

Hanoi thus had the initiative entirely — to strike when, where and how it wished. It was only a matter of waiting until communist victory in Cambodia left the road to Saigon wide open. All was ready by March 1975. The North Vietnamese had learned from their dreadful experiences of 1972 and 1968. They began on 10 March with a powerful probing thrust in the Central Highlands, as the first move in a planned two-year campaign. ARVN commanders attempted to move in reinforcements with helicopters, which suffered disastrously from NVA anti-aircraft fire. Thieu then ordered a withdrawal, supposedly to concentrate on a counter-attack. But the withdrawal became a rout, and the North Vietnamese Political Bureau concluded on 24 March that there was an opportunity of ending the war right away, and not two years later. The divisions advancing in the Highlands were ordered to swing south to Saigon. Their progress was slowed by the heroic resistance of ARVN 18th Division at Xuan Loc, north of the capital. But that was the only effective opposition. Thieu resigned on 21 April. NVA tanks rolled through the gates of the Independence Palace in Saigon on 30 April. Vietnam was now a communist country, but it was to be many years before peace returned to the area of Indochina.

It could be scarcely be harder, but it would have to be even longer. The human and material costs of the armed struggle had been dreadful. Some 95 000 French and 64 000 United States and Allied military personnel had lost their lives in the two Vietnam wars. Vietnamese military and civilian dead numbered over two million. American aviators dropped 7.8 million tonnes of bombs on North Vietnam between 1965 and 1972, nearly three times the total amount dropped on the whole of Axis-occupied Europe during World War II, in incomparably the most massive operation ever undertaken to devastate a nation's ecology as well as its economy and its morale. The effect was to destroy virtually all the industrial, transportation and communication facilities constructed in North Vietnam since 1954, wiping out some fifteen years of economic development and leaving Vietnam by far the poorest country in Southeast Asia, apart from its fellow Indochinese disaster areas, Laos and Cambodia. Recovery was retarded by sanctions imposed by the United States, on the grounds that the Vietnamese had not been sufficiently co-operative about investigating the whereabouts of 2253 Americans still listed as missing in action in Vietnam. The Vietnamese of course number their MIAs in hundreds of thousands, and it was noteworthy that the United States did not adopt the same policy towards Germany after the World War II, although far more American personnel were missing in action in that conflict. President Clinton indeed lifted the nineteen-year embargo on commercial exchanges with Vietnam on 3 February 1994, but insisted that this did not constitute a normalisation of relations, and that the United States would be seeking settlement of claims against Vietnam totalling US$230 million, largely representing United States investments in South Vietnam seized by the communists after unification.

The Vietnamese might well be inclined to launch counter-claims for fifteen years of economic development destroyed by American bombing and defoliation. But in fact the market and investment opportunity spurned by the United States in pursuit of a macabre vendetta have been exploited enthusiastically by Taiwan and Hong Kong; by Australia, which a Vietnamese official surprisingly described as having something of a 'family relationship' with her country; and especially by France, which lost nearly twice as many troops in Vietnam as the United States, with a quarter of its population. France is aiming to become again the dominant presence in Indochina, economically and culturally; 32 classes in French are operating in primary and secondary schools; the Alliance Francaise is established in Hanoi and Ho Chi Minh City, formerly Saigon; and projects are currently being negotiated with a projected value of $2 to $3 billion. The game might seem worth the candle, even were *la grandeur de la France* not at issue. Vietnam now has a population of 74 million, the second largest in Southeast Asia, and 27 million more than in 1975; it achieved a growth rate of 8 per cent in terms of Gross Domestic Product in 1992; it has been commended by the International Monetary Fund for the success of its reform and stabilisation programs; and the Asian Development Bank expects it to set the pace for economic growth in Southeast Asia in 1994. It is a shame about the fifteen lost years and the 2 million dead.

Guide to further reading

It would be easy to become lost in the mass of material already generated about the Vietnam War. Fortunately, some of the shortest studies are the most helpful. One could not do better than to start with Sir Robert Thompson's brilliantly succinct summaries in his edited work, *War in Peace*, Orbis, London, 1981.

The best one-volume study of the war as a whole is still Bonds, Roy, *The Vietnam War*, Salamander, London, 1979.

The most comprehensive, accessible and even-handed discussion of the origins, course and immediate consequences of the 30-year struggle must be the multi-volume series *The Vietnam Experience*, compiled by the editors of the Boston Publishing Company over 1981–82.

The official histories of the United States Armed Forces in Vietnam written by Ronald H. Spector and Robert H. Whitlow are comprehensively researched, excellently written and quite uninhibited in the opinions they express. But one cannot pretend to any serious understanding of the conflict without having read the United States Defense Department history, at least in the potted version edited by Neil Sheehan and others, and preferably in the far fuller form compilation edited by Senator Mike Gravel, or the full-length original, *United States–Vietnam Relations, 1954–1967*, US Government Printing Office, Washington DC, 1971.

Also invaluable are the memoirs of Lyndon B. Johnson, *The Vantage Point: Perspectives of the Presidency, 1963–1969*, Holt, Reinhart & Winston, New York, 1971; Ball, George W., *The Past Has Another Pattern*, Norton, New York, 1982; Nixon, Richard M. , *RN: The Memoirs of Richard Nixon*, Warner, New York, 1979; and Kissinger, Henry A. , *The White House Years*, Little, Brown, Boston, 1979.

Notes

1   Memo, C of SA for JCS, 2 Aug 54, sub: US Assumption of Training Responsi bilities in Indochina, JCS 1992/367, in Spector, Ronald H., *United States Army in Vietnam: Advice and Support: The Early Years, 1941–1960*, Centre of Military History, United States Army, Washington, DC, 1983, p. 224.

2   Warner, Denis, *The Last Confucian*, Macmillan, New York, 1963, p. 71.

3   Spector, *Advice*, p. 336.

4   Maitland, Terence, et al., *The Vietnam Experience: Raising the Stakes*, Boston Publishing Company, Boston, 1982, p. 56.

5   Hotham, David, 'South Vietnam, Shaky Bastion', *New Republic*, 25 November 1957.

6   Lyndon B. Johnson to John F. Kennedy, 23 May 1961, 'Mission to Southeast Asia, India and Pakistan', Vice President Security File, Vice Presidential Travel, LBJ Library, Austin, Texas.

7 Memo for Record of Meeting at State Department, August 31, 1963, Senator Mike Gravel (ed.), *The Pentagon Papers: the Defense Department History of United States Decision-Making in Vietnam. The Senator Gravel Edition*, Beacon Press, New York, 1971, vol. I, pp. 203–5.

8 Whitlow, Robert H., *U.S. Marines in Vietnam: The Advisory & Combat Assistance Era, 1954–1964*, Department of the Navy, Washington, DC, 1977, p. 166.

9 McNamara, Robert S., Memo for the President, 'Actions Recommended in Vietnam', 14 October, 1966, in Sheehan, Neil et al. (eds), *The Pentagon Papers*, Bantam Press, New York, 1971, pp. 542–51.

10 MacDonald, Charles B , 'Communist Thrust — the Tet Offensive of 1968', in Bonds, Ray (ed.), *The Vietnam War*, Salamander Books, London, 1979, p. 148.

23 | The challenges of independence

The Pacific War marks a turning point in the history of the countries of Southeast Asia. Before the outbreak of the war, of all the states in the region, only one — Thailand — was independent. All the others were under the colonial domination of a foreign power — Britain in the case of Malaya, the Straits Settlements, Burma and the Borneo territories of Sarawak and North Borneo (Sabah); the Netherlands in Indonesia; Portugal in East Timor; France in Indochina; and the United States in the Philippines. In all these states, perhaps with the exception of East Timor, there were active nationalist movements demanding independence. When war broke out, however, none of these nationalist movements was on the verge of success, of throwing off the colonial regime. The closest to success was the nationalist movement in the Philippines, where the Americans had granted a limited form of self-government in 1936, with a promise that full independence would be granted ten years later.

Within a decade of the ending of the Pacific War, virtually the whole of Southeast Asia was independent, with North Vietnam and Indonesia leading the way in 1945, followed by the Philippines (1946), Burma (1948), Laos, Cambodia and South Vietnam (1954) and Malaya (1957). The paths that these states followed to independence were varied. In some cases, they were violent, marked by revolution and bloodshed. In other cases, independence came after negotiations with the colonial powers. Throughout the region, however, the new states were faced with a series of problems and challenges which had much in common.

Most obviously, there was the question of how to organise the political life of the newly independent state. Sweeping away the colonialist political system — which is what independence entailed — was one thing, but erecting something acceptable in its place was something else again. However, political change was not the only thing implied by the achievement of independence. As one leading Australian scholar of Southeast Asia has noted:

> if as outsiders we concentrate exclusively on the political changes involved in the attainment of independence we shall certainly fail to appreciate, however

imperfectly, the almost magical and certainly spiritual quality that was felt by many Southeast Asians, leaders and their followers alike, when either willingly or otherwise the colonial rulers departed.[1]

To talk about independence in these terms, as having magical or spiritual qualities, may seem strange to people who have never experienced colonialism first hand. But it is clearly the case that the peoples of Southeast Asia, like ex-colonial subjects around the world, had high expectations of independence. Colonialism had meant deprivation in all kinds of fields — certainly political, but also economic, religious, educational, even medical. With colonialism removed, and independence achieved, it was expected that these deprivations would be swept away as well. Unfortunately, as we will see, the high expectations that many people had of independence were not always fulfilled.

Let us look first at the political challenges posed by the achievement of independence, and then at some of the other non-political ones. Perhaps the most important political questions faced by all these nations concerned the political structure of the state: what kind of governmental system it should have; what the relationship between the central government and outlying regions should be; how competing ethnic and religious interest groups should be accommodated.

On becoming independent, all the countries of Southeast Asia inherited at least something of the political systems of their former colonial rulers. This legacy was strongest in the case of those states which had achieved their independence through negotiation, rather than through armed struggle or revolution: most obviously, perhaps, the Philippines and to a lesser extent Malaysia. In North Vietnam, in contrast, where Ho Chi Minh's revolutionaries had seized power from the French by military means, very little of the French governmental system was taken over.

In many states of the region, though, the political institutions put in place at independence underwent substantial modification, either formally or simply in practice, within a fairly short period of time. This was usually because, in some way or other, the imported political institutions were found to clash with local, indigenous political traditions and customs. There was also a conscious effort in many places to localise or 'indigenise' those systems, to make them resemble more closely the systems which were believed to have been in place before the colonial era. President Sukarno in Indonesia and Prince Norodom Sihanouk in Cambodia were perhaps most adept at calling on tradition to justify changes to the post-colonial political order.

One result of these modifications is that we quite often find that political terms familiar to the West have quite different meanings when used in the Southeast Asian context. All the states of the region, for instance, have political parties; in most countries, more than one. But very few of them correspond closely to political parties as they are known in the West, in the sense of representing a defined interest group, having a specific ideological orientation, articulating a set of policies across a wide political spectrum and so forth.

However, simple modifications to state political structures established in the immediate post-colonial era did not satisfy the demands of all the citizens of the new states. Most of these states found, very soon after the achievement of independence, that their national unity was challenged by dissent from within. In some cases, the source of this dissent was ideological. Given that, with the exception of North Vietnam, all the newly independent states of Southeast Asia were either anti-communist or neutral towards communism, it is not surprising that many of the political challenges to state authority came from the left. Indonesia, Malaya and the Philippines all experienced communist-led revolts against their post-independence governments in the late 1940s or early 1950s. However, in none of these countries have the communists yet managed to come to power. Their success has been limited to the three states of Indochina: Vietnam, Laos and Cambodia.

Regional dissatisfaction with central governments has also proved to represent a significant challenge to the authority of the state in some parts of the region, although only in Indonesia and Burma have these challenges taken on serious military overtones. Regional dissent, though, has often had overtones of religious or ethnic dissatisfaction as well.

Southeast Asia is a particularly heterogeneous place, inhabited by a great variety of peoples with different ethnic, linguistic, religious and cultural backgrounds. When the colonisers were drawing the boundaries of their possessions, they often paid scant attention to these factors. And, with few exceptions, the boundaries of the independent states of the region followed those of the colonial powers. As a result, these states frequently found that their boundaries encompassed divergent communities of peoples whose only common factor was the accident of having being colonised by the same foreign power. The struggle against colonialism had often provided a focal point bringing these peoples together, but once that struggle had been won, the centrifugal forces in many of these states came into play.

Both religion and ethnicity have been powerful divisive forces in different parts of the region. Religious differences were prominent in Indonesia, although ironically the conflict here was not over the status of a minority religion, but rather the status of the majority religion: Islam. From the declaration of independence in 1945, successive Indonesian governments took the view that the state should not be based formally on Islam, even though that was the religion of the majority of the population. They believed that to make the state an Islamic one would cause grave concern amongst the numerically small but economically important non-Islamic communities. Moreover, making Islam the state religion could have had the effect of giving Islamic religious leaders direct political authority, which could only have been at the expense of the established state leadership. However, from the late 1940s to the early 1960s, Indonesian governments faced a concerted challenge to their authority from Muslim groups who wanted to see Indonesia established as an Islamic state. The main organisation which took up arms against the central government with this goal was called the Darul Islam (the House or Abode of Islam), which was established in West Java in 1948 and which had spread to South Sulawesi by the early 1950s. The Darul Islam was not finally eliminated as a military force until the early 1960s.

In the Philippines, too, Muslim opposition to the predominantly Christian central government based in Manila has also been evident, particularly in the south of the country on the island of Mindanao. In Malaysia, in recent times at least, the strongly Islamic regions on the east coast of the Malay Peninsula have also been pushing the government in Kuala Lumpur for Islam to be accorded greater status, even though it is in fact the official state religion.

In other states, ethnicity has presented the major challenge to central authority. In Malaya, the struggle between the Communist Party of Malaya and the central government, euphemistically referred to as 'The Emergency' (1948–60), was ethnic, not just ideological in nature. Most of the supporters of the Communist Party were ethnic Chinese, while the emerging government was clearly dominated by Malays. The Burmese government faced even greater ethnic problems in dealing with the non-Burmese peoples of the north and east of the country: the Shan, the Kachin and the Karen, amongst others. Their dissatisfaction with the central government has resulted in a civil war which has been in progress, to a greater or lesser extent, since Burma became independent in 1948.

Various means were employed by local governments to try to address these challenges and to create a sense of unity where previously none has prevailed. Language, and communication generally, was an important issue. After all, peoples who cannot converse with each other are unlikely to feel any great sense of sharing the same identity or future. In some cases, the independent government effectively chose the language of the former colonial power to be the language of the independent state. The Philippines is perhaps the most obvious example of this, closely followed by Malaysia. But even in both these places, English has begun to be phased out in favour of a local language: Tagalog (renamed Pilipino) in one case and Malay (renamed Malaysian) in the other. In other cases, though, local languages were recognised from the outset of independence as national languages, and the use of the language of the former colonial power was discouraged.

Closely linked to this use of a national language was the expansion of educational opportunities. Again with the possible exception of the Philippines, during the colonial period, education had been the prerogative of the few — chiefly the rich and those of noble birth. For most ordinary Southeast Asians, education had been virtually impossible to get under colonial rule. As a result, once independence had been achieved, the demand for education was strong, from the ordinary people as well as from many leaders of government. The latter saw an educated population as being a crucial element both for creating a sense of national identity and unity, and also more materialistically for the purposes of economic development. The result in all countries of the region was massive campaigns to promote education. One scholar has remarked that 'the expansion of educational opportunities and facilities in Southeast Asia was one of the most dramatic changes to affect the region after World War II'.[2]

There were, however, several major problems resulting from this massive push for education, problems which in many countries became more acute as the educational programs became more successful. Firstly, as people became better educated, in many cases they also became more politically sophisticated and more critical of their governments. This had certainly been true during colonial times; we have already noted that many of the leaders of Southeast Asian nationalist movements had been people who had managed to achieve quite high levels of education under colonial rule. It was equally true after the achievement of independence. Students, primarily from the universities, have been a major source of opposition to established governments in Thailand, Indonesia, South Vietnam and Burma.

Secondly, most of the people with access to education saw it as a means of achieving social and economic advancement. At the end of their period of education, they expected to be able to find rewarding employment. Unfortunately, though, in many cases governments have found it very difficult to ensure that there are sufficient jobs to satisfy the numbers of newly educated people wanting them. The result in many countries was the emergence of a group of people with relatively high educational qualifications, but no real prospects of getting jobs commensurate with their education.

Economic integration and development, too, were seen as having important roles to play in promoting national unity by way of linking regions together via trade, and by providing local producers and traders with the opportunity to participate in the national economy. During the colonial era, such opportunities had been greatly restricted, the local economies being dominated, in the main, by colonial and other foreign economic interests (primarily at the large-scale level) and by local minority interests, chiefly Chinese, Indian or Arab (at the small-scale level).

However, in their rapid nationalisation of French economic interests, the North Vietnamese were unusual in the region; other states tended to move much more slowly against the economic interests of the former colonial power, if at all. It was a decade or so after independence before Indonesia and Burma, for instance, took widespread action against Dutch and British capital; and to the present day American and British capital continues to play important (albeit gradually declining) roles in the Filipino and Malaysian economies. Most regional countries undertook programs to encourage local businesspeople to fill the gaps gradually being opened by the elimination of foreign economic interests. In many cases, though, these programs failed to have the desired impact, because of the economic power still wielded by local ethnic minorities such as the Chinese. These minorities were then themselves subjected to campaigns to weaken their hold on the local economies, but with comparatively little success. In any event, taking action against them, while it may have served important purposes in trying to secure a more prominent position in the state for local business interests, and thus promoted a degree of economic integration, had the opposite effect in terms of government efforts to integrate various resident ethnic minorities into the mainstream of the state.

Another aspect of economic policy which was important in virtually all the countries of Southeast Asia was land reform. Agriculture is still the source of livelihood of the majority of Southeast Asians. And for farmers, access to land is crucial. Yet during the colonial era in most regional countries, large tracts of land had come into the hands either of foreigners, or of members of the local elite allied to the colonialists. After achieving independence, many landless farmers expected that their governments would take steps to give them access to land by taking land away from major landlords, whether foreign or local. Most regional countries saw land reform campaigns being undertaken with official backing, but the results were generally disappointing; although much fuss was made of the campaigns, in fact little land was redistributed. The sticking point was not so much foreign-owned land as land owned by wealthy locals. While virtually all citizens of the new state might be able to agree that foreign landholdings were an affront to national pride and dignity and thus ought to be abolished, there was no such consensus on the question of local landlords. Only in the countries where the communists came to power — Vietnam, Laos and Cambodia — did any substantial redistribution of land take place, and even here it was primarily a redistribution into collective farms rather than to individual owner-cultivators.

Finally, we need to look at the relations which states in the region enjoyed with their former colonial overlords. There were perhaps two contradictory pressures here. On the one hand, there was clearly a feeling that independence meant cutting most of the ties with the former colonial power, getting rid of everything which reminded them of past humiliations and defeats. On the other hand, there was also the pragmatic view that these links ought to continue, albeit in a much-revised form — economic assistance, or continued military support, or perhaps simply a maintenance of social and cultural ties. The tendency to want to sever formal ties with the ex-colonial power was strongest in those states which had had to fight wars for their independence: North Vietnam in particular, but also (to a lesser extent) Indonesia. On the other hand, the states which negotiated their way to independence were much more willing to see ties retained. Malaysia and Singapore opted for membership of the Commonwealth, and to permit the retention by the British of military bases on their soil; when these bases were finally closed in the 1970s, it was as much the result of the British wanting to go as the Malaysians or the Singaporeans wanting them out. The Philippines, to the present day, still has American military bases on its territory. In July 1991, the United States and the Philippines agreed to close down Clark Air Base, which had anyway just been rendered inoperable through the eruption of the Mt Pinatubo volcano, but to retain Subic Bay for a period. In late 1991, the Philippines Senate demanded an early closure, but the American and Philippines administrations are pushing for an extension and the future remains unclear.

Conclusion

In concluding this chapter, we could observe that, although the Southeast Asian states' experiences of colonialism varied considerably, all were faced with similar challenges on attaining independence. These challenges were broad — social and economic as much as political. But perhaps the underlying challenge they all faced was to create a sense of unity and nationhood amongst their heterogeneous peoples. This was no easy task; many obstacles lay in their paths. The highest expectations or hopes that the people of the region held for their independent future might not have been met in full. However, for the most part, as we will see in the following chapters, the states of the region have not only survived the challenges of independence rather well but most cases they have done so very successfully.

Guide to further reading

The comments on further reading at the end of the next chapter are equally applicable to this chapter. See also the following:

Leifer, Michael, *Dilemmas of Statehood in Southeast Asia*, Asia Pacific Press, Singapore, 1972

A little dated now, but still an excellent introduction to the range of issues Southeast Asian leaders faced in the quarter-century following the end of the Pacific War.

Steinberg, David Joel (ed.), *In Search of Southeast Asia*, Allen & Unwin, Sydney, 1987

Probably the best comprehensive introduction to the development of Southeast Asian societies since the eighteenth century, though more accessible to teachers than students. Pays as much attention to social and economic developments as political ones. Has a very valuable annotated bibliography.

Southeast Asian Affairs, published annually by the Institute of Southeast Asian Studies, Singapore

Contains articles focusing on individual countries in the region, and on the region as a whole. Good for up-to-date analysis of recent developments in Southeast Asia.

Smith, Roger M. (ed.), *Southeast Asia Documents of Political Development and Change*, Cornell University Press, Ithaca, 1974

Presents translated extracts from important documents from all parts of Southeast Asia, with a useful introduction to each country and to each document.

Notes

1 Osborne, Milton, *Southeast Asia: An Introductory History*, Allen & Unwin, Sydney, 1979, p. 164.

2 Steinberg, David Joel (ed.), *In Search of Southeast Asia*, rev. edn, Allen & Unwin, Sydney, 1987, p. 454.

24 Southeast Asia: The search for political form

The previous chapter's focus on the independence of Southeast Asian countries after World War II is here narrowed to the problem of the political forms those newly independent states adopted.

Southeast Asia in the twentieth century was swept by new movements for political and social change which took much of their inspiration from Western precedents. These new nationalist movements, usually led by Western-educated elites, sought not only to expel Western colonialism from Southeast Asia, but to create *nations* which had little or no regional precedent as such, and which were based on territorial boundaries originally imposed by the colonial powers. The meteoric rise of charismatic nationalist personalities like Sukarno in Indonesia, Ho Chi Minh in Vietnam, Tunku Abdul Rahman in Malaysia, Lee Kuan Yew in Singapore and Ramon Magsaysay in the Philippines took place within a context shaped by the Western colonial powers. In fact, it took the humiliating destruction of this Western colonial structure by the Japanese military successes in 1941 and 1942 to provide a favourable environment in which the Southeast Asian nationalist leaders could come into their own.

Successful struggles against Western colonial rule produced intense emotional euphoria in the Southeast Asian region after 1945. However, the achievement of formal independence did little in itself to eradicate the basic political, social, religious and economic issues that confronted the peoples of the region in their daily lives. Independence, whilst of undoubted symbolic significance, was little more than a declaration of intent, and often the intentions of newly independent governments were anything but clear, even to themselves. All governments inherited territorial boundaries which had been established in earlier times by colonial powers, with little or no regard for geographical, ethnic, religious or linguistic circumstances. The Malay people left in Southern Thailand provided one example of awkward boundaries; the Muslim peoples of Mindanao in the Southern Philippines were another. All the new states adopted political and administrative systems which bore scant relationship to traditional norms and structures. All inherited diverse plural societies with conspicuous and economically aggressive alien minorities, especially overseas Chinese. All were confronted with a popular 'revolution of rising expectations', and with demands for immediate economic development, educational opportunity and social justice. All discovered the existence of wide disparities in the distribution of goods and services between rich and poor, as well as enormous gaps in communication between urban and rural dwellers, and between the people of the mountains and the people of the coastal plains and river deltas. It is highly doubtful, for instance, whether the concept of 'Malaysia', centred on Kuala Lumpur, had substantive meaning in 1963 for the distant, jungle-dwelling Iban groups of Sarawak 450 kilometres away, or whether the Montagnard tribespeople of the Annamite Mountains were terribly excited about the communist reunification of Vietnam in 1975. There are also refugees from the island of Timor, now living in Darwin, Australia, who have chosen not to remain in Indonesia.

Above all else, the new governing Southeast Asian elites had the task of building nations where none had previously existed, at least in the modern Western sense. In such circumstances, it was quite easy for the new urban ruling groups to emphasise the forms and symbols of statehood rather than its substance, to see political power as an end in itself, and eventually to provoke resentment from dissident rural, ethnic or military groups. These dissident groups in turn found solace in radical, populist movements for political change, such as communism, brigandage or religious revivals. In addition, all the new states found themselves to be sought-after members of the international community, to be part of the awesome struggle between Western and Eastern blocs for strategic and ideological advantage on a world scale. The stakes in this 'Cold War' were high. Some Southeast Asian states, like Thailand, the Philippines, Malaysia, Singapore and Brunei, chose to align themselves closely with Western powers such as the United States or Britain in this global struggle. Others, like Burma, Cambodia and Indonesia, hopefully opted for non-alignment and neutrality, while the North Vietnamese found strength in alignment with various communist powers. Whether aligned or non-aligned, all countries in the region came to depend heavily on foreign economic aid, military hardware and financial investment, much of which had direct or indirect 'strings' attached. They found that the hidden costs of formal independence were high indeed. Again, some of the new states found themselves confronted by predatory, expansive neighbours who were mindful of old rivalries and territorial claims, and able to pursue them now that the old colonial 'umbrella' had been lifted. Frontier conflicts have been a persistent feature of Southeast Asian life during the past 40 years — for example, between Cambodia and Vietnam, Malaysia and the Philippines, Indonesia and Papua New Guinea.

While virtually all the states in the Southeast Asian region have chalked up significant achievements in terms of raising popular living standards, expanding educational venues and imbuing a sense of national consciousness amongst their inhabitants, there have been some casualties in the process. Among these casualties of nation-building has been the notion of constitutional democracy in the liberal Western sense. The inappropriateness of Western-style democracy to Southeast Asian conditions has been a constant theme in government pronouncements throughout the region during the past few decades, and especially from political elites who have found themselves threatened by the parliamentary electoral process.

A brief regional survey will illustrate the basic point. In Indonesia during the 1950s, an experiment in parliamentary government brought forth dozens of bickering factions and parties, and resulted in sufficient chaos and confusion for President Sukarno to get rid of most of them and proclaim a 'guided democracy' in which essential authority rested with himself. Admittedly Sukarno had to operate in delicate tandem with the main Indonesian 'functional groups' of the army (which had been useful in crushing regional rebellions), the Muslims and the Indonesian Communist Party (PKI), and this fragile web eventually fell apart. Still, when Sukarno faded from the scene after the abortive coup attempt of 30 September 1965, his authoritative role was assumed by General (now President) Suharto and the Army High Command. Both the left, in the form of the PKI, and the notion of active popular participation itself henceforth had no legitimate place in Indonesian political life. It is difficult to conceive of Indonesia surviving in its present form of 13 000 islands in the one country without the organisational structure provided by the armed forces.

In the Philippines, an American-type Congressional political system persisted from 1946 until 1972, when President Ferdinand Marcos, denouncing a pervasive corruption and subversion of the national body politic, proclaimed martial law and rule by presidential decree in pursuit of a 'New Society'. But corruption and perversion persisted, and eventually trapped even the redoubtable Marcos. The crude, officially inspired assassination of Filipino Opposition Leader Senator Benigno Aquino on the tarmac of Manila Airport in 1983 provoked a formidable coalition of the Roman Catholic Church, dissident members of the military elite and an emotive display of 'people power' to support the accession to the Presidency of Aquino's widow, Corazon. But the Madonna-like Cory Aquino soon began to lose some of her popular magic. The endemic social and economic problems of the Philippines, such as poverty and landlessness, a series of six attempted military coups in three years, as well as breakdowns in provision of basic services like electricity and telephones, all prompted President Aquino to seek more personal as distinct from popular power. On 6 December 1989, she declared a state of national emergency.

North Vietnam achieved independence from France in 1954 under the control of the Vietminh's communist totalitarian regime, while the American-sponsored rule of President Ngo Dinh Diem south of the seventeenth parallel collapsed at the hands of a military coup in 1963. A succession of military juntas were no more successful in leading South Vietnam than President Diem, and by 1975, South Vietnam, together with neighbouring Laos and Cambodia, was the subject of a successful communist revolutionary takeover (see Chapter 22). By 1976, all of Vietnam was reunified under one government centred on Hanoi in the North. About one million Vietnamese subsequently fled the country to seek refuge in the West. Meanwhile the national government of Thailand has see-sawed between brief flirtations with parliamentary forms and a more enduring rule by generals, all in the name of revered monarch King Bhumibol, whose status is near godlike. In Burma, a successful military *putsch* in 1962 brought General Ne Win to a position of national power which, as of 1995, he had not yet finally relinquished. Instead, attempts by Burmese pro-democracy groups in 1988 and later were ruthlessly suppressed. In the year following July 1989 alone, 2000 critics of the Burmese government were arrested, including former Prime Minister U Nu and President of the National League for Democracy Aung San Suu Kyi. The latter won a national election while under arrest, but the military refused to release her, let alone hand over power. In 1991, still in prison, she was awarded the Nobel Peace Prize.

Even in Malaysia and Singapore, former British colonies where the forms of parliamentary government remain, and where regular elections are held, there are tight restrictions upon freedom of public utterance, the role of the media and the capacity to form political organisations. Malaysian leaders have described these curbs as a small price to pay for more urgent tasks of social and economic reconstruction. According to Tan Sri Ghazali Shafie, 'one of our major miscalculations at the time of Merdeka [freedom from Britain in 1957] was to welcome uncritically the concepts and precepts of a Westminster-type democracy . . . We did not realise how irrelevant it was to our society.'[1]

Significantly, the Sultan of the small, oil-rich state of Brunei refused to join neighbouring Malaysia in 1963, at least in part because he would have been compelled to adopt some practices of popular sovereignty. Even at independence from Britain in 1984, the Sultan kept most of the key posts in his government in the hands of the royal family.

Overall, the post-1945 political systems in Southeast Asia have been characterised not by openness, civil liberties or democracy, but by varying degrees of authoritarian direction. For a national leader who has and enjoys power, the main problem with an election is that he may lose it. In regional terms, it has proved relatively easy to discard Western-derived luxuries such as constitutional parliaments, and to revert to more familiar, traditionalist patterns of elite control. Indeed, the term 'bureaucratic polity'[2] has been devised to capture the essential form of political system in the region, where participation in the political process is the prerogative of senior public officials, and the rest of the population is 'motivated' by the established elite. Notwithstanding the effects of economic growth, education and improved communication systems, political change in Southeast Asia seems unlikely to follow Western models. Family, bureaucracy and the military have proved more durable institutions than parliaments.

By the early 1990s, there were encouraging signs of openness in several Southeast Asian countries. In 1990, Singapore's national patriarch, Lee Kuan Yew, voluntarily stood down as Prime Minister and was replaced by the liberal technocrat, Goh Chok Tong, though Lee undoubtedly continued to orchestrate policy directions as Senior Minister in the Singaporean Cabinet. Over in the Philippines, Cory Aquino survived to fulfil her constitutional term as President, and was able to ensure that comparatively clean and fair national elections ensued to select her successor. Former Armed Forces Commander, Fidel Ramos, emerged victorious from a multi-candidate poll in 1992, though with something less than an absolute majority of votes. Awesome poverty and crippling inefficiency combine to plague the Philippines under the Ramos government. In May 1992, the urban middle class and university students stood firm in the streets of Bangkok against another military usurpation of power in Thailand. With King Bhumibol again acting as national umpire, a civilian parliamentary leadership was installed under Prime Minister Chuan Leekpai. In other countries, however, military domination continued to characterise the political system. Former general Suharto was re-elected President of Indonesia for a sixth five-year term in 1993, with former Armed Forces Commander Try Sutrisno as his Vice-President. The organisational clout of the Armed Forces (ABRI) remains essential to the continued coherence of the Indonesian archipelago. In Myanmar (Burma), the military officers of the State Law and Order Restoration Council (SLORC) survived to taunt and haunt their population, especially the minorities in the hills, and deny Aung San Suu Kyi her popular mandate. So the regional see-saw between democracy and oligarchy persists.

Guide to further reading

Informative, analytical overviews of postwar Southeast Asia include Bloodworth, Dennis, *An Eye for the Dragon: Southeast Asia Observed*, rev. edn, Times Books International, Singapore, 1987; Osborne, Milton, *Southeast Asia: An Illustrated Introductory History*, Allen & Unwin, Sydney, 1988; Steinberg, D.J. et al., *In Search of Southeast Asia: A Modern History*,

Allen & Unwin, Sydney, 1987; and Higgott, R. & Robison, R. (eds), *Southeast Asia: Essays in the Political Economy of Structural Change*, Routledge & Kegan Paul, Melbourne, 1985.

Particular regional viewpoints may be found in Lubis, Mochtar, *Indonesian Dilemma*, Graham Brash, Singapore, 1988; *Sukarno, An Autobiography as told to Cindy Adams*, Bobbs-Merrill, New York, 1965; Penders, C.L.M. (ed.), *Milestones on My Journey: the Memoirs of Ali Sastroamijojo, Indonesian Patriot and Political Leader*, University of Queensland Press, St Lucia, 1979; Fall, B.B. (ed.), *Ho Chi Minh on Revolution*, Signet, New York, 1967; Truong Nhu Tang, *A Vietcong Memoir*, Harcourt, Brace, Jovanovich, New York, 1985; and Thumboo, Edwin (ed.), *Literature and Liberation: Five Essays from Southeast Asia*, Solaridad Publishing House, Manila, 1988.

Jackson, Karl & Pye, Lucien, *Political Power and Communication in Indonesia*, University of California Press, Berkeley, 1978, affords an excellent political analysis.

Notes

1 Tan Sri Ghazali Shafie, *Democracy: The Realities Malaysians Must Face*, Ministry of Information, Kuala Lumpur, 1971, p. 7.
2 Jackson, K.D. & Pye, L.W. (eds), *Political Power and Communication in Indonesia*, University of California Press, Berkeley, 1978.

25 | Revolution and reform in China

Unlike almost all the countries of Southeast Asia considered in the previous chapters, China was never a formal colony of a European state. Its counterpart of 'independence' was the accession to power of a radical Marxist-Leninist party. This was the Chinese Communist Party (CCP), which established the People's Republic of China (PRC) on 1 October 1949 and, despite the collapse of its Soviet counterpart, remained in power as of 1995. Since 1949 the CCP has consistently made the assumption that 'only socialism can save China'. Its 'guiding ideology' has been consistently based on Marxism-Leninism, for most of the period being named Marxism-Leninism-Mao Zedong Thought.

The effective first leader of the PRC was Mao Zedong, who was chairman of the CCP until his death on 9 September 1976. After a brief interregnum lasting until the end of 1978, the main power-holder was Deng Xiaoping. Although he retired his last official post in March 1990, he remained extremely influential in the Chinese polity.

Broadly speaking, the history of the PRC can be divided into two periods, with the dividing point at the end of 1978. They are the periods of revolution and of reform. Although both are called socialist, and both have been guided by a communist party, the CCP, they are in general extremely different from one another. On the other hand, there are years in the 1950s with striking similarities to the 1980s. In general, there has been a consistent dominating issue running through the entire history of the PRC: how to use Marxism-Leninism for the most effective political, economic, social and cultural development of China — in other words, precisely what kind of socialism can save China? Both the period of revolution down to 1978 and that of reform which followed have witnessed debate and conflict within the CCP, at times expressing themselves in very serious power struggles.

In China there is a party and government hierarchy. Following Leninist principles, the CCP is in theory the vanguard of the proletariat and quite clearly exercises 'leadership' over the Chinese government and people. The highest organ of the CCP is the National Congress, of which, as of 1995, there have since 1949 been seven, in 1956 and 1958 (Eighth), 1969

(Ninth), 1973 (Tenth), 1977 (Eleventh), 1982 (Twelfth), 1987 (Thirteenth) and 1992 (Fourteenth). Each Congress elects a Central Committee, which frequently meets in full session. These plenums, as they are called, often make policy decisions and leadership selections of crucial importance.

The leader of the government is the premier of the State Council. The first man to occupy this position — until his death in January 1976 — was Zhou Enlai. He was succeeded by Hua Guofeng (1976–80), Zhao Ziyang (1980–87) and Li Peng, who retained the position as of April 1995. The highest government body is the National People's Congress, of which, as of 1995, there have been eight, the first sessions meeting in 1954, 1959, 1964–65, 1975, 1978, 1983, 1988 and 1993. For most of the period since 1949 there has also been a president of the PRC but, though in principle senior to the premier, the president normally wields considerably less power and influence on the work of the government.

The period and process of revolution
Liberation to Cultural Revolution, 1949–66

At the time it set up the PRC, the CCP was a highly revolutionary party. Apart from strengthening its control over the whole of China, its first tasks lay in implementing measures for revolutionary socioeconomic change. Among these, the most important were land reform, which involved the destruction of the landlords and rich peasants as classes, and the takeover of the major foreign-controlled industries, including the destruction of the big and foreign-connected bourgeoisie as a class. In addition, the CCP instituted marriage reform, which was designed to abolish the old system by which parents arranged the marriages of their children, and to move towards equality between the sexes.

By 1952 the CCP had successfully consolidated its power throughout the country. This was a difficult and bloody process. Not surprisingly, there was much resistance to CCP rule, especially among those who stood to lose from it and had strong foreign backing. The United States early made it clear that it had no intention of recognising the PRC and would continue to help the overthrown Guomindang led by Chiang Kaishek to return to power if it could. From 1950 to 1953, the newly established PRC was involved in an expensive and bloody war in Korea, which diverted away from construction the efforts, and in many cases even cost the lives, of some of the best young men (see Chapter 21).

Yet, despite the difficulties, the CCP's first years also saw some major successes. Inflation was controlled and the economy stabilised. The social fabric which had been torn apart by wars and invasions lasting intermittently for well over a century was undergoing renewal. A new political system was set up.

Newly established large-scale industrial enterprises were state owned. In 1955, the CCP moved to collectivise the economy more thoroughly, by bringing many sectors, especially agriculture, under collective owner-ship. In 1958, the CCP at Mao Zedong's instigation pushed this process of collectivisation much further in a large-scale movement called the Great Leap Forward. This was designed to inspire the Chinese people to increase industrial and other output enormously within a very short time by relying on CCP-led mass mobilisation and ideological or moral incentives. The most important and longest-lasting result of the Great Leap Forward was the establishment of the rural people's communes. Although private plots remained significant in society and the economy, the communes collectivised the land more thoroughly than had ever been done before (see Chapter 30).

The Great Leap Forward did not actually last long, yet its effects were generally disastrous. In the years immediately following 1958, there was a serious downturn in the economy, one of the results of which was a major famine which took millions of lives. It was, in fact, so devastating that figures for 1960 and 1961 actually show a decrease in China's total population. Specialists still argue about the reasons for the catastrophe, but it seems very likely that the Great Leap Forward policies were at least partly responsible. By 1962 the country had begun to recover and the situation improved quite rapidly in the following years.

On the whole, the CCP leadership had remained fairly united in the early and mid-1950s. Soon after the Great Leap Forward began, Mao was forced to resign the post of president of the PRC which he had held since 1949. His successor, appointed to the post in April 1959, was Liu Shaoqi, whom Mao saw as a bitter rival. However, Mao certainly did not resign his position as chairman of the CCP and determined to use it to imple-ment his radical policies when he got the chance again.

The Great Leap Forward brought on a major split within the CCP leadership. Many of Mao's colleagues disapproved strongly of the Great Leap Forward and the people's communes, believing them hasty and totally inappropriate for China's peasantry. The policies' most important and outspoken critic was Peng Dehuai, the Minister of National Defence. Peng had enjoyed a very distinguished military career and led the Chinese troops as Commander-in-Chief during the Korean War. He was also a man of strong opinions which he did not hesitate to express forcefully, regardless of whose feelings he might hurt in the process. A showdown between him and Mao Zedong came on Lushan, a scenic mountain in Jiangxi Province, which was the site of major meetings in the summer of 1959, climaxing in the Eighth Plenum of the Eighth Central Committee, usually called simply the Lushan Plenum.

Peng Dehuai denounced the policies of the Great Leap Forward and blamed Mao for them. Mao responded by threatening to raise his own army and throw the country into civil war unless he got his way. As it turned out, the Lushan Plenum ousted Peng and reaffirmed the Great Leap Forward policies. Peng's successor as Minister of National Defence was Lin Biao. Many leaders had certainly sided with Peng over the Great Leap Forward, but they were not prepared to risk a major public split. What happened in fact was that Peng became the scapegoat, but despite the plenum's rhetoric, most of the Great Leap policies were discontinued. The communes survived, but in a somewhat diluted form.

By the early 1960s, Mao Zedong had decided that the development model China had been following since the failure of the Great Leap Forward was not nearly radical enough. He believed that revisionist leaders of the CCP, headed by Liu Shaoqi and Deng Xiaoping, were infecting the work of the CCP or, as Chinese propaganda was later more colourfully to put it, that 'the bourgeoisie was worming its way into the Party'. The CCP was forming itself into an elite which would in time become just as divorced from the masses as the Guomindang had been. Its members were no longer 'serving the people', as he believed they ought, but were more interested in serving themselves and seizing privileges.

The Cultural Revolution decade, 1966–76

Mao's answer to this trend, which he believed must in time destroy his vision of revolution, was a mass class struggle called the Great Proletarian Cultural Revolution. He most certainly saw it as a power struggle against Liu Shaoqi, Deng Xiaoping and other 'capitalist roaders', or class enemies within the CCP. Whether he was genuine in seeing it also as an ideological struggle is unclear, and may not now matter much anyway. Certainly at the time the Chinese media presented it as both an ideological issue and one of power, and the Chinese masses appeared to accept both interpretations.

In August 1966 the Eleventh Plenum of the CCP's Eighth Central Committee formally decided in favour of launching the Cultural Revolution, even though many of the main leaders thought it not only destructive but totally crazy. On 8 August, the plenum adopted the 'Sixteen Points', which were to be the guidelines for running the movement. The first of these points declared that the Great Proletarian Cultural Revolution was 'a great revolution that touches people to their very souls'. In other words, this was to be no ordinary campaign, but vast in scale; it was intended to profoundly influence the whole attitudes of the Chinese masses to life and revolution.

The ideological guidelines of the Cultural Revolution were 'Mao Zedong's Thought'. A little red book containing his most revolutionary sayings was published. A very common image of the Cultural Revolution is people waving this little red book out of ideological loyalty to Mao's thought. In 1967 alone, some 350 million copies of the book were printed in China. Unfortunately, the Cultural Revolution's ideological obsessions also resulted in the application of savage censorship to any non-Maoist literature, so that the publication of works not written by Mao and his close followers was seriously curtailed.

Because Mao's targets were within the CCP, he chose the youth, and especially the students, as the vanguard for his revolution, terming them the Red Guards. Immediately after the Eleventh Plenum, Mao and his chosen revolutionary deputy Lin Biao held a series of gigantic rallies in Tiananmen Square at the centre of Beijing. These launched the Red Guards to 'destroy the four olds and establish the four news', meaning that the young people were to attack and get rid of old ideas, old culture, old customs and old habits, and replace them with new ones. The implications of such an injunction were serious. Young people went round destroying anything connected with the old society. They forbade traditional opera, closed down churches and temples, sending monks off to do physical labour, destroyed old art objects and humiliated former landlords and old-style intellectuals. Class struggle was 'the key link' on which everything else depended, so anybody who came under the category of 'class enemy' was fair game.

The Red Guards and the supporters of the Cultural Revolution also attempted to 'seize power'. This meant they had to overthrow supposed revisionists, who had in theory refused to work with the masses but sought only to dominate them, and replace such people by genuine revolutionaries. Among the earliest and most important 'power seizures' was in early 1967 in Shanghai, where Zhang Chunqiao led a revolution against the municipal authorities and set up a regime modelled on the Paris commune of 1871, which Karl Marx had praised so effusively at the time. Although Mao failed to support the model of the 'Shanghai commune', Zhang Chunqiao did emerge as one of the most important proponents of the Cultural Revolution.

The trouble was that the 'revisionists' whom the Red Guards and the supporters of the Cultural Revolution were attempting to overthrow did not necessarily agree that they had done their job badly. They saw themselves as having devoted their lives to the Chinese revolution and were not too impressed with the sight of young people demonstrating and waving little red books at them. They became even more alarmed when the students' armoury came to include not only insults, books and ideology, but also weapons. Naturally they resisted attempts to overthrow them. The result was that the struggle became very fierce and in many places violence erupted. Red Guard groups frequently factionalised in futile attempts to be seen as the purest and most Maoist revolutionaries. This merely made the violence even more severe, because Red Guard groups were quite prepared to fight against each other as well as against power-holding class enemies.

In quite a few places, full-scale civil war broke out. One particularly serious case was in and near Wuhan, capital of Hubei Province, in the summer of 1967. During the Wuhan Incident, as it has become called, armed conflicts lasted about two weeks between the forces of Chen Zaidao, who was the commander of the Wuhan Military Region, and those of Red Guard groups.

The central government was alarmed at this development, which seemed to presage the return of the warlord days. The months following Chen Zaidao's defeat and dismissal saw a period of uneasy calm, but early in 1968 Mao made a final attempt to implement his mass-line policies and 'purify' the ranks of the CCP of 'bourgeois elements'. The result was the outbreak of even more serious clashes, amounting to civil war, in several parts of China, especially Guangxi and Sichuan in the southwest. In Guangxi the seizure of arms from trains bound for Vietnam, where the war against the United States had reached a high point, was to exercise a lasting, embittering influence on relations between China and Vietnam.

In July 1968 Mao decided to call off the Red Guards. He had many of the leaders of his 'mass organisations' shunted off to the countryside for physical labour. They were to take the blame for the evident failure of the Cultural Revolution to achieve his objectives. However, he did not concede defeat by any means. He succeeded in implementing to some degree several of the policies of the Cultural Revolution. These included the institution of 'revolutionary committees' everywhere, which were supposed to give good representation to the masses and the proletariat against the bourgeoisie; the 'barefoot doctor' system, which was designed to provide cheap but effective medical delivery to all, and especially the peasantry; a new system theoretically aimed at providing education supportive of a Marxist-Leninist and revolutionary political culture to all people; and the development of revolutionary and 'anti-bourgeois' arts based on eight 'model dramas' devised by his wife and ardent supporter Jiang Qing.

In terms of leadership, Mao got his way in the short run. In October 1968, the Twelfth Plenum of the Eighth Central Committee dismissed Liu Shaoqi from all posts and expelled him from the CCP, calling him 'the No. 1 Party person in power taking the capitalist road' as well as 'a renegade, hidden traitor and scab' and other insulting names. Liu died in prison in November 1969. However, in February 1980, a few years after Mao himself had died, the Fifth Plenum of the Eleventh Central Committee for the first time revealed the imprisonment and death of the hapless Liu Shaoqi and rehabilitated him posthumously, cancelling the 'erroneous' resolutions of the Twelfth Plenum concerning him.

The Ninth CCP Congress, which took place in April 1969, appeared to consolidate the Cultural Revolution's line and in particular saw the high point of the power of its main supporters. Lin Biao was actually named as 'Chairman Mao's closest comrade-in-arms and successor' in the Party Constitution. At the Second Plenum of the Ninth Central Committee, held on Lushan from 23 August to 6 September 1970 (the second Lushan Plenum), Mao even got support for his plan to abolish the position of president of the PRC. This had been one of Liu Shaoqi's major posts; Mao was so obsessed with Liu's 'revisionism' that he determined to go beyond having his colleague dismissed from all positions, even to the point of abolishing the post itself.

However, despite these appearances that Mao was getting his way, the difficulties of the Cultural Revolution were by no means over. In 1971, yet another major split occurred within the CCP. This time, Mao's enemy turned out to be none other than Lin Biao, who was accused of mounting a plot to assassinate Mao Zedong and seize power himself. Although absolutely nothing was said about the fate of Lin Biao at the time, official sources alleged from July 1972 that on 12 September 1971 he had fled on board an aeroplane bound for the Soviet Union after the failure of his conspiracy against Mao and been killed when it crashed in Mongolia.

The story has never been properly confirmed and there are other theories about what happened, including one that Mao invited Lin Biao to a banquet and there had him assassinated. But certainly the 'Lin Biao affair' did immense damage to the line of the Cultural Revolution. The Chinese people, who so recently had been asked to adore Lin Biao as Chairman Mao's successor, were suddenly told to excoriate him as a vile conspirator against the chairman. The whole episode was more like something from a spy-thriller or the machinations of the courts of ancient emperors than from a serious political system.

Mao and his main supporters, especially Jiang Qing and Zhang Chunqiao, responded by instituting a series of campaigns in favour of the Cultural Revolutionary line. One of these castigated Lin Biao as a bourgeois conservative equivalent in his reactionary mould to Confucius. Not all were quite as ridiculous as this, but all made it crystal clear that the supporters of the Cultural Revolution knew that they still faced intense opposition both within the CCP and from ordinary people. The implementation of policies deriving from the Cultural Revolution did not mean that the people as a whole had really been 'touched to their very souls', let alone that they were prepared to regard class struggle as the 'key link'.

The Fourth National People's Congress met in January 1975, for the only time during the Cultural Revolution decade. Two points concerning this meeting are worthy of note. One is that the main speech was given by Premier Zhou Enlai, who repeated a plan he had put forward ten years earlier 'to accomplish the comprehensive modernisation of agriculture, industry, national defence and science and technology before the end of the century, so that our national economy will be advancing in the front ranks of the world'.[1] The second is that the Congress adopted a new state Constitution which, following the recommendation made by the second Lushan Plenum in 1970, made no reference to the post of president of the PRC and thus accepted its abolition.

A climax came in 1976. At the beginning of the year, Zhou Enlai died. Many people, both in China and elsewhere, expected his replacement to be Deng Xiaoping, who after disgrace and humiliation during the height of the Cultural Revolution had come back to public life in 1973. Instead, Mao orchestrated yet another campaign against Deng as the 'arch unrepentant capitalist roader still on the capitalist road' and other absurd appellations. The man to succeed Zhou was Hua Guofeng, a comparatively unknown figure who had risen to be Minister of Public Security and one of twelve vice-premiers in 1975.

On 5 April 1976, violence broke out in Tiananmen Square when mourners for Zhou Enlai celebrating the Qingming Festival of the Dead clashed with police. Jiang Qing and her main supporters immediately had the disturbance castigated as a 'counter-revolutionary political incident'. Hua Guofeng was appointed as premier in succession to Zhou Enlai and also as first deputy chairman of the CCP, putting him in the ideal place to succeed the ageing and ailing Mao Zedong.

On 28 July an enormous earthquake, among the worst in human history, struck the major coal-producing city of Tangshan, killing several hundred thousand people. Not only were serious physical effects felt in Beijing, which is not very far from Tangshan, but there were major political ramifications as well. Jiang Qing, Zhang Chunqiao and their supporters used the earthquake to prosecute the campaign against Deng Xiaoping, but Hua Guofeng actually visited Tangshan and witnessed the human misery and economic dislocation caused by the earthquake. In this writer's opinion it was this experience which turned him against Jiang Qing and other main supporters of the Cultural Revolution. He realised it was just not possible to keep the incessant ideological campaigns going and that political stability and the economy would have to take precedence if China was to progress.

Traditionally earthquakes in China symbolised a coming dynastic change. With Mao clearly in his last days, no amount of revolutionary thought remoulding could convince the Chinese masses that the Tangshan earthquake had no symbolic significance. When Mao died on 9 September, the people expected something dramatic to follow in the political arena.

The interregnum of Hua Guofeng

They were not to be disappointed. Late on 6 October 1976, on the instructions of Hua Guofeng, People's Liberation Army Bodyguard Force 8341 arrested Jiang Qing, Zhang Chunqiao and two other senior supporters of the Cultural Revolution at their residences as they were shortly to leave for a meeting of the Politburo. This crucially important happening quickly came to be termed 'the smashing of the gang of four'. The

Politburo meeting went ahead without them and in the early hours of 7 October appointed Hua Guofeng as CCP chairman.

Hua Guofeng now had the task of legitimating his own regime in the shadows of the giants Zhou Enlai and Mao Zedong. Among his policies, two stand out as being of supreme importance. The first was that he wished to continue the basic policies of the Cultural Revolution, but blamed the 'gang of four' for its excesses, as a result of which he abandoned or moderated the purges of opponents of the Cultural Revolution and pushed relentlessly to discredit the 'gang of four'. The other was the 'four modernisations' of agriculture, industry, national defence and science and technology, the notion which Zhou Enlai had already pushed at the Fourth National People's Congress in 1975 but which had up to 1976 been totally subordinated to the Cultural Revolution and its 'key link' of class struggle.

Of course, Hua Guofeng discontinued the campaign against Deng Xiaoping, but it was not until July 1977 that the Third Plenum of the Tenth Central Committee actually restored him to the senior echelons of the CCP, including deputy chairman of the CCP under Hua Guofeng. At the Eleventh Congress of the CCP, which followed the next month, Hua Guofeng declared the first Cultural Revolution had finished with the overthrow of the 'gang of four' the previous October and continued to denounce this noxious quartet, but stuck to the idea of the central importance of class struggle and suggested that there would be more cultural revolutions in the future.

With Deng Xiaoping back in a position of power, his influence grew rapidly and enormously. Many of the political and social institutions which had characterised the 1949–66 period, but which had been downgraded or suppressed by the Cultural Revolution, came back to prominence again. The result was a series of major meetings of various political, cultural and social bodies in 1978, most of them the first of their kind since before the Cultural Revolution. They included the First Sessions of the Fifth National People's Congress and of the Fifth National Committee of the Chinese People's Political Consultative Conference late in February and early in March, a national conference on education in April and May, one of the Chinese National Federation of Literature and Art Circles in May and June, the Fourth National Women's Congress in September, and National Congresses of the Trade Unions and Communist Youth League in October.

The period and process of reform
The early successes of reform, 1978–mid-1980s

By the latter half of 1978, intellectuals were already very critical of the Cultural Revolution and unhappy with Hua Guofeng's continued support for it. In November 1978, a 'democracy movement' occurred in Beijing, urging a greater opening up of the system and more comprehensive criticism of the Cultural Revolution. It expressed itself through big-character posters in central Beijing. One of the most sensitive issues raised was the role of Mao in the years 1966 to 1976. The 'gang of four' could not possibly have done as much damage as it in fact had without the support of Mao. To condemn the four but continue the lavish praise of Mao was inconsistent and unreasonable.

Meanwhile, the senior echelons of the CCP were also locked in meetings to thrash out a whole range of important issues relating to revolution and reform. The climax came at the Third Plenum of the Eleventh Central Committee, held from 18–22 December 1978. It is from this meeting that the whole process of reform in the PRC is dated, which makes it arguably the most significant plenum any central committee of the CCP has ever held.

The main decision was to shift the emphasis of all work to economic modernisation and away from ideological concerns:

> Now is an appropriate time to take the decision to close the large-scale nationwide mass movement to expose and criticise Lin Biao and the 'gang of four' and to shift the emphasis of our Party's work and the attention of the people of the whole country to socialist modernisation. Socialist modernisation is therefore a profound and extensive revolution.[2]

The implication was that the 'key link' was no longer class struggle but economic development. The 'revolution' was no longer important, except insofar as it meant economic transformation. The Third Plenum did not yet actually take the logical step of condemning the Cultural Revolution. It specifically postponed a decision on this matter. But it did open the lid on public criticism of the Cultural Revolution, so that formal CCP negation of that vast movement was only a matter of time.

The Third Plenum took two other decisions which were highly important from a symbolic point of view. One was a re-evaluation of the Tiananmen Incident: from the 'counter-revolutionary political incident' of the last days of Mao Zedong to a series of 'entirely revolutionary actions'. The other was to rehabilitate Peng Dehuai, who had put up such strong opposition to Mao at the first Lushan Plenum of 1959. Both decisions implied a strong downgrading of Mao's influence within the CCP.

Hovering over these decisions was a power struggle between Hua Guofeng and Deng Xiaoping. Although Hua Guofeng was not formally demoted until later, his influence suffered a severe setback at the Third Plenum to the advantage of Deng Xiaoping. It is valid to date from the Third Plenum not only the era of reform, but also that of Deng Xiaoping.

Following the Third Plenum, a whole series of measures was taken which amounted to the total dismantling of the political system which Mao had set up during the Cultural Revolution. In the middle of 1979 new laws were adopted by which revolutionary committees were abolished at government level. This meant, for example, that a province was now headed by a governor, not by the chairperson of a revolutionary committee. The move was the end of the revolutionary committees altogether, and a return to the more efficient system of former times. It was also symptomatic of a generally greater emphasis on the role of directors, executives and experts, as opposed to mass participation.

One particularly important area was the countryside. The people's communes counted as government, so the revolutionary committees were abolished there too. The collective model of rural development was replaced by a contract system by which individual groups or people signed contracts with the village government for particular products. Far greater emphasis was placed on individual initiative and hard work, as a result of which the standard of living in the countryside rose dramatically, especially in the first half of the 1980s. Dazhai Brigade, which Mao had declared the model of collective farming, was discredited. Its hero Chen Yonggui, who had risen from being a simple peasant to become a vice-premier, was dismissed in September 1980, and the county where Dazhai is located was accused of having grossly falsified production figures. From being the primary example of excellence to all peasants in China, Dazhai plummeted to the status of near-fraudulence.

Another arena with extraordinarily wide social ramifications was the law. China's tradition is to focus power on persons rather than institutions, and the Cultural Revolution had in theory accorded enormous privileges to 'the masses'. But the Third Plenum quite explicitly demanded a formal law system before which all were equal and which would be independent of government or party dictates. Although the ideal of legal independence has suffered many breaches, including some very serious ones, in the years since 1978, the ideal of equality before the law remains alive and is a major feature of the reform period.

In the education, health delivery and arts fields, the tendency in the period of reform has been very strongly in favour of expertise as opposed to 'the mass line'. No longer should students criticise their teachers, as during the Cultural Revolution days, but respect and learn from them. Research, higher learning and key institutions are the order of the day. Doctors are now judged by how much they know and by their skills, not by their accessibility to the masses.

Underlying the entire process of reform in China was the policy of 'openness to the outside world', in which the advanced, industrialised countries of the world took priority. Modernisation depended on speedy industrialisation, which in turn had to take its cue from those who led the world in this area, primarily the West and Japan. It was these countries from which China could learn the vital skills of modernisation, and thus import the necessary advanced technology and know-how. Generally speaking, it was the same countries which had developed the legal, educational and health delivery systems, the methods of management and administration and the spirit of scientific inquiry which had in the first place led to the Industrial Revolution and the concomitant features which make up the modern world.

As all these processes were gathering momentum in the wake of the Third Plenum, the political trends for about five years all pointed in one direction, away from the Cultural Revolution and towards reform. At the end of 1980, as if to show off the newly established legal system, the 'gang of four' was put on trial, together with six other living and six dead persons, sixteen in all. In fact what was principally on trial was the Cultural Revolution itself. Jiang Qing made a spirited defence of her conduct, arguing that she was following the dictates of the late Chairman Mao. Of course, the four were all found guilty, Jiang Qing and Zhang Chunqiao being sentenced to death with a two-year reprieve. (Both were let off execution in 1983; Jiang Qing committed suicide in mid-1991.) The issue of Mao's guilt was confronted, but he was claimed to be a great revolutionary with good intentions, as opposed to the criminals who deserved to be condemned.

Hua Guofeng was replaced as premier of the State Council in September 1980. The new premier was Zhao Ziyang, who had been tremendously successful in the implementation of reform policies since 1975 in China's most populous province, Sichuan. The Sixth Plenum of the Eleventh Central Committee, held late in June 1981, finally saw Hua ousted from his other main post, the chairmanship of the CCP, and replaced by Hu Yaobang. Hu Yaobang was an ardent reformer and opponent of the Cultural Revolution. He had been head of the Youth League for many years before Mao both destroyed it and disgraced him as revisionist in 1966. In September 1982, the Twelfth CCP Congress changed the head position of the CCP from chairman to general secretary and the First Plenum of the Twelfth Central Committee appointed Hu Yaobang to that position.

The Sixth Plenum of the Eleventh Central Committee saw the first fully official denunciation of the Cultural Revolution and Mao's role in it by an authoritative CCP organ. It issued an enormously long document assessing the CCP's and Mao's performance as leaders of the PRC. In essence, it declared that the CCP had done an excellent job down to the late 1950s, but had then been infected by 'Left errors', which had assumed total dominance by the time of the Cultural Revolution. Mao had likewise begun to go seriously off the rails by the late 1950s, and was more or less totally crazy by 1966. The main blame for the Cultural Revolution should be sheeted home to him.

From the point of view of 'revolution and reform', two other points stand out from the Sixth Plenum, the impact of which was hardly less significant than that of the Third Plenum. The first is that the Sixth

Plenum redefined Mao Zedong Thought as 'a crystallisation of the collective wisdom of the Chinese Communist Party'. Mao Zedong had previously been the only creator of Mao Zedong Thought, but under the new formulation he became only one of many.[3] The second is that it gave heavy emphasis to the Third Plenum as a turning point in PRC history. It was the Third Plenum which had discarded class struggle as 'the key link' and begun 'to correct conscientiously and comprehensively the "Left" errors of the "cultural revolution" and earlier'.[4] Above all, it had redefined the revolution in terms of the economy.

The Sixth Plenum's negation of the Cultural Revolution and demotion of Mao's role in the PRC's history were aimed at cleansing China of the memory of his last years. Now China should get on with modernisation and forget about any other kind of radical ideology. One last major political move against Mao and his Cultural Revolution was the reinstatement of the office of presidency of the PRC. In December 1982, the National People's Congress adopted an altered PRC constitution, the fourth since 1949, but only the first since the Third Plenum. One of quite a few changes was the insertion of a long section dealing with the roles and duties of the president and vice-president. In mid-1983, the National People's Congress elected Li Xiannian as president of the PRC.

Reform in decline and student protest, mid- to late 1980s

The second half of the 1980s failed to fulfil the hopes or expectations of the first half. Although the standard of living continued to improve, it did so at a much slower rate. Inflation became a serious problem, assuming alarming proportions in 1988 and the first half of 1989. Grain production actually fell from its 1984 peak and did not surpass it until 1989.

Corruption had been a major issue for the CCP since the early 1980s and the CCP had responded by setting up a Commission for Discipline Inspection to combat it. Corruption was as old as Chinese civilisation itself, but had been substantially curbed in the early days of the PRC. Its major regrowth in the 1980s was partly caused by reform itself, because the policies of reform gave officials the incentive to use their power for economic and other gain at the expense of the people. In the late 1980s, the incidence of corruption grew alarmingly, despite all efforts to prevent it. Between 1983 and 1986, some 40 000 CCP members were expelled for corrupt practices, but in 1987 alone, the number rose to 109 000.

After contributing to the 'democracy movement' at the end of 1978, the student movement was quiescent for several years. However, disillusionment at China's failure in the second half of the 1980s to match its progress in the first half was widespread among students. Moreover, no matter how hard they worked, they often did not get the best jobs where they could contribute to modernisation most effectively, because the children of high-ranking cadres could use family connections to defeat them.

Students were deeply influenced by Western, and especially American, values and political ideas. Many came to believe strongly that a principal reason why China was so backward was because it lacked freedom and a democratic political system, and that the same factors went a long way towards explaining the prosperity and progressiveness of the West. Many Chinese students who went to study in the West either elected to stay there or returned to China deeply disillusioned with their own country. Japan, and even South Korea and Taiwan, were other models.

The students' attitude towards Japan was admiration for its industrial and economic strength and democratic system, mixed with hatred for its domination of China in the past and the fear that the Chinese government was again just a bit too eager to encourage Japanese investment and corresponding political influence in China. In November and December 1985 there were fairly large student demonstrations in Beijing, one of the motives being to commemorate the fiftieth anniversary of the anti-Japanese 9 December movement of 1935. The students opposed what they saw as excessive Japanese economic and political muscle in China, although they made clear that they did not oppose the open-door or reform policies in general.

Late in 1986 the student movement reached a high point and for the first time became a major embarrassment for the government, with ramifications affecting the highest level of the CCP's leadership. The demonstrations began early in December in Hefei, the capital of Anhui province, where the vice-president of the Chinese University of Science and Technology (Keji daxue), Fang Lizhi, emerged as a key opponent of the government. He gained enormous popularity and support among students for urging a struggle for democracy, for supporting Western political and other values and for attacking authorities in China for the slow pace of political reform.

On 19 December large-scale rallies for greater democracy began in Shanghai, and a few days later spread to Beijing. Despite the extremely cold weather at that time of the year, thousands of students were willing to get up well before dawn and march quite a few miles from their university campuses in the northwest of the city towards Tiananmen Square. The students denounced authoritarianism and called for greater democracy. They lauded the United States as a political system which China should be prepared to admire and in many respects follow. They even held up as a model the Philippines, where in February 1986 a revolution based on 'people's power' had overthrown the corrupt dictator Ferdinand Marcos and brought Corazon Aquino to power.

Both in Shanghai and Beijing, the municipal authorities quickly banned the student demonstrations, which ceased without much resistance. The authorities claimed that the people wanted stability and that 'turbulence' was not possible because of the generally favourable situation. They argued that only about 1 per cent of China's total student population had taken part in the demonstrations, but while they applauded the demands for freedom and democracy, they reiterated that these ideals must be met under the leadership of the CCP. It was made quite clear that student protests independent of the CCP would not be tolerated.

Official reaction to the student demonstrations was actually trying to cover up the immense damage which the student movement was doing to the authority of the CCP and its government. This was made clear very quickly when at the beginning of 1987, the CCP began a campaign against 'bourgeois liberalisation', a phrase meaning excessive Western influence and corresponding negation of socialism in its current Chinese form. The other side of the coin was the maintenance of the 'four cardinal principles', which can be summed up as adherence to Marxism-Leninism-Mao Zedong Thought and to the leadership of the CCP.

There were, of course, casualties of this campaign against 'bourgeois liberalisation' and in favour of the 'four cardinal principles'. Several leading liberals and dissidents, including Fang Lizhi, were expelled from the CCP. Most important of all, at Deng Xiaoping's insistence, the general secretary of the CCP, Hu Yaobang, was dismissed for allowing the spread of 'bourgeois liberalisation' within the CCP, and replaced by Zhao Ziyang.

The Thirteenth National CCP Congress was held late in 1987. In most ways it was a victory for the reform wing of the party. Certainly there was no more than lip service paid anywhere to 'bourgeois liberalisation'. The old guard withdrew from the leadership. Deng Xiaoping retired even from the Central Committee itself, though it should be added that he retained the crucially important position of chairman of the CCP's Military Commission. Zhao Ziyang was confirmed as general secretary. The new Standing Committee of the Politburo included known ardent reformers such as Hu Qili, but also Li Peng, a Soviet-trained engineer who was very much more concerned about curbing inflation than pursuing reform too rapidly.

The student movement of 1989 and reaction

On 15 April 1989 Hu Yaobang died. His dismissal had made him a hero-figure among the students and immediately demonstrations flared again. The *People's Daily* printed a hostile editorial on 26 April, written under the strong influence of Deng Xiaoping, which accused the students of creating political turmoil. This only inflamed the situation and caused well over 100 000 students to take to the streets the following day in spite of a government ban against demonstrations.

The issues of concern to the students were based on the old concepts of freedom and democracy. However, there were also more concrete demands as well. These included an end to corruption and 'genuine dialogue' with the students, meaning with independent bodies set up by the students themselves and not those which merely represented the government's wishes.

Soviet leader Mikhail Gorbachev was due to visit China in mid-May for the long-delayed 'normalisation' of relations between China and the Soviet Union. The students used the large-scale presence of the foreign media occasioned by the visit for their own purposes. On 13 May they occupied Tiananmen Square and indicated their intention to remain there until their demands were met.

Among the measures to attract the most concerned official reaction was a hunger strike by about 1000 students. The following was among the handwritten signs put up at the time. It is dated 13 May 1989 and signed simply by an 'oath-taker':

Hunger Strike Pledge

I hereby vow that in order to push forward the process of democratization in my motherland and for the sake of the country's prosperity, I am voluntarily going on hunger strike. I am determined to obey the discipline of the hunger striking group, and pledge not to give up until our goals are reached.[5]

The occupation of the square, and especially the hunger strike, sharpened a fierce power struggle already going on within the leadership between Zhao Ziyang and Hu Qili and their supporters, who were sympathetic to the students, on the one hand, and Li Peng, strongly supported by Deng Xiaoping and most of the old guard, who had absolutely no time for the kind of instability and 'turmoil' they believed the students were creating, on the other. The students had on many occasions since the beginning of the movement in April attacked both Deng Xiaoping and Li Peng, publicly calling on them to resign. Both Li Peng and Zhao Ziyang visited fasting students in hospital, but whereas Li was rather peremptory with them, Zhao was willing to linger and give signs that he took them seriously.

With Gorbachev's departure on 18 May, events began to move faster. The same evening, Li Peng appeared on live television with several of the student leaders in an attempt at dialogue. Li behaved in a condescending manner towards them and demanded that only one issue be discussed: 'how to get the fasting students out of their present plight'. The students would have none of this, and one of them in particular, Wuerkaixi, not only behaved and spoke quite arrogantly and aggressively to Li Peng, but made a whole catalogue of demands, including that Li Peng should immediately affirm the student movement and retract the editorial of 26 April. Of course, Li had no intention whatever of taking either action (nor the ability to do so), and the interview ended without positive result except that both sides 'agreed that the talks were only a meeting rather than a dialogue'.[6]

The next morning Zhao Ziyang went out into Tiananmen Square to express sympathy with the students, but also to inform them that a power struggle was in progress and they were not doing him any good with their hunger strike or occupation of the square. As it turned out, Zhao had either already lost the power struggle or was about to do so, and as of April 1995 this was to be his last major public appearance.

Li Peng immediately declared martial law and troops moved towards the square. However, the students put up barricades and persuaded many to withdraw. There was no violence. It looked as if martial law was going to be ineffective, with the students having won the victory. They had successfully flouted government authority. However, a few days later Li Peng appeared on television to assert his control of the government.

The students had already called off their hunger strike on 19 May and many began to leave the square. The trend until the end of the month was for the student movement to dwindle. At the end of the month, the students erected their Statue of the Goddess of Democracy, clearly modelled on the American Statue of Liberty in New York. Shortly afterwards, another hunger strike began in the square and demonstrations started again.

This time the government reacted very strongly. Despite the failure to implement martial law on the days following 20 May, the army had in fact been hovering on the outskirts of Beijing. On the evening of 3 June it pounced and over the next few hours forced its way into Tiananmen Square, clearing it of all demonstrators by dawn the next day. Casualties were heavy in this military action which in the West is usually known as 'the Beijing massacre', but in China as 'the June 4 incident'. The exact number of deaths is unknown, but was probably at least a thousand. The student movement had been crushed.

On 9 June Deng Xiaoping appeared with quite a few of the leadership on television congratulating the armymen who had cleared the square. Deng and the government were now claiming that the 'turmoil' of the student movement had turned into a 'counter-revolutionary rebellion' over the night of 2–3 June. The army had done well to nip this rebellion in the bud before it could do serious damage. Had it not carried out this action, the CCP would have been overthrown and the PRC replaced by a 'bourgeois republic',[7] meaning a political system modelled on that of the United States. At the same time, Deng Xiaoping was adamant that reform and 'openness to the outside world' would continue.

Later in June 1989, the Fifth Plenum of the Thirteenth Central Committee dismissed Zhao Ziyang as general secretary of the CCP and replaced him by Jiang Zemin who, as secretary of the Shanghai Communist Party, had been able to avert in Shanghai the disaster which had struck Beijing. In November 1989, Deng Xiaoping retired as chairman of the CCP's Central Military Commission, Jiang Zemin taking over that position also.

A savage crackdown on student and other dissent got underway. The regime of Jiang Zemin and Li Peng consolidated itself. It pushed its line about the quelling of the counter-revolutionary rebellion endlessly. It subjected the loyalties of those who entered universities or went abroad to study to greater surveillance and checks. It also went to greater lengths to curb corruption within the CCP and government.

The government's case that 'a counter-revolutionary rebellion' had occurred perhaps gains weight in the light of the collapse of several communist parties in Eastern Europe later in 1989 and of the Soviet Communist Party itself in August 1991. However, to this writer the evidence produced by the government in favour of the eruption of a counter-revolutionary rebellion is not compelling. Although both students and government agree that arms passed from the military to forces hostile to Deng Xiaoping and Li Peng on the night of 2–3 June, neither side claims the numbers as great. Moreover, government sources make no reference to an intensive military campaign, nor do they point to organised leadership of the sort which could seriously qualify as a counter-revolutionary rebellion. Very few of the students or their demonstrations called for the overthrow of the CCP.

To this writer, the students were extraordinarily unwise to push their occupation of the square so far and to demonstrate for so long, in such large numbers and so intensely. It was naive in the extreme for them to go out of their way to humiliate the government in general and Deng Xiaoping and Li Peng in particular. But a more competent government would have refused to panic and handled the matter much more sensibly and with much less brutality. It was not necessary to carry out a massacre to suppress the student movement. A much better thought-out action late in May would probably have produced the same result but without the bloodshed. And it was stupid in the extreme not to import enough teargas or water cannons to make tanks and guns unnecessary. The whole process of the student movement and the military suppression which followed it did incalculable damage to China's political culture, its economy, society and image in the world.

This writer's visit to China in October 1991 convinced him that the new government had stabilised. The process of reform has survived, albeit in a somewhat diluted form. The CCP showed no sign of being overthrown in the near future, or of giving up its monopoly of power. But the basic problem of the educated youth was not even nearly solved. Reform involves drastic opening to the outside world. It is inevitable that the values of the rich and industrialised countries of the West and Japan will gather influence in China. Controls on this influence are inevitably going to create resentments among the educated young, the skilled people who are going to make up the very personnel who implement modernisation. The government wants them on side, not resenting everything it does. Indoctrination of the youth has worked in the past, but the fact that the student movement and massacre occurred proves that it was not working from the mid-1980s on. It is unlikely that such indoctrination can function effectively in the aftermath of so traumatic a crisis.

Conclusion

The period of the PRC has seen enormous achievements but also enormous mistakes. It has so far kept China united, strong and important on the international scene. However, the problem of just how to use Marxism-Leninism to solve China's immense problems has not been solved. It is for this reason that we see vast swings in China's political pendulum, even while the same party remains in power.

One point is fairly clear. In the process of undergoing a period of revolution and then one of reform which can validly be dubbed post-revolutionary, China has changed enormously since 1949. Admittedly the post-revolutionary period of reform has seen the return of many traditional values and practices, and Jiang Zemin's government has gone out of its way to laud Confucianism. However, the whole texture of society and the political culture, not to mention the economy, is totally different now from what it was in 1949. The changes in the class and ownership structure within society, the types of people who hold power, the ideals of the people, and the level of prosperity have undergone enormous transformations under the influence of the CCP. Many of these changes are probably permanent, and it is most unlikely that even an unforeseen disaster could take China back to where it was before the triumph of the revolution in 1949.

Guide to further reading

Baum, Richard, *Burying Mao: Chinese Politics in the Age of Deng Xiaoping*, Princetown University Press, Princetown, 1994
   A highly scholarly and accessible account of Chinese politics in the age of Deng Xiaoping by a leading authority in the field.
Dietrich, Craig, *People's China, A Brief History*, Oxford University Press, New York, Oxford, 1986; 1994
   This is a concise and excellent general history of the PRC, beginning with some background on pre-1949 history and revolutionary personalities, and ending in the mid-1980s. Though basically chronological, it includes detailed discussion of important topics and issues. The second edition includes an account of the crisis of 1989.

Gittings, John, *China Changes Face, The Road from Revolution, 1949–1989*, Oxford University Press, Oxford, 1990

The new edition of this book, which was first published in 1989, contains an excellent chapter on the 1989 crisis and its aftermath. The book argues that the CCP has lost its mandate with the failure of its revolution.

Mackerras, Colin & Yorke, Amanda, *The Cambridge Guide to Contemporary China*, Cambridge University Press, Cambridge, 1991

This book aims to present information about all periods of the PRC, especially the 1980s, in an accessible form. It consists of a detailed, categorised chronology, bibliography and gazetteer, as well as chapters on politics, biographies, foreign relations, the economy, population, the minority nationalities, education and culture and society. The bibliography contains an analytical list of all works focusing most or all their attention on the PRC period in China published in the English language down to the northern autumn of 1989.

Townsend, James R. & Womack, Brantly, *Politics in China*, 3rd edn, Little, Brown & Co., Boston, Toronto, 1986

This is a political science, rather than historical, work. It focuses on ideology, governmental processes and political frameworks. Its period of coverage is all of the PRC, but there is a good deal of emphasis given to the changes brought about by the period of reform. There are several useful appendixes, mainly on population and the economy.

Notes

1 'Report on the Work of the Government', *Peking Review*, vol. 18, no. 4, 24 January 1975, p. 23.

2 'Communique of the Third Plenary Session of the 11th Central Committee of the Communist Party of China', *Peking Review*, vol. 21, no. 52, 29 December 1978, pp. 10–11.

3 'On Questions of Party History', *Beijing Review*, vol. 24, no. 27, 6 July 1981, p. 29.

4 ibid., p. 26.

5 This was among a number of documents collected in China at the time of the student protest movement, and given to Colin Mackerras, who translated it into English.

6 See the account of the televised interview, including much direct quotation from it, in 'Li Peng Meets with Student Leaders', *Beijing Review*, vol. 32, no. 22, 29 May–4 June 1989, pp. 16–20.

7 'Deng Hails Armymen', *Beijing Review*, vol. 32, nos 24–25, 12–25 June 1989, p. 4.

26 | Sukarno to Suharto

Another major example where a radical phase was succeeded by a more conservative reform age was Indonesia. However, the processes of development and change were very different from those in China.

In Chapter 18, we examined the Indonesian revolution, which ended when the Dutch formally recognised Indonesia's independence on 27 December 1949. For many Indonesians, the final lowering of the Dutch flag in Jakarta on that day seemed to promise the end of a long period of struggle, and the start of a new era of peace and prosperity. They soon found, however, that the struggle to maintain and to give substance to their hard-won independence was just as difficult a task as the fight against colonialism itself had been.

Most historians divide Indonesian history since 1949 into three broad periods:

1 *1949–late 1950s:* parliamentary or constitutional democracy;
2 *late 1950s–mid- to late 1960s:* guided democracy;
3 *mid- to late 1960–present:* New Order period.

Parliamentary democracy

For nearly a decade, from 1949 until the last years of the 1950s, Indonesia's political system was strongly influenced by European models: it had a parliament whose members belonged, in the main, to political parties; a cabinet responsible to that parliament; and a military which was subordinate to the civil power. The presidency — held by Sukarno — was a largely ceremonial post, with day-to-day political power resting with the prime minister as head of government. In practice, however, these institutions often did not work as effectively as their European counterparts. Eventually, they were abandoned in favour of ones which seemed better suited to indigenous Indonesian political culture.

The first major political problem the Indonesian state faced after the recognition of its independence concerned its formal structure. Under the terms of the Round Table Conference Agreements, the state whose independence the Dutch recognised in 1949 was the federal Republic of the United States of Indonesia (RUSI), led by Prime Minister Hatta. The Republic of Indonesia, with its capital at Yogyakarta, was just one out of fifteen states or provinces in the RUSI.

However, many leading Republican politicians, most notably Sukarno himself, saw this situation as intolerable in the longer term. They saw federalism as something which had been inflicted upon Indonesia by the Dutch; something which served chiefly to prolong Dutch influence in Indonesia by ensuring divisions in the Indonesian state. Thus, immediately after Dutch acknowledgment of Indonesian independence, a carefully orchestrated campaign began to bring this federal system to an end.

During the first seven months of 1950, the governments of the federal states one by one resolved to amalgamate their territories into the Yogyakarta-based Republic of Indonesia. On 17 August 1950, the fifth anniversary of the proclamation of independence, Sukarno announced that the federal system had been abolished, and the unitary republic restored. A temporary constitution was drawn up and adopted, on the understanding that a Constituent Assembly would shortly be elected and charged with writing a permanent constitution for the country.

These developments did not mean, however, that the Indonesian nation was now firmly united. Many people in the outlying regions remained concerned at what they saw as the centralisation of power in Jakarta. As we shall see later, this concern was to erupt in a civil war in the late 1950s. Debate about the role of Islam in the state continued as well. In 1948, as was noted in Chapter 18, a group of Muslims wanting to see Islam made the official religion of the country had formed the Indonesian Islamic State, usually called the Darul Islam (meaning literally 'Abode of Islam'). The Darul Islam was never a serious military threat to the Indonesian state. However, its continued existence was a constant reminder to Jakarta that the problem of the position of Islam in the state had still not been resolved.

From 1950–53, Indonesia had three different governments, led by Prime Ministers Natsir, Sukiman and Wilopo. They were drawn from different coalitions of parties, but in their platforms all three cabinets placed the highest priority on restoration of the country's economic stability and prosperity. They believed that unless and until this was done, nothing else could be achieved.

This may seem a very sensible and responsible policy to follow. However, it was one which brought those governments into conflict with particular interest groups within the community. We can see this happening in several different policy areas.

Firstly, all three cabinets were in principle committed to asserting Indonesian control over the economy, ousting non-Indonesians — chiefly Dutch and Chinese — from the positions of strength they had occupied during the colonial period. However, in practice they moved only slowly in this direction. They reasoned that the swift and wholesale replacement of these elements with Indonesian entrepreneurs and capital would only lead to a very substantial disruption to the economy. But their reluctance to move more swiftly brought all three governments into conflict with local Indonesian businesspeople, who of course would have stood to benefit from any actions taken against their Dutch or Chinese competitors.

Secondly, the cabinets wanted to reduce the size of both the public service and the army, in an attempt to rationalise and reduce the cost of government and administration. Not surprisingly, both resisted the government's moves.

In the case of the bureaucracy, the government was faced with the fact that most of the major political parties had actively sought recruits in the public service, and many had succeeded in converting one or more departments into their own little fiefdoms. Having done this, they naturally did not want to see their pet departments cut back — this would have been a direct attack on their power bases.

The army presented an even greater problem. Government attempts to reduce its size and raise its professionalism implied getting rid of those officers and soldiers with the least technical military training and education. The people who seemed likely to benefit most from this policy were those who had received formal training from the Dutch. This included men like Colonel Abdul Haris Nasution, who had served in the KNIL before the revolution, but who had joined the Republican army in 1945. However, it also included Indonesians who had fought *with* the Dutch and *against* the Republicans during the revolution, and who had only transferred to the Indonesian army in 1950. Naturally this did not sit very well with those revolutionary army officers and men who believed they were likely to be demobilised or passed over for promotion because, in comparison, they had little formal military training.

The net result of these pressures was that, despite their best intentions, these first three governments were able to achieve little by way of rationalising the economy and the infrastructure of the state and making them more efficient.

Wilopo's successor as prime minister was Ali Sastroamidjojo, usually referred to simply as Ali. Ali's priorities were somewhat different from those of his predecessors. Rather than emphasising economic rationality and recovery, he pressed instead for the assertion by Indonesians of full political and economic sovereignty over their territory. This was to be done even thought it was recognised that there would be economic costs attached to it.

A first priority was to repudiate the economic clauses of the Round Table Conference agreements which gave Dutch business interests a privileged position in Indonesia. Ali also moved to try to strengthen the position of indigenous businesspeople, as compared with Chinese entrepreneurs. He proposed to do this through an elaborate system of licences and permits which would have been available only to indigenous businesspeople. However, as he himself was later to acknowledge in his autobiography, this policy ran into problems. The speed with which this policy was implemented:

> resulted in a lack of detailed examination [and] in the issuing of commercial licences to people who had no experience in trade and commerce. The result was that many Indonesians sold their licences to Chinese businessmen, and became scornfully known as 'briefcase businessmen'.[1]

It was, however, in the field of foreign policy — a field to which his predecessors had paid comparatively little attention — that Ali made his most important mark. Two particularly important initiatives stand out.

First, there was the struggle for West Irian. The Round Table Conference agreements had left the Indonesian–Dutch dispute over control of the territory unresolved. As a result, it developed into a major bone of contention between Indonesia and the Dutch. Previous Indonesian governments had sought to gain control over the territory through negotiations with the Dutch, but had failed. Ali decided to internationalise the issue by taking it to the United Nations in 1954. The Indonesian position was supported by more than half the members of the General Assembly — but by less than the two-thirds majority necessary to commit the UN to taking action. It was, however, an important moral victory for Indonesia, and certainly drew the attention of the international community to the dispute.

Ali's second important initiative was in the formation of the Asian–African bloc of states — now known as the Non-Aligned Movement. By the middle of the 1950s, a growing number of Asian and African countries had achieved their independence. In April 1955, they came together in Bandung, West Java, for their first-ever conference. The conference attracted a plethora of distinguished visitors: Nasser, Nehru, Zhou Enlai, Tito. Ali and, of course, Sukarno were at the centre of things. The conference marks the beginning of a decade in which Indonesia was to play a major role in world affairs.

Unfortunately for Ali, however, while he was preoccupied with foreign affairs, domestic affairs got out of hand. He ill-advisedly sought to appoint an unpopular man to the position of commander of the army. Other senior army officers organised a very effective boycott of the swearing-in ceremony; the reactions, both military and civil, to this clash were vigorous and they led to Ali's downfall in June 1955.

The formation of a successor cabinet took place in an atmosphere of steadily increasing excitement and expectation as the country moved closer to the September 1955 deadline for the holding of its first general elections. It was widely hoped that these elections would show clearly which political parties had the confidence of the people, and thus a mandate to govern, thereby bringing to an end the political instability which had seen the country governed by no fewer than five different prime ministers since 1949. Eventually a coalition cabinet was stitched together under the leadership of Burhanuddin Harahap, a rather conservative politician not at all in the Ali mode.

The elections were duly held, and by all reports were well organised and honest. But instead of stabilising politics by producing a clear result, with one party or coalition of parties getting a clear majority of the vote, the reverse happened: the popular vote was widely dispersed among no fewer than 28 parties. The Nationalist Party of Indonesia (PNI) proved to be the most popular, securing 22 per cent of the vote. This was followed by two Islamic parties, Masjumi (21 per cent) and Nahdatul Ulama (NU, 18 per cent), and the Communist Party of Indonesia (PKI, 16 per cent). It would have taken a coalition of three of these four major parties to command a simple majority of the vote and thus claim a mandate to govern — a most unlikely occurrence.

But the election results not only failed to produce any clear political winner; they also starkly revealed the extent to which regional geographical divisions were politically powerful. The ethnic Javanese heartlands in central and east Java were the strongholds of the PNI, the NU and the PKI, which between then controlled 141 of the 257 seats in the parliament. The regions outside central and east Java — the western third of the island, and the Outer Islands — had only one major party to represent their views: the Masjumi. Many non-Javanese feared that this would mean that their interests would be subordinated to those of Java and the Javanese. This consternation was made worse the following year, 1956, when Hatta resigned as vice president. As a Sumatran, Hatta had long been seen by non-Javanese as an important guarantor of the political balance in Jakarta.

Rather than uniting Indonesia, then, the elections confirmed the divisions in the country. And as if to confirm that nothing had really changed, the Burhanuddin cabinet fell and was replaced by one led, again, by Ali Sastroamidjojo. From this point onwards, Indonesian politics moved rapidly towards conflict and crisis, a situation which gave Sukarno the opportunity to take a much more active role in national politics.

Sukarno had never made any bones about the fact that he was no supporter of parliamentary democracy, with its political parties and its emphasis on reaching decisions by majority votes. To him, this system was inherently divisive, alien to Indonesian political culture and the prime cause of the country's political instability. In October 1956, he made a speech strongly critical of the political parties, and calling for the establishment of a new form of democracy. He explained:

> [T]he democracy I crave for Indonesia is not liberal democracy such as exists in Western Europe. No! What I want for Indonesia is a guided democracy, a democracy with leadership. A guided democracy, a guided democracy, something which is guided but still democracy.[2]

Just exactly what he meant by 'guided democracy, democracy with leadership' was not entirely clear. But he subsequently urged a return to what he described as traditional Indonesian values, which were typically to be found in the nation's villages. In the villages, he said, decision-making was a co-operative process, involving all adult members of the community, under the leadership or guidance of the village head. Proposals or suggestions for action were discussed at length (*musyawarah*), until eventually consensus (*mufakat*) was reached. In this way, harmony within the village was maintained. And what was good for the village was also good for the nation.

Sukarno made two specific proposals to give effect, at least in part, to his ideas: the formation of a cabinet in which representatives of all the major political parties would sit, and the establishment of a National Council, its membership based on what he termed 'functional groups' in Indonesian society. These included farmers, women, artists, religious leaders, the military and so forth.

The political parties were divided over these proposals. Support for them came chiefly from the PKI and the PNI, with opposition from the Muslims. The latter were particularly concerned that the effect of these proposals was to give the communists access to much greater power than they had ever previously had; up to this point, despite their strong electoral showing, the communists had always been kept out of the cabinet. Clearly, if Sukarno's proposals were to be accepted, this situation could not continue. Over the next few months, the sense of crisis deepened, in both Java itself, and in the Outer Islands.

In the Outer Islands, increasingly strong feelings of neglect and exploitation by Java were being expressed by military and business leaders. These people were concerned about the increasing strength of the PKI in national politics. They were also strongly religious — either Muslim or Christian — and saw secularism increasing in political influence in Jakarta. Many were also exporters of estate crops, who believed their business activities were being crippled by the protectionist economic policies being pursued by Jakarta.

In late 1956 and early 1957, regional military commanders in Sumatra and Sulawesi seized power from the local civilian administrations. These developments posed a major challenge to the authority of the government in Jakarta. It was a challenge that Prime Minister Ali Sastroamidjojo was simply unable to meet. He resigned his office on 14 March 1957, immediately after which Sukarno accepted the advice of Army Commander General Nasution, and proclaimed a state of martial law across the country. This move, however, failed to dissuade the Outer Islanders: on 15 February 1958 they proclaimed a rebel government, the Revolutionary Government of the Republic of Indonesia (Pemerintah Revolusioner Republik Indonesia: PRRI) in west Sumatra. Two days later, they were joined by the rebels in Sulawesi. Indonesia was by now split in two, with the sides divided by political ideology, religion, economic philosophy and geographical location.

This move demanded a direct and forceful response from Jakarta. Sukarno authorised Nasution to take military action against the rebels. The ensuing war was perhaps not very costly or bloody as civil wars go, but it was damaging enough. The end result, though, was a clear victory for the forces of centralism, the forces of Jakarta, and a defeat for the rebels.

On the one hand, this victory strengthened Sukarno's position. He no longer had to worry about the political and economic repercussions which would have followed from either a protracted civil war or, worse, from a victory by the rebels. Moreover, victory brought Sukarno the opportunity to move forcefully against his opponents in Jakarta. The Masjumi and the Indonesian Socialist Party, two parties which had expressed strong opposition to his proposals for a reorganisation of the country's political system, had been compromised by the involvement with the rebels of many of their most prominent leaders. In 1960, Sukarno announced that both these parties had been banned.

The other major victor was clearly the army under Nasution. The army was now firmly established as a major political actor. In 1958 Nasution set out a political doctrine for the armed forces which he termed the 'Middle Way'. He argued that the Indonesian armed forces had a unique role to play in society:

> We do not and we will not copy the situation as it exists in several Latin American states where the army acts as a direct political force; nor will we emulate the Western European model where armies are the dead tools (of the government) or the example of Eastern Europe.[3]

Rather, the army stood in the middle, having both a military and a civil–political role to play in the life of the nation, just as it had done during the revolution. But the army could not play this role unless the political system were altered: parliamentary democracy had no place for an army wanting to wield direct political influence. Sukarno's emerging guided democracy, though, did offer such an opportunity, so long as it could be moulded in the right direction. Nasution thus had an interest in the establishment of guided democracy; he and Sukarno were drawn into an alliance, though it was one of convenience rather than conviction.

His position now secure, and with Nasution's support, Sukarno moved to put in place his guided democracy. A crucial element was the reinstatement of the 1945 constitution, which gave the president far greater powers than the provisional constitution of 1950. On 22 April 1959, Sukarno formally proposed to the Constituent Assembly, elected in 1955, that it adopt the 1945 constitution. In light of the Assembly's failure to write a new constitution, there was a good deal of sympathy for Sukarno's proposal among its members. However one major and long-standing problem loomed over consideration of the issue: whether the state should be based constitutionally on Islam or on the Five Principles of the State philosophy (Pancasila — see Chapter 18).

Three times in mid-1959 the Assembly voted on whether to accept the 1945 constitution, which makes no formal reference to Islam; three times a simple majority of members favoured this course of action, but the two-thirds majority required to make a decision binding was never achieved. Finally, on 5 July 1959, his political patience having been exhausted, Sukarno stepped in and unilaterally declared that the constitution of 1945 had been reinstated.

Many politicians protested at Sukarno's unilateral action, arguing that it was illegal and unconstitutional. Formally, it may have been both those things. But in practical terms, Sukarno had made the decision, and he was able to enforce it: he was able to secure the active support of sufficient people to ensure that his decision stuck. With this decisive, albeit rather risky, action he had seized the political initiative and thus ushered in the era of guided democracy.

Guided democracy

Guided democracy was a system of government in which the parliament was to play a relatively small role, as were most political parties with the increasingly important exception of the Communist Party. It was one which saw the emergence of a major new political force in the Indonesian army. It was in many respects a very populist political system, in the sense that political leaders — Sukarno in particular — encouraged mass popular participation in political rallies, parades and so forth, something early leaders had assiduously avoided. And perhaps most importantly of all, the system was one in which Sukarno was to play a pivotal role.

Many of these features of guided democracy can be seen in the campaign to force the Dutch to relinquish control over West Irian. We have already noted that Ali Sastroamidjojo had adopted a more activist line on this issue than his predecessors, giving up bilateral negotiations with the Dutch in favour of internationalising the dispute through the United Nations. Four times the matter went before the General Assembly; four times it secured the support of a simple majority of members, but never the required two-thirds majority. The campaign certainly raised international awareness of the Indonesian position, but it still left the Dutch in control of the territory.

In late 1957, though, after the General Assembly had once more failed to give its full support to Indonesia, Sukarno announced that Indonesia would now follow a new course in trying to recover the territory, putting direct pressure on the Dutch. This meant, first of all, a campaign against Dutch business interests in Indonesia. In late 1957, major Dutch businesses were taken over, in most instances by their employees, although all eventually came under government or military control. Dutch nationals were subjected to public harassment, and most finally expelled from the country. Mass rallies and parades were held in cities, towns and villages across Indonesia, demanding that the Dutch get out of the territory.

The next step in this 'new approach' was taken at the end of the decade, when Indonesian troops and volunteers were landed in West Irian, by boat and by parachute, to challenge the Dutch militarily. In one sense, these military actions were a defeat for the Indonesians: the vast bulk of their troops were quickly either captured by the Dutch, or killed. But the Dutch soon found that their military victory was being won at enormous political and financial cost. It was easy enough, and cheap enough, for the Indonesians to infiltrate small groups of troops at places and times of their own choosing. But for the Dutch to adequately defend the territory was vastly more difficult and more expensive.

In 1962, with the assistance of a retired American diplomat, Ellsworth Bunker, the Dutch and the Indonesians came to an agreement under which control over the territory would be transferred to Indonesia in 1963, via a United Nations Temporary Executive Authority. The one condition placed on this agreement was that by 1969 an 'Act of Free Choice' was to be undertaken in West Irian, to give the people there the opportunity to say whether or not they wanted to remain within the Indonesian Republic.

With his new approach to the West Irian issue, Sukarno had given the people the sense that they were participating in a great crusade against colonialism — a crusade which was not just national, but also international in its reach. The campaign was also important in bringing the people of Indonesia together. Virtually no identifiable group in the community opposed it: communists, Muslims, military leaders, and politicians all participated in the struggle. The contrast with the divisive politics of the parliamentary democracy period was striking. Sukarno tried the same strategy between 1963 and 1965, in his campaign against the formation of the Federation of Malaysia. This time, however, he was spectacularly less successful.

In the early 1960s, in collaboration with the leaders of the Federation of Malaya and of Singapore, the British had worked out a plan for the formation of a new state of Malaysia, which would be made up of the already-independent Federation of Malaya and the British-controlled territories of Singapore, Sabah and Serawak.

At first this proposal aroused little interest in Indonesia. However, in January 1963, Foreign Minister Subandrio announced Indonesia's opposition to the plan, proclaiming:

> The President has decided that henceforth we shall pursue a policy of confrontation against Malaya . . . We have always been pursuing a confrontation policy against colonialism and imperialism in all its manifestations. It is unfortunate that Malaya, too, has lent itself to become tools of colonialism and imperialism. That is why we are compelled to adopt a policy of confrontation.[4]

Sukarno's argument was that the Malaysia proposal was an attempt by the conservative leadership of Malaya on the one hand, and the British on the other, to preserve the regional economic and political status quo after the withdrawal of formal British colonial and military power. As such, the scheme was a classic illustration of the global conflict between what Sukarno called the New Emerging Forces and the Old Established Forces, that is, those seeking radical changes and those for conservatism and colonialism.

Not all observers accept that Sukarno's motives for opposing Malaysia were those he himself cited. Some have seen his policy as a reflection of an adventurist and aggressive foreign policy, or an attempt to divert the attention of the people away from increasing internal economic and political turmoil and towards another foreign issue, or a reflection of Sukarno's pique at not having been consulted on a major regional political issue. There is undoubtedly at least an element of truth in all these suggestions. By the same token, Sukarno's own explanations for his actions are clearly consistent with his general political reasoning at this time, and should be taken seriously as reflecting, at the least, an important part of a rather complex story.

On 16 September 1963, despite Sukarno's opposition, the new Federation of Malaysia was officially established. This brought an immediate reaction in Indonesia: diplomatic relations with Malaya were severed, the British embassy in Jakarta burnt down and British firms seized. On 25 September, Sukarno formally announced that Indonesia had embarked on a campaign to 'crush Malaysia'.

This 'crush Malaysia' campaign attracted widespread popular support in Indonesia, as political and other groups manoeuvred to align themselves with the president. The PKI, the political party with the clearest ideological objection to Malaysia, was the most active in supporting, organising or participating in scores of mass rallies and parades, and leading the way in the seizure of British-owned business enterprises.

The army, however, was in a much more difficult position. On the one hand, like the PKI, it needed to be seen to be supportive of the president. On the other, many of its anti-communist leaders felt politically threatened by the campaign, given the mileage being obtained from it by their opponents, the PKI. Thus, while giving public support to Sukarno, the army leadership in fact maintained clandestine contacts with the Malaysians and the British, and ensured that loyal troops were kept away from the battlefront in Kalimantan, and close to Jakarta.

Malaysia, however, turned out to be no West Irian. Its internal political cohesion and strength were considerable, its military backing clearly a match for the Indonesians, and its degree of international legitimacy high. Outside Indonesia, Sukarno's position was supported only by China and a handful of like-minded states, such as North Korea. At the end of 1964, Sukarno withdrew Indonesia from the United Nations in protest at the organisation's election of Malaysia to a seat on the Security Council. By the time of the fall of the New Order regime in 1965, despite having been in progress for two years, the 'crush Malaysia' campaign was to all intents and purposes stymied. When the military came to power under the leadership of General Suharto, one of its first acts was to end confrontation, and to establish friendly relations with Malaysia.

On economic matters, Sukarno's position was the complete reverse of the nation's leaders in the early 1950s. No economist himself, Sukarno looked down on those who were. He took the view that political reform was a higher priority than economic development; indeed, without political reform there could be no meaningful economic development. In particular, it was more important to raise the people's political consciousness and morale, to make them proud of themselves and their nation, than to worry about mundane things such as the reform of the bureaucracy and making manufacturing industry more efficient. Thus guided democracy saw the erection around the country of numerous statues, skyscrapers, stadiums and other buildings symbolising the greatness of Indonesia and its peoples. Sukarno described critics of his expenditure on such monuments as 'chicken-hearted souls with a grocer's mentality'.[5] Unfortunately, while it might indeed have been important to raise the self-esteem of the people after decades of colonial rule, the economic cost to the country was high. By the mid-1960s, Indonesia's annual inflation rate was over 650 per cent, and the nation's coffers were virtually empty.

We have already noted that, although Sukarno may have been the most powerful symbol of guided democracy, he shared power with at least two other groups of people: the communists and the military.

During the early years of guided democracy, while martial law was still in force, the army was probably more powerful than the PKI. But when martial law was lifted in 1963, and most of the restrictions on civilian political activity were removed, the balance of power began to shift.

Theoretically, all political groups could have taken advantage of the opportunities this development offered; in practice, though, only the PKI had the organisational capacity, the discipline, the ideological training and the popular support to take full advantage of it. It was the largest political party in the country, with about 3 million members.

The army did establish a number of civilian functional groups or associations under its de facto leadership, which could operate on its behalf after the ending of martial law. It also established a secretariat to co-ordinate the activities of these functional groups, known as Sekber Golkar. By and large, however, the leadership of these functional groups showed far less flair for propaganda and organisation than did the leadership of the PKI; the army-linked groups proved to be unable to compete very effectively with the PKI in the political arena.

By the mid-1960s, this conflict between the army and the PKI had become the dominant theme in Indonesian politics. The Indonesian political system seemed to be heading for a major clash between these two powerful but contradictory political forces. In fact, just this kind of clash did take place, starting in the second half of 1965. It saw a shattering of the PKI, its leaders killed or imprisoned or in exile; it saw Sukarno on a steady downward slide from office; and it saw the army firmly entrenched in power.

The catalyst for these events occurred on the night of 30 September–1 October 1965 when squads of troops and members of the PKI-affiliated youth and women's organisations kidnapped six of the country's most senior army officers and killed them. Though he was on the murder list, General Nasution managed to escape from his would-be assassins. Other troops seized control of the centre of Jakarta and broadcast a statement in the name of what they termed the '30th September Movement', saying that they had acted to protect the president from a *coup d'etat* being planned by rightwing generals in the pay of the CIA.

However, the troops had failed to capture General Suharto, the commander of the Strategic Reserve, a sizeable, well-trained and well-equipped force stationed in the capital. Suharto used these troops to confront the rebels; by nightfall on 1 October, Jakarta was firmly in his hands. Although there were demonstrations of support for the 30th September Movement in a number of cities and towns in central and east Java, the movement was effectively dead by 2 October. The PKI itself was banned on 12 March 1966.

Suharto moved cautiously but firmly to take over authority from Sukarno. He secured a mandate to exercise temporary authority in Sukarno's name on 11 March 1966, became acting president in 1967 and then finally displaced Sukarno as full president in 1968. By the end of the 1960s, the displacement of Sukarno was virtually complete. Held under virtual house arrest, and in bad health, he eventually died in Jakarta on 21 June 1970.

Suharto saw Sukarno as at best a not-unwilling dupe of the communists, and at worst as an open collaborator with them. He wanted to distance himself and his new administration from Sukarno as much as possible, to emphasise the break with the past. Thus, for instance, he called his administration the 'New Order', in contrast to the 'Old Order' as represented by Sukarno.

To describe the events of 1965–66 in the bald terms we have just used is quite easy; to do so, though, is to gloss over the huge human tragedy which they represented. In the aftermath of the victory of the forces of the New Order, hundreds of thousands of people were killed or imprisoned, on the grounds that they were allegedly supporters of the 30th September Movement. Most of those imprisoned without trial had been freed by 1979; many who had been sentenced to long terms of imprisonment, or to death, were still in gaol in 1990.

The New Order

The conflict which had brought the New Order government to power involved not only the army and the PKI. The army was supported in its fight against the communists by a loose coalition of civilian groups: at least two major ones, and a host of minor ones.

One important group consisted of politically active Muslims, and especially those who were inclined towards the reformist rather than traditionalist stream of Islam. They included former leaders of the strongly anti-communist Masjumi party, banned since 1960. But some traditionalist Muslims, too, rallied to the support of the Suharto government. Indeed, in many parts of central and east Java, killings of communist party members were carried out not by the army but by members of the youth wing of the conservative and traditionalist Muslim party NU.

The second major group supporting Suharto consisted of students and intellectuals. In the early weeks after the coup attempt, university and high school students formed action groups which launched a series of massive street demonstrations in support of what they called the 'Three Demands of the People': the lowering of prices, the banning of the PKI and the purging from the cabinet of PKI members and sympathisers, including the Foreign Minister, Dr Subandrio. Student groups were involved in violent attacks on a number of public buildings, including the Department of Foreign Affairs; student demonstrations and attacks also spread to other cities, including Surabaya, Ujung Pandang (Makassar) and Medan.

While there is no doubt that these demonstrations did genuinely reflect the views of their participants, they were also carried out with the tacit approval of the army leadership. Indeed, some authors have suggested that in fact the army leadership was the key element in their organisation, which it saw as a convenient and effective way of mobilising popular civilian opinion in their struggle against the PKI, and ultimately against Sukarno.

For the students and the Muslims, the Sukarno regime had come to mean moral, intellectual and economic bankruptcy; the New Order government was seen as offering a way out of that bankruptcy. By and large, however, they did not see the military solution as being a long-term one. Rather, they tended to see it as a short-term remedy only, as something which would facilitate a return to what they saw as normalcy and order, after which the army would return to its barracks and leave politics to the civilians once more. As we will see, though, on this point they were to be sorely disappointed.

The New Order government set the achievement of political and economic stability and then development as its major broad policy objectives. Economic recovery headed its priority list. Guided democracy had been disastrous for the economy, with inflation running at greater than 650 per cent annually by 1965. If the inflation rate could not be brought down, and prices and wages stabilised, then the country would very quickly be literally bankrupt. Suharto moved rapidly to arrest and then turn around this situation. Public-sector expenditure was cut down, foreign investment attracted back, and the collection of taxes revitalised. Investments were also made in the productive, revenue-earning sectors of the economy, such as commercial agriculture and mining, so as to boost export earnings. Wages were controlled and strikes, if not formally outlawed, were at least strongly discourag ed. A new *Foreign Investment Law* was enacted in 1967, offering foreign investors substantial incentives — legal and financial — to bring money into the country. Once again foreign aid was actively sought. In 1967 a group of Indonesia's major Western creditors, including Japan, the United States and Australia, formed the Inter-Governmental Group on Indonesia (IGGI), an organisation aimed at co-ordinating the flow of aid to Indonesia. In combination, these policies had the desired effect, with the national inflation rate falling to single figures by the start of the 1970s.

In the political field, Suharto's prime objective was to create a political system which maintained a fine balance between allowing a degree of public debate on political issues, and ensuring that his government's control over political power was not threatened.

A major challenge to Suharto was posed by elements of the non-communist and anti-communist political forces which had initially allied themselves with the military in 1965. These forces were now expecting that they would be able to take over the reins of government, and to reassert civilian control over the nation. To counter these groups would not be easy; certainly the brutal and repressive measures used against the PKI and its members could not be used against them. Two major strategies were evolved.

First, a political machine had to be established to mobilise support for the government, in competition with the existing political parties. In fact, the shell of such an organisation already existed: Golkar. So far it had not been particularly effective. The late 1960s and early 1970s, however, saw the government make enormous efforts to boost Golkar's fortunes. Many civilian supporters of the government were co-opted into its leadership, and civil servants were required to give it their support. These efforts were rewarded when, at the first post-1965 elections held in 1971, Golkar won over half the votes cast, and well over half the seats contested. Although there may well have been an element of vote-rigging in the elections, there is little doubt that the government had been remarkably successful in turning Golkar into a slick vote-gathering machine. In subsequent elections, in 1977, 1982 and 1987, Golkar has continued to capture the majority of the popular vote.

Second, the Suharto government also acted to ensure that its political opponents would have their activities strictly circumscribed. After the 1971 elections, the government announced that a rationalisation of the parties was to take place. Their number, which then stood at nine, was to be reduced to two. One party was to be a Muslim one, formed by amalgamating all four Muslim parties, and the other was to be secular, encompassing all the other parties, including the Catholic and Protestant ones. The rationale for this action was that there were too many political parties operating in Indonesia; the plethora of parties unnecessarily complicated the political process and made it less efficient and less capable of reflecting the wishes of the people.

The parties themselves naturally objected to this amalgamation, but they had nothing like the popular support to enable them to successfully defy the government's plans. In 1973, the two new parties were inaugurated: the Development Unity Party (Partai Persatuan Pembangunan, PPP) formed from the Muslim parties, and the Indonesian Democratic Party (Partai Demokrasi Indonesia, PDI).

In the first elections it contested, in 1978, the PPP managed to attract around 30 per cent of the popular vote. Since then, though, its share of the popular vote has been falling. At the last elections, held in 1987, it failed to win a majority of the vote in any province — even the most strongly Muslim ones such as Aceh.

The other party, the PDI, for a long time seemed politically irrelevant, struggling to maintain sufficient votes to retain any kind of popular legitimacy. To the surprise of a number of observers, though, its support went up noticeably in the 1987 elections, to around 15 per cent. This may not seem much, but it was nearly twice what many had expected it to be. The PDI had campaigned very strongly on a range of moral issues: anti-corruption, rights of the individual, the environment and so forth. What this says for its long-term prospects is not clear, but they certainly look a little healthier than they did five years ago.

Overall, Suharto has been remarkably successful in controlling Indonesian political life. The only serious challenge to his rule came in 1974, at the time of the visit to Indonesia by Japanese Prime Minister Tanaka. Riots and demonstrations took place in the streets of Jakarta, ostensibly by students protesting at increasing Japanese control of the economy. There is clear evidence, though, that there were other forces involved in the riots as well, and other issues. Elements of the army leadership engaged in a leadership struggle with Suharto gave tacit support to the students; many of the urban poor also joined in, in protest at the growing gap between rich and poor. However, by a combination of political and military force, Suharto was able to ride out this storm. Subsequent expressions of opposition to his rule have been more muted, though there is no doubt such opposition still exists.

In foreign affairs, as much as in domestic politics, Suharto has been keen to draw a clear dividing line between his government and that of his predecessor. Sukarno's foreign policy had been activist, global in its scope and, in the later years of guided democracy, increasingly aligned with China. Sukarno saw himself as a world figure, and as the leader of Southeast Asia.

Suharto's foreign policy has been much less visible, and regionally rather than globally directed. Soon after taking power in 1965–66, the new directions in Indonesian foreign policy were made clear. We have already noted that the Suharto government ended confrontation with Malaysia. It also broke off diplomatic relations with China, alleging that Beijing had supported the PKI's coup attempt. Relations with China were not normalised until August 1990, and in 1967 Indonesia joined with Malaysia, Thailand, Singapore and the Philippines to form the Association of Southeast Asian Nations (ASEAN). Brunei joined the group when it became independent in 1984. There is little doubt that most Indonesian politicians saw their country as the natural leader of ASEAN; nonetheless, the government has gone out of its way on most issues to avoid the appearance of dominating the association.

One issue, however, seemed to bring seriously into question the New Order's determination to be seen as a responsible, peaceful state in its relations with its neighbours: the invasion of the former Portuguese colony of East Timor in 1975, and its incorporation into the Republic as its twenty-seventh province in 1976.

The history of the incorporation of East Timor is a confused and complicated one. By mid-1975, the two major political forces in East

Timor, UDT and Fretilin, were struggling for control of the territory, the Portuguese colonial authorities having virtually abandoned it following the 1974 coup in Lisbon which brought an anti-colonialist government to power. Although it is simplifying a complex matter, we may characterise UDT as favouring East Timor's incorporation into Indonesia and Fretilin as wanting full independence. Fretilin was by far the most popular party. There is no doubt that Indonesia was contributing to this conflict by infiltrating troops into the territory in the guise of 'volunteers' supporting the UDT. On 16 October 1975 some of these troops shot and killed five journalists from Australia at a town called Balibo.

Despite this assistance, by late 1975, the Fretilin forces were getting on top of their opponents. On 28 November, Fretilin proclaimed the independence of the Democratic Republic of East Timor. Nine days later, on 7 December, Indonesia officially landed troops in the territory. On 17 December pro-Indonesian forces established the Provisional Government of East Timor on board an Indonesian warship. Six months later, on 31 May 1976, the Indonesian-nominated regional assembly formally applied to have the territory incorporated into Indonesia.

This incorporation did not go unchallenged, either in East Timor or outside it. Forces loyal to Fretilin have continued the armed struggle against the Indonesians to the present day, though they currently pose little military threat to the Indonesian administration. The United Nations continues to regard Portugal as the legitimate authority in the region, as do the Portuguese themselves. Most other countries have come to accept that the territory is now Indonesian, though they might well express regret at the way in which it was incorporated into Indonesia, and in particular at the horrific loss of life this process entailed. Australia falls into this category.

Indonesia's motives in invading and incorporating East Timor have been widely debated. Jakarta was certainly concerned that an independent East Timor would be politically unstable, and liable to domination by a leftist, if not communist, regime which might unsettle neighbouring parts of Indonesia or even encourage latent secessionist movements. Some critics of Jakarta have argued that the Indonesians had strategic and economic reasons for wanting to incorporate East Timor, including the desire to control the seas around the territory, which are strategically important because of their depth, and may be economically important as sources of oil and gas. Others have drawn parallels between East Timor and Irian Jaya, seeing in them both evidence of some deep-seated Indonesian expansionism which might later threaten Papua New Guinea. This latter fear seems most unlikely, for a variety of reasons. For one thing, Indonesia has never evinced any interest in absorbing Papua New Guinea, nor does it have the military, economic or administrative capacity to undertake such an absorption. For another, Papua New Guinea is an independent, sovereign state, recognised as such by the world community, which is unlikely to stand by and witness its forcible conquest by Indonesia.

Conclusions: The last great challenge?

One of the words being heard frequently around Jakarta in recent years is *keterbukaan*, the Indonesian equivalent of *glasnost*. Indonesia is most unlikely to become a liberal democracy very quickly. However, the signs are that the country is moving away from the rather suffocating blanket which the New Order of Suharto has previously placed over it, towards a greater degree of openness in both the political and economic arenas. This openness is discussed in more detail in Chapter 32.

If there is one particular area of domestic politics where greater openness may be crucial, it is the succession to the presidency. Suharto is currently into his fifth five-year term as president, having last been re-elected in 1993. Attention is now focusing on when he will retire. He has already been president for longer than Sukarno. Indonesia has only ever had two presidents and both of them came to office under extraordinary circumstances. There are no precedents for a peaceful and planned transition from one president to another. Creating such a precedent may well be the last great political challenge awaiting Suharto.

Guide to further reading

Jenkins, David, *Suharto and His Generals*, Cornell University Modern Indonesia Project, no. 64, Ithaca, 1984
> An excellent discussion of the position of the military in Indonesian politics.

Legge, John, *Sukarno: A Political Biography*, Allen Lane, London, 1971
> The best of the available biographies of Sukarno.

Reeve, David, *Golkar Of Indonesia*, Oxford University Press, London, 1985
> A detailed account of the emergence of Golkar, and at the same time a good commentary on postwar politics in Indonesia in general.

Ricklefs, M.C., *A History of Modern Indonesia*, Macmillan, London, 1981
> Written in a clear, narrative style, this book provides a detailed coverage of Indonesian history since the coming of Islam. Chapters 18–20 deal with independent Indonesia.

Notes

1 Sastroamijoyo, Ali, *Milestones on my Journey*, ed. C.L.M. Penders, University of Queensland Press, St Lucia, 1979, p. 268. Sastromijoyo is an alternative spelling of Sastroamidjojo.

2   Sukarno, *An Autobiography, as Told to Cindy Adams*, Bobbs Merrill, Indianapolis, 1965, p. 82.

3   Quoted in Sundhausen, Ulf, *The Road to Power, Indonesian Military Politics 1945-1967*, Oxford University Press, Kuala Lumpur, 1982, p. 126.

4   Subandrio, 'Speech to the Mahakarta Regiment in Yogyakarta, 20 January 1963', in Peter Boyce (ed.), *Malaysia and Singapore in International Diplomacy*, Sydney University Press, Sydney, 1968, pp. 69–70.

5   Sukarno, *An Autobiography*, p. 293.

27 | Japanese politics

Japan under Allied occupation

Political development in Japan since the end of World War II could hardly have been more different in most respects from the other two enormous countries of East and Southeast Asia, China and Indonesia. Although defeated in the war, Japan has in general been more successful. Yet in 1945, Japan was forced to undergo foreign occupation which it had itself forced upon a range of countries, including both China and Indonesia. The occupation forces, largely American, arrived in Japan in September 1945 with three specific tasks — democratisation, demilitarisation and decentralisation of the economy. The last of the three objectives was to dismantle the large economic combines known as the *zaibatsu* on the grounds that these combines were inordinately powerful and exercised too much influence in the political sphere and also incompatible with the ideals of market competition. The fundamental American objective was to democratise both the political and the economic systems.

Under the direction of the occupation authorities and General Douglas MacArthur, the Supreme Commander of the Allied Powers (SCAP), a new constitution was promulgated in 1947. The new constitution removed the special position of the emperor and acknowledged the people as sovereign. The emperor's divinity was revoked and he became merely 'the symbol of the state'. However, while the Meiji Constitution was a gift from the emperor, this new constitution has been perceived as a 'gift' of the American occupation forces to Japan. Its foreignness is betrayed by the style and language of the constitution. Like the American Constitution, which begins with 'We, the people', the new Japanese Constitution begins with 'We, the Japanese people'. Even so, the level of popular commitment to the constitution has remained high throughout the postwar period, despite early efforts by successive governments to revise it. The new constitution contained full guarantees of human rights, made the judiciary independent and made the two Houses of the Diet elective bodies, abolishing the House of Peers in the process. Also, to ensure that the new political order would not be tainted by the old system, most of the political leaders were purged and forbidden from participating in political activities for a number of years.

The ease with which the reforms were implemented belies the initial fears of the occupation authorities about resistance to the reform measures. The easy implementation perhaps reflects the historically demonstrated willingness of the Japanese people to learn from other countries, despite the 250 years of forced isolation under the Tokugawa system. In the ancient period, Japan had borrowed aspects of its culture and writing system from China and in the period after the Meiji restoration, the Japanese people had shown a similar willingness to learn from the West in pursuit of political and economic modernisation. After Japan's second forced opening, following its defeat in World War II, the horrors of war and the desire not to allow militarism to become dominant again once more created the conditions for borrowing from the West to strengthen democracy and ensure that the military would be controlled by, rather than controlling, the political process.

The reforms carried out by the occupation authorities were intended to democratise Japan but also, perhaps unwittingly, they remade Japan as a country unlike any other country in the world, at least in terms of constitutional principles. This was the result of Article 9 of the constitution, also known as the 'peace clause'. This clause prohibits the use of force by Japan but has since been loosely interpreted by successive governments to allow for the maintenance of a self-defence force. The official policy has been to differentiate between offensive and defensive uses of force and Article 9 has been interpreted as forbidding only the offensive use of force.

Not all the early reform measures were pursued to their logical conclusion by the occupation forces. One area where the achievements fell short of original intentions was the field of economic decentralisation. This happened as a result of the growing tensions between the United States and the Soviet Union and the division of the world into two opposing blocs. Instead of the wartime alliance, great power rivalry and mutual suspicion of the other's intentions foiled any hope that the alliance relationship might be continued in the postwar period. The United States adopted a policy of containing the Soviet Union and preventing any further spread of communism under Soviet sponsorship. As the nature of global politics changed, so did American policies in Japan. Rather than promoting economic decentralisation, it was now believed that it was more important to promote economic reconstruction and development as a way of checking the spread of communism in Japan. This 'reverse course' in SCAP economic policies began in 1947 and emphasised economic growth and prosperity. An economically strong Japan, it was believed, would prevent the further spread of communism, especially after the communist forces took power in mainland China. The reverse course signified that the original missionary goals had been replaced by a more pragmatic set of objectives.

Party politics in postwar Japan

The purge of political leaders in the early postwar period created a political vacuum in Japan. The effect of the purge was particularly strong for the conservative forces, the Progressive Party and the Liberal Party and it was particularly beneficial for the left-leaning parties whose leaders were now released from incarceration. The occupation forces also removed all restrictions on labour unions and on the establishment of socialist and communist political parties. The first free national election was held in April 1947 and resulted in a plurality for the Japan Socialist Party (JSP). As a result, Katayama Tetsu formed the first socialist government in coalition with the conservatives. Socialist participation in government lasted only until October 1948, partly because of left–right tensions within the socialist movement, but mainly because of the inherent difficulty of maintaining a socialist-conservative coalition intact over a period of time. Because of internal divisions, the socialist party eventually split into the left and right factions over the issue of the peace treaty that brought an end to the occupation of Japan in 1952.

From 1948 to July 1993, the rule of the conservatives remained unbroken and the socialist forces became increasingly marginalised. From November 1955 until its defeat in the 1993 election, the Liberal Democratic Party (LDP) was the only party to exercise political power in Japan. It was formed when the different conservative parties decided to merge, in response to an earlier (October 1955) unification of the right socialists and the left socialists which created the Japan Socialist Party. For a time it looked as though Japanese politics might settle down in the comfortable mode of two-party politics, but the JSP failed to present itself as a credible alternative to the conservatives. Apart from the absence of a viable alternative, the continuied dominance of the LDP is no doubt due mainly to its enviable track record in promoting economic growth and industrialisation, and to its flexibility in adapting to changing circumstances.

The electoral gerrymander also helped in maintaining the LDP in power in the postwar period. The LDP's main support was in the rural areas where the value of the vote was considerably greater than in urban areas because of demographic changes, such as internal migration from the rural areas to the urban centres, that have taken place since the electoral boundaries were first formed. The LDP ensured its dominance in the rural areas by its commitment to pro-farm policies and the protection given to the farm sector of the economy from foreign competition.

During this period the party acquired an image as a 'party of farmers'.[1] The policy of protecting the farm population is changing as a result of American pressure on Japan to liberalise agriculture, but also because of the embarrassment caused to the government as a result of the growing foreign trade surpluses. While support for the farming population has not been abandoned completely, it is being eroded at the margins. Imports of primary commodities are being liberalised despite continued opposition from the nation's farmers. Rice remains the only major agricultural product where a ban on imports remains in place, but even here Japan is under intense pressure from the United States to guarantee access to foreign producers. The policy of liberalising agriculture has been facilitated by the ability of the LDP to extend its support base to urban areas at the expense of the JSP.

The LDP's staunch support for the farming sector through much of the postwar period is especially interesting given the financial indebtedness of the party to its financiers in big business. For example, on the basis of reported figures, Keidanren, the national federation of big businesses, provided the LDP with Y12 billion in political donations in 1990 which represented about 31 per cent of total revenue raised by the LDP that year of Y38.9 billion. Big business, however, acquiesced in the LDP's support for agricultural sectors because these policies were initiated in times of domestic political crisis, and it was in the interest of both the LDP and big business to try to maintain political stability. Government support for the farming sector was based precisely on the need to create a wide and stable social coalition as an insurance against domestic instability. Calder has termed the Japanese public policy formation process the crisis-compensation model, signifying the prevalence of crisis-induced policies of social compensation.[2] Within this model, it is possible to attribute the ongoing process of agricultural liberalisation to the markedly reduced perception of crisis as the economy has matured and gained in strength. Liberalisation of agriculture trade has also been influenced by big-business interests which now see this as a small price to pay for resolving trade disputes between Japan and the United States and, at the same time, for ensuring continued access to the American market for Japanese industrial products.

The LDP also benefited from its ability to put together a shifting and fluid support base. Rather than be rigidly commited to any particular group, the party (it is alleged) was able to marry a degree of rigidity with flexibility and this has allowed it to capture a wide support base and change its electoral strategy depending on circumstances. There are a number of reasons that have been identified as contributing to flexible rigidity on the part of the LDP, including that of Calder which suggests that flexibility is induced by a sense of crisis, such as that which pervaded Japanese politics, especially in the early years. Another explanation for

LDP flexibility is the level of factionalism within the LDP. According to Baerwald, factions are not simply personality cliques, but also a source of policy competition. He finds that, 'In the case of the LDP, it is the factions that have . . . enable[d] the party to respond flexibly to changing circumstances.'[3] A third reason for LDP flexibility was its role in producing the economic miracle and rapid growth and industrialisation. It cannot be denied that the Japanese government/LDP has actively intervened in the economy with its industrial policy and indicative planning. The result of such state intervention was to produce winners and losers within the economy, and the ability to identify and create such winners and losers in turn allowed the LDP to secure the support of the relevant sectors. This particular advantage was not due to any intrinsic quality of the LDP, but simply because it was the party in power and was in a position to create, as well as respond to, the needs of the winning groups within the domestic political economy. This was essentially the advantage of incumbency. Related to this was the entrenchment of 'money politics' in Japan. Because of huge campaign financing requirements, the LDP had to shift its appeal to growth sectors, which were necessarily better able to provide the necessary political funds. The nature of political campaigns in Japan means that the LDP cannot afford to be too principled in its stand.

In a sense this makes the LDP an unprincipled and opportunistic political party, but where this has rebounded to the success of the party, the JSP on the other hand has become a party in perpetual opposition since it has decided to remain firmly committed to its original principles. However, even though the JSP was in opposition from 1955 until a socialist became prime minister in 1994, it has still had some influence in public policy-making in Japan. It is large enough to be able to extract concessions from the ruling conservatives and one area where the JSP has had a significant, and moderating, impact is the field of defence and military policy. In addition, on the issue of constitutional reform, the JSP has been able to thwart early LDP attempts to amend it. The LDP has wanted, with varying intensity through the postwar period, to 'Japanise' the constitution as well as remove or change the peace clause (Article 9), but the JSP's commitment to established constitutional principles has denied the LDP the opportunity to secure the numbers to see an amendment through the Diet.

However, if the *raison d'etre* of any political party is to form a government, then the JSP has been a complete failure. The socialist who took over as prime minister in 1994 actually did so through a coalition with the LDP. The fact that the JSP was in opposition for such a long time has no doubt hurt its ability and the motivation to formulate realistic and practical policy alternatives, and where the LDP has been both flexible and rigid, the JSP has become rigidly tied to the original policy objectives.

The JSP's chances of coming to power were further undermined when, in 1960, the socialists once more split along the left–right cleavage. The moderate members of the JSP split to form the Democratic Socialist Party (DSP). This time the split was over the revision of the Security Treaty with the United States which Japan had signed immediately after the peace treaty restoring Japanese sovereignty. The Security Treaty allowed for the continued stationing of American forces in Japan as a guarantee of Japanese security in the context of the Cold War, which the JSP opposed as violating the constitution. The split at the party level parallelled a division within the labour movement and the JSP received the backing of the Sohyo, largely representing public-sector employees, while the DSP received the support of the more moderate Domei, composed mainly of private-sector employees. The JSP's chances of coming to power were further undermined by the proliferation of smaller opposition parties which have fragmented the opposition. The JSP also undermined its chances by painting itself into an ideological corner. With the LDP emphasising the pragmatic economic policies that have been so successful for it in the postwar period, the JSP has made itself into an irrelevant party largely as a result of its rigid commitment to socialist principles. In recent years, the party has been trying to project a more likeable image. In a world of male-dominated politicians, the JSP selected a woman to be its leader. Also, in February 1991, the party changed its English-language name to the Social Democratic Party of Japan, suggesting a sort of Europeanisation of the party. The Japanese name of the party is still the same and it remains to be seen whether these changes signal real moderation.

The two other main opposition parties are the Komeito and the Japan Communist Party (JCP). The Komeito started as a political wing of the religious group known as the Soka Gakkai. Because of the links to the Soka Gakkai, the Komeito has maintained relative stability in Diet representation through the years. However, also because of this link, it has failed to broaden its electoral base since there is lingering suspicion towards the Soka Gakkai, seen as an aggressive proselitysing creed. Although the links between the Soka Gakkai and the Komeito now are de-emphasised, the Komeito still receives most of its electoral support from members of the Soka Gakkai. This fact enables it to predict its electoral fortunes fairly precisely. Like the Komeito, which mobilises the support of the Soka Gakkai, the JCP has been very successful with its cell-like organisation structure although, like the Komeito, its popular appeal is also limited.

Until 1993, the multi-party system made it relatively easy for the LDP to continue to attract a plurality of votes and thereby form the government. This is not to suggest that the opposition parties were completely irrelevant to the policy regimes instituted by the LDP. Within the crisis–

compensation model discussed above, the LDP pursued domestic political stability by consciously co-opting some of the policy programs of the opposition parties. We have already considered the policy-oriented feature of the LDP that have enabled it to form a broad support base; at an institutional level, the gerrymander was also useful to the LDP's long stay in power. Besides the gerrymander, the electoral system also worked to the advantage of the LDP. The electoral rule is 'first past the post' so that within each district the highest vote-getters are declared elected even though there may be a large disparity in total votes for each of the successful candidates. With the opposition vote split between several parties, the LDP cleverly optimised its chances by standing only as many candidates as were likely to be elected given the percentage of conservative voters in the district, without wasting precious votes.

A result of all this is that, in most districts, LDP candidates not only competed against the opposition parties, but also had to compete with other LDP-endorsed candates. In the December 1983 House of Representatives election, the total number of LDP candidates was 250, or roughly two for each electoral district. The party did this for the obvious reason that it was better, where possible, to have two members, rather than one, elected from an electoral district for the total available number of conservative votes in that district. Thus if, for instance, the total number of conservative votes in an electoral district was estimated to be 100 000 and the minimum number of votes needed to win a seat was 40 000, then the LDP could, with 100 000 votes, elect two members rather than only one member from that district.

The consequence of this multi-member, first-past-the-post system has been that it has led to the LDP's becoming factionalised and that it has engendered the growth of money politics, or *kinken seiji*. The total financial outlay of the LDP in 1990 was Y38.5 billion. While this was the highest expenditure ever recorded, it no doubt understates the total expenditure incurred, since many of the expenses are hidden and not accounted for. To generate the necessary financial resources, the party, the faction and the individual politicians have devised a host of fund-raising techniques, legal and otherwise. The result has been periodic financial scandals that have rocked the political world, the most recent being the Recruit scandal which was revealed in 1988 and which forced the fall of the Takeshita government.

The strength and persistence of LDP factions has led to an image of the party as a coalition of minor parties. Faction members are carefully recruited to ensure that there will be no competition for seats within the faction. The same faction will not stand more than one member of its faction in the same district and, because of the inter-factional competition, each member has tried to outbid the other with increasingly lavish election campaigns in the absence of real policy differences between candidates from the same party. Within this cycle of ever-increasing financial requirements, faction leaders had come to play a very important part in collecting and disbursing funds, on top of party funds. In the mid-1970s, however, changes to the electoral laws forced individual Diet members and new candidates for election to be responsible for their own fund-raising. While this has altered the relationship of dependency between faction leader and faction members, the faction leader still remains important to direct faction members to sources of political funds. Nevertheless, as Gerald Curtis suggests, this has increased the relative independence of Diet members and transformed factions into 'collegial bodies'.[4]

Factions within the LDP increase their size and influence by recruiting new candidates to the Diet. Switching factional allegiance is extremely uncommon, and there is no conscious attempt to poach from other factional groups, given the emphasis on loyalty within Japanese society. At the same time, a Diet member who switches factional membership loses seniority, which is an important criterion in securing ministerial appointments. Factions have, historically, been useful in selecting and determining the party president and prime minister. The selection of president has been based on the candidate forging together a coalition that would give it a majority of the LDP votes. Thus, up until the 1970s, the LDP would normally be split between the mainstream faction, the coalition that formed the government of the day, and the anti-mainstream faction that was not included. Since the late 1970s, however, the distinction between mainstream and anti-mainstream coalition has become blurred as cabinets have included members of nearly all factions. This has partly been the result of party presidents being selected from one of the smaller factions rather than the large ones, as was usually the case. In turn, this was the result of various scandals that tainted the image of the larger factions. Prime Ministers Miki Takeo (1978–79), Nakasone Yasuhiro (1982–87) and Kaifu Toshiki (1988–91) were all members of relatively small LDP factions and would not normally have been selected to lead the party. As a result of internal changes, the LDP today is less a party of parties (factions) and a more a party in its own right.

The first major change in the political system came in the summer of 1992 when Morihiro Hosokawa broke away from the LDP over its slowness in suppressing corruption and founded the Japan New Party. He was followed by several others who set up splinter parties as rivals to the LDP. In July 1993, a coalition led by Hosokawa actually defeated the LDP in a general Lower House election. The coalition proved unstable and the next year was itself replaced with two others in quick succession. The second saw the LDP come back to power, but this time — a supreme irony — led by a socialist, Tomiichi Mirayama. The nature of Japanese politics had changed, the long period of stability was over.

In January 1994, legislation was adopted to change the electoral system. The system which replaced multi-member constituencies was a combination of single-member constituencies (300 members) and those chosen by proportional representation (200 members). After a great deal of negotiation, the Diet adopted the electoral boundaries for the single-member constituencies in November 1994. The reform changed the balance of power in favour of urban voters, thus eliminating the gerrymander in favour of the countryside. However, as of 1995, it is far too early to say to what extent the corruption driving money politics can be removed.

Policy-making in Japan

The constitution designates the Diet as the supreme legislative body of the Japanese government. The Diet is composed of two chambers. The more powerful Lower House of the Diet, the House of Representatives, has 511 seats and the Upper House, the House of Counsellors, has 252 seats. The representatives are elected from 130 electoral districts, each electing between three and five members, except for the electoral district of Amami Islands, which elects only one member. There is also one electoral district which elects six members. The counsellors are elected from a combination of national constituencies and prefecture-wide multi-member constituencies.

While, in a formal sense, the Diet has lived up to its role as the law-making body, analysts have tended to see the Diet as little more than a rubber stamp for the bureaucracy which has been identified as the real locus of policy-making within Japan. This has led some political analysts to conclude that Japan is, in some ways, an imperfect democracy, since democracies are characterised as being dominated by elected representatives of the people rather than by unelected bureaucrats.

The dominance of the bureaucracy in the postwar period has roots going back to the Meiji period when one of the official slogans of the time, *kanson mimpi* (revere officials; despise the people), gave bureaucrats an exalted position within the society. The origins of this slogan may be traced to the hierarchically structured society with the *samurai* at the top of the social order. After the Meiji restoration, the different social classes were abolished and the *samurai* were stripped of their various privileges. They also lost their traditional way of life and increasingly moved into bureaucratic and administrative positions. They formed the core of the new national bureaucracy and *kanson mimpi* was another way for the ex-*samurai* to separate themselves from the ordinary people.

However, in the prewar period, the bureaucracy had to compete with other organised groups, particularly the military, for influence. In the postwar period, the bureaucracy became even more powerful than it was previously. The occupation authorities not only removed the military establishment from the scene, but also purged many of the prewar politicians while leaving the bureaucracy relatively intact. The occupation forces decided to govern Japan through the existing bureaucracy rather than by establishing direct rule as they had done in Germany. The SCAP opted for this course because it lacked trained personnel to establish direct rule. With the party structure weakened by SCAP purges, it is not surprising that the bureaucracy has been very powerful. According to Baerwald:

> If an army of occupation with close to dictatorial powers could not undermine the all-pervasive influence of the Japanese bureaucracy, then it is hardly surprising that domestic political leaders have not met with great success whenever they have tried to mount an assault against those who walk the corridors of power in Kasumigaseki, Tokyo's ministry row.[5]

Other factors behind bureaucratic dominance in the postwar period included the active recruitment of bureaucrats into the Liberal Party by Prime Minister Yoshida in the late 1940s, to fill the depleted ranks of the party. Yoshida did this in the belief that the bureaucracy represented the best talent in the country, but it also gave the bureaucracy direct access to and control over the political process through bureaucrats-turned-politicians. At the same time, the political parties, unlike the bureaucracy, did not have the necessary research facilities at their disposal to take the initiative in policy-making. It was natural, in these circumstances, for politicians to rely on bureaucrats for their specialised knowledge and technical expertise.

In recent years, however, the balance of power between bureaucrats and politicians has undergone some changes. This is most closely associated with the emergence of '*zoku* (policy tribe) politicians', or politicians with specialised interests who have acquired a level of expertise in that issue area. This expertise is developed, for example, through a lengthy involvement in one of the many divisions of the Policy Affairs Research Council, the main policy-making body of the LDP, or through membership in the various Diet sub-committees. While the *zoku* politicians may not always override the influence of the bureaucucracy, they are nonetheless able to participate in policy-making as relatively equal partners, together with the bureaucracy. The emergence of the *zoku* politicians is not restricted to the LDP but is also true of the Social Democratic Party (SDPJ). As a way of insulating the party from bureaucratic influence, it is interesting to note that, since 1968, no bureaucrat-turned-politician has chaired the Policy Affairs Reseach Council.

As mentioned, the emergence of the *zoku* politicians does not mean that bureaucratic influence has been completely removed from the policy-making process or that politicians dominate policy-making in all issue areas. It should be noted that the policy expertise that has been acquired by the *zoku* politicians has been in areas that would normally be beneficial to their re-election prospects. Politicians have not been very keen to develop expertise in those areas of policy-making that are unpopular with the Japanese electorate. One such issue area is that of defence policy-making. Thus the balance of power between bureaucrats and politicians depends also on the issue areas.

Foreign policy and the nature of Japanese democracy

Throughout much of the postwar period, successive Japanese govern-ments have focused their attention towards the realisation of rapid economic growth. The basis for this was laid under the prime minister-ship of Yoshida Shigeru during the late 1940s and early 1950s. For Yoshida, the task of economic reconstruction after the war meant that all available resources had to be devoted to the task of economic develop-ment. Yoshida believed that Japan could not afford the luxury of pro-viding for its own defence and successfully resisted American demands that Japan develop a credible military establishment. He argued that an active defence program would be an unnecessary drain on the limited economic resources available and that Japan should instead rely on the United States for its security guarantees. This formed the basis of a domestic consensus that politics and economics should be kept separate and that the Japanese government should assume only an economic role and a minimal political role. The Yoshida Doctrine was sustained by the fact that Japan had renounced the use of force to settle international disputes and also because domestic public opinion was strongly against major defence expansion. The result was that Japan, through the years, allocated only a small proportion of its total GNP to defence expenditure. In 1975, this objective was further strengthened by a decision taken by the Miki government that defence expenditure should not exceed 1 per cent of GNP on an annual basis. The policy of separating politics and eco-nomics meant that Japan chose to avoid entanglements in international political issues and crises for fear that a larger political role would jeopardise its international economic interests, mainly the security of raw materials and of access to foreign markets for Japanese-manufactured products. Despite being a major economic power, Japan remained a virtual non-player politically and chose to keep a low profile on the international stage.

It is not difficult to see why this should have become a source of friction between Japan and the United States over a period of time. The United States complained of a Japanese 'free ride' on American defence efforts, an anachronism at a time when Japan had emerged as an economic super-power and especially as the American economy itself was in a state of relative decline. The tensions between the two countries became particularly acute in the early 1980s as Japanese trade surpluses against the United States and against the rest of the world continued to expand each year while Japanese defence spending remained under the self-imposed limit of 1 per cent. When Nakasone Yasuhiro became Prime Minister in 1983, he tried to lay the foundation of a more internationally assertive Japan. He believed that Japan's political status should mirror its economic power and that Japan should play an international role commensurate with its economic strength. He argued that it was necessary to overcome the confines of both the Yoshida Doctrine and the nature of the postwar settlement, which had turned Japan into a unique country unlike any other in the state system. Nakasone argued that it was necessary to overcome the confines of being a unique country and become, instead, a normal country. He chose to do this gradually by chipping away at the existing consensus rather than by suggesting constitutional reform, even though he had been known to favour the latter alternative. He had some success in enhancing Japan's international profile and in overcoming the image of Japan as a free-rider on the international stage. His main achievement was the removal of the ceiling on defence expenditure, which had long been a thorn in United States–Japan relations. He also initiated a program of active military co-operation with the United States and himself enjoyed a relatively high international profile through the celebrated 'Ron–Yasu' dialogue with the American president. If some of the regional countries were worried that the removal of the ceiling on defence spending would lead to rapid remilitarisation, that did not happen. Nevertheless, in absolute dollar terms, Japan currently ranks third in total defence spending.

Under Nakasone, Japan also tried to cultivate a new image as a responsible economic player globally and shed the image of a neo-mercantilist trader. The mid-1980s saw significant liberalisation of the Japanese economy and government-sponsored efforts to increase the level of imports and reduce exports so as to avoid trade frictions. At the same time, the Japanese yen was revalued to facilitate trade adjustment. The most dramatic changes have been in Japan's trading relations with the countries of the Asia-Pacific region. Beginning in the mid-1980s, the Japanese economy has been progressively opened up to imports and the principal beneficiaries have been the Asian countries. As an indication of the changes, while in 1985 Japanese imports from the newly industrialising economies (South Korea, Taiwan, Hong Kong and Singapore) had posted a negative growth over the previous year, in 1987 it increased by 59.7 per cent and in 1988 by 46.4 per cent over the previous years.

Japanese imports from the ASEAN countries also posted similar high increases. The result of all this has been a growing international division of labour in the Asia-Pacific region, which works to the advantage of both the regional countries and Japan. Unlike in the past, when Japan was identified more with the West, it is today playing a useful economic role within the region. Japan is also the largest donor of foreign aid and much of it is dispensed within the region.

Despite the growing role and influence of Japan within the region, and partly because of it, there is some concern and fear expressed by the regional countries about economic domination by Japan. The fears are rooted in the wartime experiences of these countries and the crude and cruel face of Japanese imperialism. That the fears should linger so long after the event is evidence of the harshness of Japanese colonialism, but equally it alludes to perceived flaws in Japanese democracy and the prospects of a militaristic revival.

Democracy is often equated with alternation of political power and, on this criterion at least, Japan ranks very low in the scale of political democratisation. From 1955 to 1993, the LDP monopolised political power. Within this structure, the JSP/SDPJ presented itself as the defender of democracy in Japan, which tended to suggest that democracy had a precarious existence under LDP rule. This made democracy in Japan appear fragile, but as far as political alternation is concerned, it cannot be denied that elections were free and that LDP rule was based on popular mandate. The gerrymander certainly helped, but it should also be pointed out that the opposition parties were not united in their demands for major electoral overhaul.

Another working definition of democracy is based on the processes of government, on governmental responsiveness to the electorate and a decision-making process that is open to popular in-fluence. There is no evidence to suggest that the LDP is a closed political party without grassroots links or influence.

The defeat of the LDP at the 1993 election demonstrated the solidity of the democratic system. Even when they were forced to compete in the same electorate with others of the party, LDP politicians competed to be responsive to the needs of their electorate. This process ensured a close link between the party and the electorate, and was very different from the militaristic prewar period when governmental policies were based not on popular wishes, but on the dictates of the military. To fear Japanese militarism today is to deny the important structural differences between prewar and postwar Japan and to denigrate the level of popular influence within the policy-making process. Certainly, Western ideals of democracy have been adapted to suit Japanese conditions, but that should not be taken to mean that Japanese democracy is fragile and susceptible to the dangers of militarism.

Guide to further reading

Calder, Kent E., *Crisis and Compensation: Public Policy and Political Stability in Japan, 1949–1986*, Princeton University Press, Princeton, NJ, 1988
A good study of Japanese public policy-making in the postwar period. The basic argument is that policies have been driven by a sense of political crisis and threat of domestic instability which has forced the government to provide compensation in the interests of ensuring stability.

Curtis, Gerald L., *The Japanese Way of Politics*, Columbia University Press, New York, 1988
This book is a study of Japanese domestic politics and is good as an introductory overview of the Japanese party system. Looks at the dominance of the LDP in the postwar period and attributes this to the capacity of the party to adapt and to respond to change in a flexible manner.

Baerwald, Hans H., *Party Politics in Japan*, Allen & Unwin, Boston, 1986
This book is recommended to those readers who wish to explore the functioning of the Japanese Diet in some detail. It also looks at factionalism within the Japanese political parties.

Stockwin, James A.A., *Japan: Divided Politics in a Growth Economy*, Weidenfeld and Nicolson, London, 2nd edn, 1982
This book provides a good overview of postwar Japan, beginning with the occupation period. It argues that, despite LDP dominance and political stability, Japan remains a divided polity.

Woronoff, Jon, *Politics the Japanese Way*, Macmillan, Basingstoke and London, 1986
This book is recommended to those who are interested in obtaining an alternative perspective on Japanese politics. It argues that Japanese democracy is, at best, incomplete and, more correctly, a superficial facade. Woronoff argues that policies are made not on the basis of popular support, but rather determined by the power position of groups within the society.

Notes

1 Curtis, G., *The Japanese Way of Politics*, Columbia University Press, New York, 1988, p. 54.
2 Calder, K., *Crisis and Compensation: Public Policy and Political Stability in Japan 1969–1986*, Princeton University Press, Princeton, 1988.
3 Baerwald, H., *Party Politics in Japan*, Allen & Unwin, Boston, 1986, p. 17.
4 Curtis, G., *The Japanese Way of Politics*, p. 180.
5 Baowald, H., *Party Politics in Japan*.

28 | The Japanese model of economic growth

During the period from the end of World War II to the mid-1970s, Japan experienced a remarkable economic transformation. In the late 1940s it was a defeated nation with rampant inflation and massive unemployment; by the 1960s it was a rapidly growing industrial power, the performance of which was attracting nervous admiration from its Western competitors; by the 1980s it was the second largest economy in the world, and a technological leader in many key branches of industrial production. This 'economic miracle' (as it is often called) has fascinated observers in many parts of the world. From the early 1970s onwards, Asian industrialising nations have looked to Japan as a source of inspiration for their developmental policies. More recently, the governments and businesses of industrialised nations in Europe and North America have also shown growing interest in learning the secrets of Japan's impressive industrial performance.

Certain scholars of Japan's growth suggest that there is a single cornerstone which provides the basis for the Japanese 'miracle'. Some, for example Morishima, identify that cornerstone with Japan's religious and cultural traditions.[1] Others such as Johnson prefer to emphasise the role of government policy in promoting industrial growth.[2] Careful consideration of the Japanese experience since the mid-twentieth century, however, suggests that high growth was not the consequence of any one factor on its own, but rather resulted from the fortuitous combination of a number of factors — social and political as well as narrowly economic. This chapter will outline some of the most important of those factors, and also go on to consider the impact which Japan's high-speed economic growth has had upon the lifestyles and living standards of Japanese people.

First of all, though, it is necessary to look a little more closely at the overall pattern of growth in Japan since World War II. Roughly speaking, Japan's recent economic history can be divided up into three main phases. The years from 1945 to 1955 were a period of postwar recovery. Wartime disruption and bombing had reduced the economy to a state of chaos. Almost 3 million Japanese people had been killed during the

Pacific War, and millions of refugees and demobilised soldiers had to be resettled into the peacetime economy. About one-third of Japan's industrial machinery, one-quarter of its buildings and more than three-quarters of its shipping had been destroyed by bombing. In these circumstances, it was not surprising that the level of economic activity immediately after the war should have been very low. It was also predictable that, as conditions returned to normal, Japan (like other war-devastated nations) would experience relatively rapid economic growth.

By the mid-1950s, the process of postwar recovery was virtually complete. Japanese industry had regained the levels of production achieved during the late 1930s, and many Japanese economists were predicting a slowing of the unusually rapid growth achieved during the recovery phase. This pessimism proved ill-founded. After a dip in the years 1953 to 1954, growth rates recovered and, during the 1960s, reached an average of 10 per cent a year — the highest level of sustained growth recorded in any country up to that time (see Figure 28.1). The high growth period, which lasted from 1956 to 1973, was not just one of quantitative economic expansion; it was also a time in which the structure of the Japanese economy underwent major changes. Agriculture and light industry declined in importance, while heavy industries such as steel, aluminium, petrochemicals and machinery production experienced particularly vigorous development. New heavy industrial estates, known in Japanese as *kombinato*, began to appear along the coastal fringe of Japan, their red-and-white chimneys dominating the skylines of districts which had once housed little more than a few fishing or farming communities.

The expansion of these industries made Japan's resource-poor economy more dependent than ever on imports of raw materials such as iron-ore, bauxite and crude oil. As a result, when Arab oil-producing nations curtailed output and sharply increased their prices, Japan was one of the countries most severely affected. Although (as we shall see) the first oil crisis of 1973 was only one reason for the fall in Japan's growth rates, it provides a convenient milestone for marking the end of Japan's high growth era. The period from 1974 onwards is generally known in Japan as the 'low growth era', but the term 'low' is of course a comparative one. Although the average rate of economic growth from 1974 to 1987 was only 4 per cent — far below the 10 per cent level attained in the 1960s, this was still above the level achieved by Japan's major industrialised competitors, including the United States, Britain and West Germany.

During the 1970s and 1980s, attention in Japan switched from promoting basic heavy industries such as steel and petrochemicals to encouraging the development of new so-called 'knowledge-intensive' industries, among them microelectronics and biotechnology. Japan, so long regarded as an imitator of Western industrial techniques, now began to be recognised as a world leader in some of the most complex branches of manufacturing technology. The rapid expansion of Japan's exports and, even more notably, of its foreign investment, caused friction and hostility in some foreign countries, but at the same time firmly established Japan as a dominant force in the world economy of the late twentieth century. Meanwhile, however, Japan was beginning to experience the economic and political stresses which often accompany international power. The first years of the 199s marked a period both of economic instability — with sharp falls in real estate and share prices — and of political change. The general election of 1993 brought an end to 38 years of continuous rule by the Liberal Democratic Party and opened the way to a phase of greater flexibility and uncertainty in Japanese political and economic life.

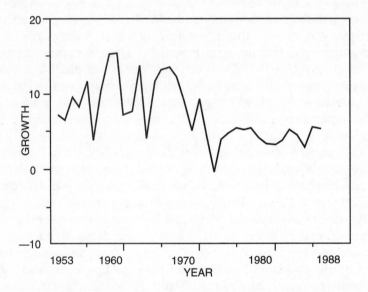

Figure 28.1 Real GNP growth rates: Japan, 1953–88

Source: Allen, G.C., *A Short Economic History of Modern Japan*, Macmillan, London, 1981, p. 285; Keizai Kikakucho (Economic Planning Agency, Japan), *Keizai Yeran*, Tokyo, 1990, p. 14

The historical background

The origins of Japan's economic strength, of course, have deep historical roots. Japanese industrialisation had begun in the latter part of the nineteenth century, and by the 1930s the country was already producing large quantities of steel and chemicals, as well as light industrial goods like silk and cotton cloth. Despite the enormous damage inflicted by wartime air-raids, much of this industrial legacy survived intact. Bombs could destroy buildings and machinery, but they did not destroy the business expertise of managers, the skills of factory workers or the knowledge of scientists and technicians. In particular, some of the organisational structures which had supported prewar growth were virtually unaffected by the war. The most important of these was the bureaucracy, which had played a crucial part in developing industrial policies immediately before the war, and which drew on this prewar experience in formulating policies for economic development in the 1950s and 1960s.

At the same time, the reforms introduced during the Allied occupation from 1945 to 1952 helped to remove some of the obstacles which had hindered economic change in the earlier part of the century. The most important of these reforms was probably the redistribution of farm land. During the 1920s and 1930s, rural poverty had led to hardship and social unrest (see Chapter 15). Most Japanese farmers were tenants, who lacked the wealth and incentive to invest in order to improve the land they farmed. The occupation authorities were swift to recognise that land redistribution was essential both to ensure political harmony and to provide a basis for Japan's economic recovery, and in 1946 they ordered the Japanese cabinet to prepare a plan for agrarian reform. When the Japanese proposal proved too cautious, the Allied command forced them to revise the plan until it was acceptable.

The scheme which was eventually implemented obliged all absentee landowners to sell their land to the government at very low prices, while those who lived in the villages were allowed to keep only a small plot of land, suitable for their own family's needs. All other farmland was sold at cheap rates to the tenants, who received government loans to enable them to buy the fields which they had once rented. As a result of this measure, about 80 per cent of all leased land was redistributed to tenants. In the words of the leading occupation advisers on agriculture, land reform 'provided a basis for increasing production' while at the same time creating a large class of landowning farmers whose presence made the Japanese countryside 'almost impervious to communism'.[3]

The changes which the occupation brought to factory work were equally dramatic. Trade unions were legalised and labour standards legislation enacted, with the aim of protecting the health and safety of Japanese workers. At the same time, the occupation authorities turned their attention to the giant corporations — the *zaibatsu* — who were widely seen as having misused their enormous economic power before and during the Pacific War. The powerful holding companies which had provided the focus of control within the *zaibatsu* were dissolved, and new laws were introduced to prevent their re-emergence.

The reforming zeal of the occupation authorities, however, was only part of the story. While trying to rid Japan of political oppression and militarism, they were also concerned to prevent the emergence of a radical left wing in Japan, and this concern became increasingly intense as the international tensions of the Cold War heightened. By 1947, the Allied command was already moving to prohibit strikes by public servants and to purge those suspected of being communist sympathisers from government employment. At the same time, proposed measures to prevent the concentration of economic power in the hands of large enterprises were watered down.

The overall achievements of the occupation period, both political and economic, remain a topic of considerable controversy. However, it is clear that a combination of wartime destruction, occupation reforms and rampant postwar inflation reduced the size of many of Japan's great private fortunes, and created a more equal distribution of wealth between different sections of the population. This meant that, as the economy grew, Japanese producers could take advantage of a big domestic market for a whole range of goods which had previously been beyond the reach of most consumers: in the 1960s for items like electric stoves, irons and refrigerators, and later for colour televisions, videos and private cars.

The workforce and labour relations

During the 1950s and 1960s, foreign observers frequently attributed Japan's economic success to its cheap labour. Nowadays, emphasis is more often placed on the hard work, discipline and dedication of Japanese employees. Both of these explanations contain an element of truth, but both of them have also been the source of much mythologising and misunderstanding.

The postwar Japanese economy undoubtedly benefited from an abundant supply of labour. In the late 1940s, almost half the workforce was employed in agriculture, where technology was still relatively simple and productivity low. The effect of land reform and rising prosperity, however, was to encourage greater investment in agricultural chemicals and simple farm machinery, and to reduce the need for farm workers. Labour released from agriculture flowed in a steady stream to the newly expanding industrial sectors, enabling these to grow rapidly without facing serious shortages of employees. During the first part of the 1950s, the easy availability of employees did help to ensure that wages remained relatively low, and that Japanese labour was cheap by comparison with other industrialised countries. From 1953 to 1972, however, wages in Japan rose faster than in any of Japan's major competitors, but the really significant fact is that productivity increased *more rapidly still* (see Table 28.1). It was because of this that Japanese companies could hold down their prices and increase their competitiveness, even at a time when their wage bills were rising.

Table 28.1 Days lost in labour disputes, 1978–88^a (1000 person-days)

	USA	Italy	UK	France	Japan^b	Germany, F.R.
1978	23 774	10 177	9 405	2 200	1 353	4 281
1979	20 409	27 530	29 474	3 172	919	483
1980	20 844	16 457	11 964	1 511	998	128
1981	16 908	10 527	4 266	1 442	543	58
1982	9 061	18 563	5 313	2 257	535	15
1983	17 461	14 003	3 754	1 321	504	41
1984	8 499	8 703	27 135	1 318	354	5 618
1985	7 079	3 831	6 402	727	257	35
1986	12 140	5 644	1 920	568	252	28
1987	4 481	4 606	3 546	501	256	33
1988	4 417	3 315	3 702	1 132	163	42
1989	16 996	4 436	4 128	805	176	100

^{a} Based on data from each country. Labour disputes, as a rule, involve protest action.
^{b} Japanese figures include days of disputes involving protest action and factory closure.

Source: Keizai Koho Center, *Japan 1990: An International Comparison*, 1989, p. 71 and 1992, p. 70.

The high productivity of Japanese industry is partly the result of a skilled and disciplined workforce, although an even more important factor has been the large scale of investment in equipment and technology (discussed in the next section). Although industrial skills are usually acquired through training and experience at work, most Japanese workers have a strong background of general school education, which provides an important basis for later technical training. Even before the beginning of industrialisation in the Meiji period, education was regarded as a vital path to social success, although only a select few managed to enter the elite imperial universities. After World War II, secondary and tertiary education were greatly expanded, and by the early 1970s almost all Japanese students were completing high school, with about 30 per cent going on to college or university. Although the Japanese education system is widely criticised for its emphasis on rote learning and examinations, the relatively high levels of literacy and numeracy achieved by students have undoubtedly helped to make the Japanese workforce well prepared for the challenges of contemporary high-tech society.

The media outside Japan have fostered a popular image of the Japanese worker as being a highly motivated and loyal employee, who stays with the company for life and rarely if ever goes on strike. In fact, the picture is a little more complicated than this. The Japanese manufacturing workforce (like the workforce of most other industrialised countries) is made up of various groups. One section is the core workforce of large companies, consisting mostly of male white-collar, skilled or semi-skilled workers. In Japan, these employees are paid a salary which increases steadily the longer they stay with the company. Their pension entitlements also rise sharply with seniority. This means that they have a strong incentive to stay with one firm for their whole career, rather than swapping employers at frequent intervals. Although movement from one company to another is not unknown, workers in this position often do choose to stay with the same enterprise for life. This has considerable advantages from the company's point of view. Knowing that their core workers are likely to be with them for many years, the company's managers are willing to invest quite substantially in training. Workers are usually rotated from one position to another within the factory, so that they gradually gain skill and experience in a range of different productive tasks. Many experts believe that this process, known as 'multi-skilling', makes the workforce better able to adapt to technological change.

Besides the core workforce, however, many large companies also employ temporary or part-time workers. Young women workers, who perform a large part of the factory work in the electronics industry, for example, are usually taken on by the company when they leave school, but expected to resign when they get married or become pregnant with their first child. Many big corporations also subcontract some of the simpler parts of their manufacturing work to small companies. All in all, temporary and part-time workers and those employed in small firms make up some 75 per cent of Japan's manufacturing workforce. The pay and conditions of these workers usually compare unfavourably with those of the core workforce in large firms, and the workers themselves are more likely to change jobs several times in their career.

During the 1950s and 1960s an important source for the recruitment of temporary labour was agriculture: farmers would often go to work in the factories during the winter months and return to the farm when the rice-growing season began in spring. By the 1970s, however, the percentage of the workforce remaining in agriculture had fallen to about 10 per cent, and the pool of labour to be recruited from the farms had almost dried up. As a result, employers were forced to look elsewhere for temporary employees. One particularly important new source of labour has proved to be married women who choose to return to work once their children are at school. These women can rarely find employment as core employees in large companies, and therefore often take factory or service sector jobs on a part-time basis. During the late 1980s some companies, particularly in the service and construction areas, were also beginning to recruit labour from other Asian countries, despite strict laws limiting the inflow of foreign workers into Japan.

The existence of temporary workers and the practice of subcontracting work to smaller companies provides large firms with a degree of adaptability which is important to them in an age of rapid economic and technological change. If times are hard, temporary employees and subcontracting can be cut back, while the core workforce, with its valuable skills, is preserved for future recovery and expansion.

Although employees of small firms and part-time workers are usually non-unionised, trade unions do exist in most large firms, and have played an important role in certain phases of Japanese history. During the immediate postwar period, trade union membership in Japan rose to high levels, and a number of prolonged industrial conflicts occurred in various sections of Japanese industry. In 1960, too, plans to close coal mines and switch to oil as the major source of Japan's energy production provoked fierce conflicts with miners' unions. In general, however, the most militant Japanese unions have been those in the public sector. Private-enterprise unions are usually organised on a company basis, with all company employees up to and including the lower levels of management belonging to the same union organisation. Because they are so closely identified with a particular enterprise, these unions may be relatively cautious about taking drastic action which could damage the company's viability. Brief strikes over pay disputes are quite common in Japan, particularly in spring when the annual round of wage bargaining takes place, but prolonged stoppages in private industry are relatively rare. In recent years, Japan has lost fewer working days to strikes than most of its major industrial competitors (see Table 28.2).

Table 28.2 Growth rates of wages and productivity (%)

	Annual average growth of industrial productivity 1935–72	Annual average growth of real wages in manufacturing 1953–75
Japan	8.9	5.4
USA	2.7	1.5
UK	3.0	3.4
West Germany	5.0	5.3
France	5.4	4.0
Italy	5.0	7.0

Source: Morris-Suzuki, T., *Beyond Computopia: Information, Automation and Democracy in Japan*, *Kegan* Paul International, London, New York, 1988, p. 43

Wealth for growth

An abundant and skilled labour force, however, is not the only necessary ingredient for rapid growth. It is also essential to have the capital with which to build new factories, buy new machinery and acquire the latest technical knowhow. Unlike many other Asian industrialising countries,

Japan did not rely heavily on foreign investment for its industrial growth. On the contrary, the Japanese government tended to be cautious of excessive dependence on overseas capital and maintained tight restrictions on foreign investment until the early 1970s.

Instead, the supply of capital for high growth in Japan came mainly from savings within the Japanese economy — above all from the savings of ordinary Japanese households. In 1970–72, the average Japanese household was saving about 26 per cent of its disposable income, compared with a figure of about 15–17 per cent for Western European countries like West Germany, France and Italy.[4] The reasons for these very high levels of saving in Japan are something of a puzzle, and many different explanations of the phenomenon have been put forward. During the 1950s and 1960s, one factor may have been the rather underdeveloped state of Japan's welfare system. Employees of small companies in particular had little protection against sickness, unemployment or old age, and therefore felt a need to develop a nest-egg of savings to provide for times of crisis. Improvements in welfare benefits, however, have made this a less important motive, and it seems likely that other influences are also at work. One point to be noted is that consumer credit is less widespread in Japan than in other countries, and that Japanese consumers have therefore needed to save towards the cost of expensive items like furniture or cars. In recent years, large savings have also been necessary to enable the average Japanese family to make a down-payment on a house (since high land prices make urban housing exorbitantly expensive), or to pay the costs of their children's education (because many Japanese universities are private and charge high fees).

Whatever the reasons for this frugality, the savings of Japanese families have proved a powerful engine of industrial growth, and the banking system has acted as an efficient means of channelling these savings into corporate investment. During the high growth era in particular, Japanese industrial enterprises relied very heavily on the banks for loans to purchase new machinery or expand their factories. This was rather different from the behaviour of British or American corporations, which were much more likely to raise capital by selling shares on the stock market.

Reliance on the banks in Japan reflects a further peculiarity of the Japanese business system which has had very important implications for the country's postwar economic growth. Many major Japanese companies are parts of larger groups of firms, which are called in Japanese *keiretsu* or *kigyo shudan*. Unlike the great prewar conglomerates or *zaibatsu* (from which some of them are descended), the postwar business groups are not highly centralised organisations, but are held together by a number of loose and informal links. Every group, for example, is centred on a bank, which will often hold some shares in group companies and also provide them with loans when needed. Senior managers of one group company will often sit on the board of directors of another group company. Most groups also include one or more general trading companies *(sogo shosha)*, which may handle the products of group companies or provide them with information on market conditions and technological developments around the world.

The corporate groups help to provide Japanese big business with a source both of strength and of flexibility. It is often argued that the nature of the Japanese system enables Japan's big companies to pay more attention to long-term growth than to short-term profits. Because much of their capital comes from banks and other large institutions, Japanese corporations do not have to worry so much about attracting investors with promises of quick returns, and can concentrate instead on reinvesting their profits in continuous expansion.

During the high-growth era much of that invested wealth went into improving the capacity of Japan's manufacturing equipment. The war years had cut Japan off from the technological advances which were occurring in Europe and America in the mid-twentieth century, and in the early 1950s the technological level of Japanese industry was far behind that of its main competitors. Paradoxically, this gave Japan an important advantage. Since few Western companies regarded Japanese firms as serious rivals, many were quite willing to sell or license their latest technical knowhow to Japan. As a result, Japanese firms were able to obtain new technology quickly and relatively cheaply, without having to conduct their own lengthy research projects, and were able to equip their new or expanded factories with the very latest machinery.

The consequence was a dramatic improvement in the quality of Japanese production. In 1952, for example, Japan's steel factories were only half as productive as their counterparts in Britain; by the beginning of the 1970s, the situation had been reversed. Similarly impressive productivity gains were also made in areas such as the chemicals industry and the production of household electrical goods. The advantage, however, could not last indefinitely. As Japan caught up with the technological levels of one competitor after another, it became increasingly difficult to import knowhow from other countries, and Japanese firms were obliged to put more effort into their own research and development programs. Most responded swiftly to the challenge. In 1967, only about 1.7 per cent of Japan's national income was devoted to research and development, but by 1988 the figure had risen to 3.3 per cent — higher than West Germany, France or Britain, and about the same as the figure for the United States. By this time Japan, although still a major purchaser of technology from overseas, was also emerging as an increasingly important *exporter* of technology, particularly to other Asian countries.

Foreign trade and investment

During the late 1970s and 1980s, Japan's exports, particularly of goods like cars and electronic equipment, made increasing inroads into foreign markets. Japan also emerged as a leading international investor, establishing or buying factories, banks and tourist resorts overseas. The very visible international role of the Japanese economy caused concern and antagonism in some quarters: one American political adviser even described the growth of Japanese industrial competition not just as 'a threat to our economy', but as 'a threat to our nation'.

Despite this image of Japan as an aggressive trader, however, it is important to remember that the postwar Japanese economy has not been particularly heavily dependent on exports. In 1965, for example, Japan's total exports were only equivalent to 11.1 per cent of the county's total gross national product (GNP). The comparable figure for West Germany was 19 per cent, and for the United Kingdom, 23.3 per cent.[5] Nevertheless, exports did play a significant part in Japan's high economic growth. Because of its lack of natural resources, Japan is obliged to import many of its key industrial raw materials, and the rapid expansion of manufacturing would have been quite impossible if Japan had not been able to earn the foreign exchange necessary to pay for these imports.

From this point of view, the international economic environment of the postwar world was very advantageous to Japan. The United States, as the leading world economy, was eager to prevent a repetition of the events of the 1930s, when countries had responded to the economic crisis by raising high tariff walls around their own economies — a policy which only served to prolong and intensify the world depression. At the same time, the United States government was also keen to encourage the recovery of the Japanese economy, for it saw Japan as a vital bulwark against the spread of communism in East Asia. Until the early 1960s, therefore, Japanese goods were allowed relatively easy access to the markets of the United States and Western European nations, while Japan itself was allowed to retain considerable protective barriers (such as tariffs and foreign exchange controls) around its own economy. Japanese exporters also benefited from the relatively low value of the yen. The exchange rate of Y360 to the US dollar, set in 1947, remained unchanged until 1971, but by the late 1960s this value was unrealistically low, making Japanese goods artificially cheap on world markets.

As high growth gathered momentum, however, the attitude of the United States and Western Europe to Japan began to change. Japan started to be seen as an increasingly serious international competitor, and the Japanese government came under pressure to open its country's market to imports of foreign manufactured goods. From 1961 onwards, the government reacted to these demands by gradually lowering tariffs and by relaxing controls on foreign exchange. The result is that Japan's economy overall now has one of the lowest levels of tariff protection in the industrialised world (though its market for agricultural products has remained quite highly protected). This, however, has not solved all the problems. Many foreign manufacturers still find it hard to sell their goods on the Japanese market, and the Japanese government has sometimes been accused of using backdoor methods to keep out foreign products. For example, many medicines and cosmetics have to undergo a very long process of screening before they can be sold in Japan. Such 'non-tariff barriers' (as they are called) have become a topic of controversy between Japan and other industrialised nations in recent years, with the Japanese government claiming that the measures are necessary to protect Japanese consumers, and other governments claiming that they discriminate unfairly against foreign goods.

Meanwhile the United States and European countries have sometimes responded to influxes of Japanese exports by creating barriers of their own. In 1971, for example, the United States introduced restrictions on the import of textiles from Japan, and the Nixon administration also brought in new economic policies which resulted in a drastic revaluation of the yen against the dollar. Increasing trade friction with industrialised countries has not been the only problem faced by Japanese producers since the early 1970s. The emergence of new industrialising Asian countries such as South Korea, Taiwan and Singapore has also posed a challenge to some of Japan's traditional markets, particularly for light industrial goods. Meanwhile, the oil crises of 1973 and 1979 led to sharp increases in the price of crude oil, and sent shock waves through the Japanese economy, which imports more than 99 per cent of its oil, most of it from the Middle East.

These international problems, together with the emerging shortage of labour within Japan itself, were major reasons for the decline in Japan's economic growth rates after 1973. With slower growth and stagnating incomes at home, Japanese companies have put increasing effort into expanding the foreign markets for their goods, and by 1983 the ratio of Japan's exports to GNP had risen to just over 15 per cent. This in turn has helped to intensify competition and fuel the growth of trade friction with the United States and other industrialised economies.

One way of dealing with these frictions has been for Japanese companies to set up factories overseas. Since the beginning of the 1970s, many Japanese manufacturing companies have established subsidiaries in other Asian countries such as South Korea, Taiwan, Thailand, the Philippines and Indonesia, where they can take advantage of lower labour costs. During the 1980s there was also increasing Japanese manufacturing investment in the United States and Western Europe, as Japanese com-

panies tried to allay fears that their products were undercutting local industries and causing bankruptcies and unemployment in these countries.
At the same time, high land prices in Japan and the rising value of the yen
encouraged some Japanese firms to invest in foreign real estate, or in
tourist ventures to serve the rapidly rising number of Japanese holiday-
makers travelling abroad. Between 1980 and 1988, the annual outflow of
Japanese direct investment increased tenfold, prompting complaints by
some politicians and journalists of a Japanese 'economic invasion'. To put
this in perspective, though, it is worth noting that the accumulated total
of Japan's foreign investment up to 1988 was only about the same as the
figure for Dutch foreign investment, and was still far behind the levels
achieved by the United Kingdom and the United States.

The role of the state

The role of the state has been perhaps the most hotly debated aspect of
Japan's postwar growth strategy. Some writers have argued that the
economic influence of the government has been far greater in Japan than
in other non-communist countries, and has played a decisive role in
determining the speed and direction of Japan's industrial development.
Others claim that the crucial factors in Japan's high growth have been the
abundance of labour, the supply of capital and the initiative of Japanese
business leaders, and suggest that the role of the government has been
greatly over-estimated.

Clearly, Japan's economic policies are far from being wholly unique.
Throughout the industrialised world, the postwar era saw the evolution
of new forms of government economic management. Anxious to avoid
the disastrous experiences of the 1930s, governments used a combination
of adjustments to the money supply and adjustments to government
spending in an effort to promote stable and continuous growth. In Japan,
during the high-growth era, the main emphasis was placed on monetary
policy. The powerful Ministry of Finance ensured that interest rates were
kept relatively low to stimulate growth, but were raised at times when
excessively rapid growth threatened to cause imbalances and bottlenecks
in the economy.

Until the 1960s, the Japanese government managed to keep its budgets
more or less balanced, with revenue roughly covering government
expenditure. From 1965 onwards, however, increased government
spending was used to stimulate growth, and substantial budget deficits
began to appear. These grew particularly sharply in the period immediately following the first oil crisis of 1973, and by the end of the 1970s
Japan had one of the highest levels of public debt in the industrialised
world. In the decade which followed, the Japanese government, like

governments in many other countries, made strenuous efforts to reduce this debt by privatising state-owned enterprises (including the national railways), cutting back on public spending and also (in 1989) introducing a controversial consumption tax.

For many foreign observers, however, the most interesting facet of economic policy in Japan is not fiscal or monetary policy but industrial policy, which is largely under the control of the Ministry of International Trade and Industry (MITI). In the postwar period, MITI, the successor to the prewar Ministry of Commerce, developed and refined a complex set of strategies for encouraging the growth of selected key industries in Japan. American academic Daniel Okimoto describes MITI not as defying the laws of the market economy, but as striving to influence and modify those laws in the same way that a Japanese gardener seeks to mould nature into aesthetically pleasing shapes.[6]

The broad framework for Japanese industrial policy is provided by the government's economic plan, the first of which was drawn up in 1955. The plan (usually a five-year plan, but sometimes covering a seven- or ten-year period) is produced by the officials and professional economists of the Economic Planning Agency, which is an autonomous agency but whose head is generally appointed from MITI (indeed, the agency is sometimes referred to as MITI's 'branch store').[7] Unlike the economic plans of communist countries, the Japanese plan does not direct enterprises to act in a particular way; it merely indicates the speed at which the government expects the economy to grow and provides predictions on the performance of various branches of industry.

In order to help fulfil the predictions of the plan, MITI may introduce policies to encourage the growth of certain industries, or to help others to readjust to a changing economic climate. In 1958, for example, it brought in measures to promote the Japanese electronics industry by offering cheap loans and tax concessions for companies investing in this new and promising area of technology. These gave considerable impetus to Japan's emergence as a leading producer of transistor radios, televisions, cassette recorders and other household electrical goods. MITI also seeks to influence the development of private enterprise, not just through direct financial incentives, but also through more informal advice or 'administrative guidance' — advice which is often effective because of the close personal and organisational links which have developed between big business and the bureaucracy in Japan.

During the high-growth era, MITI's assistance was generally directed towards basic heavy industries like steel, chemicals and machinery production, but by the early 1970s it was becoming obvious that a new approach would be needed. Shortages of labour, competition from other industrialising Asian countries, worsening pollution problems and the rising cost of raw materials all threatened the basis of Japan's industrial strength. In 1971, one of MITI's key advisory bodies issued an influential report in which it was argued that the only course for Japanese industry was to shift its focus from basic heavy industry to 'knowledge-intensive' industries, such as computer hardware and software, robotics and biotechnology. These industries, it was argued, were less polluting and energy consuming than traditional heavy industries and, because of their technological sophistication, they were less vulnerable to competition from newly industrialising countries.

Under its new strategy, MITI not only supported the development of high-tech industries, but also took steps to strengthen Japan's own research and development capacity. One widely publicised move was the establishment, in 1981, of the Fifth Generation Computer Project, which brought together major corporations and academic scientists in an attempt to hasten progress towards the next stage in the evolution of computer technology. Government schemes to promote knowledge-intensive industries have clearly had considerable effect. Japan is now a leading force in areas like the production of microchips and industrial robots: indeed, in the mid-1980s, Japan was estimated to have over 60 per cent of the non-communist world's 'population' of robots.[8] Most observers, however, feel that the power of MITI itself has declined since the late 1960s. The reduction of tariffs and the removal of exchange controls have deprived the ministry of some of its most powerful instruments of economic influence, while the increasing international status of Japan's big corporations has made these firms less willing to heed the bidding of their home government.

Lifestyles and living standards

The rethinking of industrial policy in the early 1970s reflected not only changes in Japan's economic circumstances, but also changes in public attitudes to economic growth. During the high-growth phase, there had been little questioning of the desirability of rapid industrial expansion. New industries, it was believed, would provide better job opportunities for ordinary working people and, by increasing the nation's prosperity, would improve the living standards of the whole country. By the late 1960s, however, this optimistic approach was subject to growing sceptical scrutiny. Some critics — adopting the slogan *'kutabareta GNP'* (down with GNP) — were even calling for a wholesale rejection of economic growth as a solution to the country's social needs.

The main trigger for this anti-growth sentiment was awareness of the severe environmental pollution caused by quarter of a century of unfettered industrial expansion. Pollution had not only harmed the economic interests of some sections of the population — for example, by destroying traditional fishing grounds — but had also caused ill-health and, in extreme cases, even death. The incident which, for many people, symbolised the dark side of the economic 'miracle' was the tragedy of Minamata, a small town in southwestern Japan whose population was ravaged by chronic mercury poisoning caused by effluent from a local chemical factory. Cases like this not only led to calls for tighter environmental controls on Japanese industry, but also prompted widespread debate on the social costs and benefits of rapid economic growth.

Attempts to measure the quality of human life, as opposed merely to the size of the Gross National Product, are fraught with great difficulties. In some areas, the evidence certainly does suggest that economic growth has brought marked improvements to the living standards of Japanese people. Perhaps the most dramatic indications of improvement are to be found in the increase in life expectancy. Although pollution may have caused great harm to the health of some people in Japan, the overall health of the population has improved remarkably since World War II. At the beginning of the 1950s, the average life expectancy of a Japanese child at birth was about 60 years for men and 63 for women; by 1988 it was 76 for men and 81 for woman, and Japan had the longest life expectancy of any country in the world. Improved diet, which is a major reason for the rise in life expectancy, has also affected Japanese society in other ways: by 1976 the average 17-year-old Japanese boy was almost 7 centimetres taller than his counterpart in 1950.

High levels of industrial productivity have meant that Japanese shops are crammed with an abundance of electronic gadgets at reasonable prices, and consumer products such as microwave ovens, stereos and videos are common in Japanese houses. (The most common of all are colour televisions, of which, by the late 1980s, there were over 190 for every 100 homes in Japan.) On the other hand, despite the busting of the real estate 'bubble' in the early 1990s, the cost of housing itself remains high, and its quality is often relatively poor.

During the 1970s government controls were introduced to curb the worst excesses of industrial pollution. Japan's welfare and social security system was also extended, so that, for example, Japanese pension benefits are now similar to those of Western European countries. Welfare spending as a percentage of GNP in Japan is still low by international standards (see Figure 28.2), but this is partly because Japan has a relatively small number of unemployed and other welfare recipients. The figure can be expected to rise very sharply in the early twenty-first century as the number of elderly people in the population rises — a prospect which is viewed with alarm by the Japanese government's economic advisers.

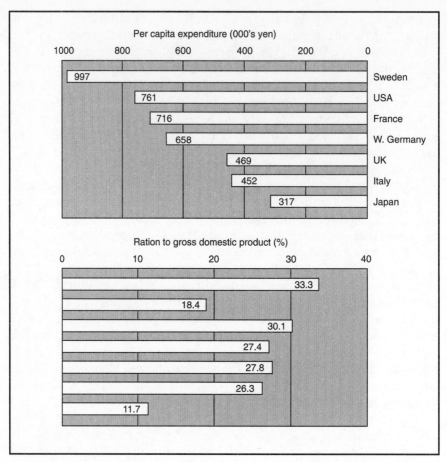

Figure 28.2 Comparison of social security expenditures (Fiscal 1984–86)

Source: Tsuneta Yano Memorial Society, *Nippon: A Chartered Survey of Japan 1989–90,* Kokusei-Sha, Tokyo, 1989, p. 320

Despite developments in environmental and welfare policy, however, many areas of concern remain. Working hours are still longer in Japan than they are in most other advanced industrialised countries, and many Japanese workers also have to face lengthy journeys to and from work each day. There is a popular feeling, not that growth has made people worse off, but that a disproportionate share of the benefits of growth have gone to large corporate organisations rather than to ordinary individuals. Among the older generation, with its memories of wartime defeat and postwar hunger, there was a widespread willingness to make economic sacrifices in the hope of a better future, but as those memories fade, the emerging generation of Japanese workers seems likely to expect a greater share in the fruits of Japan's new-found economic might.

Guide to further reading

Nakamura, T., *The Postwar Japanese Economy*, University of Tokyo Press, Tokyo, 1981, gives an excellent overview of Japan's economic growth since World War II.

The role of industrial policy in Japanese growth is discussed in C. Johnson's well-known study, *MITI and the Japanese Miracle*, Stanford University Press, Stanford, 1982. While Johnson emphasises the importance of government guidance, Kosai, Y. and Ogino, Y., *The Contemporary Japanese Economy*, Macmillan, London, 1984, takes a more 'free market' approach to the analysis of Japanese growth.

Patrick, H. & Meissner, L. (eds), *Japanese Industrialisation and its Social Consequences*, University of California Press, Berkeley, 1976, contains essays on the social, as well as the economic, aspects of Japanese development both before and after World War II.

A further useful collection of essays on the contemporary economy is contained in Yamamura, K. & Yasuba, Y. (eds), *The Political Economy of Japan: Vol. 1, the Domestic Transformation*, Stanford University Press, Stanford, 1987.

Notes

1   Morishima, M., *Why Has Japan 'Succeeded'? — Western Technology and the Japanese Ethos*, Cambridge University Press, Cambridge, 1982.

2   Johnson, C., *MITI and the Japanese Miracle: The Growth of Industrial Policy 1925–1975*, Stanford University Press, Stanford, Cal., 1982.

3   Quoted in Teruoka, S., 'Land Reform and Postwar Japanese Capitalism' in Morris-Suzuki, T. & Seiyana, T. (eds), *Japanese Capitalism Since 1945*, M.E. Sharpe, Armonk, NY, 1989, p. 89.

4   Boltho, A., *Japan: An Economic Survey 1953–73*, Oxford University Press, Oxford, 1975, p. 86.

5   Komiya, R., & Itoh, M., 'Japan's International Trade and Trade Policy 1955–1984', in Inoguchi, T. & Okimoto, D.I. (eds), *The Political Economy of Japan: Vol. 2 — The Changing International Context*, Stanford University Press, Stanford, Cal., 1988, p. 187.

6   Okimoto, D.I., *Between MITI and the Market: Japanese Industrial Policy for High Technology*, Stanford University Press, Stanford, Cal., 1989, p. 49.

7   Johnson, C., *MITI and the Japanese Miracle*, p. 76.

8   Schodt, F.L., *Inside the Robot Kingdom: Japan, Mechatronics and the Coming Robotopia*, Kodansha International, Tokyo and New York, 1988, p. 15.

29 | The rise of the East Asian NIEs: Theory and evidence

Introduction

The East Asian newly industrialised economies (NIEs) — consisting of South Korea, Taiwan and the two city-states of Hong Kong and Singapore — represent an exclusive club of super-performers dubbed the 'miracle economies' by the World Bank.[1] Certainly the East Asian NIEs have been characterised by persistently rapid growth rates that have, in recent decades, been well above the norm for most developing economies. More importantly, if one applies the fundamental criterion of development — namely poverty alleviation and basic needs fulfilment — then there is little doubt that the East Asian NIEs have been phenomenally successful. There has been a sustained reduction in poverty and satisfactory provision of basic needs within a relatively short period of time.

Perhaps the key aspect of the growth process in these economies is their ability to emerge as significant players in international markets. This can be gauged from the fact that their combined share in world exports rose from 4.1 per cent in 1980 to 7.6 per cent in 1990. This is particularly impressive when judged against the fact that over the same period the share in world exports of all developing economies fell from 29 per cent to 22 per cent. A focus on specific countries within the NIEs suggests an even more remarkable story of success in penetrating global industries. Consider, for example, the case of Korea. Prior to 1973, Korean firms were non-existent in the global shipbuilding and steel industries. In the 1980s, Korean firms gained significant market shares in these industries.

What accounts for the ascendancy of the East Asian NIEs in international markets and their corresponding success in attaining rapid, persistent and equitable growth? Explanations vary, but they can be broadly classified into two groups: those that emphasise the importance of exogenous factors and those that highlight the role of endogenous variables. In the case of the former, there is a tendency to interpret the superior economic performance of the East Asian NIEs as the product of fortuitous historical and geo-political circumstances. Many observers would also argue that these societies were blessed with a value system (Confucianism) that was highly compatible with rapid economic growth. Those who emphasise the importance of endogenous variables typically note that, while exogenous factors (history, geo-political circumstances, value systems) played a role, an appreciation of the rise of the East Asian NIEs is crucially incomplete without a deep understanding of the enterprise, initiative and creativity of policy-makers and their interaction with a dynamic private sector.

While an endogenous theory of the economic success of the East Asian NIEs is now well entrenched in the relevant literature, considerable disagreement continues to exist between economists who emphasise the importance of a market-oriented policy environment and academic practitioners who highlight the central role played by an interventionist state in guiding economic development. This debate is a fundamental feature of the literature pertaining to the East Asian NIEs.

The position adopted by this chapter is eclectic. It recognises the complex, multi-causal nature of the growth process in the East Asian NIEs and accepts the view that a satisfactory explanation of the emergence of the 'miracle economies' must take account of the interaction between exogenous and endogenous variables.

The rise of the East Asian NIEs: The impact of exogenous factors

In terms of exogenous factors, one needs to focus on the historical origins of modern economic growth in the East Asian NIEs, the impact of geopolitical circumstances and the role of cultural and social values. More specifically, the following propositions will be critically examined. Firstly, these countries benefited enormously from a favourable colonial experience. Secondly, they generally gained from being strategic allies of the United States. Thirdly, the superior economic performance of the East Asia NIEs has deep cultural roots.

The colonial experience and its relevance to modern economic growth

It is an undeniable fact that Hong Kong and Singapore prospered as entrepôts long before their era of export-oriented manufacturing. It is also an undeniable fact that the evolution of the city states as entrepôts is really the product of British colonial rule. More generally, the British brought to these economies the notion and practice of modern capitalism, with all its paraphernalia of a well-functioning system of property rights, an efficient legal system and so forth.

It appears that if one takes a historical perspective, one could suggest that Hong Kong and Singapore have prospered because of their favourable historical experiences. The trouble with this interpretation is that it is static in nature, failing to explain how a set of initial favourable conditions were converted into a phase of sustained success. Certainly the city states were subjected to periodic entrepôt crises and by the 1950s were facing insurmountable limits to maintaining rapid growth by relying on the traditional economic structure. The take-off in their economic development really came when policy-makers in Hong Kong and Singapore made a deliberate transition to export-oriented manufacturing.

Korea and Taiwan need to be discussed separately as they bear the imprint of Japanese, rather than British, colonial rule. The prevailing wisdom seems to be that modern economic growth in former Japanese colonies owes much to the era of Japanese imperialism. This thesis apparently finds much support in the experiences of Taiwan and Korea. The subsequent discussion focuses critically on this point.

As is well known, Korea was a Japanese colony from 1910 to 1945, while Taiwan was a Japanese colony from 1895 to 1945. Cumings[2] is perhaps the strongest advocate of the view that one cannot really understand postwar growth in Korea and Taiwan without appreciating their development as colonial economies. He suggests that '. . . both Korea and Taiwan experienced higher GDP growth rates than Japan between 1911 and 1939'.[3] Elsewhere he notes '[t]he period from 1935 to 1945 was when Korea's industrial revolution began'.[4]

Wade also offers a rather favourable interpretation of the Japanese colonial period. This is evident in the following remarks on Taiwan: 'some evidence suggests that the welfare of the Taiwanese peasant in the first half of the twentieth century may have exceeded that of the Japanese peasant'.[5]

Two points need to be clarified in the wake of the above observations. First, is the evidence really so favourable? Second, if it is, how can one explain the evidence? It appears that Ho is the definitive account of Korea and Taiwan as Japanese colonies.[6] His analysis provides a more balanced perspective on this sensitive issue and the discussion that follows largely draws on this key source.

To start with, it is necessary to emphasise that estimates of economic growth during the colonial period vary quite significantly, so it is not really possible to make the confident assertions that Cumings does (see above). For instance, one estimate in Taiwan suggests growth of GDP to be 4.3 per cent in the 1927–37 period, while another estimate suggests a growth rate of only 1.4 per cent over the same period.[7] Subject to this significant reservation, the data seem to suggest that total product grew between 3.6 per cent and 2.7 per cent in Korea over the 1912–37 period and between 4.3 per cent and 3.9 per cent over the same period in Taiwan. In per capita terms, the growth rates were more modest, probably no higher than 1.5 per cent.

Secondly, one has to take account of the changing pattern of colonial development. Initially, Korea and Taiwan grew as 'agricultural appendages' of Japan, but the growth of agriculture was more rapid and sustained in the latter than in the former. More importantly, in both economies there were periods of slow growth juxtaposed with periods of rapid growth. Thus, in Korea, agricultural value added grew only at 1.3 per cent in the 1927–37 period, but at 1.9 per cent in the 1912–27 period.[8] In Taiwan the comparable figures are 3.0 per cent (1927–37) and 2.0 per cent (1912–27). Furthermore, Japanese policy towards its colonies changed during the 1930s, and it is over this period that major efforts towards industrialisation took place. The outcomes were divergent, being more evident in Korea than in Taiwan (in the sense that Korea experienced more rapid growth in manufacturing than Taiwan).

The Japanese colonial state did not limit its efforts to agriculture and industry. Most observers maintain that the Japanese made substantial investments in infrastructure, health and primary education in Taiwan and Korea. For instance, in 1900 Taiwan had very few roads or railroads, but by 1920 it had more than 600 kilometres of public railways, 3553 kilometers of roads and significant harbour facilities. Although the Japanese colonial state apparently made a modest allocation of its expenditure to health and medical services, its heavy reliance on preventive measures against infectious disease led to significant drops in mortality. In Taiwan, the death rate declined from 33 to 19 deaths per thousand between 1906 and 1940.[9] In Korea, the death rate fell from 35 to 23 per deaths per thousand between 1910 and 1935–40.[10]

In the sphere of education, one can observe impressive advances. Primary school enrolment increased from 20 000 in 1910 in Korea to 901 100 in 1937.[11] In Taiwan the improvement was even more impressive. By the end of the colonial rule, the primary school enrolment ratio stood at 71 per cent.[12]

Despite these impressive achievements, one should be cautious about exaggerating the contributions of Japanese colonial rule to the economic development of Taiwan and Korea. It has already been noted that the estimates on growth performance in the two ex-Japanese colonies are subject to wide variations. The growth performance was also uneven, being more sluggish in some periods and sectors than others. More importantly, the Japanese state developed the colonies to meet the short-term needs of its economy. In some cases, as in health and infrastructure, this strategy produced tangible benefits. In other cases, the results were inefficient and inequitable. Thus, for example, the efforts of the Japanese colonial state to industrialise Korea and Taiwan primarily developed as a result of the objective of meeting specific Japanese needs.

One could argue that the Japanese left behind an industrial structure which was inefficient and thus not the basis upon which one could build the export-oriented manufacturing revolution of the 1960s. In any case, the industrial base of the Japanese period hardly remained intact, given the destruction of World War II, the splitting up of Korea and the calamities of the Korean War. Indeed, the postwar dislocation was so severe in the case of Taiwan that 'total domestic product . . . on a per capita basis had not recovered to the 1937 level until 1953'.[13] In the case of Korea, the partition meant that, at one stroke, south Korea lost the bulk of her heavy industry and electricity generation to the north. This was not surprising given the regional concentration of industry during the colonial era. Thus, 85 per cent of the hydroelectric power, 95 per cent of iron and steel, 80 per cent of the coal industry and 85 per cent of the chemicals industry were located in the north.[14]

The ultimate test of development is the extent to which it leads to an improvement in the welfare of the population. The available indicators of welfare suggest a rather uncertain picture in the colonial era in Korea and Taiwan. If one looks at daily per capita food availability in Korea, it fell from 2133 in the 1910–14 period to 1812 in the 1930–34 period.[15] Data on real wages in Taiwan show that they remained constant between 1910 to 1919, rose between 1920 to 1934 but fell significantly after that. In other words, while Korea and Taiwan certainly did not stagnate during the colonial era, indicators of welfare suggest a possible paradox of growth without development.

Confucianism and Eastern Asian economic development

One could argue that cultural and social values represent fundamental historical parameters that need to be understood as part of the dynamics of development. Obviously the NIEs have cultural affinities. Taiwan, Hong Kong and Singapore are predominantly Chinese and are influenced by Confucian values. Korea has historically been strongly influenced by the Chinese and Confucian values. There is little doubt that political leaders in these countries (with the possible exception of Hong Kong) have periodically invoked Confucianism as a means of political and social mobilisation. A typical example is offered by Cho and Kim on Korea.[16] They note: 'Park made explicit efforts to inculcate in the Korean populace the Confucian value of "chung hyo" (loyalty to the state, filial piety, and harmony).'

Given the cultural similarities of the East Asian NIEs, and given the evidence of the government in these economies making use of Confucian values for the purpose of political and social mobilisation, it is tempting to make a connection between Confucianism and economic success. Certainly there is an enduring perception among many scholars that such a connection exists.[17] What is Confucianism and how does it promote growth? The discussion that follows draws upon O'Malley[18] and Pye.[19]

Confucianism has gone through considerable transformation over the course of two and a half millennia. Despite such metamorphosis, key elements of it have endured the passage of time to the extent that one can suggest a recognisable post-Confucian culture.

The Confucian value system generates particular institutional outcomes that are reflected at the level of the political system, in the arena of industrial organisation and in the interaction between the government and the private sector. Firstly, it imparts a 'strong ethical-moral basis of government . . . that both sets the limits on the pragmatic uses of power and requires that authority act with compassion for the people'.[20] Secondly, it justifies the existence of hierarchical political systems. More specifically, given its emphasis on leadership based on the highest standards, it suggests the need for a centralised, meritocratic bureaucracy that operates within an authoritarian political tradition. Thirdly, the stress on respect and loyalty to superiors gets translated into a demand for consensus and conformity. This in turn implies that 'Confucian political cultures places obstacles on . . . challengers of the status quo'.[21] Fourth, it breeds a particular type of industrial organisation in which:

> companies . . . are organised in community-like, almost family-like ways, with a strong emphasis on team spirit and mutual respect. In the larger and more successful firms, employees . . . are almost guaranteed life-long employment and predictable advances in rank and salary . . . The result . . . is a highly developed sense of loyalty . . . for the good of the collective effort which is the company.[22]

Finally, the Confucian value system leads to the evolution of a cooperative relationship between the government and corporate interests.

Apart from encouraging the development of particular institutional outcomes, the Confucian value system encourages hard work, diligence and a reverential attitude towards education, given that such traits are widely perceived to be the most acceptable means of career progression in a hierarchical system. This in turn implies that Confucianism encourages rapid human capital formation.

Such a framework of interpreting the impact of Confucianism on economic development is very much in line with more standard interpretations of East Asian economic success. At a subsequent stage, it will be noted that there is a well entrenched body of scholarship which maintains that the fundamental source of East Asian economic success is a set of particular institutional arrangements — centralised, meritocratic bureaucracy, 'insulated' political systems that are able to withstand the pressures of sectional interests, close government-business interactions — which facilitates the implementation of coherent economic policies. In addition, it will be noted that the East Asian economic miracle has also been characterised by a rapid rate of human capital formation. What this interpretation has done is to extend this analysis by suggesting that East Asian-style institutional arrangements have culturally specific, Confucian origins.

Perhaps the major problem with the notion that economic success has strong cultural roots is its inability to cope with the standard critique that while Confucianism has been around for centuries, East Asian success is of 1960s vintage.[23] Economists resolve this puzzle by offering a simple, but effective, interpretation of East Asian success.[24] They emphasise that the 1960s represented a turning point in the economic development of the East Asian NIEs because at that juncture the NIEs managed to implement a set of broad-based policy reforms. Pye obliquely admits this to be the case:

> . . . [T]he Confucian tradition had to be coupled with advances in economics as an intellectual discipline in order to produce the economic miracles of East Asia. The new mandarins had to be schooled in the wisdom of Western economic theories and practices.[25]

Given such analytical limitations of the Confucian model of economic development, can one draw any firm conclusions concerning its relevance to East Asia? Perhaps the most appropriate position to take is the one suggested by Little.[26] He notes: 'cultural factors cannot be more than contributory factors, which may play their part, but only when other conditions are favourable'.

Geopolitical realities: The impact of United States aid and the Vietnam War

There is an enduring perception that the East Asian NIEs benefited from the United States' perception of the region and that the United States used its aid leverage to reinforce the position of pro-American elites and to cement strategic ties with economic ties. It is alleged that these geopolitical realities go a long way towards an understanding of the dynamism of the region. Haggard offers a clear expression of this view:

> [I]nternational political conditions . . . have had an important bearing on East Asia's economic development. Japan's defeat in the Second World War made the United States the pre-eminent political power in the region. The outbreak of conflict on the Korean peninsula extended the Cold War to Asia, altering the United States' strategic perception of the region and creating expanded political

and economic commitments to the Republic of Korea and Taiwan. The growth of a regional economy in the Pacific Basin cannot be understood without reference to this underlying strategic context.[27]

The immediate outcome of this 'strategic context' was the massive influx of United States aid to Korea and Taiwan during the 1950s and 1960s. Woo highlights the magnitude of this aid inflow in the following manner:

> From 1946 to 1976, the United States provided $12.6 billion in American economic and military aid to Korea (for Taiwan, it was $5.6 billion) . . . No other country in the world received such large sums . . . with the exception of Israel and South Vietnam.[28]

Little recognises the importance of the aid inflow to Taiwan and Korea, but notes that it tapered off by the early 1960s, at which point other countries were more significant aid recipients.[29] The shifting importance of United States military and economic assistance can be gauged from the fact that in Taiwan aid as a proportion of GNP was 6–7 per cent in the 1958–61 period but became negligible by 1968.[30] In the case of Korea, United States military assistance fell from well over 10 per cent of GNP in the late 1950s to under 5 per cent in the second half of the 1960s.[31]

Wade emphasises that the aid inflow assisted Taiwan in several important ways.[32] His arguments are general and broadly apply to Korea as well. Thus:

1 The aid inflow met the immediate need of stabilising the economies in the wake of postwar dislocation.
2 It gave local and foreign investors confidence in the viability of the regime.
3 It helped finance land reform, dampen inflation and act as an important channel of technology transfer.
4 It allowed the economies to maintain large military establishments without them becoming a major drain.
5 American aid advisers played a role in the shift towards export-oriented industrialisation — a point which is also emphasised by Haggard.[33]

Despite these important contributions which United States aid made to the economies, Wade recognises that aid cannot really be taken as a sufficient condition for superior economic performance of East Asia.[34] Little emphasises this point by observing that '[h]eavy aid coincided roughly with their [Korea and Taiwan] period of slow growth, and they became miracle economies when aid dwindled away'.[35] Riedel makes a similar point and emphasises that 'Hong Kong did not receive much aid . . . Singapore borrowed heavily in the early 1960s from the World Bank and the Asian Development Bank, but on relatively hard terms'.[36]

It thus appears that one can easily exaggerate the importance of United States aid to the East Asian NIEs. Ultimately, the impact of aid inflows depends on the absorptive capacity of recipients. Aid dependency is a well known syndrome. The East Asian NIEs escaped from this syndrome because of their capacity to utilise the aid inflow in a productive manner.

Several authors have also emphasised the importance of the Vietnam War to the development of the East Asian NIEs. Cole and Lyman have called it 'Korea's El Dorado'.[37]

Woo offers an in-depth analysis on the impact of the Vietnam War on Korea. Her point is that the Vietnam War acted 'as an incubator of new industries before testing the fires of international competition'.[38] These industries (steel, transport equipment, etc.) subsequently became the leaders of the 1970s and 1980s. In addition, the Vietnam War offered an avenue for large Korean firms to gain experience in international construction projects by undertaking large-scale construction work in South Vietnam.

The Vietnam War was, in retrospect, a fortuitous event for the East Asian NIEs (particularly Korea). However, its implications have to be set in a broader perspective. A lucky event can only become a launching pad for sustained industrialisation if the country (or countries) in question has the initiative and enterprise to exploit the event to its advantage. The East Asian NIEs demonstrated that they could do so. Otherwise one would have seen a deceleration of growth after the termination of the Vietnam War.

The rise of the East Asian NIEs: The role of endogenous factors

While external events have shaped the unfolding of the East Asian 'miracle', an adequate explanation for this phenomenon must take account of the role of endogenous factors. In particular, two hypotheses deserve closer scrutiny: the role of appropriate economic policies and the nature of the East Asian state that guided economic development.

The impact of the policy environment

Economists — particularly those adhering to the neoclassical tradition — have placed considerable emphasis on the role that appropriate economic policies have played in the rise of the East Asian NIEs. In particular, such practitioners note that these economies embarked on period of reforms around 1960 that shifted the production structure away from import substituting industrialisation (ISI) and provided the basis for export-oriented industrialisation (EOI). This is summarised by Little in the following terms:

> Starting in the years around 1960, these countries (i.e. Korea, Taiwan and Singapore) made policy changes that by the middle of 1960s combined selective protection for certain import competing sectors with a virtual free trade regime for exporters — by which we mean that exporters could obtain inputs . . . at

world market prices, while the effective exchange rate for exporters was close to that which would have ruled under free trade. Overall effective protection for industry was zero for Korea, and, of course, Hong Kong, and low for Taiwan and Singapore. The consequential growth of exports was phenomenal, far exceeding what anyone could have predicted or did predict.[39]

Advocates of EOI argue that such a strategy yields substantial benefits to society. The primary advantage of EOI, according to its supporters, is that it promotes both allocative and dynamic efficiency. Resources are allocated according to the principle of comparative advantage so that one attains maximum production from a given stock of resources and a given state of technology. Perhaps more crucial are the additional benefits that are supposed to flow from the implementation of export-oriented policies: exploitation of economies of scale in the wider export market and enlarged technological and social capabilities as a result of the exposure to foreign know-how. In addition to allocative efficiency gains, advocates of EOI also claim that the strategy generates higher savings which in turn provides an additional boost to economic growth. The higher savings take place through several channels: higher household income generated by increased exports, a less distorted capital market compared with ISI in the sense that interest rates at least keep pace with the rate of inflation, and the greater inflow of foreign capital that seems to be associated with EOI.

It has also been suggested[40] that EOI provides for self-correcting mechanisms for efficient macroeconomic management. The argument seems to be that misaligned macroeconomic variables, such as over-valued exchange rates and persistently high inflation rates, become quickly obvious because of their direct influence on a key performance target, the current account of the balance of payments.

Finally, advocates of EOI argue that it promotes equitable growth.[41] This argument depends on the link between employment growth and EOI. The strategy by its very nature focuses on the growth of labour-intensive exports. This increases the demand for semi-skilled labour and thus allows the poorer sections of society to participate in the growth process.

The East Asian success stories, in fact, first came into the limelight through this protracted debate on the relationship between trade regimes and economic development. Supporters of the EOI strategy felt that the experience of East Asia vindicated their position. The following observation is typical:

> The evidence is quite conclusive: countries applying outward-oriented development strategies had a superior performance in terms of exports, economic growth, and employment whereas countries with continued inward orientation encountered increasing economic difficulties.[42]

The more recent literature on the impact of export-orientation (or trade liberalisation) urge a circumspect view on the link between the trade regime and economic development. Cross-country evidence typically show a realtively weak relationship between the trade-orientation of a policy regime and its economic performance. As Rodrik argues:

> [a] reasonable hypothesis is that trade policy plays a rather asymmetric role in economic development: an abysmal trade regime can perhaps drive a country into economic ruin; but good trade policy cannot make a poor country rich. At best, trade policy provides an enabling environment for development.[43]

Whether entrepreneurs will take advantage of this environment to stimulate investment and growth depends on the existence of an appropriate institutional framework. The state can play an important role in providing an appropriate institutional environment for facilitating both economic growth and export expansion. Thus the particular nature of the state in East Asia might be regarded as the missing 'third factor' in the observed positive correlation between exports and economic growth (see subsequent discussion).

It must also be emphasised that EOI is only one element of a range of policy reforms that the East Asian NIEs implemented. The World Bank thus emphasises the 'policy fundamentals' that combined to create the 'East Asian miracle': sound macroeconomic policies, relatively efficient microeconomic policies and, most importantly, aggressive intervention in human capital formation through education and training policies.[44]

The role of the state

It is now widely acknowledged that in emphasising the impact of the policy environment on the rise of the East Asian NIEs, economists have overlooked the central role that the state has played in producing rapid growth. Advocates of this view are are keen to point out that the East Asian NIEs have been as interventionist as some of the less successful developing countries. A searching analysis of regulatory mechanisms in East Asia (e.g. the regulation of the financial sector) suggests an equally pervasive presence of the state.[45] This has led to the growing realisation that what matters to the process of economic development is not the extent of intervention but the quality of such intervention.

According to the literature on East Asian political economy, it is necessary to distinguish between different types of state as a means of analysing the circumstances in which policy activism will yield social benefits. As a first approximation, one may distinguish two generic types: the 'weak' and the 'strong' state. The former is captive to a wide array of distributional coalitions and thus exposed to the ravages of rent-seeking activities. The latter, on the other hand, is able to develop a considerable degree of insulation (or relative autonomy) from the ravages of rent-seeking groups.[46] The emphasis on 'relative autonomy' is important: no state operates in a vacuum. The ideal-type strong state may in fact develop durable links with some modernising interests but exclude or restrict the access of more narrowly based and fractious groups to the policy-making process. Given these distinctive features, the 'strong' state is able, on average, to formulate and implement policies that are broadly in line with societal interests. Thus, for example, the strong state is more likely to resist protectionist measures and adopt policies that facilitate export-oriented industrialisation.

What are the institutional mechanisms that allow a state to develop 'relative autonomy'? Initial work in this area was influenced by the Japanese experience in the postwar period. Hailed by many as a shining example of state-led industrialisation, the characteristic features of the Japanese policy-making process are seen as providing the archetypical institutional mechanisms of the 'strong, developmental state'.[47] These ideas have also been used to analyse the nature of the policy-making regime of the East Asian NIEs.[48] The East Asian state is supposedly characterised by:

1 an elite bureaucracy staffed by the best managerial talent in the system;
2 an authoritarian political system in which the bureaucracy is given sufficient scope to take policy initiatives;
3 close government–big business co-operation in the policy-making process.

Some observers regard the third of these as being the most important element of the Eastern Asian state.[49] According to this view, the close government–big business co-operation converts the state into a 'quasi-internal organisation'. The QIO is productive for two main reasons. Firstly, it creates an atmosphere of trust and co-operation which allows a substantial agreement on an agenda of economic development to emerge. Secondly, it allows the state to fend off or modulate pressures from other elements of society where it is perceived that these pressures might deter or impair critical elements of the economic development agenda. Once the crucial steps of goal-setting and consensus are completed, the centralised bureaucracy can in fact actively pursue interventionist economic policy. Seen in these terms, the state can indeed become an 'engine of growth'.

The literature on East Asian political economy has made a significant contribution to the greater understanding of the policy process and politics that underpin any successful development strategy. In making such a contribution, it has exposed the misleading nature of the more strident and uncritical policy-oriented interpretations of East Asian economic success. Yet, in some important respects, this literature over-states its case. Two points are worth noting.

Firstly, the validity of the political economy approach to economic development cannot be separated from the role of foreign trade and the way it shapes state autonomy. In their eagerness to construct the hypothesis of the state as an engine of growth, political economists sometimes imply that foreign trade — in the specific form of export-oriented policies — plays a superficial role in economic development. Yet they also argue that the reason why policy-makers in Eastern Asia managed to maintain efficient policies had to do with the foreign trade dependence of their economies. In other words, once policy-makers became aware that domestic economic fortunes were closely linked to export growth, they were constrained from making persistent policy mistakes. If this is the case, then export-orientation plays a primary role in East Asian economic development, with state activism playing a supplementary role — an implication that runs contrary to the central arguments of Eastern Asian political economy!

Secondly, it is worth emphasising that advocates of QIO are aware that the state, even when organised as a QIO within an export-oriented regime, can make episodic, but significant, policy mistakes. This is evident in the following observations:

> It is important to point out here that the quasi-internal organization is not relatively efficient under all circumstances. As the economy grows and as the number of enterprises increases within the organization, it will run into more of 'internal organizational failures', increasing the cost of policy implementation. Moreover, as the economy graduates from producing simple labour-intensive products, choosing right industries to promote will become more difficult. Consequently, the quasi-internal organization is more likely to make mistakes of choosing wrong policies than before.[50]

Given the above observations, is it possible to draw firm conclusions about the role of the state in Eastern Asian economic development? It is tempting to suggest that the issue should be resolved by making use of the available evidence. The problem is that the evidence is equivocal, supporting elements of both the statist and policy-oriented interpretations.[51] This is perhaps to be expected. The extreme versions of the statist as well as the policy-oriented models of East Asian success lack analytical and empirical credibility. One must move away from the idea that the 'strong, developmental state' in East Asia produced error-free policies. Equally, one must move away from the naive notion that East Asian success vindicates the efficacy of *'laissez faire'* policies. The truth probably lies in a synergestic interaction between the state and the market. More importantly, while the state in East Asia may not have played the role of an 'engine of growth', it has certainly played the role of a 'handmaiden of growth'. Policy-makers in such countries fulfilled an important developmental function by carrying out necessary policy reforms which created and maintained an environment conducive to rapid economic growth. They have also fulfilled an important task by making necessary investments in essential infra-structure. In cases where policy-makers moved to the much more ambitious and risky realm of industry-specific interventions, the limits to their potency became evident.

Concluding remarks

This chapter has discussed a range of of explanations that can account for the remarkable ascendency of the East Asian NIEs in international markets. The survey shows that a combination of exogenous (history, culture and geopolitics) and endogenous (appropriate economic policies, state activism) factors have played a role in the graduation of Hong Kong, Singapore, Korea and Taiwan into NIEs. As the survey shows, the relative contributions of each of these factors are not fully clear. Thus the lesson is to take a cautious approach and to avoid ready generalisations.

A more fundamental question is whether the East Asian NIEs can continue to prosper in the future. This depends on how they adjust to their success. In particular, it depends on the ability of policy-makers to restructure the economy towards one which is driven by innovation. It may well be that the institutional structure which was conducive for their initial sucesses may not help the politics of policy-making at this juncture. The recent political unrests in Korea and Taiwan are indications of likely frictions arising from the problems of adjusting to success. Thus whether or not the East Asian NIEs can graduate to an 'innovation-driven' stage of development depends on the ability of national governments in creating an institutional environment which encourages diversity and creativity.

Guide to further reading

The literature on the East Asian NIEs is now voluminous and continues to grow rapidly. Here is a selection of some recent surveys:

Chowdhury, A. and Islam, I. (1993) *The Newly Industrialising Economies of East Asia*, Routledge, London and New York

World Bank (1993) *The East Asian Miracle: Economic Growth and Public Policy*, Oxford University Press, New York

Dixon, C. and Drakakis-Smith, D. (1993) *Economic and Social Development in Pacific Asia*, Routledge, London and New York

Chow, P.C.Y. and Kellman, M.H. (1993) *Trade: the Engine of Growth in East Asia*, Oxford University Press, New York

Note that the World Bank (1993) covers the South-east Asian economies of Indonesia, Malaysia and Thailand. Dixon and Drakakis-Smith (1993) cover Japan, South-east Asia, Burma, China. Laos and Vietnam. They are useful in comparing the East Asian NIEs with other countries in the region.

Two widely cited studies that utilise an overt political economy framework in understanding the East Asian NIEs are:

Wade, R. (1990) *Governing the Market: Economic Theory and the Role of Government in East Asian Industrialization*, Princeton University Press, New Jersey

Haggard, S. (1990), *Pathways from the Periphery: Politics of Growth in the Newly Industrialising Countries*, Cornell University Press, Ithaca, New York

One study in particular takes a rather dim view of the future of the East Asian NIEs unless wide-ranging political and social reforms are carried out. It is a departure from the 'mainstream' literature, but worth reading:

Bello,W. and Rosenfeld, S. (1992), *Dragons in Distress Asia's Miracle Economies in Crisis,* Penguin, London

All the studies cited here have extensive references on in-depth, individual country studies.

Notes

1   World Bank, *Economic Growth and Public Policy,* Oxford University Press, Oxford, 1993.

2   Cumings, B., 'The Origins and Development of Northeast Asian Political Economy: Industrial Sectors, Product Life Cycles, and Political Consequences', in Deyo, F.(ed.), *The Political Economy of the New Asian Industrialism,* Cornell University Press, Ithaca and London, 1987.

3   Japan: 3.36%; Korea: 3.57%; Taiwan: 3.85%: Cumings, B., 'The Origins and Development', 1987, p. 45.

4   ibid., p. 57.

5   Wade, R., *Governing the Market: Economic Theory and the Role of Government in East Asian Industrialization*, Princeton University Press, New Jersey, 1990.

6   Ho, S.P.S. 'Agricultural Transformation Under Colonialism: The Case of Taiwan', *Journal of Economic History,* vol. XXVIII, 1968; Ho, S.P.S., *Economic Development of Taiwan,* Yale University Press, New Haven, 1978; Ho, S.P.S., 'Colonialism and Development: Korea, Taiwan, Kwantung', in R. Myers and Petrie, M.R. (eds), *The Japanese Colonial Empire, 1985–1945,* Princeton University Press, Princeton, 1984.

7   Ho, S.P.S., 'Colonialism and Development: Korea, Taiwan, Kwantung', in Myers, R.H. and Petrie, M.R. (eds), *The Japanese Colonial Empire, 1895–1945*, Princeton University Press, Princeton, 1984, Table 1.

8   Ho, ibid., Table 1.

9   Ho, S.P.S., *Economic Development of Taiwan*, Yale University Press, New Haven and London, 1978, Table A11.

10 Kwan, T.H. et al., *The Population of Korea*, Seoul National University, Seoul, 1975, Table 11.4.

11 Gradzanzev, A.J., *Modern Korea,* Institute of Pacific Relations, New York, 1944, p. 261.

12 Ho, S.P.S., 'Colonialism and Development: Korea, Taiwan, Kwantung', in Myers and Petrie M.R. (eds), *The Japanese Colonial Empire, 1895–1945*, Princeton University Press, Princeton, 1984, p. 353.

13 Little (1979), 'An Economic Reconnaissance', in Galenson, W. (ed.), *Economic Growth and Structural Change in Taiwan*, Cornell University Press, Ithaca and London, p. 454.

14 Woo, J.E. (1991), *Race to the Swift: State and Finance in Korean Industrialisation*, Columbia University Press, New York, p. 41.

15 Ho, S.P.S. , 'Colonialism and Development: Korea, Taiwan, Kwantung', in Myers, R.H. and Petrie, M.R. (eds), *The Japanese Colonial Empire, 1895–1945*, Princeton University Press, Princeton, 1984, Table 5.

16 Cho, L.J. and Kim, Y.H., 'Political and Economic Antecedents of the 1960s' in Cho.L.J. and Kim, Y.H. (eds), *Economic Development in the Republic of Korea: A Policy Perspective*, Honolulu University, Hawaii, 1991, p. 29.

17 For example, Berger, P.L., 'An East Asian Model' in Berger, P.L. and Hsio, M. (eds), *In Search of an East Asian Development Model*, Transaction Books, New Brunswick, 1988; Pye, L., 'The New Asian Capitalism: A Political Portrait', in Berger, P.L. and Hsiao, H.M. (eds), *In Search of an East Asian Development Model*, Transaction Books, New Brunswick, 1988; O'Malley, W.J. 'Culture and Industrialisation', in Hughes H. (ed.), *Achieving Industrialization in Asia*, Cambridge University Press, Cambridge, 1988; Hofheinz, R. and Calder, K.E., *The Eastasia Edge*, Basic Books, New York, 1982; Kahn, H., *World Economic Development: 1979 and Beyond*, Croom Helm, London, 1979.

18 O'Malley, 'Culture and Industrialisation'.

19 Pye, 'The New Asian Capitalism'.

20 ibid., p. 86.

21 ibid.

22 O'Malley, 'Culture and Industrialisation', p. 341.

23 Pang, P.E., 'The Distinctive Features of Two City States' Development: Hong Kong and Singapore', in Berger, P.L. and Hsiao, M.(eds.), *In Search of an East Asian Development Model*; Papanek, G. 'The New Asian Capitalism: An Economic Portrait', in Berger, P.L. and Hsiao, H.M. (eds), *In Search of an East Asian Development Model*.

24 For example, Little, I.M.D., 'An Economic Reconnaissance', in Galenson, W. (ed.), *Economic Growth and Structural Change in Taiwan*, Cornell University Press, Ithaca and London, 1979; Little, I.M.D., 'The Experiences and Causes of Rapid Labour-intensive Development in Korea, Taiwan Province, Hong Kong and Singapore and The Possibilities of Emulation', in Lee, E. (ed.), *Export-Led Industrialization and Development*, ILO-ARTEP, Bangkok and Geneva, 1981.

25 Pye, 'The New Age Capitalism', p. 86.

26 Little, 'The Experiences and Causes', p. 463.

27 Haggard, S., 'The Politics of Industrialisation in Korea and Taiwan', in Hughes, H. (ed.), *Achieving Industrialisation in East Asia*, Cambridge University Press, Cambridge, 1988, p. 265.

28 Woo, 'Race to the Swift', p. 45.

29 Little, 'The Experiences and Causes', p. 456.

30 ibid., note 31, p. 458.

31 ibid., p. 459.

32 Wade, *Governing the Market*, p. 83.

33 Haggard, 'The Politics of Industrialisation'.

34 Wade, *Governing the Market*.

35 Little, 'The Experiences and Causes', p. 457.

36 Reidel, 'Economic Development in East Asia: Doing What Comes Naturally?' in Hughes, H (ed.), *Achieving Industrialisation in East Asia*, Cambridge University Press, Cambridge, 1988, p. 25.

37 Cole, D. & Lyman, P., *Korean Development: The Interplay of Politics and Economics*, Harvard University Press, Cambridge, Mass., 1971, p. 135.

38 Woo, 'Race to the Swift', p. 97.

39 Little, 'The Experiences and Causes', p. 141.

40 World Bank, *World Development Report*, Oxford University Press, New York, 1987.

41 Little, 'The Experiences and Causes'; Papanek, G., 'The New Asian Capitalism: An Economic Portrait', in Berger, P.L. and Hsiao, H.M. (eds), *In Search of an East Asian Development Model*, Transaction Books, New Brunswick, 1988.

42 Balassa B., *The Newly Industrializing Countries in the World Economy:*, Pergamon, New York, 1981, pp. 16–17.

43 Rodrik, D., 'The Limits of Trade Policy Reform in Developing Countries', *Journal of Economic Perspectives*, vol. 6, no. 1, 1992, p. 103.

44 World Bank, *Economic Growth and Public Policy*, Oxford University Press, Oxford, 1993.

45 Wade, R., 'The Role of Government in Overcoming Market Failure: Taiwan, Republic of Korea and Japan', in Hughes, H. (ed.), *Achieving Industrialization in Asia*, Cambridge University Press, Cambridge, 1988.

46 Haggard, S., 'The Politics of Industrialisation'; Haggard, S., *Pathways from the Periphery: Politics of Growth in the Newly Industrializing Countries*, Cornell University Press, Ithaca and New York, 1990.

47 Johnson, C., *MITI and the Japanese Miracle: The Growth of Industrial Policy, 1925–1975*, Stanford University Press, Stanford, 1982.

48 For example, Wade, 'The Role of Government'; Johnson, C.,'Political Institutions and Economic Performance in Japan, South Korea and Taiwan', in Deyo (ed.) *The Political Economy of the New Asia Industrialism*, Cornell University Press, Cornell, 1987.

49 Lee, C. and Naya, S., 'Trade in East Asian Development with Comparative Reference to Southeast Asian Experience', *Economic Development and Cultural Change*,vol. 38, no. 3, pp. S123-S152.

50 Lee and Naya, 'Trade in East Asian Development', p. 5147.

51 Wade, *Governing the Market*.

30 | Socialist economies

After the end of World War II, the countries of East and Southeast Asia embarked on a process of political and economic transformation. Some of the main manifestations of this have been the subjects of the previous four chapters. Among the most important elements in this transformation was the introduction of a new ideology — Marxism — which heralded the beginning of a new era in social, political and especially economic organisation of society in China and later in other countries.

In 1949, China became the first East Asian country to begin the process of social and economic transformation under the leadership of a communist party. Since the Chinese Communist Party (CCP) had come to power after a protracted and violent struggle, it was able to put into practice many Marxist ideas in the areas under its control, even before the formal establishment of the People's Republic of China. Vietnam, North Korea and Cambodia have also followed a similar path. The focus of this chapter will be on China, although the experience of Vietnam will also be discussed.

Although there are wide differences in the natural resource endowments, levels of technological and economic development and in the economic institutions of the various socialist countries, they nonetheless share fairly similar patterns of economic organisation, the genesis of which can be found in the economic organisation of the Soviet Union. The main common features of this system are:

1 *Public ownership of the means of production*. This is achieved through the socialist transformation of private industry, agriculture and commerce, and takes the form of state, co-operative or collective ownership. Private ownership need not be totally excluded from the socialist system; it can play a minor role in some sectors of the economy, but strict limits are imposed on the hiring of labour by private entrepreneurs. The banking system and commerce, including most domestic and all foreign trade, are also nationalised.
2 *The existence of a market for consumption goods*. The vast majority of consumption goods (as against production goods) are exchanged in the market, where transactions take place in cash, although non-cash instruments of exchange such as food coupons are also used. The

market for production goods (e.g. machinery, industrial raw materials, etc.) is severely restricted and, where it does exist, it is separated from the market for consumption goods.

3 *Centralised control of the rate of accumulation and the direction of economic growth.*

4 *Drastic reduction in the role of prices as informational signals.* Prices and price-limits for all goods sold through the state-controlled commercial channels are decided by the planning authorities. Prices cannot change spontaneously.

The actual mix of these features in a given country depends on a number of factors. The features described above present a highly generalised picture of a socialist economy. In practice, however, there are no 'pure' systems. As the noted Hungarian economist, Kornai, has said, every real system is built upon the practical compromises of mutually contradictory principles and requirements.[1] What differentiates between socialist systems, and indeed between one phase and another in the same economy, is the role accorded to the markets and the degree of centralisation. In China, for example, the periods of greater decentralisation have often been accompanied by greater tolerance in the market. Socialist economies are never completely free of markets, just as capitalist systems are not totally free of regulation by governments.

Because of the central role of planning in socialist economies, they are also referred to as 'centrally planned state socialist' or 'command' economies. All such economies derive from a common source which Prybyla calls 'Stalinplan', introduced in Russia in the late 1920s.[2] In the Soviet Union itself, despite many problems, no significant changes were made to the institutional arrangements and goals of the Stalinplan until Stalin's death in 1953. China also faithfully followed a model of the Stalinplan until the late Chinese leader, Mao Zedong, rejected some of its important features in favour of his own mass-based strategy of economic development in 1958. Even then, many of the essential aspects of the Stalinplan continued to be dominant in the Chinese economic system. The changes which were designed to overcome the weaknesses of the Stalinplan produced results which were far worse than those achieved during the First Five-year Plan (1953–57) when the Stalinplan was used. Since 1978, however, significant changes have been made to China's economic system which are vastly different from the leftward adjustments of the Stalinplan carried out during the late 1950s and 1960s. The 'economic reforms', as such changes are routinely called in socialist countries, have sought to broaden the scope of market forces in the economy. Vietnam has embarked on a similar program of reform. The following section looks at the process of development of the Chinese and Vietnamese economic systems.

The Chinese economic system, 1949–78

When the CCP came to power in 1949, about 67 per cent of the total industrial capital was already in the public sector under the Guomindang government, and this was later inherited by the new government. But of the total industrial output value, the state sector accounted for only 34.7 per cent, while the joint state–private sector contributed 2 per cent and the private sector 63.3 per cent.[3] The Chinese economy as a whole was still overwhelmingly agrarian, with the output value of modern industry accounting for only about 10 per cent of the total output value of the nation's economy. Therefore, the new government was faced with the difficult tasks of reviving the national economy and creating a modern agricultural and industrial infrastructure.

During the 22-year armed struggle in the rural areas, the CCP had gained considerable experience in organising the peasants and directing the small peasant economy in the areas under its control. It organised 'supply and marketing co-operatives' in these areas which exchanged farm produce for manufactured goods with the peasants. In addition to making the communist-controlled areas self-sufficient in food production, this strategy also helped the CCP in its war effort and rallied the peasants around it. After 1949, similar co-operatives were also established in the newly liberated areas. Based on the Marxist principle that socialism can only be built on the basis of large-scale socialised production, some in the CCP felt that Chinese agriculture must be mechanised before it was collectivised. This view, however, failed to sway Mao Zedong, who was in favour of putting collectivisation before mechanisation, mainly because, in his opinion, the average size of land holdings was too small to produce substantial benefits from mechanisation. After several years of agrarian reform, the process of agricultural collectivisation was declared basically completed in 1956.

Meanwhile, the First Five-year Plan (FFYP) began in 1953 (although it was not officially adopted until July 1955) and with it the market as a means of co-ordination was progressively rejected and replaced by the plan. With the implementation of the FFYP, a new hierarchically ordered decision-making structure began to take shape. All the major decisions regarding production and distribution were concentrated in the hands of the central planning authorities. The planning process started at the top of the hierarchy with the party's top leadership deciding what was in the general interest of the society and, based on this perception, dictating long-run goals to the State Council. That body, which consisted of the ministers in charge of functionally defined bureaucratic bodies, assigned the actual task of elaborating economic plans to the State Planning Commission, set up in 1952. The Planning Commission would then work out detailed long-term plans on the basis of submissions from the various ministries. In this, and in short-term planning, it was assisted by the State Statistical Bureau, the State Construction Bureau, the People's Bank of China and other agencies under the State Council. The duties of the Planning Commission included 'drafting of the national economic plan, including the integration, revision, and appraisal of all the partial plans of the individual central government ministries and of local, provincial, and municipal governments'.[4]

After the creation of the State Economic Commission in May 1956, the State Planning Commission was relieved of responsibility for the preparation of annual plans, which were formulated to facilitate the fulfilment of five-year plans in a systematic and easy-to-monitor way. At this stage, the decision-making powers were shared by these two commissions. Their authority was, however, constrained by the major targets set for them by the CCP leadership, but since these targets were few in number and stated in highly aggregated terms, the commissions had great scope for interpretation. As such they were powerful bodies, but within certain definite limits. The next stage in the decision-making process involved various other government agencies. The State Economic Commission, based on CCP directives and information supplied by the Statistical Bureau, would set 'control figures' concerning output targets in both physical and value terms, input and cost coefficients, and other indicators. These figures were then transmitted to the industrial ministries of the central government and the provincial or municipal authorities. They in turn translated these figures into output targets and input coefficients for the major enterprises, most of which were then directly under their supervision. Only the smaller units producing routine commodities for local use were managed by local (provincial and sub-provincial) governments.

The third stage involved the basic units of economic activity: the enterprise in the industrial sector and the collective unit in the agricultural sector. At this stage, an enterprise had to look into its own internal conditions and formulate a bid for its own production plan on the basis of output targets and input and cost coefficients provided to it. Individual enterprise plans were formulated through 'consultations' between the enterprise managements and ministry officials, which in reality took the form of defensive bargaining, wherever the enterprises tried to resist the planners' imposition of ever higher output targets and to secure additional material and labour inputs. Once a compromise had been worked out between the ministry and the enterprise, the plans were then submitted to the higher authorities for approval and integration into the national plan. What is notable in this is the sharp conflicts of interest between the ministry and the enterprise; from this flowed much of the low quality of information in the system.

Ideally, the formulation of the national plan, according to the above description, should have provided each enterprise with exactly enough working capital, materials and labour inputs to produce the required quantities of goods, and all resources would have been deployed with maximum efficiency. The actual experience of the FFYP, however, showed that this was not the case. This plan was one of the most detailed long-term plans adopted by China to date. Because the majority of the investment projects, and all the 156 projects built with the help of the Soviet Union, were covered by it, the central authorities exercised the greatest degree of control during this period. The greater control resulted in what was widely seen as over-centralisation of the decision-making powers in the hands of the central authorities. Despite all the powers of resource and factor allocation in their hands, the central planners still found it difficult to determine capital-output ratios and material requirements for each individual enterprise with any degree of accuracy.

Such weaknesses of planning notwithstanding, the FFYP marked the beginning of a period of sustained economic growth. China's national income during this period (1953–57) grew at an annual average rate of 8.9 per cent. Great emphasis was placed on the development of certain basic industries. The development of heavy industry in particular paved the way for further development of other sectors of the economy. The energy, metallurgical and machine-building industries absorbed nearly 67 per cent of total investment funds during this period. But giving priority to heavy industry began to adversely affect the growth of light industry and agriculture. Moreover, the bulk of investment funds could only come from the peasantry. The one-sided emphasis on heavy industry not only reduced the potential of agriculture to support industrialisation, but it also failed to meet the rising needs of China's urban population. Under these circumstances, further development of heavy industry became increasingly difficult.

Even before the completion of the FFYP, Mao Zedong had repeatedly called for early collectivisation of industry and commerce, for measures to reduce the role of heavy industry in economic development, and for decentralisation of the economy. His dissatisfaction with the slow rate of growth in agriculture and light industry led him to believe that a faster rate of growth could be achieved only by complete, rapid public ownership of the economy, and by the relaxation of central control over planning. These views of Mao reflected his belief that the 'command economy' model that China had borrowed from the Soviet Union was unsuitable for its needs and conditions. In his 1956 speech entitled 'On The Ten Major Relationships', Mao called upon China's economic planners to readjust the ratio between agriculture and light and heavy industries.

His frustration with the existing state of affairs led Mao to launch the extraordinary Great Leap Forward of 1958. In agriculture, the framework for the Leap was a new form of organisation — the people's commune.

The creation of communes 'larger in size and having a high degree of public ownership', to use Mao's words, was indicative of his desire to spread the 'communist wind' across China. They were part of an attempt to hasten the process of transition from socialism to communism. In launching the Great Leap Forward campaign, Mao exhorted the local party leaders to take the initiative for developing small-scale industry into their own hands. The new Maoist economic strategy which emphasised 'more, faster, better, and cheaper' production of goods, however, did not ignore the heavy industrial sector, and the targets for production in this sector were also raised. A significant outcome of the Leap was that the centralised bureaucratic economic planning apparatus was partially dismantled in favour of relative autonomy and decision-making powers for provinces and localities.

The beginning of the Leap marked the start of a cycle of decentralisation and recentralisation. Of over 9300 enterprises under central control in 1957, about 87 per cent were transferred to provincial or local governments in 1958, leaving less than 1300 under central control. Many of the central enterprises not transferred to provincial or local control were also subjected to varying degrees of local influence. Another important implication of the Leap was the growth of labour-intensive, small-scale industries in the rural areas, the most extreme example being the 'backyard furnaces', which proved to be economically counter-productive. Consequently, the Leap's unco-ordinated pursuit of higher output threw the centralised decision-making structure into disarray. Instead of increasing agricultural production, the Leap succeeded in producing a massive famine which some observers estimate claimed as many as 10 to 20 million lives.

It was not until 1965 that the grain output increased to its 1957 pre-Leap figure. Once the failure of the Leap had become painfully obvious, a process of re-centralisation of state enterprises was started, and by 1963 the number of central enterprises had again jumped to over 10 000.[5] With the abandonment of the Great Leap Forward, planning through material balances was restored to its old glory. The Bureau of Material Supply, which was absorbed by the State Economic Commission in 1958, again became an independent body in 1963. The adjustments made to the system during this period were, however, reactive in nature. It was an attempt to rebuild the channels of decision-making and information that were seriously damaged during the Leap. As the old institutions were restored, the emphasis among the targets shifted away from output maximisation towards expert supervision and quality control in production. Although a significant change from the Leap period, it did not mean the disappearance of output quotas and material balances, but rather their restoration.

By 1966, Mao Zedong and his supporters had renewed their accusations that the chains of authority had become too rigid, charging that technocrats and bureaucrats had focused all their efforts on running the economy, to the neglect of the cause of revolution. Economic rationality was seen as taking precedence over revolutionary politics, which was in their view contrary to the principles of the CCP. Thus the industrial and party leaders who had emphasised production were denounced as 'capitalist roaders'. Deng Xiaoping, the undisputed leader of China since 1978, was one of them. These were the early days of what was officially designated as the Great Proletarian Cultural Revolution, and a section of China's youth, the Red Guards, took upon themselves the task of 'toppling' the capitalist roaders. The planning authorities and the bureaucrats responsible for the implementation of the plan were accused, doubtless with some justice, of dealing with numbers and not reality. 'Popular initiative' replaced administrative order in the first two years of the Cultural Revolution, resulting in a sharp decline in industrial production. Although the chaos of the Cultural Revolution was in the main brought to an end by 1969, its spirit continued to live on until the death of Mao Zedong in September 1976 (see Chapter 25).

Post-Mao economic reform and systemic changes

Nearly two years after the death of Mao, the reform-minded leaders within the CCP (the erstwhile capitalist roaders) forged an alliance in favour of economic changes aimed at making China one of the fastest growing economies in the Asia-Pacific region. Just as in the political field discussed in Chapter 25, the Third Plenary Session of the Eleventh Party Central Committee of December 1978 is regarded as a major turning-point in communist China's economic development. It was at this meeting that the decision was made to adopt a more pragmatic approach to economic development, shedding some of the old Marxist and Maoist dogmas that had prevented the reformers from implementing more market-oriented policies. A program of all-round modernisation known as the 'Four Modernisations' was implemented to modernise China's agriculture, industry, science and technology and defence.

In agriculture, modernisation meant not only the technological transformation of this vital sector of the economy, but also the reintroduction of material rewards for increases in output and the allocation of arable land to individual households for cultivation under the 'household responsibility system'. It also marked the beginning of a process of dismantling of the 'people's communes', which have now been stripped of almost all their economic functions, with their political functions also severely curtailed. The 'household responsibility system', which has undergone several modifications since it was first introduced, allows peasant families to contract a piece of land with the state, which they can use to grow their own crops. In return, the state collects a part of their output at state-fixed prices; the rest they are allowed to sell on the free markets, often at higher prices. The major difference between this new system and the previous system is that it offers an incentive to those peasants who work harder, whereas the old system rewarded everyone more or less equally regardless of their contribution to the output.

The reform of the agricultural production system has undoubtedly boosted China's farm production and helped to improve peasants' living standards. Simultaneous reform of the industrial system has also boosted the production of farm machinery, further contributing to the productivity of agriculture. But the reform of China's agriculture has not been without problems. Grain production peaked in 1984, and did not better that figure until 1989. In a country where the population had already reached 1.13 billion (according to the 1990 census) and where many senior leaders have consistently emphasised the importance of grain self-sufficiency, the failure of the agricultural sector to produce enough grain to meet local needs is indeed worrying. The critics of the reform policy see it as a major failure of the new policies. As far as grain production is concerned, their complaints do contain an element of truth. Because of the parallel but limited reform of China's agricultural price system, some fruits, vegetables and other cash crops command much higher prices in the marketplace than grain. Consequently, the peasants prefer to grow crops that will bring in greater monetary rewards.

The government's initial policy of encouraging people to 'get rich' fast has also generated income disparities in both rural and urban areas. The rural reform policy has been successful in creating a new class of rich peasants in Chinese society where only a decade or so ago it was a curse to have such a background. Today many rich peasants and entrepreneurs openly flaunt their newfound wealth, much to the disgust of many old revolutionaries, who see it as a sign of the political degeneration of society. Their wealth and prosperity are also resented by the vast majority, who have not benefited from the new policies to the same extent. These problems are compounded by the re-emergence of many of the old social vices that were thought to have been eradicated during the first three decades of the revolution.

If changes in the agricultural sector have been far-reaching, the reform of the industrial sector has been no less spectacular. The market-oriented reform of China's domestic industrial structure has been accompanied by an eagerness (or necessity) to open up to foreign trade and investment on a larger scale. Whereas in the 1950s and 1960s, China's attitude to foreign trade was moulded by the thinking that regarded foreign trade merely as a 'means of balancing surpluses and shortages', in the late 1970s the Chinese authorities decided to substantially expand the role of foreign trade in the country's economy. As part of their search for new sources of investment to modernise China's industry, the central authorities granted considerable decision-making powers to the provincial and other sub-national governments to deal directly with foreign companies. A major plank of the new policy was to focus on the development of coastal regions. In 1980, the central government formally approved the establishment of Special Economic Zones (SEZs) in the southern Guangdong and Fujian provinces. Based on the concept of Export Processing Zones in Taiwan, South Korea and other Southeast Asian countries, which had at best produced mixed results, the SEZs were designed to attract foreign investment in the country and to improve the quality of China's own products through the transfer of technology and skills.

Apart from the two functions mentioned above, the SEZs were to serve as 'laboratories' where the government could try out changes to the economic organisation of the country as a whole. Accumulating dissatisfaction with the performance of the Soviet-style command system had combined with changes in the configuration of political forces in the country to make reform of the economic system a necessity. It was, however, feared that attempting to change the command economy system by introducing uncontrolled market forces throughout China could lead to a serious dislocation of the economy and to political upheaval. The SEZs were, therefore, to serve as sealed-off enclosures for experimentation with market economy practices. As confidence developed, fourteen other coastal cities were opened up to foreign investment in 1984. In the early 1990s, foreign investment can be found in almost every sector of the Chinese economy.

The year 1984 was also important for the reform of China's industrial economic structure. A document approved at the Third Plenary Session of the Twelfth Party Central Committee, held in October 1984, contained the formal articulation of many of the reform policies covering the industrial sector. Since then, many unprecedented changes have been made to China's economic system. Prominent among them are the devolution of substantial powers related to input–output decisions to individual state-owned enterprises and the concomitant weakening of the powers of the central bureaucracy; the partial reform of the price system; the introduction of such capitalistic institutions as the stock and money markets in some parts of the country; and the slow but steady growth of a private economy in some sectors.

The Vietnamese experience

Immediately after the end of French colonial rule and the creation in the northern part of the country of the Democratic Republic of Vietnam (DRV) in 1954, the Vietnam Workers' Party (renamed the Vietnam Communist Party in 1976) was faced with the formidable task of reconstruction and development. By 1954, the share of modern industry had been reduced to less than 2 per cent of the total material output in North Vietnam by years of wartime destruction. Although the DRV was rich in mineral resources, much of its industrial infrastructure had been destroyed by the French prior to their departure. To meet this challenge, the government of the DRV adopted the same system of economic organisation that had been chosen by the CCP only five years prior to that — the centrally planned command economy. Since the two governments shared common ideological goals, the choice of the command economy system by the DRV was not surprising. The main features of this system have already been outlined above; the section will therefore focus on some similarities and differences between the Chinese and the Vietnamese experiences.

Like the CCP, the Vietnamese Workers' Party had also launched a comprehensive program of social and economic transformation of areas under its control before coming to power. In 1953 it implemented a rent-reduction program as part of its agrarian reform campaign. The formal founding of the DRV paved the way for the launching of land reforms in 1954, aimed at eradicating the economic power and political influence of landlords and rich peasants. The process of land reform was completed in 1956, but the North Vietnamese leadership took a more cautious approach to agricultural collectivisation than their Chinese counterparts. Whereas in China the process of 'co-operativisation' was 'basically completed' in three years, the DRV authorities took nine years (1958–66) to accomplish the same result. Forced collectivisation was rejected by the Vietnamese leaders from very early days and, with the exception of some cases of use of force, this policy was generally maintained even after the reunification of the country in 1975. Moreover, the Vietnamese never considered the creation of collective units of the size of China's people's communes.

But until the late 1970s, like Mao Zedong, the leaders of Vietnam also believed that collectivisation should be achieved before mechanisation in agriculture, ignoring Lenin's warning that large-scale agricultural collectivisation should not be pursued without industrialisation. In Vietnam, collectivisation did produce increases in agricultural output in the early 1960s, but some scholars such as Beresford have argued that these increases can be attributed to the 'one-off effects' of the large-scale construction of irrigation schemes, etc. by the collective units.[6]

Encouraged by the initial success of the collectivisation program, the North Vietnamese leaders shifted their attention to industrialisation. As in most other socialist countries, the emphasis of the DRV's First Five-Year Plan (1961–65) was on the development of heavy industry. Even before the achievements of agricultural collectivisation and early industrialisation could be properly assessed, North Vietnam was heavily involved in a war with the United States (see Chapter 22). The incessant American bombing caused widespread destruction of industrial capacity and forced the removal of many factories to rural areas. Unable to direct the development of agriculture and industry, the leadership was compelled to transfer much of its control over the economy to local authorities.

At the end of the war in 1975, the victorious communist government decided to follow the northern model in the south as well. The party leadership decided in 1976 to press ahead with agricultural collectivisation in the south, which was to be completed by 1980. In order to facilitate the process of collectivisation, the government took control of the trade in agricultural inputs and outputs from private merchants. Meanwhile, the northern and southern parts of Vietnam were officially reunified in July 1976 as the Socialist Republic of Vietnam (SRV). The socialist transformation and collectivisation of agriculture in the south met with resistance from peasants in the more prosperous Mekong Delta, but the provinces of Central Vietnam achieved the goal of collectivisation relatively smoothly after 1976. The Second Five-Year Plan (1976–80) presented rather belatedly at the Fourth Party Congress in December 1976, outlined several tasks for the country, which included the rapid development of agriculture to provide food and to accumulate capital for industrialisation and the development of heavy industry.

However, the transfer of the northern (DRV) model to the south was not easy for a variety of reasons. To begin with, external constraints such as the United States economic blockade, conflict with China and Vietnam's involvement in Cambodia seriously undermined the leadership's ability to direct and organise economic development. Moreover, the fact that South Vietnam had until then followed a completely different path to economic development had created special social and economic conditions which could not be easily undone. Aware of these difficulties, the Vietnamese leaders simultaneously began to look for other ways of stimulating development. A foreign investment law was passed in 1977 with a view to attracting overseas investments to revitalise the country's moribund economy. However, in the absence of any significant re-adjustment of domestic trade and investment policy and with the United States-led Western economic blockade still in force, Vietnam's half-hearted plans to integrate into the international economy did not meet with much success.

The August 1979 Plenary Session of the Party Central Committee adopted new policies to overcome economic difficulties. The main thrust of the new policies was to expand the role of the market and material incentives. As in China, the changes in agricultural sector were designed to bring into full play the initiative and energies of individual rural households. A system similar to the 'household responsibility system' in China was implemented. Under this system of 'product contracts', an area of land is allocated to households to carry out some of the more labour-intensive phases of the production process. In return for agricultural inputs, seeds and other services, households agree to a target quota of grain to be supplied to the collective. The above-quota output can be retained by the household for personal consumption or for sale on the free market where prices are determined by the market forces. The state also purchases surplus quantities of grain from individual households at negotiated prices which are above the normal quota price, but generally below the prevailing market price.

Despite many similarities with the Chinese system, the 'product contract' system is different in some respects from its Chinese variant. The Vietnamese system does not usually involve sales of previously collectively owned assets to individual households, as is widely reported in China. Another important difference between the two systems is that, unlike in China, Vietnamese households are not given responsibility for the entire production process on a contracted piece of land. Jobs requiring mechanised tools and equipment and other technically advanced aspects of production are retained by the collective. Thus the Vietnamese peasants take part in collective as well as individual labour.

Conclusion

The economic reforms of both China and Vietnam have stimulated agricultural and industrial production, but both seem to be halfway between planning and market. While market forces have gained ground in both countries, the governments' half-hearted attempts at price and ownership reforms have left the fledgling groups of entrepreneurs wondering about the future direction of reforms. The collapse of the political power of communist parties in Eastern Europe and the emergence of pro-democracy movements, especially in China, have forced the ruling communist parties in Asia to take a fresh look at their economic reforms, for the success of economic reforms, which invariably involve greater interaction with the outside world, also generates demands for political pluralism and human rights.

Guide to further reading

Beresford, Melanie, *National Unification and Economic Development in Vietnam*, Macmillan, London, 1989
    An excellent up-to-date account of the Vietnamese economy.
Chow, Gregory C., *The Chinese Economy*, Harper and Row, New York, London, 1985; World Scientific Publishing Company, Teaneck, NJ, 1987
    This book is designed as an economics textbook and aims to apply the basic tools of economic analysis to the PRC's economy. There are chapters on the organisation and performance of the various sectors of the economy.

Feuchtwang, Stephan, Hussain, Athar & Pairault, Thierry (eds), *Transforming China's Economy in the Eighties*, 2 vols entitled *The Rural Sector, Welfare and Employment* and *Management, Industry and the Urban Sector*, Westview Press, Boulder, Col., 1988

A comprehensive account of China's economy. Although the emphasis is on the first part of the reform period, from 1978 to the mid-1980s, there is also treatment of the period from the 1950s to 1978.

Howe, Christopher, *China's Economy: A Basic Guide*, Paul Elek, London, Basic Books, New York, 1978

An excellent introduction to China's economic system before the period of reform, covering such areas as population, agriculture, industry, foreign trade and incomes, prices and the standard of living.

Porter, Ian et al., *China, Long-term Development Issues and Options*, Johns Hopkins University Press, Baltimore and London, 1985

A World Bank country study covering agriculture, energy development, international economic strategy, industrial technology, human development and other factors.

Prybyla, J.S., *Market and Plan under Socialism: The Bird in the Cage*, Hoover Institution Press, Stanford, 1987

This is a theoretical book on the nature of socialist economies. There are two parts, concepts and cases, the latter being the Soviet Union, China, Hungary and Yugoslavia.

Notes

1 Kornai, J., 'The Dilemmas of a Socialist Economy: The Hungarian Experience', *Cambridge Journal of Economics*, vol. 4, no. 2, 1980, p. 156.

2 Prybyla, J.S., *Market and Plan Under Socialism: The Bird in the Cage*, Hoover Institution Press, Stanford, 1987.

3 Xue Muqiao, *China's Socialist Economy*, Foreign Languages Press, Beijing, 1986, p. 19.

4 Wu Yuan-Li, *The Economy of Communist China*, Pall Mall Press, London, 1965, p. 32.

5 Lyons, T., *Economic Integration and Planning in Maoist China*, Columbia University Press, New York, 1987, p. 213.

6 Beresford, M., *National Unification and Economic Development in Vietnam*, Macmillan, London, 1989, p. 142.

31 | Thailand and Indonesia: The transformation of the bureaucratic polity

Introduction

In strong contrast to the socialist economies considered in the previous chapter are two Southeast Asian countries whose histories are often compared: Thailand and Indonesia. The argument of this chapter is that a fruitful way to understand politics in both countries is to view them as bureaucratic polities in transformation. The essay begins by explaining the concept of bureaucratic polity and then moves on to discuss its application to Thailand and Indonesia. Importantly, however, it is argued that both countries have undergone a process of political pluralisation in recent years which has seen groups or institutions outside the bureaucratic realm coming to play a larger role in politics. In short, both Thailand and Indonesia appear to be in the process of evolving away from bureaucratic polities. For a number of reasons, this transformation seems to be taking place somewhat more rapidly in Thailand than in Indonesia.

Bureaucratic polity explained

The concept of bureaucratic polity was first developed to explain Thai politics between the 1930s and the 1960s by the American scholar Fred Riggs.[1] Subsequently his ideas were taken up by other scholars working on Thailand as well as Indonesia. Riggs and many other observers noted the minimal role of representative institutions such as parliament, political parties and interest groups in public policy-making in both countries. Key decisions were taken by senior officials — military or even civilian — who rose to executive power as a result of successful coups or because of the support they received from the armed forces. Political and bureaucratic power in these two nations was often fused as government leaders came mostly from the ranks of military or civil bureaucrats, not professional politicians as in Western democratic countries or socialist states. It should be pointed out, too, that whereas a bureaucratic polity shares features of an authoritarian rule, not all kinds of modern authoritarianism are bureaucratic polities. A number of developing countries have authoritarian regimes which are headed by official mass-mobilising parties or charismatic leaders, not the military-bureaucratic elite.

Underpinning the bureaucratic polity is the weakness of extra-bureaucratic forces. These include both societal actors (classes and groups) as well as non-bureaucratic institutions within the state itself (such as the monarchy, the judiciary or the official party). Of particular interest here is the position of the bourgeoisie or the business class. With the European experience of industrialisation and democratisation in mind, many Western scholars expected that the business and middle classes created in Indonesia and Thailand by the process of economic development would quickly assert themselves politically, forcing government to become more accountable to their interests. And yet, for the most part, businesspeople in both countries shied away from active involvement in politics; the business elite commanded considerable wealth, but little political influence. The explanation for the disjunction of wealth and power was intimately bound up with the ethnic and religious composition of the business classes in these countries.

In both Indonesia and Thailand, business activity came to be dominated by the immigrant community of ethnic Chinese. Although Chinese people had been spreading into Southeast Asia for several centuries, the major waves come in the late nineteenth century. In both Indonesia and Thailand, the immigrant Chinese were concentrated in the commercial world for lack of other alternatives. Indigenous Thais and Indonesians overwhelmingly worked as peasants, while the socially privileged were absorbed into the feudal and colonial bureaucracies. The Chinese were therefore a distinctive minority and their de facto monopolisation of commercial activity earned them some suspicion and resentment from the native people. In Indonesia, the distinction between the Chinese minority and the local population was accentuated by religious differences, as the majority of indigenous Indonesians were Muslims. In Thailand this was less of a problem, as both the immigrant Chinese and the indigenous Thais shared the same Buddhist religion. The integration of the Chinese into Thai society was, however, retarded in the early part of this century by the sheer number of Chinese immigrants arriving. In addition to communal resentment, the Chinese minorities in both Thailand and Indonesia also had to contend with the fact that the governments which emerged in the wake of colonial or monarchical rule adopted nationalist economic orientations and thus sought to promote indigenous entrepreneurship at the expense of Chinese or other foreign businesses. Faced with popular resentment and governmental discrimination, the Chinese communities kept a low political profile and sought to defend their interests by developing clientelistic links with powerful indigenous officials in the upper echelons of the civilian and military bureaucracies. Riggs was so struck by the position of the Chinese-dominated business class that he coined the term 'pariah entrepreneur' to convey a sense of the low social status of businesspeople and their relative political weakness.[2]

Thailand

Thailand is among the few developing countries never to have fallen under Western colonialism. Its modern political history began in 1932 when a group of Western-educated, middle-ranking civilian and military bureaucrats successfully seized power from the centuries-old absolute monarchy. Although these young officials aimed to install a democratic constitutional monarchy, in reality the post-1932 regime succumbed rapidly to the rule of the bureaucratic polity. Once established, the political supremacy of the military-bureaucratic elite continued almost uninterrupted for over four decades from 1932–57. It is helpful to divide these classic bureaucratic polity years into two periods: the first from 1932–57, in which some electoral activities were tolerated; and the second from 1957–73, when even the trappings of democracy were dispensed with.

The first quarter-century following the end of the absolute monarchy saw Thai politics dominated by the leaders of the 1932 coup, especially by two chiefs, Pahon and Pibun, who together served for about twenty years as prime ministers. During this period, coups and counter-coups became a regular feature of political life, as different factions with the bureaucratic and military elite jostled for advantage. (Between 1932 and 1954 there were thirteen coup attempts, or on average one attempt every two years.) Gaining and holding power depended upon a leader's ability to maintain the support of rival factions within the military and civilian bureaucracy. Extra-bureaucratic groups were for the most part politically apathetic, so the question of public support was of little significance to political leaders. Although there was a House of Representatives (whose major role was to elect a prime minister) and competitive elections took place regularly, political parties played no real role and were in fact banned for much of this period. Even the so-called People's Party formed by the leaders of the 1932 coup against the monarchy failed to develop into a coherent organisation. Apart from a few years, only half the members of the House of Representatives were popularly elected, the other half being appointed by the government. In addition, serving military and civilian officials were permitted to hold political offices. As a result, the cabinet and the appointed half of the House of Representatives were overwhelmingly staffed by bureaucrats and soldiers rather than elected or professional politicians. In this situation, politics was organised on the basis of contending factions made up of individuals grouped informally around particular leaders.

Governments during the first phase of the bureaucratic polity in Thailand had little need to resort to brute force to preserve their position. Between 1932 and 1957 the political dominance of the military-bureaucratic elite was founded more upon the passivity and under-organisation of extra-bureaucratic forces than upon repression and exclusion. The absence of political parties and interest groups to challenge the position of the governing elite can be traced back to the fact that Thailand had not been colonised and, as a result, had not produced a mass nationalist movement. (The overthrow of the monarchy in 1932 had involved only a handful of military and civilian officials.) In many other Third World countries the struggle against colonialism served to mobilise much of the population, stirring people into mass political action and providing the foundations for popular political participation following independence. In Indonesia, for example, there was a range of political parties vying for power during the 1950s. In Thailand, however, as late as 1955 a foreign observer could say:

> The contented Siamese, traditionally uninterested in politics and with an ingrained talent for obedience, have never shown the slightest desire for democracy — a phenomenon disconcerting to well-intentioned western visitors. If they are now to enjoy the benefits of democracy it is clear that these will have to be imposed from above.[3]

Rivalry within the ruling elite led to yet another military takeover in 1957 by Marshal Sarit, the first important army chief who did not belong to the generation of the People's Party. Under Sarit and his successor, Thanom, the character of the bureaucratic polity in Thailand became decidedly more authoritarian. Between 1957 and 1973, the military simply dispensed altogether with any notion of encouraging democratic institutions. For most of the period, political and civil liberties were discarded, political parties and elections were banned and the parliament was made up entirely of government appointees — most of whom came, of course, from the bureaucratic and military elite. In order to legitimise his highly authoritarian regime, Sarit set about promoting rapid economic growth and deliberately moved to revive the dignity and public role of the monarchy. Paradoxically, however, these moves — stimulating rapid economic growth and rehabilitating the monarchy — unleashed forces which ultimately come to challenge the very foundations of the bureaucratic polity in Thailand.

Through its integrity, commitment to the public interest and dedication to the improvement of the welfare of the common people, the royal family regained within a decade the overwhelming respect and admiration of the nation and, in so doing, became an effective rallying point for democratic forces working in opposition to the authoritarian regime. In 1973, in the face of massive anti-government demonstrations, the revered king succeeded in persuading the military to give up the control of the country and then proceeded to appoint a caretaker prime minister in his own right. Equally spectacularly, in 1981 the royal family managed to gather enough loyal troops around them to save the democratically installed government from attempted coups.

If the revived monarchy has turned out to be an extra-bureaucratic force capable of checking the bureaucratic polity from above, then students and businesspeople have worked similarly from below. The emergence of these two modern urban forces has been caused to a great extent by the exceptionally high economic growth initiated by Sarit. During the 1960s and 1970s Thailand enjoyed an average annual GDP growth of 8.4 per cent.[4] Between 1965 and 1986 the Thai average GNP per capita grew 4 per cent annually; only thirteen countries in the world outranked Thailand in this respect.[5] Importantly, expansion of the private sector (rather than the public sector) was the main engine for this spectacular rate of economic development. Sarit and his colleagues gave up anti-Chinese nationalism of the previous regimes, turning instead to a policy of gradually integrating the ethnically Chinese middle class and business community into the mainstream of Thai society.

College students, many of whom had a Chinese ancestry, were the first of the new groups spawned by the processes of rapid socioeconomic change to become politically assertive. In 1973 they led a popular uprising which, with the previously mentioned help of the king, succeeded in toppling the regime that had been founded by Sarit. In the wake of the demise of the military regime there was an extraordinary growth in the level of mass political participation. One manifestation of this was that in the following three years there were 1333 strikes and 322 demonstrations,[6] as activist students, in co-operation with emerging associations of peasants and workers, pressed for a multitude of social reform measures. The military viewed these developments with mounting alarm, seeing the instability as a threat to national security. In a dramatic move, the army seized power again in 1976 and ruthlessly suppressed the popular movement. Since then, the students, peasants and workers have been unable to regain the same political prominence.

The repressive government that came into being as a result of this bloody coup could not, however, return the country to a bureaucratic polity format for long. Following widespread resistance from the educated urban elite, the new military was itself deposed by yet another coup. Recognising that the days of the bureaucratic polity were now gone, the succeeding regime accepted the need to move towards sharing power with extra-bureaucratic forces. Under the arrangements which subsequently unfolded, although military support continued to be a prerequisite for political survival, it was accepted that governments should come to power on the basis of free and competitive elections. However, because three or more parties were usually needed to construct a parliamentary majority, party leaders were often unable to decide who among themselves would serve as prime minister. Consequently, until 1988 the ruling parties opted to invite respected retired generals to serve as prime ministers and as ministers in selected portfolios.

In this more open and stable political environment, business began to emerge as a major political force. Responding to the unprecedented opening of political and electoral opportunities, a legion of highly educated and 'Thaiified' Chinese businessmen poured into parliament and the cabinet. Between 1983 and 1988 there were more than three times as many parliamentarians with business backgrounds as with bureaucratic backgrounds. Even more evident of the business strength was the fact that, among the 206 cabinet members serving under Prime Minister Prem between 1980 and 1988, as many as 88 members (i.e. about 43 per cent) came from the business community.[7] By contrast, of the 174 men who served in all cabinets of Pahon and Pibun between 1933 and 1944, only five were non-bureaucrats;[8] of the 85 men serving as cabinet members under Sarit and Thanom between 1959 and 1973, only five had a business background.[9]

But the emergence of business as a political force did not centre only around political parties; the 1980s also saw business interest groups increase markedly in number and importance within the policy-making process. In part, this greater willingness among business leaders to undertake open and collective political action reflected the successful integration of ethnic Chinese into Thai society. By 1973, some 87 per cent of presidents of trade associations already held Thai citizenship. The assimilation of ethnic Chinese was also indicated by the fact that by the early 1970s, children of businessmen, presumably mostly of Chinese origin, constituted almost one-third of the bureaucratic elite (special grade officers). Conversely, a substantial number of the offspring of bureaucrats have entered the traditionally Chinese-dominated business executive ranks. A 1979 survey found that one-fifth of the business elite were children of government officials.[10] However, the increased importance of business associations was also stimulated by the economic crisis which confronted Thailand in the early 1980s. The economic downturn at this time was so severe that the government needed to consult with and seek the support of business groups in reforming the country's regulatory environment and making the Thai economy more internationally competitive.

While the history of trade associations in Thailand goes back to the nineteenth century, in 1975 there were only 75 trade associations in Bangkok. By 1979, however, this number had risen to 124 and by 1987 to 177. Even more striking was the proliferation of provincial chambers of commerce. In 1979 there was only one chamber in each of four provinces; by 1987 chambers of commerce had spread to all 73 provinces of the country. A content analysis of *Prachachart turakij*, an established business newspaper, reveals that between 1979–81 and 1985–87, the frequency of reports on activities of trade associations and chambers increased by about 87 per cent. Moreover, there are numerous cases demonstrating the effectiveness of business associations in initiating, deflecting or blocking import public policies.

Generally, the growing cohort of business associations operated independently of each other and dealt directly with the relevant government agencies. Significantly, however, the 1980s also saw the emergence of corporatist-style links between government and peak business associations with the establishment of the Joint Public and Private Sector Consultative Committees (JPPCCs). At the national level, this high-calibre committee is headed by the prime minister and brings together representatives of the largest business associations and senior government officials. A similar pattern operates at the provincial level, with the governor heading the committee. Since the early 1980s the JPPCCs have played a decisive role in bringing about reforms keenly sought after by business, such as the reduction of bureaucratic red tape, the elimination of double taxation and the promotion of economic deregulation. There can be little doubt that business associations emerged the strongest of all interest groups in Thailand during the 1980s, far surpassing student, farmer and peasant associations.

The introduction of more democratic political institutions and the emergence of new societal forces — especially business forces — meant that Thailand was gradually moving away from its bureaucratic polity past. The power of the military-bureaucratic elite declined further during the late 1980s, when Chatichai Choonhavan, the elected leader of Thailand's largest political party, succeeded Prem Tinsulanond (an army man) as prime minister. Under Chatichai, for the first time since 1976, virtually all cabinet positions were filled with elected politicians. Even the Interior Ministry, which had long been a military fiefdom, was occupied at one point by an ethnic Chinese businessman-turned-politician. The Chatichai government is generally regarded as having performed well, although there was concern about the extent of corruption and log-rolling that had been allowed to develop under Chatichai's free-wheeling style of leadership. Serious problems began to emerge, however, in late 1990 as a result of a series of quarrels between the government and the military establishment. Then, in a surprise move, the military launched a successful coup, forcing Chatichai from office and reinstating martial law.

While the 1991 coup clearly runs against the flow of developments of the 1980s, it seems unlikely that military leaders in Thailand will again been be able to reinstitute the bureaucratic polity of old. As of mid-1991, the military junta undoubtedly reigns supreme through its appointment of the prime minister and members of the legislative assembly in the interim regime. However, people with non-bureaucratic backgrounds, especially those from backgrounds in business, make up a substantial component of the current cabinet and the legislative assembly. Most importantly, the new prime minister, Ahand Panyarachun, was, at the time of his appointment, president of the Federation of Thai Industries (FTI), the most powerful peak business association. Other important cabinet positions are also taken by former FTI directors, Ajva Taolanon (now Deputy Minister of Agriculture) and Arsa Sarasin (now Minister of Foreign Affairs). Several independent business and banking technocrats have been included in the cabinet as well. On the basis of currently available evidence, although martial law prevails, the new regime does not vest all power in the hands of the military-bureaucratic elite, unlike the classic bureaucratic polity regimes of the past. Businessmen and technocrats are at least junior partners in the interim government. Moreover, the inclusion of prominent technocrats such as Snoh Unakal, the architect of the JPPCC system, suggests that the inclusion of business associations within the policy-making processes of the state will be maintained.

The 1991 coup reminds us that the military remains a potent force in Thai politics and democratic institutions still occupy a precarious position. Yet, in spite of this, it is also clear that the days of the classic bureaucratic polity in Thailand have now passed. The central position of the monarchy and the rise of societal forces — especially business forces — means that political life is now considerably more complex and pluralised, and not easily susceptible to control by a small clique of army officers and civilian bureaucrats. Regardless of whether future Thai governments take an authoritarian or semi-democratic form, power is very unlikely to be monopolised by a narrow military and bureaucratic elite again.

Indonesia

Despite important differences in the two countries' political and economic make-up, as in Thailand, the bureaucratic polity occupies a central place in Indonesia's modern political history. Indonesia did not begin to move in the direction of becoming a bureaucratic polity until the late 1950s when President Sukarno abandoned parliamentary democracy and returned the country to the earlier 1949 constitution which provided for a strong presidency and more centralised form of government. During the so-called guided democracy period which followed, power became concentrated around Sukarno and senior military officers. However, in 1965 a coup and counter-coup brought Suharto to power, as discussed in Chapter 26.

Suharto's rise to the presidency in March 1968 marked the beginning of what has been called the 'New Order' period. While the movement towards a bureaucratic polity began in the late 1950s under Sukarno, it was under Suharto that power became more tightly concentrated at the apex of the state structure and the exclusion of societal groups from effective political participation became more systematic. During the near quarter-century that Suharto has been in power, Indonesia has been seen by many scholars to come to resemble Riggs' bureaucratic polity model quite closely.

In the early years, Suharto was supported by a broad coalition comprising sections of the military and civilian bureaucracy, student groups, political party leaders, and business and Muslim groups. This picture began to change, however, as Suharto moved steadily to centralise power around the presidency. Before long, extra-bureaucratic groups were disabused of any illusions that they might come to share in power; effective influence was concentrated in the hands of a relatively small group of senior military officers and civilian officials (particularly the so-called 'technocrats' or Western-trained economists) surrounding Suharto.

With the support of the military, Suharto and his key advisers were able to restructure the political landscape in Indonesia, implementing institutional changes which minimised the scope for political participation by extra-bureaucratic groups. Much attention was directed to the political parties and the nascent interest groups. In the case of the former, although the Communist Party had been destroyed in the wake of the 1965 coup (see Chapter 26), New Order leaders remained very wary of the remaining political parties, fearing their potential to mobilise large sections of the population and challenge the authority of the new regime. As a result, in the early 1970s the government developed a new party framework which ensured that they would not develop any independent momentum. The nine remaining political parties were forced to merge into two new parties, one (the PPP) amalgamating former Muslim parties and the other (the PDI) former nationalist and Christian parties. By a variety of means, the government was able to make certain that these two parties remained weak and compliant. At elections the PPP and the PDI have always been swamped by the very much larger state political party, Golkar. However, even Golkar has lacked any real life of its own, tending instead to function as little more than an electoral vehicle for the government. While it has been able to secure ever-larger majorities at elections, it has had no real role in the development of policy.

Political parties were not the only representative organisations to be brought to heel. Just as the government secured a very tight grip on the political parties in the 1970s, so it also moved to limit the scope for interest organisations to develop significant political capabilities. Government strategists adopted what amounted to a corporatist system for the containment of interest groups under which gradual steps were taken to create, sponsor or designate particular organisations as the official body to represent the interests of almost all segments of the social and economic spectrum. Many of these organisations (or functional groups) were gathered under the umbrella of Golkar, which ostensibly served to aggregate public demands. The government maintained a close watch on the largest such organisations (e.g. the peak trade union and business bodies, the teachers' association and the civil servants' organisation) and was able to ensure that those who rose to leadership positions within them were amenable to 'guidance'. Though in formal terms the corporatist bodies were important advisory and consultative organs, in practice they were peripheral to power. What emerged over time was a pattern in which officially sanctioned interest organisations tended to become formalistic and docile, and to play little role at all in terms of feeding membership demands into the policy process.

The efforts of Suharto's New Order government to minimise the scope for political participation by extra-bureaucratic groups have not been in vain; from the early 1970s onwards, power has become ever more concentrated in the hands of the president and the circle of senior officials surrounding him. Importantly, not even the business elite, with the very considerable financial resources at its disposal, was able to secure a significant share of power. A number of factors explain the ability of the government to exclude even business leaders from the policy process.

The first and most obvious is that the government has consistently worked to keep business organisations from developing any real political momentum. In the same way as it has kept interest groups in other sectors on a tight leash, the government has kept a close check on the activities of business associations. And it is widely recognised that most of the organisations nominally responsible for representing the interests of business people are in fact lame and unwilling to push business demands in the face of government opposition. This is particularly true of the peak organisation, the Indonesian Chamber of Commerce and Industry.

A second, and probably more important, factor explaining the political weakness of business relates to the structure of the Indonesian economy. Put simply, the political overshadowing of business by the state has roughly corresponded to the relative importance of the state and the private sector in the economy. The state has had a massive involvement in the economy, both as macroeconomic manager and as financier and investor in the economy. Indonesia has historically had a relatively small local private sector, with state-owned enterprises dominating many key sectors of industry. Direct state involvement in the economy was extended in the 1970s and early 1980s as a result of the OPEC-induced boom in oil prices which resulted in vast sums of money flowing into the government's coffers. With up to two-thirds of its revenue coming directly from oil and gas at the beginning of the 1980s, the state enjoyed a high degree of fiscal autonomy. Because the state did not rely on the private sector to generate taxation revenue, there was, correspondingly, little need to heed its grievances. Without economic leverage, it has been difficult for business activists to bargain with policy-makers.

A third factor which can be seen as having impeded the development of organised business influence is the ethnic composition of the local business class. This concerns the already-mentioned fact that the business class in Indonesia is largely made up of ethnic Chinese, something which has stimulated persistent communal resentment. At times, hostility towards Chinese Indonesians from the indigenous majority has exploded into violence. The political vulnerability of the Chinese minority has for many years ensured that few Chinese businesspeople have been willing to involve themselves in the public promotion of business causes. Instead, individual businesspeople have pursued their own personal interests by cultivating covert links with senior military and civilian figures within the government. While clientelistic links of this sort enabled some to amass great wealth, they did not afford them the opportunity to influence broader policy decisions.

The final major factor contributing to the traditional political weakness of business is a long-standing ideological ambivalence, if not antipathy, towards the principles of capitalism in Indonesia. Reflecting the country's colonial past, notions such as free-market competition and profit-making have for many years been ritually derided by political leaders who have branded capitalism as a Western phenomenon alien to Indonesia. Even though official rhetoric has often been a poor guide to political practice, the reality of an ideological climate unsympathetic to capitalism has served as a significant constraint on the political advancement of business interests.

While some of the factors contributing to the inability of business to secure effective representation in the policy process do not apply to other sectors of society, one can readily identify a general pattern of political exclusion and monopolisation of power by the state elite. Firm government control has been one of the hallmarks of political life in Indonesia since the 1960s. It has been achieved through close government oversight of political parties, the parliament and interest groups. In addition, the press has had to operate within certain boundaries, avoiding politically sensitive matters with a bearing upon the country's leadership or national security. The government has been able to sustain its firm grip on politics through a combination of 'carrots and sticks'. The carrots have been the very real economic benefits which have been brought to most of the population as a result of the country's rapid economic development. In addition to a general increase in living standards, the government has been able (thanks largely to the oil boom revenue) to 'buy' political stability by distributing special resources to particularly disgruntled segments of the community. At times, however, the government's economic carrot has proved insufficient compensation for some groups in society. In these situations when political demand-making has broken out of the structures designed to contain it, the government has been able to rely on the armed forces to suppress any unrest.

And yet, while this picture remains accurate in important respects, there is reason to believe that the government's ability to control political life is beginning to dissipate. In other words, there are signs that the bureaucratic polity image of political life in Indonesia is of diminishing value. As has become well known in recent years, there have been sweeping political changes in many parts of Asia, Eastern Europe and Latin America, with authoritarian regimes of various types giving way to more democratic forms of government. Indonesia has not been entirely insulated from this trend. As speculation has mounted about the possibility that President Suharto may step down when his current term expires in 1993, there has been an unusual level of public discussion concerning the prospects for greater political openness and even democratisation in Indonesia.

One sign that the government's ability to limit political participation may be beginning to ebb is the restiveness that has been evident in the national parliament since about 1988. While the party system itself remains feeble, some sections of the parliament are evidently increasingly dissatisfied with the effective exclusion of the legislature from the political process. Interestingly, it has been the parliamentary members of Golkar and the armed forces (that is, the sections of the parliament most closely aligned with the government), rather than members of either of the non-government parties, who have been most effective in articulating demands for the parliament to be permitted to perform the executive oversight and legislative responsibilities which, in theory, are vested in it by the constitution. While at this stage the actual impact of this parliamentary restiveness has been limited, it is a clear example of political behaviour which runs counter to the traditional bureaucratic polity pattern of political exclusion and the centralisation of power.

An even more conspicuous indicator of growing uncertainty about the government's ability to maintain its strategy for political containment has been the recent upsurge in political debate under the rubric of *keterbukaan*, or openness. One of the most interesting features about this wave of open political debate about the existing political framework and implicit criticism of the government is that it has emanated from a wide variety of sources. Not only have we seen student groups voicing critical demands, but also parliamentarians from both Golkar and the armed forces blocs, the press and other politically articulate elite groups and individuals have been outspoken. The open political debate surrounding the notion of *keterbukaan* is remarkable both because of the vein of dissatisfaction it reveals and, more fundamentally, because of the protracted and public manner in which it has taken place. And here there can be little doubt that the persistence of open discussion about the country's political future has taken place with, at the least, the acquiescence of the military leadership. Responding to these pressures, in his Independence Day speech in August 1990, President Suharto attempted to regain the political initiative by speaking himself of the need for political reform, more open debate and a relaxation of press censorship.

Less conspicuous than either of these developments, though probably of greater long-term significance, has been the gradual transformation in the character of a number of the state-sponsored interest groups. From having been compliant and docile bodies serving primarily to restrict demand-making, some of these organisations are coming to take on a more active role and are assertively projecting the demands of their members into the policy-making process. This is especially apparent in some sections of the business community, as well as in a number of the professions. While a number of factors have been involved, the key to the newly emerging political assertiveness of these groups appears to have been the sharply deteriorating economic circumstances of the mid-1980s. Squeezed by the depressed economic conditions, some sections of business have become more assertive and more determined to ensure that their problems are adequately communicated to policy-makers. Equally, however, the tougher economic climate has forced the government to slash its own expenditure, reduce the level of direct state involvement in the economy and rely to a much greater extent on the private sector both as a source of tax revenue and as an engine for growth.

As emphasised earlier, far from being effective mouthpieces for business concerns, many of the bodies officially responsible for promoting business interests have for many years been rather placid institutions sponsored by the government. However, activist business leaders have become increasingly dissatisfied with the fact that these bodies provide little or no capacity to promote business causes and project specific demands into the policy-making process. This has led in some cases to moves by reform groups to overhaul particular industry associations in order to bolster their capacity to secure a voice in policy-making debates. While many business organisations remain docile — including the Chamber of Commerce and Industry — a number of the smaller industry-specific business associations have become increasingly energetic and outspoken. This represents a fundamental change from the old pattern in which such organisations would basically absorb and contain member demands rather than promote them.

These various developments all raise questions about the government's ability and willingness to maintain its firm grip on political participation. Emerging societal groups are becoming more assertive and more determined to ensure that their grievances are lodged on the political agenda; simultaneously, competition within the state elite is producing cracks in the barriers previously insulating the policy process and facilitating the concentration of power in the hands of a relatively small number of people. While political life in Indonesia clearly remains very restricted, there is reason to believe that, unless the government resorts increasingly to brute force, its capacity to limit demand-making and political participation by groups with organisational resources seems to be receding. As in Thailand, political and economic life has become too complex to permit power to be monopolised by a small group of army officers and civilian officials.

Conclusion

The bureaucratic polity model is a useful guide for interpreting Thai and Indonesian politics for much of the period since World War II. Certainly there have been important differences between the two, most notably the fact that in Indonesia the bureaucratic polity has been consistently associated with an authoritarian style of government. This has not always been the case in Thailand. Although hardly democratic, the various governments during the early bureaucratic polity years in Thailand (1932–57) were not particularly authoritarian. During this period, the bureaucratic polity in Thailand was based on the weakness of societal groups and classes rather than straightforward repression. In Indonesia, by contrast, the nationalist struggle against the Dutch resulted in a relatively high level of political mobilisation in the early post-independence years. Consequently, when Sukarno and the army ended democratic government in the late 1950s and began the transition to a situation in which effective power was confined to the bureaucratic elite, an authoritarian style of rule was necessary in order to exclude groups and institutions which had previously played a significant role in political life.

The central argument of this chapter is that while Thailand and Indonesia have indeed approximated the bureaucratic polity for many years, they are currently going through a period of transition and their resemblance to Riggs' model is declining. In both countries there is a process of political pluralisation taking place, the result of which is that new forces are coming into play and the bureaucratic elite is no longer able to monopolise influence over the policy-making process as it once did. As emphasised, this process has gone considerably further in Thailand than in Indonesia. There appear to be three broad sets of reasons for this: the pace of economic change, the extent of Chinese assimilation and the structure of the political system in each country.

Undoubtedly the impact of rapid economic development has been central to processes of political change in both countries. Economic development has resulted in the emergence of a national bourgeoisie and, more broadly, the creation of an increasingly educated middle class. This, in turn, has resulted in demands by groups within these new classes for increased political participation. However, if we compare the economic profiles of the two countries, it is evident that the processes of industrialisation have gone further and that income per capita is higher in Thailand than in Indonesia. Table 31.1 shows clearly that agriculture remains more important than manufacturing (a sub-sector of industry) in Indonesia. In Thailand, however, manufacturing has already surpassed agriculture. In short, Thailand is both more economically advanced and more prosperous than Indonesia. A corollary of this is that the development of a local business and middle class has gone further in Thailand than in Indonesia.

Table 31.1 Thailand and Indonesia:
Comparative economic indicators

	GNP per capita (US$)	Distribution of GDP (%)							
		Agriculture		Industry		(Manufacturing)		Services	
	1988	1965	1988	1965	1988	1965	1988	1965	1988
Thailand	1000	32	17	23	35	14	24	45	48
Indonesia	440	56	24	13	36	8	19	31	40

Source: World Bank

Another variable relating to economic structure, which helps explain the fact that the transition away from a bureaucratic polity is more advanced in Thailand, is the larger economic role played by the Indonesian state. As noted earlier, the fact that the state sector overshadowed the private sector in Indonesia until recently has been an important check on the expansion of the political muscle of business in Indonesia. While the Thai state has certainly not pursued a *laissez faire* strategy, it is clear that it has involved itself much less extensively in the economy than its Indonesian counterpart and, equally, that distrust of private enterprise and the market have dissipated more quickly in Thailand than in Indonesia. In structural terms, then, the private sector in Thailand is of considerably greater significance and this has facilitated its more rapid entry into the political limelight. Significantly however, since the mid-1980s, state intervention in the Indonesian economy has been gradually pared back and the private sector is now coming more to the fore.

Closely related to the more limited economic role of the Thai state is the fact the social integration of the Chinese minority in Thailand has proceeded much more rapidly than in Indonesia. While the Indonesian business class continues to be widely stigmatised as a Chinese enclave by the indigenous majority, this problem has largely passed in Thailand. As a result, business is less politically defensive and more willing to participate openly and collectively in political life. In short, the breakdown of ethnic barriers has facilitated moves by the Thai business elite to challenge the bureaucratic elite's grip on power. Broad-based indigenous resentment towards Chinese Indonesians has been an important factor contributing to the enduring support for extensive state intervention in the economy; it has long been recognised by the bureaucratic elite in Indonesia that if market forces prevailed, wealth would become even more concentrated in the hands of the Chinese.

The final key variable accounting for Thailand's more rapid movement away from a bureaucratic polity concerns differences in political structure between the two countries. Put simply, for most of the bureaucratic polity period, Indonesia's political system has been more centralised than that of Thailand. In Thailand, the emergence of the monarchy as a key political institution has, at crucial junctures, served as a counterbalance to the power of the cabinet and, in particular, the military. Although part of the state structure, the Thai monarchy has been politically distinct from the bureaucratic elite. Lacking any parallel to the Thai monarchy, power in Indonesia has been centred to a very great extent around the presidency. A second consideration here is the fact that in Indonesia, particularly under Suharto, there has been an extensive campaign of political engineering to construct pliant institutions which would contain any demands for political participation by nascent societal groups. In other words, rather than simply relying on military force to repress any extra-bureaucratic opposition, under Suharto there has been a wide-ranging proactive strategy of channelling politically active groups into toothless political parties and state-dominated corporatist institutions. In Thailand there was no comparable effort to preserve the bureaucratic polity on the basis of pre-emptive political restructuring.

For a variety of reasons, then, Thailand has moved more rapidly — if fitfully — away from a bureaucratic polity than Indonesia. Nevertheless, despite the difference in the pace of change, the longer term trend in both countries is that the grip of the military and civilian bureaucratic elite on power is being challenged by the emergence of new societal groups seeking greater scope for political participation.

Guide to further reading

The bureaucratic polity model has been the dominant framework for Western and Thai scholars of Thai politics. The model also gains wide currency among scholars of Indonesian politics. For examples of works on Thailand using this framework, see Girling, J.L.S., *Thailand: Society and Politics*, Cornell University Press, Ithaca, 1980, and Chai-anan Samudavanija, 'Democracy in Thailand', in Diamond, L., Linz, J. & Lipset, S.M., *Democracy in Developing Countries: Asia*, Lynne Reiner, Boulder, Col., 1989.

For works on Indonesia, see Jackson, K.D., 'Bureaucratic Polity: A Theoretical Framework for the Analysis of Power and Communications in Indonesia', in Jackson, K.D. & Pye, L.W. (eds), *Political Power and Communications in Indonesia*, University of California Press, Berkeley, Cal., 1978; Crouch, H., 'The New Order: The Prospect for Political Stability' in Fox, J.J. et al. (eds), *Indonesia: Australian Perspectives*, Research School of Pacific Studies, ANU, Canberra, 1980; and MacIntyre, Andrew, *Business and Politics in Indonesia*, Allen & Unwin, Sydney, 1991.

John Girling has done the pioneering work in comparing Southeast Asian nations on the basis of the bureaucratic polity model; see his *The Bureaucratic Polity in Modernizing Societies: Similarities, Differences and Prospects in the ASEAN Region*, ISEAS, Singapore, 1981.

Notes

1   Riggs, Fred W., *Thailand: The Modernization of a Bureaucratic Polity*, East-West Centre Press, Honolulu, 1966.

2   ibid.

3   *The Economist*, vol. CLXXVI, no. 5854, 3 September 1935, p. 779, as quoted in Emerson, Rupert, *From Empire to Nation*, Beacon Press, Boston, 1960, p. 271.

4   World Bank, *Thailand: Managing Public Resources for Structural Adjustment*, World Bank Publication, Washington DC, 1984, Table 2.1, p. 7.

5   World Bank, *World Development Report 1988*, Oxford University Press, New York, 1988, Table 1, pp. 222–23.

6   Samudavanija, Chai-anan & Bunbongkarn, Suchit, 'Thailand', in Ahmad Zakaria & Crouch, Harold (eds), *The Military–Civil Relations in South-East Asia*, Oxford University Press, Singapore, 1985, p. 89.

7   See Loathamatas, Anek, 'Business and Politics in Thailand', *Asian Survey*, vol. 28, no. 4, April 1988, Table II.

8   Calculated from data given in Riggs, *Thailand*, Table 30, p. 316.

9   Calculated from data given in Pipatseritham, Krirkkiat, *Economic Change and the Human Rights Issue in Thailand* (in Thai), Thammasat University Press, Bangkok, 1985, Table 9.3, pp. 472–75.

10 Prasartset, Suthy, *Thai Business Leaders*, Institute of Developing Economics, Tokyo, 1980, p. 36.

32 | The prospects for regional economic integration

> Separate economic blocs, and all the friction and loss of friendship they bring
> with them are expedients to which one may be driven in a hostile world where
> trade has ceased, over wide areas, to be co-operative and where are forgotten
> the healthy rules of mutual advantage and equal treatment. But it is surely
> crazy to prefer that.

So British economist John Maynard Keynes told the House of Lords in
1945. Perhaps policy-makers in Western Europe and the United States
believed that their world was in fact hostile enough to warrant such
expedients. Belgium and Luxembourg had already formed their own
separate economic bloc in 1921. They had chosen then the form of a
customs union, abolishing tariffs and all other restrictions on trade with
each other and adopting a common tariff against imports from other
countries. They joined with the Netherlands to establish the Benelux
Customs Union on 16 April 1946. Then the sixteen European countries
receiving financial aid from the United States under the terms of the
Marshall Plan set up a study group on 12 July 1947 to examine the
prospects of forming a customs union among any or all of their members.
United States spokespeople encouraged their efforts in increasingly
peremptory terms. Senator Henry Cabot Lodge told the United States
Senate Foreign Relations Committee on 20 January 1948 that the incidence
of American aid to Europe should be determined by the rate of progress
of economic integration among the recipient countries. Under-secretary
of State John Foster Dulles said that there was a vital need for a customs
and monetary union in Europe. And Administrator of the European
Recovery Program Paul G. Hoffman made it clear in October 1949 that
what Washington understood by economic integration in Europe was
nothing less than the creation of a huge customs union such as that
represented by the then 48 states of the United States itself.

There were obvious problems with such a model. It was one thing for
the former American colonies to abandon sovereignty in matters of trade

when they agreed to form a single nation. It was quite different for the independent states of Western Europe to do the same thing. But economic considerations were not the prime factors here. Planners in Washington found it easy to believe that the only way for the Europeans to recover from the devastation of World War II, to be preserved from communism and to be deterred from fighting one another again was for their economies to be integrated inextricably. It was also all too easy to believe that the economic system of the United States was the ideal pattern for the rest of the world to follow, given the enormous disparity in terms of prosperity between the United States and most of the rest of the world at the time.

The Europeans had an even more convincing incentive. European economic recovery depended in the first instance on the recovery of Germany, as the most dynamic element on the Continent. But the leaders of those countries which had been victims of German aggression were determined that Germany should never again be in a position to act in such a manner towards its neighbours. This meant that the Germans would have to learn to identify the interests of the rest of Western Europe with their own. And this meant that German economic development would have to be linked with that of other European countries so intimately that war among them would be seen to be mutually ruinous and indeed made physically impossible.

All this led to an incentive without precedent in the history of international relations. On 9 May 1950, French Minister for Foreign Affairs Robert Schuman launched a proposal for the integration of the coal and steel industries of France and West Germany and other European countries willing to participate, under the direction of a High Authority of International Civil Servants, charged primarily with ensuring that the liberalisation of trade in coal and steel products among the members did not lead to unemployment or a decline in living standards for the workers in the industries involved.

Italy and the Benelux Union joined with France and Germany to set up the European Coal and Steel Community on 12 March 1951. The same six then committed themselves under the terms of the Treaty of Rome on 25 March 1957 to extend their association to encompass the establishment of a United Europe by the development of common institutions, the progressive fusion of national economies, the creation of a common market and the progressive harmonisation of their social policies. It was the genesis of what was to emerge as the most awesome concentration of economic power in human experience. And the daring, vision and sheer originality of the European initiatives could not fail to inspire similar ventures among other countries in the world outside the European continent.

All this, of course, did not mean that what the West Europeans were doing would necessarily have beneficial results if practised by people in very different situations, or even that it was necessarily beneficial to the Europeans themselves. Economic integration is like prayer, in that it is impossible to prove that anything which might come about after it has been put into operation would not have come about anyway. Its basic idea derives from customs union theory, which argues that removing restraints on trade within an enlarged common market enhances productivity by maximising opportunities for competition and reducing unit costs. What, however, cannot be calculated in advance is how far any gains in productivity thus accruing would offset the social costs of business failure and consequent unemployment and whether enhanced trade among members would compensate for diversion of trade from partners outside the union. Such factors cannot be demonstrated one way or another, and it is difficult to argue rationally about what cannot be demonstrated. The fact is that European economic integration was not motivated primarily by economic calculations. Its essential impetus came from considerations far more emotional and even irrational, conveyed brutally in the words of *Combat*, once the underground broadsheet of the French Resistance and later the voice of Democratic Socialism in postwar France, which declared on 21 February 1957 that:

> [the] movement towards European economic integration is now irreversible
> . . . At a time when the disunited countries of Europe are the playthings of the
> hostile forces that divide the world, it is not presumptuous or utopian to think
> of bringing about the union of the oldest civilised peoples on earth.

There are a few reasonable guidelines, however. It might be impossible to be certain in advance whether any proposed form of economic integration would be worth embarking upon or not. But it is reasonable to assume that it would be more likely to be rewarding if the economies of the countries concerned were at comparable levels of development and not too disparate in size, with similar wage levels, unit costs and social welfare policies; if they imposed significant tariff restrictions on imports from one another and if foreign trade accounted for a high proportion of their Gross Domestic Products (GDP); if they had similar or at least familiar and mutually comprehensible languages, customs and legal systems; and if they could rely on the expertise of competent and honest public servants and managers to handle the administration of their union. They would also have to be basically free-market economies, accepting the general principle of free competition, or there could be no mutual benefit accruing from their association; and it would seem essential for them to be similarly aligned in foreign policy and committed to remaining so.

These guidelines would narrow the field of prospective candidates down a good deal. Canada and the United States might seem obvious prospects. So would the Latin Americans, at least in some respects, though attempts to form a Central American Free Trade Area and a wider

Latin American Free Trade area foundered on mutual distrust, disinterest and what appeared to be a failure to agree on the simple arithmetic of tariff harmonisation. There were, however, two countries which possessed almost every possible qualifications as partners in some form or other of economic union, and which were also sufficiently interested to embark on such a venture. Australian Minister for Primary Industries John McEwen and New Zealand Minister for Overseas Trade John R. Marshall announced on 11 April 1963 that they had been examining trends in trade between their two countries; that they had considered measures which might be adopted to check this trend and encourage a mutually beneficial expansion of trade; and that it had accordingly been decided to set up a Joint Standing Committee to devise proposals for 'a free trade area in forest products and other items suitable for inclusion in a free trade arrangement, either from the outset or subsequently'.

A free trade area differs from a customs union primarily in that the member countries retain their separate tariff regimes against outsiders. Nor is it assumed that social policies will be harmonised or any other steps taken towards actual political integration. It is, however, the case that there are so few working examples of either form of association, and those examples are so different in their circumstances, that very little in the way of general rules can be assumed about either. A free trade arrangement between Australia and New Zealand nonetheless seemed, *prima facie*, a very reasonable proposition. Their traditions, social policies and wage structures differed as little as those of any two other countries on Earth, and external trade accounted for an impressive 20 per cent of New Zealand's GDP and 16 per cent of Australia's. Trade between them was admittedly not too substantial. Australia took a little less than 5 per cent of New Zealand's exports and supplied some 19 per cent of its imports, while New Zealand took 6 per cent of Australia's exports and supplied fractionally less than 2 per cent of its imports. But Australia's share of trans-Tasman trade included 87 per cent of New Zealand's exports of manufactures and New Zealand's share included 26 per cent of Australia's, which were very significant figures indeed.

They did not become much more significant during the first few years of the New Zealand–Australia Free Trade Arrangement (NAFTA). Fear had been expressed that economic union between the two countries might be seized on as an excuse for them both to ignore Asia. This was not happening. Exports to Australia indeed rose over the first five years from 4.8 to 8 per cent of total New Zealand exports, but New Zealand imports from Australia increased only marginally from 18.5 to 20 per cent. Trade with New Zealand actually declined as a proportion of total Australian external trade, and the increase in importance of New Zealand exports to Australia might well have reflected merely the impact on the direction of New Zealand trade of diminishing access to the British market, consequent on the entry of the United Kingdom into the European Community.

Another modest experiment in regional economic co-operation was meanwhile achieving even more modest progress. Indonesia, Malaysia, the Philippines, Singapore and Thailand signed the Declaration of the Association of Southeast Asian Nations (ASEAN) in Bangkok on 8 August 1967. Trade liberalisation among the members was not even listed among its aims and purposes. These were merely to 'accelerate the economic growth, social progress and cultural development in the region through joint endeavours in the spirit of equality and partnership'. Committees were instituted and annual meetings of Foreign Ministers called for, but no administrative machinery set up and no timetables prescribed.[1]

Integration was evidently not on the order of the day for the ASEAN five. It was not surprising that co-operation did not seem all that much in evidence, either. Bernardo M. Villegas concluded that 'after twenty years of ASEAN's existence . . . economic co-operation within ASEAN has proceeded at a snail's pace'.[2] Zakaria Haji Ahmad similarly observed that attempts at practical measures of co-operation as in 'the ASEAN Industrial Projects (AIP), ASEAN Industrial Joint Ventures (AIJV), in the reduction of tariff barriers . . . and even a private-sector effort in the form of the ASEAN Finance Corporation (AFC), have all foundered'. He considered that there was a very simple explanation for all this. It was that 'ASEAN is a grouping of economic competitors trying to sell to the same external markets', which was a prescription for a cartel, rather than for any kind of economic union. And in any event there was, 'as also seems clear, official resistance to any major step towards a common market arrangement'.[3]

A flurry of new initiatives emerged on this rather dispiriting scene in 1980. Australia and Japan staged the Pacific Economic Co-operation Conference in Canberra, for non-official discussions on regional economic issues among businesspeople, academics and officials participating in a private capacity. Meanwhile, the Australian and New Zealand governments publicly recognised the self-evident truth that their free trade arrangement was not providing sufficient impetus to the kind of co-operation likely to serve best the interests of their two countries in the changing conditions of the world economy. They announced on 4 June 1982 that NAFTA would be replaced on 1 January 1983 by a Closer Economic Relationship (CER), having as its central objective the gradual and progressive liberalisation across the Tasman of all goods produced in either country. Export incentives were to end by 1987 and import restrictions by 1995.

New Australian Prime Minister Robert J. Hawke pursued the notion of regional economic co-operation further in a visionary address to the Australia–Thailand Chamber of Commerce in Bangkok on 22 November 1983, claiming that Australia was 'committed to building a strong, mutually beneficial economic relationship with its neighbours in ASEAN and the wider region of Asian and the Pacific'. He was supported by Japanese Prime Minister Nakasone Yasuhiro. It appears that their immediate practical objective was to organise pressure within the region for the liberalisation of trade so as to be able to negotiate more effectively with the European Community. Such a concern became even more urgent when the Europeans agreed in July 1987 on the Single Act to bring about, by 1992, a unified market that would constitute the greatest agglomeration of economic power on earth. This in turn prompted the Americans and Canadians to agree, on 1 January 1989, to form a North American Free Trade Area by the end of the century. *Asiaweek* warned its readers (on 13 December 1988) that 'within five years most of the world's wealthiest nations will be presenting common economic fronts to each other and the rest of the world'.

Regional economic co-operation might well have seemed to be an idea whose time had come. Prime Minister Hawke told a luncheon of Korean Business Societies in Seoul on 31 January 1989 that he had directed Australian missions in the region to canvass opinion on 'the possibility of creating a more formal inter-governmental vehicle for regional co-operation'. Their approaches had in fact already elicited a bewildering variety of responses, some more attractive than others. Nakasone proposed a Pacific Forum for Economic and Cultural Co-operation; United States Secretary of State James Baker favoured an organisation of key regional powers to co-ordinate broad economic policies; and some State Department officials spoke frankly of what amounted to an alliance to protect, perpetuate and promote American values. What nobody was suggesting was anything along the lines of European-style economic integration. Mr Hawke recognised this reality when he assured the Korean businesspeople that nothing that he had said should be 'interpreted as suggesting by code words the creation of a Pacific trading block'.[4] And Australian Minister for Foreign Affairs and Trade Senator Gareth Evans insisted in London that it has been 'firmly agreed by all those in the region that we are not seeking to create an Asia/Pacific trading bloc. Nor would we support such a development.' He considered nonetheless that 'none of the existing structures quite met the requirement for a broad regional dialogue . . . aimed at identifying — across a wide front — common economic interests'.

Twenty-seven ministers representing the putative United States/ Canada Free Trade Area, the ASEAN five, the Australia/New Zealand

CER, Japan, South Korea and Brunei Darussalam assembled in Canberra over 6–7 November 1989 for the first meeting of the Forum on Asia/ Pacific Economic Co-operation (APEC). Australian diplomat Richard Woolcott hailed the event as 'one of the most important international meetings since Bretton Woods', which was the genesis of the International Monetary Fund.[5] Its practical achievements were not quite of that order. Members agreed to review data on regional trade flows and technological and economic developments; to institute procedures to assist such reviews; to meet again in Singapore in 1990; and not to form any kind of regional trading bloc. This might well have been the limit of agreement possible among what the *Australian Financial Review* (on 16 November 1989) categorised as an 'odd combination of members, which are otherwise united by neither geography, history nor culture'. 'What of India?' the *Financial Review* asked. 'And if it is the Pacific, where are the Island States of the Ocean itself, or Mexico, Venezuela and Chile?'

It might have been more pertinent to ask, where the Soviet Union, China and Taiwan were, since they were all in or on the Pacific, whereas Venezuela of course was on the Atlantic. But the *Review's* geographical confusion was not surprising: the fact was that the whole logic of the original project had been eroded by its being extended to the 'American Hemisphere'. The term 'Asia-Pacific' has meaning as a distinct concept only if restricted to those Asian countries the shores of which are washed by the Pacific Ocean, and by extension to island states actually in the Pacific (see also Chapter 2). These obviously would include Japan. They might reasonably include Australia and New Zealand. But the term loses all meaning if stretched to include countries which are neither part of Asia nor actually in the Pacific, such as those composing the continents of North and South America.

Problems of identity might seem intangible, but they are quite important: one cannot very well know what one is supposed to do if one does not know what one is supposed to be, or where one is supposed to be, as in this instance. And it would have been difficult enough to discover elements of common identity even among the strictly limited group of Northeast Asian, Southeast Asian and South Pacific countries which Mr Hawke had originally envisaged as participants in APEC. Soviet Foreign Minister Eduard Shevardnadze, speaking for the country with the longest Pacific coastline in the world, called for an Asian summit to be hosted by the United Nations in Vladivostok in 1993, for the purpose of laying the groundwork for European-style integration in the region. But the obvious response was made by Chairman of the Nissho Iwai Corporation, Mr Masaru Hayami, who warned the Australia–Japan–Canada Economic Issues Symposium that the world economy was moving towards a tri-polarisation of Europe, North America and Asia, but that it would be difficult to create an Asian trading bloc of any kind because of the 'considerable differences among countries — in racial make-up, religions, languages, customs, history and culture, not to mention economic power'.

Such differences indeed made the prospects for Asia-Pacific economic integration incomparably less propitious than had been the case with the Europeans. It was possible to talk sensibly of a common European culture, a common European religious tradition and a common European historical experience resting on the tangible basis of a common European geographical contiguity, as implied in the claim of a Vatican spokesman that 'the Europe of history, of culture, of the faith, goes as far as Vladivostok'. It was also the case that the founding members of the European Community had all ben parliamentary democracies; they had comparable wage levels and production costs; they all had highly developed manufacturing industries and substantial agricultural sectors; they traded largely with one another already; and their respective levels of economic output were roughly similar, both overall and per head. But such unifying factors were markedly absent from the Asia-Pacific region. What were strikingly present by contrast were factors for disunity. Economically, Australia and New Zealand are major resource and commodity exporters, with relatively small and uncompetitive manufacturing sectors; Japan, Korea, Taiwan and Singapore have massive and highly competitive manufacturing sectors, with minimal natural resources; the other Southeast Asian nations could be described as basically primary producing countries in the process of developing highly productive manufacturing industries; and China is both an industrial power and a producer of resources on a continental scale. Disparities of national wealth are best indicated by noting that Japan's GDP overall is ten times that of Australia, while Australia's GDP per head is 37 times that of Indonesia and 60 times that of China.

Culturally, Australia and New Zealand are predominantly European and formally Christian; the Philippines is a volatile amalgam of Austronesian/Malay, Spanish and North American elements, with the Christian religion overwhelmingly predominant; Malaysia and Indonesia are secular Islamic states; and China, Japan, South Korea, Taiwan and Thailand all reflect in varying degrees the traditional cultures of the Middle Kingdom. Politically, Australia and New Zealand are model Western-type parliamentary democracies, while most of the other members of the region might be categorised as dominant-party states, either institutionally or in effect, or as democracies tempered by coups. And this is not to mention the abiding ethnic and historical tensions among the regional countries, one of the effects of which is to make it impossible for Japan to presume to the kind of leadership role which Europeans are positively pressing Germany to exercise in their part of the world.

It might well have seemed hardly promising to pursue any form of economic integration among countries so disparate, culturally, ethnically, politically and geographically, even if they did in fact transact a large part of their external trade with one another. But the difficulties could only be multiplied by involving in the process countries from other continents and totally different cultures which also transacted the greater part of their external trade outside the region. Only 29 per cent of United States exports went to Northeast and Southeast Asia; only 9 per cent of Canadian; and only 5 per cent of Mexican. And most of the exports of the North American group to the region went to Japan anyway.

Australian Minister for Foreign Affairs and Trade Senator Gareth Evans nonetheless suggested at the 5th APEC Ministerial Meeting in Bangkok on 12 September 1992, that the association might become 'as integrated, harmonised and coherent economically and possibly politically as the European Community'. Japanese representative Mr Nobuthoshi Akao maintained more realistically that APEC should remain as originally conceived, in no sense a formal union of any kind, the members of which were bound to act in a certain way, but 'merely facilitating consultation'. It was agreed admittedly that 'institutionalisation could further strengthen APEC's role and enhance its efficiency in promoting regional economic cooperation'; but that meant no more in practice than setting up a permanent secretariat in Singapore.[6] However, a Re-Report of the Australian Senate Standing Committee on Foreign Affairs, Defence and Trade submitted in December 1992 proposed that APEC could also have a significant function as 'an important tool in reducing the risk of fracture in economic relationship across the Pacific'.[7]

This was the first official recognition of the fact that extending the concept of Asia-Pacific to include countries which were in no sense part of that region incurred problems more substantial than those of mere logic, identity, geography or direction of trade. The risk of fracture to which the Senate Committee alluded arose out of the fact that the United States government had since late 1984 been seeking to remedy the mushrooming United States trade deficit by pursuing a variety of economic strategies deliberately aimed at subverting the economic interests of a number of Asian countries, including fellow members of APEC. Four distinct strategies were being employed to this end. First was the Export Enhancement Program, under which the President was required to subsidise United States agricultural exports so as to undercut traditional suppliers in global markets, particularly affecting Australia, the initiator of APEC. Second was the MOSS, or Market-Oriented, Sector-Selective strategy, in terms of which Washington had been pressuring Japan under threat of sanctions to guarantee American exporters agreed percentages of the Japanese domestic market in sectors in which the

Americans represented themselves as being competitive, regardless of indicated consumer preference. That this had nothing to do with free trade principles as such was indicated by the testimony of United States Commerce Secretary Ron Brown that removal of barriers will not be the ultimate measure of our success — sales will. Third was the North American Free Trade Agreement (NAFTA), which economist Milton Friedman said should be called the North American Managed Trade Agreement because it retained so many restrictions on free trade. This had been conceived by the Bush Administration as a means of frustrating attempts by Asian and European companies to gain access to the United States market by establishing subsidiaries in Mexico. The Clinton Administration has since proposed that it should also be employed to extend the MOSS strategy of managed trade to other regional countries as well as to Japan, by involving them in bilateral arrangements with NAFTA through a system of 'hubs and spokes', which Australian Ambassador to Japan Rawdon Dalrymple said would mean 'the hub getting the best arrangements for itself, and complex and costly arrangements among the spokes'.[8] And finally there was the application or threat of various economic and other sanctions on alleged human and animal rights grounds against Asian countries with which the United States was running trade deficits, as with China, Indonesia and Taiwan, or pursuing a macabre vendetta, as with Vietnam.

These developments posed particular problems for Australia, as the countries against which Washington was pursuing these strategies were in fact Australia's major trading partners and the regional countries which were achieving the highest rates of economic growth, and were in consequence precisely the ones which the APEC project had been introduced to enhance Australian relations with in the first place. The hope was expressed, however, that APEC might represent 'the concept around which those fearing further US efforts to manipulate world trade can rally' in defence of the principles of free trade which all its members pretended to espouse. Senator Evans said that there was no thought at the present stage 'of moving to anything so ambitious as an APEC-wide free trade agreement'; but that the organisation was nonetheless 'taking the first tentative steps towards exploring the possibility of tariff reduction or removal in individual sectors', which of course would have meant moving towards a free trade agreement. What he was really thinking of was made clear by his further comment that such regional trade liberalisation measures were best pursued in the first instance in sectors where trade was heavily concentrated within the region, such as steel, which happened to be a sector that the Clinton Administration was preparing to subject to new protective measures.

Senator Evans' aspirations for APEC failed to thwart the advance of United States neo-mercantilism, carried out behind the smokescreen of an unreserved commitment to universal free trade in general and to APEC in particular. President Clinton affirmed that the United States 'would continue to welcome foreign goods and services into our markets, but insist that our products and services be able to enter theirs on equal terms'. United States Trade representative Mickey Kantor put it more forthrightly, declaring that the overall trade policy of the Administration was 'to expand [US] trade through market-opening measures backed by rigorous enforcement of US laws'; his office published a 275-page report, accusing 44 countries of unfair trade practices, with fellow APEC member Japan singled out as the biggest perpetrator; anti-dumping duties of up to 109 per cent were imposed on imports of steel from nineteen countries including fellow APEC members in Japan and Australia; and regional concerns were heightened by Mr Kantor's assurance to a Congressional Committee that the Administration was going to try to use the opportunity provided by chairing APEC 'to really open up and put a framework around APEC'.[9]

Malaysian Prime Minister Dr Mahathir evoked against this possibility of an American takeover of his project an East Asian Economic Caucus (EAEC), comprising the ASEAN countries, Japan, China and South Korea, which would be only a consultative body, but would at least have the advantage of precise geographic boundaries, as well as being unambiguously Asian in identity. Australian Prime Minister Paul Keating, whose country was specifically excluded by Dr Mahathir from EAEC, insisted that Australia was committed to APEC precisely because it embraced the main economic linkages between the Western Pacific and the United States. And Singaporean Prime Minister Goh Vok Tong thought that there was a possibility of developing a Pacific-Asia Free Trade Area (PAFTA) big enough to develop its own trade even without Europe, if NAFTA could reach out to countries in Asia through APEC, although he did not think it would make much difference either way so long as GATT remained at all effective. Waves of German and French trade delegations were in any case providing more than sufficient evidence that there was no question of the region ever having to develop its trade without Europe.

An Australian cartoonist suggested that what was really achieved at the much-heralded December 1993 APEC meeting in Seattle was that the national leaders agreed that they all agreed to agree again on their agreements when next they agreed. That might indeed have been a sterling effort for an association which had been looking progressively more amorphous and incoherent since its inception. What they did in fact agree on was to hold another informal meeting the following year in Jakarta; to take the first steps towards a regional investment agreement; to analyse avenues towards free trade in the region; and to admit Papua New Guinea and Mexico as members, with Chile to be considered for membership in 1994. What was more important than what they agreed to do was what they agreed *not* to do, which was to convert the association into any kind of a discriminatory trading bloc, to suit the interests of its non-Asian members. Japanese Minister for Foreign Affairs Mr Tsutomo Hata insisted that the association should never degenerate into exclusive regionalism. Chinese President Jiang Zemin declared that it should remain an open, flexible, fairly loose forum for economic co-operation and an organisation for consultation, reminding the impatient Australians and Americans of the old Chinese proverb that 'a meal should be eaten one mouthful at a time'. And the Malaysians and Indonesians rejected an Australian–American proposal that the 'C' in the acronym should be understood to stand for 'Community', asserting that 'community' was a rather elastic word and they were very happy with 'Co-operation'.

It was not surprising that the Asians should have been unresponsive to manifestly self-serving attempts by Washington and Canberra to exploit regional economic success to their own national ends. Nor was it surprising that extending the concept indefinitely on both sides of the Pacific would not only have the effect of making it looser as it became wider, but would also positively encourage the development of smaller, more coherent groupings within its framework, as had in fact also been happening in Europe.[10] It might in any event be questioned whether the very notion of economic integration based on the existing nation-states was not itself an anachronistic concept, whose time had perhaps gone before it had ever really come.

A secret report of the 'Eminent Persons Group' of APEC, fully circulated before the Seattle Meeting, had recognised that 'the Asia-Pacific has not needed regional institutions' to achieve an advanced level of economic co-operation. What was actually emerging in the Asia-Pacific as in Europe was a 'soft' regionalism, with 'geo-economic patterns rapidly replacing existing geo-political alignments'.[11] This trend manifested itself first in the informal 'sister' relationships between cities, states, provinces and areas in different countries. These informal relationships were now evolving into more elaborate structures of 'growth triangles' of contiguous regional zones of common economic interest, overlapping national frontiers. Best established was that of Singapore, the Malaysian State of Johore and the Riau Islands of Indonesia. Work had also started on the Northern Triangle linking southern Thailand, northwestern Malaysia and northern Indonesia. Further north still, officials of the Asian Development Bank were encouraging the development of the Mekong region, linking China, Burma, Laos, Vietnam, Cambodia and Thailand. Indonesia and the Philippines had agreed to study a further triangle, straddling eastern Indonesia, the southern Philippines and the Malaysian State of Sabah.

Overwhelmingly the most spectacular in terms of current growth is the emerging association of Guangdong Province in China with Hong Kong and Taiwan. And greatest in its potential significance would be the proposed Tumen River Scheme, linking the northern provinces of China, Russia Far East and Korea, with Vladivostok serving as a major Asian gateway for Europe as well as a European gateway to the Asia-Pacific. It might seem prudent to suppose that processes of this kind could be the wave of the future of Asia-Pacific economic integration in a postmodernist world, rather than notions from the past introduced from outside the region, to serve the interests of countries which are not in it.

Guide to further reading

Discussion of customs union theory and of other concepts of international economic theory is of necessity abstruse, technical and speculative in the extreme. It is also somewhat irrelevant, since no models exist which have any bearing on the current situation, and since political considerations invariably dominate economic ones in this issue anyway. The shortest and most intense theoretical analysis is provided by Tinbergen, Jan, *International Economic Integration*, Elsevier, Amsterdam, 1965. Krauss, Melvyn B. (ed.), *The Economics of Integration*, George Allen & Unwin, London, 1973, is a more extensive and less abstract study. Woronoff, Jon, *World Trade War*, Praeger, New York, 1984, presents a more helpful survey of the dislocations in global commerce resulting in the main from confrontations between the European Community and other major agricultural exporters.

Essential background reading from an Australian perspective is Garnaut, Ross, *Australia and the Northeast Asian Ascendancy*, AGPS, Canberra, 1989, and National Pacific Co-operation Committee, *Report to the Australian Government on Australia and Pacific Economic Corporation*, Australian National University, Canberra, 1985.

Notes

1   Thailand, Ministry of Foreign Affairs, *Foreign Affairs Bulletin*, vol. 7, no. 1, August–September 1967, pp. 74–76.

2   Villegas, Bernardo M., The Challenge to ASEAN Economic Co-operation', *Contemporary Southeast Asia*, vol. 9, no. 2, September 1987, pp. 120–28.

3   Ahmad, Zakaria Haji, 'Introduction', *Contemporary Southeast Asia*, vol. 9, no. 2, September, 1987, pp. 79–85.

4   Australia, Department of Foreign Affairs and Trade, *Monthly Record*, vol. 60, no. 1, January 1988, pp. 5–7.

5   Woolcott, Richard, 'Australia's Role in a Changing World', Address to the Australian Institute of International Affairs, Brisbane, 10 August 1990.

6   Australia, Department of Foreign Affairs and Trade, *Backgrounder*, 19 October 1990.

7   Australia, Department of Foreign Affairs and Trade, *Insight*, vol. 1, no. 5, 21 September 1992, p. 3.

7   Australia, Parliament, Senate Standing Committee on Foreign Affairs, Defence and Trade, *Implications of United States Policies for Australia*, Canberra, Australian Government Printing Service, 1992, pp. 83–87.

8   Rawdon Dalrymple, 'Current Situation and Future Perspectives of the Asian and Pacific Economies', Speech to the EXIM Bank of Japan Symposium, 28–29 October 1992.

9   See *inter alia* 'Clinton Explains His International Program', United States Information Agency, Official Text, 5 April 1993; 'Lord Lays Out 10 Goals for U.S. Policy in East Asia', United States Information Service, Official Text, 5 April 1993; 'Barshefsky Addresses Asian, Latin American Trade Policy', USIA, Wireless File EPF 511, 21 May 1993.

10 Glen St J. Barclay, 'Breathing with Two Lungs: Australia and the New Order in Europe', *Meanjin*, vol. 52, no. 1, Autumn 1993, pp. 117–33.

11 Mark J. Valencia, 'Economic Cooperation in North-east Asia: The Proposed Tumen River Scheme', *Pacific Review*, vol. 4, no. 3, 1991, pp. 263–71.

33 | Family change in postwar Japan and China

The political and economic changes in Asia since the end of World War II have had major social and cultural implications for the region. Among them there are few which affect ordinary people as much as those with an influence on the family.

Social change refers to change in social structure, social institutions and customs. Social change may or may not accompany modifications to values, ideals and attitudes held by the majority of people in a society. This latter change is called cultural change and is conceptually distinguished from social change, although they are closely related. This chapter deals with both types of change, and focuses on the change that has occurred in the family organisation. It aims to investigate the nature and the extent of change in the family organisation in postwar Japan and China.

Japan

The end of World War II marks a break with the past in terms of the legal and political systems of Japan. Transformation of the society, however, was not initiated nor accomplished by these postwar politico-legal alterations. The postwar constitution and other legal changes definitely facilitated a process of social change by giving a direction and legal support to the changes which had been generated much earlier in the Meiji era (1868–1911), when Japan began to industrialise its economy.

It has been argued that industrialisation brings about certain changes in family organisation. Although the relationship between the two has not been systematically demonstrated, it is generally accepted that industrialisation accompanies a change in the family structure from an extended family type to a nuclear family type where the central relationship is the tie between a husband and a wife. Whether this sort of change has also occurred or is now underway in non-Western societies has not been empirically established. The following pages try to show, firstly, what changes have occurred in the Japanese family organisation in the postwar era; secondly, to what extent the changes have been promoted by industrialisation; and thirdly, how the values and ideology of the society have interacted with the process of change.

Size and structure of household

The baseline against which we assess the nature and the extent of change is the prewar *ie* organisation discussed in Chapter 4. The size of the prewar Japanese household was on average not very large, with the mean number of persons per household having been around five.[1] This is firstly due to the *ie* system itself, because the ideal form of the *ie* household was a stem family household. Secondly, high infant and premature mortality rates and short life expectancy prevented the family from growing in size in prewar times.

A first sign of decline in the household size appeared after 1955. In the ten years between 1955 and 1965, the Japanese household size had fallen from 5.0 to 4.1 (see Table 33.1). This is an extremely rapid decline, as it took the United States 50 years from 1880 to 1930 to record a drop of the same order. The Japanese household size has steadily declined since, and in 1985 the average size was 3.2 persons. This shrinkage in household size has resulted from two factors: lower birth rates and changing household structure.

Table 33.1 Change in household size in Japan 1920–85

Year	Number of persons per household
1920	4.99
1930	5.07
1940	5.10
1950	5.02
1955	4.97
1960	4.52
1965	4.08
1970	3.44
1975	3.32
1980	3.25
1985	3.17

Source: Institute of Population Problems, *Nihon no jinkohendo no gaikan* (An Outline of Demographic Trends in Japan), Ministry of Health and Welfare, Institute of Population Problems, Tokyo, 1988, p. 106

Birth rates began to decline in prewar days with the advent of industrialisation, as young women started to participate in the non-agricultural and non-domestic labour force (e.g. factory work), after finishing six years of compulsory education. This delayed their marriage, and hence reduced the proportion of child-bearing women in the population. Real decline in fertility, however, is a postwar phenomenon. After the postwar 'baby boom', a drastic fall in birth rates was recorded in 1950 and 1955. The rates stabilised in the 1960s and 1970s, but in the 1980s the decline in birth rates further accelerated, as Table 33.2 indicates.

Table 33.2 Change in birth rates in Japan, 1920–85

Year	Birth rates (per 1000 persons)
1920	34.9
1930	31.7
1940	30.7
1947	33.8 (postwar baby boom)
1950	23.8
1955	18.2
1960	17.3
1965	18.7
1970	18.8
1975	17.1
1980	13.6
1985	11.9

Source: Institute of Population Problems, *Nihon no jinkohendo no gaikan* (An Outline of Demographic Trends in Japan), Ministry of Health and Welfare, Institute of Population Problems, Tokyo, 1988, p. 20

Why have Japanese couples decided to limit the number of their children? Firstly, it has become extremely costly to raise children in the postwar society. Whereas before the war children contributed to the household economy from a young age, in postwar Japan children do not participate in the labour force until they have finished at least nine years of compulsory education, and in most cases three more years of senior high school education. This period is further extended when children receive post-secondary or tertiary education. Education beyond the compulsory level is not free in Japan, and increasingly costly educational expenses must be borne by the family. Secondly, Japanese couples no longer need to fear that they might lose some or all of their children before they reach maturity, thanks to the advances in medical technology, public health and nutrition. Thirdly, more and more Japanese women remain in the labour force longer as job opportunities open up to them, thus delaying marriage and shortening the child-bearing period. And fourthly, people in general aspire to a higher standard of living.

All of the above act against having and raising many children. Industrialisation has changed the lifestyle of Japanese people and their attitudes towards family, education and other matters. Children are still desired, but only a small number of them. Thus means of birth control available in postwar Japan have been widely used. Limiting births by contraception or abortion does not go against the religious or other traditional values held by the people, and this has also encouraged the trend. As a result, most Japanese couples today have only one or two children.

Reduction in household size is also attributed to the increasing proportions of nuclear-family households and single-person households in postwar Japanese society (see Table 33.3). Abrogation of the *ie* system and the associated practices in the 1948 Civil Code have facilitated the trend, but the process was fundamentally due to the changes which occurred in the occupational structure and to the resultant extensive urbanisation. Migration to urban centres existed in prewar days as some of the non-inheriting sons and daughters of rural *ie* moved to urban centres for non-agricultural employment, but extensive urbanisation did not occur until after Japan had recovered from the defeat of the war and had begun to expand its industries.

Table 33.3 Distribution of households in Japan by type of household (%)

Year	Nuclear-family households	Extended-family households (stem family households)	Single-person households
1920	54.0	39.0 (31.0)	6.6
1955	60.6	36.0 (32.6)	3.4
1965	62.6	29.6 (24.3)	7.9
1975	64.0	22.4 (22.2)	13.6
1985	62.6	19.9 (19.7)	17.5

Source: Yuzawa, Yasuhiko, *Gendai Nihon no kazoku mondai* (Problems of the Contemporary Japanese Family), Nippon Hoso Kyokai, Tokyo, 1987, p. 7

Note: 'Household' in these statistics is defined as a group of people sharing a domicile and a living, or a person forming an independent domicile. It excludes those who are living in boarding houses, dormitories and institutions.

The urban population grew rapidly in the 1960s, which were a time of unprecedented industrial development in Japan. Changes in farming technology after the postwar land reforms (1946–47) were an integral part of this process, contributing to wide-scale migration of people from the rural areas to urban centres. Having become owners of small pieces of land, Japanese farmers eagerly adopted mechanical and other technological devices available to improve their yield. This dramatically cut the need for labour. Despite heavy investment in farming technology, however, the agricultural growth rates were much lower than those of the expanding industrial sector. This has made agriculture a less rewarding and unattractive enterprise to the majority of the Japanese. Young people who saw no future in remaining in the rural areas chose to migrate to cities to obtain a wage/salary-earning job or to further their education and training. Most of these young people stayed in the city, married and established a nuclear-family household there.

The proportion of nuclear-family households (parents and unmarried children only) has increased in postwar Japan but, as Table 33.3 shows, over 50 per cent of households were already nuclear-family households in the prewar years. This indicates that nuclear-family households were not directly produced by postwar industrialisation; rather, it can be argued that certain features of the Japanese family organisation (e.g. stem-family system and single-heir inheritance) have facilitated the process of urbanisation, by providing necessary labour for industrialisation. (A stem family consists of parents, an only child and his or her spouse and children.) We can also note from Table 33.3 that in recent decades the proportion of nuclear-family households has changed little, after having reached a plateau in the mid-1970s. The rate of decline of extended and stem-family households has also slowed down since 1975. Recently, we have seen the proportion of single-person households increasing. This is partly due to an increasing proportion of the elderly now living alone. Stem-family households still persist, however. At present, one out of every five households is a stem-family household, although the present-day stem family households differ in their organisation from the traditional *ie* households, as will be explained later.

Marriage and mate selection

Marriage was universal in prewar Japan. Nearly every man and woman married at least once before they reached middle-age. As marriage was indispensable for the perpetuation and expansion of the *ie*, it was not a matter left to two inexperienced individuals, but the concern of the entire *ie*. The extensiveness of marriage has continued in postwar Japan, despite the abolition of the *ie* system. Reasons for this lie in the significance Japanese people attach to marriage. The Japanese believe that marriage is a necessary step for a man to be recognised as a socially responsible adult and for a woman to have children and become socially and economically stable. Motherhood is intimately tied to the Japanese feminine identity. Until recently, it was also difficult, if not impossible, for a single woman to lead an independent life in Japan.

It is therefore considered undesirable to remain unmarried beyond a certain age. This implies that social pressures exist in Japan for a person to be married before he or she passes a suitable period for marriage. This period is known as *tekireiki* (marriageable age). *Tekireiki* applies to both women and men in Japan, but the pressure to be married while one is at *tekireiki* is felt much more heavily by women than men, because a suitable timespan for marriage is set shorter for women than men. In this respect there has been very little change in the postwar era.

Nonetheless, there have been a few important changes regarding marriage and mate selection since the end of the war. Firstly, marriage has become the basis for establishing a new household in postwar Japan. In prewar days, most marriages were aimed at joining a husband's or wife's parental *ie*. Even those who established a branch household were under the control of the parental household. The postwar Civil Code changed this by abolishing the *ie* system and adopting a separate house registry system for each new marriage.

A second change concerns the age of marriage. The average age at first marriage for men and women was recorded as relatively high in prewar Japan. This is partly due to the fact that the statistics were based on the year in which marriage was registered and not the year in which marriage was consumated. Some marriages were undoubtedly registered later in prewar years, sometimes after the wife conceived or gave birth to a child. If we take the figures in Table 33.4 as they are, the average age at first marriage for men has not changed very much except for a drop of a few years in 1950, while the marriage age for women has steadily risen since 1950. In 1985, Japanese women married on average at 25.5, two or more years later than in prewar times. As a result, the age difference between a wife and a husband has narrowed. The rising average marriage age for women results directly from the fact that women now receive post-secondary or tertiary education and become gainfully employed after finishing formal education.

Table 33.4 Average age at first marriage in Japan

Year	Wife	Husband	Age difference
1920	23.2	27.4	4.2
1930	23.2	27.3	4.1
1940	24.6	29.0	4.4
1950	23.0	25.9	2.9
1960	24.4	27.2	2.8
1970	24.2	26.9	2.7
1980	25.2	27.8	2.6
1985	25.5	28.2	2.7

Source: Institute of Population Problems, *Nihon no jinkohendo no gaikan*, p. 17

Another change which has occurred is in the method of finding a marriage partner. With several years of work experience outside the home and recreational and other extra-work activities, Japanese women today have more opportunities for meeting men and finding a marriage partner on their own than they did a few decades ago, although some people still marry through *miai*. This term literally means 'mutual viewing', and is a formal occasion for marriage candidates to be introduced. It constitutes an essential component of Japanese arranged marriages. Japanese people distinguish *miai* marriage from *renai* marriage. The latter is commonly translated into 'love match', but the fundamental difference between the two does not lie in the presence or absence of 'love', but depends on whether marriage partners have found each other with or without the formal intervention of a third party.

Japanese people enthusiastically welcomed an idea proclaimed in the postwar constitution that marriage should be based on the mutual consent of the two individuals concerned, but in practice most people had to rely on *miai* for finding a marriage partner in the earlier postwar decades, owing to the lack of appropriate opportunities for meeting members of the opposite sex. *Miai* still plays an important role in contemporary Japan, in particular among self-employed people and individuals who have passed *tekireiki*. A little over a quarter of marriages were made through *miai* in the 1980s, while the rest found their marriage partners in other ways, with workplaces and the introduction of friends being two of the most common.

A similar shift in mate selection from arranged marriages to marriages based on individual selection of partners has occurred in other countries which have gone through modernisation and industrialisation. In the case of Japan, however, this is not an entirely new phenomenon, as arranged marriages were not the norm among the ordinary people before the turn of the century. In any case, this shift signifies that today more Japanese people decide to marry after having been acquainted with each other for some time. This fact, along with the previously mentioned narrowing age difference between a wife and a husband, has contributed to the formation of a more egalitarian and communicative relationship between a wife and a husband in the contemporary Japanese family.

Family roles and relationships

One of the principal changes associated with industrialisation is a shift in the labour force from primary industries to secondary and tertiary industries. At the time of the Meiji restoration (1868), approximately 80 per cent of Japan's working population was engaged in agriculture. This percentage gradually fell as industrialisation progressed, but it was not until the postwar recovery was completed in the mid-1950s that the percentage of people who were engaged in agriculture began to drop markedly. With this shift in labour force composition, the workplace was separated from the home for most people. Now the majority of Japanese workers commute to their workplaces, and spend long hours away from home every working day.

As the separation of the two spheres has become established, earning a living has become primarily the husband's responsibility, whereas a domestic and nurturing role has been allocated to the wife. Division of labour by gender certainly existed in prewar Japan, but before the technological advances had reduced the labour need drastically, both men and women participated in farming. In addition, the domestic and nurturing role was not the responsibility of one individual, but was shared by two or more adults in the household. For instance, grand-parents, a mother and possibly a young aunt looked after the children, and a junior wife and a senior wife were both engaged in domestic work, the former being supervised by the latter. In prewar days it was only among a small minority of emerging new middle-class families in cities that the division of labour and the separation of spheres by gender was practised, as it is at present. The division of labour and separation of spheres by gender was the ideal of the *samurai* class during the Tokugawa era, when the *samurai* class constituted a small but prestigious minority. After the Meiji restoration, this *samurai* model was further fortified by the ideal of the Western middle-class family which was introduced to Japan while it was eagerly catching up with the West.

The segregation of gender roles in the postwar era has created the status of the fulltime housewife in urban Japan who devotes her attention and time to running and managing the household and looking after the family members' well-being. Most salary-earning husbands in Japan give their monthly earnings to their wives to be managed. This practice discourages the husband's active involvement in household decision-making, and is used to justify his reluctance to participate in domestic work. As a matter of fact, few Japanese men participate in cleaning, washing, preparing meals, tidying up the kitchen, grocery shopping or managing the household finances. On the whole, the household authority rests with the wife.

The education of children is also considered to be primarily a wife's or mother's role, although about a third of the people surveyed in 1985 believed it should be carried out jointly by a wife and a husband. In prewar days, the education of children was not such a central issue to the average Japanese family. At that time the head of the *ie* was responsible for supervising and training the offspring of the *ie*, and all adult members of a household were involved in child-rearing and disciplining. In contemporary Japan, however, a high school diploma is a bare minimum to obtain a stable job, and in order to succeed in a career, higher educational qualifications are often considered essential. Thus keen competition exists in contemporary Japan for passing an entrance examination to a good high school and to a respectable university. Most Japanese believe that going through this 'examination hell' is a necessary ordeal to gain or retain middle-class status, and that mothers are primarily responsible for supervising their children's studies and making appropriate arrangements for improving and promoting their chance to pass the ordeal. This also enhances the wife's power and authority in the family.

Since the 1960s the model of gender role segregation has been widely propagated through the mass media and school textbooks. As a consequence, most Japanese take it for granted. The model has become so pervasive in contemporary Japan that even mothers with full-time jobs are compelled to follow the same pattern. Most of them manage the double load by obtaining help from a trusted kin member, their mother or mother-in-law. Survey results indicate that there is little difference between the husband of a full-time housewife and the husband of a working wife in terms of the tiny amount of time (several minutes a day) the Japanese husband spends on domestic work and child care.

Turning to family relationships, the emotional distance which previously existed between a wife and a husband has narrowed or disappeared altogether in the majority of today's couples. This results from the fact that most people today choose their marriage partners by themselves on the basis of mutual attraction and affection. The fact that young couples now start their married life in a nuclear-family household further reinforces the degree of closeness between the two. Despite this, however, the conjugal relationship is not the most emphasised or central relationship in middle-class Japanese families. As fathers are away from home until late on working days, children naturally spend more time with their mothers. This fosters a close, affectionate bond between a Japanese mother and her children. This mother–child relationship outweighs the conjugal relationship in the Japanese family.

The segregation of gender roles is not the only reason for a Japanese mother's close emotional alliance with her children. The fact that a Japanese husband and wife rarely share social or leisure activities or common friends also contributes to it. Husbands spend their after-work hours with their workmates or friends, whereas wives associate with a totally different circle of people. Before the birth of a child, a couple may dine out or spend leisure hours together, but after the arrival of a child, such a practice is most unlikely to be maintained, because leaving small children with a babysitter is not regarded as a proper thing to do. A close, affectionate tie, of course, also existed between a mother and her children in the prewar *ie*, although the circumstances were quite different. The degree of the mother's emotional investment is more intense in the contemporary mother–child relationship than it was before the war, since the number of children is now only one or two and there are no other individuals in most contemporary Japanese households.

The elderly and the Japanese family

The traditional Japanese *ie* performed a number of functions. The *ie* was a production unit as well as one which looked after its members' physical, social, emotional and welfare needs. For example, a woman gave birth at home with the help of a midwife and other experienced women, and the mother and the newborn baby were taken care of by the members of the *ie* after her confinement. Similarly, the sick, the handicapped and the aged were all looked after by the *ie*. It was part of the normal responsibilities of the *ie* to provide necessary care and assistance for those who needed them. The contemporary Japanese family is no longer a production unit. Its most important function is that of socialisation and social reproduction. In addition, the family is also expected to perform some of the welfare functions in contemporary Japan, including the care of elderly parents and parents-in-law.

Until 1970, Japan was not an ageing nation. Its elderly population constituted only 4.9 per cent of the total population in 1950, but the percentage rapidly grew in two decades, reaching 7.1 per cent in 1970.[2] The speed of ageing is far greater in Japan than in any Western nation, and this is one of the worrying problems that contemporary Japanese society faces. Early in the postwar era, nearly all elderly people lived with one of their children in the same household. In 1960 the ratio of 'living together' was 87 per cent. This percentage has gradually declined, but in 1985 two-thirds of elderly Japanese still lived with one of their children.[3] The contemporary 'living together', however, is different from the prewar *ie* arrangement. Most young couples today establish their own nuclear-family household upon marriage, and later in their middle age they incorporate their parents or parents-in-law in their household. They form a stem family household, but the younger generation is the centre of the household and the older generation is not necessarily fully integrated, since the household members no longer share the same interests or lifestyle.

Although the above statistics show that the percentage of elderly Japanese living with one of their children has been decreasing in contemporary Japan, it would be premature to conclude that this practice will soon disappear. Over 60 per cent of the adults surveyed nationwide in 1985 considered 'living together with a son's or daughter's family' to be desirable. Only 20 per cent of those surveyed responded that 'parents and married children had better live separately'.[4] Some argue that since Japan's welfare system is inadequate at present, elderly parents are bound to live with one of their children. Nonetheless, the ratio of living with one of their children is higher among the better-off families. Does this mean that if economic circumstances permit, Japanese people prefer to live together with their children? It certainly suggests that factors other than economics are also involved in the decision of whether or not to 'live together'. We must also bear in mind that the present government is promoting the traditional ideal of the family looking after its members' welfare. Further studies are required to gain insight into this issue.

China

We turn next to China, where overall conditions have been extremely different from those prevailing in Japan. Some of the most obvious differences are that China remains much bigger in area and population, even though the population density is very much smaller. China is far more diverse in ethnic and geographical terms than Japan. It is far less prosperous and less industrialised. Another extremely important difference is that China is much less urbanised than Japan, as a result of which those trends towards the kind of modern family values which first grew so extensively as a result of the Industrial Revolution in the West have proved far slower to develop in China than in Japan. The following account has reason to emphasise the differences between the Chinese countryside and cities.

Since 1949, China has undergone a revolution led by the Chinese Communist Party (CCP), which claims adherence to Marxism-Leninism. The CCP has made several sustained attempts to impose this ideology everywhere, but has met with some opposition, especially in the countryside, where passive resistance to rapid change has for centuries been firmly embedded in the social fabric. The family revolution was high on the agenda of the CCP in the early years of the People's Republic of China (PRC). On 1 May 1950, the *Marriage Law of the PRC* was promulgated, which banned arranged marriages, concubinage, polygamy and interference in the remarriage of widows, and laid down equal rights for both sexes. Although the implementation of this law was very much more thorough than earlier laws with similar ideals, it was by no means totally effective. The period of the Cultural Revolution from 1966 to 1976 saw a quickening of the pace in terms of demands for such social changes as a rise towards equality between the sexes. However, the greater freedom which accompanied the thrust towards modernisation in the period after 1978 has, ironically, also brought with it a revival of some traditional forces, including the rural patriarchal family.

One of the main aspects of modernity since 1978 is the attempt to create a properly constituted and implemented legal system. One of the laws introduced has been a second *Marriage Law*, adopted by the National People's Congress in September 1980. It laid down minimum marriage ages as 22 for men and 20 for women and encouraged late marriage. It allowed divorce 'in cases of complete alienation of mutual affection', and forbade a husband to apply for divorce when his wife was pregnant or within a year after the birth of a child, but specifically waived this restriction for a pregnant wife. The law banned infanticide and any discrimination against children born out of wedlock. Article 8 stated that after marriage, 'the woman may become a member of the man's family, or the man may become a member of the woman's family', as the couple agreed.[5]

The fourth, and as of 1995 current, state constitution of China, which was adopted in December 1982, devotes some space to family matters. Under Article 48, 'the state protects the rights and interests of women, applies the principal of equal pay for equal work for men and women alike and trains and selects cadres from among women'. Article 49 confirms that the state protects marriage, the family and mother and child; that parents must bring up and educate children, but that people who have come of age 'have the duty to support and assist their parents'; and that the freedom of marriage is inviolable. It also affirms the policy of family planning and states that the duty to practise it rests with both husband and wife. Equality between the sexes is a clearly guaranteed constitutional right, and the family holds a high priority as a social institution.

Who actually decides on marriage partners for young people? Is there in fact freedom of choice as both the constitution and the *Marriage Laws* declare there must be? A researcher who interviewed 300 women in two cities and four rural areas in 1980–81 found that urban people in general do indeed choose their own spouses according to the law. However, in the countryside, change has been far less rapid and thorough. Her finding was that only 27 per cent of the rural women married since 1950 had known their husbands before becoming engaged to them, 29 per cent met them only after becoming engaged, and 33 per cent did not meet them until their wedding day.[6] An official survey carried out in two counties in Anhui province in the early 1980s found that only 15 per cent of recent marriages were by free choice, 10 per cent had been parentally arranged, and the remainder, or three-quarters, had been 'agreed upon' — in other words, the couples had not actively opposed their parents' choice.[7] These figures sit comfortably with a belief (which is widespread both in the West and in China, and accords with my own explorations in the 1980s and 1990s in China) that in general the choice of rural marriage partners is made by the parents but subject to veto by the people involved, whereas in the cities it is the other way around — in other words, the spouses initiate the choice of partners, which their parents may veto. To be fair, this is an enormous advance since the days when rural women were not even consulted about their spouse, but it falls far short of the real freedom of choice in marriage which the CCP has been trying to put into effect. As a factor in deciding on a marriage partner, family convenience is much slower to yield to love or other factors in the countryside than in the cities.

Courting patterns changed drastically in the 1980s. Love, courtship and marriage are now talked about in the press more than at any time in the past, with the possible exception of the liberal 1915–20 period. On many issues, debate is very intense, but young Chinese, especially men, tend to tie love to the practicalities of furthering their own, and their family's, interests. The point is well illustrated by a cartoon in the newspaper *Chinese Youth News* (23 September 1982) which shows a young man with a piece of paper in his hand reading 'three-part melody'; he has jumped from an oval called 'good work unit' to another entitled 'good job' and is finally, through a larger leap, landing in a third bearing the words 'good girl'.

On the other hand, to marry without love merely for social or material advancement will nowadays arouse disapproval in Chinese cities. One young female correspondent of *Chinese Youth News* (5 September 1982) had fallen very much in love with a man living in a different city, but had been persuaded by her parents to marry someone else whom she did not love so that she could register the marriage and be allocated housing, for which there is always a long waiting list in overcrowded Chinese cities. Then her first love had unexpectedly come to live in her city. Since she was not yet living with her registered husband, she sought advice on whether she should break it off with him and instead marry the man she really loved. She received a stern public rebuke from the editor, who accused her of rashness in having married just to get housing and of a frivolous and selfish attitude towards a serious matter. What she did in the end is not reported, but it does appear such manipulations as hers are not acceptable for men either, and that love, or at least serious mutual affection, competes with convenience as a real factor in urban Chinese marriages.

The age of first marriage of women in China gives some indication of family change. For the Han nationality who made up 92 per cent of the Chinese population, according to the 1990 census, the figures are as follows: 1940 — 17.86; 1950 — 18.5; 1960 — 19.45; 1970 — 20.3; and 1980 — 23.17.[8] This last mean is just over three years higher than the minimum legal age for women under the 1980 *Marriage Law*. The figures show that the rise in age accelerated decade by decade from 1940 to 1980, except in the 1960s, but it is doubtful that the acceleration continued to the 1990s. A Western researcher found that the age of women at marriage stood at just over 25 in 1980–81. In the countryside, however, it was about 23 in the same years. Another interesting finding is that newly-wed men are about four years older, on average, than their wives in Chinese cities and about three years older in the countryside. Both these figures have fallen substantially in recent years.[9] One implication of this is that the number of young women married off to much older men has fallen drastically.

Although the very early years of the CCP's rule saw a rise in the divorce rate over the preceding era, as people were encouraged to escape from arranged and loveless marriages, divorce again became very rare indeed until the late 1970s. In the 1980s and 1990s divorce again developed into a feature of social life in China, especially in the cities. In 1991 there were 9 509 849 registered marriages nationwide, and 828 449 divorces. These figures would mean a divorce rate of 1 in 11.5 marriages,[10] low by the standards of many Western countries, but much higher than in China's past. Another significant change is that it is nowadays usually the woman who files for divorce, whereas in the

Chinese tradition there were several grounds on which men could divorce their wives, but women enjoyed no reciprocal rights.

It appears that the family as an institution is considerably stronger in its impact on the lives of individuals in the countryside than in the cities, where changes have been greater and deeper. In other words, the CCP's attempts to wrest control over the lives of people from the family have been far more successful and thorough among urban than rural Chinese. The years since the early 1980s have probably strengthened the family as an institution in the countryside even more, because the commune system has collapsed. As a result, the authority of the CCP has declined markedly, with the family stepping in to fill the partial power vacuum created.

Another question which has a bearing on the importance and power of the family within society is household composition. The ideal in the past was the extended family, which included parents, married children and their children as well under one roof. The more married children there were, the greater was the prestige which accrued to the family. In practice, only a small minority could afford to implement this ideal, which endowed great authority on the patriarch.

A survey carried out in 1936 in a Chinese village by the famous Chinese anthropologist Fei Xiaotong showed that 10.3 per cent of families were extended, 38.4 per cent stem, 23.7 per cent cent nuclear and 27.6 per cent other. An urban and a rural survey, each carried out by Chinese scholars in 1982, showed a drastic increase in the proportion of nuclear families, and a decline in both of the other types. The findings are shown in Table 33.5. The extended family will probably disappear within a couple of decades simply because of the policy of one child per couple, which is discussed in more detail in Chapter 34.

Table 33.5 Types of Chinese family, 1982

Pattern	Percentage in urban survey	Percentage in rural survey
Nuclear family	74.8	67.7
Stem family	22.0	31.7
Extended family	3.2	0.6

Source: Guo Xuan, 'Changes in Chinese Family Structure', *Women of China*, no. 5, May 1984, pp. 8–9

In traditional times many sons were the ideal. The famous Confucian philosopher Mencius (371–289 B.C.) stated that the most unfilial of all acts was to die without progeny. The function of children, was to carry on the family line and to look after parents if and when they reached old age. So to have a family became a kind of insurance policy. Mortality rates were high and low standards of living with periodic famines were taken for granted for all but the elite, so controlling population growth never became a high priority in government policy.

The new family planning policy, which is discussed in Chapters 34 and 35, has been fairly successful in the cities, but much less so in the countryside. One reason for this is the continuing desire for sons in a context where only one is allowed. Most peasants prefer their only child to be a boy and are willing to pay heavily in terms of fines to 'try again' if it is a girl. Although such practices are of course illegal, some will refuse to register or even kill a girl in order to get another chance for a boy. Despite the law which specifically allows either pattern, the tradition by which most women move into their husband's family when they marry, not the other way around, remains the norm in contemporary China. Thus the expense of raising a girl merely benefits another family in the long term, whereas a boy will grow into a more valuable labour unit than a girl, not only because of his greater muscular strength but because he will attract another productive labour unit in the form of a wife. This means that economic and social factors conspire to favour boys in the countryside.

The rapid rise in the status of women in the first three decades of the PRC thus appears to have been to some extent reversed in the 1980s, at least in the countryside. One Western scholar writes that 'though the revolution for women has never been repudiated, it has been postponed all too many times'.[11] The image of the 'revolution postponed' suggests that it is at the expense of women that the thrust towards modernisation has been carried out. In an interview early in 1989 with an official magazine, the president of the All-China Women's Federation, Chen Muhua, complained that women had been 'the big job losers' in the 1980s, 'since many enterprises sacked women with the belief that they will be an economic burden after they give birth'.[12] Following the mid-1989 crisis in China there was a serious campaign against 'the six evils', which included pornography, prostitution and even the buying and selling of women. These phenomena, which had been widespread before 1949 but appeared to have been more or less eliminated in the first decades of the PRC, were thus officially acknowledged as having revived to an extent alarming enough to require major government action.

However, the picture is not uniformly grim. Women face considerably less discrimination than they did before the CCP came to power. The proportion of cadres (that is, administrators or people in decision-making positions of various kinds) who were female stood at 26 per cent in 1982, incomparably higher than when the CCP took power.[13] The sample census of 1987 found that, since the national 1982 census, more and more women had moved from manual labour to white-collar jobs in commercial services, social welfare, finance and government administration.

'Many women have also found employment in high-tech industries and research, the legal profession, further education and business management,' it claimed. In economic business, the proportion of women rose from 38.92 per cent in 1982 to outnumber men at 50.75 per cent in 1987.[14]

Conclusion

We have examined the Japanese and Chinese family systems in the postwar period from various angles. In certain respects the postwar Japanese family is like the family in the industrialised West. It is small in size and nuclear in structure. Individuals choose their marriage partners mostly on the basis of mutual attraction and compatibility. In other respects, however, the Japanese family is rather different from the Western conjugal family. In the contemporary middle-class Japanese family, the household authority rests with the wife/mother, the mother–child relationship predominates over the husband–wife relationship, and the division of labour and sphere segregation by gender are quite pronounced. Many families also look after their elderly parents or parents-in-law by living with them in the same household.

The existence of these features in the contemporary Japanese family may be interpreted as evidence of a historical link between the present family organisation and the prewar *ie* organisation. This contention is not supported, however, because most of the today's young and middle-aged families have no experience of living in the traditional *ie*. As demonstrated in this chapter, the contemporary Japanese family organisation is fundamentally different from the traditional *ie* in its internal dynamics.

Despite the enormous differences between the two societies, China demonstrates some similarities with Japan. As in Japan, the overall picture to emerge in China is of the continuing strength of the family, and of substantial and fairly rapid change, but with some continuities as well. Probably the changes are greater and the continuities slighter in Japan than in China. In Japan, the changes are due primarily to industrialisation, urbanisation, democratisation and Westernisation, whereas in China they are due more to Marxism-Leninism. Urbanisation and industrialisation, though far from negligible factors in China, have been very much less significant there than in Japan.

The suggestion which was quite frequently made in the 1950s and 1960s that the CCP was attempting to destroy the family in China as an institution has proved to be unfounded. At the same time, the changes in family patterns, including the status of women, have been very far-reaching over the more than four decades since the PRC was established. It is true that there was a revival of some aspects of tradition during the 1980s, including a 'postponement' of many aspects of the women's revolution. But even that reversal, which affected the countryside far more than it did the cities, did not bring the overall situation back to anything like that existing before 1949. Moreover, the standard of living is far higher and the general fabric of society is somewhat stronger than it used to be. The changes wrought by the CCP's revolution in family matters do not look nearly as significant in the early 1990s as they did in the late 1970s, but they are pretty substantial all the same.

Guide to further reading

Goode, William J., *World Revolution and Family Patterns*, The Free Press, New York, 1963, 1970
    This is a classic work on family change. It first presents theoretical issues regarding the universal change in family organisation and family changes in the West, and then examines the family organisation in the non-Western world, including in China and Japan.

Hooper, Beverley, *Youth in China*, Penguin, Harmondsworth, 1985
    This excellent study focuses on the 1980s and the changes in youth over the period. It is based on interview work and experiences in China, as well as copious written material. There are chapters on femininity, love and marriage and other aspects of family life.

Parish, William L. & Whyte, Martin King, *Village and Family in Contemporary China*, University of Chicago Press, Chicago and London, 1978; and Whyte, Martin King & Parish, William L., *Urban Life in Contemporary China*, University of Chicago Press, Chicago, 1984
    This pair of books by the same authors and publisher focuses on what is probably the principal dichotomy of social and family life in China today, namely that between the rural and urban areas. They have a great deal to say about change, and the lack of it, in Chinese society. The first of the two books concludes that peasants are best seen not as traditionalists, modernisers or socialists, 'but as flexible, family-oriented individuals striving to deal with the unique set of problems and opportunities existing in their local village environment' (p. 337).

Rohlen, Thomas P., *For Harmony and Strength*, University of California Press, Berkeley, Cal., 1974
    This is an anthropological study of a Japanese bank organisation. The final chapter deals with marriage and family among the bank employees. Although the focus is on the bank employees, the discussion is equally relevant to the family life of other white-collar employees in Japan.

Vogel, Ezra F., *Japan's New Middle Class*, University of California Press, Berkeley,1963, rev. edn, 1971
    This book is based on fieldwork conducted in a suburb of Tokyo where six 'salaryman' families were closely studied. The book discloses the importance of salary, how to become a 'salaryman', the family and its relations to the outside world, and internal family dynamics. It is indispensable for anyone wishing to study the postwar Japanese family.

Wolf, Margery, *Revolution Postponed: Women in Contemporary China*, Stanford University Press, Stanford, 1985
This is an excellent example among a number of studies of women in China with the focus on the 1980s. It sees the position of women as having risen greatly under the CCP, but is pessimistic about the future and concludes that the reforms of the 1980s have sacrificed the interests of women.

Notes

1   Institute of Population Problems, *Nihon no jinkohendo no gaikan (An Outline of Demographic Trends in Japan)*, Ministry of Health and Welfare, Institute of Population Problems, Tokyo, 1988, p. 106.

2   Institute of Population Problems, *Nihon no jinkohendo no gaikan* , p. 67. When the proportion of the elderly (those who are 65 years old and above) reaches 7 per cent of the total population, a nation is categorised as an ageing nation.

3   Yuzawa, *Gendai Nihon no kazoku mondai*, p. 155.

4   Sorifu Kohoshitsu (ed.), '*Kazoku — katei* (Family and home)', *Gekkan Yoron Chosa*, vol. 18, no. 10, 1986, pp. 50–53.

5   See the text of 'The Marriage Law of the People's Republic of China (1980)', among other places, in *Pacific Affairs*, vol. 57, no. 2, Summer 1984, pp. 266–69.

6   Wolf, Margery, 'Marriage, Family, and the State in Contemporary China', *Pacific Affairs*, vol. 57, no. 2, Summer 1984, pp. 227–28.

7   See Hooper, Beverley, *Youth in China*, Penguin, Harmondsworth, 1985, p. 190.

8   See these figures in Deng Zhixian (ed.), *Minzu renkouxue sanlun (Papers on the Demography of the Nationalities)*, Guizhou Nationalities Press, Guiyang, 1990, p. 52.

9   Wolf, Margery, 'Marriage, Family, and the State in Contemporary China', pp. 222–25.

10 State Statistical Bureau, *Zhongguo tongji nianjian Statistical Yearbook of China 1992*, China Statistical Press, Beijing, 1992, p. 801.

11 Wolf, Margery, *Revolution Postponed: Women in Contemporary China*, Stanford University Press, Stanford, 1985, p. 26.

12 *Beijing Review*, vol. 32, no. 13, 27 March–2 April 1989, p. 9.

13 *China Daily*, 7 March 1983, p. 1.

14 *Beijing Review*, vol. 31, no. 49, 5–11 December 1988, p. 28.

34 | Population: Growth and mobility

Introduction

In many instances the overall development of a country is directly linked to the size of its population, and thus a country's population is generally its most valuable resource. At the same time, for some countries a large population can be their greatest liability. For this reason, the larger Asian countries frequently attempt to restrict their population size, since they believe that if their population is too large, this will inhibit the country's economic development. On the other hand, larger populations have also been perceived as leading to increased power for a country, a view which was maintained by countries such as Indonesia and North Vietnam in the late 1950s, and Cambodia during the reign of Pol Pot in the late 1970s. At the other end of the population spectrum, some of the smaller Asian countries desire to enhance their populations in the belief that a larger population is a prerequisite for future economic development.

Demographically, the Asian region is very diverse, ranging from regions of extremely high population density, such as the islands of Bali and Java in Indonesia and the Red River Delta region of northern Vietnam, to the sparsely populated mountainous countries of Bhutan and Laos. Some of the countries and regions of high population density, such as Bangladesh and northern Vietnam, have a great deal of difficulty in feeding their populations, while other Asian countries, such as Thailand, are net exporters of food.

Countries in the Asian region have had a variety of population policies in recent times. While some countries, such as Indonesia, the People's Republic of China (PRC), Malaysia and Singapore, have perceived that a large population will hinder their economic development, other countries, such as Thailand (in fear of a communist threat) and Cambodia under Pol Pot (for military advancement) have, at times, encouraged population growth.

This chapter seeks to provide a brief discussion of population growth and mobility in the Asian region. The following section on population growth will consider some of the factors which influence changes in population size, and will devote particular attention to one important factor: family planning programs. The next section of the chapter will discuss the issue of population mobility — or, as it is more generally referred to, migration. This particular section will discuss factors influencing migration within Asian countries, migration between Asian countries and emigration out of the Asian region. Table 34.2, at the end of the chapter, provides some basic demographic statistics, some of which will be referred to in the chapter.

Population growth

Population growth results from changes in the three principal demographic variables — fertility, mortality and immigration — as well as changes in the standard of health care. An increase in the fertility rate — that is, the number of babies a woman bears during her lifetime — leads to an increase in the population, if it is assumed that the levels of mortality, emigration and immigration remain constant, and that natural and human-made disasters, such as earthquakes, famines, floods, wars, etc., do not occur. On the other hand, if such disasters do not occur, and the levels of mortality, emigration and immigration remain constant, then a reduction in the level of fertility will result in a decrease in the population size of a country. Under similar assumptions, an increase in the level of mortality or emigration, or a decrease in immigration, will lead to a reduction in population size, while a decrease in the level of mortality or emigration or an increase in immigration will lead to an expansion of the population size. Changes in the direction and magnitude of these three demographic variables, when they are all taken into account at the one time, directly influence variations in population size.

Most of the population growth in Asia since the middle of this century has been a direct result of a fall in the level of mortality, brought about by a rise in the standard of health care, as well as in the nutritional intake and the standard of living of the population. As few countries in the Asian region have a significant level of emigration, a reduction in the level of fertility is thus the only viable means by which most Asian countries can hope to reduce their level of population growth. Another factor which has contributed to rapid population growth in the Asian region over the past few decades is the heavy concentration of women (over one-third in many countries) in the child-bearing age group — that is, between the ages of 15 and 44.

There are essentially five means by which governments may directly influence the extent of population growth:

1 the dissemination of information about population growth and its effects on the country through community education;

2 the implementation of voluntary family planning programs;
3 the stimulation of change in social institutions which will indirectly change the direction and magnitude of population growth;
4 the manipulation of various types of incentives and disincentives which will directly change the direction and magnitude of population growth; and
5 coercion.

Other indirect policies in the economic or social realm may also be implemented with the aim of influencing the level of population growth.

An increase in population size directly results in an increased demand on the infrastructure of a country. If there is a rise in the number of births, then this directly leads to an increase in the demand for medical and educational facilities, as well as in the amount of food that the country must produce or import in order to feed the additional population. There are thus increased economic costs to a rising population. While some of the more developed and prosperous Asian countries, such as Brunei and Japan, are able to meet these increased economic costs without too much difficulty, other less developed and larger countries, such as the PRC, India and Vietnam, cannot meet these increased costs, and thus these countries have adopted national family planning policies which aim to limit their population size.

However, some countries have adopted a mixed (and at first glance apparently contradictory) national population policy. In the mid-1980s, Singapore introduced a selective policy of encouraging population growth amongst citizens who had graduated from university, while at the same time encouraging the poor and the not so well educated to restrict their family size. The aim of this policy was to enhance the overall intelligence of the Singaporean population, which in turn (it was maintained) would contribute to the economic development of the country. If they had more children, those couples who were well educated were given priority access to good educational facilities for their children and to the best welfare services, as well as tax incentives and other financial advantages. On the other hand, the uneducated and the poorly educated were not given these incentives, and disincentives were implemented in order to discourage this group from having large families. Malaysia has also adopted a similar policy of encouraging population growth, but in this case it is limited to the native ethnic Malay population, at the expense of the minority Chinese and Indian communities. The racially based policies of the Malaysian government, especially those initiated under the Third Malaysian Plan (1976–80), were implemented due to the high income and wealth inequalities between the three main ethnic groups, as well as the inequitable occupational distribution of the main ethnic groups, and were aimed at giving more power and wealth to the ethnic Malay population.

Any attempts which are made to change people's attitudes to the number of children they want are often a very difficult enterprise, especially in communities where large families have been the norm for generations. This is particularly the case in rural communities, where it is frequently believed that the more children a couple has, the more people there will be in the family to work the fields, and thus the greater the family wealth. It is often a difficult task to explain to poorly educated farmers that probably the economic cost of having a large family will not be matched by an eventual rise in household income to counter the increased expenditure. At the same time, many people in the general community cannot understand that rapid population growth retards the economic development of the country, and thus brings down the quality of life of the entire population though reduction of the per capita Gross National Product (GNP) of the country.

Other than economic factors, there are also cultural factors that impinge upon the desire of couples to limit the number of children they have. An excellent example of this is in Confucian societies, such as in the Chinese communities and in Korea and Vietnam, where traditionally parents desire to have at least one male heir to carry on the family name. In the PRC, there is a fairly strict family planning policy of restricting couples to one child, except in some special cases. Since the early 1970s, the desire for a male heir has meant that if the first child born was a girl then some couples would either kill or fail to register the baby so that they could then legally have another baby, who would hopefully be a boy. An examination of the age–sex pyramid for various regions of the PRC reveals that these practices were reasonably widespread. From the early 1990s ultrasound techniques, which enable the sex of the unborn child to be ascertained, have circulated widely enough in China to influence the sex ratio at birth of the country as a whole, because some parents want a son strongly enough to abort a female foetus.

The government of the PRC has implemented a number of different programs over the past few decades to limit the size of its population. During the mid-1970s a two-child-per-family policy was introduced, but the current policy calls for one child per couple. The current policy aims at promoting the termination of childbearing after the first child is born, and provides incentives such as longer maternity leave for women who agree to have only one child, as well as priority in housing, job assignment, food ration and education for the child for those couples who agree to have only one child.

Overall, the multitude of family planning programs implemented in various Asian countries since the 1960s have made some contribution to the decline in fertility in the region. But the most important factor has probably been the improvement in the standard of health care, which in turn has lead to a fall in mortality, especially infant mortality; thus the need to have a large number of births has been reduced. The decrease in infant and child mortality has been the main contributing factor to the fall in fertility levels in Asia. However, despite this, family planning programs are generally expanding within the Asian region.

The general population trends in Asia over the past few decades indicate that women want smaller families than their mothers, and that in general urban people wish for smaller families than rural dwellers. The number of children in Asian families has been declining steadily since the beginning of the twentieth century. At that time, the average completed Asian family consisted of about ten children; by the middle of the century it had fallen to about seven children, and by the 1980s to about four. As of the early 1990s, in Bangladesh, Laos, Nepal and Pakistan the total fertility level is approximately six births for each women, while in India, the Philippines and Vietnam, women are averaging about four and a half births. On the other hand, women in Indonesia and Thailand average slightly more than three births, those in Singapore and Taiwan just below two births, and women in Japan and South Korea just over one and a half births each. In the mid-1960s the fertility level in the PRC was about six births per woman, while by the end of the 1980s this had decreased to about 2.3 births per woman. Of all the Asian countries, the PRC has experienced the most significant reduction in the fertility level.

However, fertility decline should not be considered in isolation, as in many countries where fertility decline has occurred, economic and social events which have had both direct and indirect influences on the fertility rate were taking place at the same time: increases in the level of industrialisation and urbanisation, greater employment possibilities for women, real increases in incomes, rises in the standards and level of education of the population, easier access to better health care facilities, and the changing attitudes of people to what they consider to be the optimum family size. However, apart from an improvement in the standard of health care, one of the most important factors which has led to a reduction in the fertility levels of Asian women has been the implementation of family planning programs.

Family planning

Most Asian countries have adopted policies which aim to limit the size of their populations, while at the same time enhancing the health and welfare of children and mothers. In general, many Asian countries believed that lower birth rates would lead to improved economic and social conditions. The two Asian countries with the largest populations, the PRC and India, have for several decades implemented strict policies to limit the size of their populations. On the other hand, some of the smaller Asian countries, such as Cambodia and Laos, currently encourage families to have more children, while other countries, such as Brunei, have no specific official population policies. Although official family planning programs aimed at limiting the size of families became official government policy in most Asian countries during the 1970s, some countries have had small private or semi-official programs since the late 1950s. The family planning organisations which developed these programs generally had three principal objectives:

1 educating the community about the family planning philosophy;
2 providing information to couples on the different methods of contraception available; and
3 the provision of family planning services to couples as required.

The family planning policies in the Asian region have been implemented in a variety of ways and with varying degrees of pressure. The governments of the Philippines and Thailand have not placed any pressure on couples to restrict the size of their families. On the other hand, the Indonesian and Vietnamese governments have, at different times, threatened to restrict families' access to educational and medical services, or to inhibit employment prospects. They have also offered financial rewards or privileges to couples who agree to restrict the number of children they have to meet the government's guidelines. At the other extreme, officials in the PRC and India have been known to kidnap people, inflict abortions on pregnant women and force them to undergo sterilisation operations.

Due to the activities of the various family planning organisations throughout Asia, there is a significantly greater knowledge of methods of contraception today than there was two decades ago, which in turn has contributed to a reduction in the size of Asian families. In most Southeast Asian countries, the Pill is the most widely known method of contraception, followed by IUDs.

The main shortcomings of the family planning programs in Asia vary from country to country, and are often directly related to the relative wealth of the countries concerned. However, as a generalisation, the major problems can be summarised as:

1 limited ability to reach the smaller rural communities where significant proportions of the population reside;
2 the poor relationship between knowledge about family planning and contraception, and the ability to put this knowledge into practice;
3 the lack of financial and qualified personnel resources to conduct educational programs and to implement programs effectively; and
4 the inability of bureaucracy and bureaucrats to administer and co-ordinate programs.

An additional difficulty has been the complex inter-relationship between the determinates of fertility and the economic and socio-cultural characteristics of the population. The frequent inability to obtain empirical knowledge of these inter-relationships within a particular country or cultural context has restricted the ability of family planning organisations to implement large-scale effective family planning programs. However, despite these shortcomings, many governments in the region have attempted to integrate their family planning and population programs with national economic development plans.

While some programs have realised their desired goals, many have been only partially successful, while others have been total failures. Yet, overall, the various family planning programs implemented in Asia over the past few decades have contributed to a lowering of the rate of population growth. Whatever the outcomes of the family planning programs, it is certain that the family planning philosophy in Asia has had a significant impact on reducing the rate of population growth in the region.

Population mobility

The movement of people from one location to another is referred to as migration. Movement solely within a country is called *internal migration*, while movement between countries is termed *international migration*. People move from their place of residence generally because they are dissatisfied with their current situation.

There are two types of factor which influence people's decisions to migrate: *push factors* which force people away from where they currently reside, and *pull factors* which may attract people to alternative locations. The push factors include such situations as civil unrest, drought, famine, flood, poverty (perceived or real), war, etc. The pull factors are generally beliefs that the quality of their physical and social life, and their future happiness, would be more readily assured if they lived in another location, city or country.

Mobility may be short-term or long-term. Those who move for a short term may move from one location to another seasonally due to the demands of employment, such as farmers or people involved in the tourist industry, or due to human-made or natural disasters, such as war or flood. On the other hand, long-term movements are primarily made for the long-term benefit of the individual or family. The decision-making process involved in determining whether to move or not, as well as where to resettle, is complex and variable. The patterns of mobility may be expected to vary not only among individuals, but from country to country. The variations are due both to differing economic, political and social situations between countries, and to cultural differences. Thus the decision to move from one location to another is based on a complex amalgam of economic, political and socio-cultural environmental factors, together with those related to individual personality.

Internal migration

Individual movements within a country may be initiated by individuals, or their families, or by governments. There are a number or reasons why governments may want people to move from one location to another, but the two main ones are for security/military considerations, or over-crowding, with the government desiring to ease the burden on the over-populated region by moving people to a less densely populated region.

Voluntary internal migration

Most of the population movements in the Asian region during the first half of the twentieth century may be described as movements to frontier regions. In other words, these movements were to open up and exploit virgin lands, and most of these movements were rural–rural movements. During the past four decades the trend has been more towards rural–urban movements, especially migrations to capital cities. The rapid urbanisation of many Asian countries has been due to large-scale rural–urban migration, rather than an increase in the level of fertility of city dwellers. Table 34.1 provides an indication of the degree of urbanisation in selected Asian countries since 1965 by providing data on the pro-portion of the population that resided in urban areas in 1965 and 1993. This table shows that the most rapid urbanisation has occurred in Bangladesh, Nepal, the PRC and South Korea, while little urbanisation has occurred in Japan and Sri Lanka since 1965. The data in this table indicates that there is no necessary link between the economic develop-ment of a country and the degree of urbanisation it experiences.

One of the main reasons for the migration from rural to urban areas is that the cities are frequently the centre of the economic and educational institutions of the country. At the same time, most capital cities are the principal entry-point of Western ideas and technology, generally per-ceived (not necessarily correctly) as being superior to those of the East.

At times there was a belief by some Asian politicians and economists that the greater the degree of urbanisation of their countries, the more rapid their economic development and growth would be. This philo-sophy was rooted in the economic development and demographic evolution of some Western countries, a philosophy which is not neces-sarily transferable to the Asian environment, as Table 34.1 indicates. In Asia, the city, or rapid urbanisation, has not been the key to economic development, except in the unique situation of Asia's two city-states, Hong Kong and Singapore. An examination of social and economic indicators of the rural and urban populations of the poorer South Asian countries of Bangladesh, India and Pakistan reveals that there are few differences between the values of these indicators in the rural and urban areas for these three countries, suggesting that the cities are not en-hancing the economic development of these countries; the belief that

Table 34.1 Proportion of the total population in urban areas in
selected Asian countries

Country	Percentage in urban areas in 1965	Percentage in urban areas in 1993
Bangladesh	6	17
Bhutan	NA	6
Brunei	NA	64
Cambodia	NA	12
China	18	60
Hong Kong	NA	94
India	19	26
Indonesia	16	31
Japan	67	77
Laos	NA	19
Macau	NA	100
Malaysia	26	44
Mongolia	NA	58
Myanmar	NA	25
Nepal	4	10
Pakistan	24	33
Philippines	32	43
Singapore	NA	100
South Korea	32	74
Sri Lanka	20	22
Taiwan	NA	75
Thailand	13	23
Vietnam	NA	20

Source: Asiaweek, vol. 17, no. 2, 11 January 1991, p. 11; and vol. 19, no. 50,
15 December 1993, p. 50. NA = data not available

urbanisation always leads to economic development is thus unfounded.
The variables examined included family size and structure, fertility rates,
household size and structure, and mortality rates. The influence of
Western culture, the level of individual and household incomes, and the
occupational distribution of the labour force were found to be the main
differences in the characteristics of the rural and urban populations in
these three countries. Indeed, the strongest economic power in contemporary Asia, Japan, developed economically not through rapid large-
scale urbanisation, but rather through agricultural advancement in the
rural areas, which subsequently led to an expansion in commercial and
industrial areas, later enhancing the overall economic development of the
country.

Voluntary internal migration is thus generally seen from the individual's perspective as being of immediate or future benefit to the

individual and his or her family. The capital cities are perceived by a significant proportion of rural people, especially youth, as being somewhere where employment is easier to find, wages are higher and life is easier. This may be true, but many of the rural people do not possess the occupational skills or knowledge required in order to obtain employment in the large cities. At the same time, the capital cities generally do contain the best educational, health and welfare services in a country, and for some these conditions are a strong enough magnet to encourage movement to the cities.

Government-initiated internal migration

A number of countries in Asia have developed and implemented policies of population redistribution for a variety of reasons, such as to enhance economic development, reduce pressure on infrastructure in densely populated regions, and for security or military considerations. Those policies aimed at enhancing economic development have generally taken the form of land resettlement programs and have been undertaken very actively in the last few decades in countries such as Indonesia, Malaysia and Vietnam.

Indonesia has had a policy of population redistribution since the early 1900s, implemented by the Dutch colonial rulers. This policy was developed due to the unfavourable population distribution in Indonesia, rather than because of a high fertility rate. This imbalance in the population distribution of Indonesia resulted in what has been termed the *transmigration program*, which called for the movement of people from regions of high population density, such as the islands of Bali and Java, to areas of low population density. In the early 1970s the island of Java contained about 65 per cent of Indonesia's population, while occupying approximately 7 per cent of Indonesia's total land area, thus leading to a substantial imbalance between the country's population and natural resources. This imbalance made it difficult for the labour force to exploit Indonesia's natural resources efficiently. This is because there was a labour surplus, as well as unemployment and underemployment, in Java at the same time as there were labour shortages in other regions of the country. Currently about 60 per cent of Indonesia's population lives on Java, and the economic imbalances still remain.

A policy similar to the Indonesian transmigration program was adopted by the Vietnamese government after 1975. This policy aimed to move people from the densely populated Red River Delta region of northern Vietnam and Ho Chi Minh City (formerly Saigon) to the less populated provinces bordering Cambodia, China and Laos, as well as to the central highland region of the country. This redistribution policy was aimed not only at relocating people from areas of high population density to regions that were sparsely populated, but also at increasing the population in strategically important areas, such as the border regions with Cambodia and China.

The rapid growth in the urban areas of some Asian countries, especially in the capital cities, has created many problems for most Asian nations. In an effort to reduce population pressures on the capital cities, a number of countries have implemented programs which aim to encourage the rural population to remain in rural areas and recent immigrants to the capital cities to return to their previous abodes in the countryside, or to go and reside in provincial or state capitals rather than in the larger capital cities. Thus in some countries, such as Malaysia and Thailand, policies of regional development and decentralisation have been developed in an effort to restrict the massive expansion in the size of capital cities. In other countries, such as the PRC, Indonesia and Vietnam, people have had to obtain the permission of government officials before being able to move to live in the capital city. However, these policies have rarely been effective in achieving their goal, either due to government corruption or people moving into the cities and squatting.

Policies of population redistribution are frequently not clearly thought through. Often little attention is given to the important question of why people do not live in the sparsely populated regions in the first place. In some cases people do not live in these areas because of security problems — this is especially the case with border regions. On the other hand, mountainous regions may not be habitable, due to malarial infestation, climatic conditions or lack of infrastructure. In other situations, soil infertility or an inadequate water supply may be the reason. Even if these difficulties are overcome, it may still be difficult for people to be successfully moved to sparsely populated regions. The forcible redistribution in the late 1970s and early 1980s of people who had lived in Ho Chi Minh City to provinces bordering Cambodia failed not only due to security problems and the lack of facilities, but also because the soil was so barren that farmers could not produce crops without fertilisers, which were not sufficiently available in the country.

One method of developing an effective program of population redistribution is to develop attractive decentralised centres of employment opportunities, as has been attempted in the Albury–Wodonga region of Victoria–New South Wales in Australia. Frequently, the main reason for migration from the rural regions to capital cities is that some rural people believe such cities provide better employment opportunities, and the chance to make more money. In order to counter this, it is necessary to develop decentralised employment opportunities, a policy that is currently being attempted in Bangladesh, Indonesia, Japan, Malaysia, Thailand and several other Asian countries. However, politicians in many Asian countries have yet to take the hard political decisions and create the necessary incentives to implement an effective decentralisation policy.

International migration

Asian people have been migrating from their homelands to other countries for centuries. However, the largest population movements commenced in the middle of the nineteenth century, with tens of thousands of Chinese going to Australia, Canada and the United States in search of gold and employment. Migration from other Asian countries to the West continued, but at a lower level, during the first half of the twentieth century. However, the largest movement of people from Asia to the West occurred after the communist victories in the three Indochinese countries (Cambodia, Laos and Vietnam) in 1975. Since early 1975, over 2 million Cambodian, Lao and Vietnamese nationals have migrated, most of them as refugees, from their homelands to Western countries. Currently, over 40 per cent of the immigrants arriving annually in the major immigrant settlement countries of Australia, Canada and the United States were born in Asia.

While most of the migration from Asian countries has been to the developed Western countries, there has also been a significant amount of temporary migration between countries within the region. Hardly any Asian countries have immigration programs similar to that in Australia, and they do not encourage immigration. On the other hand, some Asian countries, such as the Republic of Korea and Pakistan, have had policies of encouraging their population to emigrate to other countries as a means of controlling population growth. Other countries, such as Indonesia, the Philippines, Thailand and Vietnam, have encouraged the temporary short-term emigration of workers so as to increase their foreign reserves and trade balances.

Intra-regional international migration

Over the past few decades there has been an increase in the amount of temporary international migration between Asian countries. Nationals from Japan, South Korea and Taiwan follow their companies, which establish operations in Asian countries, generally for periods of up to about five years. At the same time, workers such as domestic maids and labourers, especially from Indonesia, the Philippines and Thailand, go to work in the more advanced economies in the region, especially in Hong Kong, Japan, Singapore and Taiwan, and to a lesser extent Malaysia. In many instances there are formal agreements between Asian countries to let in nationals from other countries in the region on temporary work permits. These agreements are seen to be mutually advantageous to the countries concerned.

While most of the intra-regional international migration is temporary, there is also some permanent migration. There has been a long history of Chinese migration from the PRC to other countries in the Asian region.

Currently some of the Chinese residents of Hong Kong are attempting to migrate to countries such as Malaysia, Singapore, Taiwan and Thailand, as well as to Western countries such as Australia. In addition, many of the countries currently providing refuge to Indochinese refugees have provided permanent residency to some of the refugees who landed in their country. The main countries in this endeavour have been Hong Kong, Japan, Malaysia, the PRC and Thailand. In the past, Hong Kong has also provided residency to hundreds of thousands of refugees from the PRC.

Inter-regional international migration

Inter-regional migration accounts for most permanent international migration involving the Asian region. As noted at the beginning of this section, there is a large amount of permanent migration from the Asian region to other countries. Currently over half a million Asian nationals annually migrate on a permanent basis to countries outside the region, most going to the European and North American continents.

At the same time, there is also large-scale temporary inter-regional migration. Over 100 000 students from Asian countries are studying at educational institutions in Western countries, as well as in Eastern and Central Europe. At the same time, more than 2 million Asian workers have work permits to be employed in countries outside their region, mostly in West Asia and the Middle East. In the late 1980s, approximately 100 000 Vietnamese workers were temporarily employed in factories in Eastern European bloc countries, while a similar number of Indonesian and Filipino workers were employed as domestic workers and labourers in West Asia. There is also an increased level of temporary international migration into Asian countries, especially Hong Kong, Malaysia, Singapore and Thailand, where professionals from Australia, Britain and the United States obtain employment.

Short-term population prospects

The enhancement of economic and social development, as well as expected improvements in welfare services, in most Asian countries in the immediate future will result in the continuing demographic transformation of the region. Over the next decade or so, most of the countries in the Asian region will experience a decline in their fertility rates. This will come about as family planning programs expand and become more effective. At the same time, health care standards will rise, as will the level of education of women, which in turn will lead to an increase in the age of first marriage and a fall in family size. The rate of family formation is also expected to increase as a greater number of younger people reach marriageable age. Additionally, with the expansion of health care programs and advances in health technology, people may be expected to live longer, and thus the number of aged people will grow.

The increased level of urbanisation within the region will also result in societal changes, such as a reduction in the prominence of extended family living arrangements, and thus an increase in the significance of nuclear family households. Also, more women will join the labour force; as economies expand, women will increase their level of education; and families will want more consumer goods. Currently there is a strong, but inadequate, demand for skilled, and especially technically competent, labour in many Asian countries, especially in Hong Kong, Singapore, South Korea, Taiwan and Thailand. A significant amount of this demand will be met by women who attain a high level of education and enter the labour force upon graduation.

The future of migration affecting the region is complex, and heavily dependent upon economic and political factors. As of the early 1990s, it appears that there will be increased emigration from Hong Kong, as it is due to return to the control of the PRC in 1997, and the Philippines, due to increased poverty and possible political unrest. Migration out of the region is also likely as well-educated professionals seek higher incomes and greater security in the West, and Asians currently outside the region attempt to sponsor family members out of the region. However, some Asian people who previously migrated to the West are now considering returning home as the standards of living in their homelands rise. For example, each year a significant number of Indochinese refugees return to their homelands for visits, with some deciding to remain as they realise that their life in the West is much more difficult than they originally believed. The coming decades are likely to provide more interesting and unexpected demographic changes in the Asian region.

Guide to further reading

Fawcett, James T. & Carino, Benjamin V. (eds), *Pacific Bridges: The Immigration From Asia and the Pacific Islands*, Centre for Migration Studies, Staten Island, New York, 1987
This edited volume addresses migration from the Asian and Pacific Island countries to Australia, New Zealand and the North American continent. The book provides a brief historical overview of this migration and the restrictions on the free movement of peoples between these geographic regions, and information on the Asian communities in Australia, New Zealand and the North American continent. The chapters in this volume provide an excellent general overview of migration from the Asian region to the locations of the main expatriate Asian communities in the West.

Hugo, Graeme J., Hull, Terence H., Hull, Valerie J. & Jones, Gavin W., *The Demographic Dimension in Indonesian Development*, Oxford University Press, Kuala Lumpur, 1987

This recent volume by some of the leading Western experts on Indonesian demography relates the changing nature of Indonesia's population and its contribution to Indonesian development. This work is probably one of the best contemporary works available in English on Indonesian demography.

Jones, Gavin W. & Richter, H.V. (eds), *Population Mobility and Development: Southeast Asia and the Pacific*, Occasional Paper No. 29, Development Studies Centre, Australian National University, Canberra, 1981; Jones, Gavin W. & Richter, H.V. (eds)., *Population Resettlement Programs in Southeast Asia*, Occasional Paper No. 30, Development Studies Centre, Australian National University, Canberra, 1982

These are very useful monographs on the issues of population mobility, resettlement and development in the main countries of Southeast Asia, with particular attention being directed towards the ASEAN countries. Although these two volumes only cover the period up to the early 1980s, they do provide important contemporary information on the demographic position of the Southeast Asian region and, just as importantly, they are not over-engrossed in technical terminology and are thus readily comprehensible to the intelligent reader.

Kane, Penny, *The Second Billion: Population and Family Planning in China*, Penguin, Harmondsworth, 1987

A highly accessible and informative account of policy and practice towards population matters in the PRC. It focuses on the differences between the urban and rural areas.

Table 34.2 Selected demographic characteristics of Asian countries

Country	Estimated pop. size at end of 1993 (millions)	% average annual growth 1984–91	Projected pop. size in the year 2010 (millions)	Number of years until the current pop. doubles	Urban pop. as a % of the total pop.	Death rate per 1000	Birth rate per 1000	Infant mortality per 1000	% of pop under 15 years of age	Life expectancy at birth	% of women using contraception
Bangladesh	124.6	2.0	161.0	36	15.7	11.0	31.6	101	46.5	51	25
Bhutan	0.6	2.5	1.0	35	5.0	17.0	39.1	133	40.3	48	NA
Brunei	0.3	2.5	0.4	27	59.0	3.3	27.2	8	35.8	74	NA
Cambodia	8.7	3.0	NA	NA	12.0	16.0	38.0	120	47.0	50	NA
China	1187.2	1.4	1498.1	48	26.4	7.0	19.7	22	27.2	69	74
Hong Kong	5.9	0.9	6.5	NA	NA	5.0	12.0	5	20.4	78	72
India	890.8	2.3	1178.2	34	27.7	10.0	31.0	80	35.4	61	35
Indonesia	189.5	**1.9	++275.0	NA	31.0	9.0	26.0	61	37.0	60	45
Japan	125.0	0.5	129.5	NA	77.3	6.7	10.0	5	17.7	79	64
Laos	4.3	2.9	4.9	30	15.0	18.0	42.0	101	47.0	50	NA
Macau	0.4	1.6	0.5	50	98.0	3.8	15.3	7	25.0	73	NA
Malaysia	19.0	***2.5	27.0	27	60.0	4.6	28.0	15	37.0	71	51
Mongolia	2.4	+2.7	3.5	25	58.0	8.0	33.0	62	44.0	63	NA
Myanmar	44.8	2.5	58.6	36	24.0	8.9	28.5	85	35.6	59	NA
Nepal	20.7	2.1	27.3	32	9.6	16.0	47.0	102	27.7	53	15
North Korea	*22.1	1.7	24.9	32	62.0	5.6	24.1	31	28.7	69	NA
Pakistan	123.8	+3.1	203.3	23	28.0	11.0	41.0	94	44.5	59	11
Philippines	64.6	2.4	76.5	30	48.4	5.4	26.0	34	40.0	65	44
Singapore	3.1	1.4	3.2	55	100.0	4.2	19.0	5	23.2	74	67
South Korea	44.2	1.0	49.6	70	74.4	5.8	15.4	16	24.8	72	70
Sri Lanka	17.7	1.4	NA	NA	21.5	5.5	20.6	16	35.2	71	62
Taiwan	20.9	1.1	23.7	60	80.0	5.0	16.0	5	26.3	74	NA
Thailand	59.2	1.5	75.8	46	27.0	7.0	22.3	28	34.0	69	66
Vietnam	72.3	2.3	110.0	30	19.8	8.4	30.3	39	46.0	67	58

Sources: Far Eastern Economic Review, Asia 1993 Yearbook, Far Eastern Economic Review, Hong Kong, 1993, pp. 6–7; Asiaweek, vol. 17, no. 2, 11 January 1991, p. 11; and vol. 19, no. 50, 15 December 1993, p. 50

Note: NA = Data not available   * 1992 Figure   ** 1988–92 figure   *** 1981–88 figure   + 1983–90 figure   ++ estimate for the year 2025

35 | Class, status and gender

Introduction

Asian societies throughout their histories have shown significant social stratification. This covers three dimensions of social relations: relations of rewards, relations of prestige and relations of power. When access to rewards, prestige or power is systematically differentiated, hierarchy is produced in terms of statuses and roles, accompanied by greater rewards, prestige or power. Inequality is produced when movement into such statuses or roles is restricted. Such social stratification may be discussed in terms of *class*, *status* and *gender*. Status distinctions divide persons principally according to prestige, deference granted to them on the basis of such criteria as birth into a prestigious family, clan or ethnic group, on the basis of wealth, or on the basis of knowledge or educational mastery. Class can overlap with status, as in the case of premodern class societies like Japan during the Tokugawa era (1600–1868), when the nation was formally divided into four classes, distinct groups which did not ordinarily intermarry or cross occupational lines: warriors *(samurai)*, peasants, artisans and merchants. Below the four classes was a group of persons associated with such stigmatised occupations as slaughtering and leatherwork. The four major divisions defined a hierarchy of prestige, with the *samurai* carrying the highest prestige, but this prestige was not necessarily accompanied by great rewards in the form of wealth, and frequently the merchants — lowest in the four-class hierarchy of prestige — accumulated much greater personal fortunes than did the *samurai*. The term 'class' is used to define the relation of social groups to the means of production within capitalist economies, so that capitalists — those in control of the means of production — are fundamentally different, having greater prestige, rewards and power than workers, who sell their labour. This crudest of distinctions — workers and capitalists — is further nuanced by the development of professional and middle classes, and these divisions of class exist alongside older status distinctions emerging from other criteria.

Both status and class divisions are further cross-cut by distinctions on the basis of gender. The term 'gender' refers to culturally constructed categories of masculinity and femininity and is distinguished from the biological fact that individuals have the reproductive organs of one sex or the other. Within any status group or class, a further division exists on the basis of sex and gender, generally yielding a tendency towards subordination of women to men within the group, though there is wide variation in the degree to which gender stratifies Asian societies and in the precise nature of that stratification. In most Asian societies, a division of labour on the basis of sex may be observed, so that certain tasks associated with domestic life (cleaning, cooking, child care) are considered uniquely appropriate to women, and thus to be associated with the feminine gender, while men dominate in such areas as political life, which becomes associated with the masculine gender. The more clear-cut the division of labour by sex, the greater the resistance to either sex's crossing the boundary into the activities deemed appropriate to the other gender. Generally these divisions are hedged about with religious, philosophical and moral justifications used to prevent such crossover. In modern times these are used especially to prevent women from entering advanced sectors of the economy in capitalist societies.

Over time, we can see an increasing division between the realms of productive and reproductive labour, so that greater prestige, rewards and power are accorded toparticipation in activities resulting in the production of tangible goods, especially those that can be exchanged for currency. There is a concurrent progressive devaluation of those activities associated with maintaining the capability for productive labour and with group reproduction. The persistent association of men with productive labour and women with reproductive labour is linked to a devaluation of women's work in capitalist societies, where labour leading to cash rewards tends to be valued more highly than that which does not. Thus the entry of men and dominant-status or ethnic groups into roles and statuses carrying high rewards, prestige and power is mirrored in the exclusion of men in subordinate status or ethnic groups, and of women from such rewards, prestige and power.

In modern times, Asian societies have initiated policies aiming to erase status inequalities and to result in more equal access to opportunity. Various societies have tried to equalise opportunities for different ethnic groups living within their boundaries, for members of traditionally stigmatised occupations, and for women. Among these various policies, the franchise is perhaps the most important, giving such groups the right to elect representatives to promote their interests; legislation to guarantee equal access to education and employment is also extremely significant. The gains produced by the franchise can be limited, however, by provisions excluding such groups as non-property-holding men and women.

Furthermore, social equality across the lines of class, status and sex tends to be promoted by situations of peace and development and retarded by war and civil unrest.

A major topic of scholarly inquiry on Asian societies in recent times concerns the effects of economic development upon divisions of class, status and sex. Asian societies have generally accepted the view that their standard of living will improve if they emulate the industrialised world, and thus development has meant industrialisation first and foremost, though processes of urbanisation and integration into the world market economy are also involved. Planners directing their attention to industrialisation, rural development and education have generally tended to assume that development will promote increased opportunity and social equality for all. Where improvements have been slow or have not occurred for particular ethnic groups, status groups or women, the response has frequently been that these problems will be solved gradually, as such groups are more fully integrated into various schemes of national development.

Since about 1970, however, it has become apparent that while development may readily bring about improvements for some groups, its results are not necessarily or uniformly positive. In particular, industrialisation, urbanisation, colonial rule and participation in the world economy can remove women from traditional positions of status and authority, deprive them of access to and control over resources, and exclude them from rights and privileges. Development itself is not the same everywhere, and specific development programs bring different cultures into contact (as in the case of the entry of transnational corporations into developing economies) and involve complex negotiations between capitalist interests and members of indigenous elite or bureaucratic classes over the labour of subordinate classes and women. These phenomena can produce new classes and new constructions of gender in the societies involved. In the following sections we examine how changing patterns of land tenure have impacted on issues of class and gender in Indonesia and Thailand, how incorporation into the world economy (in the form of transnational corporations) has affected Malaysian women, and how development has affected class and gender relations under a government led by a Marxist-Leninist party in the case of Vietnam. Special sections are devoted to the People's Republic of China (PRC) and Japan.

Southeast Asia
Changing rural society: Thailand and Indonesia

Southeast Asia covers a vast area of land, and the several countries of the region each have distinct histories and contemporary social patterns. Each one has within it local cultures of ethnic, religious and tribal groups, yielding a great mosaic of patterns from which it is very difficult to generalise. Nevertheless, in Thailand and Indonesia we can observe shifting dynamics of class and gender brought about by a growing shortage of land which is producing pressure for migration to the cities.

In both societies, growing populations and the intensification of agriculture have led to a shortage of agricultural land, so that the majority of rural families must take up secondary occupations to supplement their income from agriculture. Large families have traditionally been favoured as a means to ensure the care of the elderly, for religious reasons (to perpetuate the worship of ancestors, for example) and because indigenous gender constructions accorded high status to women who bore many children. Secondary occupations that can be undertaken near a family's land include day-labour in agriculture, such as harvesting or construction work. Many women as well as men take up such work, commuting daily or seasonally. Also, women have traditionally been involved in small-scale trade.

Because alternative sources of cash income are limited in rural areas, people migrate to the cities in search of wage labour to supplement what their families earn from agriculture. As this workforce is generally not highly educated, the available occupations are limited, with men finding work as carpenters, day-labourers and in such miscellaneous occupations as musicians and traditional healers, while women become employed as hairdressers, dressmakers, domestic servants or prostitutes.

The progressive separation of people from the land contributes to the stagnation and impoverishment of the countryside and tends to produce a polarisation of urban and rural people. In rural society, class divisions become more pronounced as prosperous peasants are able to acquire land from cultivators in need of cash, who then may become tenants, share croppers or day-labourers, caught in a cycle of unending debt. Class thus remains an important element in rural society, and it is further cross-cut by gender. Women have traditionally inherited land, but as land becomes scarce, women lose this resource, and when they migrate to urban areas, they may lose their position on the land entirely. Rural areas come to depend upon remittances of cash from people who have migrated to the cities. Although this urban labour provides new access to cash income for some groups who would not otherwise have this resource, such as unmarried women, often their families retain strict control over that income, while lower class men may be more free to use their income for personal consumption. Thus traditional inequalities of class and between women and men may be exacerbated in the decline of rural areas.

Changes in class, status and gender arising through the influence of transnational corporations

Since the 1970s, a new form of transnational enterprise has arisen, characterised by the manufacture of goods in less developed countries for sale overseas. The industries involved in Southeast Asia, particularly microelectronics and garment work, are labour-intensive and depend primarily upon young, unmarried women workers. From the corporations' point of view, the attraction of setting up factories in developing countries lies in the availability of cheap labour. From the point of view of governments of developing nations such as Malaysia, the Philippines and Singapore, the incentive to attract foreign transnational corporations is in the prospect of improved foreign exchange earnings and greater employment for their large unemployed populations, themselves formed as rural areas and agriculture have stagnated or declined. Thus governments seek to provide conditions favourable to the corporations: a stable political climate, tax incentives, little or no labour unrest, and few barriers to maximum use of the indigenous labour force.

Malaysia's social policy, the New Economic Plan, which is intended to prevent an unbalanced concentration of employment and assets in the hands of Chinese and Indian ethnic groups by promoting the indigenous Malaysian population, has set the stage for the formation of a new class of female labourers: new school-leavers, largely recruited from rural areas, who are young and unmarried. In order to address the imbalance in the distribution of wealth by ethnic groups, and also to redress the general problem of poverty, the Malaysian government promoted export-oriented industrialisation, creating a free trade zone within which transnational corporations could operate freely.

The microelectronics industry, dominated by United States and Japanese corporations, manufactures semiconductors, parts used in calculators, watches, computers, communications equipment and strategic missile-guidance systems. The semiconductor industry is highly competitive and demands extremely high production standards. A semiconductor is either perfectly manufactured or completely unusable; there is no use for imperfect chips. Thus the pressure to work swiftly and accurately under conditions of steadily increasing production quotas is inherent to the industry. The Malaysian government has sought to attract the transnational corporations of the electronics industry by advertising the skills of its female labour force, as in a brochure titled *Malaysia: The Solid State for Electronics:*

> The manual dexterity of the oriental female is famous the world over. Her hands are small and she works fast with extreme care. Who, therefore, could be better qualified by nature and inheritance to contribute to the efficiency of a bench-assembly production line than the oriental girl?[1]

This advertising appeal establishes that factory work in the electronics industry will be generically 'female', thus excluding men from it and assuring also that such work will be defined as less skilled and so be intensely supervised. In order to assure that these female workers prove satisfactory to the transnational employer, in 1970 the Malaysian government made exceptions to the provision previously protecting women from night-shift work.

Most of the workforce in the free trade zone consists of semi-skilled workers, the majority of whom are single women, unmarried new school-leavers, chosen because of their docility and dexterity, unlikely to cause strikes and highly capable in the production of semiconductor chips, manufactured under a microscope. During the period of employment, young women workers generally remit money to their parents, often residing in rural areas, so that the countryside comes to depend upon this remittance economy fuelled by young women's labour. Because employers maintain that single women do not need to earn as much as men, since they are not the sole supporters of families, low wages are justified. Similarly, married women are not typically employed, thus making provisions for maternity leave and child care unnecessary. Women's jobs in the electronics industry last about four years on average, because the workers' sight deteriorates after continuous work with a microscope for that long, and they become unable to continue. Companies claim that it is then time for the woman to 'retire' to get married. The skills learned in the electronics industry cannot be applied to any other form of labour, and thus the women 'retirees' do not take usable skills back to their homes. Instead, scholars point out that export processing leads to the formation of a large-scale female proletariat which derives little long-lasting benefit from its labour in the electronics industry. Prevented from organising to improve their conditions of labour, Malaysian factory women have experienced a phenomenon of mass hysteria, described as spirit possession; first one woman and sometimes whole factories of women will fall into fits of uncontrollable screaming. These outbursts would appear to be symbolic appeals by the women concerned.

Vietnam

The recent history of Vietnamese society has been dominated by war, producing an uneven demographic pattern in which women outnumber men, because so many men have died in war, and in which children under 15 years of age comprise about half the total population. The nation as a whole idealises a classless society, but while much progress towards that goal has been made, many inequalities between women and men remain.

During the Vietnam War, women were called upon to take men's places in industrial production, to maintain homes and families, and also to fight in actual combat. Women entered many occupations traditionally defined as men's work during the war, but after 1975, women were expected to vacate these jobs for men returning from military service. Whereas women made up about one-third of all elected members of the

National Assembly in 1971, and while they comprised about the same proportion of membership in the Communist Party of Vietnam at that time, those figures have declined significantly since then. At present, women form about two-thirds of the workforce across all sectors of the economy, with the exception of heavy industry.

Agriculture in the north was collectivised by the mid-1960s, and this change went far towards equalising former class inequalities between land-owners and poorer peasants, as well as contributing to equality between women and men. Collectives provided opportunities for women to have solidarity with each other, pooling resources for child care, giving them training in new skills, and providing health benefits and conditions of labour compatible with parenthood. A system of work points allowed women an opportunity to prove by objective measures that they were at least as productive as men, and often more so. Collectives thus helped transform male–female power relations from personal problems to political matters amenable to public, political intervention.

While the benefits of collectivisation have been significant, however, it has not been free of problems. Greater capital investment is allocated to men's agricultural tasks, such as ploughing, while women's tasks such as transplantation remain unmechanised, giving the false impression that men are more productive than women. There is a tendency for men to dominate higher positions of leadership in the collectives and a continuing resistance to women in positions of authority. There has been little alteration to traditional expectations that women will bear nearly full responsibility for housework and child care, and thus 'parenthood' is equated with 'motherhood', giving the father few of the burdens of maintaining the family home. Because of the demographic shortage of men and the high positive value placed on having children for women, a problem of polygamy has appeared. Because women, with little or no assistance from men, carry the triple burden of employment as well as maintaining the home and child care, men are freed to devote leisure time to education, training and political activities. These various activities are directly linked to rewards, prestige and power, thus creating inequalities between themselves and women.

China

Premodern Chinese society was rigidly stratified according to four classes: the scholar-gentry, peasants, artisans and merchants. Mobility across class lines was strictly limited, although a system of examinations leading to bureaucratic positions afforded one exceptional opportunity for males. Women were restricted by an inflexible sexual division of labour in the household that cut across class lines, as did Confucian religious and cosmological ideology supporting the notion of female inferiority. Women had little freedom in marriage and divorce, and such practices as foot-binding further curtailed the scope of their social participation.

In the late nineteenth and early twentieth centuries, rebellion against social inequality became widespread. The May Fourth Movement criticised older, Confucian social institutions and upheld values of humanism and individualism in their place, advocating a reform of repressive class restrictions and marriage codes, and promoting the introduction of education for women. Soon a movement for women's suffrage emerged, along with the newly formed Chinese Communist Party (CCP), espousing the ideals of socialism and the liberation of the proletariat.

As a means to achieve a classless society, Mao Zedong sought to overturn the feudal powers of landlords, the clans and religion, and he perceived that for the liberation of women to be achieved, it was further necessary to break down hierarchical relations between the sexes. Women were recognised as having played significant roles in the struggles of the Chinese Revolution, and the emancipation of women was one of the first platforms of the CCP. Thus Mao's analysis identified a close connection between general economic and social oppression based upon class and unequal relations between women and men, and he recognised women as equal partners in the struggle for national liberation.

The legal basis for the achievement of much greater social equality was established during the first years of the PRC through land reform and the partial collectivisation of industry and commerce. But the small peasant economy remained unchanged, and the rural areas ended up preserving far more aspects of pre-revolutionary China than did urban areas, especially those aspects which affected the status of women.

The Great Leap Forward of 1958 was a movement to expand the economy and increase rural and industrial production. For women it represented an opportunity to actualise the principle holding that women's entry into production was the key to their liberation. Under the Great Leap Forward, women became involved in all aspects of rural production, swelling China's labour force dramatically. This incorporation of women into the labour force was made possible through the collectivisation of cooking and child care; these factors, combined with women earning individual wages for their own labour, facilitated some breakdown in the traditional sexual division of labour.

By the 1960s, however, it was understood that these changes in the economic realm did not automatically produce corresponding changes in relations between women and men. Sexuality remained a tabooed, unresolved issue for many men and women, who had little guidance in overcoming pre-revolutionary ideas stigmatising this entire aspect of human life. Furthermore, birth control had only just begun to be tolerated, owing to Confucian ideas condemning it as immoral and advocating that women bear as many children as possible. Especially in the countryside, children were viewed as an informal type of 'old age insurance', and in the absence of social policy to guarantee support for the elderly, many couples continued to view large families as economically desirable.

Like other developing nations, China anticipated that development and modernisation would be accompanied by a decline in fertility, but it is also held that modernisation and development themselves would depend upon a reduction of population growth. It was estimated that China's total population would reach 1.3 billion by the year 2000 if it continued to grow at the 1979 level. It was concluded that if the nation did not take draconian measures to curtail this population growth, it would simply be unable to feed its massive population, and many would starve. Thus in 1979 the PRC initiated a policy of limiting all families to one child.

It is difficult to overstate the importance of this policy. It represents massive state intervention into one of the most intimate areas of life, enforced by direct regulation of reproductive life through a system of incentives and disincentives. Social equality is directly linked to the control of population increase, because a rapidly increasing, uncontrolled growth of population severely strains a society's resources in terms of employment, food, housing and social services. The results of un-controlled fertility weigh unevenly upon women and men, however, firstly because women bear the physical burden of pregnancy and childbirth, and secondly because of the persistence of the idea that women should take the major responsibility for child care, cooking, housework and care of the elderly, making it difficult for mothers to participate in the workforce on terms equal with fathers.

Since about 1985, rewards for compliance with the one-child policy have been standardised, giving couples applying for a one-child family certificate a cash subsidy. These subsidies are accompanied by various additional privileges, such as priority admission to nurseries, schools and hospitals for the single child, and the reduction or waiving of fees for education, medicine and job allocation. Single-child families receive priority in housing and larger grain allocations and, in addition, parents of single children receive special financial assistance after retirement.

Acceptance of this radical policy has varied significantly across the country, but the cities have generally seen a much higher rate of compliance than rural areas. In some Beijing neighbourhoods, the rate exceeds 90 per cent. Urban areas are more easily supervised by cadres who record residents' reproductive histories and current practice minutely, and urban families face severe housing shortages and employment limitations which act as an informal incentive to limit family size. In rural areas it is clear that an increasing population decreases the available arable land per capita, which means a decreasing share of food, and this recognition has facilitated acceptance of the policy. As rural collectives are obliged to pay the subsidies mandated for single-child families, however, they encounter financial strain in the short run, which does not make compliance easy.

There has been resistance to the one-child policy, however, and this has been particularly strong in the countryside. Everywhere there is a strong preference for sons, for reasons which are discussed in Chapter 33.

According to Chinese family-planning experts, the implementation of the one-child policy was particularly difficult in the years 1979–80, when the population was first asked to accept the basic concept. A rising age at marriage, lengthening of the average lifespan and recognition of the physical, economic and emotional burdens of large families have facilitated compliance with the policy, as has a mammoth educational campaign aimed at convincing the nation of the policy's necessity. The universalisation of contraceptive availability and the encouragement of sterilisation for couples who have had one child have also played a role, as has the nation's choice of the IUD (a type which, once inserted, can only be removed by a medical procedure) as the principal means of contraception. Thus there is little problem of compliance with the actual use of contraception. Barrier methods (the condom and diaphragm) are also in use, but the Pill is generally used only to achieve a desired timing of conception.

While it is too early to assess the effect of policy after only fifteen years of implementation, it promises to contribute a great deal to the achievement of social equality across Chinese society, and especially to the equality of women and men.

Japan

Since around 1970, surveys of Japanese public opinion have shown that the great majority of the Japanese population — sometimes as high as 90 per cent — believe that they are members of the middle class. This is not to say that all inequalities have disappeared from the society by any means, but the belief of so many that they belong to the middle class is striking within the larger context of Asian societies, where extreme disparities in the distribution of prestige, status and power are marked. This phenomenon is the more striking in that it should appear after a long history of class stratification in premodern times (mentioned above) and so soon after the formal abolition of hereditary nobility status, which came shortly after the end of World War II.

The standard of living has risen steadily in Japan since 1945, and while there are disparities in the distribution of wealth, almost no one lives in destitution. Literacy is nearly universal, and more than 90 per cent of young people complete high school, which represents three years beyond compulsory education; increasing proportions go on to some form of tertiary education as well. Thus, relative to the prewar period when inequalities of opportunity were very marked, and to the immediate postwar period, when the nation's economic infrastructure was in ruin and many were in poverty, the present situation represents a truly dramatic improvement. These various improvements have come about as part of postwar Japanese economic development and growth, the so-called 'economic miracle'.

When Japanese overwhelmingly respond to survey-takers that they belong to the middle class, they are to some extent making a comparison with the prewar and immediate postwar periods. They are also affirming the nation's solid commitment to economic expansion as the principal means of raising the standard of living for all. Rising levels of educational achievement, as well as confidence in the nation's international position as an economic superpower, are also reflected.

There is a strong belief in the country that education is the most important means to personal prestige and security, and that educational attainments can only be achieved through the merit of the individual, the will to study diligently over the entire period of primary and secondary education. Universal access to public education of a very high quality reinforces this belief, though it is recognised that many of those who succeed at the highest levels have frequently had the benefit of private tutors and academies, which can represent a major expense. Thus dependence upon these supplemental forms of education has the potential to create social inequalities.

Perhaps the greatest stratifying feature of Japanese society is gender. While women were enfranchised as a result of occupation reforms, the number of women elected to public office fell steadily over the postwar decades, at least until the defeat of the Liberal Democratic Party in the 1993 general elections. Women achieve high levels of educational achievement through high school, but they are far more likely than men to attend a two-year, rather than a four-year, college, or not to go on to tertiary education at all. Wage differentials are among the worst in the developed world, with women earning about 60 per cent of a man's wage for equivalent work. More than half of all married women are engaged in waged work, but many of these work part-time, in conditions carrying far less benefits than full-time work, though the differences in hours worked may be negligible. Japanese women face barriers to entering managerial work of any kind, due to a strong prejudice against women in positions of authority over men, and because the division of labour in the home for married women is quite inflexible, leading to the double-burden problem examined above. Similarly, traditional images of femininity are closely linked to marriage and motherhood, and women who choose careers face social disapproval (see Chapter 33).

Guide to further reading

Croll, Elisabeth, *Feminism and Socialism in China*, Routledge and Kegan Paul, London, 1978

Croll, Elisabeth, Davin, Delia, & Kane, Penny (eds), *China's One-Child Family Policy*, Macmillan, London, 1985
These works take up the topics of class, status, and gender in Chinese society, and the second, which is devoted to the one-child family policy, provides a good introduction to the overlapping quality of issues of class and gender in China.

Pearson, Gail & Manderson, Lenore (eds), *Class, Ideology and Woman in Asian Societies*, Asian Studies Monograph Series, Asian Research Service, Hong Kong, 1987
This useful collection of articles includes a good introduction to the topic of class in Asian societies as this affects women and issues of gender. It makes a distinction between involvement in productive and reproductive labour which has wide applicability.

Sacks, Karen, 'Toward a Unified Theory of Class, Race, and Gender', *American Ethnologist*, vol. 16, no. 3, 1989, pp. 534–50
An influential article setting out theoretical considerations for examinations of class, status and gender.

Stevens, Rob, 1983, *Classes in Contemporary Japan*, Cambridge University Press, Cambridge
A provocative and polemical examination of class in contemporary Japan.

Notes

1 Quoted in Grossman, Rachael, 'Women's Place in the Integrated Circuit', *Southeast Asia Chronicle*, no. 66, Jan.–Feb. 1979, p. 8.

36 | The role of religions in modernising Asia

Chapter 5 presented the history of religions in Asia and pointed out some basic comparisons amongst them. In this chapter we survey the present distribution of religions in Asia and assess the strength of those traditions in competition with secular views. Secular philosophies are not new to Asia, but cogent new systems of secular thought came to Asia from the West in the nineteenth and twentieth centuries, together with the political philosophies and technical knowledges which have contributed so much to the transformation of Asian countries into modern societies. In the West, both industrialisation itself and the social processes associated with it, such as urbanisation, have promoted a secular outlook, although atheism and agnosticism have by no means completely supplanted religious belief. Church attendances in the major denominations in most Western countries have fallen over the last century, and more and more areas of life have been removed from the influence of organised religion. Is Asia going the same way as it adopts Western forms of education and political institutions and industrialises? We shall see that, while there are signs of this in some countries, there are also signs of the continuing and even growing importance of religion elsewhere in Asia. First, however, we must consider which religious traditions continue to play at least some part in the lives of people in the countries of present-day East and Southeast Asia.

The distribution of major religions in Asia today

The historical and cultural processes through which religions have developed and spread in Asia make the map of present-day religious affiliations extremely complex. Both indigenous religions and religions imported from other parts of Asia (whether from Southwest Asia, Eastern Asia or both) are present in all the countries of Eastern Asia. Also, people in cities and in many parts of the countryside profess several different religions. While maps of religious affiliation tend to be either impossibly complex or misleadingly oversimplified, a table showing percentages of major religious groups country by country can be of some use in forming a quick impression of which religions are important in individual countries (see Table 36.1). We must be aware, however, that bodies which compile statistics for cross-national comparison often rely on information of different types from the countries they cover. (For example, they may use census data from one country and a survey based on a sample of the population from another. They may even use notoriously unreliable claims to memberships from individual religious organisations for other countries.) In addition, they may use data from different years for different countries. From this sort of data we can only form a rough picture; we cannot draw precise conclusions. Yet, with these reservations in mind, we may make use of the chart provided to sketch an overview of the distribution of religious commitments in the Asian region.

The most reliable impressions we can form from data presented in the chart concern which traditions presently form the dominant cultural influences in each of the countries listed. Thus we can readily see that the most important religious tradition in mainland Southeast Asia today (see listings for Thailand, Vietnam, Laos and Cambodia) is Buddhism. We know from our study of the history of religions in Asia (see Chapter 5) that the dominant form of Buddhism practised in this region is Theravada Buddhism. Mahayana Buddhism, or the Buddhism of the northern schools of China, Korea and Japan, is present in Southeast Asia today only in northern Vietnam, which has a heritage of Chinese domination and cultural influence, and among immigrant or 'overseas' Chinese who live as minorities within the Southeast Asian region.

The East Asian countries to the north appear to have mixed affiliations as the dominant religious preference. This reflects the close association of Confucianism, Daoism and Buddhism in the religious, political and cultural lives of East Asian peoples for more than a thousand years. While priests and scholars learned in these traditions have preserved the separate and distinct heritage of each, in the everyday lives of people in China, Korea and Japan, all of the traditions have played a part. The word 'traditional', used to designate the religion of 90 per cent of the people of Hong Kong, should thus be read as 'elements of Confucianism, Buddhism and Daoism'. Seventy-two per cent of South Koreans appear to be 'Buddhist/ Confucian', but it is well to remember that elements of Daoist practice have survived in Korean tradition, even if they are not explicitly recognised as such. The same might be said for Japan, where the indigenous folk religion, Shintoism, has been supplemented not only by Buddhism but also substantially by Confucianism, and in a minor way by Daoism.

Islam is the religion of the majority of the people of Indonesia and Malaysia, as shown in the table, and a minority religion in the Philippines, Thailand and (not shown) China (PRC). A smaller percentage of Malaysians than Indonesians profess Islam, owing to the large number of non-native peoples in that country whose ancestors came from China and India. The smaller percentage of Muslims in Malaysia is also due to the amalgamation of the eastern states of Sabah and Sarawak, with their many tribal peoples, into the Federation. Some of those tribal peoples have become Muslims, but many have become Christian or have continued to hold to their indigenous community religions.

Table 36.1 Religious affiliation in East and Southeast Asia
(based on data from PCGlobe, 1988)

Country	Religious category	Percentage
China	Atheist/eclectic	97
	Other	3
Japan	Shinto/Buddhist	84
	Other	16
Indonesia	Islam	88
	Protestant	6
	Roman Catholic	3
	Hindu	2
	Other	1
Malaysia	Islam	58
	Buddhist	30
	Hindu	8
	Christian/Other	4
Thailand	Buddhist	95
	Islam	4
	Christian	1
Republic of Korea (South)	Buddhist/Confucian	72
	Christian	28
Republic of China (Taiwan)	Buddhist/Confucianist/Daoist	93
	Christian	5
	Other (some would be Muslim)	2
Vietnam	Buddhist	60
	Confucianist	13
	Daoist	12
	Roman Catholic	3
	Other	12
Laos	Buddhist	85
	Animist/Other	15
Cambodia	Buddhist	95
	Other	5
Hong Kong	Traditional	90
	Christian	10
Republic of the Philippines	Roman Catholic	83
	Protestant	9
	Muslim	5
	Buddhist/Other	3

Source: These figures are based on the PCGlobe, Comwell Systems 1988, which is a computer data base covering the world's countries.

The Philippines is the only Asian country to have a Christian majority. Due to its heritage of Spanish colonialism, the Catholic Church is still the strongest denomination there (claiming 83 per cent of the population), but Protestant denominations have made substantial numbers of converts in the last century. There are Christian minorities in all of the other countries of East and Southeast Asia, but their numbers are mostly small in comparison with those of other religions. South Korea, however, constitutes a striking exception, with nearly a third of its population now Christian.

While the chart gives us a reasonably accurate picture of which religious traditions colour the cultural landscapes of the Asian countries most dramatically, it is less useful in suggesting the relative strength of religious as opposed to secular outlooks on the world. For example, the educational and propaganda drive of the Marxist government of China (PRC) to expose religion as 'false consciousness' appears to be reflected in the listing of 97 per cent of Chinese as 'Atheist/eclectic'. However, 'eclectic' can mean anything, and might well suggest bits and pieces of the classic 'three religions' (Confucianism, Daoism and Buddhism). Further, highly industrialised Japan is often described as secularised, like its Western industrialised counterparts, yet the figures on the chart give no indication of this. Clearly more information must be provided if we are to form an accurate picture of the extent to which secular philosophies and values have been adopted in Asian countries. That is the task to which we turn in the next section.

Religions and secularisation in the modern societies of Asia

Research and writing in any field of science is guided by theoretical paradigms, sets of guidelines, assumptions and beliefs which shape the way scientists think things work. In the 1950s and 1960s, when what we now call Third World or developing nations had just become or were becoming independent and their governments began to industrialise their economies, the dominant paradigm affecting Western sociology, anthropology, economics and political science was *modernisation theory*. This paradigm was based on the analysis of social scientists of what had happened in Western nations in the course of the Industrial Revolution. They said that Western societies and peoples were once bound up in 'irrational' and 'unscientific' beliefs, many of which were based in the supernatural explanations of religion, and also in equally 'irrational' social relations with kin and community that obligated people to value kin and community ties over 'rational' ways of making money. However, as Western societies industrialised, they observed that secular, rational and scientific thought became predominant, and democratic institutions replaced autocratic ones. Indeed, they postulated that these qualities which Western societies had developed were necessary to any modern nation-state with an industrialised economy. So they predicted that, as Third World nations modernised, they too would follow a like path: formerly traditional countries would evolve into democratic nation-states, social relations in the public sphere would become based on merit and economic need, and religion would fall into disuse.

This view, however, has been embarrassed by more careful studies of what was going on in Western societies at the time modernisation theory was developed, as well as by subsequent events, both in Western societies and in the developing countries of Asia. In the 1950s, 1960s and 1970s, all of the Western countries experienced falls in mainstream church attendances, but from the 1960s they began to experience upsurges in religious or spiritual activities outside the mainstream churches. One of these phenomena, Pentacostalism, which started in sectarian groups, flowed into established churches, buoying up their sinking memberships. Then, in the 1980s, Christian religious groups in the United States and Eastern Europe entered national politics as a major force. In the 1990s all sorts of religious communities are making come-backs in the countries of Central and Eastern Europe as independence movements and other forces transform those societies. And most countries of Asia have nothing like the Western history of falling church attendances followed by resurgence of religious and spiritual interests in a variety of novel and established institutions.

We can understand why the modernisation theorists failed to analyse their own societies accurately and made inadequate predictions for developing societies in Asia and elsewhere when we examine their assumptions. One assumption is that a church-like institution exists in and is equally important to all religions. The universalistic religions all have buildings in which rituals are performed by members, but they may not expect everyone to attend ceremonies regularly. Muslim women typically practise religious observances at home rather than at the mosque. Hindu rituals in Bali require some family member to attend, but other members of the household need not attend. In Southeast Asian Buddhism, it is much more important for people to support the monks and send male family members to live in the monasteries for a period of time than it is for individuals to join in ceremonials. Clearly we cannot measure the importance of religion to people in the same way everywhere.

When we readjust our measures and look at changing patterns of participation in ritual activities of various sorts in Asia, we find no single trend. Japan itself appears to be a maze of contradictions. Official statistics from the 1970s, far from showing that participation in religious organisation was declining, actually showed that the number of persons belonging to religious groups was greater than the entire population!

Clearly this could not be true, but what was going on? Initially this apparent oversubscription was explained by the fact that in Japan it is not regarded as inconsistent for a person to be a member of more than one religion. (In contrast to those which originated in West Asia, most Asian religions are not exclusivist in orientation, and revelation from many sources is accepted.) However, it is now recognised that the error came from over-reporting by religious organisations that were the source of the figures. This was not necessarily bald misrepresentation. For example, some shrines and temples saw themselves as serving a particular geographical area, so they reported the number of persons actually living there, ignoring the fact that not all residents participated in the activities of that shrine or temple and that the area was also served by Shinto shrines, Buddhist temples, Christian churches and New Religion congregations. Moreover, national shrines often counted up the number of visitors or purchasers of charms and amulets and reported all as representing memberships. Thus the numbers originally supplied were highly inaccurate. In fact, when people are asked individually, fewer than half the Japanese population say they belong to any denomination or sect.

If we look at the numbers of festivals and visits to shrines, we see another complicated picture. Over the past two to three decades, participation in activities of local shrines has declined. This seems to be related to the massive population shift Japan has experienced from rural to urban areas in the last century. There are not so many people left in the villages to visit the old shrines. Also, villagers remaining in the country (many of them older people with less energy to devote to community affairs) are finding it difficult to put on traditional Shinto festivals and have given some up. In the cities, people are not building enough new shrines to keep up with the rise in the urban population. However, major shrines still draw large numbers of visitors from a wide area. The festivals are perhaps not less popular, but are celebrated in fewer locations. Yet people question whether visits to these shrines represent genuine religious motives or whether they are simply popular holiday activities. The latter interpretation appears more plausible in the light of surveys which show that only very small percentages of people profess a high regard for religion or believe in supernatural entities.

Quite different is the situation in Java, where for centuries the majority of Javanese Muslims, both male and female, have made little use of Islamic ceremonial, using it only at a boy's circumcision, at marriage and at death. This was not the Muslim ideal, but it was common practice, even the norm. For this reason, many villages did not have even a *langgar* (small chapel). But things are changing, and interestingly the trend is the reverse of what is happening in Japan. Today few Javanese villages lack a *langgar* or mosque, indicating an actual increase in Islamic devotions. At the same time, some traditional non-Muslim rituals that Javanese used to perform regularly are now falling into disuse as the economic base of rural life changes. Thus the ceremonies in honour of the rice goddess, Dewi Sri, are dying out as the old, local varieties of rice are replaced by Green Revolution varieties that do not have the sacred aura of the old ones. The situation in Java, then, is not one of religious decline but of changing emphasis in religious practice.

Another gauge of secularisation (in addition to participation in religious ritual) is how much influence religions have in social life, particularly political life. A hallmark of industrialised Western societies is a more or less thorough-going 'separation of church and state', whereby the state is prohibited from establishing a state religion or supporting religions (as in the United States) or has ceremonial links with a church but otherwise remains neutral towards religions (as in the United Kingdom). Modernisation theorists considered separation of church and state the only 'rational' arrangement for a modern society, and expected all the developing countries to eventually evolve such an system. They did not realise that it was the product of quite specific, even peculiar, historical circumstances. In the eighteenth and nineteenth centuries, Western societies, in order to disengage themselves from rule by monarchs, had to dismantle the special relationships that had existed between the Christian churches and the European states in the feudal past. Because the churches had legitimated the authority of kings, the new republics had to sever relationships between church and state when sovereignty was lodged in the people. Churches were allowed to continue, but the state was not to support them, nor was any one of them designated as the sanctifier of the state.

Some Asian societies do indeed have such arrangements. Japan, whose present constitution was imposed upon it by the Americans at the end of World War II, is a case in point. Clearly in that case, the separation of church and state was meant not simply to provide the Japanese with a modern institutional structure, but to crush the emperor cult, which had played a major role in Japanese imperialism. Religions are allowed to flourish in Japan, but not to be linked to the state.

The communist countries of Asia provide somewhat different examples of the principle of separation of church and state. These countries, based on Marxist philosophy, are officially atheist but may allow some religions to be practised. Thus the constitutions of the PRC and the Democratic People's Republic of Korea (north Korea) stipulate that religious activity should be tolerated. This is counterbalanced by the state educational systems teaching people that religions give false understandings of the world. Also, there have been long periods in these countries in which religion has in fact been heavily suppressed. Despite this, especially among the peasants, many people have carried out folk rituals and observances in secret. Thus, in spite of official disapproval and the periodic strict suppression of religious behaviour in China, religious observances are still important in the lives of many. This is especially so among the Islamic minorities of northwestern China and the Tibetans.

Elsewhere in Asia, however, states have actually forged official links with religion. In Malaysia, Islam has been made the state religion. We can understand this as an action on the part of the indigenous Malays (who are Muslims) to see that their values are dominant in a society where they feel threatened by migrant communities (Chinese and Indian), who together make up almost half of the population. Indonesia has not made Islam the state religion, even though about 87 per cent of the population claimed to be Muslims on the last national census. But at the time the nation was founded its leaders did acknowledge the intense feeling on the part of Muslims that their religion was basic to the national identity by making 'belief in God' one of the five basic principles of the state (see Chapter 18). That formula also acknowledged the religious feelings of Christian and other minority groups. At the same time it protected Muslims who felt their indigenous customs might be threatened by over-zealous neighbours if the state were declared Islamic. The net effect of this formula was to enable the Indonesian state to call upon the loyalties of people from all over the archipelago who belonged to several religions and more than 250 different ethnic groups, and who were left with little to motivate allegiance to a common centre once their common enemy, the Dutch colonialists, were expelled. Many other 'new nations' — that is, nations formed out of former colonial empires of ethnically diverse populations since World War II — have faced a similar need to construct a common national identity that would inspire loyalty to the state. It is not surprising that some of these should choose not to separate church and state, but rather to enlist religious ideas and institutions in support of the state.

Just as Asian states sometimes find it useful to support religion or specific religions to express a national identity and inspire solidarity with the nation, so too may smaller units of society express their distinctiveness and provide mutual support through religions. This is the case, for example, for Indonesia's Christian Bataks who have moved in substantial numbers to predominantly Muslim cities outside their Sumatran homeland and are famous for their vigorous church life. Another case of religion supporting ethnic cohesiveness is provided by the Teochiu migrants in Hong Kong. The Teochiu and the native Cantonese are both Chinese, but they differ in language, in customs, in cuisine and in the deities they worship. By establishing temples to Teochiu deities and participating in Teochiu religious festivals, the migrants are able to maintain their community.

The power of religious symbols to represent ethnic distinctiveness and to command extraordinary loyalty and sacrifice can, of course, be manipulated in political rivalries between groups and have marked disruptive, even revolutionary, effects. For example, in northern India, Hindus incited by the leaders of the Bharata Janata Party are attempting to build a temple on a site occupied for some centuries by a Muslim mosque. At least one aim of the party leaders appears to be to gain support by focusing on religious differences and to exploit the threat that many Hindus feel from Islam.

Another example is Taiwan. There, particularly in the 1950s and 1960s, there was much bad blood between the native Taiwanese and the Mainlander Chinese. While both groups are ethnically Han Chinese, they were separated by language (Hokkien as opposed to Modern Standard Chinese or Mandarin) and history (Taiwan had been colonised by the Japanese in 1895 and thus was on the Japanese side in World War II). Moreover, in Taiwan the Mainlanders were a numerical minority, but they monopolised political power. During the push for economic development in Taiwan beginning in the early 1950s, the Taiwanese government attempted to suppress local religious festivals and celebrations, ostensibly because it regarded the relatively large amounts of money spent on feasting, firecrackers and religious items as wasteful and better invested in reconstruction. This gave many Taiwanese an added reason to participate in these festivals and the desire to register a (thinly) disguised protest against the government; it also strengthened the symbolic meaning of participation in local religious festivals.

Another weak assumption in modernisation theory was that religions are essentially sets of intellectual propositions about the nature of the universe (and for this reason are particularly vulnerable to the 'march of science'). Dogma and its intellectual justification were indeed the predominant emphasis in European Christianity, especially Protestantism, as it developed a defensive stance in the face of the growing influence of science. Yet Christianity was not always so narrow, nor have other religions given so much emphasis to dogma. Islam, for example, has always placed far more emphasis upon sets of laws governing family and community life. And Buddhist monastic traditions emphasise spiritual practices that are to be used in an open-ended exploratory way to understand, in a non-intellectual, experiential mode, the nature of mind and nature. Further, all religions can have value in ways other than describing the world, and in ways that are not undermined when it is found that science has a different account of how things work: the poetic and evocative power of religious symbols enhances people's emotional lives; the ethical systems within religions may moderate the harsh impact of political and economic forces on people's lives and the environment; and mystical practices can be used to expand the range of human experience and understanding.

Finally, modernisation theorists failed to appreciate that, no matter how much we understand about how the world works from a scientific point of view, uncertainty concerning our individual fates cannot be eliminated. This is felt not only by the 'person in the street' but by businesspeople who manage large personal fortunes and even people who hold the fortunes of nations in their hands. Beliefs in the supernatural are attractive supports to people in such situations. Sometimes they encourage people to believe they can manipulate fate and sometimes they console people for a fate suffered. They may also help people justify extraordinary good fate to themselves when others around them are not so fortunate. So it is not surprising rumours were reported about American President Reagan's wife consulting an astrologer for him and about Indonesian President Suharto engaging in a seance in which he called upon Semar, the guardian spirit of Java, to counsel him and stand behind his power. And when people are asking spirits for power and financial success, we can expect to see them expressing their thanks by making donations to religious institutions and sponsoring religious celebrations, especially when supporting a shrine or ceremony is itself a public declaration of success that wins status. This is indeed found in Penang, where the general rise in the level of prosperity in the 1920s was accompanied by the building or restoration of several imposing Chinese temples. In Taiwan, too, economic development has been accompanied by more, not less, religious display, as those positioned to benefit from economic growth thank the gods for their good fortune by refurbishing old temples or building new ones, by participating in pilgrimages, or by holding bigger, more expensive festivals. For example, the primary religious festival in honour of the goddess Mazu (the patron saint of Taiwan) in the town of Beigang has burgeoned from an event attracting people in south-central Taiwan to one drawing people from all over the island, and in much greater numbers. There are now several rival Mazu festivals which compete for the honour of the biggest and most bustling.

The enthusiasm we see in both industrialised Western countries and industrialising Asian countries for 'tips' and assistance from unseen beings does not deny the expanding scope of rational calculation in business and productive activities. An enormous range of technical expertise is available to national leaders and businesspeople in both East and West that was not available a hundred or two hundred years ago. And even then, most tasks in all societies, even those with the simplest technologies, were accomplished simply with the aid of technical knowledge. The trend we have seen over the last centuries is that, as the area of scientific expertise expands, the range of situations in which people make use of apparently supernatural forces has diminished proportionally. The use of the supernatural has not, however, been eliminated. We must also leave open the possibility that our science is not complete. Some practices which today appear to have no scientific basis may tomorrow be proven efficacious and understood in scientific terms. Acupuncture appears to have gone part way along this route. A Chinese healing practice once thought to be entirely superstitious by Westerners, it is now used by many Western-trained physicians because its efficacy has been demonstrated. However, there is as yet no satisfactory scientific explanation for how it works.

Thus in many Asian countries religion has so far not declined in popularity or attraction as was thought to have happened in the West. Why? There are several reasons. Firstly, religions are useful in symbolising group solidarity, and both new Asian nations and smaller communities within the Asian nations have made use of this. Secondly, many Asian people associate prosperity with supernatural assistance and, as they become better off, show their gratitude by making donations — or giving return gifts — to their gods. Thirdly, religious activity, whether it be donations to a temple or a sect, sponsorship of a ceremony, or acting in a support or leadership role in the local religious community, confers prestige on the actor. Many persons, as they reach middle age and are financially more comfortable and have fewer responsibilities around the home, become part of a temple committee or equivalent organisation. Fourthly, not all elements of religion are effectively challenged by science, and Asians, like people elsewhere, continue to find value in the genuinely spiritual and ethical dimensions of their faiths. Curiously, many Asians are learning a new appreciation of these values through religions originating to the west of their homeland, Islam and Christianity, whilst many Westerners have rediscovered an appreciation of religion through East Asian religions — Hinduism, Buddhism and elements of Daoism — that are in the vanguard of the Western religious revival.

Guide to further reading

Caldarola, Carlo (ed.), *Religion and Societies: Asia and the Middle East*, Mouton, The Hague, 1982

A country-by-country survey of the development and present state of religious life in Asia, including West Asia, edited by a sociologist. This work contains both historical and sociological perspectives on Asian religious life.

Eliade, Mircea, *A History of Religious Ideas*, University of Chicago Press, Chicago, 1982

An exploration of the development of religious thought from the beginnings of human history to modern times by a doyen of the history of religions. This multi-volume work covers both universalistic religions and reflections on the nature of the community religions which preceded them.

Kendall, Laural, *Shamans, Housewives and Other Restless Spirits: Women in Korean Ritual Life*, University of Hawaii Press, Honolulu, 1985

A study of folk beliefs and practices in modern Korea, with a focus on women's roles.

Kitagawa, Joseph (ed.), *The Religious Traditions of Asia*, Macmillan Publishing Co., New York, 1989; excerpts from *The Encyclopedia of Religion*, Mircea Eliade, editor in chief
Comprehensive historical treatment on selected topics from the *Encyclopedia* by prominent authors. Emphasises institutional and political history rather than the history of religious thought.
Norbeck, Edward, *Religion and Society in Modern Japan: Continuity and Change*, Tourmaline Press, Houston, 1970
A standard anthropological source on the place of religious beliefs and practices in postwar Japan
Smart, Ninian, *The World's Religions: Old Traditions and Modern Transformations*, Cambridge University Press, Cambridge, 1989
A leading historian of religion provides an historical overview of religious history taking regions rather than universalistic religions as the main organising device for his discussion. Much contemporary material.
Yang, C.K., *Religion in Chinese Society: A Study of Contemporary Functions of Religion and Some of their Historical Factors*, University of California Press, Berkeley and Los Angeles, 1970
A classic anthropological study of religion at the folk and the official levels in traditional Chinese society.

37 | Cultures under pressure

Asian arts and literatures have changed dramatically during the last two centuries under the impact of several forces. European colonialism and imperialism introduced new cultural forms and transformed the socio-economic and political context within which Asian cultures operated. In addition, Asian nationalism profoundly transformed what Asians themselves expected of culture. In those countries ruled by Marxist-Leninist parties, we must add a further factor: the political imperatives of Marxism-Leninism, which have imposed very special demands on artists and the kind of work they produce. Marxist thinking has even exercised influence over the literature and arts of countries which never underwent leftist revolutions, such as Japan.

Along with guns and trade goods, European colonialists brought elements of their cultures to Asia. For many, this was merely an incidental aspect of profit-making, while for some — Christian and secular missionaries — it was a major goal. The French in particular talked of a *mission civilisatrice*, or civilising mission, which involved spreading French culture as widely and deeply as possible. Europe's introduction of new and challenging ideas to Asia, of course, was matched by Asia's gift to Europe of ideas just as challenging and just as new. The history of European and Asian cultural cross-fertilisation is a fascinating story in its own right. The exchange, however, was never equal, not because Asian cultures were less in quality or refinement, but because changes in the society and politics under the impact of colonialism demanded far greater cultural adaptation on the part of Asians than they did of Europeans. New niches for cultural expression opened while others closed, leaving Asian cultures deeply transformed. The process was immensely complex, varying from era to era and from country to country. Many of the cultural traditions we described in Chapter 6 continued to thrive and develop well into the colonial era without any appreciable European influence; others took elements of European culture and forged new, hybrid forms; still others began to crumble and decline. These processes continue to this day and we can only sketch their broadest lines here.

While Japan was subject to major influences from Western imperialism, it also imposed its own brand on the countries of East and Southeast Asia for a longer or shorter period. Japanese colonialism exercised a profound impact on Korean and to a lesser extent Chinese culture, but also provoked serious nationalist responses. Japan modernised itself far more quickly and successfully than any other Asian country, which meant that its adoption of Western and international trends in the arts was much more from a position of strength than in any other country of East or Southeast Asia. On the other hand, its situation was different from other countries in that it had to sustain the humiliation of defeat in World War II, a fact which was reflected in its cultural life during the post-1945 period.

The rise of a new nation-state in Indonesia and the transformation of old nations in Thailand and Vietnam into equally new nation-states put further pressure on culture. Right from the start, nationalists turned to traditional forms of cultural communication in order to spread their ideas, and once the new nation-states were established, they began to demand greater cultural orthodoxy to reinforce state identity. These demands of orthodoxy fell especially hard on ethnic minorities whose cultures were valued less than those of the dominant centre. The cultural diversity of small ethnic groups has been in steady retreat across the whole of Southeast Asia since the start of this century. Even where minority and majority cultures are preserved in institutes of national culture, the vitality of these cultures has often been stifled. In Indonesia and Vietnam, the demand for orthodoxy fell also on forms of culture associated with particular social classes. Both countries saw extensive debate on the correct place of literature and the arts in the national struggle.

In China, the May Fourth Movement of 1919 included a quest for a new culture. It wanted to change or uproot traditional Chinese culture, which was seen as a relic of a Confucian and reactionary past. Although firmly anti-imperialist, it was also heavily influenced by Western cultural and literary patterns. There was simply no way around the dilemma that if China was going to modernise and reject Confucianism, it would have to adapt itself to Western influence.

Marxist-Leninist parties have had no monopoly of censorship of the arts in Eastern Asia. But they have been much more direct in their demands that the arts should serve the state and socialism as a vehicle of propaganda. Marxist-Leninist parties in China, north Korea and Vietnam have attempted to build up a cultural cadre which can create a 'proletarian' mass culture. However, these cultures' attachment to a class does not mean they are not nationalist. All Marxist-Leninist parties have demanded that the arts remain 'patriotic' and build creatively on the traditions of their particular nation. In theoretical terms, an important landmark in Asian Marxist-Leninist thinking on the arts was Mao

Zedong's account put forward at a major forum held in the CCP head-quarters, Yan'an, in 1942. Mao's focus was on the propaganda and revolutionary functions of the arts and the creation of works which would appeal to the masses, not merely to an educated elite. Both Korea and Vietnam experienced savage wars (see Chapters 21 and 22), during both of which the arts were used by both sides, especially the left wing, for propaganda and nationalist causes.

In China, Marxism-Leninism took on an extreme form during the Cultural Revolution (1966–76) in which class struggle was to take precedence at all times. The arts had to give play to the CCP and Chairman Mao as the sources of all that was positive and good. Content was to be modern, socialist and patriotic. The pure traditional arts were all but wiped out, with the tradition surviving only in certain aspects of form.

Music and drama

In Southeast Asia, European cultural influence was first noticed in music. European traders and sailors brought their musical instruments with them, and in the turbulent port cities of Asia's great trade routes, a hybrid musical culture quickly developed. European administrators brought their own musical tastes, and the generations of Asian performers whom they recruited to provide Western music at official and social occasions took their instruments and techniques into the musical world of the cities of the region. We know tantalisingly few details about these hybrid musical forms; because they drew from Western traditions, most European observers described them as 'debased' and left it at that. One or two descendants of these early forms, however, still survive in Indonesia and they suggest the kind of musical blending which took place. *Kroncong* music, for instance, emerged among descendants of the Christianised slaves of Portuguese merchants in the Jakarta area. The *kroncong* itself is a kind of ukulele or small guitar, based originally on Portuguese models, but the name also stands for a larger ensemble of guitars and violins, with a cello, a tambourine and triangle, and an occasional flute. *Kroncong* music follows Western conventional harmonies and chord progressions, but its style draws much from the *gamelan*: the stringed instruments are plucked to provide a percussive, somewhat interlocking base, over which the flute, one of the violins or a voice languidly embroiders a crooning melody.

In the court cities of Java, another kind of musical development took place. Dutch rule on the island operated through an indigenous aristocracy called the *priyayi* whose function was not so much to administer as to preserve the illusion of indigenous rule and to carry out the political and religious rituals traditionally expected of a ruling class. Deprived of political power, many members of the *priyayi* channelled their energies into cultural pursuits, refining and complicating central features of Javanese culture such as *gamelan* and batik-making, and thus creating an increasing distance between aristocratic and folk art. The effect of this was to make *gamelan* music, which had once been shared by all levels of society, something closer to being the cultural property of the old elite. *Gamelan* became less receptive to outside influences, and its further development now came less from vibrant local cultures than from the more intellectual reflections of court musicians. Something similar happened in Vietnam, where courts from the fifteenth to the eighteenth centuries followed Chinese musical styles increasingly closely, isolating them from popular tradition.

Neither *gamelan* nor traditional Vietnamese music died as a result of this refinement — in both countries, aristocratic arts remained in demand amongst those who held or aspired to aristocratic status. In both countries, however, nationalism largely rejected these compromised musical forms and turned instead to popular traditions. In Indonesia, the *kroncong*-style of Ismail Marzuki (1914–58) became the principal vehicle for nationalist songs, while in Vietnam a whole repertoire of patriotic songs was crafted out of the folk tradition of peasant songs. Thai court music was never rejected in this fashion, but its close dependence on court musicians kept it at a distance from folk music.

The commercialisation of music in Southeast Asia began in the early twentieth century with the introduction of jazz. A Western musical form with no pretensions to status, jazz appealed alike to European settlers and increasingly Westernised local elites. Jazz clubs and professional jazz groups proliferated; King Bhumibol Adulyadej of Thailand is an accomplished jazz musician. The postwar development of recording technology led to further change: the hit, a relatively short-lived song with romantic lyrics and a catchy tune, became the most widespread musical form in all three Southeast Asian countries. Some hits were virtually indistinguishable from their Western counterparts — indeed, in the absence of significant copyright laws, many were virtually identical — while others drew to varying extents on local folk traditions. Because of their popularity and their similarity to Western forms, however, they often drew the hostility of conservative traditional musicians and other cultural brokers.

Recording technology, however, has also encouraged experimentation with other styles. The most successful of these has been Indonesia's *dangdut* music, a dynamic blend of *kroncong*, West Asian music and Western heavy rock, whose heavy irregular beat and sinuous compelling melodies command an enormous following amongst the poor of Indonesia's cities. Even the more traditional styles have been influenced. Bali's strong *gamelan* tradition was never affected by the process of court-centred refinement which took place in Java, Thailand and Vietnam and it remained a vibrant and constantly developing part of village tradition.

Since World War II, however, it has responded to commercial demands with more lively and catchy tunes and by emphasising the personalities of individual 'star' performers.

None of these developments severed Southeast Asian music's close relationship to drama. Traditional drama, of course, continued, with Europeans occasionally appearing in traditional stories as comic or frightening extras. A series of new dramatic forms also appeared, each incorporating a strong musical line. Vietnam's *tuong cai luong*, or reform drama, was a variety of musical drama which developed around the time of World War I and became enormously popular, not just as a variety of entertainment but as a means of disseminating new ideas. Plays without music in the Western style were presented from time to time, but until well after World War II these were either drawing-room imitations of European models or stiff political pieces. Only with the advent of the Indonesian dramatist W.S. Rendra and his *Theater Bengkel* (Workshop Theatre) has a strong indigenous dramatic interpretation begun to emerge.

After the Meiji restoration of 1868, Japan introduced Western music very quickly and with great enthusiasm, beginning with military band music but soon spreading to many other areas. Japan quickly became a centre which famous European and American musicians wished to visit, and it spawned its own Western-style composers from early in the twentieth century. The leading early example was Yamada Kosaku, a German-trained musician who made the first major attempts in Japan to compose orchestral works and operas in the Western idiom. Since World War II, Japan has retained its reputation as the main centre for Western-style music in Asia. It has become a major manufacturer of musical instruments derived from Western music and the method of violin teaching devised by the educational philosopher Suzuki Shinichi has been introduced all over the world. Traditional Japanese music has tended to decline at the expense of Western music. However, it shows absolutely no signs of disappearing. One example illustrating this point is the Japanese Imperial Household Agency, which still employs musicians for the preservation of the old court music. Some attempts have been made to integrate Western with traditional music. Michio Miyagi (1894–1956) was a leader in this field who introduced some Western elements into his own traditional compositions and also was the first to use traditional instruments in a European-influenced style. This latter trend has become a prominent feature of postwar Japanese music.

In the early years after the Meiji restoration, there was a move to reform the traditional *kabuki* theatre by modernising it in line with Western practices. On the whole, this was not a great success. The reason, as one noted authority puts it, was that 'trams and telephones proved totally incompatible with *kabuki*'s elaborately conceived patterns of non-realistic movement and style of elocution'.[1] One feature of this new-style *kabuki* which did remain permanent was that literary figures outside the theatrical world, such as Mishima Yukio (1925–70), wrote new scripts for the *kabuki*. But even this has rarely inspired great enthusiasm among theatre-goers, and these newly written *kabuki* rarely run for very long. Brandon describes the *kabuki* of the 1980s as 'a classical, orthodox theatre in which little change occurs'.[2] Despite this lack of creativity, its early demise is extremely unlikely. In 1966 the enormous new state-run National Theatre was opened in Tokyo for *kabuki* and other traditional Japanese theatre forms. There is still an excellent acting tradition and many young people among the audiences.

In 1906, Tsubouchi Shoyo (1859–1935) established the Literary Arts Society and thus began a new form of Japanese literary drama known as *shingeki*, which literally means 'new drama'. He was a great admirer of Shakespeare and other Western dramatists. He translated all Shakespeare's works into Japanese and expressed his belief that 'research into Shakespeare might be the most useful means of improving the Japanese drama, not only for me personally, but for the Japanese as a whole'.[3] The point of the 'new drama' was to adopt Western drama for Japan, to translate many of its items into Japanese, but more importantly to use its structure, emphasis on conflict, characterisation and literary and performance conventions for a new Japanese drama. The 'new drama' has never had an enormous audience, but it has exercised substantial influence in the twentieth-century Japanese theatre. Alone among the arts, it never succumbed to the dictates of the militarist government. Indeed, Kubo Sakae (1900–1957), one of the most famous of Japan's playwrights, was a Marxist whose aim was to create a proletarian theatre. His *Region of Volcanic Ash* (*Kazambaichi*), from the late 1930s, is an extremely long play which describes the society of an impoverished area of Japan in great detail. Kubo himself described it as 'anti-capitalist realism', but in 1940 the government suppressed the left-wing theatre and Kubo was imprisoned.

The period since Japan's defeat has seen something of a reaction against excessive dependence on Western forms in the 'new drama' and, since 1960, even what one writer has described as 'the return of the gods'. By this he means that in order to escape 'the debilitating sense of enforced passivity and stasis' they had experienced in the preceding period, including their failure to reflect the problems of Japanese society in the years immediately following Japan's defeat, the playwrights of the years following 1960 engineered 'moments when gods once again came to populate the Japanese stage',[4] just as happened in the traditional *no* drama. There has been a trend also for the main troupes to abandon the major cities for smaller towns. They work out of trucks and perform in tents. Brandon sums up their work and the post-1960 'new drama' as follows:

These new theatre artists are not so much specifically Japanese as they are part of the international theatre of the young who see a performance as a participatory experience, a communication enveloping actor and spectator (and hopefully eliminating the usual barriers between them), a direct social action, valued not for its ideological message *per se*, nor for its cognitive or rational statement about society, nor indeed for its beauty of form, but for the momentary, but intensely real, human contact which, hopefully, can occur when the artificial conventions of theatre, Western or Asian, no longer apply.[5]

Just as in Southeast Asia and Japan, music in twentieth-century China has been subject to severe pressures and contradictions. Some of these contradictions are expressed in the career of its most famous composer, Xian Xinghai (1905–45). Trained in the Western classical tradition at the Paris Conservatory, he was also a communist and held to the belief that the function of music was to spread revolutionary activism among the people. He composed China's first symphony but he was also the leading musician of the CCP in its headquarters in Yan'an. As such he wrote revolutionary marches and strongly nationalistic music such as the *Yellow River Cantata*, which aimed to express in music the river which above all others symbolises the Chinese nation and psychology. As one Western writer puts it, 'Xian attracts interest merely by the juxtaposition of such cultural antitheses in a single career'.[6]

The Chinese were from the start highly ambivalent about Western music. Some Chinese thought it very much superior to their own, but ordinary people certainly did not give up their own folk or theatrical music, and the traditions of aristocratic music also remained very much alive. Based on Mao's ideas as expressed at the Yan'an Forum in 1942, the CCP saw music, like all other arts, as a weapon to be used on behalf of the revolution and the proletariat. During the Cultural Revolution, there was a strong tendency to condemn classical Western music as well as contemporary American popular music as bourgeois. However, the 1980s have seen a strong revival of interest in Western music of all kinds, and in the 1990s young people, especially those in the cities, are far more likely to admire disco than traditional Chinese music. Moreover, since the 1970s China has been a major producer and exporter of Western musical instruments. 'Lark' brand oboes, violins and so on dominate the bottom end of this particular market.

The 'spoken drama' (*huaju*) is the term applied in China to dramas which have spoken dialogue, but very little or no music or singing. The origins of the Chinese spoken drama were actually not in China but in Japan, where in 1907 Chinese actors performed in Chinese a dramatisation of Harriet Beecher Stowe's novel *Uncle Tom's Cabin*. Called *The Black Slave's Cry to Heaven (Heinu yutian lu)*, it was strongly hostile to slavery and to all kinds of oppression. The spoken drama was later to play a highly progressive political role in China, especially during the May Fourth Movement and during the 1930s. China's most famous dramatist of the twentieth century, Cao Yu, wrote several very important plays during the 1930s and 1940s on progressive and nationalist themes. His most famous item is probably *Thunderstorm* (*Leiyu*), a tragedy which attacks the traditional family system in very strong terms.

Under the People's Republic, the spoken play has generally flourished as a dramatic and literary form, except during the Cultural Revolution decade (1966–76). In the 1950s the propaganda and nationalist emphasis was very strong. However, during the 1980s and 1990s, the trend has been for playwrights to oppose excessive propaganda, in the knowledge that their audiences find it boring. The emphasis placed on the role of the CCP has declined more and more while greater influence has been accepted from the West in terms of both content and form. Numerous dramas have been set in the present (i.e. in the China of the 1980s or 1990s), and have often criticised it severely.

At first, traditional drama was only marginally affected by the revolutionary tide sweeping China in the first half of this century. Many young people may have opposed such reactionary culture during the May Fourth Movement, but it nevertheless retained a substantial following. The CCP's policy was to retain and patronise traditional drama on the grounds that this had always been the entertainment of the masses, but to revolutionise it so that the heroes it presented were proletarian. A form favoured by the CCP was the 'newly arranged historical drama'. The style of such a drama was traditional and the story was set in the dynastic past, but it expressed the Marxist theme of struggle and rose to a denouement which should ideally show the wretched of the Earth victorious over the rich and powerful of the feudal ruling classes, or Chinese patriotism winning out over treachery. Dramas about peasant rebellions of the past, lovers who overcame the feudal system of arranged marriages, or patriotic wars against foreign aggressors were all very popular.

However, during the Cultural Revolution, Mao Zedong's wife Jiang Qing seized control of the Chinese theatre and in effect banned all but a very few of her own 'model dramas'. One of the main features of these models was a very stark characterisation according to which positive and negative characters were sharply delineated by class. The proletarian characters had to be very good indeed, selfless and strong supporters of the CCP, while the bourgeois were evil. Western musical instruments were added to the orchestra and the music made more staccato on the grounds that it thus became more revolutionary and heroic, but some of the traditional melodies were retained.

The period of reform has seen a large-scale revival of traditional drama and 'newly arranged historical dramas'. In the 1990s the government has even run an officially sponsored campaign to try to revive the traditional theatre as an art-form of which the Chinese can be proud. The themes of the traditional items in the 1980s and 1990s are far more nationalistic than they used to be, with very little concern for the lower classes or the plight of the poor. The hero is more likely to be a famous and distinguished emperor than a peasant rebel. However, young people are nowadays simply not interested in the traditional theatre, especially in the cities. They regard it as irrelevant to their lives. Moreover, television is now very widespread in China and forms a substantial rival to any live theatre, simply because it is so convenient and obviates any need to face the highly uncomfortable transport system.

Literature and language

Changes in Southeast Asian literatures were part of a broader change in the character of Southeast Asian languages. A key development was the adoption of Roman characters for the writing of the Vietnamese and Malay languages. This took place initially for the convenience of Europeans. In 1651 a Roman Catholic missionary sought to simplify the study of Vietnamese by priests by devising a style of romanisation for Vietnamese, called *quoc ngu*, which added diacritical marks to Roman letters to indicate tones. For the next two centuries his invention remained a seldom-used curiosity, but in the second half of the nineteenth century, the French colonial government adopted *quoc ngu*, partly to avoid the old script's closeness to Chinese. Malay, which has none of the tones of Vietnamese or Chinese, was easily transcribed into Roman characters and was preferred by the Dutch as a language for trade, government and the law. These colonial impositions, however, gave the Vietnamese and Indonesian peoples a powerful linguistic tool. *Quoc ngu* was far simpler than the old Chinese and *nom* scripts and soon spread widely; for the first time people outside the ruling elite could enjoy the benefits of literacy. We have seen previously that European influence brought a general decline in literacy in Indonesia. The new romanised Malay, however, was by no means a difficult language and Indonesians gradually began to make up the lost ground.

This process both enabled and was assisted by the spread of commercial publishing, especially of newspapers, which became an established feature of public life in the second half of the nineteenth century, thanks to new print technology. Publishers also met a growing demand for creative literature amongst the merchants and bureaucrats of Hanoi, Saigon, Bangkok, Batavia and Surabaya and their increasingly educated wives. Novels and short stories became firmly established as a Southeast Asian literary form. Thai and Vietnamese creative writing is still rare in English translation, but interested readers can follow a rich tradition of

Indonesian prose composition in the translated writings of men such as Sutan Takdir Alisyahbana, Mochtar Lubis and Pramoedya Ananta Toer.

In both Vietnam and Indonesia, the change was not merely in the mechanics of writing. As the scope of literacy expanded, socio-political circumstances changed and new ideas arrived from the West, both languages began to take on new vocabulary at a rapid rate, adopting words from Asian and European languages alike and coining new terms of their own. Even grammatical structure altered, as people sought new or more effective ways to express ideas. In Vietnam, the translation of great literary works, such as the nineteenth century *Tale of Kieu* (*Truyen Kieu*), from *nom* into *quoc ngu* further sensitised Vietnamese to the role of linguistic structure and vocabulary in creative expression. Linguistic change not only enabled people to formulate concepts of nationalism, but became one of the symbols of nationalist vigour. Indonesian and Vietnamese nationalists ran literacy classes for the masses. Indonesia's 1928 Youth Congress, which formally adopted Indonesia as the framework for the struggle against the Dutch, renamed Malay *Bahasa Indonesia* (Indonesian language) and specified it as one of the central elements in the Indonesian identity.

Because language and literature were so closely associated with national revival, cultural issues occupied a central position in political debate. In Indonesia, in particular, a long-running dispute emerged. One side argued that art and literature were always political, reflecting and reinforcing the values and interests of one or other social group, and that therefore culture should be 'engaged', taking sides and acknowledging the power of art to shape the great political issues of the day. The other side argued in contrast that true art reflected universal human values which transcended specific national, political or social interests, and that any attempt to politicise art and literature was debasing and destructive. Sutan Takdir Alisyahbana, who founded Indonesia's first literary journal in 1933, was the foremost proponent of the latter view, while the former view has been backed from time to time by both the left and the right. During the late 1950s and early 1960s the debate was conducted with a venom which still disfigures Indonesian literary discussion.

One of the aims of the May Fourth revolutionaries in China was to create a new language for literature. They wanted not only the overthrow of tradition, but also the establishment of a new world based on science and democracy. This necessitated major changes in the Chinese language to make it capable of expressing the new world. Numerous new terms must be created to express new ideas and objects, and the terminology specifically related to Confucianism and other outdated doctrines must be downgraded. Up to this point, the literature most admired by the educated elite had used classical language which was very difficult for ordinary people to understand. The May Fourth Movement greatly strengthened the notion that since literature should be for the masses, it should quite properly use colloquial language instead.

The PRC has also changed the Chinese language substantially. In 1955 Chinese newspapers and magazines began using simplified characters in place of the relatively complex traditional ones. This was the first thorough-going reform of the Chinese script since the third century B.C. It has proved permanent, despite occasional moves to reinstate the old characters, and as of the early 1990s the great majority of PRC publications nowadays use simplified characters. Hong Kong and Taiwan publications, on the other hand, continue to use the old-form complex characters.

The May Fourth Movement spawned numerous literary societies, each with different theories about the nature and functions of literature. Possibly the best known of these is the Creation Society, established in July 1921, which first advocated the notion of art for art's sake, but later changed to a more left-wing espousal of proletarian literature. Among the leaders of the Creation Society was Guo Moruo (1892–1978), who was to become one of the favoured authors of the PRC and who was among the very few who survived the Cultural Revolution relatively unscathed.

The most famous of twentieth-century Chinese writers is most certainly Lu Xun, the pen-name of Zhou Shuren (1881–1936). He was an active supporter of the May Fourth Movement and the progressive literary and other movements which followed it. His most productive period ran from 1918 to 1927 — in other words, he took part in, influenced and was in turn influenced by the literary trends of the May Fourth Movement. *Call to Arms (Na han)* is a collection of fourteen short stories written between 1918 and 1922, which many in the PRC regard as 'the foundation stone of modern Chinese literature' for their strong attacks on the old society and the 'cannibalistic' or dog-eat-dog values of the people who controlled it.[7] The best known of the stories is *The True Story of Ah Q (A Q zhengzhuan)*, which is about a coolie's life over the period of the 1911 revolution. Despite the promises and his own enthusiastic support for the revolution, it makes absolutely no difference to his miserable life. In the end he is executed for a crime of which he is not even aware, let alone guilty.

The war against Japan spawned a great deal of literature aimed specifically at the defence of the nation, as well as that produced in the CCP's areas, which was both revolutionary and nationalistic (i.e. it sought not only to defend China against Japan but also to use literature to overthrow exploiting classes and change society). The early years of the PRC developed this approach, and most of the many novels written during the 1950s were heavily propagandistic in nature. As in drama, the Cultural Revolution was much narrower, far less productive and more rigid in its demand that literature should promote the banner of class struggle above all. Even the novels of the 1950s came under savage criticism for being bourgeois.

The late 1970s and 1980s saw an impressive literary revival in China. The first period focused mainly on works attacking the society of the Cultural Revolution and the wounds it had inflicted on China: the 'wound' literature. In general the trend was towards far greater liberalism and individualism in literature, with a consequent diminution of direct propaganda content. Chinese writers experimented with various literary trends in the West. A prominent example is Wang Meng, who wrote a short novel called *The Butterfly (Hudie)*, published in 1980, which was notable for its impressionism rather than the story it told. The idea that atmosphere and social questioning, not narrative, should be central to a good novel, whether short or long, was quite daring in the early 1980s. The literary world pushed against the authorities and the extent of liberalism grew, even though specific works continued to be banned. Liberals and literary innovators assumed positions of great influence and even power. However, this situation was sharply reversed with the crisis of 1989. The literary world was, in general, extremely supportive of the student movement and suffered a serious blow with the military suppression of June 1989. The career of Wang Meng exemplifies the trend of the 1980s. From literary leader he actually ascended to become the national Minister of Culture early in 1986, but was dismissed from that position in September 1989 following the June crackdown.

In Japan the movement towards a modern fiction predated that in China, simply because it was much quicker to modernise. In the 1880s the literary reformer Tsubouchi Shoyo, the translator of Shakespeare into Japanese, advocated realistic and rational writing for the novel; and Futabatei Shimei (1864–1909) wrote a novel using colloquial Japanese in place of the difficult classical language in use up to that time. These moves heralded what some have regarded as the growth of the modern Japanese novel. In the decade following Japan's victory in the Russo-Japanese War in 1905, a whole series of Japanese novelists emerged, among whom Tanizaki Junichiro was a distinguished representative. His novel of 1929, *Some Prefer Nettles (Tade kuu mushi)*, takes up the theme of conflict between traditional and Western-inspired ways. On the whole, however, Tanizaki's novels are psychological, not social, studies. They rarely deal with contemporary social phenomena. Among the generation following Tanizaki were Kawabata Yasunari (1899–1972), an enormously prolific writer who had an obsession with beauty and the aesthetic, and Kobayashi Takiji (1903–33), a good representative of the 'proletarian' school which wished to promote revolution through literature. Of these two extraordinary and very different writers, Kawabata attained to a far higher reputation in Japan and the world, and was even awarded the Nobel Prize for Literature in 1968. The proletarian school, not surprisingly, attracted the ire of the militarist government.

In the years immediately following Japan's defeat, the 'postwar group' of novelists dealt with Japan's wartime experience from a leftist point of view. On the whole they were not revolutionaries or Marxists, but rather represented a kind of attempt to expiate Japan's guilt over Japan's invasions of China, Korea and other countries. For the writers of this group, who included Noma Hiroshi and Takeda Taijun, 'the issue of war took on an almost theological significance, as they linked it to the problem of original sin'.[8]

At the same time, the old guard of novelists continued to write in a traditionalist style. During the war, Tanizaki Junichiro had begun what has become his most famous work, *Sasameyuki*, which has been translated into English as *The Makioka Sisters*, but it was not completed until 1948. It describes a great but declining merchant family over the period 1936–41. As in all Tanizaki's works, there is a feeling of gloom overshadowing the novel. The main character, Yukiko, is a highly introverted woman about to be married when the novel ends, but for whom this is anything but a happy conclusion. In this, as in his other later works, Tanizaki gives very little attention to the war. The same applies to Kawabata Yasunari, whose postwar novel *Yama no oto (The Sound of the Mountain)* presents through fiction a consciousness of beauty more appropriate to a dying past than to the postwar world.

Later novelists have focused attention not on war or the past but on the sense of crisis in Japanese postwar life. The content has included the changes in family and social life which have swept Japan in the postwar era, and which have accompanied Japan's ascension among the world's economic superpowers. Abe Kobo's works employ an abstract avant-garde style to reflect the processes of urbanisation, with its skyscrapers and concrete jungles, and its effects upon people. In the West the most famous of all postwar Japanese writers is probably the novelist and playwright Mishima Yukio, who considered himself a disciple of Kawabata, but is nevertheless more nihilistic about the modern world than an admirer of classicism. His novels 'may give an impression of vigor and self-control but not of classical harmony'.[9] His works are set in contemporary, or at least modern, Japan. Politically and socially he was extremely conservative and nationalist, and even set up a small private army to defend the emperor. He created a sensation in 1970 by committing ritual suicide in public, the traditional *seppuku* or *harakiri*, after an unsuccessful attempt to provoke a mutiny in Tokyo's military headquarters.

Visual arts

Of all the Southeast Asian visual arts, painting has been stylistically most influenced by the West. The Javanese aristocratic painter, Raden Saleh (1814–80), who studied for years in Europe, introduced a naturalistic-romantic style closely based on European models, and since then much Indonesian painting has moved with the flow of various currents in Western art. The debate over artistic engagement was at its strongest amongst painters and figures such as Affandi (1910–90), who painted in an individual style with few distinctive Southeast Asian features. Probably the most important development in the visual arts has been the emergence of 'batik painting', in which traditional batik waxing techniques are used to produce artistic works for display. The combination of traditional materials and techniques with modern dyes and a vastly enlarged range of subjects has produced a distinctive and exciting new form which has begun to find a following in the West.

In wood and stone carving, by contrast, Western stylistic influence has been minimal, largely because, in Thailand and parts of Indonesia at least, carving has retained its ritual significance, partly due to the fact that commercial demand for the Southeast Asian product has been precisely on the grounds of its distinctiveness. The enormous touristic demand for quasi-traditional artwork has tended to encourage mass production of identical pieces for sale, but the fact that fine pieces of Southeast Asian traditional art still command high prices suggests that this may not be occurring at the expense of traditional craftsmanship.

Since the time of the Meiji restoration, Japanese painting has also undergone Western influence so strong that it can now readily be classified into traditional and Western-influenced categories. At the same time, some features of painting originally associated with the West have found their way into the Japanese style. These include notions such as realism and techniques such as perspective and shading. Although interest in Japan's cultural heritage in the visual arts has remained very strong in the period since World War II, the complicated society which has emerged from Japan's defeat and economic prosperity has brought a strong subjectivist element into Japanese painting, which has made it both international and national.

As in other cultural forms, the May Fourth Movement produced a profound impact on the visual arts in China, and in particular on painting. The thrust was to create a new form of arts based on Western models, but to combine it with Chinese tradition. One approach was that of the Lingnan (or Canton) School which 'set out to create a new art for China by an arbitrary synthesis of traditional technique and modern subject matter'.[10] At the same time the decades following the May Fourth Movement saw the development of a worthwhile oil painting tradition, a form which, though dating from the seventeenth century, had never been part of the mainstream of Chinese painting. The CCP pursued its policy of using the arts as a mass medium on behalf of revolution both in terms of content and form. The most famous painter of modern China was Qi Baishi (1864–1957), who being of peasant background was much favoured by the CCP. Although already ancient by the time the CCP came to power, his reputation was such that his support was of great value to them. Yet ironically, Qi's works have nothing revolutionary about them; in style they are very traditional, and in subject matter feature such things as shrimps, flowers, fruit, small everyday objects or simple landscapes. Although the CCP was quite happy to allow the continuation of tradition, it encouraged painters to depict peasants, workers and other such ordinary people carrying out the production work of the revolution. Not surprisingly, the Cultural Revolution pushed the visual representation of the class struggle and modern production and frowned on anything too traditional — for example a landscape which did not also show a railway or some such other modern productive force. However, the period of reform has seen a very strong return to tradition and an abandonment of the directly political dimension. In addition, several worthwhile schools of avant-garde painting have arisen, based largely on experimentation with styles and forms from the West. The avant-garde is generally suspect to the authorities but the overall result is a broader, more daring and more interesting visual arts scene than China has known for a long time.

Conclusion

The cultures of East and Southeast Asia have all been under pressure to combine their own traditions with influences from outside which can very broadly be associated with modernity. The source of these outside influences has usually been the West and, in the case of the countries ruled by Marxist-Leninist parties, the Soviet Union as well. By far the most important 'modernising' influence from within the region itself has been Japan. Just as Japan has been the most successful of all Asian countries in modernising itself, so it has taken on Western and other foreign ideas in the arts with more confidence than the other countries.

The particular blend of tradition and modernity has resulted in some diminution of cultural variety in East and Southeast Asia. The American pop style of music has, with only very few exceptions, attained a high degree of popularity in all parts of the region. At the same time, it would be a grave mistake to hear or see a monoculture. Variety persists and while some of the traditions are wilting, few are dying out. The different countries have experienced various degrees of success in their amal-gamations of tradition and modernity, but all have been able to absorb their own traditions into a respectable modern culture.

Guide to further reading

Anderson, Benedict R. O'G. & Mendiones, Ruchira, *In the Mirror: Literature and Politics in Siam in the American Era*, Duong Kamol, Bangkok, 1985

The cultural history of Thailand is relatively poorly covered in published works, but this volume is a useful survey and anthology.

Brandon, James R. (ed.), *The Cambridge Guide to Asian Theatre*, Cambridge University Press, Cambridge, 1992
This splendid volume covers all the countries of Eastern Asia, as well as several others, and provides extensive coverage on the modern period.

Brandon, James R. (ed.), *The Performing Arts in Asia*, Unesco, Paris, 1971
This is an excellent and brief survey of theatre and cinema in Asian countries such as Sri Lanka, Japan and India, with accounts of theatre also in Cambodia, Indonesia, Thailand and Vietnam. It is based on a conference held in Beirut in 1969, which was organised by UNESCO.

Far Eastern Literatures in the 20th Century: A Guide, Oldcastle Books, Harpenden, 1988
Selected from the *Encyclopaedia of World Literature*, this contains introductory essays and biographical accounts of contemporary or nearly contemporary writers. Included among the biographies are those of 25 Japanese, seventeen Chinese and three Korean writers.

Holt, Claire, *Art in Indonesia: Continuities and Change*, Cornell University Press, Ithaca, New York, 1967
This is the best survey of art and cultural politics in Indonesia.

Keene, Donald, *Dawn to the West, Japanese Literature of the Modern Era*, Holt, Rinehart and Winston, New York, 1984
The first volume of this excellent and extremely detailed and scholarly study covers fiction, while the second covers poetry, drama and criticism. These two volumes are part of a multi-volume history of the whole of Japanese literature by Donald Keene, dealing with the period since the Meiji restoration.

McDougall, B.S. (ed.), *Popular Chinese Literature and Performing Arts in the People's Republic of China, 1949–1979*, University of California Press, Berkeley, 1984
This is a highly perceptive series of articles covering balladry, song, cinema, fiction, drama and poetry.

Marr, David G., *Vietnamese Tradition on Trial 1920–1945*, University of California Press, Berkeley, 1984
This is a masterly survey of trends in Vietnamese cultural politics in the closing decades of French rule.

Scott, A.C., *Literature and the Arts in Twentieth Century China*, Peter Smith, Sloucester, Mass., 1968
This work takes a look at literature, theatre and dance, the cinema, painting, architecture, sculpture and music. It is a survey account, notable for its perceptiveness and brevity.

Notes

1   Brandon, James R., 'Japan: Theatre's Response to a Changing Society', in Brandon, James R. (ed.), *The Performing Arts in Asia*, UNESCO, Paris, 1971, p. 103.

2   Brandon, James, 'Japan, I. Ancient and Traditional', in Banham, Martin (ed.), *The Cambridge Guide to World Theatre*, Cambridge University Press, Cambridge, 1988, p. 515.

3   Quoted in Keene, Donald, *Dawn to the West, Japanese Literature of the Modern Era, Poetry, Drama, Criticism*, Holt, Rinehart and Winston, New York, 1984, p. 413.

4   Goodman, D.G., 'Japan, 2. Modern Japanese Theatre', in Banham, Martin (ed.), *The Cambridge Guide to World Theatre*, p. 519.

5   Brandon, James R., 'Japan: Theatre's Response to a Changing Society', in Brandon, James R. (ed.), *The Performing Arts in Asia*, p. 105.

6   Kraus, Richard Curt, *Pianos and Politics in China, Middle-Class Ambitions and the Struggle over Western Music*, Oxford University Press, New York, Oxford, 1989, p. 40.

7   *China Handbook* Editorial Committee, trans. Bonnie S. McDougall and Hu Liuyu, *Literature and the Arts*, Foreign Languages Press, Beijing, 1983, pp. 51–52.

8   Isoda Koichi, 'The Novel', in *A Survey of Japanese Literature Today*, Japan PEN Club, Tokyo, 1984, p. 9.

9   Makoto Ueda, *Modern Japanese Writers and the Nature of Literature*, Stanford University Press, Stanford, 1976, p. 245.

10 Sullivan, Michael, *Chinese Art in the Twentieth Century*, University of California Press, Berkeley and Los Angeles, 1959, p. 74.

38 Ecology and environment in Asia

The Asian landscape has been thoroughly transformed by its contact with humankind over the last 2000 years. Forests once stretched from the Himalayan treeline in Tibet to the shores and islands of the Pacific and Indian Oceans, shading naturally in the north into the grasslands of Central Asia. Those forests are now reduced to a remnant and many of the grasslands are desert. Rivers and streams have been diverted into dams and irrigation channels, the once-teeming wildlife of Asia is on the defensive, and in place of the original landscape are cities, farms and industries.

The subjugation of nature was once seen by many historians as a noble theme in human history. The historian Arnold Toynbee liked to describe human history as the story of human response to the challenges of nature, and many scholars have followed Toynbee's approach, at least as far as their treatment of environmental issues is concerned. Now we are not so sure. Alongside such positive benefits for humankind as the provision of food and the elimination of disease, the subjugation of nature has had its costs in the loss of animal and plant species, the transformation of climates and the destruction of soils, as well as in the pernicious legacy of pollution which endangers the lives of present and future generations. The reality of environmental degradation challenges not only our policies for the future, but our understanding of the past. Although history is still largely an account of humans and human institutions, it is now becoming possible to chart the complex interaction between humankind and our natural environment in a way which not only informs us of the history of the environment, but also sheds light on the nature of human society and on humankind's capacity to respond to today's growing environmental threat.

The motives for environmental destruction — food production, industry, warfare, greed and thoughtlessness — are easy enough to establish; the motives for environmental protection, however, tell us more about Asian societies and about the future prospects for protection of the Asian environment. The focus of these efforts at protection has changed, too, over the centuries, involving different aspects of the environment and different social forces.

We can distinguish three broad phases in humankind's relationship with the Asian environment. They are not distinct eras, for they overlap considerably from place to place, but they are a useful framework for understanding human attitudes to the environment.

Early societies

The impact of the earliest Asian societies on the environment was limited both by the small size of communities and by the relatively undeveloped technology which they had at their command. Whether we imagine the hunting communities of the Japanese mountains, the fishermen of the Indonesian archipelago or the millet cultivators of northern China, we are dealing with small communities largely unable to wreak great damage on the forests or grasslands which surrounded them. The precise impact of these communities may have been greater, however, than has traditionally been thought. Comprehensive studies of the human ecology of early Asian societies remain to be done, but preliminary research points to the extinction or dramatic reduction in range of large mammals — both predators which offered competition and a threat to early communities and grazing animals which were a source of food — and changes in vegetation as result of burning for hunting, clearing for agriculture or cutting for firewood. Soil core samples dug in lakes in what is now the Indonesian province of Irian Jaya (West New Guinea) show the arrival of Melanesian cultivators during the seventh millenium B.C. in thick layers of ash and a dramatic change in the proportions of tree species, as shown by pollen deposits.

Nonetheless, archaeological and literary traces of these early societies, together with more recent anthropological studies of societies which still retain early characteristics, show that they were far from being simply predatory on the environment. In the earliest beliefs of Asian peoples, the natural world was barely distinguishable from the supernatural. Both worlds offered wealth and power to those with the strength and ability to subdue them, while wreaking a terrible punishment on those who did not. The world where prayers to the sky could bring much-needed rain was also a world where disease and natural disaster could destroy human existence. In all the major Asian traditions, therefore, an important strand of thought existed which identified the value of nature to humans and prescribed ways in which human society should in turn cherish the natural environment. Although these ways of behaving were often expressed in religious terms, we now recognise many of them as ecologically sound environmental management practices.

One of the characteristic agricultural forms in Southeast and southern East Asia, for instance, has been swidden agriculture, sometimes called slash-and-burn, in which forest-dwellers clear a stretch of jungle, allow the cut vegetation to dry before burning it to fertilise the soil, and then plant a rain-watered crop of rice or vegetables for a few years until the soil's fertility decreases or until weeds become established. The plot is then abandoned, allowing the natural succession of forest to take place. It may then be 20, 30 or more years before the land is cleared again. Although once condemned as wastefully destructive of forest, this kind of agriculture has now been shown to cause no more long-term destruction of forests than natural forces such as storms, drought and landslides, provided that the long interval between clearings is maintained. Within swidden societies, however, the motive for shifting cultivation and for leaving land fallow was often expressed in religious terms, such as the avoidance of land where tribal members had died. In China, temples were often a place of special reverence for nature, and temple groves sometimes became important reservoirs for tree species almost eliminated from the wild.

Economic growth and state power

The rise of great civilisations in East and Southeast Asia brought new pressure on the environment. The growth of population in the fertile river valleys of China, Vietnam and what was to become Thailand, the coastal plains of Japan and Korea and the volcanic slopes of Java and Bali demanded land for agriculture. Land cleared and terraced for wet-rice agriculture, unlike swidden land, has generally stayed under cultivation, because of the effort involved in preparing the land. The passing centuries have seen a gradual and then rapid expansion in the area under wet-rice cultivation. From the easily cleared and well-watered middle reaches of Asia's rivers, intensive rice cultivation has spread downstream into formerly inhospitable coastal swamps such as those of the Mekong Delta in Vietnam, as well as uphill into cooler mountain regions.

Much more forest was cleared, however, than was used for growing food. The need for firewood, sometimes used directly, sometimes turned into charcoal, has been the greatest traditional danger to forests. When we remember that every meal for every family had to be cooked on wood or charcoal derived from forests, and add all the other common domestic and farm uses of wood, from fencing to furniture, it is not hard to understand how vast areas of forest could be cleared in a piecemeal but relentless fashion. Taking place over generations, this change was often barely perceptible to people at the time. Clues to its progress often have to be sought, for instance, in the fact that a dense forest mentioned in one century as the haunt of wild animals and bandits ceases to be mentioned in later accounts. Most of the work to assemble a history of forest cover in East and Southeast Asia still remains to be done, but there is strong evidence that by the start of the sixteenth century, the indiscriminate clearing of land in China was already causing long-term ecological damage in the form of permanent deforestation and serious erosion both on the steep hillsides of the south and in the fragile dry plains of the north.

Not only population, however, but growing industry was responsible for much destruction. Even in the twelfth century, severe depletion of accessible forests in north China led Chinese shipbuilders to look at the rich forests of Manchuria and Korea for material to outfit their fleets, while the destruction of South China's forests by the fifteenth century sent Chinese timber merchants south to Borneo. Even the art of writing, which used soot as the main pigment in ink, has been accused of contributing substantially to forest destruction in China. In eighteenth-century Indonesia, the enormously lucrative market for spices, especially pepper, led to the clearing of large areas of jungle in Borneo, Sumatra and Java for short-lived pepper plantations. Today, two centuries later, many of those plantation sites are still covered with the pernicious blady grass *(Imperata cylindrica)*, a hardy species whose matted root system makes eradication difficult and whose dry leaves fuel periodic fires which hamper the regrowth of forests.

The trade in exotic jungle products from Southeast Asia also had a direct impact on unfortunate animal species which were hunted especially for parts of their bodies: the reputation of pangolin scales and rhinoceros horn as medicine ensured an unremitting pressure on animals which were never very numerous. The scale of the early trade in animal parts is hard for us now to imagine. Every year for centuries, thousands of bezoar stones, a chemical accretion collected from the stomachs of porcupines, were exported from Borneo. During the 1920s, at the height of the fashion for feathered ladies' hats in Paris, 20 000 bird-of-paradise pelts were exported each year from Dutch New Guinea. The taste for rare and exotic meats, especially amongst the Chinese, continues to put pressure on a wide range of animals.

It was in this age of population growth and increased pressure on natural resources that Asian states began to take a greater hand in environmental protection, though they certainly did not do so for what we would now recognise as environmentalist reasons. As the natural environment began to appear as a rare and precious commodity, rulers began to restrict access to it as a means of protecting their own privileges. In all the countries discussed in this book, enclosed gardens became a symbol and privilege of those with wealth and power. The imperial parks of China in particular covered enormous areas, partly protecting natural landscapes, and partly giving emperors room in which to construct symbolic artificial landscapes.

Not only gardens, but hunting forests, became the preserve of state elites. Kings and aristocrats hunted game as a status symbol, sometimes reserving large tracts of land or particular species for their exclusive use. Especially after the introduction of Islam made the hunting of wild boar religiously unacceptable on Java, deer were often reserved as the prey for rulers, and extensive areas of forest were cleared to provide pasture where deer could graze. In the European colonies of Southeast Asia, white hunters maintained the same tradition, posing for photographs with the carcasses of tigers, elephants and buffalo. A number of today's nature reserves in Indonesia had their origins in hunting reserves set aside in the early twentieth century as the exclusive preserve of either indigenous sultans or Dutch hunting clubs.

Even more important, rulers began to restrict access to forests by ordinary people in order to ensure that the state would have adequate timber to meet its own needs. In late sixteenth century Japan, for instance, the military ruler Hideyoshi embarked on a major program to construct castles, temples and ships — both warships and domestic transports. To support this construction, he installed a strict system of forest management in the favoured forests of the Akita region in the north. The Dutch colonial authorities on Java were similarly restrictive in managing the rich teak forests of the island's northern coast, reserving monopoly rights for themselves and, especially in the early twentieth century, limiting the access of local people to forests where they had once freely collected firewood and hunted game.

Serious forest management, including the replanting of trees and the development of production plans based on the time needed for saplings to grow to maturity began only in the early nineteenth century. Japan and the Dutch in Java, both of whom drew on the strong German tradition of forest management, were Asia's pioneers in this field.

Warfare, international trade and industrialisation

The political upheavals and economic change of the twentieth century have put greater pressure still on the Asian environment. First, the political turmoil which has swept through much of Asia since 1900, punctuated by the deep disruption which Japan's prolonged wars wrought on the mainland and in the Southeast Asian islands, meant occasional and sometimes chronic weakening of the power of states to enforce measures to protect the environment. Even when these measures had been formulated purely in the interests of the ruling elite, their breakdown meant that one-sided regulation was replaced by the absence of regulation altogether.

The Japanese occupation of Korea, Southeast Asia and parts of China was a source of considerable environmental damage. During Japan's 35-year occupation of Korea, the peninsula's forests were ruthlessly harvested to meet the needs of metropolitan Japan for paper, chopsticks and construction. Further afield, the insistence of Japan's military commanders on economic autarchy in each of the occupied regions meant that large areas of forest in densely populated areas such as Java had to be felled to increase food production. When Japanese policies failed, moreover, and famine ensued, as in Vietnam in 1944–45, the catastrophic results for human beings — half a million or more dead — were mirrored in a much less noticed slaughter for food of birds and small animals in the countryside.

Peasant revolutions across Asia had as their goal not only improvement in the conditions of agricultural production, but access to forests for traditional purposes — hunting, collection of firewood and cutting of timber for domestic purposes. Wherever peasant power became established or influential, even temporarily, a renewed onslaught on the forests began. The Marxism which powered many of these revolutions was committed to the removal of social inequalities and ideologically inclined to see the subjugation of nature as a measure of human progress. Marxist leaders often had difficulty in controlling the peasants' conviction that liberation also meant freedom of the forests. After its political defeat in 1965–66, the Indonesian Communist Party was widely accused of sabotaging the ecology of Java by encouraging peasants to remove state forests and plant their own crops. The Chinese communist government nationalised all forest land on taking power in 1949, but did not begin to develop a forest policy until 1953. An important part of the policy which subsequently emerged was a major propaganda campaign to encourage peasants to 'love and protect' the forests, which suggests that party leaders were aware that loving and protective attitudes were not widespread amongst the peasantry.

World War II and its revolutionary aftermath also put pressure on the wildlife of the Asian forests. This was the great age of guerrilla warfare in Asia, when large armies made a virtue of living off the land in remote and sometimes sparsely populated areas which were the main refuge of animal species already extinct in settled areas. The wars in Indochina brought the local rhinoceros close to extinction, although research in the 1990s has discovered that it is not extinct and may be reviving. The wars were also very deleterious to other species, including the kouprey, a large relative of the domestic cow once common in the forests of Cambodia. The Indonesian revolution of 1945–49 sealed the fate of the Java tiger, though a few small communities survived until the late 1980s.

Of all Eastern Asian wars this century, however, the Second Indochina War was by far the most destructive in environmental terms. American forces made extensive use of defoliants to remove the jungle which provided shelter for the Vietnamese insurgents. Widespread use of napalm and of carpet-bombing compounded the damage. The result was a sudden and catastrophic destruction of large areas of tropical rainforest, far beyond the capacity of the jungle to recover. Large areas of northern and southern Vietnam remain under stunted regrowth as a result of this destruction. The environmental effects of this war have been even more insidious in terms of the residues from chemical warfare which have remained in the ecosystem, causing appallingly high levels of birth abnormalities amongst both humans and animals. The poisoned soil of Vietnam remains one of the most serious long-term environmental problems in Asia.

In non-socialist Southeast Asia, the principal environmental threat since World War II has come from the cutting of forests for the international timber market. Struggling to obtain state revenue without placing too heavy a taxation burden on their people, the governments of Thailand and Indonesia, along with those of Malaysia and the Philippines, each found forests to be enormously useful. Although they often sold timber at what now seem to be disappointingly low prices, the sheer volume of the trade made a major contribution to national treasuries. Indonesia, for instance, embarked on a major program of forest exploitation in 1967, when President Suharto's New Order government was desperate for foreign exchange to begin a program of national development along the capitalist path spurned by his predecessor President Sukarno. Timber was well suited to this role: the technology of extraction was relatively simple and quick to install, while the major timber concessions affected remote jungle areas far from the main centres of population where the loss of a national resource might have been challenged.

Timber concessions in most Southeast Asian countries, although generally bringing in considerable state revenue, also offered a painless and lucrative means of providing rewards and kickbacks within the ruling elite. Concessions were widely granted to individuals and firms close to the elite. Concessionaires then typically dealt with foreign timber firms who provided all the expertise, and often all the capital investment, to get the logs out of the jungle, floating down the rivers and aboard ships for transport to mills for processing abroad.

All the countries involved instituted comprehensive regulations to prevent over-harvesting. Regulations in Indonesia, for instance, prescribed a 35-year logging cycle in each concession, implying that the concessionaire should log one thirty-fifth of the concession each year. Further regulations obliged the loggers to replant after the clearing of each site. In practice, however, these regulations were virtually ignored by all concerned, the timber-getters logging freely without regard for cycles or protected zones and the government declining to send inspectors into the field to supervise operations. In one celebrated instance, a large portion of East Kalimantan's main nature reserve was removed from the reserve, logged and returned to the reserve.

This cavalier attitude was partly due to ignorance of the effects of logging on rainforests. Policy-makers did not appreciate that logging operations — for instance, by compacting the soil — can hamper the regeneration of forest after clearing or that logging vehicles can be responsible for introducing previously unknown infections into jungle areas. Nor did they appreciate the significance of rainforests as a reservoir of genetic diversity which may be of enormous value to humankind in the future. On the other hand, it is probably fair to say that the forests would still have been logged even if the policy-makers had been aware of these things, so great was the lure of profit.

Important progress in forest protection has been made in the 1980s, however, at least in Thailand and Indonesia, as the result of a growing realisation of the finite nature of forest resources. Thailand, in fact, has already become a net importer of timber. Periodic floods, a direct consequence of the removal of forest cover with its capacity to absorb rainfall and release it gradually, also gave an impetus to this reorientation. In both countries, therefore, increasing attention has been given to proper forest management, to the preservation of remaining intact ecosystems and to changing the traditionally exclusivist techniques of timber production by introducing what is called social forestry, under which people live in the forest and tend the trees while also engaging in other productive activities such as keeping bees or raising deer. Illegal logging and unsuitable management practices, however, remain a major problem and both countries have a long way to go before their forests are safe.

Forest protection has become a major issue in the international dialogue between Third World countries and the rich nations of the West and Eastern Asia. The West on the one hand has urged forest conservation in order to preserve the planet's capacity to put oxygen back in the atmosphere. Countries such as Indonesia have responded by pointing out that the combustion of fossil fuels by the West and Japan is the major cause of rising carbon dioxide levels and have suggested that the West, having destroyed much of its own forest cover on the road to industrial development, should not stand in the way of similar progress in the Third World unless it is willing to compensate Third World countries for their sacrifice.

In East Asia, industrial pollution represents a greater environmental danger than deforestation. Under the capitalist systems of Japan, Taiwan and South Korea, industrial firms ignored or even concealed the level of toxic wastes which they were putting into the environment, while in China, although official recognition was given to the dangers of pollution, the emphasis on production targets often led factory managers to disregard regulations. In both capitalist and communist systems, disregard for environmental protection was based on the view that it was a luxury which developing countries could not afford. Thailand and Indonesia, both undergoing rapid industrial development in the 1990s, are showing signs of the same vulnerability to pollution damage.

Asian experience, however, has shown two significant paths towards pollution control and, by extension, other forms of environmental protection. The first has been the growing willingness of authoritarian governments to take the initiative to enforce environmental protection measures. This is partly due to the high value placed on technology and long-term planning in most of the governments under discussion. Most policy-makers are aware now that the short-term benefits of increased productivity have to be weighed against the long-term costs of environmental damage. Authoritarian governments such as Indonesia's, moreover, have even seen environmental protection as a means of tightening the network of government control over society and the economy.

Democratic institutions, too, have sometimes helped to limit pollution. Japan in particular has a long history or political and legal action by local residents in order to avert or seek compensation for the damage caused by polluting industries. Anti-pollution campaigns date from the late nineteenth century, but the most celebrated was the Minimata disease case in Nigata and Kumamoto in the late 1960s and early 1970s, when courts awarded over US$4 million to people affected by mercury poisoning.

Although its internal environmental protection measures are now working well, Japan has an unenviable reputation as an exporter of environmental problems, through the dumping of wastes in international waters in the Pacific Ocean, through the siting of hazardous industries in vulnerable Third World countries and through its predatory fishing program. Fish is the most important source of animal protein throughout the region and huge fleets set out each year from ports in East and Southeast Asia to harvest the seas. We know nothing of the ecology of the seas of the region in early times, but strong indications of overfishing come from the expanding scope of fishing expeditions. After the trepang, or beche de mer (a somewhat slug-like relative of the starfish) became a popular food in Ming China, voracious Chinese and Indonesian fishing fleets exhausted stocks in the South China Sea and then moved south, eventually fishing the northern coasts of Australia in the eighteenth and nineteenth centuries. Repeated incursions by Taiwanese, Korean and Indonesian fishing boats into Australian waters in the late twentieth century in search of trochus shells, clams and other delicacies are a part of this long-standing tradition.

Japan's fishing activities have been subject to special criticism for several reasons. Japanese vessels often use high-tech equipment, including radar and spotter planes, which take much of the guesswork out of hunting fish, making it easier to over-harvest fish populations. The Japanese have also been criticised for using unnecessarily destructive fishing techniques, including tuna nets which entrap and drown dolphins. And they have been the target of a long-standing international campaign over their continued sponsorship of whaling, despite the threat to the survival of many whale species. For many of her neighbours, Japan's willingness to show greater environmental responsibility is a major test of her acceptability as a partner in development, and this pressure shows some signs of bringing changes in Japanese policy.

Conclusion

The picture is by no means entirely grim. Asian history contains interwoven themes of environmental protection and destruction. In the modern context of intense and growing pressure on environmental resources, all Asian countries have adopted measures to limit environmental damage, and these measures, despite facing many practical difficulties, are achieving some degree of success.

Guide to further reading

Tuan, Yi-Fu, *China*, Longman, London, 1970, The World's Landscapes Series, offers a good basic summary of environmental history in China, while Totman, Conrad, *The Green Archipelago: Forestry in Preindustrial Japan*, University of California Press, Berkeley, 1989, is a path-breaking study of evolving environmental attitudes in Japan.

The ecological effects of the war in Indochina are discussed comprehensively in Lewallen, John, *The Ecology of Devastation: Indochina*, Penguin, Baltimore, 1971.

Modern environmental problems in Japan are discussed in Huddle, Norie & Reich, Michael, *Island of Dreams: Environmental Crisis in Japan*, Autumn Press, New York, 1975, while the corresponding studies for Thailand, Indonesia and China are Sternstein, Larry, *Thailand: The Environment of Modernisation*, McGraw-Hill, Sydney, 1976; Donner, Wolf, *Land Use and Environment in Indonesia*, University of Hawaii Press, Honolulu, 1987; and Ross, Lester, *Environmental Policy in China*, Indiana University Press, Bloomington, 1988.

Vaclav Smil's book *The Bad Earth: Environmental Degradation in China*, M.E. Sharpe, Armonk, N.Y.; Zed Press, London, 1984, is a thorough and very bleak view of environmental problems in China.

The political dimensions of environmental policy are discussed in McKean, Margaret A., *Environmental Protest and Citizen Politics in Japan*, University of California Press, Berkeley, 1981; Cribb, Robert, *The Politics of Environmental Protection in Indonesia*, Monash University Centre of Southeast Asian Studies, Clayton, Vic., 1988; and Hirsch, Philip, 'Contemporary Politics Of Environment In Thailand', *Asian Survey*, vol. 29, no. 4, 1989, pp. 439–51.

39 Security and political relations in Asia after World War II

Since the end of the World War II, political relations among the states of Southeast and Northeast Asia (the Asia-Pacific region) have tended to lack stability. Suspicion and mistrust rather than amity and goodwill have often characterised regional interactions. Within the region there have been relatively few strong close and enduring bilateral or multilateral relationships; instead, contacts between governments have often shifted dramatically back and forth between the poles of co-operation and confrontation. One consequence has been that political instability and insecurity have long been features of the postwar strategic environment of the Asia-Pacific area. In part this instability has been caused by issues and events within the region itself, but the active involvement in regional affairs of outside powers, particularly the superpowers, has also been important in shaping relations.

This chapter examines political and security relations in the Asia-Pacific region since 1945. The discussion divides the period into three parts: the first from the end of the Pacific War to 1950, a time of postwar recovery and reconstruction; the second from 1951 to 1975, the period of the Cold War in Asia; and the third, a period of growing regional self-confidence and dynamism, from 1976 to the end of 1991, when the Soviet Union collapsed. The years since then find some focus in Chapters 40 and 41.

The aftermath of war, 1945–50

World War II had a profound impact on the political life of Asia. The Allied victory over Japan put an end to that country's hegemonial ambitions in Asia and the Pacific and left the United States in a position of regional pre-eminence. In Northeast Asia, Japan was placed under Allied occupation and set on a course of political and economic reconstruction. Liberated from the Japanese occupation of the 1930s, China quickly declined into political and economic chaos as the long-running civil war between the Republican government of Chiang Kaishek and the communists under Mao Zedong gained in intensity. Korea was liberated from Japanese colonialism but then immediately divided into two zones occupied by Soviet and American troops (see Chapter 20). Throughout Southeast Asia, the Japanese invasion left a dismal legacy of economic devastation and political turmoil. In particular, the war contributed strongly to the rise of anti-colonialism throughout the area and left nationalism a well-entrenched force for change.

Against this background, relations between the communities of the region and more distant countries immediately after the war were highly fragmented. After 1945 the preoccupation of most Asian governments, whether they enjoyed full sovereign status or were dependencies of distant powers, was with political and economic reconstruction, and this left little opportunity for the development of wider regional relations. But there were also some clear impediments to closer contacts. At a political level, most of the states of the region lacked the constitutional capacity to establish formal diplomatic relations with other countries. In Southeast Asia, the return of colonialism left responsibility for inter-state relations not with local colonial administrators, but with home governments many thousands of miles away in Europe. Thus, while it was common for European governments to establish consular posts in other colonial territories throughout Southeast Asia, they served less as mechanisms for establishing local regional contacts than as means for protecting the home government's local political and economic interests.

European governments returned to Asia determined to continue where they had left off in the late 1940s: as masters of their imperial domains. But, as they were soon to discover, this was to be fraught with many problems. Although many were common to most European possessions in Asia, the competitive element in colonialism largely precluded the pursuit of co-operative regional responses. While most colonial governments ensured that they were well informed of political developments around the region, particularly in relation to the growing threat of communism, they pursued their own policies and were inclined to resist strongly any hint of outside interference. Particularly unwelcome was any hint of interference from the United States, whose anti-colonial sympathies were known and disparaged among the capitals of Europe. America, however, now had a substantial stake in the region and its influence in local affairs could not easily be ignored, especially in Northeast Asia. There the transitional nature of postwar constitutional arrangements in Japan and Korea limited their foreign contacts, but in both places America was a highly influential actor, as was also the case in China.

At the same time, the war had severely disrupted regional patterns of trade, thus limiting local economic linkages. Prior to the war, the Japanese economy had been the most powerful in Asia. It was now in ruins, as were most economies throughout the region. The volume of prewar intra-regional trade had not been substantial, since most of Japan's trade had been directed further afield and the trade relationships of the European colonies had been strongest with their home governments. Nevertheless, there had been a lively local economy. The economic devastation wrought by years of conflict brought the commercial life of the region to a virtual standstill and was to demand the injection of massive amounts of postwar economic aid before there were any clear signs of a recovery or significant economic growth. In summary, in the years immediately following the end of World War II, the governments in Asia were constrained in their capacity to develop extensive and closer political and economic relations and the immediate destiny of the region seemed to be largely in the hands of outside powers.

But even before the arsenal of war was fully silent, Asia and the Pacific were beginning to stir politically. As European governments returned to their prewar colonies, they confronted the twin forces of nationalism and communism which had emerged to challenge their long-entrenched imperial interests. The former was perceived as the more formidable and was to prove a potent source of opposition to colonial authorities. Indeed, nationalism preoccupied the colonial mind and attitudes to it largely dictated the course of colonial policy in Southeast Asia after 1945.

Communism often complicated the nationalist issue. Throughout Southeast Asia, communism identified itself with the nationalist aspirations of local populations and began to draw support by offering a more radical path to independence. While the appeal of communism was often very limited and the active membership of local movements quite small, its capacity for social and political disruption proved a significant and increasingly threatening problem for colonial authorities, particularly in places like Indochina and Malaya. Soon communism was also to become a powerful force for change, as the success of the communist revolution in China in 1949 was to demonstrate (see Chapter 25).

In the decade after 1945, independence movements throughout Southeast Asia gathered sufficient strength to bring about the rapid decolonisation of virtually the whole region. But for most of the new states, the attainment of independence was merely the first step towards autonomy in international politics. It was now necessary to perfect independence by complementing constitutional separation with political and economic self-reliance. Few found this an easy task. Most of the countries of the region faced severe domestic problems, for which the solutions seemed to lie in a combination of massive foreign aid, disruptive internal reform and continued reliance on the strength of former colonial masters. Politically, internal dissent continued to trouble governments in the Philippines, Indonesia, Burma, Vietnam and Malaya. From the perspective of Western governments, economic underdevelopment, internal turmoil and the emergence of alien ideologies, notably communism, all created the spectacle of Southeast Asia and the region more widely as a place of chronic instability. Thus, both for the newly independent states of the region and for interested outsiders, decolonisation and the years that followed were marked by turmoil and disarray. While old and decaying structures of empire were swept away, the forms and processes of the regime or regimes that would replace them remained unclear and in contest.

Thus the progress of decolonisation quickly began to change the character of Southeast Asian political life. Although the newly independent states of the region had few resources with which to establish elaborate overseas missions, they nevertheless sought to exercise their newly won freedom in the international arena. The new Philippines government, for example, remained heavily dependent on American economic aid after independence, but in the late 1940s it launched a diplomatic initiative to bring several states in the Pacific area together in a regional association. While the attempt failed mainly for want of an enthusiastic response from the United States, the idea that the newly emergent countries of the region had many interests in common was beginning to take root, and outsiders were quick to recognise the burgeoning political and economic importance of the area. As a consequence, there was a steady expansion of diplomatic contacts within the region and between local governments and countries outside. After 1945, the international isolation that much of Asia had enjoyed prior to the outbreak of World War II was very much a thing of the past as the region's chaotic political life increasingly drew in outside intervention.

Cold War in Asia, 1950–75

The outbreak of the Korean War in June 1950 materially increased the level of this intervention and was to polarise the region's political life for nearly 25 years. As noted in Chapter 20, tension between the divided parts of the Korean Peninsula had been building since the end of the war in 1945. Thus when war broke out between north and south in June 1950, informed observers were not entirely surprised. Few, however, could have predicted the long-term consequences for either regional or international politics.

Washington's immediate reaction to the outbreak of war in Korea was to see communism as making a decisive thrust into Asia comparable with the postwar gains it had made in Europe. Applying this overly simplified analysis to the situation, the United States made plans to defend Western, and more particularly its own, interests in the region. To this end it moved to help defend south Korea against the invaders from the north and took a range of other policy initiatives (see Chapter 21).

With the United States perceiving the government of China to be behind the invasion, relations between Washington and Beijing immediately took a turn for the worse. Henceforth, China was to be identified by Washington and other Western countries as a constant source of threat to stability in Asia. America stepped up its policy of isolating China within the international community and over the next twenty years made the containment of China's presumed desire for regional expansion the central motif of its security policy in Asia. At the same time, the progress of restoring full postwar sovereignty to Japan was advanced and, with substantial infusions of foreign aid, the process of turning Japan into a bastion of Western interests in Asia was also advanced. Under the umbrella of the American nuclear deterrent, Japan was to become one of Washington's strongest allies in Asia, though as a consequence of the war its role in regional political affairs was relatively low key. In 1951 a security treaty was signed with Japan, while another was made with the Philippines and a third was agreed with Australia and New Zealand to create the ANZUS alliance. To further reinforce Western interests in Asia, the United States greatly expanded its defence aid program in the region, offering, for example, US$133 million in military aid to the French in their struggle against the communists in Vietnam. Finally, in the early 1950s, the United States began to show an interest in regional defence consultations with Britain, France, Australia and New Zealand to develop co-operative arrangements for the defence of Asia against the further advance of communism.

Within a matter of years, the Korean War and the events that followed had profoundly changed the political landscape of Asia. The postwar struggle for political stability and economic development in the region, which had taken place largely free of the growing ideological divide between communism and capitalism developing in Europe, was now to be conducted in precisely those terms in Asia. The Cold War had arrived in Asia and it cast its chilly mantle over the whole region. Problems in Asian political and economic development were in future to be defined in ideological terms. For example, the struggle in Vietnam between the French and the communist-cum-nationalist Ho Chi Minh was viewed among Western governments less as a struggle for Vietnamese independence than as the key to defending Southeast Asia against a communist takeover. Vietnam became the first of the Asian dominoes which, if it were to fall to communism, would cause the political collapse of the whole of Southeast Asia. Reflecting this situation, the countries of the region divided largely into two opposing blocs, each reliably supported by outside interests. Firmly aligned with American interests in the region were Japan, Thailand, South Korea, the nationalist Chinese government on Taiwan, the Philippines, the French in Indochina, the British in Malaya, Australia and New Zealand. Communist China, North

Korea, the various communist movements in Indochina, Malaya and the Philippines and of course the Soviet Union, whose insatiable appetite for conquest was seen to be animating all, constituted their opponents.

While this alignment of strategic interests was to remain largely unchanged for the next two decades, at the international level as well as in Asia itself there was to emerge during the 1950s a third grouping of states anxious to resist alignment with either side in the Cold War. These countries were newly independent, underdeveloped and looked upon the Cold War as a destructive confrontation in international affairs. Inclined because of their colonial past to be anti-imperialist (meaning somewhat anti-Western), these states nevertheless contrived to pursue a more independent path in world affairs. Led by charismatic international figures such as Egypt's Gamel Abd-al Nasser and India's Jawaharlal Nehru, neutralism, as this movement was first called, attracted considerable support in parts of Asia. Aside from India, independent Ceylon, Burma and Indonesia were early adherents, to be joined later by Cambodia and Laos once they had gained independence from the French in 1954. To many Western governments, including those in Canberra and Washington, neutralism was a suspicious ideology and those countries professing it were essentially pro-communist, disingenuously masquerading as something else. But this was a misconception. Most neutralist states were not communist. Although they may at times have been fellow travellers of communism, they were unable to see any advantage for their countries in becoming involved in the poisonous struggle between East and West. Yet so blinded by their visceral hatred of communism were most Western governments that they were either unwilling or unable to appreciate their position.

In the Indonesian town of Bandung in April 1955, a large group of neutralist countries, together with some others such as the Philippines and the People's Republic of China (PRC), more clearly aligned in international affairs, met to discuss issues of common interest. Although the meeting produced little of substance beyond a very lengthy communiqué, the value of the conference to the nations participating went far beyond this modest achievement. As Knapp has pointed out, it drew together states with different histories and traditions from different parts of the world and, rather than underscoring their differences, focused attention on their common economic problems and the extent of their shared aspirations in world affairs. Bandung marked a 'watershed between neutralism as a negative refusal to takes sides in international politics and a positive policy'.[1] It laid the foundations for an international position that was to have great emotional appeal at home and growing legitimacy abroad. By the early 1960s, neutralism had gained greater form and adherents to become a non-aligned movement. The growth of this movement added another dimension to Asian politics during the

1950s as countries such as Cambodia and Indonesia sought to remain aloof from the East–West struggle. Simultaneously, the prominence of several newly independent Asian countries in the movement underscored the growing importance of the region in world affairs.

Despite the emergence of this third force in world affairs, politics in Asia during the 1950s and 1960s was dominated by the Cold War. Following the outbreak of war in Korea, each new issue on the Asian political agenda served to underscore the situation. The negotiation of a ceasefire in Korea took two years to achieve. At a conference in Geneva the following year (1954) an attempt to negotiate a final settlement of the conflict failed when both sides refused to make compromises. Korea was left as it remains as of 1995, divided between a communist government in the north and a right-wing authoritarian state in the south. The 1954 Geneva conference also attempted to resolve the long-running civil war in Vietnam. While a settlement was reached at the conference, it eventually failed to end the conflict. The elections intended to reunify the country after a brief period of partition were never held, leaving Vietnam also divided between the communists in the north and a Western-leaning government in the south. This laid the foundations for the intense struggle of the 1960s when Vietnam became the battleground between East and West.

Another notable outcome of Geneva was the creation in 1954 of the South-East Asia Treaty Organisation (SEATO). SEATO brought the governments of the United States, Britain, France, Pakistan, the Philippines, Thailand, Australia and New Zealand together in a security alliance akin to the North Atlantic Treaty Organization (NATO) in Europe. The new organisation was intended to serve as an instrument of America's policy of containing the communist threat and was significant for the fact that it was the first to bring Asian and Western countries together in an alliance for the common purpose of their security. SEATO directed its attentions to the possibility of a communist Chinese invasion of Southeast Asia and the destabilising impact of communist insurgency. To this end it undertook planning for the military defence of Southeast Asia and in the late 1950s and early 1960s became involved in the internal crises threatening Laos and Thailand. But overall SEATO lacked the internal coherence of its European counterpart and was never a particularly effective security grouping. By the time the Vietnam War began to intensify in the early 1960s (see Chapter 22), it had already begun to disintegrate and was never able to fashion a common policy over the conflict. As a result, America's intervention in Vietnam was never formally sanctioned under the SEATO treaty, a fact which severely compromised one of America's persistent justifications for its involvement in the war, namely that it was fulfilling its obligations within the alliance.

SEATO added a military dimension to the main political divide in Cold War politics in Asia and thus served to reinforce regional tensions. But the struggle between East and West was not the only source of instability in Asian affairs during this period. As the struggle in Vietnam began to intensify in the late 1950s and early 1960s, many of the traditional tensions that had existed between Asian societies, in some cases prior to the onset of the colonial era, continued to simmer below the surface of the Cold War. In some cases these tended to intensify East–West tensions, in others they served to ameliorate them, while in still others the war had relatively little impact. Notable among the former was the treatment of Chinese minority groups in many Asian countries. Traditionally resented throughout many parts of Southeast Asia, the racial tensions excited by the overseas Chinese were intensified in places like Malaya by the fact that the Chinese Communist Party (CCP) was perceived to be pursuing a policy of international subversion in the region and seeking to recruit its 'nationals' overseas to serve as instruments of its design. In Malaya the cause of independence was set back in part by the existence of a strong communist insurgency in the late 1940s-early 1950s which was Chinese based, while in Indonesia, the Sukarno government showed strong pro-communist, pro-Chinese sympathies which were underpinned by an active and influential Chinese minority in Indonesian politics. Indeed, it was this ideological persuasion within Indonesian politics that made Western governments sceptical of Sukarno's neutralism and reinforced, in particular, the unease that conservative governments in Australia felt towards Indonesian foreign policy.

At the other end of the spectrum, the Cold War served to modify some ancient tensions. The communist leadership of North Vietnam, for example, set aside centuries of hostility towards the Chinese to secure their support (albeit less substantial than that of the Soviet Union) to prosecute their war of national liberation first against the French and later the Americans. Finally, there were issues that divided the countries of Asia during the 1950s and 1960s period which were largely independent of the Cold War. Most notable among these was the split between China and the Soviet Union, which resulted in an intense rivalry for global ideological ascendency and led to the two countries' common border in north Asia becoming one of the most heavily fortified in the world. The visceral hostility between the two sides of this conflict added greatly to the security tensions and instabilities in the Asia-Pacific region. Also cutting across the East–West divide was Indonesia's (crush Malaysia) policy against the creation of the Malaysian federation between 1963 and 1965 (see Chapter 26). Sukarno's attempt to disrupt the creation of the federation led to a conflict that saw the deployment of Australian and

British military forces against those of Indonesia and a deepening of the perception that Southeast Asia was an inherently unstable region. The confrontation did not end until Sukarno was toppled from power in the coup of 1965. Yet another divisive regional issue was the dispute between the Philippines and Malaysia over Sabah in 1963.

But the overriding source of insecurity in the region in the 1950s and 1960s was the conflict between East and West. By the mid-1960s, America's deepening involvement in the Vietnam War testified to its power to shape the political agenda in Asia. From being a low-level conflict for authority against political insurgency in the south of the country, by 1965 the war had escalated to a full-scale conflict between a United States-led coalition of Asian and Pacific states and communist North Vietnam with its agents in the south strongly supported by their fraternal allies in Moscow and Beijing. The war dominated the strategic agenda in Asia in the mid-1960s, polarising local political interests in Asia just as effectively as in the United States (see Chapter 22). Yet, behind the backdrop of the war, important changes were beginning to take place in Asia and the Pacific. Over the next few years, as the war moved towards stalemate, the region was to go through a process of profound transformation. In line with changes taking place elsewhere in international politics, most notably in Europe and in superpower relations, the end of the 1960s and the early 1970s saw a series of events which was to bring the Cold War era in Asia to an end and lead to fundamental changes in the regional strategic and economic environment.

Asia in transition

By 1965, most of the countries of Southeast Asia had enjoyed a decade and in some cases nearly fifteen years of independence. They were moving more confidently on the international stage and were conscious of their emerging regional interests. Internally, the economies of most Asian states remained fragile with underdevelopment the norm, but in Japan twenty years of postwar reconstruction had produced the foundations of what was to become the world's most powerful economy in little over a decade. One reason for Japan's growing strength was the stability of its postwar political system. With China about to go through the cathartic events of the Cultural Revolution, Indochina in turmoil and a coup in Indonesia in 1965, stability was certainly not universal in Asia. As a consequence, few Western commentators were optimistic over the long-term future of the region. But in retrospect the period emerges as the start of a time of political growth and development. Over the next few years, with the turmoil that had characterised their emergence in the immediate postwar years now well behind them, Southeast Asia's new states produced a crop of leaders that were to guide the destinies of their respective countries for many years to come with Rahman in Malaysia, Suharto in Indonesia, Marcos in the Philippines and Lee Kwan Yew in Singapore being among the most obvious. Under the stability of their leadership and the ordered emergence of their successors, Southeast Asia was to make the transition from the politics of the high Cold War to that of emerging detente with growing confidence.

One of the most visible signs of this growing political maturity was the emergence of regional organisations. After the Philippines government's attempt to create a Pacific association in the late 1940s, Asian governments had shown little inclination to pursue regional institutional initiatives, though they had often been happy to participate in those proposed by others, including the British Commonwealth's Colombo Plan to provide economic assistance to Asian members of the Commonwealth, ANZAM (a British-sponsored plan to provide for the defence of Malaya) and SEATO. In short, initiatives in regional co-operation were largely in the hands of outsiders and generally reflected their narrow interests.

In 1961, Malaya called for the establishment of a 'non', if not 'anti'-communist grouping of Southeast Asian states to provide Asian solutions to Asian problems. Thailand and the Philippines joined the Association of Southeast Asia (ASA) but it soon collapsed following the suspension of diplomatic contacts between Malaysia and the Philippines over Sabah. The Philippines revived local efforts to build regional co-operation in 1963 when it proposed the creation of Maphilindo, a political grouping between itself, Malaysia and Indonesia. While this initiative was defeated by mistrust and suspicion, and by Malaysia's eventual withdrawal, another proposal four years later for a wider association led to the creation in 1967 of the Association of Southeast Asian Nations (ASEAN).

Comprising Indonesia, Malaysia, Singapore, Thailand and the Philippines, ASEAN was established ostensibly as an organisation for economic, cultural and scientific co-operation; in reality, however, security was the preoccupation of its founders. Concerned about the defence and security implications of the war in Vietnam, the leaders of the association's governments saw a regional institution as providing a framework for reconciling some of their own tensions as well as offering a foundation with which to begin shaping the environment of their own collective security. This was only spelt out in a parsimonious way in the Bangkok declaration that created ASEAN and has thus created ambiguity in the development of the association's regional aims and objectives as members have struggled on occasions to define clearly the purpose of their grouping. Until the emergence of the Cambodian crisis in the mid-1970s (see Chapter 42), the focus of ASEAN's co-operative activities had been economic, although its efforts in this area have been slow and over nearly a quarter of a century less than impressive. Nevertheless, in the context of the late 1960s, the creation of ASEAN marked an important stage in the development of regionalism in Asian being a reflection of the determination of Southeast Asia countries to take control of their own destinies independent of outside intervention.

Given the changes that were now beginning to take place in Asia, this was to be increasingly important. The first of these signs of significance for the region's security appeared when the British government announced in 1967 that it would withdraw all its defence forces east of Suez. Although the United Kingdom had all but given up its territorial possessions in Asia over a decade beforehand (it still possessed Hong Kong), it had continued to maintain a military presence in the area primarily to guarantee the security of Malaysia. Now, with its security and economic interests clearly oriented towards Europe, London decided it could no longer justify its Asian defence commitments. As the British departed, the Five-Power Defence Arrangement (involving Britain, Australia, Malaysia, Singapore and New Zealand) came into being to guarantee Malaysia's security and allay local Commonwealth concerns about the British departure.

Within a year, the perception of change was reinforced by the decision of President Johnson of the United States not to contest the next presidential election and to work during his remaining year in office to secure a resolution to America's painful involvement in Vietnam. To this end Johnson refused a request from his military advisers to undertake a further large deployment of troops to Vietnam and actively sought a way to negotiate an end to the war. After seven years of a steadily increasing American involvement in Vietnam, this marked a profound change in policy and opened the prospect of a end to the conflict. When Richard Nixon, Johnson's successor, took office in January 1969, he made a commitment to peace in Vietnam and soon began pursuing peace negotiations with the North Vietnamese while simultaneously starting the withdrawal of American forces. Nixon's determination that there should be 'peace with honour' in Vietnam meant that it took another four years before a satisfactory peace formula could be agreed upon, a period during which the fighting in Vietnam sometimes reached an intensity greater than any experienced in the previous years of conflict. Nor was America's goal achieved in the end. The peace settlement signed in Paris in January 1973 was intended by Washington to ensure the survival of the South Vietnamese government. It did not. The North Vietnamese government had never accepted that this was a legitimate aim of the peace negotiations and continued to press their objective of Vietnamese unification under communist rule. In April 1975 they eventually succeeded and, 30 years after Ho Chi Minh had declared Vietnamese independence shortly after World War II, it became a reality.

The decision to withdraw from Vietnam marked a watershed in American policy towards Asia. Bruised by its experience in Vietnam and facing a financial crisis that required economies in military spending, America, like Britain, was preparing to scale down its military involvement in the region. It would withdraw from the mainland of Asia and in future its military presence in the region would be consolidated on the offshore islands of Japan, Guam and the Philippines. Nixon's declaration of the Guam Doctrine in 1969 reflected this policy. Arguing that the United States could not continue to bear the burdens of regional defence that it had assumed since 1945, Nixon made it clear to America's friends and allies in the region that defence against conventional threats was their own responsibility and that, except in the advent of a general nuclear war, they could no longer rely on America to provide for their security.

The Guam Doctrine was one of numerous changes Nixon brought to American foreign policy during the first term of his presidency. With no less warning, he announced to a surprised international community two years later in July 1971 that he would soon make a personal visit to the PRC, where he hoped to be able to begin the task of developing friendly relations with the Chinese government. The visit took place in February 1972 and was as much welcomed by the Chinese as by the Americans. The move signalled that after two decades of hostility, during which the United States had actively sought to exclude China's participation in world affairs, Washington now accepted Beijing as having a legitimate role to play as a responsible member of the community of nations. Instabilities in the leaderships of both countries and differences over the status of Taiwan meant that it was to be another eight years before full diplomatic relations were established between Washington and Beijing, but long before that had occurred, their rapprochement had brought widespread consequences, particularly in Asia.

Washington's shift in policy towards China gave a sudden international respectability to the government in Beijing. Countries that had continued for years to recognise the nationalists on Taiwan as the legitimate government now switched their allegiance, so that between 1969 and 1981, 45 countries changed their stance. One among them was Japan, whose relations with China for over a century had been tense and hostile. The Nixon announcement of an impending visit to China caught the Japanese government by surprise and led to domestic pressures for Tokyo to normalise its relations with Beijing. Japan's newly elected prime minister, Tanaka Kakuei, eventually responded and visited China in September 1972. In Beijing he publicly referred to the 'unfortunate experiences' between the two countries and said that 'the Japanese side is keenly aware of Japan's responsibility for causing enormous damage in the past to the Chinese people through war and deeply reproaches itself'.[2]

China's rapprochement with the United States and Japan was followed by improved relations with other countries of Asia. In steady succession, Australia, the Philippines, Malaysia and Thailand all extended recognition to the communist regime in Beijing. Notable for their refusal to follow the trend until relatively recently, however, were Singapore and Indonesia, both of which established relations with the PRC in 1990. In the case of Indonesia, relations with the PRC deteriorated sharply after the 1965 anti-communist coup and subsequent leaders long remained wary of being seen to encourage closer contacts with the PRC lest it serve to revive pro-communist elements in Indonesian society. Nor of course was there an immediate improvement in relations between South Korea and China. With the communist regime in North Korea being backed strongly by the Chinese and the animosity between the two divided states of the Korean Peninsula hardly cooled in the twenty years since the Korean War, moves towards closer contact were not within Seoul's contemplation. But perhaps most directly affected by the change in China's international fortunes was Taiwan. Its relations with the communist government on the mainland had remained hostile all through the Cold War, while it enjoyed the support of the international community. Now that the winds of change were blowing through the region, it was becoming increasingly isolated. Taipei denounced Washington and the other states that had moved towards closer ties with Beijing, accusing them of abandoning a friend and being misled by communist propaganda.

After the developments of the early 1970s, the outlook for regional political stability and security in Asia looked more promising than at any time since the end of World War II. While remnants of the Cold War remained in relations between the countries of the region, the most destructive manifestations of East–West confrontation had largely faded. Yet the promise of a new and more co-operative future was not, at least in the short term, fulfilled. By the end of the decade, a new series of regional and international crises had again disrupted regional interstate relations and created a situation in which Asia once again seemed to be among the most volatile and unstable regions of the world.

The growth of regional self-confidence, 1975–91

One reason for the optimism about Asia's future stability in the mid-1970s was the promising economic outlook for many of the countries of the region. By 1975, Japan, South Korea and Taiwan all had impressive growth rates. Hong Kong's economy was also booming and there were reassuring signs that several Southeast Asian countries, most notably

Singapore and Thailand, were on the way to levels of high annual growth. Even the outlook in China was more promising than in the past. Following the death of Mao Zedong and Zhou Enlai in 1976, the CCP went through a period of uncertainty over the new leadership. By 1979, however, this had been resolved. Deng Xiaoping emerged as the new leader of the party and soon began implementing a series of ambitious economic reforms which opened the Chinese economy for the first time to substantial outside investment. Over the following years the rapid expansion of intra-regional trade and investment in Southeast and North Asia has been one of the key factors encouraging closer contacts among the countries of the area. While the level of this growing economic interdependence has been uneven, it has persisted despite renewed threats to political security.

The most important of these new threats was to emerge in Indochina. After the reunification of Vietnam, the country's communist leadership moved swiftly to try to build friendly relations with the states of Southeast Asia. Up to a point its initiatives were successful. The member states of ASEAN, particularly Thailand, responded to Vietnam's overtures. Political contacts were re-established and there was even contemplation that Vietnam might become a member of the association. However, the progress of rapprochement was brought to an end when Vietnam invaded and occupied Cambodia in December 1978.

Cambodia's plight in the 1970s was one of the ruinous legacies of the Vietnam War (see Chapter 41). American and communist intervention during the course of the conflict had compromised the country's neutrality and left rival Khmer groups contending for power. In 1975 the communist Khmer Rouge, led by Pol Pot, came to power and in an effort to purge the political system of its reactionary elements began the systematic elimination of his regime's opponents. The Vietnamese invasion was motivated less out of concern for the genocidal impact of Pol Pot's policy on the Cambodian people than out of a perception that his policies challenged Vietnam's political and security interests in the region. Thus, despite the relief it brought to the Cambodian people, the invasion was widely condemned by the international community as a breach of international law and as politically destabilising; it resulted in Vietnam being branded a pariah among the states of the region.

The members of ASEAN viewed the Vietnamese invasion as a direct threat to their regional interests and quickly became strong opponents of the occupation. Their resolve to force a Vietnamese withdrawal, as well as that of opponents from outside the region, was reinforced by the fact that Vietnam's main ally, the Soviet Union, supported its actions. Within the region and outside it, this immediately raised the spectre of a Soviet thrust into Southeast Asia and possibility of Moscow gaining an important strategic foothold in the area. The politics of the situation were further complicated by the fact that China was also a strong opponent of Vietnam's actions. From Beijing's perspective, the invasion established Vietnam as a hegemonial power in Indochina, an area of traditional concern to Chinese foreign policy. At the same time, the Chinese saw Moscow's sinister hand seeking to encircle their country as part of the struggle for strategic and ideological supremacy that the two countries had been waging since the late 1950s. To reinforce China's opposition to the Vietnamese occupation of Cambodia, Beijing armed and supported the ousted Pol Pot and his followers who had retreated to the northwest corner of the country near the Thai border. There they established a base and proceeded to prosecute a guerilla war against the Vietnamese-installed government of Heng Samrin.

To the very conservative government of President Ronald Reagan in Washington, the Soviet Union's backing of Vietnam at a time when it had itself recently invaded Afghanistan marked the revival of new era of East–West confrontation. There were other governments inclined to see the conflict in these terms, such as that of Malcolm Fraser in Australia, but in Asia the perspective was somewhat different. Out of deference to the role of the United States as the balancer of Soviet power, and to an extent Chinese power, in Asia, Asian countries such as Japan and the members of ASEAN publicly supported America's inclination to a Cold War analysis of the situation in Cambodia, but they were far less convinced of it than in the past and far less prepared to allow Washington to make all the running on the issue. Circumstances had changed in Asia since the height of the Cold War, as China's position on the issue demonstrated. Indeed, Japan, the members of ASEAN and other Western-leaning countries in Asia and China now all found themselves on the same side. Among the members of ASEAN at least there was a new confidence in dealing with issues such as Cambodia that directly affected them. While Japan, as it had throughout much of the postwar period, tended to stay clear of the conflict diplomatically, ASEAN sought to establish itself at the forefront of the campaign to remove the Vietnamese and thus as a central player in any attempt to secure a resolution of the problem.

In June 1991 a lasting ceasefire was reached and, on 23 October 1991, an agreement was signed resolving the situation. However, in the eighteen years that it has been on the Asian political agenda it has made Indochina once again a focus of regional conflict with widespread consequences. At one level it helped to fuel a series of long-standing tensions among states of the region: Vietnam and its non-communist neighbours; Vietnam and China; China and the Soviet Union. At another, it served to isolate Vietnam, Cambodia and to some extent Laos from many of the mainstream contemporary developments in Asian affairs. While none of the states of Asia could easily ignore the conflict taking place on their doorstep (just as they could not easily ignore the crackdown on the democracy movement in China in 1989), for most of them the political agenda in Asia continued to change, evolving specifically in the direction of giving greater attention towards economic issues. The countries of Indochina were caught in something of a time warp. Preoccupied with military confrontation, the expanding regional political agenda seemed to have passed them by. While Vietnam's withdrawal from Cambodia in 1989 and normalisation of relations with China in November 1991 eased its diplomatic isolation, over the thirteen years from 1978 to 1991 Vietnam and Cambodia were not only denied much-needed Western aid to stimulate their economic development, but were excluded from regional initiatives such as the Asia Pacific Economic Cooperation (APEC) movement which could well be among the factors that will shape the destiny of Asia into the next century (see also Chapter 40).

The settlement in Cambodia came at a time when there were signs of movement on some other long-running problems in the area. The issue most conspicuously left over from the Cold War, the division between north and south Korea, is an example. In the late 1980s, Pyongyang and Seoul began a tentative dialogue with one another. Though they did not reconcile their differences, it was a mark of the change that was taking place that Seoul was not waiting for full reconciliation before broadening its bilateral contacts. Overtures were made towards old Cold War enemies. South Korea established full diplomatic relations with the Soviet Union in August 1990, which continued with the successor states after the Soviet Union collapsed, and with China two years later. South Korea's near century-long hostile relationship with Japan also eased. Similarly, Soviet relations with Japan have improved. In May 1989, Soviet leader Mikhail Gorbachev visited Beijing and formally normalised relations with the PRC, thus ending a conflict of three decades' standing.

These developments reflected the changes that had come over the security environment in the Asia-Pacific region. There, as elsewhere around the globe, international politics entered an era in which the United States was the only military power. In Europe this new era was characterised by the collapse of the communist governments in the East, though in general not in Asia. In China and Vietnam, communism has been closely identified with nation-building and political liberation, and did not come under threat despite the changes that had been taking place in both countries. Much the same can be said of north Korea, though here the situation was vastly more complicated because of the division with the south. On the other hand, in Mongolia the communist People's Republic was replaced by the State of Mongolia at the end of 1991, while developments in Cambodia are considered in Chapter 42.

In any event, the changes that were taking place in international politics go well beyond the collapse of communism, important though that was. They were firstly changes of a systemic nature: reshaping the structure of world politics through developments such as the emergence of a global economy, expanding democratisation and new threats to the authority of the nation-state. Secondly, they were dispositional, affecting the distribution of power among states and between states and other actors in international affairs such as transnational corporations. Finally, they were instrumental in affecting the processes and means of international politics through developments such as expanding international organisations and the rising utility of economic power.

With varying degrees of intensity, these changes were already visible in Asia. As improving relations between South Korea and China, among others, demonstrated, ideology was no longer important in determining the direction of a country's foreign policy, as it had been during the Cold War. The United States continued reappraising its role in the region. We also saw the steady rise of economic issues on the regional policy agenda. The Asia-Pacific region became host to some of the world's most dynamic economies and has become a new centre of economic power in terms of world affairs. The rising importance of international organisations can be seen in new regional initiatives such as the Asia Pacific Economic Co-operation (APEC) movement and the attention now being given to the possibility of a new regional multilateral security arrangement. More than at any time in the postwar era, the resolution of Asian problems, along with the destiny of the whole region, came into the hands of Asian leaders and their increasingly articulate peoples, rather than the outsiders who for so long actively intervened in their affairs.

Guide to further reading

Herring, George C., *America's Longest War: The United States and Vietnam, 1950–1975*, 2nd edn, Alfred A. Knopf, New York, 1986
  The best brief scholarly account of America's involvement in Vietnam that is available. Contains a very comprehensive annotated bibliography.

Iriye, Abira, *The Cold War in Asia: A Historical Introduction*, Prentice Hall, Englewood Cliffs, N.J., 1974
  An examination of the origins of the Cold War in Asia which explains the impact of World War II and postwar events in Europe on security in the Asia-Pacific area.

Gaddex, John Lowes, *Strategies of Containment: A Critical Appraisal of Postwar American Security Policy*, Oxford University Press, New York, 1982
  A thoroughly researched and documented account of the evolution in American security policy during the Cold War. Covers both Europe and Asia.

Fitzgerald, C.P., *China and Southeast Asia Since 1945*, Longman, London, 1973

A short but well-focused account of China's relations with the countries of Southeast Asia during the height of the Cold War.

McWilliams, Wayne C. & Piotrowski, Harry, *The World Since 1945*, 2nd edn, Lynne Rienner Publishers, Boulder, Col., 1990

A general study of postwar international relations with several good chapters on the impact of the Cold War on Asia.

Notes

1 Knapp, Wilfrid F., *A History of War and Peace 1939–1965*, Oxford University Press, London, 1967, p. 260.
2 McWilliams, Wayne C. & Poitrowski, Harry, *The World Since 1945: A History of International Relations*, 2nd edn, Lynne Reinner, Boulder, Col., 1990, p. 218.

40 Regional institutions, regional identities

'Cultural differences lay the powder train for international conflict.'
John K. Fairbank

The rapid transformation of international relations in Eastern Asia since the mid-1980s has produced some surprises. Economic growth and integration; technological revolutions in production, transport and communications; and vastly improved bilateral diplomatic and political relations among almost all of the countries of the region have been set in place as the normal prerequisites for the establishment of formal regional institutions and organisations on a multilateral basis. But a comprehensive multilateral organisations in Eastern Asia has yet to materialise. Why is this the case?

The absence of such institutions is less surprising if we consider the historical context of the region, especially its East Asian component. East Asia has been traditionally resistant to multilateralism for a combination of attitudinal and geo-political reasons. The long-standing dominance of Imperial China produced a hierarchical tribute system which, at least when China was strong, functioned as the defining element of the international relations of the region until the middle of the nineteenth century. The domination of Western powers in the century that followed and Sino-Japanese conflict made systematic intra-regional co-operation impossible into the Pacific War. And during the Cold War which followed, ideological and military conflict had a similar effect in dividing the countries of the region.[1] In security and economic matters, China in particular, and to a lesser extent Japan, continued to prefer unilateral and bilateral instruments for expanding regional contacts.

The nature of regional co-operation and institutions has changed fundamentally in the decade from the mid-1980s to the mid-1990s. No dominant power — whether that power be China, Japan or the United States — now has the capacity to single-handedly shape the regional order. The ghosts of the Greater East Asia Co-Prosperity Sphere and such

Cold War organisations as the Southeast Asia Treaty Organisation (SEATO) and the Asia and Pacific Council have been vanquished, if not forgotten.

Compared with Europe and most other parts of the world, East Asia and Eastern Asia are institutionally underdeveloped. But this should not blind us to the vast array of informal networks which have recently been created or the proliferation of institutional activities which are occurring both at the sub-regional level (especially in Southeast Asia) and at the broader trans-Pacific level in which several Eastern Asian countries are playing leading roles. What are the prospects of a new era in East Asian, and Eastern Asian, regional co-operation? What processes, material and attitudinal, are already in motion which will influence the shape and direction of the institutional structures that are likely to emerge in future? What kind of regionalism will accelerated regionalisation produce?

Sub-regional institutions[2]

Asia and the adjoining Western Pacific — or at least its sub-regions — are not allergic to multilateral institutions. Two much-analysed examples are the South Asian Association for Regional Co-operation (SAARC) and South Pacific Forum. In the context of Eastern Asia, it is ASEAN that has been by far the most important. Since its creation in 1967, its agenda has focused on social, political, security and economic affairs. In the 1980s it frequently functioned as a bloc in regional and global forums, proving capable of limiting and obstructing proposals it found contrary to the interests of its members. More recently it has played an activist role in launching new initiatives. Some of these have related specifically to Southeast Asia, such as the movement to create an ASEAN Free Trade Area (AFTA). Others have engaged the broader regional agenda in the areas of both economic and security matters. The ASEAN Post-Ministerial Conference is a major forum for discussion of regional matters, involving the participation of the six members of ASEAN plus seven dialogue partners (Australia, Canada, the European Union, Japan, New Zealand, South Korea and the United States). It has also been a leading force in regional security matters, hosting the annual ASEAN Regional Forum.

At the non-governmental level, ASEAN is also playing a pivotal role in regional affairs. The ASEAN Institute of Security and International Studies (ASEAN ISIS) has been an active catalyst in creating forums for discussion of sensitive political, economic and security issues and also organising meetings to deal with emerging issues and problems ranging from preventative diplomacy measures to conflicts over human rights and good governance.

The trans-Pacific setting

Another sphere of action has developed on a trans-Pacific basis. The level and pace of institution building in the Asia-Pacific in the past two decades, and especially in the past five years, has been impressive. Governments around the Pacific have found it in their interest to accelerate a process of dialogue and co-operation extending far the initial efforts promoted by such organisations as the Institute of Pacific Relations in the period before World War II. Underlying these formal governmental initiatives has been a legion of foundations, businesses, universities and research institutes, and non-governmental organisations that have spun an extensive web of contacts across the Pacific.

In a region born of commerce, it comes as little surprise that the main line of activity has been economic. On the non-governmental side, three institutions deserve particular attention.

- The Pacific Trade and Development Conferences (PAFTAD) began in the mid-1960s. Primarily composed of economists, it convenes a meeting every twelve to eighteen months for what one Australian academic has described as 'intelligent consideration of economic policy issues of importance to Pacific countries'.[3] All participants attend in their private and personal capacities and the definition of the Pacific also extends into Latin America.

- The Pacific Basin Economic Council (PBEC) was created in 1967 as a private organisation with five national committees (Australia, Canada, Japan, New Zealand and the United States). It expanded after 1974 and by 1994 involved business leaders from ten countries in Eastern Asia and fifteen others.

- The Pacific Economic Cooperation Council (PECC) is the most comprehensive of the non-governmental organisations. Formed in 1980, it now includes 26 member committees from around the Pacific. Promoted by academics and officials in Australia and Japan, its objective has been to promote trans-Pacific co-operation, primarily on economic matters. Its composition is tripartite, involving government officials serving in their private capacities, academics and business leaders. It operates a standing committee, a rotating secretariat and approximately twelve specialised task forces.

Three formal governmental organisations are especially important.

- The Economic and Social Commission for Asia and the Pacific (ESCAP). Created in 1947 as the Economic Commission for Asia and the Far East and renamed in 1974, it is one of the regional commissions of the United Nations. Its members include governments from Asia (including South Asia, Afghanistan and Iran) as well as four from

Europe and the United States. It has approximately ten committees with a special focus on human resource development in the region.

- The Asian Development Bank (ADB). Created in 1965–66, it now has almost 50 members. Its membership includes most of the countries of Eastern Asia plus those in South Asia, thirteen from Europe plus Canada and the United States. Not included are Australia, New Zealand and the island nations of the South Pacific. In connection with the World Bank, the International Development Association and the International Monetary Fund, the ADB provides the bulk of multilateral development assistance programs to the less developed countries of the region.

- The Asia-Pacific Economic Co-operation (APEC). The newest and highest profile governmental organisation, APEC was formed in 1989. Its membership now includes eighteen countries from around the Pacific including Eastern Asia, Australasia, North America and Latin America. It has a permanent secretariat based and and has established more than a dozen working groups. Connected to APEC is the 'Leaders Summit' which it has developed. First held in the United States in November 1993, the summit is a gathering of heads of state to discuss regional economic issues.

In the post-Cold War setting, the need and opportunity for new forms of multilateral co-operation in political security matters have also increased substantially. The leading edge in much of this co-operation has again been non-governmental institutions and processes. The proliferation of unofficial and 'track two' channels for discussion of regional political and security issues has been considerable. In 1989 there were only two or three channels for multilateral dialogue and consultation on regional security matters; by 1994 there were more than 30. Two are particularly important as ambitious efforts at creating regularised, inclusive and comprehensive discussion of regional matters:

- The Council for Security Co-operation in Asia Pacific (CSCAP). Created by a consortium of research institutes around the Pacific in November 1992, its objective is to provide a non-governmental, inclusive mechanism for discussion of regional security issues. It is currently composed of twelve-member committees (the sensitive matter of the membership of Taiwan and mainland China has not yet been resolved) and is aiming at including all countries and territories from Eastern Asia, Australasia and North America. It has established four working groups.[4]

- The ASEAN Regional Forum (ARF) was first announced in July 1993 and held its first ministerial-level meeting in July 1994. Like CSCAP, its objective is to create a region-wide, inclusive forum for discussion of regional political and security issues. Unlike CSCAP, it is a formal governmental process. The participants at the July 1994 meeting represented sixteen Asia-Pacific countries including the members of ASEAN, the formal dialogue partners (Australia, Canada, the European Union, New Zealand, South Korea and the United States), plus China, Russia, and Papua New Guinea. The meeting of ministers occurred at the same time as the ASEAN Post-Ministerial Conference. It is planned as an annual meeting at the ministerial level with Senior Officials' Meetings conducted on an inter-sessional basis.

The institution-building process across the Pacific has developed considerable momentum. Judged on the basis of the high-level governmental and intellectual attention this process has received, Asia-Pacific is now a significant part of the global agenda. Yet, despite the level of recent activity at both the official and unofficial levels, the current institutional framework is far less developed than in a European or trans-Atlantic context. There are no Asia-Pacific equivalents of the Organisation for Economic Co-operation and Development, the North Atlantic Treaty Organisation, and the Conference for Security and Co-operation in Europe, much less a European Union.

It should not be assumed that the end destination of institution building in Asia will be the same as in Europe or in Asia-Pacific as across the Atlantic. Institution building in the context of Asia and the Pacific has its own distinctive pace and style, and perhaps endpoint. Firstly, it tends to be cautious, incremental and pragmatic, inspired less by grand visions than immediate problem-solving. For some, the Asia-Pacific process is a step toward the eventual creation of a Pacific community. For most, however, it is a useful and forward looking mechanism for expanding co-operation. Secondly, it works on the basis of consensus rather than more formal processes for voting and ratification. There is considerable resistance to the creation of permanent bureaucratic structures to advance the work of international organisations. Thirdly, it frequently features 'track two' or non-governmental forms rather than exclusively governmental and official channels. Finally, although it depends on the consent and support of the great military powers of the region (the United States, Russia and China), its prime movers have been such 'middle powers' as Australia, Canada and South Korea, the ASEAN countries and Japan. The process has the markings of a species of non-hegemonic leadership.

Pan-Asianism

The countries of Eastern Asia have a continental as well as an oceanic connection. How significant have been exclusivist pan-Asian efforts at building new institutions and networks? The simple answer is: very little.

The formal institutions that focus on Asia, including ESCAP, the ADB and the Colombo Plan, all have considerable and influential non-Asian participation.

Where pan-Asianism is important is less in building institutions than in building ideas and identities. Since the period at the turn of the century when Asian intellectuals flocked to Meiji Japan, several important Asian writers and activists including Rabindranath Tagore, Sun Yatsen, Okakura Kakuzo and Nitobe Inazo have explored the positive values in Asia which could be presented to the world as universals. The disaster that was the Greater East Asian Co-Prosperity Sphere wrecked any pan-Asian attempts until after the defeat of Japan. Indian and Chinese efforts at the time of the Bandung Conference in 1955 quickly split apart in the face of Cold War rivalries and Sino-Indian competition.

It has only been in the 1990s that the prospect of pan-Asian values has again received widespread attention. The concept has been packaged in a variety of different ways. Among them are the New Asianism, the Asian way, the Asian restoration, the Asianisation of Asia, and the Asian renaissance. The common objective is to identify and build upon a set of shared values, accomplishments and challenges, and to create what Yoichi Funabashi has called 'a cohesive Asian worldview'.[5]

One approach has been to trace commonalities in the developmental experience of Asian countries (almost always focusing on Eastern Asia and excluding South Asia!), among them an emphasis on education, political stability and export-oriented industrialisation. As Funabashi notes, 'Philosophical and theoretical frameworks are forming around these models.'[6] Several Western scholars have indeed identified a distinctively East or Eastern Asian variant of capitalism.

On the political and philosophical front, new groups have been formed such as the 'Commission for a New Asia'. An intellectual forum, it is attempting to create a framework for discussion of what one author has called the 'issues of beliefs, principles, and codes of ethics, and to explore the potential for what might be called an Asian "New Asia", one which is not obliterated by Western culture and values'.[7] At the level of popular culture, Star Television based in Hong Kong now transmits across Asia and there is discussion of Asian co-operation in satellite technology. A small number of rock stars have generated an Asiawide following.

Another approach is much more closely identified with a revived and reconstituted Confucianism. Several writers, including Lee Kuan Yew, speak of distinctly 'East Asian' values. One formulation by another Singaporean identifies ten: balancing individual interests with those of family and society; strong family; education; the virtues of saving and frugality; hard work; national teamwork; an Asian version of a social contract; communitarian societies built on making citizens stockholders; moral wholesomeness; a free but responsible press.[8] A Japanese writer adds three additional 'Asian' virtues: diligence, courtesy, discipline and creating harmony between nature and mankind.[9]

Finding 'Asian values' as distinct from Hindu, Buddhist, Islamic or Confucian ones is, correctly notes one influential publication, 'a tall order'.[10] It is less difficult to identify a common attitude. One theme which connects much of the new Asianism is a shared resistance to perceived imposition of values and standards from outside Asia. This has emerged with particular intensity around three issues: human rights, democracy and environmental concerns. The Bangkok Declaration of March 1993 was produced by 49 Asian states attending the regional preparatory meeting before the United Nations-sponsored World Conference on Human Rights in Vienna. It insisted that human rights must be:

> considered in the context of a dynamic and evolving process of international norm setting, bearing in mind the significance of national and religious particularities and various historical, cultural and religious backgrounds.

Behind the search for an Asian alternative and arguments about cultural differences and state sovereignty often lie the immediate political interests of ruling elites and regime legitimation. Cultural differences can be and sometimes are the last refuge of a desperate government. But the debate is about ideas and identity, not just power. One of the strongest unifying forces has been the Asiawide experience with Western imperialism. However difficult it is to define Asian values, there is a readiness to rally against imposition of standards from the outside.

The degree of unanimity among Asian governments and societal groups on specific issues like the definition of human rights should not be overestimated. The Bangkok Declaration was not endorsed by all 49 states. The Japanese government, for example, issued a special statement objecting to the Declaration's rejection of aid conditionality. A number of Asian non-government organisations (NGOs) vocally rejected large elements of the Declaration. But in an era of swelling universalism and activism among many Western-based NGOs and at least some governments, there reside possibilities for a sharp and prolonged confrontation. Beyond philosophical principles, the policy matters of aid and trade conditionality will remain contentious and emotional issues into the foreseeable future.

Implications for Eastern Asia

But what of an Eastern Asia that combines the diverse cultural and civilisational influences of East and Southeast Asia? In matters of institution building, the most obvious point is that there are few Eastern Asian-wide processes or organisations. Several of the countries of Eastern

Asia, especially Japan, South Korea, Taiwan and the members of ASEAN have been active in a variety of regional and global fora. China has rarely been an initiator of multilateral institutions but has demonstrated an abiding interest in participating in regional institutions that are created.

The most important proposal for an intra-regional organisation was offered in December 1990 by Prime Minister Mahatir of Malaysia for the creation of an East Asia Economic Grouping or Caucus. His concept of 'East Asia' corresponds to what we have labelled Eastern Asia. Conspicuously absent from his proposal are the other members of APEC — Canada and the United States which are members of the North Atlantic Free Trade Association, but also Australia and New Zealand. First suggested in 1991, the precise nature of the Caucus remains vague, but the idea resonates with a variety of policy groups and interests in Asia as a potentially defensive organisation should Europe and North America become continental fortresses.

One of the peculiarities of Eastern Asia is that an astonishing amount of economic co-operation has occurred without formal organisations or formal international agreements. The driving forces of regional economic integration and growth have been in the private sector. The role of government has been to create macro-economic stability domestically and an attractive regime for investment and trade. Instead of creating formal instruments for policy co-ordination, individual countries have engaged in a process of unilateral and tacit adjustments to one another. Even the newly emerging trans-boundary economic zones are being managed with a minimal regulatory framework.

The constraints on institution building in Eastern Asia, like a broader Asian region, are formidable. Chief among them are the size and diversity of the region, conflicting national interests and a strong commitment to nationalism. Latecomers to the process of state formation, few if any governments are willing to delegate sovereignty to larger political units. This sets limits on the scope and effectiveness of any kind of regional organisation. Not surprisingly, none of the Asian, Asia-Pacific or sub-regional proposals for expanded co-operation have run in the direction of supra-national organisations or political integration.

Yet the deepening economic interdependence and a more fluid and multipolar security environment make new forms of co-operation essential. In looking to the future, there is little immediate danger of Eastern Asia becoming an inward-looking bloc. Though it is not the case in Southeast Asia, the structures of Eastern Asian multilateralism appear to depend upon a significant trans-Pacific core. Instead of pursuing formal organisations, the preferred option remains a form of what Robert Scalapino has referred to as 'soft regionalism'.[11]

In matters of identity building, one particular hazard is projecting East Asian values across all of Eastern Asia. This does injustice to the complex and rich weave of non-Confucian elements which have shaped societies and cultures in Southeast Asia. The dangers here are political as well as intellectual. Citizens of Southeast Asian countries who are of Chinese descent (the so-called overseas Chinese) have in many instances enormous economic power. Some estimates indicate that ethnic Chinese represent about 5 per cent of the population of Southeast Asia but control as much as 70 per cent of non-state commercial and manufacturing activity. Treating them as extensions of Confucian and Chinese society overestimates their cultural influence and runs the serious risk or exacerbating deep-seated ethnic tensions.

Living with Eastern Asia

For the first time in 150 years, the future of Eastern Asia sits principally in Eastern Asian hands. Comparative domestic stability and unprecedented economic growth in combination with a positive security environment have produced a region which is growing in self-confidence and assertiveness.

From the perspective of governments and peoples lying across the Pacific, the lines of our connection with Asia are diverse and expanding. They take several forms ranging from trade and investment to immigration and defence co-operation.

One obvious challenge is to expand relations with a portion of the world of major economic and social consequence. The doubling and redoubling of efforts to create profitable business ventures in and with Asia is a consistent pulse in modern approaches to Asia among almost all of the advanced economies.

A related challenge is to sustain the vibrant economic growth of the region. This demands continuous engagement and the improvement of institutional mechanisms for managing regional conflict. One of the necessary items in this process is the creation and strengthening of multiple networks — governmental and unofficial — for linking policy elites within Eastern Asia and across the Pacific. Nowhere is this clearer than in the complex relationship between the United States and Japan. Should it deteriorate substantially, the consequences would be devastating on both sides of the Pacific. Equally serious is the management of value differences in the divisive areas of human rights, democratic development and the environment. A 'clash of civilisations' would be far more dangerous than a clash of nation states, even as it evolved in the 1930s.

All of these problems call out for political and economic as well as institutional responses. But the greatest challenge remains that of understanding. If cultural differences do indeed have the power to ignite international conflict, the central task must be to increase cross-cultural understanding. Here education about Eastern Asia is the key.

No country is more acutely aware of the dilemmas and opportunities of closer contact with Eastern Asia than Australia. Australia's future is inextricably linked to Asia. Unlike Eastern Asia's other European and trans-Pacific partners (including Canada and the United States), Australia and New Zealand have no realistic options except deeper integration into Asia. Fully 70 per cent of Australia's exports already go to Asia.

For much of the past decade Australia has been in the vanguard of forging a trans-Pacific, Asia-Pacific nexus. It has been Australian academics, business leaders and government officials who have taken a leading role in most of the institution building that has occurred. Yet there are now voices that suggest that Australia's future lies less in an Asia-Pacific formula than in direct enmeshment in Asia. One step in this direction would be Australian membership in ASEAN. Another would be the creation of Western Pacific processes which intentionally exclude participants from the Europe and North America.[12]

Australian thinking and action may not be the determining factors in setting the future of Eastern Asia and trans-Pacific relations, but they will tell a great deal about the possibilities and limitations of cultural and political convergence. Considering the vast gap in values and institutions that separates Australia from Asia, the processes it helps put in place will be testament to one of several different possibilities about dealing with Eastern Asia in future: co-operation, complementarity, convergence or community.

Guide to further reading

Palmer, Norman D., *The New Regionalism in Asia and the Pacific*, Lexington Books, Lexington, 1991
> The descriptive sections are now slightly out of date, but this is still a useful inventory and analysis of regional institutions.

Mack, Andrew & Ravenhill, John (eds), *Pacific Cooperation: Building Economic and Security Regimes in the Asia-Pacific Region*, Allen & Unwin, Sydney, 1994
> A collection of eleven essays attempting to connect recent developments in the region with some of the ideas related to regime theory.

The Pacific Review, vol. 7, no. 4, 1994, edited by Richard Higgott
> A special issue devoted to 'Ideas, Policy Networks and International Policy Coordination in the Asia-Pacific'.

The eight papers in the Australia-Asia Perceptions Project, produced by the Academy of Social Sciences in Australia and the Australia-Asia Institute of the University of New South Wales present a thoughtful examination of several of the complex issues which accompany closer integration of Australia and Asia. Topics covered include national security, democracy, human rights, business ethics, labour practices, citizenship, media and education.

Notes

1 Segal, Gerald, *Rethinking the Pacific*, Oxford University Press, London, 1990, Ch. 1.

2 The most useful, though now slightly out of date, compendium of institutions in Asia and the Pacific is Norman D. Palmer's *The New Regionalism in Asia and the Pacific*, Lexington Books, Lexington, 1991.

3 Peter Drysdale, quoted in Palmer, *The New Regionalism*, p. 135.

4 Evans, Paul M. 'Building Security: The Council for Security Co-operation in Asia Pacific (CSCAP)', *Pacific Review*, vol. VII, no. 2, Summer 1994.

5 See Yoichi Funabashi in 'The Asianization of Asia', *Foreign Affairs*, vol. 72, no. 5, November/December 1993.

6 ibid., p. 78.

7 FitzGerald, Stephen, 'Ethical Dimensions of Australia's Engagement with Asian Countries: Are There Any?', *Asia-Australia Institute Newsletter*, no. 4, December 1993, p. 5.

8 Koh, Tommy, 'The Ten Values that Undergird East Asian Strength and Success', *International Herald Tribune*, 11–12 December 1993.

9 Ogura Kazuo, 'A Call for a New Concept of Asia,' *Japan Echo*, vol. XX, no. 3, Autumn 1993.

10 *The Economist*, 28 May 1994.

11 Scalapino, Robert A. 'Regionalism in the Pacific: Prospects and Problems for the Pacific Basin', *The Atlantic Community Quarterly*, vol. 26, no. 2, Summer 1988.

12 One such organisation already exists, the Confederation of Asian Chambers of Commerce and Industry.

41 | The security architecture of Eastern Asia

Although Eastern Asia is a region of significant diversity, three common factors have shaped its overall security environment in the post-World War II period. First, the region is a hub of Great Power interaction, locating four of the major powers of the contemporary international system — the United States, Russia, China and Japan. As a result, it has rarely been possible to insulate local and regional conflicts from Great Power dynamics and intervention. Second, in contrast to Europe, Eastern Asia was never divided into two neat ideological blocs during the Cold War. The Sino-Soviet rift in the 1960s introduced a complexity to the region's security structure at variance with the bipolar international system. Important historical, cultural and political differences between subregions, as well as the region's geographic division into maritime and continental segments, made it difficult to duplicate European-style alliance structures in Eastern Asia. Third, the postwar United States security role in the region, including its alliance commitments and direct military presence, has been more extensive and deep-rooted in this region than in any other area outside of Western Europe. As the dominant Pacific military power after the defeat of Japan in World War II, the United States established a network of military alliances as part of its strategy of 'containment'. In the first decade after the end of World War II, bilateral security treaties were concluded with Japan, South Korea, the Philippines and the Republic of China (Taiwan). In addition, the trilateral ANZUS treaty, involving Australia and New Zealand, and the Manila Pact, which formed the basis of the Southeast Asia Treaty Organisation, constituted what Dulles described as a 'defensive bulwark for freedom in the part of the world'.

No other external power could match the scope of the United States security system in the region. The Five Power Defence Arrangement involving Australia, New Zealand, Singapore, Malaysia and the United Kingdom was essentially a stop-gap and loose arrangement designed to smooth the departure of British forces from the region as part of its 'East of Suez' policy. While the Soviet Union did develop a significant alliance relationship with Vietnam, which included acquisition of military bases in Cam Ranh Bay, it did not alter the power projection balance which remained firmly in favour of the United States.

In contrast to bilateralism, multilateral regional security arrangements did not flourish in the Eastern Asian milieu. The Soviet Union's efforts to float a collective security concept in the 1970s — the so-called Brezhnev plan for an Asian collective security system — were met with widespread regional suspicion and rejection. The United States seemed far less interested in security multilateralism in Asia than it was in Europe. For the United States, a multilateral system like NATO made little sense in Asia in view of the weak military resources and capabilities of its Asian allies. While SEATO was of some symbolic value in projecting an American Commitment to Asian stability against communist expansion, the United States involvement in the alliance was kept deliberately weak and was in no way intended to match the significance of its bilateral alliances.

The primary United States security objective in the region in the twentieth century has remained remarkably consistent. It may be described as a policy of 'counter-hegemony' — that is, to deny any other power an opportunity to achieve preponderant influence. To this end, the United States pursued a balance-of-power framework as the core element of its security strategy. Such a strategy did not, however, address the range of local and regional conflicts that emerged in post-colonial Eastern Asia. These included conflicts stemming from weak national integration, lack of government legitimacy, and domestic political struggles reflecting the global ideological divide. Instead, the United States–Soviet–China competition contributed to the internationalisation, escalation and prolongation of many of these conflicts. Conflicts in Korea, Vietnam and Cambodia all begun as domestic political struggles, but escalated into major flashpoints of the Cold War due to the intervention by major powers. Although the two superpowers on occasion did exercise a degree of restraint on their clients so as to prevent their direct involvement in a regional conflict (which risked developing into a nuclear Armageddon), this did not contribute to the resolution of the local/regional conflicts.

The Cold War security architecture was marked by the absence of indigenous regional security frameworks to promote the pacific resolution of local conflicts. The interstate system in Eastern Asia had no previous experience in such regionalism. This was in sharp contrast to other regions such as Europe (with the Council of Europe and the European Economic Community), the Middle East (with the Arab League), Africa (with the Organisation of African Unity) and Latin America (with the Organisation of American States). In 1967, the formation of the Association of Southeast Asian Nations (ASEAN) introduced the first successful experiment in regional political co-operation. While the United States supported the formation of ASEAN, ASEAN's formation actually signalled the weakening of United States' credibility among its allies (especially Thailand and the Philippines) which saw indigenous regionalism as a politically more credible alternative to alliances within Great Power orbits. ASEAN survived early intra-mural tensions and was strengthened by the common fear of communist expansion in the wake of the United States' withdrawal from Vietnam. It also played a major role in seeking a negotiated settlement to the Third Indochina Conflict (1978–91). But ASEAN's interest in regional conflict management remained limited to Southeast Asia and it did not develop a full-fledged security role until after the end of the Cold War. Its policies towards external powers, such as its proposal for a Zone of Peace, Freedom and Neutrality (ZOPFAN) in Southeast Asia, were constrained by the continued dependence of its members on external security guarantees and the overlying dynamic of Great Power competition.

The end of the Cold War has created serious uncertainties about the regional balance of power in Eastern Asia. Superpower retrenchment, including the Soviet withdrawal from its military bases in Vietnam and United States withdrawal from the Philippines, has allowed a greater scope for local actors, especially China and Japan, to assert themselves in regional security affairs. China appears to be the major beneficiary of this situation. Its improved relations with Russia have lessened China's concern with the strategic nuclear threat and allowed it to devote greater attention and resources to regional conflicts, especially in the South China Sea. Its armed forces have embarked on a major modernisation drive. This modernisation is of long-term significance for an important reason. Unlike the Soviet military buildup during the Cold War, China's is backed by a booming capitalist economy. Unlike the pre-Gorbachev leaders of the former Soviet Union, China's military build-up has followed a successful phase of economic and technological modernisation. Now the potent combination of annual double-digit economic growth rates and double-digit increases in military spending (since 1990) places China in a position to dictate the regional balance of power.

At the same time, a more independent Japanese security posture seems to be emerging. Japan continues its long-term military buildup with the development of a credible sealanes defence capability. If the health of the United States–Japan security relationship deteriorates further from trade disputes, a unilateral Japanese effort to counter China's military buildup could usher in a new era of Great Power rivalry in Eastern Asia. This prospect, especially in the absence of a counterveilling American military presence, has emerged as a principal source of security concern for the lesser regional actors.

The shift in the regional balance of power assumes further significance in the light of several other potential sources of conflict in the region. The first is the proliferation of territorial disputes in the region, including the

South China Sea disputes over the Spratly and Paracel Islands involving China, Taiwan, Vietnam, the Philippines, Malaysia and Brunei, the East China Sea dispute between China and Japan, and the dispute between Russia and Japan over the Northern Territories. Additionally, a number of maritime disputes exist in Southeast Asia, such as the Singapore–Malaysia dispute over the Pedra Branca Island, the Malaysia–Indonesia dispute over Sipadan and Ligitan Islands and the Vietnam–Indonesia dispute over Natuna. Of these, the South China Sea dispute may be the next major flashpoint of conflict in the region. Not only does it involve a multiplicity of actors, but its strategic significance is magnified by its potential for oil and other maritime resources and the impact of any armed conflict in disrupting the security of the sea lanes through much of the region's commerce passes.

A second security challenge is the region's growing militarisation. The threat of nuclear proliferation is evident in North Korea's attempts to develop a nuclear capability. If it succeeds, a nuclear North Korea might provide the catalyst for the nuclearisation of its neighbours, especially Japan, South Korea and Taiwan, all of which possess an advanced civilian nuclear industrial base that could produce nuclear weapons within a relatively short time. At the same time, defence expenditures throughout the region are on the rise, and large quantities of sophisticated conventional weapons are entering the inventory of regional states. According to an estimate by the International Institute for Strategic Studies, the rise in defence spending during the 1985–92 period was 12.6 per cent for China, 28.5 per cent for Japan, 22.4 per cent for North Korea, 63.5 per cent for South Korea, 31.2 per cent for Malaysia, 36.2 per cent for Singapore, 29.9 per cent for Taiwan and 27.6 per cent for Thailand. Moreover, the growth of indigenous arms industries makes the regional states less reliant on external suppliers. The arms buildup is fuelled by a number of factors, such as uncertainty about the strategic environment, shifts in the balance of power, the growing affluence of regional countries, prestige and domestic influence of the military. Whether these trends constitute a regional arms race is not yet clear, but the possibility of such a race developing cannot be ruled out.

The militarisation of Eastern Asia compounds the threat of violence involving divided states. Nuclear tensions between the two Koreas and the arms race between China and Taiwan at a time of growing Chinese concerns over demands for Taiwanese independence not only make peaceful reunification a remote (although not inconceivable) possibility but also increase the destructive potential of any outbreak of conflict geared to unilateral reunification efforts.

A third challenge to security in Eastern Asia stems from the pressures towards political liberalisation. Authoritarian regimes which sought legitimacy by virtue of their strong economic performance are facing demands for political openness from a rapidly growing middle-class population. During the Cold War, the Western powers tolerated, even defended, brutal authoritarianism in their client regimes; such tolerance has now given way to a campaign for human rights and democratisation. The bloodshed in Thailand in May 1992 and the Beijing massacre of June 1989 attest to the potential violent domestic conflict linked to demands for political openness. The other socialist regimes in the region, Burma and Vietnam (and possibly north Korea), can be expected to face similar pressure if they continue in the path of market-oriented economic development. Civil–military relations continue to be an important factor in the political balance in Thailand, Indonesia and the Philippines. The military establishments in Thailand and the Philippines remain opposed to political openness and could usurp power from a civilian government made vulnerable by corruption and inefficiency, despite growing political constraints on the military's coup-making potential. In Indonesia, tensions between the military and the Suharto regime threaten political stability at a time of leadership transition.

Finally, insecurity in Eastern Asia derives from the problems of national and political integration faced by its numerous weak states. Cambodia's failure to develop a viable polity despite the efforts of the United Nations Transitional Authority in Cambodia, one of the largest peacekeeping operations in United Nations history, has opened the door to renewed civil war and a possible return to power of the Khmer Rouge, which committed genocide during its years in power from 1975 to 1978. The refusal of the military regime in Burma to transfer power to the elected civilian government and the problem of insurgency among its myriad ethnic minorities are other sources of regional concern. Indonesia faces insurgencies in a number of provinces, Aceh, East Timor and Irian Jaya. The Philippines might have won the war against communist insurgency, but they are a long way from pacifying the troubled Mindanao region where armed separatist campaigns persist. Thailand has a similar separatist problem in its southern provinces, while in Malaysia, the emergence of radical Islamic groups poses a serious threat to national security.

The emerging threats to regional stability in Eastern Asia did not, as of 1994, threaten the centrality of the United States bilateral relationships in the region's security architecture. The ASEAN members, Japan, South Korea and Taiwan continue to see these arrangements as a fundamentally stabilising factor in the region. Despite their military buildup, few of these regional countries can claim self-reliance in security and defence matters. The United States alliances are seen by them as key to its role as a 'regional balancer', providing a guarantee against the ambitions of regional powers and preventing an all-out arms race in the region. Thus, while some bilateral relationships have been weakened after the end of the Cold War (such as the United States–Philippines relationship), others have been strengthened. In fact, with the dismantling of large United States military bases in the region, several Southeast Asian countries have quietly moved to establish access arrangements with the United States.

But the United States role as a regional balancer faces a number of uncertainties. Three sets of problems are particularly noteworthy. Military-strategic uncertainties relate to the status of United States regional military presence, the decline of which has created doubts about United States credibility. Economic-trade frictions threaten the stability and longevity of the United States–Japan alliance. Political-diplomatic problems relate to the United States' policy on human rights and demo-cratisation, which could seriously strain relations between the United States and some of its regional allies. Managing these problems would be a key test for American policy-makers in the post-Cold War era and would be vital to the preservation of a balance-of-power security struc-ture in the Eastern Asian region.

In view of these uncertainties, there has been a growing debate on the need for multilateral security approaches in the region. Multilateralism in the Eastern Asian context involves more than a question of the number of actors. It is defined *substantively* in direct opposition to the 'exclusive bilateralism' of America's post-World War II security strategy in the region. While the United States strategy focused primarily on a balance-of-power approach maintained by a regional network of bilateral military alliances, multilateralists promise 'common' or 'co-operative' security institutions which would be 'inclusive' in scope and political (non-military) in content.

Multilateralism is viewed as a *desirable* long-term alternative to bilateralism because threats to the region's stability have become much more complex and multi-faceted. Advocates of multilateralism embrace a comprehensive notion of security, including a number of non-military and non-ideological issues, such as environmental degradation, illegal migration and resources scarcity, as important concerns for a new security system. Furthermore, multilateralists advocate a notion of common and co-operative security, the original inspiration for which was provided by the success of the Conference on Security and Co-operation in Europe in bridging the East–West ideological and military rivalry in Europe. Indeed, the first to call for security multilateralism in the Asia Pacific region, the former Soviet President Mikhail Gorbachev in his famous Vladivostock speech in July 1986, invoked the need for an Asia Pacific version of the Conference on Security and Co-operation in Europe. (This proposal received little support from within the region due to prevailing suspicions of the Soviet Union.) A number of other countries, notably Australia and Canada, have proposed multilateral approaches to security which challenge the Cold War logic of balance-of-power and deterrence. After initial reluctance and opposition, the United States and the ASEAN countries have endorsed a similar conception of multilateralism as the basis for a new era of security co-operation in the region.

Approaches to security multilateralism in Eastern Asia have been extensively debated. Some advocates would prefer a new, broad-brush security institution to facilitate confidence-building and conflict resolution within the region, while others have stressed the need to build on existing subregional and bilateral mechanisms that do not undermine the relevance of United States security relationships. While some would like to see a standing multilateral institution with formal procedures for decision-making, others want multilateralism to be flexible and ad hoc in the sense that multilateral action would only be organised when specific security problems arose and would be undertaken only by those countries most immediately affected by it.

The result has been a compromise based on an initiative by the ASEAN members to develop a region-wide dialogue on security issues which would follow their annual multilateral consultations (called the ASEAN post-ministerial conferences, or ASEAN-PMC) with a number of non-member dialogue partners. This process, which has been expanded to cover eighteen countries (the six ASEAN members — Indonesia, Malaysia, Brunei, Singapore, Thailand and the Philippines — plus South Korea, Japan, Australia, New Zealand, the United States, Canada, China, the European Commission, Papua New Guinea, Vietnam, Laos and Russia), is called the ASEAN Regional Forum (ARF). By building on an existing and indigenous institution, the ARF avoids any controversy associated with attempts to form a brand new regional security institution. By requiring no binding commitments from members and relying instead on ASEAN's preferred ways of consultations and consensus, the ARF has proved to be most acceptable, if limited, path to security multilateralism in the region.

Through its consultative agenda, the ARF aims to contribute to regional security in three important ways:

1 by promoting transparency in strategic intent and threat perceptions;
2 by building confidence on military postures and deployments; and
3 by developing the 'habit' of co-operation which might pave the way for more specific and concrete measures of conflict control and security co-operation in the future.

As a framework for regional reordering, multilateralism is unlikely to offer an adequate system of security. The kind of multilateralism being envisaged under the ARF is different from the traditional alliance variety, in the sense that it does not presuppose common defence against a designated enemy. Nor does it aspire to be a full-fledged collective security system in which aggression by one member would be punished through joint action by other members of the collectivity. The rather limited and uncertain objective of the ARF is to promote dialogue and consultations on security issues, with the hope that this would enable countries to dispel mutual suspicions in strategic and defence postures. Such dialogues are primarily an exercise in preventative diplomacy, rather than an instrument of collective security.

The prospects for a genuine and effective multilateral regional security arrangement in Eastern Asia are constrained by lingering interstate suspicions, territorial and political conflicts, and an aversion to transparency in the region's strategic culture. China, the biggest security concern for its Asian neighbours, rejects multilateralism which it sees as a device directed against its own regional interests and objectives by the lesser powers of the region. None of China's neighbours sees multilateralism as a substitute for its security linkages with great powers. While multilateral dialogue is good for confidence-building in peacetime, the weaker regional countries are likely to seek protection from external powers to 'balance' the threat from their powerful neighbours at the time of a serious regional crisis.

The logic for an inclusive multilateral forum might be undermined by two other possible directions in Eastern Asia's security relations. Firstly the region's weaker states might 'bandwagon' with its emerging regional powers, China and Japan, leading to the exclusion or isolation of the United States and the further enhancement of the political and military position of the former. But neither China nor Japan is politically acceptable in the region as a partner to bandwagon with. While Japan is an established economic superpower and China is an emerging military superpower in the regional context, neither has the ability to provide the combination of military and economic security to its lesser neighbours in the foreseeable future.

A second alternative is the development of a concert system in which all the major powers in the region would assume the responsibility for order-maintenance. Such an arrangement involving China, Japan, Russia, India and the United States was once proposed by Mikhail Gorbachev. But a formal concert system (of the Concert of Europe type) would be (and indeed was) strongly resisted by ASEAN, and can only be attempted by the Great Powers at a serious risk to intra-regional cohesion. Furthermore, the existing rivalries between China and India and China and Japan would make the development of a concert system difficult.

Against this backdrop, the region's post-Cold War security architecture remains extremely uncertain. Security dialogues and consultations are useful, but not adequate guarantees of regional peace and stability. By themselves, they do not amount to a multilateral security system. A concert system in which major powers would co-operate in managing regional conflicts is unlikely to develop because of existing antagonisms among those included and resistance from those excluded. At the same time, the United States' role as a regional balancer will become less important as regional countries develop more self-reliant military postures. While a balance-of-power architecture based on existing United States alliances retains considerable relevance for the maintenance of regional order, it might not prevent the emergence of a highly volatile regional security environment marked by uncertain alignments and weak management mechanisms.

Guide to further reading

Iriye, Akira, *The Cold War in Asia: A Historical Introduction*, Prentice Hall, Englewood Cliffs, 1974

A historical survey of United States–Soviet rivalry in Asia, including the development of their alliances and application of the 'Yalta System' to Asia.

Gordon, Bernard K., *Toward Disengagement in Asia: A Strategy for American Foreign Policy*, Prentice Hall, Englewood Cliffs, 1974

An analysis of the role of bilateralism and multilateralism in the United States' security policy towards Eastern Asia, and the prospect for multilateral institutions in the region.

Acharya, Amitav, *A New Regional Order in Southeast Asia: ASEAN in the Post-Cold War Era*, Adelphi Paper no. 279, International Institute for Strategic Studies, London, 1993

A survey of ASEAN's security concerns and policy responses with regard to the development of a multilateral security system in Eastern Asia in the post-Cold War period.

Simon, Sheldon, *East Asian Security in the Post-Cold War Era*, M.E. Sharpe, Armonk, New York, 1993

A collection of essays on major regional security challenges and trends with a focus on regional conflicts in Southeast Asia and the Korean Peninsula and the changing role of the Great Powers.

42 | The agony of Cambodia

Among the countries of Eastern Asia, Cambodia occupies a very special place for the ravages and agony it and its people have undergone since the 1970s. It has been the pawn of world powers, the leaders of which have rarely cared about the fate of its people. Its tragic history requires detailed treatment for an understanding of the Eastern Asian region since the 1970s, and especially of the international relations of the period.

Cambodia was the only one of the three countries of Indochina that was not divided as a result of the Geneva Agreements of 1954. While Vietnam was separated into North and South at the seventeenth parallel, and in Laos two northeastern provinces were set aside for the regroupment of pro-communist Pathet Lao forces, the Cambodian government of Prince Norodom Sihanouk was able to argue that it alone exercised power in Cambodia. This was because in Cambodia the Khmer Issarak (Free Cambodians) who fought the French were never dominated by communists as were similar moments in Vietnam, and Laos (after 1949). When Sihanouk proclaimed himself leader of the Cambodian independence movement in 1953, and succeeded in negotiating full and final independence from France for his country, the Khmer Issarak broke up. Moderate nationalists believed Sihanouk had obtained what they were fighting for, while communists who still opposed the monarchy suspended guerrilla activity in order to reorganise.

Radical left-wing activists in Cambodia were thus left with three choices at the end of 1954: to withdraw with their Vietminh allies to North Vietnam; to remain underground in Cambodia; or to form their own political party to contest elections against Sihanouk's own broad-based political organisation, the Sangkum Reastr Niyum (Popular Socialist Community). More than a thousand Issarak guerrillas went north; most of those who stayed in Cambodia became politically inactive; while a few leftwing intellectuals in Phnom Penh formed the radical socialist Pracheachon (People's) Party.

The late 1950s were a time of repression for the radical left in Cambodia. Aided by defections and betrayal, Sihanouk's secret police sought out and imprisoned or executed many former Issarak activists, including members of the Pracheachon Party, which failed to win a single seat in either the 1955 or 1958 elections. By the time the Khmer People's Revolutionary Party (KPRP) held its Second Party Congress in 1960, the communist movement in Cambodia was at a low ebb. Its membership was divided — both geographically between Cambodia and North Vietnam, and over what policies to adopt in its political struggle against the Sangkum. Sihanouk, by contrast, was at the height of his popularity. Before the 1955 elections he had abdicated as king and placed his father on the throne while he became the unchallenged political leader of the Sangkum. Among the most popular of his government's policies were the new emphasis given to education and Cambodia's proclaimed neutrality. As a national leader, however, Sihanouk lacked an understanding of economics. He was proud, petulant and hypersensitive to any criticism of himself, his political movement or his country.

In the late 1950s, a number of Cambodian students returned from France where, in addition to their studies, they had become ardent Marxists. Thanks to Sihanouk's repression and the absence of other KPRP cadres in North Vietnam, these young urban intellectuals were able to gain effective control of the Central Committee of the party. Their leader was a school teacher by the name of Saloth Sar, better known by his later revolutionary alias of Pol Pot. Within three years, following the disappearance of the party's Secretary-General (presumably killed by Sihanouk's secret police), Pol Pot had taken over the leadership of the KPRP.

Within months of the hastily called Third Congress that confirmed Pol Pot's leadership, he and a number of his close supporters, including Ieng Sary and their wives, the sisters Khieu Thirith and Khieu Ponnary, fled Phnom Penh to the relative safety of the mountainous northeastern provinces at the southern terminus of the Ho Chi Minh trail. There they made contact with Vietnamese communist leaders directing the insurgency in southern Vietnam. Their requests for Vietnamese support in launching a communist insurgency in Cambodia aimed at overthrowing Sihanouk's government were not, however, to be met. For the next five years, with growing frustration and annoyance, Pol Pot was forced to subordinate his plans for a Cambodian revolution to the strategic requirements of the insurgency in Vietnam. It was something Pol Pot neither forgot nor forgave.

The reason for Vietnamese communist reluctance to back a revolutionary movement in Cambodia was simply that Sihanouk was too valuable to them. As the war in Vietnam escalated, Sihanouk was determined to protect the neutrality of Cambodia. To this end, he was prepared to turn a blind eye to the occasional use of Cambodian territory as a resupply route or a sanctuary for National Liberation Front (Vietcong) guerrillas. Sihanouk's decision in 1965 to sever diplomatic relations with the United States, and secretly to permit arms and ammunition for the Vietcong to be shipped through the port of Sihanoukville in return for a Vietnamese pledge to respect the territorial boundaries of Cambodia, made him even more valuable to the leadership in Hanoi. For Sihanouk, this tilt towards North Vietnam was essential to keep Cambodia out of the Vietnam War, and in this he was largely successful.

Internally, however, Sihanouk's policies were not as effective as his international diplomacy. With Sihanouk's blessing, a number of young leftist intellectuals had won seats representing the Sangkum in the 1962 elections, but the economic reforms introduced in 1963 were ineffective in solving Cambodia's growing economic crisis. The problem was twofold, due both to the corruption and greed of the Cambodian elite, and to the Vietnam War. Cambodia's exports consisted of two crops: rice and rubber. The nationalisation of rice exports under a government monopoly effectively concentrated wealth and economic power in the hands of a few people who, to increase their own profits, depressed the official purchase price of rice paid to the peasants. At the same time, the Vietcong were buying Cambodian rice through Chinese merchants at a higher price than the government purchasing monopoly. Peasants stopped selling to the government. Revenue to the state thus declined just at a time when Sihanouk's neutralist foreign policy and the break in diplomatic relations with the United States resulted in a reduction of foreign aid, and when the education system had produced a generation of young university graduates who could find no employment.

Criticism of Sihanouk and his policies increased. The Prince responded by withdrawing from politics, and in the 1966 elections first-past-the-post voting tipped the balance of political forces in the Sangkum in favour of the right. The new government of former Defence Minister General Lon Nol then used the army to forcibly collect rice from the peasantry and prevent its sale to the Vietcong. This provoked a peasant rebellion in the Samlaut area of western Cambodia in April 1967, which the army brutally repressed. The government seized upon the revolt as evidence of communist agitation. A new wave of repression followed, and a new band of recruits left Phnom Penh to join the maquis — including former Sangkum deputy and later nominal leader of the Khmer Rouge, Khieu Samphan.

In 1966 Pol Pot had changed the name of the KPRP to the Communist Party of Kampuchea (CPK). Two years later, following the Samlaut rebellion, the party decided the time was ripe for armed struggle, the Vietnamese not withstanding. During the rice harvest that year, party activists exploited continuing peasant discontent in the Samlaut area to provoke renewed opposition to the army. This decision of the party was severely criticised by the Vietnamese, who still refused to provide military assistance to the Cambodian insurgency — a position endorsed by Cambodian communists who had gone to Vietnam after 1954. However, deteriorating economic conditions, the brutality of the army, and the propaganda and political mobilisation of the party were all having their effect. By the end of 1968 the Resistance Front in Cambodia numbered perhaps 10 000 activists, fewer than half of them armed. Sihanouk, who remained Chief of State, referred to them scathingly as the Khmer Rouge (Red Cambodians).

By the end of 1969, tensions in Cambodia were coming to a head. Even though Sihanouk's foreign policy had begun to swing back towards the United States, discontent with his arbitrary authoritarianism and the corruption of those around him, the ambition of his political enemies and anger directed against the Vietnamese, whom many Khmer blamed for their own problems, all came together early in 1970. While Sihanouk was on vacation in France, the political right orchestrated a number of anti-Vietnamese demonstrations which soon turned violent and became critical of Sihanouk. When Sihanouk nonchalantly refused to cut short his vacation, the National Assembly deposed him as Chief of State and proclaimed the Khmer Republic, with General Lon Nol as president.

The overthrow of Sihanouk removed every reason the Vietnamese communist leadership in Hanoi had for refusing to support the Cambodian insurgency. Lon Nol immediately established close relations with both the United States and with the government in South Vietnam. It was obvious to the North Vietnamese that their former sanctuaries in Cambodia would no longer be safe from American and South Vietnamese attack. It was therefore in their interest to provide every assistance to the CPK. Vietnamese communist forces moved back from the vulnerable border areas deep into Cambodia, sweeping before them the small scattered garrisons of the Khmer National Army and turning vast areas over to the administration of the Khmer Rouge. When the anticipated United States–South Vietnamese invasion came in May, it failed to accomplish any of its military goals, let alone destroy the Vietnamese communist command centre for the war in the south.

Relations between the Khmer Rouge and their Vietnamese communist allies were, however, far from good. Pol Pot felt that he had received a much more sympathetic hearing in Beijing than he had in Hanoi when he sought support for the Cambodian revolution.

The Khmer Rouge leadership deeply resented the Vietnamese determination to put their own revolution first. Assurances that once the Saigon regime had been destroyed, Cambodia would fall like a ripe fruit were not welcomed by the Khmer Rouge, who had no wish to be beholden to the Vietnamese. In fact the Khmer Rouge leaders were highly suspicious of long-term Vietnamese intentions where Cambodia was concerned. Whatever their ideological differences, they were united in their determination not to permit Cambodia to fall under the political domination of a powerful, communist Vietnam. Proletarian solidarity was all very well, but not at the expense of Cambodian independence.

The civil war that wracked Cambodia from early 1970 to April 1975, when Phnom Penh finally fell to the Khmer Rouge, was an appallingly brutal conflict. No quarter was given on either side. Few prisoners were taken, and the foolhardy bravery shown particularly by Lon Nol soldiers secure in their belief in the protective powers of magic amulets meant that casualties were tragically high. American involvement took the form not of ground forces at a time when President Nixon was intent on disengaging from South Vietnam, but of massive use of air power based on minimal intelligence, resulting in heavy civilian casualties in areas under Khmer Rouge control.

The corruption, inefficiency and sheer incompetence of the Lon Nol regime in Phnom Penh goes a long way towards explaining the remarkably rapid success of the Khmer Rouge. But another reason has to do with the extent of popular support for the Khmer Rouge. Propaganda to the effect that the cities were parasitically consuming the wealth of the country ('The fruit grows in the countryside, but is eaten in the cities')[1] generated a ready response among peasant farmers well aware of how they had been exploited. The civil war in Cambodia was one of country people against the cities.

In the early years of the war, popular support for the insurgents was in part due to the appeal of Sihanouk. After his overthrow, the Prince flew to Beijing where he met with the Khmer Rouge and issued a call for popular resistance against the Lon Nol regime. Sihanouk and his followers formed a common National United Front with the Khmer Rouge, and a government-in-exile which obtained recognition from a number of countries (though not the Soviet Union or its Eastern European allies). As the Khmer Rouge progressively gained the upper hand in Cambodia, however, Sihanouk's name was less and less invoked, and the Khmer Rouge actively repressed the few Sihanoukist military units that had been formed. Within two years of his overthrow, Sihanouk was no more than a powerless figurehead for the Khmer Rouge.

The rapid military success of the Khmer Rouge in confining Lon Nol's army to the towns and in cutting all major roads (including that from the port of Sihanoukville to Phnom Penh) convinced the leadership that victory would be possible in 1973. This led them to reject United States-North Vietnamese negotiations for a ceasefire. By contrast, in Laos the Pathet Lao insurgents agreed not only to a ceasefire but also to the formation of a third coalition government with the political right. The decision of the Khmer Rouge to keep fighting, and their tightening encirclement of Phnom Penh, made them the sole targets for the full concentration of American air power. The attack on Phnom Penh was beaten back with horrifying losses. Between the February 1973 ceasefire in Vietnam and Laos and August when the American Congress ordered the termination of all bombing of Cambodia, over 250 000 tonnes of bombs were dropped, more than one and a half times the total weight dropped on Japan in the entire course of World War II.[2]

The events of 1973 secured only temporary respite for the Lon Nol regime, but were crucial for the evolution of Khmer Rouge policies and power relationships. The Vietnamese were never forgiven for concluding an agreement with the United States to the detriment of the Cambodian revolution. In the rural areas, the Khmer Rouge resorted to forced labour and forced recruitment to make up their losses. The party saw the struggle in apocalyptic terms: Cambodia stood alone; all was to be sacrificed for the victory of the revolution. Propaganda was intensified and controls over movement strictly enforced. Tens of thousands of peasant refugees fled in fear to the cities as whole villages were relocated as part of the Khmer Rouge mobilisation of the rural population for total war.

The end came on 17 April 1975 when, Lon Nol having fled shortly before, surly lines of black-clad Khmer Rouge guerrillas snaked into Phnom Penh to take power in the name of Angkar, the organisation responsible for directing the Cambodian revolution. Meanwhile, a 'Special Assembly' of the CPK Central Committee had been held, at which future Khmer Rouge policies were decided. These included immediate evacuation of all cities, abolition of money and markets, abolition of religion (all Buddhist monks to be defrocked and put to work), execution of all leaders of the Lon Nol government, administration and army, formation of communes, expulsion of all Vietnamese, and despatch of the army to guard the country's borders. Eventually all these policies were put into effect, but by no means uniformly throughout the country, for in April 1975 the party (Angkar) may have been supreme, but it was hardly monolithic.

During the civil war the country had been divided by the Khmer Rouge into five operational zones. In each, a party committee made local political decisions and directed military operations. Communications between zones was rudimentary and a considerable degree of regional autonomy existed. Instructions from the Party Centre, when they were received, were interpreted as local officials saw fit, so regional variation was considerable. Controls were harshest in the Northeastern Zone where Pol Pot had his party headquarters, but relaxed in the Eastern Zone where the leadership was influenced by techniques of mobilisation successfully applied by the National Liberation Front in South Vietnam.

Various attempts have been made to define different factions or ideological tendencies within the Khmer Rouge when they seized power in 1975. Broadly speaking, three such groupings may be differentiated. To begin with, there were the radical nationalists led by Pol Pot and Ieng Sary. They believed in the uniqueness of the Cambodian revolution, and indeed of the Khmer race, distrusted the Vietnamese, and were convinced of the need for rapid socialist transformation of Cambodian society and for a tightly disciplined party to bring that transformation about. A second group tended to be less nationalistic and more prepared to learn from the experiences of other revolutions, particularly China's. They too wanted to bring about rapid socialist transformation, but by mass popular mobilisation as in the Chinese Cultural Revolution rather than through party-imposed discipline. Both these groups were dominated by younger intellectuals. The third tendency, by contrast, comprised mainly older leaders who had fought in the Khmer Issarak, were more in touch with peasant thinking, and who favoured a slower transition to socialism with the party leading and teaching the masses. Though they had no love for the Vietnamese, they recognised that much could be learned from the Vietnamese revolution, and saw the need to maintain at least correct relations with Hanoi. Over the next three years these divisions became more marked and murderous as the radical nationalists pursued their goal of creating a totally unified Stalinist-style party unquestioningly obedient to the leadership, and all dissent was progressively eliminated.

The first move in creating the 'new' Cambodia was to decree the complete evacuation of the cities. More than three million people, refugees and those who had lived in cities all their lives took whatever possessions they could carry and moved to the countryside. The sick and wounded, the very old and very young died by the roadside in this terrible exodus to which no exceptions were permitted. The reasons given by the Khmer Rouge were that the Americans were about to bomb Phnom Penh, and that in any case the people could not be supplied with food after the United States airlift of rice had been terminated. In fact the evacuation had more to do with the imposition of party control through personal disorientation and disruption of social networks that might have challenged the party's monopoly of power; and with ideological commitment to creation of a one-class state of collectively productive worker-peasants.

Instead of creating a single class, however, new social divisions were introduced. At the summit of the new social hierarchy stood the Khmer Rouge cadres who abrogated to themselves a total monopoly of power. Every order was to be obeyed on pain of death. Next came the 'old people', those who had stayed and supported the Khmer Rouge during the civil war. And below these again came the evacuees, the 'new people', whether former peasant refugees or city dwellers. The new people, once they had written their 'confessions' or personal histories, were given the dirtiest and most difficult tasks to perform. Progressively over the next three years, however, the distinction between new and old people broke down as stricter policies of communal eating and living, longer working hours, harsher discipline and deteriorating standards of health and welfare affected both categories alike.

Of the policies outlined by Pol Pot to the April 'Special Assembly', most were applied immediately. Along with evacuation of the cities came the abolition of money and markets. Movement between villages was forbidden to all but Khmer Rouge cadres. Villages had to be self-sufficient, each producing for its own needs. Surplus production was taken away to be used by Angkar. Buddhism was entirely suppressed. All former Lon Nol officials were systematically sought out and executed. All Vietnamese were expelled. The army, sent to seal the country's borders, almost immediately clashed with Vietnamese troops. Both sides agreed to negotiations over delineation of the frontier which continued into 1976, but subsequently broke down. Border skirmishes then continued throughout most of 1977. A major Vietnamese military response at the end of 1977 only led to the severance of diplomatic relations, and did nothing to deter further Khmer Rouge border raids throughout much of 1978.

Deteriorating relations with Vietnam only served to convince the Khmer Rouge leadership of the need to push forward the transition to socialism with the utmost despatch against all internal opposition. The party decided on the need to reduce population pressure in areas near Phnom Penh that had received most evacuees, and open up new land in the underpopulated Northern, Northwestern and Western Zones. Thousands of people were transferred to 'new villages' which they were forced to carve out of the jungle in malarial areas unsuited to rice production. The resultant death toll from disease and starvation was up to 80 per cent in some of these areas, and elsewhere lack of any modern drugs, poor food, long hours of work and the draconian discipline of the Khmer Rouge, whose only punishment for any even insignificant 'crime' was death, all contributed to a tragically high death rate. Overall figures can be no more than an estimate, but best estimates are that as many as a million people died during almost four years in which the Khmer Rouge were in power.[3]

The Khmer Rouge tried to reshape Cambodia, not just socially but even physically, through huge mass construction projects such as dams and irrigation canals on which thousands of people were forced to toil for up to eighteen hours a day. In fact agricultural production actually increased under the Khmer Rouge, while food available in the communal kitchens decreased as more and more produce went to pay for Chinese weapons. As production increased so did repression. Non-Khmer minorities, such as the Chinese and the Muslim Cham, suffered with particular severity. Anyone who had had any previous contact with Vietnam, had worked for the Lon Nol administration, was foreign educated, or could be counted as an intellectual was executed. Those who survived did so by hiding their identities and doing what they were told.

As popular discontent grew (even if it was hidden) and the failures of Khmer Rouge policies became apparent, differences developed within the party. All opposition, however, was interpreted by the Party Centre (Pol Pot and his close associates) as treason. An apparent attempt to replace Pol Pot as leader in September 1976 led to the first of what became a series of increasingly bloody purges of party cadres as the radical nationalist faction tightened its grip on the party. Thousands of high-ranking cadres were secretly arrested and incarcerated in the notorious prison of Tuol Sleng on the outskirts of Phnom Penh. There they were systematically tortured, forced to write false confessions, and killed. More than 10 000 dossiers detailing each case remain as mute testimony to the terrible deaths of those who had given their lives for the Cambodian revolution.[4]

As relations with Vietnam deteriorated in 1978, and the Party Centre became increasingly paranoid, cadres in the Eastern Zone were believed to be contaminated through contact with the Vietnamese and thus disloyal to the Centre. All but a few who managed to flee across the border into Vietnam were systematically killed. As the loyalty of 'new people' resettled in the Eastern Zone was also suspect, they too were either moved further west or slaughtered en masse. New murderous attacks were mounted across the border with Vietnam.

By mid-1978, the Vietnamese had had enough, and the decision was taken to overthrow Pol Pot. On Christmas Day 1978, the Vietnamese army drove deep into Cambodia. By 10 January 1979, Phnom Penh was in Vietnamese hands, the Party Centre had fled to the Thai border, and a new Cambodian government had been proclaimed — the People's Republic of Kampuchea (PRK) — composed of Cambodians who had fled the murderous excesses of the Khmer Rouge and taken refuge in Vietnam. In response to this invasion of what they accepted as their client state, the Chinese determined to 'teach the Vietnamese a lesson' by invading border areas of northern Vietnam in February 1979. This did not, however, affect the situation in Cambodia.

Both the new government and the Vietnamese were welcomed by the people of Cambodia. Personal freedoms, Buddhism, markets and money were all restored. Almost immediately the PRK concluded a Treaty of Friendship and Co-operation with Vietnam similar to the one already signed between Vietnam and Laos. With Vietnamese and Soviet assistance, the PRK began the massive task of reconstructing a shattered society, economy and country.

The overthrow of the Khmer Rouge was the signal for yet another vast movement of people. The decimated urban population returned to their previous houses, sought missing family members, or took the opportunity to flee to Thailand. Huge refugee camps grew rapidly on the Thai side of the border. Inside Cambodia, the country's new leaders set about rebuilding the administration from scratch with the few technicians, civil servants and former party cadres who had survived and were prepared to serve the Vietnamese-dominated regime. The first priority was food production. In the chaotic weeks following the Vietnamese invasion, people who had been hungry for three years ate whatever they could find, including in some places the draught animals and seed rice needed to produce the next harvest. To add to their woes, Cambodians faced the spectre of starvation. That a famine was averted was largely thanks to Vietnam and the Soviet Union.

Both the defence and reorganisation of the country in the early years of the PRK depended heavily on Vietnamese assistance. Progressively, however, a new administration took shape, an army was recruited and power was transferred to the Kampuchean People's Revolutionary Party, a communist party which, like its Lao equivalent, was closely aligned with the Vietnamese Communist Party. By 1980 a government had been established composed of former Cambodian revolutionaries who had spent the years from 1954 to 1970 in North Vietnam, former Khmer Rouge who had split with the Party Centre, and 'technocrats' with no previous political affiliation. Both KPRP Secretary-General Heng Samrin and the man who became Prime Minister in 1985, Hun Sen, were former Khmer Rouge officials from the relatively benign Eastern Zone. In 1981 a constitution was adopted and elections held. Within three years, the PRK had become a viable state.

The Vietnamese invasion and change of government in Cambodia had, however, radically altered the strategic balance in Southeast Asia. The Vietnamese army, the largest and most battle-experienced in Southeast Asia, had advanced to the Thai–Cambodian border, and as the Thais themselves joked, the only thing likely to stop it if the Vietnamese chose to invade Thailand would be the Bangkok traffic. The historical role of Cambodia and Laos as buffer states separating Thailand from Vietnam had been destroyed. The Thais felt threatened. The government responded by concentrating every diplomatic, economic and military means available to force a Vietnamese withdrawal. To this end, Thailand sought the support of China, the United States and the Association of Southeast Asian Nations (ASEAN). Vietnam was condemned in the United Nations as an aggressor, and the overwhelming majority of member states denied recognition to the Vietnamese-installed PRK regime. On the economic front, Vietnam was denied badly needed aid and investment capital to repair its war-devastated economy. And militarily, Thailand provided assistance to any Cambodian resistance organisation opposed to the Vietnamese — including the Khmer Rouge.

All these measures took time to organise. Thailand provided sanctuary for the exhausted and shaken remnants of the Khmer Rouge under their notorious leaders, permitting them to be rearmed and supplied by China.

The Bangkok government also encouraged the establishment of two anti-communist and anti-Vietnamese resistance factions: one on the political right led by former Cambodian Prime Minister Son Sann; the other more politically moderate and led by Prince Sihanouk who had survived the Khmer Rouge years under house arrest in his palace in Phnom Penh. In June 1982 these three groups came together at ASEAN and American urging to form an unlikely and potentially unstable Coalition Government of Democratic Kampuchea (CGDK), which continued to retain Cambodia's seat at the United Nations.

Recognition of the CGDK as the lawful government of Cambodia meant no recognition of the PRK. United Nations agencies and international development funds were denied the government in Phnom Penh. Desperately needed foreign aid came from Vietnam, the Soviet Union and Eastern Europe, with assistance from India (the only major neutral state to recognise the PRK) and Western non-governmental and church aid organisations. American pressure prevented loans being made to either the PRK or Vietnam by international lending organisations, such as the World Bank or the Asian Development Bank.

Meanwhile, extensive assistance was given to the three resistance factions. While over 100 000 Cambodian refugees were resettled in third countries — mainly the United States, France, Canada and Australia — over 300 000 more were denied refugee status by the Thai authorities and instead were housed in vast camps along the Thai–Cambodian border.[5] There they served as reservoirs of recruitment for the resistance armies. Camps of the two non-communist factions were open to international aid agencies, but those under control of the Khmer Rouge were closed camps, supplied and financed by China via the Thai military. In these camps, Khmer Rouge techniques of population control continued to be enforced, as the Party Centre, still under the leadership of Pol Pot and Ieng Sary, rebuilt an ideologically committed and disciplined guerrilla army. With as many as 40 000 men under arms, the Khmer Rouge became and remained the dominant faction within the CGDK — the more so after the rightist faction all but disintegrated into mutually hostile personal followings, and Sihanouk's organisation remained militarily insignificant.[6]

In retrospect, the Vietnamese military offensive of 1984–85 marked a turning point in the Cambodian crisis. In a purely military sense, the offensive was a complete success. All the bases of all three resistance factions inside Cambodia were overrun. But the guerrillas merely retreated into Thailand where they were rearmed by the Chinese and resupplied by the Thais. Success on the battlefield neither destroyed the CGDK militarily nor changed the political situation. It was brought home to the Vietnamese that an alternative approach was needed.

The conclusion of the offensive coincided with two other developments that were to exert a profound influence on Vietnamese thinking. In the Soviet Union, Mikhail Gorbachev came to power, and in Vietnam the plight of the economy was moving from serious to desperate. In the international arena, Gorbachev's priorities were to cut Soviet losses abroad, especially in Afghanistan, improve Sino-Soviet relations and end the Cold War. The Soviet withdrawal from Afghanistan and China's determination to link improvement of Sino-Soviet relations to the withdrawal of Vietnamese forces from Cambodia placed great pressure on the Vietnamese. So too did the need to end Vietnam's isolation from sources of economic investment and aid, especially as it became clear that the Soviet Union would be unlikely to maintain its previous level of assistance. There was nothing for it, therefore, but to seek a political solution in Cambodia. The 1985 meeting of Indochinese Foreign Ministers in Phnom Penh dramatically announced that all Vietnamese forces would be withdrawn from Cambodia by 1990, and called for negotiations between the PRK and the CGDK with a view to the formation of a popularly elected government.

In response, the CGDK demanded the dissolution of the PRK and formation of a quadripartite government to be responsible for drawing up a constitution and holding free and fair elections. Neither proposal was acceptable to either the PRK or Vietnam, for fear that this would open the way for the return of the Khmer Rouge. Nevertheless the Vietnamese went ahead with their promised military withdrawal. In late 1987 and again in early 1988, Sihanouk attempted to capitalise on the changed international environment by meeting with PRK Prime Minister Hun Sen in France. These talks broke down over irreconcilable views as to the future role of the Khmer Rouge. Both China and the more inflexible members of ASEAN, notably Thailand and Singapore, were determined to dissolve the PRK in order to punish Vietnam and to ensure some political influence for the virulently anti-Vietnamese Khmer Rouge — irrespective of their previous atrocities. Vietnam and the PRK were equally determined to prevent any return of the Khmer Rouge to power. On this point, all negotiations foundered.

The Vietnamese military withdrawal, together with the collapse of the Sihanouk–Hun Sen talks, galvanised more concerned members of the international community into more actively seeking a political solution to the Cambodian problem — if only to avert the real possibility that if Vietnam did withdraw without any political settlement being reached, the Khmer Rouge could again seize power. Australia, Indonesia and France all sought not only to bring the three CGDK factions and the PRK together, but also to convince other interested powers to support a compromise agreement — one that would disarm the Khmer Rouge and permit it to participate in the political process where its own record would ensure its electoral demise. Additional impetus in the search for peace came from election of a new Thai government dedicated to turning Indochina from a battleground into a marketplace.

A month-long conference was eventually convened in Paris in August 1989, under the auspices of the United Nations, only to end in deadlock and disarray. Even so, some softening of attitudes did seem to have occurred. The United States subsequently withdrew recognition from the CGDK while still refusing to recognise the government in Phnom Penh, a position which brought it into line with Australia and Britain. China accepted that Vietnamese military withdrawal had occurred, thus clearing the way for improved relations between the two states. The next step came with agreement by the five permanent members of the UN Security Council on draft proposals for a comprehensive peace settlement to include a ceasefire, disarmament of all four factions, and formation of an interim administration to oversee elections — all to be supervised by the United Nations. All that was necessary was for four Cambodian factions to agree on the composition of an interim administration or Supreme National Council.

In June 1991, the four factions reached agreement on a ceasefire. The following month, Beijing hosted a meeting of all four factions, the first time the Chinese had received Prime Minister Hun Sen of the PRK. Prince Sihanouk was endorsed as chairman of the Supreme National Council, with Hun Sen as his deputy. With these breakthroughs, conditions at last existed for a comprehensive political settlement. Further negotiations led to the signing in Paris on 23 October 1991 of a Cambodian peace agreement committing all four factions to work together under United Nations supervision to bring an end to the Cambodian conflict. Under its terms, a two phase disarmament plan was to be carried out, while an interim administration in Phnom Penh comprising all four factions was to prepare for multi-party general elections, scheduled for May 1993.

To plan for peace and to carry through the procedures were, however, two different things. The ceasefire that was supposed to go into immediate effect took some time to enforce. Peace keeping forces of the United Nations Transitional Authority in Cambodia (UNTAC) did not reach full strength until October 1992. By then the second phase of the plan, the grouping and disarmament of 70 per cent of the armed forces of the four rival factions, should have been all but complete. In fact, it had completely stalled through the refusal of the Khmer Rouge to co-operate with UNTAC on the grounds that the withdrawal of all Vietnamese forces stipulated under the first phase of the plan had not occurred. United Nations assurances that no Vietnamese troops remained were rejected.

Khmer Rouge recalcitrance was made possible both because they had thoughtfully stockpiled considerable quantities of weapons, and because they were able to finance their activities through the export of timber and gemstones to Thailand, courtesy of the Thai military. As the peace process began to falter, UNTAC came in for increasing criticism — for being too accommodating to the Khmer Rouge, for failing to control political violence, and for undermining the Cambodian economy as its high level of spending generated massive inflation and encouraged corruption. But the United Nations could claim two considerable achievements: the return of almost all the 370 000 Cambodian refugees from camps along the Thai border; and the registration of new political parties and 4.5 million prospective voters to contest the coming elections.

Political manoevring and intimidation marred the early months of 1993, but the elections for a National Assembly were held as planned on 26 May, despite a Khmer Rouge boycott. The large voter turnout heartened United Nations officials, and resulted in a surprising victory for Sihanouk's party (known as Funcinpec) with 45.2 per cent of the vote and 58 seats over the previously ruling Cambodian People's Party (CPP) of Hun Sen with 38.6 per cent and 51 seats. The remaining eleven seats went to minor anti-communist parties.

The response of the CPP threatened to plunge the country into war, but a brief 'secession' movement in the eastern provinces soon collapsed and the CPP agreed to formation of an interim Provisional National Government co-chaired by Funcinpec leader Prince Ranariddh and Hun Sen. The first actions of the National Assembly were to endorse Sihanouk as head of state and draw up a new constitution. When this was adopted on 21 September 1993, Cambodia reverted to the constitutional monarchy it had been prior to 1970, with Sihanouk as King. A new twenty-member cabinet was endorsed with power continuing to be shared between Funcinpec and the CPP, under the joint prime ministership of Ranariddh and Hun Sen.

Formation of the new government both brought UNTAC's mission to a successful conclusion, and effectively excluded the Khmer Rouge from power. But with as many as 30 000 guerrillas under arms and in control of as much as a quarter of the national territory, the Khmer Rouge remained a formidable military and political force. Attempts by Sihanouk to hold 'round table talks' with the Khmer Rouge to bring about national reconciliation foundered on Khmer Rouge refusal to recognise the legitimacy of the new government. Limited battlefield victories against Khmer Rouge forces depleted by desertions emboldened the Cambodian army to attack Khmer Rouge strongholds in Western Cambodia. Within days a Khmer Rouge counter-attack routed government forces.

Thus, after more than two decades of conflict and misery, the outlook for Cambodia was more uncertain than ever. UNTAC had withdrawn, precipitating a financial crisis which would require massive international aid to alleviate. The new government could, thanks to the US$2 billion

UN peace process, claim democratic legitimacy, but it lacked either the financial or military means to defeat the Khmer Rouge. Only the intervention of Sihanouk seemed to offer any hope of national reconciliation, through some compromise such as appointing a few Khmer Rouge officials as government advisors. But the King was a sick man and time was not on his side.

Guide to further reading

The best general history of Cambodia is Chandler, David P., *A History of Cambodia*, 2nd edn, Westview Press, Boulder, Col., 1992 and for the modern period, Chandler, *The Tragedy of Cambodian History: Politics, War and Revolution Since 1945*, Yale University Press, New Haven, 1991.

On the Sihanouk period (from 1954 to 1970), see Osborne, Milton, *Politics and Power in Cambodia*, Longman, Melbourne, 1973, and his *Before Kampuchea*, Allen & Unwin, Sydney, 1979.

For American intervention in Cambodia following the overthrow of Sihanouk, see Shawcross, William, *Sideshow: Kissinger, Nixon and the Destruction of Cambodia*, Andre Deutsch, London, 1979.

The best study of the origins of the Cambodian communist movement and the rise of the Khmer Rouge is Kiernan, Ben, *How Pol Pot Came to Power: A History of Communism in Kampuchea, 1930–1975*, Verso, London, 1985. Two useful collections are Kiernan, Ben & Boua, Chantou (eds), *Peasants and Politics in Kampuchea, 1941–1981*, Zed Press, London, 1982, and Chandler, David P. & Kiernan, Ben (eds), *Revolution and its Aftermath in Kampuchea*, Yale University Press, New Haven, 1982.

On the Khmer Rouge years in power, see, in addition to the Finnish Inquiry Commission Report cited in the endnotes, Etcheson, Craig, *The Rise and Demise of Democratic Kampuchea*, Westview, Boulder, Col., 1984; Vickery, Michael, *Cambodia 1975–1982*, Allen & Unwin, London, 1984; Becker, Elizabeth, *When the War Was Over: The Voices of Cambodia's Revolution and its People*, Simon and Schuster, New York, 1988; Burgler, R.A., *The Eyes of the Pineapple: Revolutionary Intellectuals and Terror in Democratic Kampuchea*, Verlag Dreitenbach Publishers, Fort Lauderdale, 1990; and Jackson, Karl D. (ed.), *Cambodia 1975–1978: Rendezvous with Death*, Princeton University Press, Princeton, 1989. Jackson provides translations of four Khmer Rouge documents, a collection of which can be found in Chandler, David P., Kiernan, Ben & Boua, Chantou, *Pol Pot Plans the Future: Confidential Leadership Documents from Democratic Kampuchea 1976–1977*, Yale University Press, New Haven, 1989. A most readable biography of Pol Pot is Chandler, David P., *Brother Number One: A Political Biography of Pol Pot*, Westview Press, Boulder, Col., 1992.

Personal records of life under the Khmer Rouge include Haing Ngor, *A Cambodian Odyssey*, Macmillan, New York, 1987; Pin Yathay, *Stay Alive,*

My Son, Free Press, New York, 1987; and May Someth, *Cambodian Witness*, Faber and Faber, London, 1986. The experiences of the artist Bunheang Ung, illustrated with many of his remarkable drawings, are recounted in Stuart-Fox, Martin, *The Murderous Revolution: Life and Death in Pol Pot's Kampuchea*, Alternative Publishing, Sydney, 1985.

On events leading up to and following on from the Vietnamese invasion of Cambodia, the best study is Chanda, Nayan, *Brother Enemy: The War after the War*, Harcourt, Brace, Jovanovich, New York, 1986. An account sympathetic to Vietnam is Evans, Grant & Rowley, Kelvin, *Red Brotherhood at War: Vietnam, Cambodia and Laos since 1975*, rev. edn, Verso, London, 1990.

On the People's Republic of Kampuchea since 1979, see Ablin, David A. & Hood, Marlowe (eds), *The Cambodian Agony*, M.E. Sharpe, Armonk, NY, 1987. A good study of the issue of international recognition of the PRK is Klintworth, Gary, *Vietnam's Intervention in Cambodia in International Law*, AGPS, Canberra, 1989.

Notes

1 Kiernan, Ben, *How Pol Pot Came to Power*, Verso, London, 1985, p. 284.

2 Shawcross, William, *Sideshow: Kissinger, Nixon and the Destruction of Cambodia*, Simon and Schuster, New York, 1979, p. 297.

3 This estimate is arrived at in Kiljunen Kimmo (ed.), *Kampuchea: Decade of the Genocide: Report of a Finnish Inquiry Commission*, Zed Books, London, 1984, no. 33. For a discussion of various other estimates, see Vickery, Michael, *Cambodia 1974–1982*, Allen & Unwin, London, 1984, pp. 184–88.

4 For a description of Tuol Sleng, see Boua, Chantou, Kiernan, Ben & Barnett, Anthony, 'The Bureaucracy of Death: Documents from Inside Pol Pot's Torture Machine', *New Statesman*, 2 May 1980, pp. 669–76.

5 For the situation and numbers of refugees, see Kiljunen Kimmo, *Kampuchea*, pp. 46–53.

6 Estimates differ over the forces of the coalition factions, but see Kiljunen Kimmo, *Kampuchea*, pp. 54–56.

Index